Method Effects in Psychological Measurement

About the Authors

Stefan J. Troche (PhD) is Professor of Personality Psychology, Individual Differences, and Psychological Assessment at the University of Bern (Switzerland). He previously held positions and conducted research at the Georg-August-University, Göttingen (Germany), where he studied psychology and earned his doctorate, as a research fellow at the St. Thomas University in Fredericton (Canada), as a lecturer at the University of Bern, and as Professor for Personality and Psychological Assessment at the Witten/Herdecke University (Germany).

Samuel Greiff (PhD) has been Professor of Educational Monitoring & Effectiveness at the Technical University of Munich (TUM) since October 2024. There, he heads the Center for International Student Assessment (ZIB) and is responsible for the national implementation of the PISA study. Previously, he was head of the Educational Psychology & Artificial Intelligence working group at Goethe University Frankfurt and, from 2012 to 2024, head of the Cognition, Learning, & Educational Assessment research group at the University of Luxembourg. From 2017 to 2020 he was Editor-in-Chief of the *European Journal of Psychological Assessment*.

Karl Schweizer (PhD, Dr. habil.) was educated in psychology, mathematics, and philosophy. The professional career includes positions at Goethe University Frankfurt, University of Freiburg, and University of Tübingen as well as teaching appointments at Zhejiang University (PR China). He was president of the European Association of Psychological Assessment (EAPA) and Editor-in-Chief of the *European Journal of Psychological Assessment* (2009–2012).

Method Effects in Psychological Measurement

Stefan J. Troche
University of Bern, Switzerland

Samuel Greiff
Technical University Munich, Germany

Karl Schweizer
Goethe University Frankfurt, Germany

hogrefe

Library of Congress Cataloging in Publication information for the print version of this book is available via the Library of Congress Marc Database under the Library of Congress Control Number 2026945659

Library and Archives Canada Cataloguing in Publication

Title: Method effects in psychological measurement / [editors] Stefan J. Troche (University of Bern, Switzerland), Samuel Greiff (Technical University Munich, Germany), Karl Schweizer (Goethe University Frankfurt, Germany).

Names: Troche, Stefan, 1975- editor. | Greiff, Samuel, editor. | Schweizer, Karl, 1951- editor.

Description: Includes bibliographical references.

Identifiers: Canadiana (print) 20260222453 | Canadiana (ebook) 20260222461 | ISBN 9780889376304 (softcover) | ISBN 9781616766306 (PDF) | ISBN 9781613346303 (EPUB)

Subjects: LCSH: Psychological tests—Design and construction. | LCSH: Psychometrics.

Classification: LCC BF176 .M48 2026 | DDC 150.28/7—dc23

www.hogrefe.com

Publishing Offices

USA: Hogrefe Publishing Corporation, 44 Merrimac St., Newburyport, MA 01950
Phone 978 255 3700; E-mail customersupport@hogrefe.com

EUROPE: Hogrefe Publishing GmbH, Merkelstr. 3, 37085 Göttingen, Germany
Phone +49 551 99950 0, Fax +49 551 99950 111; E-mail publishing@hogrefe.com

Sales & Distribution

USA: Hogrefe Publishing, Casemate Publishers & Book Distribution, 22835 Quicksilver Drive, Dulles, VA 20166
Phone 610 853 9131; E-mail customersupport@hogrefe.com

UK: Hogrefe Ltd, Hogrefe House, Albion Place, Oxford, OX1 1QZ
Phone +44 186 579 7920; E-mail customersupport@hogrefe.co.uk

EUROPE: Hogrefe Publishing, Merkelstr. 3, 37085 Göttingen, Germany
Phone +49 551 99950 0, Fax +49 551 99950 111; E-mail publishing@hogrefe.com

Other Offices

CANADA: Hogrefe Publishing Corporation, 82 Laird Drive, East York, Ontario, M4G 3V1

SWITZERLAND: Hogrefe Publishing, Länggass-Strasse 76, 3012 Bern

Printed and bound in the Czech Republic

ISBN 978-0-88937-630-4 (print) • ISBN 978-1-61676-630-6 (PDF) • ISBN 978-1-61334-630-3 (EPUB)
https://doi.org/10.1027/00630-000

Contents

Chapter 1

Introduction

Stefan J. Troche, Samuel Greiff, and Karl Schweizer

An essential aim of psychometrics is to provide reliable and valid measures of psychological attributes (and processes) such as cognitive abilities (e.g., general intelligence, reasoning, memory), achievements (e.g., knowledge of math or classical Latin), and personality traits (including traits, attitudes, motives, goals, and interests). Therefore, psychometrics is concerned with constructing, evaluating, and applying psychological instruments to measure those psychological attributes, allowing for an adequate interpretation of data collected with these instruments. In this introductory chapter, we provide a brief overview of some conceptualizations of psychological measurement, to explain how and why method effects are an unavoidable challenge for interpreting data collected through psychological measures.

Criticism of the concept of measurement in psychology is almost as old as the first efforts at psychological or psychophysiological measurement (for a review, see Michell, 1997). The main criticism relates to the fact that, as Hölder (1901) defined it, a quantitative structure of an attribute is the precondition for that attribute's measurement. In other words, a structure that is not quantitative cannot be measured. We will not detail all of the conditions that must be met for an attribute to be considered quantitative (for a detailed discussion, see Michell, 1997). Instead, we limit the discussion here to the required additive structure of the attribute. This additivity is necessary to build ratios between two magnitudes of the attribute, so that the one magnitude can be expressed in units of the other magnitude (or vice versa). This condition holds for many natural scientific attributes such as length or weight, but hardly at all for psychological attributes such as extraversion, narcissism, or intelligence. Assume, for example, the difference in intelligence between an individual with intellectual disability and an individual of average intelligence: Can their difference in the attribute "intelligence" (NB: not only in their measured IQ scores) be compared, so that the ratio of their intelligence magnitudes becomes comparable to the ratio of the intelligence magnitudes of a gifted individual and an individual of average intelligence? The answer to this question is most probably no.

Nevertheless, it is helpful in psychological practice to measure individuals with intelligence tests and to assign IQ scores to individuals. For example, individuals assigned an IQ score of 75 or more can quite surely deal with the challenges of daily life (even when taking into consideration confidence intervals). However, for individuals with IQ scores of 60 or less, the need for help with everyday life requirements should be checked carefully (e.g., Tassé et al., 2017). Thus, measuring IQ and knowing the meaning of different IQ scores (or their ranges) is helpful, and the same can be said about scores on an anxiety or depression scale.

However, assigning IQ scores to individuals (or anxiety scores) is not a measurement in Hölder's (1901) sense. It is an "assignment of numerals to objects or events according to rules" (Stevens, 1946, p. 677).

In the case of intelligence testing, the rule could mean that an individual's intelligence test performance is computed, for example, by counting the number of correct responses in several subtests, averaging and weighting these numbers, and transforming the mean into an IQ norm score. This approach to measurement is also referred to as *representationalism* (Suppes & Zinnes, 1963). The assignment of numerals to objects and events is often helpful for practitioners to draw conclusions about individuals' abilities, personalities, or health issues.

It is, however, challenging to avoid the numerals being assigned arbitrarily to attributes when nothing (or not enough) is known about an attribute's structure (let alone whether it is quantitative). Therefore, an isomorphism should exist between the numerals assigned to objects and the empirical relations between the objects (Krantz et al., 1971). In other words, measurement should represent these empirical relations between objects.

Even these requirements, however, might still be too strict for most psychological measurements to fulfill them. For example, the requirement of *transitivity* (e.g., if "A < B" and "B < C," then "A < C") can easily be violated because psychological observations are "noisy" due to measurement errors and often influenced by more than one attribute (Markus & Borsboom, 2013).

According to Markus and Borsboom (2013), *latent variable theory* provides an "interface between data and attributes, when empirical relational systems are indirectly assessed through the examination of noisy data" (p. 77). Thus, through latent variable modeling, a conclusion is drawn from empirically observed behavior (such as item responses) to a latent variable as a representation of a psychological attribute. Indeed, such modeling is always an idealization that is never the "true" representation of a relational system but only an approximation. However, the models can be tested for validity and rejected when they fail to describe the empirical data accurately. For example, in testing for local (stochastic) independence, it can be checked whether the responses to the items of one specific test depend on one and only one latent variable (unidimensionality) as a representation of the attribute under investigation. Also, assumptions about the scale level (e.g., nominal, ordinal, interval, ratio) can be tested to decide how the data can be described most appropriately.

Thus, according to Markus and Borsboom (2013), investigating a test's measurement model provides a way to represent empirical relational systems and an explanation that connects the psychological attributes to observed behavior (responses to items). However, this interpretation of test and item scores requires identifying a measurement model to describe the data appropriately. As noted by Markus and Borsboom (2013), if "no measurement model can be found to hold for the data, then there is little evidence for the thesis that the test scores can be interpreted as measurements, and hence this interpretation is unsupported" (p. 78). Therefore, understanding the measurement model of a given test (or psychological measure) is mandatory for interpreting the test scores as measures of an attribute, regardless of whether the test is used in research or in practice.

A measurement model is, however, frequently found to fit the observed data less well than expected in test construction and in studies on test evaluation. Sometimes, the reason can be found in an inappropriate conceptualization of the psychological attribute, when, for example, subdomains need to be considered, instead of a single uniform construct. Other reasons for measurement models not fitting empirical data are response styles, such as social desirability, impression management, or acquiescence (Prodsakoff et al., 2024). These can be considered confounding attributes that are not intended to be measured, but affect the response behavior. In this case, the latent variable is no longer an unbiased representation of the attribute intended to be measured.

Method effects are a third group of influences on psychological measurements (i.e., the observed data), which lead to a deviation of such data from the theoretically expected measurement model. These effects can be caused by the psychological measure itself (e.g., the manner of item composition, the way of (standardized) administration and instruction, the response format, etc.), the situational context under which the psychological measure is used, and how the resulting data are interpreted. These method effects are sometimes difficult to disentangle from response styles, as several chapters in the present book will demonstrate (e.g., Chapter 6 by Ortner et al., or Chapter 7 by Hernández et al., in this book). A more detailed discussion of the nature of method effects and more perspectives on these phenomena can be found in Chapter 2.

The present work compiles "state of the art" information on a broad range of these method effects, but is by no means comprehensive. For each chapter, recognized experts in the field offer a definition of the respective method effect, as well as an overview of the current knowledge on how and under what conditions the effect can impair the validity of a psychological assessment. Most chapters also provide information on the (primarily statistical) ways the method effects can be identified and considered in measurement models, improving the representation of the attribute to be measured. The representation of method effects allows for further investigations of their nature. This enables researchers, for example, to investigate whether the method effects have a differential influence on the data of specific individuals or groups of individuals.

Most of these effects are inherently linked to the method used (e.g., the item position effect in reasoning tests with many homogeneous items). This might require control of these method effects when establishing an appropriate measurement model or interpreting test scores. For this purpose, many authors who have contributed to the present work have made additional material available at the repository of the Center for Open Science (https://osf.io/z8c5u) with example data and scripts in R (RStudio Team, 2023) or Mplus (Muthén & Muthén, 1998–2023). This should enable interested researchers to investigate the respective method effects with their own data.

Other method effects, however, can be minimized or even avoided by decisions in the design of the method, the approach to administration, or the selection of appropriate samples. Hence, knowledge of these method effects can be very helpful when selecting a measurement procedure for a specific application.

From this perspective, we hope that the chapters of this book will be helpful for test constructors, researchers, and practitioners. Test constructors will find recommendations for avoiding measurement distortions already at the test development stage. Furthermore, the stage of test evaluation may be enriched by the overview of why expected measurement models fit the observed data less well than expected. This might also be important for researchers who aim to represent and examine a psychological attribute as purely as possible. They can find several tools to improve this representation by controlling for method effects.

Finally, practitioners can use their knowledge about method effects to select an appropriate test among those available, by balancing advantages and disadvantages due to possible method effects. The standardized administration of most tests is necessary to use information about reliability, validity, and norm scores reported in the manual of that standardized test. After such a test has been selected, changing the test material (e.g., response format, phrasing) or eliminating single items is impossible when the above-mentioned information is to be used. Therefore, method effects are inevitable in psychological assessments. However, knowledge about possible method effects can guide the careful interpretation of test results. In the case of high-stakes decisions, practitioners might also consider using more than one source of information about a specific attribute, in order to estimate possible distortions of a given measurement.

In the following, we will summarize the chapters in the present book. We will also emphasize how the knowledge of the respective method effect can be used in psychological research and practice.

Chapter 2 discusses different perspectives on method effects. The measurement perspective adopted above is the most general. The validity perspective offers insight into the fact that measurement models and correlations with other constructs and criteria can be distorted by method effects, exacerbating their proper interpretation. With the seminal work of Campbell and Fiske (1959) on *multitrait-multimethod* (MTMM) *analysis*, researchers became increasingly interested in method effects per se, and their underlying mechanisms – and not only in the pure representation of the psychological attribute. This enables us today to look at method effects from the perspective of a rich research tradition. From a more specific perspective, method effects are conceptualized as common systematic variation unrelated to the attribute to be measured. This perspective is closely linked to the *confirmatory factor analysis* (CFA) approach. In summary, the various perspectives that can be taken on method effects should aid readers in orienting themselves within the following chapters and recognizing the connections between them.

Ziegler and Horstmann explain in Chapter 3 the method effect, as it can be investigated through MTMM analyses (Campbell & Fiske, 1959). Thereby, it becomes clear at the beginning of the book that any psychological measurement of an attribute contains a method-specific distortion. They also describe how method effects can be disentangled from the constructs under investigation. This might be particularly interesting in research on attributes (and method effects) to represent the attribute unaffected by the method-specific bias. Practitioners might find results from MTMM analyses informative because they help them interpret individual test scores against this background, when, for example, different sources of information about the same psychological attribute (such as a questionnaire and a behavioral observation) lead to divergent results.

The relevance of a psychological measure's *unidimensionality* for research and practice is emphasized in Debelak and Strobl's Chapter 4. The challenges of assigning numbers to a test result to represent the strength of an attribute (trait or construct) in a person is particularly emphasized here. In the case of multidimensionality, local dependence of items, or differential item functioning the relationship between the assigned numbers and the pronunciation of the attribute is distorted. This makes it difficult or even impossible to interpret the test scores as a pure representation of the attribute. In this chapter, the authors also describe how violations of unidimensionality can be investigated in the framework of item response theory, how the estimation of person parameters for more than one attribute can help disentangle the multiple dimensions, and how insights into the unidimensionality of a psychological measure and its violations can be used to interpret individual test results correctly and fairly.

Numbers assigned to a test result (i.e., test scores) can have a different meaning for different groups, contexts, or testing processes. This challenges the interpretation of psychological measurements when, for example, the same number is assigned to two individuals with different levels of the measured attribute. As outlined by Iliescu and Ion in Chapter 5, such a pattern of results is referred to as the *nonequivalence of psychological measurements* and is closely linked to their validity. The authors provide an overview of different reasons for nonequivalence and how different types of nonequivalence (e.g., construct, method, or item bias) can be differentiated and detected. They also remind us that detecting nonequivalence does not mean that nonequivalence has been eliminated. Researchers may use statistical procedures such as invariance analyses using CFA to detect and consider nonequivalence, for which the authors provide examples from the Personality Inventory for DSM-5. These examples illustrate that findings of nonequivalence can also be highly relevant for practitioners if they want to avoid treating their clients unfairly.

In Chapter 6, Ortner, Breuer, and Badstuber collate findings on how *item arrangement* (fixed-item testing, computerized adaptive testing, and mixed scale arrangement), *response format* (closed-ended vs. open-ended response formats), and *testing situation* (high- vs. low-stakes assessments, characteristics of the examiner, and stereotype threat) can affect test scores in an unintended way. For all of the method effects discussed here, the authors emphasize the interaction with characteristics of the test takers (e.g., test anxiety, motivation, metacognitive competence, sex, age, and ethnicity), revealing how strongly method effects (elicited by the test) and response styles (elicited by characteristics of the test takers) can be interwoven, making them challenging to disentangle. Researchers may be well-advised to consider these effects when implementing psychological measures in their studies. For practitioners, the chapter provides important information about differential responses of test takers to item arrangement, response format, the design of the test situation, and characteristics of the test administrator – depending on the test takers' characteristics – so that test scores might be overestimations or underestimations of the actual level of an attribute to be measured.

Different *item response formats* (IRF) can distort the measurement of an attribute by facilitating the selection of extreme options (extreme response style [ERS]) or the middle option (midpoint response style [MRS]), as outlined in Chapter 7 by Hernández, Tomás, and Cuevas. This chapter describes the mechanisms of these IRF-induced method effects (caused by the psychological measure) in their close interaction with the dispositions of the test takers and their meaning for the IRF design at the test construction stage (e.g., number and labeling of response categories and their visual presentation in graded response formats as well as continuous response and forced-choice formats). Methods to quantify and control for ERS and MRS are presented primarily from the perspective of the item response theory. They can help researchers check their data for those method effects and biases. Practitioners are well-advised to consider these effects when selecting an appropriate psychological measure attuned to the background of the individuals being assessed and the test situation.

In Chapter 8, DiStefano, Go, and Odero present research on the *wording effect*, which can be elicited by including positively and negatively phrased items on the same survey to avoid the response tendency of acquiescence. The authors compare different approaches to representing the wording effect within the framework of CFA and demonstrate these differences in an empirical example. This example illustrates that test score interpretation can be distorted when controlling for the wording effect is neglected. Researchers can benefit from these insights when representing an attribute as a latent variable extracted from positively and negatively phrased questionnaire items. The attribute is better represented, and the model fit increases. Practitioners would be well-advised to interpret individual test scores against the background of possible biases due to the wording effect, because this effect can be more pronounced in individuals with less emotional stability, lower self-esteem, and lower levels of cognitive abilities and education, as well as in individuals suffering from depression.

In many research settings, test or item scores from psychological data are not available for all individuals of a sample. Thus, the data used to investigate, for example, a measurement model are incomplete. In Chapter 9, Rose introduces Rubin's (1976) *comprehensive statistical theory of missingness*. He explains the differences between model and imputation-based methods, their advantages and pitfalls, enabling researchers to decide how they can handle missing values in their data sets and which kind of distortion can be avoided, respectively. These reflections are crucial for accurately interpreting the data – for example, within measurement models or in their correlation with other attributes and variables.

A special case of *missingness* is caused when psychological measures, such as performance tests, are administered with a time limit. Schweizer, Ren, and Wang demonstrate in Chapter 10 how the distortion in the item responses can be controlled when a second latent variable is included in the measurement model, which represents individual differences in the speededness with which the test is completed. With this approach, researchers can build measurement models that include both the attributes to be measured (e.g., reasoning ability) and the effect of speededness. When the two latent variables are not disentangled (e.g., in total test scores), the measurement probably reflects a type of efficiency related to the attribute of interest rather than a "pure" representation of the attribute itself. This is important for investigations of the structural validity of scales and can also be informative for interpreting total test scores in psychological research and practice.

A similar approach, as that described for the representation of the effect of speededness, is frequently used to identify and control the item position effect. Troche and von Gugelberg describe the item-position effect in Chapter 11 primarily from the perspective of CFA and with a focus on reasoning tests. However, they also explain item response theoretical approaches to the item position effect, which are most frequently applied to educational achievement tests. The psychological meaning of this effect is discussed in detail. The chapter also highlights the fact that repeated test administration leads to *carryover effects* in terms of score gains. These effects should be considered whenever the same individuals are repeatedly measured with the same performance test, as test scores can change without a change in the psychological attribute to be measured, which is a challenge to the measure's validity in this context.

Birney and Morris emphasize in Chapter 12 that the degree and direction of associations between variables should be interpreted against the background of the level of data aggregation. They provide examples of distorted data interpretations due to the level of data aggregation, from psychology, education, and business. They also show how multilevel modeling can address these problems and deal with repeated within-individual observations (such as items) to make between-individual comparisons in a latent construct.

In Chapter 13, Ostermann, Anheyer, and Appelbaum focus on distorted results when psychological measures are used in specific settings and samples. For example, correlational statistics will be restricted in samples with a restricted variance in the measured attribute due to bottom or ceiling effects. These effects can result from a misfit between the psychological measure and the examined sample, a systematic decrease of variance in intervention studies, or from response biases. *Scale shrinkage*, *range restriction*, and the phenomenon of the *regression to the mean* are explained in detail to direct the reader's attention to the fact that even data obtained by "good" psychological measures can be distorted due to the study design and the samples under investigation.

Finally, Schweizer, DiStefano, and Troche (Chapter 14) highlight the history of research on the *difficulty effect*, describing conditions that may foster the presence of a difficulty factor such as the binary or dichotomous nature of data, a broad range of difficulty levels, and items with extreme difficulty levels. However, it is hard to predict the presence of a difficulty factor in empirical data, as difficulty factors seem to be unstable phenomena. They propose that a combination of *difficulty-dependent random processes* and a *booster mechanism* underlies difficulty factors. Empirical evidence and evidence from a simulation study support this proposition. Examining whether a difficulty factor is present in a given dataset may help researchers establish a sound measurement model for a given psychological measure.

Summary

Proposing, designing, testing, rejecting, and revising psychometric measurement models for psychological measures help improve our understanding of measurement and the structure of the measured attribute. In one way or the other, researchers must approach these attributes by empirical observations. In psychometrics, the deployed measures are most often responses to items in performance tests or questionnaires. The measurement models based on these items allow for investigating a latent trait as a representation of the attribute by circumventing the problem of noisy data. Method effects play a crucial role in establishing well-fitting measurement models. Their consideration can provide a better representation of the psychological attribute by the latent trait, and allows for an appropriate interpretation of the measured data, in the sense of validity against the background of the situational context of the measurement.

Measurement models also open a path to combining the latent trait with further experimental, cognitive, psychophysiological, or daily life observations. This is mandatory to learn more about the validity of the psychological measure and the psychological attribute represented by the latent trait. Method effects can distort those validity results. However, knowledge about their presence in specific contexts can help avoid or control them to arrive at a more appropriate estimation of the psychological measure's validity.

Given the large number of method effects described in the chapters of this book, it seems unlikely that any latent variable will ever be a pure representation of a psychological attribute. However, the endeavors to control for method effects described here (and for further biases elsewhere) are a promising avenue to improve psychological measurement, step by step.

References

Campbell, D. T., & Fiske, D. W. (1959). Convergent and discriminant validation by the multitrait-multimethod matrix. *Psychological Bulletin, 56*(2), 81–105. https://doi.org/10.1037/h0046016

Hölder, O. (1901). Die Axiome der Quantität und die Lehre vom Mass [The axioms of quantity and the doctrine of weight]. *Mathematisch-Physische Klasse, 53,* 1–46.

Krantz, D. H., Luce, R. D., Suppes, P., & Tversky, A. (1971). *Foundations of measurement* (Vol. I). Academic Press.

Markus, K. A., & Borsboom, D. (2013). *Frontiers of test validity theory – Measurement, Causation, and Meaning.* Routledge.

Michell, J. (1997). Quantitative science and the definition of measurement in psychology. *British Journal of Psychology, 88,* 355–383. https://doi.org/10.1111/j.2044-8295.1997.tb02641.x

Muthén, L. K., & Muthén, B. O. (1998–2023). *Mplus* [Computer software]. Muthén & Muthén. https://www.statmodel.com/

Prodsakoff, P. M., Prodsakoff, N. P., Williams, L. J., Huangshan, C., & Yang, J. (2024). Common method bias: It's bad, it's complex, it's widespread, and it's not easy to fix. *Annual Review of Organizational Psychology and Organizational Behavior, 11,* 17–61. https://doi.org/10.1146/annurev-orgpsych-110721-040030

RStudio Team. (2023). *RStudio: Integrated Development Environment for R*. Posit Software, PBC. https://posit.co/

Rubin, D. B. (1976). Inference and missing data. *Biometrika, 63*(3), 581–592. https://doi.org/10.1093/biomet/63.3.581

Stevens, S. S. (1946). On the theory of scales of measurement. *Science, 103*(2684), 677–680.

Suppes, P., & Zinnes, J. L. (1963). Basic measurement theory. In R. D. Luce, R. R. Bush & E. Galanter (Eds.), *Handbook of Mathematical Psychology* (Vol. 1, pp. 1–76). Wiley.

Tassé, M. J., Bertelli, M. O., Simon, E. W., Kates, W. R., & Navas, P. (2017). Intellectual disability (intellectual developmental disorder). In R. Fletcher, J. Barnhil, & S.-A. Cooper (Eds.), *DM-ID-2: Diagnostic manual, intellectual disability: A textbook of diagnosis of mental disorders in persons with intellectual disability* (pp. 75–90). NADD Press.

Chapter 2

Method Effects: Conceptual Considerations

Karl Schweizer, Samuel Greiff, and Stefan J. Troche

Abstract

This chapter gives an overview of different conceptualizations of *method effects*. From the measurement perspective, as the most general perspective, a method effect is conceptualized as a distortion of measurement originating from characteristics of the measure or the situational context of measurement. From the perspective of quality assurance in measurement, a method effect is considered an impairment of the measure's validity against the background of established quality standards. From the research perspective, method effects are nonaccidental anormal results such as overly large correlations, specific mean patterns, specific factors, and other parameter estimates contradicting expectations based on knowledge of the subject matter. Finally, according to the model-fit approach of *confirmatory factor analysis* (CFA), a method effect is specific common systematic variation – that is, common systematic variation associated with the assessment method instead of the to-be-measured attribute.

This chapter covers method effects in general. Like physicists, who nowadays inform us about the nature of light, alternatively conceptualizing it as either waves or particles, we describe method effects from different perspectives. The preferred perspective is that provided by CFA, which associates method effects with common systematic variation for which the method latent variable accounts (Maul, 2013; Schweizer, 2020; Sechrest et al., 2000). However, this is only one of several perspectives that have been taken or can be taken. Since other perspectives also give valuable insights into what method effects are, we make the reader aware of these as well.

General Perspective

Measurement is the general framework for discussing method effects. The basic measurement theory proposed by Suppes and Zinnes (1963) describes measurement in psychology as mapping a human attribute to a numerical scale. This description of measurement outlines measurement as a simple transfer of information from the human mind to a number that receives its meaning from the available scale. But the reality of measurement is much more complex. Based on a theoretical analysis of the demands on cognitive processing, Jensen (1987a, 1987b) listed five cognitive processes required for completing a choice reaction time task, considered an elementary task measuring cognitive speed with trials serving as items. More complex tasks, such as reasoning tasks, additionally require the detection and application of logical rules (Birney et al., 2006), while memory tasks stimulate processes accomplishing the storage of information in, and retrieval from, memory (Healey et al., 2014). Thus, completing most tasks requires many (intertwined) cognitive processes. A measurement instrument must be carefully crafted to ensure that the transferred information and, as a result, the numbers assigned according to the numerical scale, reflect the attribute of interest correctly.

Since transferring information from the human mind to the score of a scale involves complex cognitive processing, it can be easily disturbed or disrupted systematically or unsystematically. Random influences lead to impairment in an unsystematic way. The outcomes of such random influences on measurement are called *random errors* (Gulliksen, 1950; Lord & Novick, 1968). Psychological tests are composed of several indicators of the attribute to be measured, to reduce these random errors, and because psychological attributes cannot be directly observed. The sum of these indicators is expected to contain less random error (i.e., is more reliable) than each single indicator. The question of whether the indicators own a sufficient degree of equivalency regarding the attribute has led to the development of measurement models such as the *Rasch* or *Birnbaum* models in the framework of the *item response theory* (IRT), and congeneric, tau-equivalent, or parallel measurement models in the CFA framework.

In both frameworks, the attribute to be measured is represented as a *latent variable*, and the quality of the indicators can be investigated empirically. Both frameworks aim to provide an answer to the question of whether the sum scores computed from the indicators reflect the latent trait correctly. If, for example, the assumptions of the Rasch model or the parallel measurement model hold, the sum scores of the test can be interpreted as *sufficient statistics*. This means that individual differences in the sum scores can be interpreted as differences in the latent trait.

Suppose the indicators are related to each other not only due to the latent trait associated with the latent variable but also due to other systematic influences. In this case, the sum score is only a biased reflection of the latent trait. An example of such a systematic bias is social desirability (see, e.g., Prodsakoff et al., 2024) in responses to the items of a questionnaire. Socially desired responses to an item include not only self-evaluation regarding the indicator of the attribute, but also a shift toward what is socially desired. Social desirability and other adverse cognitive processing styles lead to what is referred to as *response style* (Prodsakoff et al., 2024). In other words, if the test situation promotes socially desirable responses, the responses to questionnaire items as indicators of the psychological attribute not only reflect the attribute but also the tendency to respond in a socially desirable way.

Further systematic deviations of responses to indicators from what would be expected due to the psychological attribute can be elicited by the characteristics of the measure as well as the conditions and situation of measurement. This domain is under the dominating influence of the assessment methodology, which additionally includes the assessment strategy employed by the researcher. Thus, the relationship between responses to items and the psychological attribute can be distorted due to the characteristics of the measurement instrument, as well as the conditions under which, and the situation in which, the measurement is embedded. Such distortions are usually referred to as method effects.

If the historical development of the assessment methodology of measurement is perceived as an evolutionary process, method effects are a driving force in the direction of high-quality measurement. Researchers are expected to always employ the most advanced methodology to investigate research questions. However, new insights and improved methodology may already have called the employed methodology into question.

For example, when Campbell and Fiske (1959) published their seminal paper on *multitrait-multimethod* (MTMM) analyses of test scores, estimating validity by computing correlations was still an up-to-date approach. Their work revealed that correlations between measures of attributes using the same technique (e.g., self-reports) overestimated the true relationships. Since then, the CFA approach has replaced the correlational approach to MTMM analyses (Ziegler & Horstmann, Chapter 3: "MTMM Construct Validity Using SEM," this present work). Nevertheless, both approaches point to the discrepancy between (relations between) measures and (relations between) psychological attributes due to the employed measurement instruments as examples of method effects.

Therefore, taking the perspective of measurement, we can characterize method effects as distortions of the measurement of attributes, originating from characteristics of the measure used in the assessment and/or the situational context.

Quality Assurance Perspective

An essential step in the development of approaches to avoiding the problem of method effects has been the establishment of the concept of *validity*. Validity is interpreted as either "truth, accuracy, fact, or law" (American Psychological Association, 2018), or "the degree to which empirical evidence and theoretical rationales support the adequacy and appropriateness of conclusions drawn from some form of assessment" (American Psychological Association, 2018).

The second interpretation best applies to the psychology of latent constructs. It highlights the role of empirical evidence and implicitly the dangers that arise due to method effects, including impairment of the quality of empirical evidence. The older and more basic characterization of validity is that the scale measures "what it is supposed to measure" (Vogt, 2005, p. 301). This characterization states a relationship between the intended use of a scale and the performance of this scale in the context in which it is employed. A method effect can, in other words, be perceived as a disturbance of this relationship.

Various approaches focusing specific aspects of validity (convergent validity, discriminant validity, criterion validity, predictive validity, etc.) are available to check whether psychological measures and their use meet the validity requirements; these include methods, rules, and limits established by the scientific community. We refer to these as standards. These standards are described in textbooks and recommendations of assessment organizations, and are also discussed in research papers. New scales must undergo a validity check before being published and made available (International Test Commission, 2001; American Educational Research Association et al., 2014). These standards are crucial for avoiding known method effects. In this context, method effects can be understood as a disregard or violation of established standards, or insufficiency and lack of standards, regarding standards that could otherwise be selected as the basis of an assessment methodology.

Measurement models postulate relationships between the indicators (i.e., items) and the latent trait. When investigated in the framework of factor analyses, a positive outcome can establish factorial validity. Finding out whether another measure assesses the same psychological attribute requires combining the corresponding measurement models. The estimate of the correlation between the two measures is an indication of convergent validity. Concurrently, the latent trait must not represent something else not intended to be measured. If these conditions are met, discriminant validity is established. It is to the credit of the MTMM approach that today psychometricians and researchers are well aware of the possible distortion in convergent and discriminant validity caused by using similar measurement techniques.

Criterion validity is another aspect of validity and refers to the relationship between test results and external scores, such as academic or job performance, or the presence or absence of a specific disease. It is often argued that method effects reduce or obscure the relationship between the latent trait and the criterion. However, in some cases, method effects have been reported to increase this relationship, and thus the criterion validity of the instrument (Ren et al., 2015).

In sum, from the perspective of quality assurance in measurement that is organized under the auspices of validity, a method effect is an impairment of the quality of measurement, which is associated with the measure or the situational context, and is something that needs to be prevented by establishing appropriate quality standards.

Method Effect Research

While substantive psychological science aims to increase our knowledge regarding humans' abilities, emotions, and personalities, reaching this aim can be hampered by method effects. Such effects can become apparent as observed anomalies, such as overly large correlations, specific mean patterns, or factors without a rational explanation but which are related to a characteristic of the measure or the situational context. Such observations contradict available knowledge on the subject matter. The repeated observation of such anomalies is likely to lead purposeful method effect research – that is, systematic investigations expected to yield a detailed description of the anomaly, a reason for the deviation from expectation that can also be a new insight, and suggestions of provisions for avoiding it. For example, Guilford (1941) reported (probably) the first observation of a *difficulty factor*. This observation triggered numerous studies and commentaries regarding this method effect during the following decades. At the end of the century, there was still research being undertaken on *overfactoring* (e.g., Clark & Bowles, 2018; Revuelta et al., 2022), that is, the characterization of a difficulty factor as a spurious factor (McDonald & Ahlawat, 1974 ; see also Chapter 14 in this work).

Research on method effects cannot be discussed without resorting to the already mentioned MTMM approach because of its tremendous influence on the methodological developments in this area (see Chapter 3). The MTMM design of Campbell and Fiske (1959) allowed for distinguishing different types of correlations, such as correlations indicative of convergent and discriminant validity and reliability correlations. The major advantage of this design was the possibility of demonstrating in a systematic way that validity correlations surmounted method correlations.

However, conclusions based on information provided by this design required a larger number of comparisons between different types of correlations, since a comprehensive or overall test was not available. This changed when researchers started investigating the MTMM matrix by CFA (Kenny, 1976; Widaman, 1985), which took method effect research to a new level. First, it was no longer necessary to arrive at a conclusion regarding validity in a piecemeal way, because a comprehensive evaluation of a model became possible. Second, it became possible to design models according to specific assumptions, such as whether constructs and observational methods were correlated or uncorrelated. In the meantime, several specific MTMM models have become available to check for the presence of method effects (Kyriazos, 2018; see also Ziegler & Horstmann, Chapter 3: "MTMM Construct Validity Using SEM," in this present work). A typical research strategy includes the comparison of several models and a search for the best-fitting model.

Another vital avenue to investigating method effects is the IRT approach. In this framework, it is investigated whether method effects systematically influence the probability of a correct response or the endorsement of the statement of a test item. This can be examined by modeling the method effect as an influence on the *difficulty parameter* (e.g., Kubinger, 2008b) or less frequently on the *discrimination* or *slope parameter* (e.g., Nagy et al., 2018).

Alternatively, the method effect can be modeled as a *person parameter* (e.g., Embretson, 1991). Many studies have demonstrated an item position effect by IRT models (e.g., Debeer & Janssen, 2013; Embretson, 1991; Hartig & Buchholz, 2012; Kubinger, 2008a; Lozano & Revuelta, 2020; Verguts & De Boeck, 2000; see also Troche & von Gugelberg, Chapter 11: "Carryover and Item Position Effects," in this present work), while others examined *rapid guessing* (Nagy et al., 2023) or the effect of *speededness* (Bolt et al., 2002, see also Schweizer, Ren, & Wang, Chapter 10, "The Effect of Speededness" in this present work).

Additional IRT applications to identify and control for method effects can be found in the following chapters in this present work, regarding the examination of unidimensionality and differential item functioning (Debelak & Strobl, Chapter 4: "Violations of Unidimensionality and Differential Item Functioning"), the influence of item response format and response style (Hernandez et al., Chapter 7: "Item Response Format and Response Styles"), or the handling of missing values (Rose, Chapter 9: "Missing Data: How to Handle Incomplete Data").

Finally, multilevel modeling has been used to investigate method effects. Birney and Morris in Chapter 12: "Ecological Falacy and Multilevel Modeling" (this present work) provide an example for analyzing the Robinson effect. Additionally, the item position effect has been studied using multilevel modeling (Birney & Beckmann, 2022; Hartig & Buchholz, 2012).

In sum, from the perspective of method effects research, method effects are overly large correlations between test scores and/or items, specific mean patterns, method latent variables, and specific influences on parameter estimates that are not in line with knowledge about the subject matter and are associated with measurement instruments or situational characteristics.

Method Effects as Common Systematic Variation

Finally, there is the perspective that focuses on common systematic variation that is part of the model-implied covariance matrix and is basic to CFA. Although it may be perceived as part of CFA and as belonging to the method effect research perspective, we prefer to treat it as a unique outgrowth, since it combines attribute and method effect in one measurement model, and enables determining and comparing how much attribute and method effects contribute to the individual differences in the observed data. In this case, the formal foundation counts, and therefore needs to be discussed in some detail.

The starting point is provided by the CFA measurement model that is a linear one-factor congeneric measurement model (Brown, 2015; Graham, 2006; Jöreskog, 1971). It is defined as

$$\mathbf{X}=\boldsymbol{\mu}+\boldsymbol{\lambda}\xi+\boldsymbol{\delta}, \quad (1)$$

where $\mathbf{X}$ represents the $p \times 1$ vector of manifest variables, $\boldsymbol{\mu}$ is the $p \times 1$ vector of intercepts referred to as easiness, $\boldsymbol{\lambda}_{attribute}$ is the $p \times 1$ vector of factor loadings, ξ is the latent variable, and $\boldsymbol{\delta}$ is the $p \times 1$ vector of residuals. This model considers the attribute as the only source of systematic variation. A method effect, as another type of systematic variation, cannot be represented by this model. Thus, the presence of a method effect probably indicates a model misfit.

The adaptation of CFA to the MTMM design (Byrne, 2016) or the implementation of CFA as a bifactor model considering a specific method effect beside the attribute, necessitates the representation of a method effect in the measurement model. Since a method effect is assumed to be unrelated to the construct to be measured, it is treated as an independent component. (Please note that our reasoning here focuses on combining one attribute and one method effect, while a complete MTMM model requires the consideration of several attributes and several methods.)

To consider the method effect within the measurement model, a transformation of the one-factor measurement model into a two-factor measurement model is necessary. The transformed measurement model includes one latent variable for representing the attribute (see subscript attribute) and another latent variable for representing the method effect (see subscript method_effect):

$$\mathbf{X}=\boldsymbol{\mu}+\boldsymbol{\lambda}_{attribute}\xi_{attribute}+\boldsymbol{\lambda}_{method\_effect}\xi_{method\_effect}+\boldsymbol{\delta}, \tag{2}$$

where $\mathbf{X}$ represents the $p \times 1$ vector of manifest variables, $\boldsymbol{\mu}$ is the $p \times 1$ vector of intercepts referred to as easiness, $\boldsymbol{\lambda}_{attribute}$ is the $p \times 1$ vector of factor loadings regarding the attribute, $\xi_{attribute}$ is the attribute latent variable, $\boldsymbol{\lambda}_{method\_effect}$ is the $p \times 1$ vector of factor loadings regarding the method effect, ξ_{method_effect} is the method effect latent variable, and $\boldsymbol{\delta}$ is the $p \times 1$ vector of residuals.

If the factors are group factors, it is necessary to realize the model as a bifactor model (Jimènez et al., 2023; Reise, 2012). In this case, one latent variable, usually the latent variable representing the attribute, is specified as the main latent variable and the other as a specific latent variable, where at least one factor loading is fixed. This design also allows for employing the tau-equivalent model or variants of this model to represent the attribute latent variable (Lord & Novick, 1968; Alwin & Jackson, 1980) and facilitates the theory-guided decomposition of the common systematic variation of data. Fixing the correlation parameter to zero can enforce the separation of the latent variables and prevent possible adverse effects on factor variances or factor loadings (Schweizer et al., 2024).

Explaining the separation of effects requires the introduction of the concept of a *model-implied covariance matrix*. Here, we start again with the one-factor model of CFA as is conceptualized according to the model-fit approach (Jöreskog, 1970; Gumedze & Dunne, 2011). This model distinguishes between different types of systematic variation and includes the comparison of the model-implied covariance matrix with the empirical covariance matrix using fit indices. The model of the covariance matrix consists of a specific structure that reflects the measurement model. Regarding the one-factor model, this structure is given by $\boldsymbol{\Sigma}=\boldsymbol{\lambda}\phi\boldsymbol{\lambda}'+\boldsymbol{\Theta}$, where $\boldsymbol{\Sigma}$ is the $p \times p$ model-implied covariance matrix, $\boldsymbol{\lambda}$ is the $p \times 1$ vector of factor loadings, ϕ is the variance parameter, and $\boldsymbol{\Theta}$ is the $p \times p$ diagonal matrix of residual variances. Since the intercept is a constant (i.e., it does not vary), it is not considered in this model. This model only distinguishes between common systematic variation ($\boldsymbol{\lambda}\phi\boldsymbol{\lambda}'$) and unique systematic variation ($\boldsymbol{\Theta}$). The latent variable accounts for the common systematic variation in this model.

Suppose there are two latent variables – for example, the attribute latent variable and the method effect latent variable (and there is no correlation among them). In that case, each is expected to account for its own share of the common systematic variation. Adapting the model-implied covariance matrix to this situation gives $\mathbf{\Sigma}=\mathbf{\Lambda\Phi\Lambda}'+\mathbf{\theta}$, where $\mathbf{\Lambda}$ is the $p \times 2$ matrix of factor loadings (with one column for the attribute and one column for the method effect latent variable), $\mathbf{\Phi}$ is the 2×2 matrix of variances and covariances of the two latent variables, and $\mathbf{\theta}$ includes the unique systematic variation of the manifest variables.

If an investigation yields a good model fit for this model, and the factor loadings or the corresponding variance parameters are substantial, the assumed presence of common systematic variation due to a method effect is confirmed. This model can be used to investigate, for example, the wording effect (see DiStefano et al., Chapter 8: "Using Negatively Phrased Items in Surveys," in this present work) and the item position effect (Troche & von Gugelberg, Chapter 11: "Carryover and Item Position Effects," in this present work). In these examples, the factor loadings for the respective method effect are fixed according to theoretical considerations. As mentioned above, for the representation of the item position effect, the factor loading on the method effect latent variable are fixed to increase monotonically (e.g., linearly or quadratically). Finally, for the specification of the wording effect, the factor loadings on the positively phrased items are fixed to zero. In contrast, the factor loading on the negatively phrased items are freely estimated.

In this approach, method effects are perceived as common systematic variation explained by the method effect latent variable but not by the attribute latent variable. Several recent discussions have conceptualized method effects this way (Maul, 2013; Schweizer, 2020; Sechrest et al., 2000). A method effect defined in this way can be quantified in the same way as the attribute latent variable. Thus, the strength of the method effect can be estimated when the variances of the attribute and the method effect latent variables are scaled appropriately and related to each other (Schweizer et al., 2019; Schweizer & Troche, 2019). Before closing this section, a disadvantage of this perspective needs to be mentioned: It only applies to research in the framework of CFA.

In sum, taking the perspective of the model-fit approach of CFA, method effects are the common systematic variation for which the method, but not the attribute latent variable of the CFA measurement model, accounts.

Concerns With Method Effects Research Over Time

As outlined in the various examples throughout this chapter and as evidenced by the contributions in this book, the question of how different method effects systematically impact measurements and, as a direct consequence, the conclusions drawn from them, remains an important topic in the field of psychological assessment. Many details of how method effects specifically impact test scores collected in a specific context are not yet fully understood and require further investigation – for instance, on specific circumstances and conditions or individual differences on when and how method effects (substantially) impact scores that are derived from testing. As measurement theory becomes increasingly advanced and as areas of application and standards become more widespread, one would expect that the scholarly community would have given more attention to the question of method effects over the last years, from both an applied and a theoretical angle. However, literature search with "method effects" as the keyword in the period from 1959 to 2024 reveals no such pattern: The overall number of articles is low throughout that time, and there is no upward trend in the level of attention (as indicated by the number of publications) that has been paid to this topic. This is an unexpected and somewhat worrying finding. Therefore, it is all the more important to build on the existing research and the various relevant method effects as they are presented throughout this book. At the same time, rigorous methodological research is needed to better understand how method effects impact our measurement across virtually all settings.

Discussion

This chapter describes four perspectives on method effects. The general perspective presents method effects as a distortion of measurement; the quality assurance perspective, as an impairment of the quality of measurement; the method effect research perspective, as deviations from expectations based on knowledge of the subject matter; and the perspective of the model-fit approach of CFA, as common systematic variation that is unrelated to the attribute. What these perspectives have in common is that they associate a method effect with a nonaccidental imperfect outcome of measurement. It is an unintended effect that, in contrast to unsystematic random influences, does not disappear in the measurement process due to averaging out. It can be perceived as due to an assessment methodology that does not follow appropriate validity standards. Besides these commonalities, method effects are highly specific since they reflect characteristics of specific measurement situations. Given the flourishing developments in the assessment field, we hope that method research regarding method effect will also flourish further to improve the measurement models of the attributes to be measured and the estimates of validity used to interpret test scores (or, more generally, test results) in psychological research and practice.

References

Alwin, D. F., & Jackson, D. J. (1980). Measurement models for response errors in surveys: Issues and applications. In K. F. Schuessler (Ed.), *Sociological methodology* (pp. 69–119). Jossey-Bass. https://doi.org/10.2307/270860

American Educational Research Association, American Psychological Association, & National Council on Measurement in Education. (2014). *Standards for educational and psychological testing.*

American Psychological Association. (2018). *APA dictionary of psychology.* APA. https://dictionary.apa.org

Birney, D. P., & Beckmann, J. F. (2022). Intelligence is cognitive flexibility: Why multilevel models of within-individual processes are needed to realize this. *Journal of Intelligence, 10,* 49. https://doi.org/10.3390/jintelligence10030049

Birney, D. P., Halford, G. S., & Andrews, G. (2006). Measuring the influence of complexity on relational reasoning: The development of the Latin square task. *Educational and Psychological Measurement, 66*(1), 146–171. https://doi.org/10.1177/0013164405278570

Bolt, D. M., Cohen, A. S., & Wollack, J. A. (2002). Item parameter estimation under conditions of test speededness: Application of a mixture Rasch model with ordinal constraints. *Journal of Educational Measurement, 39*(4), 331–348. https://doi.org/10.1111/j.1745-3984.2002.tb01146.x

Brown, T. A. (2015). *Confirmatory factor analysis for applied research* (2nd ed.). Guilford Press.

Byrne, B. M. (2016). Using multitrait-multimethod analysis in testing for evidence of construct validity. In K. Schweizer & C. DiStefano (Eds.), *Principles and methods of test construction* (pp. 288–307). Hogrefe.

Campbell, D. T., & Fiske, D. (1959). Convergent and discriminant validation by the multitrait-multimethod matrix. *Psychological Bulletin, 56*, 81–105. https://doi.org/10.1037/h0046016

Clark, D. A., & Bowles, R. P. (2018). Model fit and item factor analysis: overfactoring, underfactoring, and a program to guide interpretation. *Multivariate Behavioral Research, 53*(4), 544–558. https://doi.org/10.1080/00273171.2018.1461058

Debeer, D., & Janssen, R. (2013). Modeling item-position effects within an IRT framework. *Journal of Educational Measurement, 50*(2), 164–185. https://doi.org/10.1111/jedm.12009

Embretson, S. E. (1991). A multidimensional latent trait model for measuring learning and change. *Psychometrika, 56*, 495–515. https://doi.org/10.1007/BF02294487

Graham, J. M. (2006). Congeneric and (essentially) tau-equivalent estimates of score reliability. *Educational and Psychological Measurement, 66*(6), 930–944. https://doi.org/10.1177/0013164406288165

Guilford, J. P. (1941). The difficulty of a test and its factor composition. *Psychometrika, 6*(2), 67–77. https://doi.org/10.1007/BF02292175

Gulliksen, H. (1950). *Theory of mental tests.* Wiley. https://doi.org/10.1037/13240-000

Gumedze, F. N., & Dunne, T. T. (2011). Parameter estimation and inference in the linear mixed model. *Linear Algebra and Its Application, 435*(8), 1920–1944. https://doi.org/10.1016/j.laa.2011.04.015

Hartig, J., & Buchholz, J. (2012). A multilevel item response model for item position effects and individual persistence. *Psychological Test and Assessment Modelling, 54*, 418–431.

Healey, M. K., Crutchley, P., & Kahana, M. J. (2014). Individual differences in memory search and their relation to intelligence. *Journal of Experimental Psychology: General, 143*(4) 1553–1569. https://doi.org/10.1037/a0036306

International Test Commission. (2001). International guidelines on test use. *International Journal of Testing, 1*(2), 95–114.

Jensen, A. R. (1987a). Process differences and individual differences in some cognitive tasks. *Intelligence, 11*, 107–136. https://doi.org/10.1016/0160-2896(87)90001-8

Jensen, A. R. (1987b). Individual differences in the Hick paradigm. In P. A. Vernon (Ed.), *Speed of information processing and intelligence* (pp. 101–176). Ablex.

Jimènez, M., Abad, F. J., Garzia-Garzon, E., & Garrido, L. E. (2023). Exploratory bi-factor analysis with multiple general factors. *Multivariate Behavioral Research, 58*(6), 1072–1089. https://doi.org/10.1080/00273171.2023.2189571

Jöreskog, K. G. (1970). A general method for analysis of covariance structure. *Biometrika, 57*(2), 239–251. https://doi.org/10.1093/biomet/57.2.239

Jöreskog, K. G. (1971). Statistical analysis of sets of congeneric tests. *Psychometrika, 36*, 109–133. https://doi.org/10.1007/BF02291393

Kenny, D. A. (1976). An empirical application of confirmatory factor analysis to the multitrait-multimethod matrix. *Journal of Experimental Social Psychology, 12*, 247–252. https://doi.org/10.1016/0022-1031(76)90055-X

Kubinger, K. D. (2008a). On the revival of the Rasch model-based LLTM: From constructing tests using item generating rules to measuring item administration effects. *Psychology Science Quarterly, 50*, 311–327.

Kubinger, K. D. (2008b). Applications of the linear logistic test model in psychometric research. *Educational and Psychological Measurement, 69*(2), 232–246. https://doi.org/10.1177/0013164408322021

Kyriazos, T. A. (2018). Applied psychometrics: The application of CFA to multitrait-multimethod matrices (CFA-MTMM). *Psychology, 9*(12), 2625–2648. https://doi.org/10.4236/psych.2018.912150

Lord, F. M. & Novick, M. R. (1968). *Statistical theories of mental test scores.* Addison-Wesley.

Lozano, J. H., & Revuelta, J. (2020). Investigating operation-specific learning effects in the Raven's Advanced Progressive Matrices: A linear logistic test modeling approach. *Intelligence, 82*, 101468. https://doi.org/10.1016/j.intell.2020.101468

Maul, A. (2013). Method effects and the meaning of measurement. *Frontiers in Psychology, 4*, Article 169. http://doi.org/10.3389/fpsyg.2013.00169 https://doi.org/10.3389/fpsyg.2013.00169

McDonald, R. P., & Ahlawat, K. S. (1974). Difficulty factors in binary data. *British Journal of Mathematical and Statistical Psychology, 27*(1), 82–99. https://doi.org/10.1111/j.2044-8317.1974.tb00530.x

Nagy, G., Nagengast, B., Becker, M., Rose, N., & Frey, A. (2018). Item position effects in a reading comprehension test: An IRT study of individual differences and individual correlates. *Psychological Test and Assessment Modeling, 60*(2), 165–187.

Nagy, G., Ulitzsch, E., & Lindner, M. A. (2023). The role of rapid guessing and test-taking persistence in modelling test-taking engagement. *Journal of Computer Assisted Learning, 39*(3), 751–766. https://doi.org/10.1111/jcal.12719

Prodsakoff, P. M., Prodsakoff, N. P., Williams, L. J., Huangshan, C., & Yang, J. (2024). Common method bias: it's bad, it's complex, it's widespread, and it's not easy to fix. *Annual Review of Organizational Psychology and Organizational Behavior, 11,* 17–61. https://doi.org/10.1146/annurev-orgpsyh-110721-040030

Reise, S. P. (2012). The rediscovery of bifactor measurement models. *Multivariate Behavioral Research, 47*(5), 667–696. https://doi.org/10.1080/00273171.2012.715555

Ren, X., Schweizer, K., Wang, T., & Xu, F. (2015). The prediction of students' academic performance with fluid intelligence in giving special consideration to the contribution of learning. *Advances in Cognitive Psychology, 11*(3), 97. https://doi.org/10.5709/acp-0175-z

Revuelta, J., Ximenez, C., & Minaya, N. (2022). Overfactoring in rating scale data: A comparison between factor analysis and item response theory. *Frontiers in Psychology, 13,* Article 982137. https://doi.org/10.3389/fpsyg.2022.982137

Schweizer, K. (2020). Method effects in psychological assessment. *Psychological Test and Assessment Modeling, 62*(3), 337–343.

Schweizer, K., Ren, X., Wang, T. (2024). Negativity of factor correlations biases the sizes of factor variances in bifactor CFA models. *Frontiers in Applied Mathematics and Statistics, 10,* Article 1423726. https://doi.org/10.3389/fams.2024.1423726

Schweizer, K., & Troche, S. (2019). The EV scaling method for variances of latent variables. *Methodology, 15*(4), 175–184. https://doi.org/10.1027/1614-2241/a000179

Schweizer, K., Troche, S., & DiStefano, C. (2019). Scaling the variance of a latent variable while assuring constancy of the model. *Frontiers in Psychology: Section Quantitative Psychology and Measurement, 10,* Article 887. https://doi.org/10.3389/fpsyg.2019.00887

Sechrest, L., Davis, M. F., Stickle, T. R., & McKnight, P. E. (2000). Understanding method variance. In L. Bickman (Ed.), *Research design: Donald Campbell's legacy* (pp. 63–87). Sage.

Suppes, P., & Zinnes, J. L. (1963). Basic measurement theory. In R. D. Luce, R. R. Bush, & E. H. Galanter (Eds.), *Handbook of mathematical psychology* (pp. 1–76). Wiley.

Verguts, T., & De Boeck, P. (2000). A Rasch model for detecting learning while solving an intelligence test. *Applied Psychological Measurement, 24,* 151–162. https://doi.org/10.1177/01466210022031589

Vogt, W. P. (2005). *The Sage dictionary of statistics and methodology: A non-technical guide for the social sciences* (3rd ed.). Sage.

Widaman, K. F. (1985). Hierarchically nested covariance structure models for multitrait-multimethod data. *Applied Psychological Measurement, 9,* 1–26. https://doi.org/10.1177/014662168500900101

Chapter 3

MTMM Construct Validity Using SEM

Matthias Ziegler and Kai T. Horstmann

Abstract

This chapter discusses the importance of construct validity in psychological measurement, specifically addressing traditional approaches to modeling the method effect in *multitrait-multimethod* (MTMM) data. It emphasizes the significance of the nomological net in setting up and interpreting such models. The chapter explores how method variance can impact measurement and presents statistical approaches to model method effects, starting with the traditional MTMM matrix and advancing to more recent techniques based on *structural equation modeling* (SEM). Through this, it provides a comprehensive guide to understanding and modeling method effects in psychological assessments.

Introduction

Psychologists strive to describe, explain, predict, and change human characteristics such as personality, intelligence, attitudes, motives, and interests. All of this requires measuring these characteristics at some point. Such measurement of human characteristics is a problem in and of itself, which has been discussed at large (for a critical stance, see Michell, 2001, 2014). Yet, the seminal definition by Stevens (1946), which builds on earlier work by the physicist N. R. Campbell (e.g., Campbell, 1928; Campbell & Jeffreys, 1938), prevails: "We may say that measurement, in the broadest sense, is defined as the assignment of numerals to objects or events according to rules" (Stevens, 1946, p. 677). A sometimes-overlooked emphasis in this definition is the accordance to rules. When looking closely, there are numerous rules to adhere to. One example, most social scientists are aware of, are the scales of measurement (i.e., nominal, ordinal, interval, or ratio). These rules define how differences between measured scores can be interpreted and how the scores can be transformed. Yet, a different emphasis can be seen in how the scores that are formed by assigning numbers to observations (e.g., referring to a response on a rating scale as 1, 2, or 3) actually reflect the ideas embedded in theories about the characteristics measured. In particular, theories define the characteristic (or latent construct) to be measured, how this characteristic relates to other constructs, and to observable variables, which are most often the items of a test as approximations of the actual behavior. This network of rules is called the *nomological net* (Cronbach & Meehl, 1955).

In test construction, a defined nomological net enables the identification of items that reflect the construct in question, thereby ensuring content validity. The nomological net also defines potential hierarchical or facetted structures and thereby enables the testing of structural or factorial validity. The defined relations with other constructs enable the testing of construct validity in the sense of convergent and discriminant validity evidence. Finally, a nomological net also contains rules regarding potential antecedents (e.g., sex differences, access to resources, or peer influence) or outcomes (e.g., scholastic success) of a construct. This allows us to derive hypotheses regarding test criterion correlations (Ziegler, 2014).

Thus, a nomological net is a set of rules which directly provides guidelines on the information needed to gather or estimate evidence for different kinds of validity (see Figure 3.1). At the core of this are the rules defining relations between the latent construct in question and observable variables, such as the items on a test. As such, the nomological net not only defines the theoretical structure of a construct but can also be seen as a roadmap for how to construct a measure and provide evidence for the validity of the interpretation for the score(s) derived from the measure.

It was recognized very early that studies on construct validity based on rules derived from theories about the constructs are actually also tests for these theories (e.g., Loevinger, 1957). For example, a theory may state that extraverts like to party, are dominant, and often experience positive affect. If three items ("I like to party," "I am dominant," and "I am happy") load on the same factor, this constitutes an initial but crucial test for the theory. Thus, it is important to keep in mind that lacking evidence for construct validity might not always reflect a failed test construction but could also imply necessary changes in one's theory (Cronbach & Meehl, 1955).

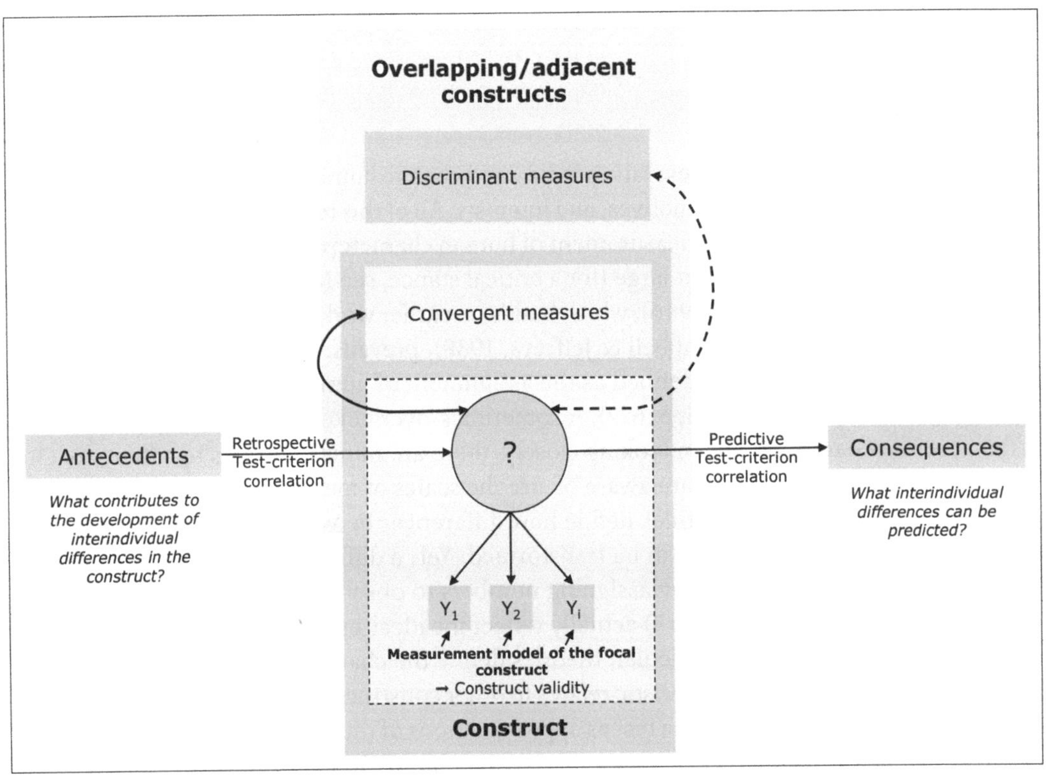

Figure 3.1 Nomological net. Y = observed variable as indicator of latent construct. i = indicator i. ? = latent construct to be measured.

Based on this, many ideas on how to provide evidence for validity have been developed, and practical guidance has been provided in numerous papers over the past decades (e.g., Condon et al., 2020; Elson et al., 2023; Schweizer, 2010, 2012; Ziegler, 2014). Utilizing these ideas and techniques, social scientists have come up with a well-equipped toolbox readily available to construct or evaluate all kinds of measurements: psychometric questionnaires and performance tests, interviews, behavior observation, psychophysiological measures, etc. While this is a cornerstone of modern psychometrics, the range of measures also raises the question of whether it matters which method the researcher applies to measure a specific construct. In other words, does it matter whether a certain personality trait (e.g., extraversion) is measured with questionnaire A or B, or as a self-rating or an other-rating, or by behavior observation or interview, or...? Thus, it seems reasonable to assume that a specific measure does not only pick up the intended differences in the measured trait but might also entail variance due to the method itself, so-called *method variance*. Campbell and Fiske (1959) laid out the problem in detail and have been cited thousands of times by test authors until today to justify the use of a MTMM approach to provide evidence for construct validity and gauge the impact of method effects. This chapter will first provide definitions for the theoretical concepts involved and then take a closer look at how method variance can be defined. The ensuing sections will explain different statistical approaches to modeling method variance, starting with the classic MTMM approach and then introducing more recent approaches based on structural equation modeling.

Defining Construct Validity

As just laid out, the concept of validity is of great importance in the social sciences, as it provides support for interpreting the result of a measurement as reflecting a certain construct. However, there is no such thing as *the* validity, which is exemplified in the following definition:

> Validity refers to the degree to which (empirical) evidence and theory support the interpretation(s) of test scores for the intended uses of those or the degree to which empirical evidence and theory support the interpretation of results derived from experiments. (Ziegler & Lämmle, 2017, p. 1)

For the present chapter, the first part of the definition is of importance, as it refers to the validity of test score interpretations. The definition emphasizes that validity means to provide empirical evidence supporting the intended uses for test score interpretations. In a more general sense, it could be said that providing validity evidence means to provide empirical support for the rules laid out in a nomological net. From a measurement perspective, the foremost intended use certainly is the interpretation of a test score as a reflection of a latent construct. Consequently, validity evidence should show that data obtained with a measure follow the assumed theoretical structure and that scores relate to other constructs as defined. In accordance with this, different kinds of validity have been proposed, each providing evidence for a specific kind of use (for a recent perspective, see American Educational Research Association, 2014; for an early perspective, see Loevinger, 1957). The most widely known kinds of validity are probably *test-criterion validity* or *criterion validity* (i.e., how well does a score correlate with outcomes that the theoretical construct that was intended to be measured should predict?) and *construct validity*. These two kinds of validity directly embody the idea of the intended uses of a test score – that is, to reflect a construct and predict behavior. In this chapter, we will have a closer look at construct validity, which has been defined as:

> The purpose of construct validation is to evaluate whether scores on a set of items build a suitable indicator for the intended construct (also known as factorial or structural validity), and whether the associations between the test score and other variables follow a theoretically expected pattern (also known as convergent and discriminant validity). To this end, the systematic testing of a-priori hypotheses regarding the relation between construct and indicators or test scores and other variables provides evidence supporting the test score interpretation. (Wehner et al., 2018, p. 1)

From this definition it becomes evident that construct validity evidence can entail three different kinds of validity: structural and/or factorial validity, as well as convergent, and discriminant validity. While factorial validity evidence supports the theoretically assumed dimensionality or hierarchical structure of data obtained with a test (i.e., the relation between a latent variable and its indicators), construct validity focuses more directly on the relations between (latent) variables in the nomological net. In this chapter we will address both aspects.

Convergent and Discriminant Validity – MTMM Approach

When providing definitions for convergent and discriminant validity as two main constituents of construct validity, the seminal paper by Campbell and Fiske (1959) must be mentioned, in which the theoretical ideas behind convergent and discriminant validity were laid out. Importantly, they noted that each test or item is a *trait-method unit*. Thus, they basically extended classical test theory by stating that an observed score Y on indicator *i*, operationalizing construct *j*, using method *k* is not only the true score plus (random) error E but actually the true score plus method impact plus (random) error:

$$Y_{ijk} = T_{ijk} + M_{ijk} + E_{ijk}. \qquad (1)$$

As discussed above, a construct can be operationalized in different ways (e.g., self- or other-rating, questionnaire, interview, or observation). Yet, to interpret scores obtained using different methods as reflecting the same latent construct, those scores are still expected to be correlated. This idea is captured in the concept of convergent validity: "Convergent validity relates to evidence whether a test score is related to test scores of the same construct ..., which were assessed with another method" (Wehner et al., 2018, p. 2).

But how large should a convergent validity be? Campbell and Fiske (1959) suggested a sequential testing process which starts with convergent validity. The simple rule here was that a convergent validity should be significant and "sufficiently large to encourage further validation" (p. 82). Clearly, this alone would not suffice, which is why construct validity evidence typically requires to consider discriminant validity evidence at the same time. Discriminant validity is defined as: "... the extent to which a test score is related to a test score capturing a distinct construct, which was assessed with the same or another method." (Wehner et al., 2018, p. 2; NB: The APA Standards (American Educational Research Association et al., 2014) and other guidelines suggest a more lenient definition, by defining convergent validity as the relation between measures for the same or similar constructs (see Ziegler, 2020, for an explanation of why it might be more prudent to stick to the less lenient definition by Campbell & Fiske, 1959).

Importantly, and as highlighted in Figure 3.1, discriminant validity should be obtained using tests that operationalize overlapping or adjacent constructs. For example, to provide evidence supporting the interpretation of a test score as verbal reasoning, convergent measures should also capture verbal reasoning, and discriminant measures could operationalize abilities close by, such as working memory or figural reasoning (for a more in depth example, see Ziegler, 2020). This shows that it is often ill-advised to expect a discriminant validity to be zero; instead, the discriminant validity estimates should be close to what is expected from theory or known from meta-analyses. Again, Campbell and Fiske (1959) provided a reasonable rule, stating that discriminant validities should be lower than convergent validities. Of importance for the scope of this book, Campbell and Fiske's approach was also designed to ascertain the influence of method variance. Following Equation 1, two observed scores can correlate because they share variance due to the same latent trait *j*, but also because of sharing method variance. To gauge evidence for construct validity, Campbell and Fiske advised that regardless of the method used to measure the traits:

> A third common-sense desideratum is that a variable correlate higher with an independent effort [i.e., method] to measure the same trait than with measures designed to get at different traits which happen to employ the same method. ... A fourth desideratum is that the same pattern of trait interrelationship be shown. (Campbell & Fiske, 1959, p. 83; comment added by chapter authors)

To better explain these and the preceding ideas, it helps a lot to make use of the method suggested by Campbell and Fiske (1959) for just this purpose: using the MTMM matrix. A schematic depiction of this is provided in Figure 3.2, which basically contains a correlation table. Importantly, the correlations allow testing of the ideas just mentioned. Three different traits were measured (e.g., neuroticism, extraversion, and conscientiousness). Each trait was

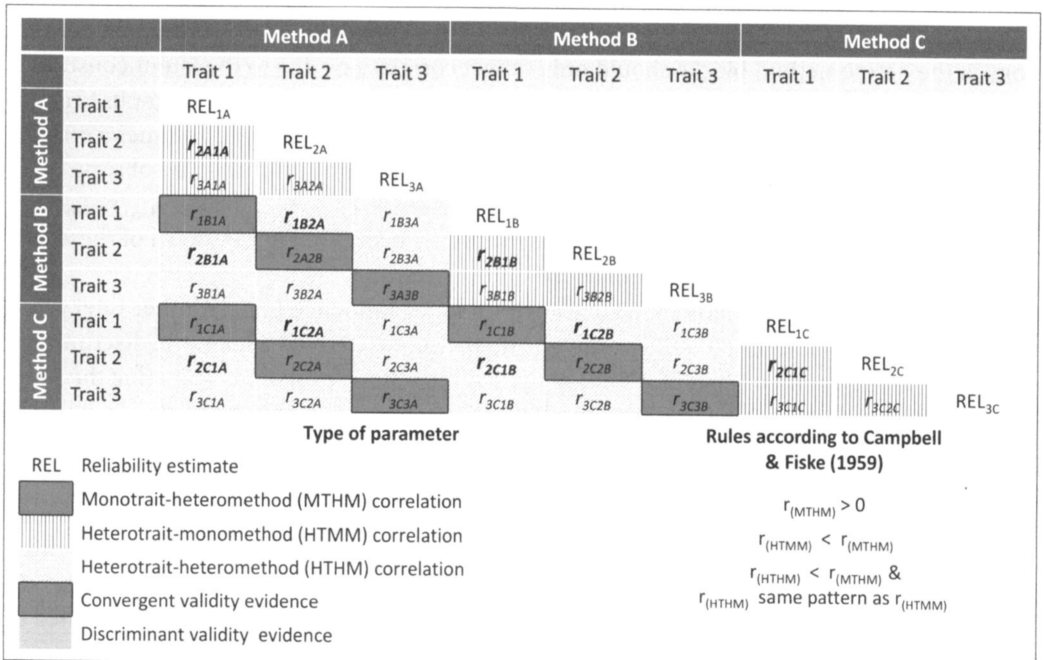

Figure 3.2 Multitrait-multimethod (MTMM) matrix; *r* = correlation coefficient. Patterned cells contain discriminant validity evidence; fully grayed cells indicate convergent validity evidence.

operationalized with one of the three methods A, B, and C (e.g., self-, friend, and parent ratings of a set of items; or self-ratings derived with questionnaires from three different test families; or self-ratings, behavior observations, and interview ratings). The MTMM matrix contains the reliability estimate for each score in the diagonal. We will come back to these later.

The rest of the matrix can be compartmentalized into three different sets of correlations. A first categorization can be made with regard to the method. There are correlations between scores obtained from the same method (monomethod blocks, e.g., correlations between all scores derived with Method A) and correlations between scores obtained using different methods (heteromethod blocks, e.g., correlations between scores derived with Method A and those with Method B). Within the heteromethod blocks, there are correlations between different operationalizations of the same trait, which is the convergent validity evidence. These diagonals (in the case of two methods, it is only one diagonal) are also sometimes called *validity diagonals* and are filled in dark gray, in Figure 3.2. The heteromethod and monomethod blocks also contain correlations between different traits, either using the same (heterotrait-monomethod triangle, here patterned with vertical lines) or different methods (heterotrait-heteromethod, here patterned with oblique lines). The figure also contains the rules set forward by Campbell and Fiske (1959). According to those rules, the convergent correlations should not only be substantial, but they should also be larger than the discriminant correlations, regardless of which method was used for the estimation of the discriminant correlations (i.e., regardless of whether they are in the monomethod or heteromethod blocks). Finally, the fourth rule cited above, requiring that discriminant validities within each method should have the same pattern, can also be elucidated with Figure 3.2.

The correlations in the monomethod blocks reflecting discriminant validity evidence can originate from a correlation between the actual constructs captured (e.g., verbal and figural reasoning, sharing the reasoning processes) but also variance originating from the method shared (e.g., verbal and figural reasoning both measured with Method A). The discriminant correlations in the heteromethod blocks should only reflect correlations due to the latent constructs, as different methods are used. Comparing corresponding correlations will then allow us to gauge the influence of method variance. If, for example, a nomological net indeed assumes a positive and moderate correlation between Traits 1 and 2, such a correlation should be observed, regardless of which method is being used. Thus, the correlations r_{2A1A}, r_{2B1A}, r_{2C1A}, r_{1B2A}, r_{2B1B}, r_{2C1B}, r_{1C2A}, r_{1C2B}, and r_{2C1C} should all be positive and moderate in size (in Figure 3.2, all of these correlations are set in bold and slightly enlarged).

If, however, one of the methods were to exert a lot of influence (e.g., another rater has a strong halo effect and rates all traits positively) on the scores derived with it, the discriminant correlation in this monomethod block might exceed the other correlations reflecting the same association. It is even possible that a method influence is so strong that a correlation reverses in direction. Such comparisons are what Campbell and Fiske (1959) were alluding to when they suggested comparing the patterns for corresponding discriminant correlations.

Despite the appealing logic and computational ease with which an MTMM matrix can be procured, its use has been criticized. An obvious critical point is that checking the rules is often done just by eyeballing the matrix (for a suggestion on how to quantify construct validity, see Furr & Heuckeroth, 2019), leaving the question open of when the rules are actually satisfied or violated (Marsh & Hocevar, 1983).

Another main argument is that, for the correlations to be comparable, they would need to be measured with equal reliability and within the same sample and sample size. To circumvent this problem, reliability estimates are reported, and sometimes correlations are corrected for attenuation. However, such corrections are only trustworthy if the assumptions for the reliability estimators used are met (i.e., tau-equivalent items for Cronbach's α, e.g., McDonald, 1970).

A final critical argument is that the variance sources assumed (i.e., traits, methods, error) are not modeled, and no model specifying and quantifying the influence of these variance sources is tested. Also, relations between different methods are not directly observable. As a consequence, a convergent validity might be large because of the trait influence but potentially also because of a correlation between the two methods (e.g., friends and parents share a positive halo effect, and both view the target positively in all traits) or a trait-method interaction (Campbell & O'Connell, 1967).

To solve these issues, it would be necessary to specify a model in which the different variance sources and the relations between them are explicitly modeled. The last two concerns can be ameliorated by employing *structural equation modeling* (SEM) or, more specifically, *confirmatory factor analysis* (CFA). With this approach, it is possible to separate the trait-method units measured, into the three variance sources defined in Equation 1. Moreover, relations between latent variables can be specified and estimated, which are then free of measurement error. The idea of using CFAs has been formalized for several decades (Widaman, 1985). Over these decades, two approaches have been very prominent: *correlated trait-correlated uniqueness* (CT-CU) and *correlated trait-correlated method* (CT-CM) models. In the next section, both approaches, with their merits and problems, will be highlighted before introducing the *correlated trait-correlated method minus one* (CT-C[M-1]) model, which directly addresses these problems.

First CFA Approaches to Modeling MTMM Data

There are many issues involved with interpreting an MTMM matrix (for a good empirical example, see Marsh & Hocevar, 1983) despite the advantages that come along with using a CFA approach. Consequently, it is not surprising that proposals have been made which allow the specification of models in which the variance sources making up the trait-method units (Y_{ijk} as defined in Equation 1) are modeled, and their influence on the score and the relations with each other are estimated. Using a CFA, model fits and measurement error-free relations can conveniently be included. In the following, we will start with the seemingly easiest approach, the CT-CU.

Correlated Trait–Correlated Uniqueness Model

As the name suggests, the Correlated Trait-Correlated Uniqueness (CT-CU) model assumes estimating latent, correlated traits, as well as correlated uniqueness. Uniqueness, in this case, refers to the residuals of manifest variables in CFA. A paper by Kenny (1976) is typically cited as being the first to propose this approach. Figure 3.3 depicts a schema of the model, which contains the same elements as the example used in the MTMM matrix in Figure 3.2. Again, we are measuring three different traits (i.e., Traits 1, 2, and 3) using the three methods A, B, and C. To highlight the different variance sources shades of gray and patterns are used. The trait variance is reflected in different shades of gray. The method variance is symbolized by patterns of dots (Method A), dashed lines (Method B), or straight lines (Method C). As the observed scores are trait–method units, they contain both a shade of gray and a pattern. An observed score Y on an indicator i for a trait j can be measured with any method k. In this schema, there is only one indicator per method and trait, to keep it simple. As is common in CFA, the variance shared by all indicators of a trait is explained by a latent variable. The remaining variance is captured by the residual variable, also called uniqueness. The shading of these uniquenesses implies that they not only contain error variance (e) but also systematic differences due to the method. To capture this variance, Kenny's (1976) idea was to add correlations between those residuals sharing the same method variance influence. Importantly, this model requires that all correlations between methods are estimated, and not only those that improve model fit.

In Figure 3.3, this is implied by the dotted (Method A), dashed (Method B), and solid (Method C) correlation arrows between residuals containing the same method variance. To gauge convergent validity, Kenny (1976) suggested looking at the model fit and the size of the trait loadings. Discriminant validity evidence can be directly taken from the correlations between the traits. Kenny even suggested fixing the correlations to 1 and comparing the fit with the model where the correlations are freely estimated. A deterioration in model fit would then suggest that the traits are not identical, and discriminant validity can be assumed. To infer the method influence, no clear suggestions have been made. One way to approach this would be to look at the size of the variance in the residuals and the correlations between residuals which provide hints at the generalizability of a method effect across traits. While this approach provides an elegant way to gauge construct validity, it seems suboptimal to satisfy more complex questions regarding the influence of a method or the relations between different methods.

Correlated Trait–Correlated Method Models

To address this problem, the CT-CM approach was formally presented by Widaman (1985) and expertly portrayed by Marsh (1989), as well as Marsh and Hocevar (1983). The general ideas are similar to the ones in the CT-CU models. They are schematically depicted in Figure 3.4. Instead of estimating the correlations between residual components for different methods, method factors are estimated to summarize these correlations. Again, the manifest observations are the starting point and reflect trait–method units. We use the same shades of gray and patterns as for the CT-CU model. Also identical is that the variance shared by all indicators of a trait is captured in a latent trait variable.

The major difference now is that the method influence is directly modeled by specifying latent method variables, which capture the variance shared by indicators for different traits but from the same method. Thus, while the trait variables capture the variance shared by different indicators of the same trait, the method variables explain the variance shared by different indicators of the same method. In such a model, the systematic variance in the trait–method units is disentangled and partitioned, leaving only error variance in the residuals. Importantly, while trait variables can correlate with each other and method variables can also correlate with each other, correlations between traits and methods are not allowed.

To evaluate construct validity, the same ideas as those proposed by Kenny (1976) can be applied. Hence, model fit and trait loadings are informative for convergent validity, and the latent trait correlations for discriminant validity evidence. The CT-CM model thereby allows us to directly estimate the amount of method variance (e.g., by estimating a construct reliability for each latent method variable or testing if the latent method variable has substantial variance)

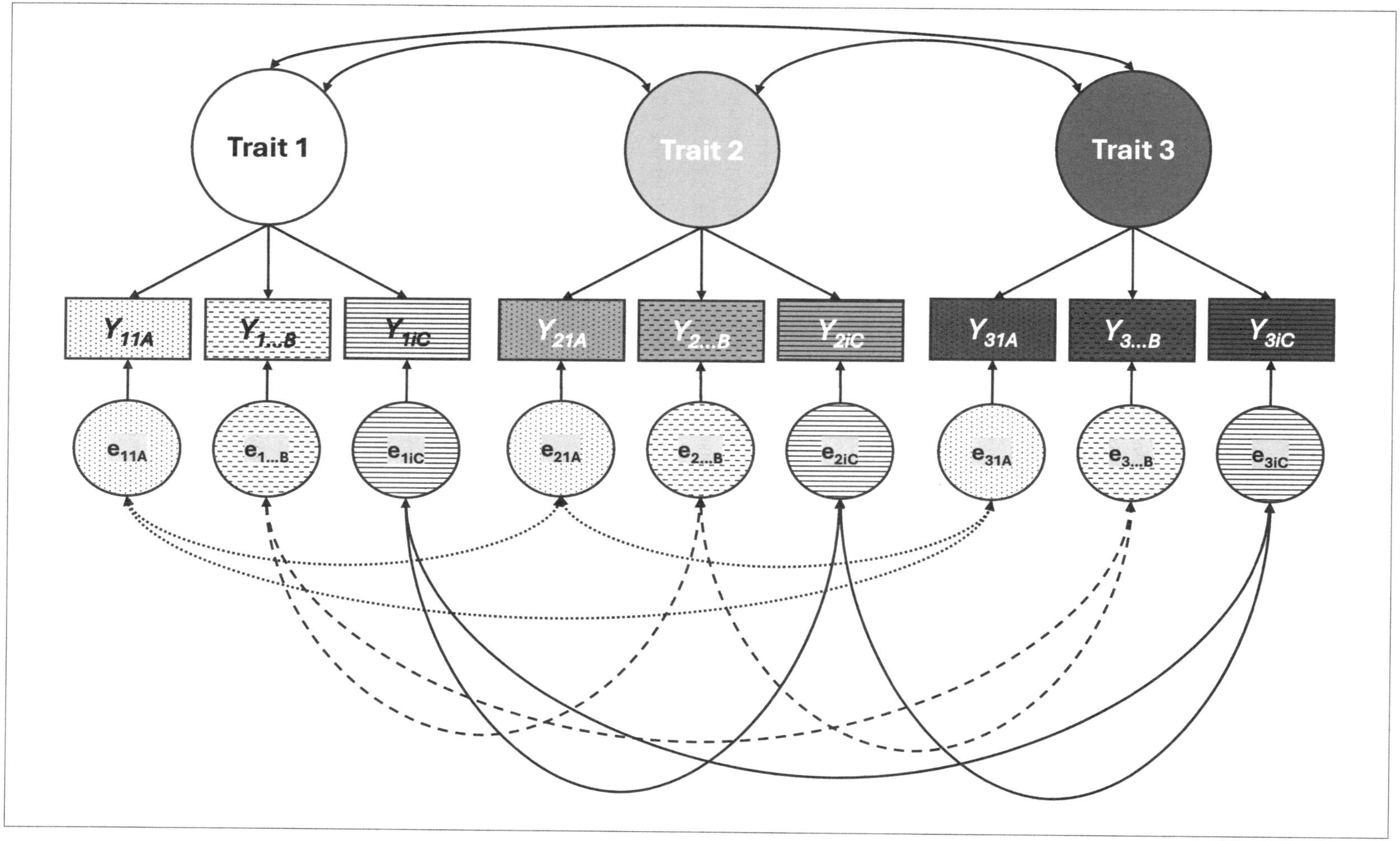

Figure 3.3 Correlated trait–correlated uniqueness (CT-CU) model. Structural model with three correlated latent trait variables and their manifest indicators. Method effects are modeled using correlations between residual components. Y = observed variable. i = indicator i.

and the relations between the method factors, at least under certain assumptions. The first assumption is that traits and methods do not actually covary; and the second assumption is that traits do not correlate highly or even form a general factor. If traits and methods covary (e.g., in a positive halo effect for extraversion when rated by parents), the disentanglement of the trait–method unit into variance due to the trait and variance due to the method will be impossible, as it assumes additive main effects only but no interaction (see Equation 1).

If the traits correlate strongly or even form a general factor, it is reasonable to assume that such a common variance will lead to convergence across methods, typically evident in strong and overestimated method intercorrelations (Marsh, 1989). This, however, would mean that the method factors capture trait and not (only) method variance.

Consider for example self-esteem and extraversion, two traits which in one study were correlated at .38 (Robins et al., 2001). A report on two indicators of these traits completed by the same person (or method) should therefore correlate as well. However, in the CT-CM model, this covariance of indicators (which is true trait covariance) would now be attributed to the method.

In fact, in his seminal paper, Marsh (1989) implied that the CT-CU approach might be more effective. He arrived at this conclusion after applying a series of different CFA models to three different data sets, looking at model fit but also plausibility. He also integrated external criteria and predicted them with trait and method variables to identify the best modeling approach. In the end, Marsh (1989) concluded:

> The most serious potential problem with MTMM models is the implicit assumption that so-called method factors represent primarily the effects of method variance. If this assumption is violated, then the interpretation of trait and method factors in most CFA studies and the detailed comparison of nested models proposed by Widaman (1985) may be unjustified. (Marsh, 1989, p. 357)

As shall be seen, this critique is not the only one brought forward against the CT-CM approach. And, despite the conclusion that CT-CU models might be more effective, CT-CU models, just like the CT-CM models, do not remain unscathed.

Critique of the CT-CU and CT-CM Approaches

As highlighted in the last section, the approaches to modeling MTMM data come with advantages and disadvantages, or even severe problems. Lance et al. (2002) summarized the major critical issues and compared the CT-CU and CT-CM models, providing a summary table, adapted here as Table 3.1. We refer the reader interested in a detailed discussion of these points to the excellent original paper and restrict ourselves to a few key observations.

An issue we have not discussed so far is the amount of variance estimated to be attributable to latent trait and method factors (the latter only in the CT-CM model). These estimates are decisive, as they reflect convergent validity (i.e., trait variance estimate is higher when loadings of different operationalizations converge) and the influence of method (i.e., method variance estimate increases if trait–method units contain increasing method variance). Thus, both estimates are vital to the goals pursued with this kind of analysis.

Lance et al. (2002) have shown that trait variance estimates are biased upwards for CT-CU models, which also means that method variance is often underestimated (for an applied example showcasing the effects of such biases on the evaluation of assessment center ratings, see Lance et al., 2004).

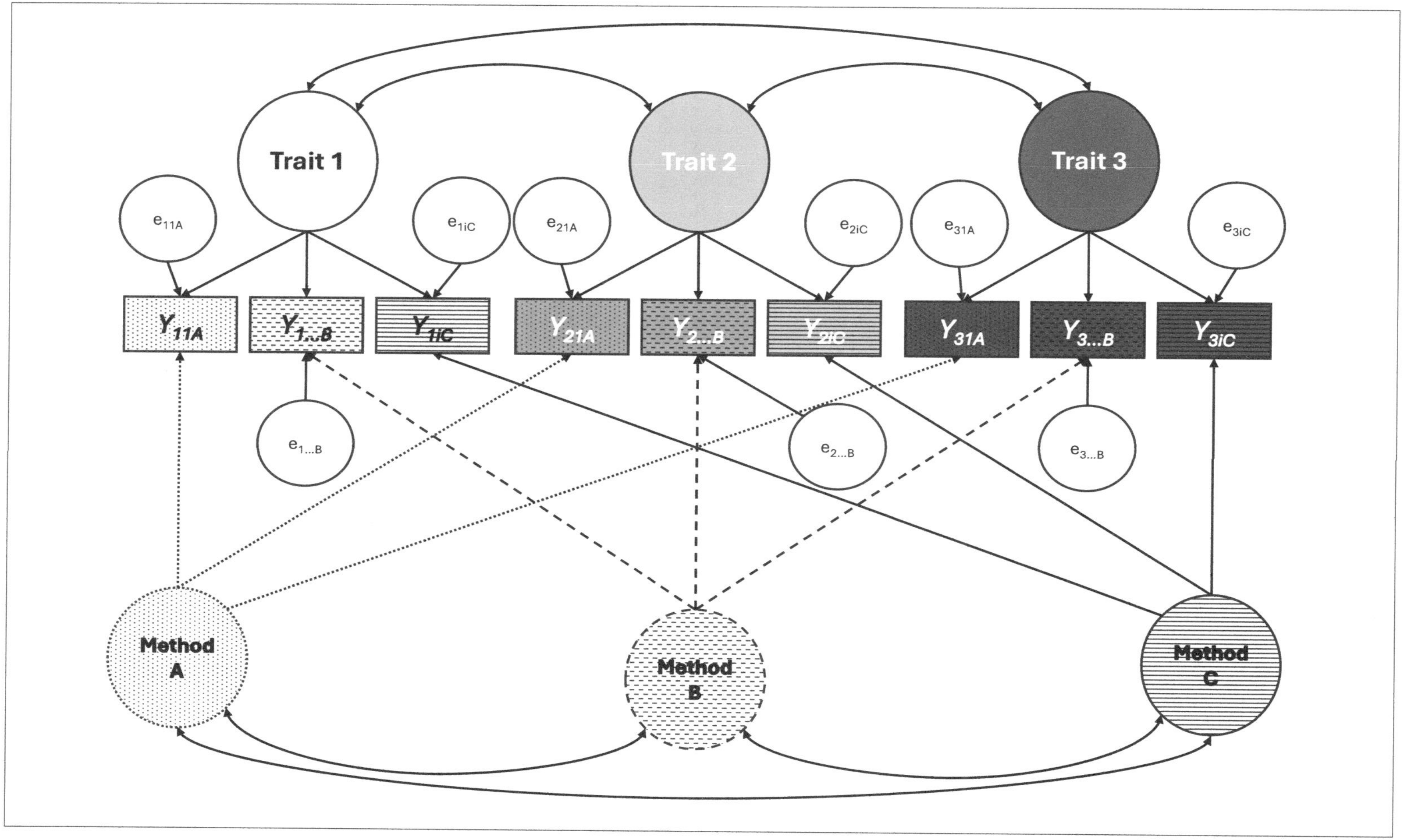

Figure 3.4 Correlated trait–correlated method (CT-CM) model. Structural model with three correlated latent trait variables and their manifest indicators. Method effects are modeled as correlated latent variables as well. Y = observed variable. i = indicator i.

Another important issue is the dimensionality and intercorrelation between method effects. While the CT-CM allows the latter, only the CT-CU allows method effects to be multidimensional (the CT-CM specifies unidimensional method variables, that assume the same method effect(s) for all indicators). Multidimensional effects in this sense mean that two residual correlations in the CT-CU model may exist for different reasons (e.g., the residual correlation between the second indicator for each trait may reflect a halo effect, whereas the residual correlation between the third indicator for each trait may reflect a wording effect). Thus, when it comes to the variance estimates and the method structure, neither approach offers a silver bullet.

Table 3.1 Comparison of correlated trait–correlated uniqueness and correlated trait–correlated methods.

Issue	Conclusion
Theoretical soundness	The CT-CM model is firmly rooted in original theoretical foundation supporting MTMM analysis. The CT-CU model is ad hoc.
Estimation of method variance components	Estimated directly under the CT-CM model but indirectly and only for heterotrait–monomethod correlations under the CT-CU model.
Relationships among methods	Method factors may be orthogonal or oblique under the CT-CM model but are constrained to be orthogonal under the CT-CU model.
Efficiency in estimation	Method effects are estimated from (a) all correlations in the MTMM matrix under the CT-CM model but (b) only the heterotrait–monomethod correlations under the CT-CU model.
Estimation of trait variance components	Estimated directly under both the CT-CM and CT-CU models; however, estimates are likely biased upward as a result of model misspecification under the CT-CU model.
Model parsimony	The CT-CU model is generally more parsimonious for "small" (i.e., $T < 3$) MTMM matrices; the CT-CM model is more parsimonious for "larger" (i.e., $T > 4$) matrices.
Range of testable models	Both the CT-CM and CT-CU models offer a wide range of trait structures; the range of method structures is very limited under the CU model.
Relationships with *external* variables	Estimable for (a) T trait factors under both the CT-CM and CT-CU models but (b) method factors only under the CT-CM model.
Model convergence and admissibility	The CT-CU model returns proper solutions more frequently than does the CT-CM model.
Dimensionality of method effects	Unspecified multidimensional method effects are estimable only under the CT-CU model; substantive method effects are estimable under the CT-CM model.

Note. CT-CM = correlated trait–correlated method; CT-CU = correlated trait–correlated uniqueness; MTMM = multitrait-multimethod; T = number of traits; M = number of methods. Adapted from Lance et al. (2002).

A final problem addressed by Lance et al. (2002) is the admissibility of solutions. Here, the CT-CM results often include Heywood cases or suppressions, resulting, for example, in loadings with unexpected directions (for a potential remedy using a Rindskopf reparametrization, see Lance & Fan, 2016). A conclusion at this point would be that using CFA to model MTMM data might require estimating a range of different models (see Widaman, 1985) and comparing the results with regard to a number of issues such as fit, variance estimates, plausibility of parameter estimates, or method correlations. It might even be necessary to include external criteria to gauge the models' plausibility (see Marsh, 1989). While this is certainly achievable, it seems to offer only a slight improvement compared with eyeballing the correlations in an MTMM matrix with the rules of Campbell and Fiske (1959) in mind. Yet, a further development has directly addressed some of these issues, offering a readily available solution.

CT-C(M-1)

In a seminal paper, Eid et al. (2008) start by pointing out that adhering to a strategy of testing multiple different models can not only be frustrating but might end up with improper solutions. Part of the solution they offer for this is to directly select a model that fits the underlying MTMM design best. For this, they refer to the "type of method considered" (Eid et al., 2008, p. 231) to determine the correct MTMM design. In their example, they choose self- and other-raters (e.g., friends and parents of a target person; students and lecturers in different lectures) but emphasize that different methods could also be item effects, assessment context, or assessment methods (e.g., different test families or questionnaires, interviews, physiological measures, etc. – any method that theoretically exerts a common method effect). The models they propose can be used to estimate such method effects as well. Another important feature of these models is the use of multiple indicators per dimension, which allows testing of whether method effects are trait-specific or general in nature. Moreover, multidimensional method effects can be specified (see Eid et al., 2008). Regardless, the key differentiation made here is with regard to the type of method – which we will outline next.

Types of Methods

Eid et al. (2008), in principle, differentiate between two different types of methods: interchangeable and structurally different methods. Additionally, there can be MTMM designs where both method types are crossed. To explain what these are, we will also use an example with self- and other-raters. Let us assume we were interested in providing construct validity evidence for scores from a new Big Five measure which is mainly used for self-ratings. Based on prior research, it is known that Big Five self-ratings and those made by friends converge to some extent (Connelly & Ones, 2010). So self-ratings can be obtained from a sample of persons from the target population. Additionally, other-ratings can also be obtained from the targets' friends. We know that our targets typically have several friends, and we can draw a random sample of friends to rate each target. Here, it should not matter much which friend is chosen for a target, as each has a highly comparable access to the target. This is what Eid et al. (2008) consider an interchangeable method. Importantly, while the friends are interchangeable within a specific target, they are not interchangeable between targets (i.e., a friend of one target cannot rate any other target). In other words, the data structure is nested (i.e., friends within targets) and requires a multilevel CFA.

Let us now assume that we are not only interested in the convergence between self- and other-ratings, but we would also have access to parent ratings. Again, prior research can be used to inform the design. It has been shown that parents and friends do not necessarily have the same access to information (Connelly & Ones, 2010; Lämmle et al., 2019), thus, it matters whether a target is rated by a friend or a parent. In that sense, the methods are structurally different and hence, noninterchangeable. In such a design, data are not nested. In our example, there is one friend and one parent for each target. Thus, each combination of target, friend, and parent is directly defined. In a data set, we would say that the data are arranged in a wide format, not a long format, as is the case for interchangeable methods.

If targets are rated by several friends and one parent, for example, the design would be a combination of interchangeable and structurally different methods. As before, friends of a target are interchangeable, but friends and parents are not. The data in such a case are nested again.

The following discussion will focus on the case of structurally different methods and refer the reader to the original paper by Eid and colleagues (2008) for excellent explanations regarding both other types, which require multilevel CFA. We are doing this because, in addition to considering the type of method, Eid and colleagues also integrated another key feature into models containing structurally different methods. As said before, a data design with structurally different methods would allow the specification of a latent variable for each method. This, however, would basically lead to a CT-CM model, with all the problems discussed above. To avoid these issues, Eid and colleagues integrated another important feature: defining the trait variable(s) by a reference method.

Reference Method – Method-Minus-One Models

MTMM designs often contain one method to assess a trait or several traits for which convergent validity evidence is wanted (e.g., scores from a new questionnaire). Alternatively, researchers might know which method might have the broadest access to relevant information (e.g., self-ratings). Thus, it is reasonable to assume that one of the methods can usually be chosen as a so-called *reference method* (Eid, 2000; Eid et al., 2003). Figure 3.5 shows a schematic depiction of a model containing the idea of a reference method for our previous example. Again, three traits are captured with three methods. As before, each trait–method unit contains systematic variance due to the trait (i.e., reflected by a shade of gray) and the method (i.e., reflected by a specific pattern). In this model, Method A is chosen as a reference method which means that no latent variable for Method A is specified. Such models are called *correlated trait-correlated method minus 1* (CT-C[M-1]) models. Each trait variable is now defined by the reference method. For example, in Figure 3.5, each of the three traits is defined by Method A. Thus, the meaning of each trait reflects the meaning as it is captured with Method A. We have patterned each latent trait variable using the pattern for Method A to signify this idea.

Choosing one method as the reference method not only means that all other methods are nonreference methods, but it also directly defines the latent method variables as residual variables, capturing the deviation between the true value in the nonreference method and the score predicted by the reference method. It follows logically that trait and method variables are uncorrelated (Eid, 2000). In other words, these method variables capture overestimations or underestimations on the observed variables compared with the value that would be expected here

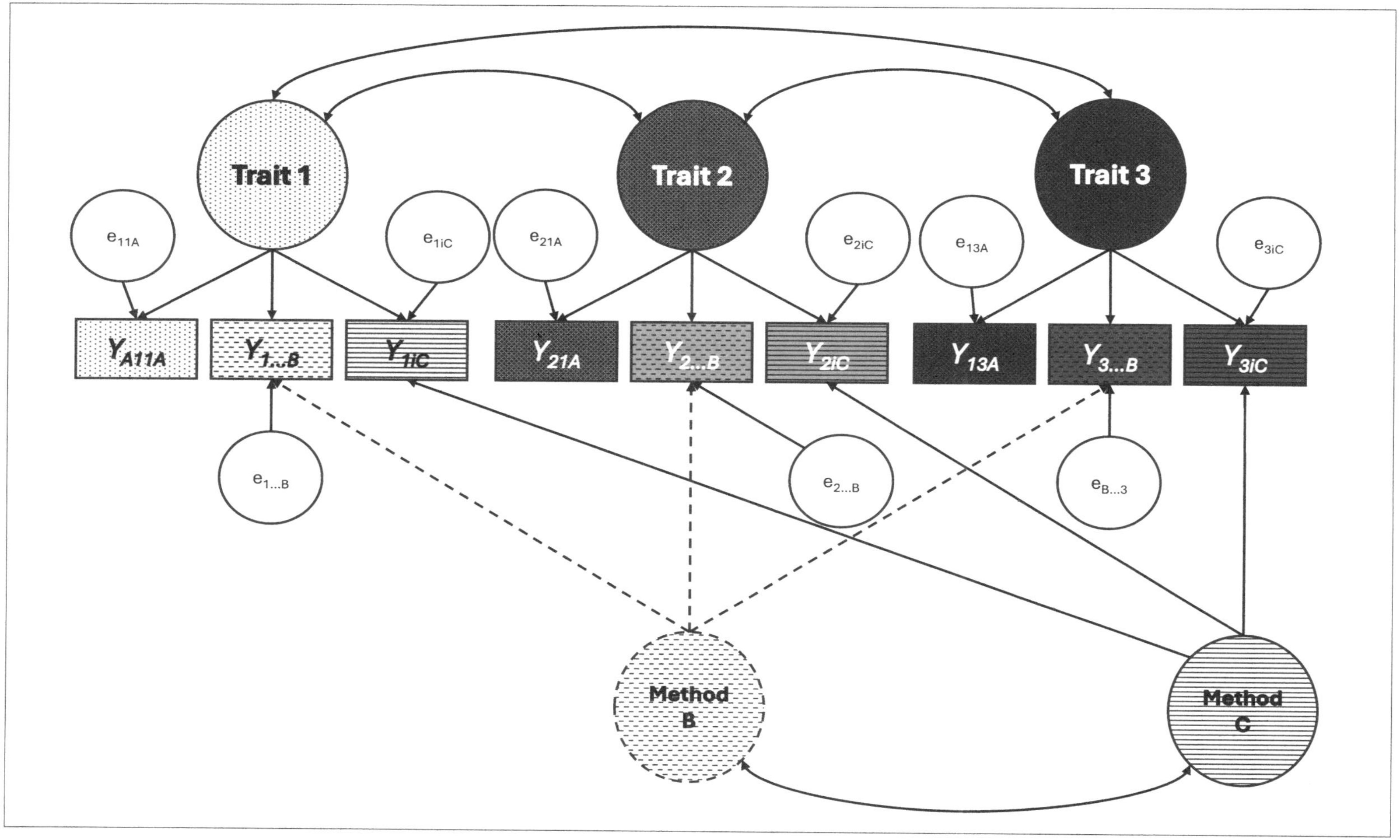

Figure 3.5 Correlated trait–correlated method minus 1 (CTC[M-1]) schema for structurally different methods. *Y* = observed variable. *i* = indicator i.

based on the trait as estimated by the reference method. Importantly, specifying a model in this way not only has the logical consequence that trait and method variables are uncorrelated, but it also solves problems with identification and biased estimates common to the CT-CU and CT-CM models (Eid, 2000).

One important issue that CT-C(M-1) models settle is the interpretation of latent variables which is an issue that hampers CT-CM models. In a CT-CM model, a trait variable explains all observed variables operationalizing this trait. When interpreting the trait, the largest loadings are the most informative. However, the size of loadings might vary between samples or when items are added or dropped. These changes automatically affect the interpretation of the trait variable. The CT-C(M-1) model solves this issue. The trait variable in such models is always defined by the reference method. Hence, the interpretation is always the same – the trait reflects the operationalization of the reference method (including its trait and its method variance). This does not change when items are added or dropped or when loadings change.

An Explanation for Structurally Different Methods

Figure 3.6 and Figure 3.7 contain schematic depictions of the general idea behind the CT-C(M-1) model for structurally different, and hence noninterchangeable, methods. In addition to the ideas outlined above, these Figures contain another important feature of CT-C(M-1) models, as suggested by Eid and colleagues (2008): the use of multiple indicators. As before, each figure contains three traits. Each trait is measured with three methods. Each method uses three items. Thus, there are nine observed variables per trait, three for each method. The difference between Figure 3.6 and Figure 3.7 is that the CT-C(M-1) model in Figure 3.7 incorporates the idea of trait-specific method factors. Let us assume that Method A is a self-rating, Method B is a parent rating, and Method C is a friend rating. The method variable Trait 1 – Method B would then be the method effect for the parent rating on Trait 1. Importantly, this variable is still a residual variable, reflecting the deviation observed in the parent ratings of Trait 1 from the true scores that would be expected based on the reference method (i.e., the self-rating of Trait 1).

Such models allow for obtaining a comprehensive idea of the method effects. Comparing a CT-C(M-1) model with and without trait-specific method effects is possible using the usual methods (e.g., χ^2-difference test, ΔCFI). If a model with trait-specific method effects fits the data better, this would mean that each method effect depends on the trait. In our example, this would mean parents might overestimate or underestimate the target, but this deviation does not generalize across traits. In a model without trait-specific method variables, such a bias does not vary with traits but is more like a general effect.

It is also interesting to use these models to explore the relations between different methods. For example, a large correlation between the method variable(s) for the parent and those for the friend would imply that both have a similar bias when evaluating the target, meaning the discrepancy compared with the self-rating is in the same direction. For an example, where these ideas are applied, see Lämmle et al. (2019), who used CT-C(M-1) models to explore the difference in self- and other- (i.e., by parent or friend) ratings of the dark triad.

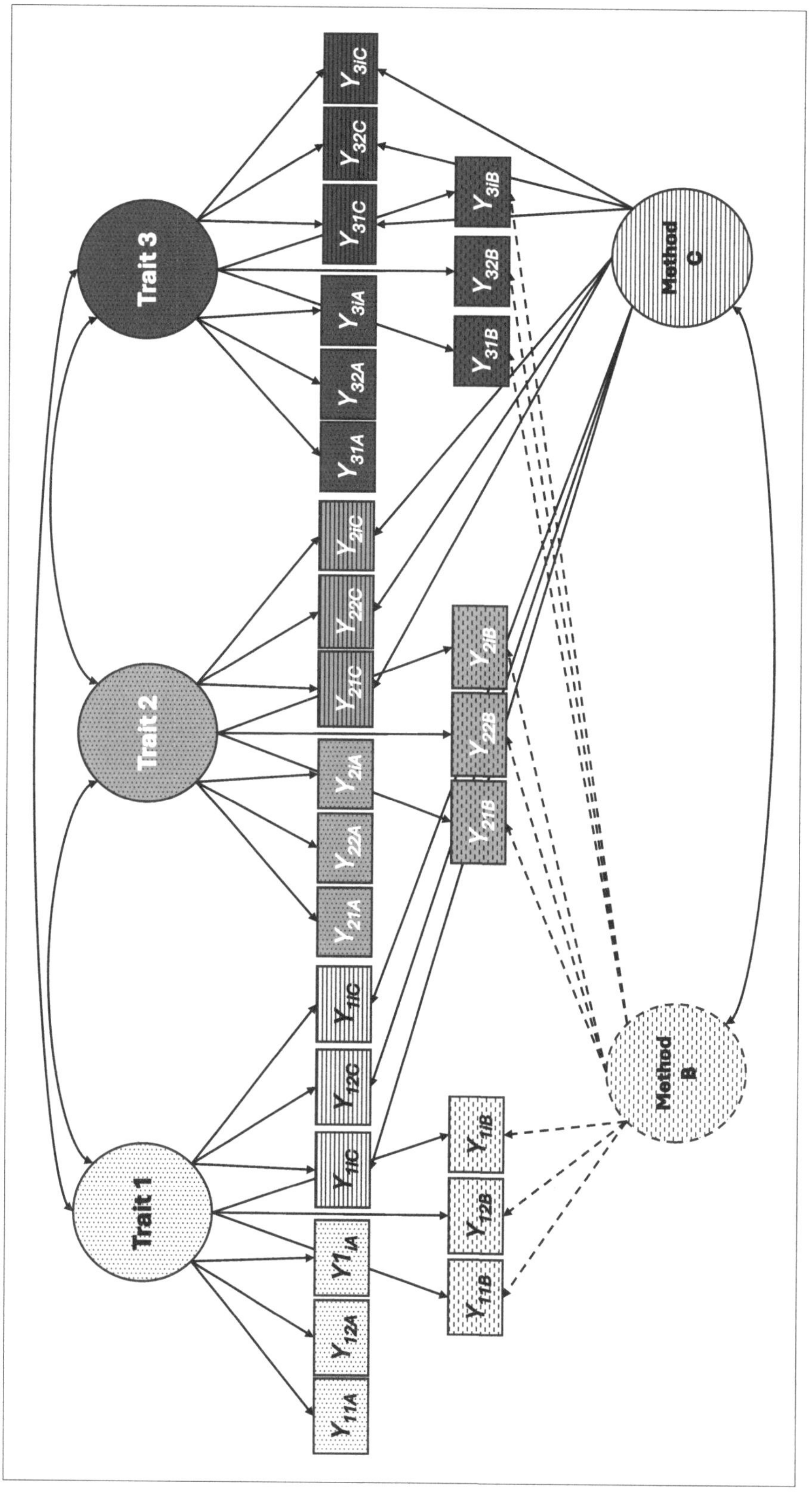

Figure 3.6 Correlated trait–correlated method minus 1 (CTC[M–1]) schema for structurally different methods. Y = observed variable. i = indicator i.

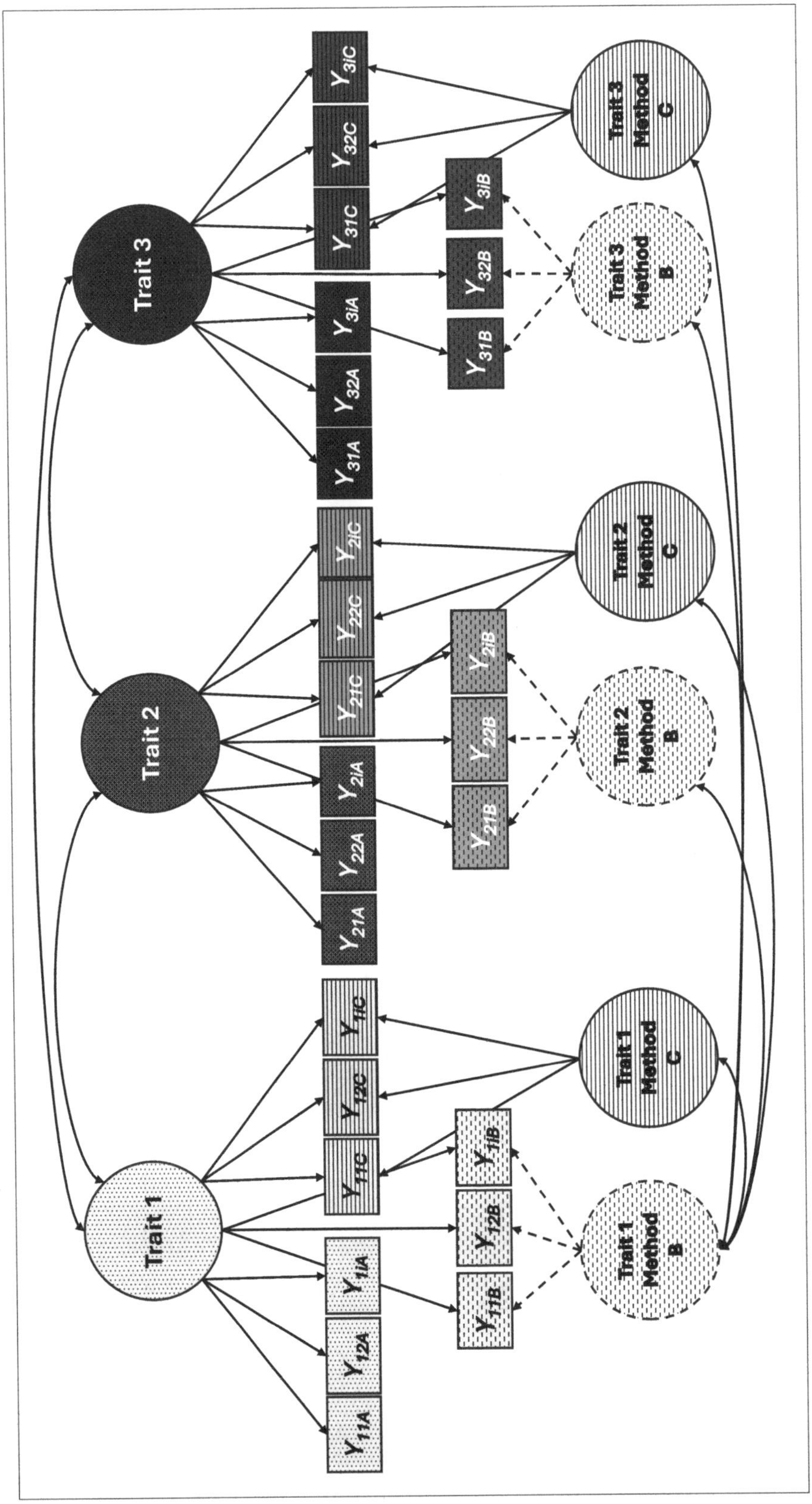

Figure 3.7 Correlated trait-correlated method minus 1 (CTC[M-1]) with multiple indicators and trait-specific method variables. Residual variables are omitted. Method correlations are only shown for Trait 1 – Method B; all other correlations are omitted to preserve comprehensibility. *Y* = observed variable. *i* = indicator i.

Construct Validity Evidence in the CT-C(M-1) Models

So far, we have shown how CT-C(M-1) models solve problems typical for CT-CM or CT-CU models. However, the initial aim in this chapter was to identify the means by which we can provide evidence for convergent and discriminant validity evidence, and also gauge the impact of method effects. As before, and as typical for all SEM approaches, model fit should be the first source of information. Discriminant validity evidence can directly be obtained from the correlations between the latent traits. As before, these are true score correlations which solves the problem of different reliabilities that hamper the classical MTMM approach by Campbell and Fiske (1959). To gauge convergent validity evidence, one could look at the sizes of the trait loadings.

Similarly, to gauge the impact of methods, one could also look at the respective loadings. However, Eid and colleagues (2008), while also using the loadings, suggest a more direct way by deriving formulae which encapsulate important variance estimates. These are the *consistency coefficient* (CO), the *method specificity coefficient* (MS), and a *reliability coefficient* (REL). All three equations for models with trait-specific method variables are listed here:

$$CO(Y_{jik}) = \frac{\lambda_{Tjik}^2 Var(T_{ji})}{\lambda_{Tjik}^2 Var(T_{ji}) + \lambda_{Mjik}^2 Var(M_{jk})} \tag{2}$$

$$MS(Y_{jik}) = \frac{\lambda_{Mjik}^2 Var(M_{jk})}{\lambda_{Tjik}^2 Var(T_{ji}) + \lambda_{Mjik}^2 Var(M_{jk})} \tag{3}$$

$$REL(Y_{jik}) = \frac{\lambda_{Tjik}^2 Var(T_{ji}) + \lambda_{Mjik}^2 Var(M_{jk})}{Var(Y_{jik})} = 1 - \frac{Var(E_{jik})}{Var(Y_{jik})}. \tag{4}$$

These equations can be applied to each observed variable *Y*. The index *jik* expresses that each of these observed variables is an indicator *i*, for a specific trait *j*, operationalized with a specific method *k*.

Each of the three equations contains the same term. For the consistency coefficient and the method specificity coefficient this term makes up the denominator while it is the nominator in the reliability coefficient equation. The term includes the variance of the trait $Var(T_{ji})$ and the method $Var(M_{jk})$ that the observed variable is an indicator for. Each of the two variances is weighted by the squared loading: λ_{Tjik}^2 and λ_{Mjik}^2, respectively. Thus, each summand in this term is an estimate of the variance in the observed variable *Y* which reflects the trait or the method. The sum of both estimates can be understood as the amount of systematic variance in the observed variable.

The equations for CO and MS differ in the nominator, though. Here, the CO shows the amount of variance in the observed variable *Y* due to the trait *j* and MS shows the variance due to the method *k*. It is important to keep in mind that the consistency for indicators of the reference method will always be 1, as there is no variance explained by any method variable. Likewise, there is no estimate for MS for any indicators of the reference method. The consistency coefficient thus captures "the proportion of true variance of a nonreference method that is explained by the reference method" (Eid et al., 2008, p. 239). Thus, a consistency coefficient larger than .5 means that more than half of the systematic variance in an observed variable is due to the trait.

Similarly, the method specificity coefficient estimates "the proportion of true variance of a nonreference method that is specific to this nonreference method" (Eid et al., 2008, p. 239). Thus, a method specificity coefficient larger than .5 means that more than half of the systematic variance in an observed variable is due to the specific method used. The reliability coefficient estimates the total amount of systematic variance in the observed variable, and its size can be interpreted like other reliability estimates. However, it has to be noted that, unlike many other reliability estimators commonly used in the classical test theory framework, this reliability estimator obviously does not assume unidimensionality. Thus, large values could be due to a lot of trait variance but also to a lot of method variance. Additionally, all three coefficients are estimated for each observed variable, not as an aggregate. So, interpretations can be made for each indicator, not necessarily a sum score.

To sum up, the procedure suggested by Eid et al. (2008) and recommended here is to define a data-generating design which is most informative with regard to the research question, meaning to consider which construct validity evidence is most informative. This includes selecting discriminant measures (for a discussion of points to consider, see Ziegler, 2020) but, importantly, also the kind of method whose influence is to be gauged. There are instances where the test family might be of interest. In other settings it might be more important to explore which role the kind of rater plays. Based on this research plan, a specific CT-C(M-1) model can be chosen, which also means that a reference method must be selected. When it comes to test construction, it is reasonable to assume that the reference method is the method for which validity evidence is to be gathered. Once the correct CT-C(M-1) model has been chosen and data collected, analyses can be conducted. It can then be tested whether there are trait-specific method effects or not. Once this has been decided, the formulae in Equations 2–4 can be used to estimate the amount of trait and method variance. Moreover, the latent trait correlations can be used to gauge discriminant validity. The correlations between method variables can be used to explore the impact of the specific methods on the measures. In sum, a comprehensive set of pieces of evidence regarding construct validity can be gathered. This is complemented by an equally comprehensive insight into the inner workings of the methods operationalized.

Outlook

This chapter is a quick journey through some of the important ideas circling around construct validity and method effects, using the MTMM framework as guiding principle. We want to emphasize that the literature on this topic is certainly larger than what has been covered here. Thus, we want to point out some interesting papers that are worth reading, which also explain and expand upon some of the content presented here, adding in-depth mathematical considerations and more sophisticated advice regarding the interpretation of parameters and variables in these complex models (see, e.g., Eid et al., 2003; Koch et al., 2017, 2018, 2015).

One interesting and for many readers potentially highly interesting development now allows the incorporation of a time perspective into the models (e.g., Holtmann et al., 2020; Koch et al.,

2014, 2022). Finally, there are numerous papers which utilize the recommended CT-C(M-1) approach. We believe that one can obtain an even better grasp of these procedures and techniques by looking at actual applications to real data. Thus, here are a few recommendations albeit not a comprehensive list: Carretero-Dios et al. (2011), Freudenstein et al. (2023), Gnambs and Appel (2017), Kupper et al. (2021), Low et al. (2014), Moersdorf et al. (2023), and Torres-Marín et al. (2021).

References

American Educational Research Association, American Psychological Association, & National Council on Measurement in Education. (2014). *Standards for Educational & Psychological Testing* (2014th ed.). American Educational Research Association.

Campbell, D. T., & Fiske, D. W. (1959). Convergent and discriminant validation by the multitrait-multimethod matrix. *Psychological Bulletin, 56*(2), 81–105. https://doi.org/10.1037/h0046016

Campbell, D. T., & O'Connell, E. J. (1967). Methods factors in multitrait-multimethod matrices: Multiplicative rather than additive? *Multivariate Behavioral Research, 2*(4), 409–426. https://doi.org/10.1207/s15327906mbr0204_1

Campbell, N. R. (1928). *An account of the principles of measurement and calculation.* Longmans, Green and Company.

Campbell, N. R., & Jeffreys, H. (1938). Symposium: Measurement and its importance for philosophy. *Proceedings of the Aristotelian Society, Supplementary Volumes, 17,* 121–151. https://doi.org/10.1093/aristoteliansupp/17.1.121

Carretero-Dios, H., Eid, M., & Ruch, W. (2011). Analyzing multitrait-multimethod data with multilevel confirmatory factor analysis: An application to the validation of the State-Trait Cheerfulness Inventory. *Journal of Research in Personality, 45*(2), 153–164. https://doi.org/10.1016/j.jrp.2010.12.007

Condon, D. M., Wood, D., Mõttus, R., Booth, T., Costantini, G., Greiff, S., Johnson, W., Lukaszewski, A., Murray, A., Revelle, W., Wright, A. G. C., Ziegler, M., & Zimmermann, J. (2020). Bottom up construction of a personality taxonomy. *European Journal of Psychological Assessment, 36*(6), 923–934. https://doi.org/10.1027/1015-5759/a000626

Connelly, B. S., & Ones, D. S. (2010). An other perspective on personality: Meta-Analytic integration of observers' accuracy and predictive validity. *Psychological Bulletin, 136*(6), 1092–1122. https://doi.org/10.1037/a0021212

Cronbach, L. J., & Meehl, P. E. (1955). Construct validity in psychological tests. *Psychological Bulletin, 52*(4), 281–302. https://doi.org/10.1037/h0040957

Eid, M. (2000). A multitrait-multimethod model with minimal assumptions. *Psychometrika, 65*(2), 241–261. https://doi.org/10.1007/BF02294377

Eid, M., Lischetzke, T., Nussbeck, F. W., & Trierweiler, L. I. (2003). Separating trait effects from trait-specific method effects in multitrait-multimethod models: A multiple-indicator CT-C(M-1) model. *Psychological Methods, 8*(1), 38–60. https://doi.org/10.1037/1082-989x.8.1.38

Eid, M., Nussbeck, F., Geiser, C., Cole, D., Gollwitzer, M., & Lischetzke, T. (2008). Structural equation modeling of multitrait-multimethod data: Different models for different types of methods. *Psychological Methods, 13*(3), 230–253. https://doi.org/10.1037/a0013219

Elson, M., Hussey, I., Alsalti, T., & Arslan, R. C. (2023). Psychological measures aren't toothbrushes. *Communications Psychology, 1*(1), 25. https://doi.org/10.1038/s44271-023-00026-9

Freudenstein, J.-P., Mussel, P., & Krumm, S. (2023). On the construct-related validity of implicit trait policies. *European Journal of Personality, 37*(1), 113–127. https://doi.org/10.1177/08902070211056901

Furr, R. M., & Heuckeroth, S. (2019). The "Quantifying Construct Validity" procedure: Its role, value, interpretations, and computation. *Assessment, 26*(4), 555-566. https://doi.org/10.1177/1073191118820638

Gnambs, T., & Appel, M. (2017). Is computer gaming associated with cognitive abilities? A population study among German adolescents. *Intelligence, 61,* 19–28. https://doi.org/10.1016/j.intell.2016.12.004

Holtmann, J., Koch, T., Bohn, J., & Eid, M. (2020). Multimethod assesement of time-stable and time-variable interindividual differences. *European Journal of Psychological Assessment, 36*(6), 1024–1043. https://doi.org/10.1027/1015-5759/a000577

Kenny, D. A. (1976). An empirical application of confirmatory factor analysis to the multitrait-multimethod matrix. *Journal of Experimental Social Psychology, 12*(3), 247–252. https://doi.org/10.1016/0022-1031(76)90055-X

Koch, T., Holtmann, J., Bohn, J., & Eid, M. (2017). Multitrait-multimethod analysis. In V. Zeigler-Hill & T. Shackelford (Eds.), *Encyclopedia of personality and individual differences* (pp. 3034–3056). Springer. https://doi.org/10.1007/978-3-319-24612-3_1331

Koch, T., Holtmann, J., Bohn, J., & Eid, M. (2018). Explaining general and specific factors in longitudinal, multimethod, and bifactor models: Some caveats and recommendations. *Psychological Methods, 23*(3), 505–523. https://doi.org/10.1037/met0000146

Koch, T., Schultze, M., Burrus, J., Roberts, R. D., & Eid, M. (2015). A multilevel CFA-MTMM model for nested structurally different methods. *Journal of Educational and Behavioral Statistics, 40*(5), 477–510. https://doi.org/10.3102/1076998615606109

Koch, T., Schultze, M., Eid, M., & Geiser, C. (2014). A longitudinal multilevel CFA-MTMM model for interchangeable and structurally different methods. *Frontiers in Psychology, 5*, Article 311. https://doi.org/10.3389/fpsyg.2014.00311

Koch, T., Voelkle, M. C., & Driver, C. C. (2022). Analyzing longitudinal multirater data with individually varying time intervals. *Structural Equation Modeling: A Multidisciplinary Journal*, 1–19. https://doi.org/10.1080/10705511.2022.2096612

Kupper, K., Krampen, D., Rammstedt, B., & Rohrmann, S. (2021). The German-Language Short Form of the Big Five Inventory for Children and Adolescents – Other-Rating Version (BFI-K KJ-F). *European Journal of Psychological Assessment, 37*(2), 109–117. https://doi.org/10.1027/1015-5759/a000592

Lämmle, L., Nussbeck, F. W., & Ziegler, M. (2019). Hello from the other side: Can we perceive others' darkness? Observers' accuracy of the Dark Triad. *Journal of Personality Assessment, 103*(1), 106–119. https://doi.org/10.1080/00223891.2019.1683020

Lance, C. E., & Fan, Y. (2016). Convergence, admissibility, and fit of alternative Confirmatory Factor Analysis Models for MTMM data. *Educational and Psychological Measurement, 76*(3), 487-507. https://doi.org/10.1177/0013164415601884

Lance, C. E., Lambert, T. A., Gewin, A. G., Lievens, F., & Conway, J. M. (2004). Revised estimates of dimension and exercise variance components in assessment center postexercise dimension ratings. *Journal of Applied Psychology, 89*(2), 377–385. https://doi.org/10.1037/0021-9010.89.2.377

Lance, C. E., Noble, C. L., & Scullen, S. E. (2002). A critique of the correlated trait-correlated method and correlated uniqueness models for multitrait-multimethod data. *Psychological Methods, 7*(2), 228–244. https://doi.org/10.1037/1082-989x.7.2.228

Loevinger, J. (1957). Objective tests as instruments of psychological theory (Monograph Supplement 9). *Psychological Reports, 3*(3), 635–694. https://doi.org/10.2466/pr0.1957.3.3.635

Low, J. A., Keith, T. Z., & Jensen, M. (2014). What predicts method effects in child behavior ratings. *Journal of Psychoeducational Assessment, 33*(2), 177-187. https://doi.org/10.1177/0734282914544922

Marsh, H. W. (1989). Confirmatory factor analyses of multitrait-multimethod data: Many problems and a few solutions. *Applied Psychological Measurement, 13*(4), 335–361. https://doi.org/10.1177/014662168901300402

Marsh, H. W., & Hocevar, D. (1983). Confirmatory factor analysis of multitrait-multimethod matrices. *Journal of Educational Measurement*, 231–248. https://doi.org/10.1111/j.1745-3984.1983.tb00202.x

McDonald, R. P. (1970). The theoretical foundations of principal factor analysis, canonical factor analysis, and alpha factor analysis. *British Journal of Mathematical and Statistical Psychology, 23*, 1–21. https://doi.org/10.1111/j.2044-8317.1970.tb00432.x

Michell, J. (2001). Teaching and misteaching measurement in psychology. *Australian Psychologist, 36*(3), 211–218. https://doi.org/10.1080/00050060108259657

Michell, J. (2014). *An introduction to the logic of psychological measurement*. Psychology Press. https://doi.org/10.4324/9781315807614

Moersdorf, L., Daum, M. M., Eid, M., & Freund, A. M. (2023). Chasing the "How" and "Why" of goal pursuit: A multimethod approach to the study of goal focus. *Journal of Research in Personality, 104*, 104371. https://doi.org/10.1016/j.jrp.2023.104371

Robins, R. W., Tracy, J. L., Trzesniewski, K., Potter, J., & Gosling, S. D. (2001). Personality correlates of self-esteem. *Journal of Research in Personality, 35*(4), 463–482. https://doi.org/10.1006/jrpe.2001.2324

Schweizer, K. (2010). Some guidelines concerning the modeling of traits and abilities in test construction. *European Journal of Psychological Assessment, 26*(1), 1–2. https://doi.org/10.1027/1015-5759/a000001

Schweizer, K. (2012). On issues of validity and especially on the misery of convergent validity. *European Journal of Psychological Assessment, 28*(4), 249–254. https://doi.org/10.1027/1015-5759/a000156

Stevens, S. S. (1946). On the theory of scales of measurement. *Science, 103*(2684), 677–680.

Torres-Marín, J., Carretero-Dios, H., & Eid, M. (2021). The fear of being laughed at, social anxiety, and paranoid ideation: A multilevel confirmatory factor analysis of multitrait-multimethod data. *Assessment, 29*(6), 1285–1300. https://doi.org/10.1177/10731911211010961

Wehner, C., Roemer, L., & Ziegler, M. (2018). Construct validity. In V. Zeigler-Hill & T. K. Shackelford (Eds.), *Encyclopedia of personality and individual differences* (pp. 1–3). Springer. https://doi.org/10.1007/978-3-319-28099-8_1288-1

Widaman, K. F. (1985). Hierarchically nested covariance structure models for multitrait-multimethod data. *Applied Psychological Measurement, 9*(1), 1–26. https://doi.org/10.1177/014662168500900101

Ziegler, M. (2014). Stop and state your intentions! Let's not forget the ABC of test construction. *European Journal of Psychological Assessment, 30*(4), 239–242. https://doi.org/10.1027/1015-5759/a000228

Ziegler, M. (2020). Psychological test adaptation and development: How papers are structured and why. *Psychological Test Adaptation and Development*, 1–9. https://doi.org/10.1027/2698-1866/a000002

Ziegler, M., & Lämmle, L. (2017). Validity. In V. Zeigler-Hill & T. K. Shackelford (Eds.), *Encyclopedia of personality and individual differences* (pp. 1–7). Springer. https://doi.org/10.1007/978-3-319-28099-8_1354-1

Chapter 4

Violations of Unidimensionality and Differential Item Functioning (DIF)

Rudolf Debelak and Carolin Strobl

Abstract

This chapter discusses violations of unidimensionality and differential item functioning as two central challenges for the construction of psychometric scales. It first provides a nontechnical introduction to these terms and their meaning for scale construction. Second, it provides a brief introduction to item response theory as a statistical framework for the interaction of respondents and test items. In this framework, violations of unidimensionality and differential item functioning can be considered as model violations. It then summarizes statistical procedures for detecting these model violations, and points to available implementations in R. Finally, there is a discussion of methods for conducting power analyses in the context of scale development.

Introduction

From a methodological perspective, a *scale* can be seen as a collection of items (i.e., tasks or questions) that aim to measure a trait of the respondent that is not directly observable. The application of scales for the assessment of cognitive abilities, personality traits, and other person characteristics of interest is ubiquitous in psychology, and related fields. Popular examples include the use of intelligence tests in psychological diagnostics (e.g., van der Ven & Ellis, 2000), educational tests such as the Program for International Student Assessment (PISA; OECD, 2020) or the IEA Trends in International Mathematics and Science Study (TIMSS; von Davier, 2020), or clinical assessments (e.g., Siegert et al., 2010) such as those for dementia or depression. Usually, these assessments consist of one or more scales that each aim to assess a single trait of interest – for instance, a specific facet of intelligence. Since the performance in each of such scales aims to be summarized by a single dimension, or a single number, we can also say that these scales aim to be *unidimensional*.

An important concept when working with psychological scales is their *validity*. Validity has been the topic of lively discussion over the last decades (Borsboom et al., 2004; Kane, 1992; Markus & Borsboom, 2013; Messick, 1989). A useful definition of validity is that a scale is valid when its interpretation is empirically justified (see American Educational Research Association et al., 2014). When considering the examples given above, it becomes obvious that scales must have a high validity to allow their application in practice, and indeed it is often seen as one of the central characteristics of a scale (e.g., American Educational Research Association et al., 2014).

In this chapter, we discuss some possible threats to the validity of a scale – namely, *violations of the unidimensionality* of a scale and *differential item functioning* (DIF; Holland & Wainer, 1993), and how researchers may address them. Violations of unidimensionality concern situations in which a scale measures not only the psychological variable (e.g., an attitude or proficiency) that it aims to measure, but one or more additional latent variables, in which the respondents taking the test differ significantly. We refer to such a scale as *multidimensional.*

From a technical perspective, violations of unidimensionality also concern situations in which some items show a mutual dependency that needs to be considered in the evaluation of a scale. Such a scale is said to show *local dependence*. Further, DIF addresses another, related, threat for the validity of a scale. It occurs if respondents of equal ability on a latent trait of interest differ in their probability for solving one or more items. As we will discuss in this chapter, DIF can result from multidimensionality (Ackerman, 1992).

Especially in the earlier psychometric literature, a violation of unidimensionality is also referred to as *scale inhomogenity* (e.g., Hattie, 1985). Likewise, DIF was referred to as *item bias* in earlier work (e.g., Angoff, 1993). Another term that is closely related to DIF is *measurement invariance*, which is defined as the degree with which a scale measures in the same way across different subpopulations (J. Liu & Dorans, 2016). In this chapter, we treat both terms as addressing the same property, so that a scale is measurement invariant if DIF is absent.

A short example based on Walker and Beretvas (2003) will make the problems of violations of unidimensionality and DIF more concrete. Consider a test of mathematical ability, which contains two types of questions: The first type are multiple-choice items, which require the respondents to select from several available written responses, and the second type are open-ended questions, which require the respondents to formulate their own responses. While both of these item types assess general mathematical knowledge, the second item type also requires proficiency in communicating about mathematical problems. If our respondents (e.g., students) can be expected to differ in both of these abilities, we would therefore need two measures to describe their abilities, the first one corresponding to general mathematical ability, and the second one representing the ability to communicate in mathematics. If we tried to treat these items as a unidimensional scale, and our respondents did differ in both of these abilities, we would risk having overall poor performance not being able to be interpreted properly: It could indicate poor mathematical knowledge, poor communication ability, or both.

We can also use this example to illustrate the problem of DIF. Consider two respondents who have the same overall mathematical knowledge, but differ in their ability to communicate regarding mathematics. For instance, one respondent could be a native speaker of the language in which the test is presented, whereas the other is not. Since our test aims to assess mathematical ability, we would expect both persons to show the same overall performance. However, open-ended items would be comparatively difficult to answer for the respondents with the lower communication ability. Again, it is necessary to consider this effect when evaluating the scale, in order not to threaten the validity of its interpretation as a test of mathematical knowledge.

The rest of the chapter is set up as follows: The next sections will give a more abstract treatment of the problems considered so far. We start with a discussion of item response theory as a statistical framework for modeling the interaction of respondents and items. This in turn allows more precise definitions of DIF and violations of unidimensionality in the section "Violations of IRT Model Assumptions." In the section "Detecting Model Violations," statistical tests will be discussed that can be used for checking these problems after data have been collected, and advice will be given regarding their practical application. The section "Sample Size Planning and Power Analysis" discusses the problem of how to determine suitable sample sizes for the application of these tests. Finally, the section "Discussion and Practical Recommendations" concludes the chapter. Supplementary material is available in a Center for Open Science (OSF) repository (see https://osf.io/juw79/).

A Modeling Framework: Item Response Theory

This section focuses on a family of statistical models to describe the interaction of respondents and items – namely, *item response theory* (IRT). Technically, IRT is closely related to factor analysis (Kamata & Bauer, 2008; Takane & De Leeuw, 1987) and therefore is sometimes referred to as *item factor analysis* (e.g., Chalmers, 2012). Its main perspective is that the responses given by a specific respondent to a set of items can be explained by their proficiency level on a latent, that is unobservable, trait. For instance, the test of mathematical ability that was mentioned in the introductory example, aims to measure a proficiency that cannot be directly observed, but has to be deduced from the given responses. We also aim to summarize the mathematical ability of the respondents by numbers, which allows us to compare different respondents. Another example would be the common evaluation of intelligence tests: These tests often lead to an ability score, which can be interpreted as an indicator for the general level of intelligence of the individual respondents.

IRT includes a wealth of statistical models for describing various aspects of the response process. Many widely known models (Birnbaum, 1968; Lord, 1980; Rasch, 1960) focus on modeling binary responses, but IRT models for polytomous responses have been developed as well (e.g., Masters, 1982; Samejima, 1969). More recently proposed IRT models allow the modeling of complex phenomena, such as the interaction of responses and response times (e.g., Klein Entink et al., 2009; van der Linden, 2007), missing data (e.g., Pohl, Ulitzsch, & von Davier, 2021; Ulitzsch et al., 2020a, 2020b, 2021), or response styles (e.g., Böckenholt, 2012; Henninger & Meiser, 2020a, 2020b).

A comprehensive introduction to all of these models cannot be provided here. Instead, this section will be confined to some basic and widely used examples. More extensive overviews of central models can be found, for instance, in the books of van der Linden (2016–2018) or De Ayala (2009).

A simple example of an IRT model is the one-parametric logistic model of Rasch (1960), which aims at describing the responses to binary items. The responses to such items are usually coded as 1 or 0, which can stand for correct or incorrect responses in ability tasks. This model further assumes that all items measure the same latent trait. The following notation is then introduced: the response given by respondent v to item i as X_{vi}. The trait level of respondent v, which stands for the proficiency of this respondent, is denoted by θ_v. We further introduce a parameter for item i which we denote as b_i and which represents the difficulty of an item. The probability that respondent v now solves item i is given by:

$$Pr(X_{vi} = 1|\theta_v, b_i) = \frac{\exp(\theta_v - b_i)}{1 + \exp(\theta_v - b_i)}. \quad (1)$$

In this equation, *exp* stands for the exponential function. It is clear from this equation that the probability of a correct response increases with $\theta_v - b_i$. This is consistent with the interpretation of these parameters as ability and difficulty parameters. Equation 1 can be extended to another well-known IRT model, the *two-parametric logistic* (2PL) model of Birnbaum (1968). This model has two parameters a_i and b_i per item. In the 2PL model, the probability of a correct response is given by:

$$Pr(X_{vi} = 1|\theta_v, a_i, b_i) = \frac{\exp(a_i \cdot (\theta_v - b_i))}{1 + \exp(a_i \cdot (\theta_v - b_i))}. \quad (2)$$

An alternative notation is given by:

$$Pr(X_{vi} = 1|\theta_v, a_i, d_i) = \frac{\exp(a_i \cdot \theta_v + d_i)}{1 + \exp(a_i \cdot \theta_v + d_i)}. \quad (3)$$

Equation 2 helps us with the interpretation of a_i and b_i: a_i indicates how much the probability of a correct response increases with $(\theta_v - b_i)$. It is referred to as the discrimination or slope parameter, or also, to emphasize the relationship to factor analytical models, the factor loading. On the other hand, b_i again indicates the overall difficulty of the item. For fixed values of a_i and θ_v, items with large values for b_i are less likely to be solved than items with small values. Therefore, b_i is called the difficulty parameter.

We can obtain Equation 3 from Equation 2 by setting $d_i = -a_i b_i$. In this parametrization, d_i is referred to as the intercept parameter. We can further generalize Equation 3 to obtain a model with more than one latent trait per respondent. The ability parameters for the different latent traits can be denoted by $\theta_{v1}, \theta_{v2}, \ldots, \theta_{vk}$, with k being the number of latent traits measured by the scale. These values can be summarized by a vector $\boldsymbol{\theta}_v$. To measure the relationship between each latent trait and the probability to solve item i, we replace a_i in Equation 3 by k factor loadings $a_{i1}, \ldots, a_{ik}$. Again, these can be summarized by a vector $\boldsymbol{a}_i$. In summary, we obtain the following equation, which underlies the *multidimensional compensatory 2PL* (M2PL) model of Reckase (2009):

$$Pr(X_{vi} = 1|\boldsymbol{\theta}_v, \boldsymbol{a}_i, d_i) = \frac{\exp(\boldsymbol{a}_i \cdot \boldsymbol{\theta}_v + d_i)}{1 + \exp(\boldsymbol{a}_i \cdot \boldsymbol{\theta}_v + d_i)}. \quad (4)$$

The name of the model refers to its characteristic that a low ability in one latent trait can be compensated by a high ability in another latent trait. In the estimation of this model, the various latent traits are usually not assumed to be independent. For instance, their pairwise correlations can be estimated as part of the model estimation, which is common in confirmatory models of factor analysis. Other, noncompensatory multidimensional variants of the 2PL model were described by, for instance Reckase (2009) as well as by Hartig and Höhler (2009). Following the definition of these models, we are now prepared to discuss DIF and violations of unidimensionality as violations of certain IRT models.

Violations of IRT Model Assumptions

Unidimensional IRT models, such as the Rasch or 2PL models, are commonly used to evaluate scales in psychology, education, and related fields. The estimation of item parameters can help with assessing the psychometric characteristics of individual items, such as their difficulty, whereas the estimation of person parameters enables an assessment of the respondents' ability. In the IRT framework, DIF and violations of unidimensionality correspond to a deviation of the true model from the model that is used for estimation. As a consequence of this deviation, the estimates for the item or person parameters can be biased, so that they do not describe the observed response data accurately. It further follows that the interpretation of these biased parameter estimates can be problematic. In the following, we discuss concrete violations of IRT models of this kind, using the 2PL model as an example. This discussion begins with two violations of unidimensionality – namely, local dependence and multidimensionality, before addressing DIF.

Local Dependence

It follows from Equation 2 that in the 2PL model the response to each item of a scale is independent from the response given to any other item or the parameters of any other item; any relationship between the responses given by a specific respondent v is modeled by the ability parameter θ_v. The responses can therefore be considered as independent outcomes, once θ_v is kept fixed. This characteristic of the 2PL model, the Rasch model and similar IRT models is also named local independence. Local dependence can now be defined as a model violation, where local independence does not hold. In non-technical terms, local dependence means that the relationship between two items is either stronger or weaker than predicted by the IRT model.

A violation of local independence occurs, for instance, if we use a unidimensional IRT model such as the 2PL or Rasch model for modeling the responses to a scale, but a model with two or more ability parameters, such as the multidimensional 2PL model, would be the true model, and the respondents also differ in all ability parameters. In this case, the true relationship between two items measuring different latent traits is weaker than would be predicted by a unidimensional model, while in the case of two items measuring the same latent trait, the true relationship is stronger. This indicates that multidimensionality leads to local dependence. As we will see, modeling multidimensional scales with unidimensional models can further lead to DIF.

Another common case of local dependence concerns the violation of local independence for individual item pairs. This type of model violation can occur if the probability of solving an item depends on the response given to another item. This can happen, for instance, if solving a previous item can help with responding correctly to a later item. In this case, the relationship between the responses to these two items will be stronger than predicted by a unidimensional model, which again results in local dependence. Statistically, local dependence for item pairs and multidimensionality are assessed with different procedures, as will be shown later in the section "Detecting Model Violations."

Multidimensionality

From a technical perspective, multidimensionality is present if an IRT model with more than one ability parameter provides a more accurate description of the response data than a unidimensional model with one ability parameter per person. Multidimensionality occurs, for instance, if a M2PL model based on Equation 4 provides a more accurate description of the data than the unidimensional 2PL model based on Equation 2.

When considering the factor loadings, one can further discern within-item multidimensionality from between-item multidimensionality. Within-item multidimensionality concerns cases where items have non-zero factor loadings on several latent traits. Between-item multidimensionality, on the other hand, concerns cases where each item has only non-zero factor loadings on a single latent trait. Practically, between-item multidimensionality means that our scale combines several scales that can each be considered unidimensional. Within-item multidimensionality, on the other hand, means the respondents differ in several traits that are necessary for solving the individual items (Adams et al., 1997). Both of these forms of multidimensionality are illustrated in Table 4.1 and Table 4.2, using factor loadings for two latent traits in 10 items: In practical applications, between-item multidimensionality can be addressed easily by splitting up the item set into suitable subgroups that can be considered as unidimensional.

Table 4.1 Between-item multidimensionality.

Item *i*	a_{i1}	a_{i2}
1	1.2	0
2	2.3	0
… 5	1.7	0
6	0	1.1
… 9	0	2.0
10	0	1.3

Note. a_{i1} and a_{i2} are item discrimination parameters.

Table 4.2 Within-item multidimensionality.

Item *i*	a_{i1}	a_{i2}
1	1.2	0.7
2	2.3	3.1
… 5	1.7	-0.1
6	1.7	1.1
… 9	0.8	2.0
10	0.4	1.3

Note. a_{i1} and a_{i2} are item discrimination parameters.

Within-item multidimensionality, on the other hand, describes a situation in which unidimensional IRT models do not provide an accurate description of the response data and can also lead to DIF, as will be described in the next subsection. In the Introduction, an example for within-item dimensionality was described, by discussing a test of mathematical knowledge, where some items also assess the ability to communicate in mathematics.

Differential Item Functioning

To understand DIF in a unidimensional IRT model on a technical level, it is helpful to consider again the Rasch or 2PL model. By its definition, DIF occurs if two respondents who have an identical ability parameter on the latent trait of interest, but belong to different respondent groups (e.g., native and non-native speakers of the test language), differ in their probability for solving a specific item. DIF is therefore not the same as an actual ability difference between the respondent groups, which is sometimes referred to as impact (e.g., Wang et al., 2012).

DIF results if item characteristics, such as the item difficulty or the item discrimination, differ for groups of respondents. This becomes immediately obvious from Equation 2: If a_i and b_i change their values between two respondents, this immediately affects their probability of giving a positive response, even if they have the same overall ability θ_v. As we will see, statistical DIF tests in an IRT framework usually aim at testing whether the estimates for item parameters such as a_i and b_i are stable over a population.

As Ackerman (1992) discusses, multidimensionality can also lead to DIF in unidimensional models. The basic idea is that, if we model a multidimensional scale with a unidimensional model, the estimated latent trait is a weighted mean of the multiple latent traits that are present in the test (such as mathematical and communication ability). If there are two or more respondent groups that differ in the distribution of the secondary traits (such as non-native speakers of the test language having lower communication ability), this can lead to DIF in the unidimensional model for the primary trait. This discussion illustrates the relationship between DIF and multidimensionality and further describes a plausible scenario under which DIF can occur.

When discussing DIF, it is important to discern specific subtypes, which affect the practical interpretation of the DIF effect. An initial distinction concerns balanced and unbalanced DIF effects. A *balanced DIF effect* corresponds to a situation where no respondent group gets an overall advantage when working on a scale, since the DIF effects for individual items cancel each other out. Otherwise, DIF effects are *unbalanced*, which may be a more common model violation than perfectly balanced DIF effects (Kopf et al., 2015a).

A second distinction concerns uniform and nonuniform DIF effects. In the context of the models discussed here, a uniform DIF effect corresponds to a situation where the DIF effect only affects the item difficulty parameters. All other DIF effects are nonuniform. In non-technical terms, uniform DIF is found in any situation where respondents from specific groups appear to be more or less able than their ability parameter would indicate, when they are working on specific items. On the other hand, a nonuniform DIF effect would correspond to a situation where the discrimination of one or more items differs between groups of respondents, possibly in addition to their difficulty. Over the years, numerous methods for DIF detection have been proposed, and several important examples will be discussed in the next section.

Detecting Model Violations

This section summarizes some techniques for detecting the model violations that were discussed in the previous section. We will also mention some software packages that help apply those techniques, and point to references in the literature for further reading. Besides these specific tests, there are some overall goodness-of-fit assessments, which allow an overall check of whether an IRT model provides a good description of the data.

Examples of techniques for detecting the model violations include the M_2 test (Maydeu-Olivares & Joe, 2005) and the *root-mean-square error of approximation* (RMSEA, Maydeu-Olivares et al., 2011), which are both available in the R package *mirt* (Chalmers, 2012). The applications of these and many of the following model tests in R are shown in Debelak et al. (2022), as well as in the supplementary material for this chapter.

Local Dependence

As was already outlined, local dependence can be considered for pairs of items or for more than two items. We will first discuss local dependence for item pairs, and then address local dependence for more than two items in the subsection on multidimensionality. Conceptually, this type of model violation can be addressed very straightforwardly using the IRT framework. We will illustrate the basic idea with a pair of binary items: In this special case, there are four possible response patterns – namely, that both items are answered correctly (or solved); that both items are answered incorrectly; and two further response patterns, where one item is solved, but the other one is not.

The estimation of item and person parameters enables a prediction of how frequently each of these response patterns should occur in our sample, if our chosen IRT model provides an accurate description of the data. A basic check of local dependence consists of comparing the observed frequencies with the values that we would expect under our IRT model.

In the case of local dependence for an item pair, two types of model violations can be discerned: First, the items can show a stronger relationship than would be expected under our IRT model. This is the case if responses where both items are either solved or not solved occur more frequently than would be expected under the IRT model. Second, two items can show a weaker relationship than expected. This is the case if response patterns where only one item is solved are more frequent than expected. Conceptually, this can indicate that the two items measure two distinct latent traits. In summary, it follows that the first model violation indicates some sort of dependence between these items, whereas the second violation can indicate multidimensionality of the item set.

A common check for this type of model violation is based on the model residuals, which are the differences between the observed and the expected response for each person–item interaction. The Q_3 statistic (Yen, 1984) is the correlation between the model residuals for both items over the sample. Values of Q_3 strongly above 0 indicate a strong positive dependence, whereas values below 0 indicate negative dependence or multidimensionality. Statistical tests for this type of model violation are, for instance, the χ^2 test of Chen and Thissen (1997) and, for the Rasch model with complete data, a nonparametric test based on the Q_3 statistic as proposed by Debelak and Koller (2020).

While the χ^2 test has been implemented in the R packages *mirt* (Chalmers, 2012) and *TAM* (Robitzsch et al., 2022), the nonparametric Q_3 test is available in eRm (Mair et al., 2020). The Q_3 statistic along with several variations is also available in *TAM* and *mirt*. In the supplementary material, we illustrate the calculation of the χ^2 test and the Q_3 statistic with *mirt*.

An important aspect of the application of these tests is that they usually assume that the person and item parameters provide an accurate description of the data. This assumption can be strongly violated if the estimated IRT model does not fit the data because, for instance, many items pairs are affected by local dependence. In this case, it is often better to consider the statistical checks discussed in the next section instead of considering individual item pairs. Y. Liu and Maydeu-Olivares (2013) and Edwards et al. (2018) present additional tests of local dependence for item pairs.

Multidimensionality

Conceptually, this type of model violation can be addressed by two families of approaches. The first approach is exploratory and assumes that the number of latent traits is unknown. It therefore aims at determining the number of latent factors from a dataset, which is a common problem in factor analysis and can be addressed using methods from this field of methods. In this context, IRT models with different numbers of latent factors are estimated and compared with regard to their relative model fit. In general, all latent factors are allowed to have non-zero factor loadings with all items. Possible criteria for comparing the individual models include information criteria such as the *Akaike information criterion* (AIC; Akaike, 1973) or the *Bayesian information criterion* (BIC; Schwarz, 1978). Assessing the fit of exploratory models is possible with R packages such as *mirt* (Chalmers, 2012) or *TAM* (Robitzsch et al., 2022). This approach is showcased in the supplementary material for this chapter.

More recent methods include variations of parallel analysis for ordinal data (Timmerman & Lorenzo-Seva, 2011). Here, the basic idea is to compare characteristics of the matrix of the pairwise correlations between the responses to the individual items, in particular its eigenvalues, with those of data generated under models with different dimensionality. Historically, some further approaches for determining the dimensionality of response data have been proposed, including approaches based on cluster analysis. Reckase (2009) provides a brief overview of these methods.

The second approach is confirmatory and compares the relative model fit of two competing models with a known number of latent traits. Here, it is important to consider the relationship between the two models. If one model results as a special case of the other model, the two models are said to be nested. An example of a pair of two nested models that differ in their dimensionality would be a unidimensional and two-dimensional 2PL model. Here, the unidimensional model results as a special case of the two-dimensional model, by setting all slope parameters (or factor loadings) of the second latent trait to 0. An example of two nonnested models would be a pair of two-dimensional 2PL models that differ in how the items are assumed to be related to the two latent traits. As an example, think of a test with 20 items: In this example, a first 2PL model could assume that items 1–10 load on the first latent trait and items 11–20 on the second latent trait. A second 2PL model could assume that items 1–15 load on the first latent trait, and items 16–20 on the second latent trait. In this case, each model is not a special case of the other. If the models are not nested, the fit of two models can again be compared using information criteria, or via the Vuong test (Merkle et al., 2016). An illustration and evaluation of these methods in the context of IRT has been provided by Schneider et al. (2020). These checks aim at comparing the relative model fit of two models, and do not assume that any of the compared models is the true model in the population.

If the models are nested, several additional tests are available, including the well-known likelihood ratio test, the score test, the Wald test, and the gradient test (Zimmer, Draxler, & Debelak, 2022). In their most common versions, these tests make the critical assumption that the more general model is correctly specified (e.g., Maydeu-Olivares & Cai, 2006). In practice, the plausibility of the more general model and its goodness-of-fit to the data can be checked, for instance using the M_2 test or the RMSEA criterion. Information criteria, the Vuong test, the likelihood ratio test, and the Wald test are available in *mirt* (Chalmers, 2012). Similar methods for model comparison are available in the R packages *TAM* (Robitzsch et al., 2022) and, for Rasch models, *eRm* (Mair et al., 2020) as well.

Differential Item Functioning

As with the detection of multidimensionality, one can discern several approaches for the detection of DIF that differ in their underlying assumptions. Consider three families of approaches: The first approach compares the relative fit of two specific IRT models, of which one model allows some item parameter to differ between predefined groups, whereas the other does not. The second and third approach are more exploratory in nature, in that they aim to find groups of respondents between which the item parameters differ. While the second approach explicitly uses available information on person covariates (e.g., sex, age) for this endeavor, the third approach does not depend on this information.

In the first family of approaches, we have two specific IRT models for our data. The first model generally assumes that all item parameters are invariant, whereas the second model allows some or all of the item parameters to differ between known groups. Statistically, this is similar to the confirmatory case discussed in the section on multidimensionality in that we want to compare the relative fit of two competing models. In the simplest case, the more general model allows all item parameters to differ, which leads to a test of whether any item shows DIF.

Alternatively, we can check the presence for DIF effects in specific items by assuming that the parameters of other items are invariant. Here, the practical problem arises that it has to be defined which item parameters are assumed to be invariant between the two groups. Items whose item parameters are considered stable over all groups are referred to as *anchor items*. Statistical tests for DIF effects are more sensitive when more anchor items are selected, if their item parameters are indeed stable. However, the selection of anchor items whose item parameters are not stable over all groups can lead to undesirable results, such as the tendency of DIF tests to show false-positive results (see, e.g., Huelmann et al., 2020; Kopf et al., 2015a; and the references therein).

Anchor items should therefore be carefully selected, either based on their item content or by suitable statistical methods. An overview on some methods for anchor selection, which are currently implemented in the R package *psychotools* (Zeileis et al., 2022a), has been provided in the studies of Kopf et al. (2015a, 2015b).

Alternative approaches that are based on optimization are the *alignment approach* proposed by Muthén and Asparouhov (2014) and the related *anchor point selection method* of Strobl et al.

(2021), available in *psychotools*, as well as the cluster-analytical approach of Pohl, Schulze, and Stets (2021). As soon as suitable anchor items have been selected, the resulting two models can be compared by statistical discussed previously, such as likelihood ratio tests, Vuong tests, and information criteria. These methods are available in *mirt* (Chalmers, 2012) and, with the exception of the Vuong tests, in *TAM* (Robitzsch et al., 2022). Some of these methods are demonstrated in the supplementary material.

For Rasch models, suitable DIF tests have been implemented in the R packages *eRm* (Mair et al., 2020) and *psychotools* (Zeileis et al., 2022a). Their usage and interpretation is illustrated in Debelak et al. (2022).

There are some related, commonly used DIF tests that are not based on IRT models. Two important examples are the Mantel-Haenszel test and a DIF test based on logistic regression (see, e.g., Magis et al., 2010). In both tests, the raw score – that is, the sum of correct responses – is taken as an approximation for the ability of each respondent, whereas the frequency of correct responses is taken as an approximation for the difficulty of a specific item. Conceptually, these tests compare the relative frequency of positive responses to a specific item for respondents from two known groups (e.g., native and non-native speakers of the test language) with the same raw score. If these frequencies differ, it is taken as an indication that the item difficulty differs between these two groups for people with the same raw score – that is, the same ability. Technically, these tests assume that the Rasch model provides a good description of the data (cf. Ackerman, 1992). Since the raw score can also be affected by DIF, we strongly recommend the use of purification strategies, which aim at eliminating DIF items from the raw score (cf., e.g., Henninger et al., 2023; and the references therein). The Mantel-Haenszel test and the logistic regression DIF test are both available in the R package *difR*, which also contains options for purification and several additional DIF tests (for an overview, see Magis et al., 2010).

In the second family of approaches, it is unknown between which groups of persons the item parameters differ, but we have a set of known person covariates (e.g., age, education, sex, and native language) that might be related to differences in item parameters. In this family, we can distinguish tree-based approaches from approaches based on regularization: Tree-based approaches find subgroups of persons that are defined by the values of covariates and in which the item parameters are stable (Henninger et al., 2023; Komboz et al., 2018; Strobl et al., 2015). There are also variations of these tests that are applicable to check the stability of individual item parameters (Debelak et al., 2022; Schneider et al., 2020).

The basic idea of regularization-based approaches (Gürer & Draxler, 2022; Magis et al., 2015; Schauberger & Mair, 2020; Tutz & Schauberger, 2015) is to first define an IRT model that includes multiple possible DIF effects. In a second step, this model is estimated while defining a penalty for any non-zero DIF effects that result in its estimation. Whereas tree-based approaches are available in the *psychotree* package (Zeileis et al., 2022b), regularization-based approaches are implemented in the R packages *DIFlasso* (Schauberger, 2020) and *GPCMlasso* (Schauberger, 2022).

The third family of approaches corresponds to a scenario where the item parameters differ between unknown groups, which do not have to be defined by known person covariates. This type of scenario is usually addressed by mixture distribution IRT models (Rost, 1990; von Davier & Yamamoto, 2007). Here, it is assumed that the respondents belong to a given number of latent groups that differ in their item parameters, but which are not necessarily related to any observed person covariates. However, it is possible to include observed covariates in such models as concomitant variables (Frick et al., 2012; Tay et al., 2011). This approach is implemented in the R packages *mirt* (Chalmers, 2012), TAM (Robitzsch et al., 2022), and *psychomix* (Frick et al., 2012).

Sample Size Planning and Power Analysis

So far, we have discussed the framework of IRT and some statistical tests for detecting important model violations that lead to local dependence, multidimensionality, and DIF for specific scales. An important question in the application of statistical tests is how large a sample size should be to detect an effect of interest – for example, with regard to the detection of DIF. A second, related question is whether a given sample size is large enough to detect a practically relevant effect – for example, a specific violation of an IRT model. In this section, some options for addressing these questions are discussed.

Statistical power is defined as the probability that a statistical test rejects an incorrect null hypothesis in favor of a correct alternative hypothesis. *Power analysis* relates statistical power to several aspects of the study, such as (a) the null and alternative hypothesis, (b) the sample size, (c) the applied statistical test and its alpha level. In the context of IRT models, power analysis addresses the question of how large a sample should be to discern between two IRT models, where one model corresponds to a violation of the other one. Using a sample size below this recommended sample size, usually leads to reduced power, so that an actual model violation is less likely to be detected. On the other hand, the use of larger samples leads to a higher power, but at the cost of a more expensive study.

In the literature, several approaches for power analysis have been proposed in the context of IRT. In this section, we discuss the main ideas, and how they can be used to detect model violations corresponding to multidimensionality, local dependence, and DIF.

A first approach proposed by Draxler (2010) and Draxler and Alexandrowicz (2015) aims at comparing two IRT models that can be estimated using a specific approach – namely, *conditional maximum likelihood estimation*. This includes Rasch models for binary and polytomous items but excludes other commonly used IRT models such as the 2PL model and its multidimensional variant. This approach can be used for planning the sample size for checking for DIF in the Rasch model, as Draxler (2010) demonstrates. This approach is implemented in the R package *tcl* (Draxler & Kurz, 2021).

A second approach was proposed by Zimmer, Draxler, and Debelak (2022). This approach is closely related to the one proposed by Draxler (2010), but was developed for the larger family of models that can be estimated using marginal maximum likelihood estimation (e.g., Baker & Kim, 2004), which includes all of the models discussed so far. This approach can be used for detecting multidimensionality by comparing unidimensional and multidimensional models and for detecting DIF in a wide class of IRT models. It is implemented in the R package *irtpwr* (Zimmer & Debelak, 2022a) and its application with the 2PL model is illustrated in the supplementary materials.

Both approaches that have been discussed so far are analytical, meaning that they are based on the theoretical distribution of a test statistic for checking the fit of an IRT model when this model is violated. The derivation of this distribution is not always possible and is also sometimes based on large sample arguments. Power estimates based on such arguments can be imprecise for small samples, although the bias is usually negligible from a practical perspective (see the simulation results in Zimmer, Draxler, & Debelak, 2022).

A third approach that addresses the limitations of such analytical approaches is a simulation-based power analysis. This approach is based on the generation and evaluation of artificial datasets where a model violation is present. It is then evaluated how reliably this model violation is detected using a specific statistical test. This evaluation might result in the recommendation of a lower or higher sample size. The repeated evaluation of various sample sizes will eventually lead to the recommendation of a suitable sample size. Some recent works have enhanced this approach with machine learning models to accelerate the search for a suitable sample size (Constantin et al., 2023; Mulay et al., 2021; Zimmer & Debelak, 2022c; Zimmer, Henninger, & Debelak, 2022). For IRT models, this approach is implemented in the R package *mlpwr* (Zimmer & Debelak, 2022b).

Discussion and Practical Recommendations

This chapter has provided a brief overview of some model violations of scale unidimensionality – namely, local dependence and multidimensionality, as well as DIF. It has addressed the practical relevance of these model violations and the statistical framework of IRT to allow their detection. It has further discussed suitable statistical procedures to detect these model violations and some implementations. Finally, it has addressed the topic of power analysis.

One practically relevant topic concerns the question of how the statistical checks outlined here can be integrated into the workflow for the psychometric evaluation of a psychological or educational scale. Several authors have recommended checking IRT models with tests that are sensitive against violations of unidimensionality (e.g., Kubinger & Draxler, 2007; Maydeu-Olivares et al., 2011; van de Winckel et al., 2022) and also checking for the presence of DIF effects (e.g., American Educational Research Association et al., 2014; Kubinger & Draxler, 2007; van de Winckel et al., 2022). These checks can be carried out with the tests presented in this chapter.

Additional checks for model violations that should be considered include graphical checks, descriptive statistics and significance tests for general model fit and model comparisons, item and person fit (i.e., whether the response patterns of individual items or respondents are expected under the assumed IRT model), etc. (see, e.g., Bond & Fox, 2007; De Ayala, 2009; Debelak et al., 2022).

A related, but possibly more difficult question is how to proceed once violations of unidimensionality or DIF have been detected. In this case, it is often useful to determine the practical significance of a model violation. This question can be partly addressed by comparing the goodness-of-fit of IRT models that do or do not model specific model violations, such as unidimensional and multidimensional models in case of multidimensionality. If both models differ strongly in how well they describe the data, it can usually be concluded that their difference is practically relevant.

Another, more refined approach would consist of the calculation of effect sizes. For DIF, suitable effect sizes have been discussed, for instance, by Steinberg and Thissen (2006), DeMars (2011), and Chalmers (2023). In general, we recommend that any revisions to scales or items should aim at reducing construct-irrelevant aspects of items while preserving the construct coverage of the scale (cf. American Educational Research Association et al., 2014, p. 82). As is also emphasized by Camilli (2006), statistical evidence of DIF does not necessarily mean that a scale is unfair. Fairness is only infringed if an item shows DIF and the source of this DIF is irrelevant to the construct the scale is intended to measure. We have argued that this is the case, for example, in a scale that claims to measure only mathematical ability, but which contains items that disadvantage non-native speakers of the test language. In such scenarios, the respective items are often excluded from the scale or modified in a new version of the scale. However, if you imagine a scale that is supposed to measure the competency for becoming a mathematics tutor, one could argue that both knowing how to solve mathematical problems and being able to communicate about mathematical concepts are relevant skills, so that keeping all items in the scale and using a two-dimensional model to capture both competencies might better reflect the intention of the scale. If a scale is found to be multidimensional, this usually indicates that multiple measures - that is, the estimated person parameters - reflect the ability level of the respondents more accurately, than would a single measure, such as the sum score. Moreover, any revisions to a scale that are motivated by the results of statistical analyses should be cross-validated with an independent sample of respondents (cf. American Educational Research Association et al., 2014, p. 89).

Author Note

The authors declare that they have no conflict of interest. There is no funding to report for this study.

References

Ackerman, T. A. (1992). A didactic explanation of item bias, item impact, and item validity from a multidimensional perspective. *Journal of Educational Measurement, 29*(1), 67–91. https://www.jstor.org/stable/1434777 https://doi.org/10.1111/j.1745-3984.1992.tb00368.x

Adams, R. J., Wilson, M., & Wang, W. (1997). The multidimensional random coefficients multinomial logit model. *Applied Psychological Measurement, 21*(1), 1–23. https://doi.org/10.1177/0146621697211001

Akaike, H. (1973). Information theory and an extension of the maximum likelihood principle. In B. N. Petrov & B. F. Csaki (Eds.), *Second international symposium on information theory* (pp. 267–281). Academiai Kiado.

American Educational Research Association, American Psychological Association, & National Council on Measurement in Education. (2014). *Standards for educational and psychological testing.* American Educational Research Association.

Angoff, W. H. (1993). Perspectives on differential item functioning methodology. In P. Holland & H. Wainer (Eds.), *Differential item functioning* (pp. 3–23). Lawrence Erlbaum.

Baker, F., & Kim, S.-H. (2004). *Item response theory: Parameter estimation techniques* (2nd ed.). CRC Press.

Birnbaum, A. (1968). Some latent trait models and their use in inferring an examinee's ability. In F. Lord & M. Novick (Eds.), *Statistical theories of mental test scores* (pp. 397–479). Addison-Wesley.

Böckenholt, U. (2012). Modeling multiple response processes in judgment and choice. *Psychological Methods, 17*(4), 665–678. https://doi.org/10.1037/a0028111

Bond, T., & Fox, C. (2007). *Applying the Rasch model: Fundamental measurement in the human sciences.* Lawrence Erlbaum.

Borsboom, D., Mellenbergh, G. J., & van Heerden, J. (2004). The concept of validity. *Psychological Review, 111*(4), 1061–1071. https://doi.org/10.1037/0033-295X.111.4.1061

Camilli, G. (2006). Test fairness. In R. Brennan (Ed.), *Educational measurement* (pp. 221–256). ACE; Praeger Series on Higher Education.
Chalmers, R. P. (2012). mirt: A multidimensional item response theory package for the R environment. *Journal of Statistical Software, 48*(6), 1–29. https://doi.org/10.18637/jss.v048.i06
Chalmers, R. P. (2023). A unified comparison of IRT-based effect sizes for DIF investigations. *Journal of Educational Measurement, 60*(2), 318–350. https://doi.org/10.1111/jedm.12347
Chen, W.-H., & Thissen, D. (1997). Local dependence indexes for item pairs using item response theory. *Journal of Educational and Behavioral Statistics, 22*(3), 265–289. https://doi.org/10.2307/1165285
Constantin, M., Schuurman, N. K., & Vermunt, J. (2023). A general Monte Carlo method for sample size analysis in the context of network models. *Psychological Methods*. https://doi.org/10.31234/osf.io/j5v7u
De Ayala, R. (2009). *The theory and practice of Item Response Theory*. Guilford Press.
Debelak, R., & Koller, I. (2020). Testing the local independence assumption of the Rasch model with Q3-based nonparametric model tests. *Applied Psychological Measurement, 44*(2), 103–117. https://doi.org/10.1177/0146621619835501
Debelak, R., Strobl, C., & Zeigenfuse, M. D. (2022). *An introduction to the Rasch model with examples in R*. CRC Press. https://doi.org/10.1201/9781315200620
DeMars, C. E. (2011). An analytic comparison of effect sizes for differential item functioning. *Applied Measurement in Education, 24*(3), 189–209. https://doi.org/10.1080/08957347.2011.580255
Draxler, C. (2010). Sample size determination for Rasch model tests. *Psychometrika, 75*(4), 708–724. https://doi.org/10.1007/s11336-010-9182-4
Draxler, C., & Alexandrowicz, R. W. (2015). Sample size determination within the scope of conditional maximum likelihood estimation with special focus on testing the Rasch model. *Psychometrika, 80*(4), 897–919. https://doi.org/10.1007/s11336-015-9472-y
Draxler, C., & Kurz, A. (2021). *tcl: Testing in conditional likelihood context* (R package version 0.1.1) [Computer software manual]. https://CRAN.R-project.org/package=tcl
Edwards, M. C., Houts, C. R., & Cai, L. (2018). A diagnostic procedure to detect departures from local independence in item response theory models. *Psychological Methods, 23*(1), 138–149. https://doi.org/10.1037/met0000121
Frick, H., Strobl, C., Leisch, F., & Zeileis, A. (2012). Flexible Rasch mixture models with package psychomix. *Journal of Statistical Software, 48*(7), 1–25. http://www.jstatsoft.org/v48/i07/ https://doi.org/10.18637/jss.v048.i07
Gürer, C., & Draxler, C. (2022). Penalization approaches in the conditional maximum likelihood and Rasch modelling context. *British Journal of Mathematical and Statistical Psychology*. https://doi.org/10.1111/bmsp.12287
Hartig, J., & Höhler, J. (2009). Multidimensional IRT models for the assessment of competencies. *Studies in Educational Evaluation, 35*(2), 57–63. https://doi.org/10.1016/j.stueduc.2009.10.002
Hattie, J. (1985). Methodology review: assessing unidimensionality of tests and ltenls. *Applied Psychological Measurement, 9*(2), 139–164. https://doi.org/10.1177/014662168500900204
Henninger, M., Debelak, R., & Strobl, C. (2023). A new stopping criterion for Rasch trees based on the Mantel–Haenszel effect size measure for differential item functioning. *Educational and Psychological Measurement, 83*(1), 181–212. https://doi.org/10.1177/00131644221077135
Henninger, M., & Meiser, T. (2020a). Different approaches to modeling response styles in divide-by-total item response theory models (part 1): A model integration. *Psychological Methods, 25*(5), 560–576. https://doi.org/10.1037/met0000249
Henninger, M., & Meiser, T. (2020b). Different approaches to modeling response styles in divide-by-total item response theory models (part 2): Applications and novel extensions. *Psychological Methods, 25*(5), 577–595. https://doi.org/10.1037/met0000268
Holland, P. W., & Wainer, H. (Eds.). (1993). *Differential item functioning*. Taylor & Francis.
Huelmann, T., Debelak, R., & Strobl, C. (2020). A comparison of aggregation rules for selecting anchor items in multigroup DIF analysis. *Journal of Educational Measurement, 57*(2), 185–215. https://doi.org/10.1111/jedm.12246

Kamata, A., & Bauer, D. J. (2008). A note on the relation between factor analytic and item response theory models. *Structural Equation Modeling, 15*(1), 136–153. https://doi.org/10.1080/10705510701758406

Kane, M. T. (1992). An argument-based approach to validity. *Psychological Bulletin, 112*(3), 527–535. https://doi.org/10.1037/0033-2909.112.3.527

Klein Entink, R., Fox, J.-P., & van der Linden, W. J. (2009). A multivariate multilevel approach to the modeling of accuracy and speed of test takers. *Psychometrika, 74*(1), 21–48. https://doi.org/10.1007/s11336-008-9075-y

Komboz, B., Strobl, C., & Zeileis, A. (2018). Tree-based global model tests for polytomous Rasch models. *Educational and Psychological Measurement, 78*(1), 128–166. https://doi.org/10.1177/0013164416664394

Kopf, J., Zeileis, A., & Strobl, C. (2015a). Anchor selection strategies for DIF analysis: Review, assessment, and new approaches. *Educational and Psychological Measurement, 75*(1), 22–56. https://doi.org/10.1177/0013164414529792

Kopf, J., Zeileis, A., & Strobl, C. (2015b). A framework for anchor methods and an iterative forward approach for DIF detection. *Applied Psychological Measurement, 39*(2), 83–103. https://doi.org/10.1177/0146621614544195

Kubinger, K. D., & Draxler, C. (2007). Probleme bei der Testkonstruktion nach dem Rasch-Modell [Problems in test construction based on the Rasch model]. *Diagnostica, 53*(3), 131–143. https://doi.org/10.1026/0012-1924.53.3.131

Liu, J., & Dorans, N. J. (2016). Fairness in score interpretation. In N. J. Dorans & L. L. Cook (Eds.), *Fairness in educational assessment and measurement* (pp. 77–96). Routledge. https://doi.org/10.4324/9781315774527-6

Liu, Y., & Maydeu-Olivares, A. (2013). Local dependence diagnostics in IRT modeling of binary data. *Educational and Psychological Measurement, 73*(2), 254–274. https://doi.org/10.1177/0013164412453841

Lord, F. M. (1980). *Applications of item response theory to practical testing problems.* Lawrence Erlbaum.

Magis, D., Beland, S., Tuerlinckx, F., & De Boeck, P. (2010). A general framework and an R package for the detection of dichotomous differential item functioning. *Behavior Research Methods, 42*, 847–862. https://doi.org/10.3758/BRM.42.3.847

Magis, D., Tuerlinckx, F., & Boeck, P. D. (2015). Detection of differential item functioning using the Lasso approach. *Journal of Educational and Behavioral Statistics, 40*(2), 111–135. https://doi.org/10.3102/1076998614559747

Mair, P., Hatzinger, R., & Maier, M. J. (2020). *eRm: Extended Rasch modeling* (R package) [Computer software manual]. https://CRAN.R-project.org/package=eRm

Markus, K. A., & Borsboom, D. (2013). *Frontiers of test validity theory: Measurement, causation, and meaning.* Routledge.

Masters, G. N. (1982). A Rasch model for partial credit scoring. *Psychometrika, 47*(2), 149–174. https://doi.org/10.1007/BF02296272

Maydeu-Olivares, A., & Cai, L. (2006). A cautionary note on using G2(dif) to assess relative model fit in categorical data analysis. *Multivariate Behavioral Research, 41*(1), 55–64. https://doi.org/10.1207/s15327906mbr4101_4

Maydeu-Olivares, A., Cai, L., & Hernández, A. (2011). Comparing the fit of item response theory and factor analysis models. *Structural Equation Modeling: A Multidisciplinary Journal, 18*(3), 333–356. https://doi.org/10.1080/10705511.2011.581993

Maydeu-Olivares, A., & Joe, H. (2005). Limited- and full-information estimation and goodness-of-fit testing in 2n contingency tables. *Journal of the American Statistical Association, 100*(471), 1009–1020. https://doi.org/10.1198/016214504000002069

Merkle, E. C., You, D., & Preacher, K. J. (2016). Testing nonnested structural equation models. *Psychological Methods, 21*(2), 151—163. https://doi.org/10.1037/met0000038

Messick, S. (1989). Validity. In R. L. Linn (Ed.), *Educational measurement* (pp. 13–104). American Council on Education; Macmillan.

Mulay, A. K., Lane, S., & Hennes, E. (2021, December 29). Simulation-based design optimization for statistical power: Utilizing machine learning. https://doi.org/10.48550/arXiv.2201.00719

Muthén, B., & Asparouhov, T. (2014). IRT studies of many groups: The alignment method. *Frontiers in Psychology, 5*, Article 978. https://doi.org/10.3389/fpsyg.2014.00978

OECD. (2020). *Pisa 2018 technical background.* OECD. https://doi.org/10.1787/1b045c06-en

Pohl, S., Schulze, D., & Stets, E. (2021). Partial measurement invariance: Extending and evaluating the cluster approach for identifying anchor items. *Applied Psychological Measurement, 45*(7–8), 477–493. https://doi.org/10.1177/01466216211042809

Pohl, S., Ulitzsch, E., & von Davier, M. (2021). Reframing rankings in educational assessments. *Science, 372*(6540), 338–340. https://doi.org/10.1126/science.abd3300

Rasch, G. (1960). *Probabilistic models for some intelligence and attainment tests.* University of Chicago Press.

Reckase, M. (2009). *Multidimensional item response theory.* Springer. https://doi.org/10.1007/978-0-387-89976-3

Robitzsch, A., Kiefer, T., & Wu, M. (2022). *TAM: Test analysis modules* (R package version 4.1-4) [Computer software manual]. https://CRAN.R-project.org/package=TAM

Rost, J. (1990). Rasch models in latent classes: An integration of two approaches to item analysis. *Applied Psychological Measurement, 14*(3), 271–282. https://doi.org/10.1177/014662169001400305

Samejima, F. (1969). Estimation of latent ability using a response pattern of graded scores. *Psychometrika Monograph Supplement, 34*(4), i–169. https://doi.org/10.1002/j.2333-8504.1968.tb00153.x

Schauberger, G. (2020). *DIFlasso: A penalty approach to differential item functioning in Rasch models* (R package version 1.0-4) [Computer software manual]. https://CRAN.R-project.org/package=DIFlasso

Schauberger, G. (2022). *GPCMlasso: Differential item functioning in generalized partial credit models* (R package version 0.1-6) [Computer software manual]. https://CRAN.R-project.org/package=GPCMlasso

Schauberger, G., & Mair, P. (2020). A regularization approach for the detection of differential item functioning in generalized partial credit models. *Behavior Research Methods, 52*(1), 279–294. https://doi.org/10.3758/s13428-019-01224-2

Schneider, L., Chalmers, R. P., Debelak, R., & Merkle, E. C. (2020). Model selection of nested and non-nested item response models using Vuong tests. *Multivariate Behavioral Research, 55*(5), 664–684. https://doi.org/10.1080/00273171.2019.1664280

Schwarz, G. (1978). Estimating the dimension of a model. *Annals of Statistics, 6*(2), 461–464. https://www.jstor.org/stable/2958889 https://doi.org/10.1214/aos/1176344136

Siegert, R. J., Tennant, A., & Turner-Stokes, L. (2010). Rasch analysis of the Beck Depression Inventory-II in a neurological rehabilitation sample. *Disability and Rehabilitation, 32*(1), 8–17. https://doi.org/10.3109/09638280902971398

Steinberg, L., & Thissen, D. (2006). Using effect sizes for research reporting: Examples using item response theory to analyze differential item functioning. *Psychological Methods, 11*(4), 402–415. https://doi.org/10.1037/1082-989X.11.4.402

Strobl, C., Kopf, J., Kohler, L., von Oertzen, T., & Zeileis, A. (2021). Anchor point selection: Scale alignment based on an inequality criterion. *Applied Psychological Measurement, 45*(3), 214–230. https://doi.org/10.1177/0146621621990743

Strobl, C., Kopf, J., & Zeileis, A. (2015). Rasch trees: A new method for detecting differential item functioning in the Rasch model. *Psychometrika, 80*(2), 289–316. https://doi.org/10.1007/s11336-013-9388-3

Takane, Y., & De Leeuw, J. (1987). On the relationship between item response theory and factor analysis of discretized variables. *Psychometrika, 52*(3), 393–408. https://doi.org/10.1007/BF02294363

Tay, L., Newman, D. A., & Vermunt, J. K. (2011). Using mixed-measurement item response theory with covariates (MM-IRT-C) to ascertain observed and unobserved measurement equivalence. *Organizational Research Methods, 14*(1), 147–176. https://doi.org/10.1177/1094428110366037

Timmerman, M. E., & Lorenzo-Seva, U. (2011). Dimensionality assessment of ordered polytomous items with parallel analysis. *Psychological Methods, 16*(2), 209. https://doi.org/10.1037/a0023353

Tutz, G., & Schauberger, G. (2015). A penalty approach to differential item functioning in Rasch models. *Psychometrika, 80*(1), 21–43. https://doi.org/10.1007/s11336-013-9377-6

Ulitzsch, E., Pohl, S., Khorramdel, L., Kroehne, U., & von Davier, M. (2021). A response-time-based latent response mixture model for identifying and modeling careless and insufficient effort responding in survey data. *Psychometrika*, 1–27. https://doi.org/10.1007/s11336-021-09817-7

Ulitzsch, E., von Davier, M., & Pohl, S. (2020a). A hierarchical latent response model for inferences about examinee engagement in terms of guessing and item-level non-response. *British Journal of Mathematical and Statistical Psychology, 73*(S1), e12188. https://doi.org/10.1111/bmsp.12188

Ulitzsch, E., von Davier, M., & Pohl, S. (2020b). Using response times for joint modeling of response and omission behavior. *Multivariate Behavioral Research, 55*(3), 425–453. https://doi.org/10.1080/00273171.2019.1643699

van der Linden, W. J. (2007). A hierarchical framework for modeling speed and accuracy on test items. *Psychometrika, 72*(3), 287–308. https://doi.org/10.1007/s11336-006-1478-z

van der Linden, W. (Ed.). (2016–2018). *Handbook of item response theory – three volume set.* CRC Press. https://doi.org/10.1201/9781315119144

van der Ven, A., & Ellis, J. (2000). A Rasch analysis of Raven's standard progressive matrices. *Personality and Individual Differences, 29*(1), 45–64. https://doi.org/10.1016/S0191-8869(99)00177-4

Van de Winckel, A., Kozlowski, A. J., Johnston, M. V., Weaver, J., Grampurohit, N., Terhorst, L., Juengst, S., Ehrlich-Jones, L., Heinemann, A. W., Melvin, J., Sood, P., & Mallinson, T. (2022). Reporting guideline for RULER: Rasch reporting guideline for rehabilitation research: Explanation and elaboration. *Archives of Physical Medicine and Rehabilitation, 103*(7), 1487–1498. https://doi.org/10.1016/j.apmr.2022.03.019

von Davier, M. (2020). TIMSS 2019 scaling methodology: Item response theory, population models, and linking across modes. In M. Martin, M. von Davier, & I. Mullis (Eds.), *Methods and procedures: TIMSS 2019 technical report* (pp. 11.1–11.25). Boston College; TIMSS & PIRLS International Study Center.

von Davier, M., & Yamamoto, K. (2007). Mixture-distribution and HYBRID Rasch models. In M. von Davier & C. H. Carstensen (Eds.), *Multivariate and mixture distribution Rasch models* (pp. 99–115). Springer. https://doi.org/10.1007/978-0-387-49839-3_6

Walker, C. M., & Beretvas, S. N. (2003). Comparing multidimensional and unidimensional proficiency classifications: Multidimensional IRT as a diagnostic aid. *Journal of Educational Measurement, 40*(3), 255–275. https://doi.org/10.1111/j.1745-3984.2003.tb01107.x

Wang, W.-C., Shih, C.-L., & Sun, G.-W. (2012). The DIF-free-then-DIF strategy for the assessment of differential item functioning. *Educational and Psychological Measurement, 72*(4), 687–708. https://doi.org/10.1177/0013164411426157

Yen, W. M. (1984). Effects of local item dependence on the fit and equating performance of the three-parameter logistic model. *Applied Psychological Measurement, 8*(2), 125–145. https://doi.org/10.1177/014662168400800201

Zeileis, A., Strobl, C., Wickelmaier, F., Komboz, B., Kopf, J., Schneider, L., & Debelak, R. (2022a). *psychotools: Infrastructure for psychometric modeling* (R package version 0.7-2) [Computer software manual]. https://CRAN.R-project.org/package=psychotools

Zeileis, A., Strobl, C., Wickelmaier, F., Komboz, B., Kopf, J., Schneider, L., Dreifuss, D., & Debelak, R. (2022b). *psychotree: Recursive partitioning based on psychometric models* (R package version 0.16-0) [Computer software manual]. https://CRAN.R-project.org/package=psychotree

Zimmer, F., & Debelak, R. (2022a). *irtpwr: Power analysis for IRT models using the Wald, LR, score, and gradient statistics* (R package version 1.0.0) [Computer software manual]. https://CRAN.R-project.org/package=irtpwr https://doi.org/10.32614/CRAN.package.irtpwr

Zimmer, F., & Debelak, R. (2022b). *mlpwr: A power analysis toolbox to find cost-efficient study designs* (R package version 1.0.0) [Computer software manual]. https://CRAN.R-project.org/package=mlpwr https://doi.org/10.32614/CRAN.package.mlpwr

Zimmer, F., & Debelak, R. (2022c, March 28). *Simulation-based design optimization for statistical power: Utilizing machine learning.* https://doi.org/10.31234/osf.io/tnhb2

Zimmer, F., Draxler, C., & Debelak, R. (2022). Power analysis for the Wald, LR, score, and gradient tests in a marginal maximum likelihood framework: Applications in IRT. *Psychometrika.* https://doi.org/10.1007/s11336-022-09883-5

Zimmer, F., Henninger, M., & Debelak, R. (2022, October 28). *Sample size planning for complex study designs: A tutorial for the mlpwr package.* https://doi.org/10.31234/osf.io/r9w6t

Chapter 5

Identifying Nonequivalence in Measurement Tools

Dragos Iliescu and Andrei Ion

Abstract

The concept of *equivalence* in psychological measurement, a form of validity, ensures comparability of test scores across different groups, contexts, or testing processes. Equivalence, often referred to as *invariance*, is essential for unbiased interpretation of scores and their use across diverse settings, such as cross-cultural assessments or varying test modalities. This chapter explores the theoretical underpinnings of equivalence, emphasizing its role in a spectrum rather than as a binary construct, and its critical connection to measurement bias. It delineates three primary categories of nonequivalence – construct, method, and item bias – each with unique detection challenges and implications for test adaptation. Statistical methods, such as *confirmatory factor analysis* (CFA) and *item response theory* (IRT), are highlighted for detecting and addressing nonequivalence. Practical examples illustrate challenges in achieving invariance across cultures, sexes, and administration formats. The discussion underscores the necessity of considering equivalence as a dynamic, context-dependent characteristic of scores, with implications for both theoretical development and practical application of psychological assessments. Recommendations for future research include advancing methodologies for detecting and mitigating bias, emphasizing the importance of partial invariance, and ensuring robust test adaptations across diverse populations.

Definition

Equivalence in psychological measurement has been described and defined in many ways. We define it here as a form of validity. This form of validity is observed when the relationship between test scores and their correlates is the same across different groups, contexts, or separate testing processes. Correlates in this sense can be observed variables that contribute to those scores (e.g., items), or latent constructs that are reflected by those scores. Separate testing processes in the sense of the above may be based on different tests or different forms of the same test (such as in the case of test adaptation), different testing contexts (e.g., low-stake vs. high-stake testing), different groups of test takers, or even combinations of these. This special form of validity is also referred to as *invariance*. Lack of equivalence is associated with measurement bias – hence equivalence, invariance, and (lack of) bias are oftentimes used as interchangeable terms.

The literature regarding equivalence is strongly grounded in the cross-cultural measurement tradition and was especially developed in such domains as test adaptation – so much so that "testing for equivalence" usually presupposes some form of test adaptation in a different language or on a different population (Iliescu, 2017). This does not, however, need to be so: Equivalence refers to the comparability of scores obtained from any two testing processes – but the association with cross-cultural measurement underscores the fact that the basic issue behind equivalence is the issue of comparability across cultures. We specifically point out that, while much of the literature regarding equivalence reflects this cross-cultural heritage, equivalence can be and oftentimes is discussed relative to modes other than language and culture, such as different modes of administration (e.g., digital vs. paper-and-pencil), different age groups (e.g., children vs. adults), different educational levels, etc. However, for brevity (and also as an acknowledgment of the fact that most of the literature is provided by those in the cross-cultural test adaptation tradition), this chapter will use mainly language referring to the comparable entities as being from "two cultures."

Equivalence "is not an intrinsic property of an instrument, but a concomitant of the application of that instrument in a particular group for a particular purpose" (van de Vijver & Poortinga, 2005, p. 41). The key point in this definition is that equivalence is not a property of an instrument, although this is how it is most often expressed in studies – for example, by referring to the measurement equivalence of the X language form of instrument Y. While we acknowledge that equivalence always employs a comparative logic (i.e., a measure cannot be simply equivalent on its own, but is equivalent to something), we insist that it is not the instrument but the scores that are equivalent. Oftentimes we compare (and test the equivalence of) scores provided by one language version of a test with scores stemming from another language version. But equivalence can also be tested for scores provided by the same form of the test in two populations (e.g., male vs. female) or in two measurement contexts (e.g., low-stake self-description vs. high-stake personnel selection settings).

Equivalence has been defined above as a source of validity (for a more detailed discussion of this view, see Iliescu, 2017), but the main arguments for this position are briefly presented below. Validity is defined as "the degree to which evidence and theory support the interpretations of test scores for proposed uses of tests" (American Educational Research Association et al., 2014, p. 11). Equivalence is the degree to which the empirical evidence supports the fact that the adapted version of the test is similar to the original version and warrants the same score interpretations. Equivalence evidence is therefore a form of validity evidence. At least five arguments can be put forward for this position:

a. Equivalence is a matter of degree, not of difference in quality. This is the dominant view about validity, too: "validity is a matter of degree, not all or none" (Messick, 1990, p. 1487), and it is valid also for equivalence. The degrees of sameness will be discussed as they arise between two forms of a test on a continuum between complete nonequivalence and complete scalar equivalence.
b. Equivalence is a property of scores, not of the instrument: It is a characteristic of the relationship between two forms of a test, each administered in a specific context for a specific purpose. Tests are not equivalent, although this is usually phrased as something like "scores provided by two forms of a test can be equivalent."
c. Equivalence is therefore contextual to specific situations: Scores are provided by the application of a test to a particular situation, in a particular context. Different forms of the same test that were adapted for use in different cultures and different professional contexts, may

show different equivalence when compared, two by two with each other. Even the same-language form of a test may not generate equivalent scores in two different contexts of administration. Statements about the equivalence of two sets of scores (or "two tests") are meaningless without the referent – that is, the contexts that provided the scores and that are ultimately compared.

d. Equivalence is directly connected with bias and error. Equivalence is placed on one end of a continuum on which the other end is "bias." Less equivalence represents more bias. Strictly applied to measurement, bias, or error, is associated with reliability more than validity. Of course, two equivalent forms of a test can be considered to be parallel forms – and this is after all a form of reliability. At the same time, reliability is a prerequisite of validity, and vice versa, reliability evidence is a source of validity evidence.
e. Equivalence is related to the capacity to generalize: How much can we generalize the conclusions drawn from a test across different contexts, with different samples, in different cultures, etc.?

If we accept these points and qualify equivalence as validity, it follows that sources that can be accepted for equivalence evidence are the same sources that are indicated for validity evidence. This describes a finer-grained picture than is oftentimes presented in the literature. Evidence for equivalence is most often given in the form of one hard statistic or another. Our position here is that several sources of validity evidence from among those initially proposed by Messick (1995) and later absorbed by the Joint Standards (AERA, APA, NCME standards, informally they are known as the Joint Standards) apply to equivalence (American Educational Research Association et al., 2014, pp. 13–16):

a. Evidence based on test content: that is, whether or not the content of tests that are compared is equivalent. This is particularly important in the case of tests adapted for use in different languages or cultures but may not be important when the same test is used on two populations in the same language and culture.
b. Evidence based on response processes: that is, whether the cognitive processes in which test takers engage are similar.
c. Evidence based on internal structure: that is, if the relationships between the different components of the test, such as test items, and test scales, are similar.
d. Evidence based on relations to other variables: that is, if the intended interpretations, defined by relations with variables not measured by the test, are similar.
e. Evidence based on the consequences of testing: that is, consequential validity, if the consequences of testing, specifically of interpretations and decisions following the testing, are similar.

Current practice related to equivalence focuses overwhelmingly on (c) evidence based on internal structure, (d) evidence based on relations to other variables is sometimes touched upon, and (a) evidence based on test content is most often mentioned in passing (though, sadly, not detailed enough) in linguistic and cultural test adaptations. The sources (b) evidence based on response processes and (e) evidence based on the consequences of testing are orphans in this context.

Finally, to complete this short introduction, it is necessary to dedicate a little space to linguistic concerns. The way in which the term "equivalence" is used in practice is connected to statistical issues – that is, it has a rather technical connotation, associated with a specific statistical instrumentation. At the same time, the realm of equivalence is much larger and covered oftentimes by other terms. Specifically, "equivalence" and "bias" are oftentimes used as antonyms – that is, nonequivalence is bias. For many purposes related to equivalence, "bias" is the term used. For example, we talk about construct bias (i.e., construct nonequivalence), method bias (i.e., method-driven nonequivalence), or item bias (i.e., item-driven nonequivalence), and not about the respective equivalences.

Categories of Equivalence

Inspired mainly by the cross-cultural research tradition, discussions of lack of equivalence (i.e., presence of bias) have been undertaken under three large categories: *construct bias*, *method bias*, and *item bias* (Byrne, 2015; van de Vijver & Leung, 1997; van de Vijver & Tanzer, 1997). These are then further subdivided into sources of bias that are typical for each of the categories. Table 5.1 presents and briefly describes these categories and sources.

Table 5.1 Three types of cross-cultural bias in test adaptation: descriptions and sources.

Type of bias	Description	Sources	Examples
Construct bias	Incomplete overlap of the measured constructs in the original and adapted versions of the test	Differences in the definition of the construct between the source and target culture	The construct is defined differently in one culture than in another
		Construct contamination: incomplete overlap of construct-relevant indicators across the source and target culture	Indicators of the construct which are valid for one culture and not valid for the other
		Construct deficiency: incomplete coverage of the construct	Not all relevant domains of the construct are sampled, or domains are poorly sampled with items studied (especially for short measures)
		Differential appropriateness of construct-relevant indicators across the source and target culture	The skills sampled do not belong to the repertoire of one of the cultural groups

Table 5.1 Continued

Type of bias	Description	Sources	Examples
Method bias	Nuisance factors arising from aspects of method		
Sample bias	Differences in sample characteristics	Lack of comparability in experimental (research) samples	The sample used for piloting the adapted test is different in some characteristics (e.g., education) from the sample used for the original version
		Lack of comparability in samples of actual test takers	The adapted version of the test is used on a sample of test takers substantively different (e.g., in terms of education, age, etc.) from the sample on which the original version of the test is used
Instrument bias	Features of the instrument (measure), not related to construct or items	Differential familiarity with stimulus material	Test takers in the target culture are not familiar with a large proportion of the items represented or described in the stimuli
		Differential familiarity with response procedures	Test takers in the target culture are not familiar with the procedures which are used in order to offer answers to the items
		Differential response styles (cultural response sets, self-disclosure)	Extremity scoring or acquiescence are significantly more or significantly less present in the target culture than in the source culture
		Differential social desirability	Some items or categories of items are significantly more or significantly less socially desirable in the target culture than in the source culture

Table 5.1 Continued

Type of bias	Description	Sources	Examples
Administration bias	Issues in communication between test administrator and test taker	Differences in language proficiency	The test administrator is not very proficient in the language of the test takers, or the test takers are not very proficient in the language the test is administered in
		Differences in the observance of target culture	The test administrator does not possess enough knowledge of the target culture (is not culturally competent)
		Differences in technological administration conditions	The technology used in the target culture for administration is different from that in the source culture or unfamiliar for the test takers (e.g., computerized testing in rural areas of sub-Saharan Africa)
		Differences in physical administration conditions	The physical environment of testing differs from the source to the target culture (e.g., thermic comfort, phonic comfort)
		Differences in social administration conditions	The social environment in which the test is administered in the target culture is different from the source culture (e.g., larger classrooms, mixed- or mono-sex composition of classrooms)
		Differential expertise of test administrators	The professionals administrating the test in the source and target cultures have different levels of expertise in test administration
		Interviewer characteristics	Characteristics of the test administrator may influence test takers

Table 5.1 Continued

Type of bias	Description	Sources	Examples
Item bias	Anomalies in items	Incorrect item translation (errors in translation)	Items are wrongly translated (incorrect meaning)
		Poor item translation (shift in meaning due to new connotations)	Translated items are tainted by unintended connotations in the target culture (lexical nonisomorphism)
		Inadequate item formulation	Translated items use complex wording (unnatural syntactic constructions)
		Item familiarity	Some (few) items are unfamiliar in the target culture
		Item appropriateness	Some item content (not large) is unknown in the target culture (e.g., a topic in an educational test may not be part of the school curriculum in the target culture)

Note. Adapted from van de Vijver & Leung (1997); van de Vijver & Poortinga (1997, 2005).

Construct bias occurs when the attribute being tested does not translate identically across cultures in a test's adaptation process. This could mean the attribute does not exist in the new culture, its components differ, or its structure varies, affecting the test's relevance and accuracy. Construct equivalence is achieved when the tested attribute fully aligns between the original and adapted cultures.

Method bias stems from factors inherent to the testing process itself, including sample, instrument, and administration aspects. It can occur even when the construct is applicable in the target culture, suggesting that testing procedures suitable in one culture may not translate well to another. This includes everything from test design elements such as layout and color, to more significant issues like question formatting and scaling. Similarly, test administration methods that work in one culture might not be effective in another, highlighting the importance of method equivalence – where both the test's format and its administration are equally appropriate and effective across cultures.

Item bias occurs when specific test items do not perform the same across cultures, independent of construct and method biases. This can happen even with perfect construct alignment and method adequacy between source and target cultures. Causes include poor translation or adaptation, and making an item unclear, inappropriate, or differently challenging, due to cultural nuances. Additionally, translations can introduce unintended connotations, as languages are not directly equivalent. Item equivalence is achieved when each test item provokes the same response with the same intensity, in both the original and adapted versions across cultures.

Neither the literature nor practitioners have the same awareness for all these three categories. The most obvious attention is almost always given to item bias: Any adaptation of a test will start from the items of that test. At the same time, item bias is most often treated in a very naive way and with little sophistication and awareness for the different intricacies. Construct bias has become the best documented category, with obligations to establish invariance relative to the construct being omnipresent requests in scientific journals nowadays. Method bias has remained behind in everyone's attention and is likely the most insidious of the three forms of bias.

What is clear is that these three categories of bias are progressively more difficult to control: Item bias is the easiest to manage, method bias presents more challenges, and construct bias might be insurmountable without investing substantial effort. We consider "difficulty" in terms of the effort required for (a) detecting that form of bias by empirical tests and (b) controlling that form of bias by modifications needed on the test. Brief explanations – hints, really – about how each of the three categories can be detected and controlled, follow, with more in-depth discussions after that.

Detecting item bias is relatively straightforward, requiring just one administration of the test in the target language and comparing item behaviors to the original. Various statistical methods can be used in this comparison, with both data collection and analysis being relatively simple. Addressing item bias typically involves reformulating or rewriting the biased items.

Detecting method bias is more complex, as it involves considering cultural, social, and other variables that may affect the test's adequacy across the two groups (e.g., cultures). This process may require investigating differential familiarity with test materials, analyzing typical response styles within the target culture, or even conducting specialized research: A simple administration of the test on both groups is rarely sufficient for the detection of method bias. Addressing method bias can be challenging, necessitating changes ranging from minor adjustments, such as modifying instructions or switching from online to paper formats, to more significant overhauls, such as rethinking stimulus materials or completely changing items to align with cultural differences.

Detecting construct bias is highly challenging, as it requires not just multivariate analyses such as CFA within a structural equation modeling (SEM) framework (which is quite straightforward, really), but also a deep dive into the construct definitions' similarities across cultures, and the associated range of behaviors in the target culture. This might necessitate separate research projects to explore the construct's correlates. Addressing construct bias is extremely difficult, and even sometimes impossible. When constructs are not equivalent across cultures, making significant modifications might be the only solution, potentially involving changes in the test's structure, such as adjusting scale structure or scoring procedures. Consequently, rectifying construct bias can necessitate alterations in both method and items.

Detecting Bias or Nonequivalence

We emphasize the difference between bias detection and bias control: Detecting nonequivalence does not mean anything in itself. The objective is always to eliminate that form of bias or to control it in some way. Of course, an important point in the elimination of bias is its detection – but it should be pointed out that, in order to control bias, detection has to be fine-grained enough to suggest why that form of bias appears – and not only that it does appear. In addition, researchers need to undertake extra steps after such bias is detected, in order to eliminate it. Bias detection is oftentimes seen as the finish line of a study: Researchers collect data, and after data collection they conduct a number of analyses that show that some form of nonequivalence in their data is visible; they report this result and draw a line.

We do wish to remark, firstly, that statistical analyses for equivalence detection are always a posteriori: They can only detect bias but cannot in themselves eliminate bias. This is something that has to be done in the early phases of the study, test adaptation, sampling, data collection, or wherever else bias may creep in. Bias detection methods in test adaptation are applied after collecting data, using a posteriori, or statistical procedures. These methods identify but do not solve the lack of equivalence. They are crucial for rigorously proving equivalence, surpassing judgmental approaches in robustness. SEM is considered by many the benchmark in this domain, but many other approaches are used – for example, IRT, *exploratory factor analysis* (EFA), analyses of reliability or difficulty – these all provide insights into the comparability between original and adapted tests.

We also wish to point out, secondly, that after detection of nonequivalence, the work should continue by going back to the drawing board, to the early phases of the study, and using the conclusions just reported, in order to eliminate bias. Of course, to this end the study designs need to be informative regarding not only the existence but also the likely source of bias.

Detecting Construct Bias

While statistical methods are to be valued for detecting construct bias in test adaptations, their limitations, particularly in pinpointing the causes of construct bias, warrant scrutiny. Construct bias occurs when there is an incomplete alignment of the constructs being measured in the original and adapted test versions. Confirmation of construct bias involves qualitative discussions about the construct across cultures, highlighting differences in their domains or expressions. Statistical techniques, regardless of their sophistication, only signal the presence of differences in data between cultures. They might suggest reasons for data nonequivalence, but these indications are not conclusive proof of construct bias, as differences could also stem from item or method bias.

Direct Versus Indirect Detection

Thus, it is useful to distinguish between *direct detection* of construct bias, which involves actual cultural discrepancies in the construct, usually shown through qualitative methods, and *indirect detection*, where statistical analysis reveals nonequivalence without concrete proof of cultural differences. Claims of construct nonequivalence based solely on statistical analysis lack solidity, without qualitative evidence demonstrating construct-related behavioral differences between cultures.

Item Level Versus Scale Level

Analyzing construct equivalence can occur at both item level and scale level, but the conclusions drawn from these two approaches differ significantly. Scale-level analysis helps understand the relationship between a construct and its dimensions, such as the facets of neuroticism in a personality inventory, but it does not provide insights into the construct's individual indicators. Item-level analysis is more suitable for short or unidimensional tests, providing detailed insights that are particularly useful and should be pursued whenever possible. However, for longer or more complex tests, item-level analysis often fails to produce acceptable fit indices, making scale-level analysis more practical. Regardless, researchers adapting tests should carefully consider whether to base their analyses on item-level or scale-level data, depending on the nature of the test and constructs in question, aiming to include item-level data in their equivalence analyses as comprehensively as possible.

How to Approach Construct Equivalence

To detect invariance in test adaptations, the procedure involves applying the same statistical techniques to the adapted version as were used on the original, then comparing the outcomes. Equivalence is inferred when the results show reasonable similarity, particularly through techniques that reveal the test's underlying structure. Typically, dimension-reduction methods are used to compare dimensions across test versions, languages, and cultures, interpreting similar dimensions as indicators of equivalence, or differences as signs of bias. Researchers are encouraged not to limit their analyses to replicating original studies but to broaden their investigation, incorporating innovative analyses to support the adapted test's validity. This could include aligning the test with underlying theories or examining predictions not addressed by the original test.

A significant challenge is that researchers often lack access to the original test data, relying instead on published statistical findings. This restriction limits the ability to apply additional useful statistical techniques not originally reported, constraining invariance testing to methods previously utilized. For instance, if the original analysis used an exploratory approach without defining a clear structure, the adapted test's comparison must follow suit, highlighting a critical limitation in detecting construct bias due to the absence of original data.

The most common technique for reducing data dimensionality is factor analysis, with EFA traditionally used to explore data structure. CFA has evolved during the past 2 decades into the preferred method, often regarded as the gold standard, gradually supplanting EFA. Yet, researchers in test adaptation should not consider CFA a cure-all. It may not be suitable for all situations, and other methods can also effectively indicate construct equivalence. These include EFA, other factor-based methods, and different grouping (e.g., cluster analysis, latent class analysis) and dimensionality reduction strategies (e.g., multidimensional scaling), as well as techniques not primarily focused on reducing data dimensionality.

Detecting Method Bias

Method bias occurs when testing differences arise not from the content or specific questions but from the test-taking process itself. This can include variations in participant demographics (sample), improper test administration (administration), or differences in test format and materials (instrument). Method bias is often considered the most challenging type of bias to address, and there are no universally accepted methods for testing it, unlike the quite well established techniques for evaluating construct and item bias. The difficulty in developing a standard approach is due to the distinct nature of method bias, requiring unique strategies for unique cases. Addressing method bias requires additional data beyond what is habitually obtained from test takers in traditional studies: It often requires a specific design focusing on that specific source of bias. Once these data are available, they can be used to assess the impact of that specific confounding variable on score comparability. However, the main challenge in studying method bias lies not in statistical analysis but in gathering relevant data.

It is therefore crucial for researchers adapting tests to proactively gather data on potential sources of method bias, which can range from demographic factors to content familiarity. However, possessing this data for only the adapted version is insufficient; comparable data for the original test version are essential. For instance, understanding the demographic makeup of participants for the adapted test is meaningless without similar information for the original test, making it impossible to accurately assess sample bias. Likewise, documenting the language proficiency of test administrators in the adapted test's language is futile without equivalent data for the original test's administrators. This underscores the fact that effective test adaptation requires collaboration between the adapting researchers and the original test creators. Researchers are advised against relying on premade solutions for assessing method bias. Instead, they should employ creativity and innovation in their approach to truly address the complexities of method bias in test adaptations.

Sample Bias

Sample bias emerges when the composition of the original and adapted test samples leads to noncomparability. Detection of sample bias is a two-step process: It requires first to identify composition differences and then to assess their impact on score differences. To spot these differences, researchers may utilize univariate methods such as chi-square tests for categorical variables (e.g., sex) and *t* tests for continuous ones (e.g., age), or multivariate methods for assessing combinations of factors (e.g., sex, age, education). The statistical analysis often involves comparing proportions or contingency tables, with alternatives such as Fisher's exact test used when standard tests are not suitable.

It is crucial not to assume that sample differences automatically imply bias in scores; a direct relationship between sample composition differences and score disparities must be established. Once a difference in sample composition is identified, it is treated as a hypothesis for potential sample bias, requiring validation through methods such as SEM or matched subsample comparisons. For example, discrepancies in sex and age distributions may prompt researchers to segment both samples into subgroups for detailed equivalence testing, or use these distributions as covariates in a multigroup analysis. This rigorous approach helps clarify the influence of identified differences on test scores, ensuring accurate bias assessment.

Instrument Bias

Instrument bias occurs when a test's format or presentation, rather than its content, unfairly advantages or disadvantages certain cultures. This includes biases from stimulus types, response methods, or how materials align with a target population's familiarity and response styles. Unlike item bias, which affects individual questions, instrument bias reflects a systemic reliance on stimuli that do not translate equally across groups. For example, a test containing items that refer to sports unknown in the target culture demonstrates instrument bias, as it embeds cultural assumptions into the test structure.

Professional judgment is needed to differentiate when item bias escalates to instrument bias. Instrument bias is confirmed when these systemic differences impact the test's measurement accuracy, leading to potential floor and ceiling effects for some of the populations, in items, groups of items, or the entire test. These effects, indicating too many test takers scoring at the extremes, compromise the test's reliability by limiting score variability. Although these effects may also occur in other conditions and do not automatically prove instrument bias, they are indicative for such a possibility.

Administration Bias

Administration bias occurs due to variances in language, culture, or test conditions between administrators and test takers. Identifying this bias is complex, as it impacts the entire target culture sample and intertwines with the test's administration, making it hard to isolate from other biases. Traditional bias testing methods, reliant on statistical analysis, struggle to address administration bias directly. One approach to investigate administration bias involves mimicking the original test's administration within a small target culture sample, allowing for controlled comparisons. However, assessing administrator expertise, especially in diverse cultural contexts, remains difficult. Despite these challenges, differences in administration quality do not inherently invalidate a test, provided they do not significantly deviate from acceptable standards. These differences are often reflective of the cultural context rather than indicative of bias.

Efforts to ensure high-quality data collection and competent administration are essential, yet adapting a test's administration to match its original conditions is not always necessary or beneficial. The focus should be on making test adaptations relevant and effective within their specific cultural context, rather than achieving strict cross-cultural comparability. This recognizes that while administration bias is a concern, especially in cross-cultural research, the primary goal in test adaptation is to ensure accurate and culturally relevant assessments.

Detecting Item Bias

At present, the term "item bias" is often used interchangeably with *differential item functioning* (DIF), but item bias represents a broader issue that requires both quantitative and qualitative evaluation. While DIF focuses on the statistical evidence for item bias, understanding item bias encompasses more, including professional judgment and multiple sources of evidence.

It is critical to note that item bias is not merely about differences in item responses between test versions. An item showing a different average response in the adapted test version does not automatically indicate bias. This variation might reflect actual differences in the measured characteristic between the populations taking the original and adapted versions. Therefore, the focus should be on how items function across groups relative to overall test scores, rather than just comparing average item scores. Simple comparisons of averages can miss nuanced biases, as items might function differently across score levels without these variations being apparent in mean scores alone.

The modern approach to assessing item bias involves examining how test items function across different score levels for various groups. This is commonly done by dividing the test takers from both the original and adapted test versions into subgroups, such as high and low scorers, to explore whether an item's behavior changes across language and score-level groups. More advanced techniques may categorize samples into more than two groups or assess item performance based on latent traits rather than observed scores, but the underlying principle remains the same.

In the context of test adaptation, bias is explored between two main groups: those taking the test in its original form and language (the *reference group*) and those taking the adapted version (the *focal group*). The focal group is often the one potentially disadvantaged by the adaptation – for instance, with second-language learners compared with native speakers in language research. This distinction helps researchers pinpoint where and how biases might occur, guiding efforts to ensure fairness and accuracy in cross-cultural testing scenarios.

Using Test Data and Supplementary Variables

Van de Vijver (2011) highlights a distinction in procedures for investigating item behavior in tests, differentiating between those relying solely on test scores and those incorporating additional variables. The first approach, exemplified by multigroup CFA, focuses on the relationship between item scores and latent variables to explore construct equivalence across test versions; it assesses items based on their correlation with scale-level scores, categorizing test takers into groups by their scores on the latent trait or observed characteristic, without considering external variables.

The second approach broadens the analysis by including variables outside the test itself, such as demographic background, and psychological or sociological characteristics, to determine their impact on item performance and potential bias. This method allows for a more comprehensive investigation into how various factors might influence the fairness and accuracy of test items across different groups.

Types of Item Bias: Uniform Versus Nonuniform Bias

The literature identifies specific types of item bias based on the relationship between item scores (observed variables) and overall test scores (latent variables), aligning with the concept of examining adverse impact through moderating effects. Following this approach, Clauser and Mazor (1998), as well as Mellenbergh (1982), differentiate between uniform and nonuniform bias, with further consideration for combined bias. *Uniform bias* occurs when the prediction slopes for two groups are parallel, indicating a consistent difference in item performance across all levels of the latent trait. This means that, regardless of trait level, one group consistently scores higher or lower on an item than the other group, but by a similar margin across all trait levels. *Nonuniform bias*, in contrast, is observed when the prediction slopes for the groups diverge, meaning the difference in item performance between the groups varies across different levels of trait. In such cases, the two groups might perform similarly at lower trait levels but diverge as trait levels increase. *Combined bias* encompasses situations where items exhibit differences in both slope, and intercept between groups. This indicates that not only does the difference in item performance between groups vary across trait levels, but the nature of these differences also changes, possibly even reversing at different points along the trait spectrum.

Distractor-Focused Assessment of Item Bias

Distractors (i.e., foils, decoys) are crucial yet often overlooked components of multiple-choice tests, playing a key role in item effectiveness by diverting test takers from the correct answer. Their inclusion in item bias analysis can provide insights into whether these alternatives serve as plausible options, thus ensuring the test's ability to accurately measure the intended skill. The quality of distractors determines an item's strength; they must be convincing enough to challenge test takers, ensuring that selecting the correct answer truly reflects the specific ability being tested, such as arithmetic skills. Weak distractors might lead test takers to the correct answer through elimination rather than knowledge, compromising the item's ability to assess the intended skill accurately.

Evaluating how often distractors are chosen in adapted test versions can reveal their effectiveness and highlight potential issues in the adaptation process that affect their utility as credible options. Distractor effectiveness can vary between cultures due to differences in knowledge, curriculum, or cultural references, making some distractors less effective in certain contexts. To assess distractor effectiveness, analyses should be conducted separately from traditional DIF studies, using discrimination indices to evaluate each answer option. Distractors that seem plausible to the target culture, indicated by positive discrimination values, may need revision. Additionally, *differential distractor analysis* (DDA) offers a sophisticated but underutilized method for examining distractor performance across cultures, suggesting an area for further exploration in test adaptation research.

Statistical Approaches to Testing for Item Bias

The exploration of DIF has led to the development of numerous statistical methods, reflecting the complexity of the issue and the variety of item formats and scaling approaches. While it is challenging to cover all these methods comprehensively, understanding their core logic and application in test adaptation is crucial. Commonly used DIF detection methods include the Mantel-Haenszel procedure, regression-based techniques (such as delta-plot and logistic regression), IRT-based methods (such as IRT area and IRT likelihood ratio), and SEM-based approaches. Each method has its context of appropriateness and notable applications, offering diverse tools for researchers to identify and address item bias effectively.

Statistical Approach to (In)Equivalence Testing

We hope to have been able to reflect the wide variety of forms of nonequivalence that can creep in when comparing scores that stem from two different testing situations (e.g., groups, cultures, languages, testing contexts etc.) and consequently the wide variety of statistical approaches that can be taken in order to detect and maybe control one or the other of these various forms of inequivalence.

In this variety of statistical approaches, two specific general approaches range supreme: SEM (specifically CFA) and IRT. Both of these are latent variable models, and while they are both able to answer some questions, they are also uniquely qualified to answer other specific questions. IRT is more often preferred in educational settings and SEM-CFA is more often preferred in psychological testing. We will, therefore, focus here only on the CFA approach to invariance, which has clearly evolved into a gold standard in psychology.

Figure 5.1 illustrates the basic components of a CFA model with two latent factors (F1 and F2), each represented by three indicators (I1 to I3 for the first factor, and I4 to I6 for the second). The regression of the indicators on the factors includes a factor loading (f1 to f6), an intercept (c1 to c6), and a residual or uniqueness (u1 to u6). The regression is modeled as I = c + fF + u. The latent factors have covariance (CovF1F2), and each latent factor has a mean (K1 and K2) and variance. In such an approach, invariance is tested by comparing the structure of the data across the two groups (i.e., *multigroup*), in a number of consecutive steps, with ever harsher constraints.

The entire process actually contains eight steps, as described by Iliescu (2017), Steenkamp and Baumgartner (1998), Vandenberg (2002), and Vandenberg and Lance (2000), but the overwhelming majority of analyses needed and used in test adaptation projects, only address three steps. First, *configural invariance* (also called sometimes *weak factorial invariance*) ensures that

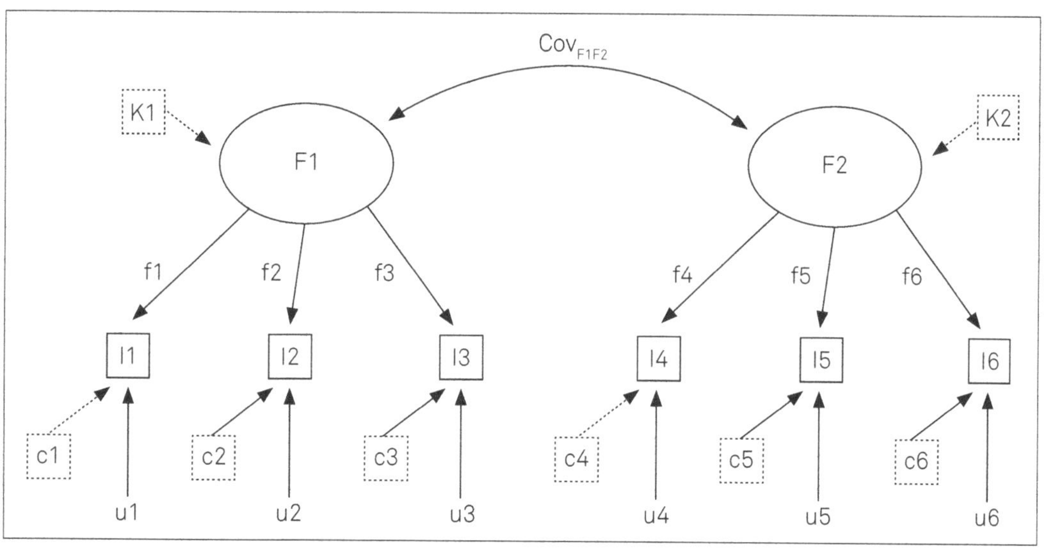

Figure 5.1 Confirmatory factor analysis model with two latent factors (F1 and F2), each represented by three indicators (I1 to I3 for the first factor, and I4 to I6 for the second). The regression of the indicators on the factors includes a factor loading (f1 to f6), an intercept (c1 to c6), and a residual or uniqueness (u1 to u6). The regression is modeled as I = c + fF + u. The latent factors have covariance (CovF1F2), and each latent factor has a mean (K1 and K2) and variance. Reproduced with permission from Schmitt & Kuljanin (2008, p. 211).

the hypothesized underlying factor structure of the measure is the same across groups. Second, *metric invariance* (also called sometimes *strong factorial invariance*) ensures that valid comparisons indicate that the relationships between constructs and their indicators (items) are consistent across the two cultures. As a rule of thumb, valid comparisons can be made if at least half of the items are invariant between the two cultures (Schmitt & Ali, 2014). Third, meeting the *scalar invariance* requirement indicates that not only the scale structure (configural) and the item loadings (metric) are equivalent, but also that the equivalence assumption extends the item intercepts as well. When the scalar invariance requirements are met, any observed differences in mean scores are more likely to be actual differences in the constructs being measured, rather than differences in how individuals from different cultures interpret the scale items. In some rare cases, especially for tests that are applied in high-stakes situations, two extra steps are tested over scalar invariance – that is, strict invariance (equality of residuals) and invariance of factor variances and means.

We draw attention to the fact that there is some confusion in these terms, with different authors labeling slightly different assumptions under these labels; we recommend that researchers apply the labels for the different levels of invariance with great care, and always only together with a clear explanation of the specific analysis and models that they actually test.

An example will now be given for how these steps can be applied. It will rely on the *alternative DSM-5 model for personality disorders* (AMPD), introduced in Section III of the Diagnostic and Statistical Manual of Mental Disorders, 5th edition (DSM-5; American Psychiatric Association, 2022, pp. 761–781) to illustrate how the various forms of invariance should be considered when a measure is used across different cultural groups. The AMPD proposed a significant shift in the conceptualization of personality disorders (PDs). This model was developed by considering the longstanding criticisms of the categorical approach traditionally used in the DSM for diagnosing PDs (Widiger & Trull, 2007). The AMPD provides a more flexible, dimensional, and empirically anchored framework for understanding PDs. The AMPD differs from older approaches in several ways: (1) The AMPD is a dimensional approach – it conceptualizes PDs as existing on a continuum rather than in discreet categories; (2) the AMPD introduces Criterion A, which assesses impairments in self (identity and self-direction) and interpersonal (empathy and intimacy) functioning; (3) the AMPD introduces Criterion B – a set of five broad domains of pathological personality: Negative Affectivity, Detachment, Antagonism, Disinhibition, and Psychoticism. These domains are further subdivided into 25 facet scales. The DSM-5 also includes a personality inventory measuring the five broad domains with their 25 corresponding facets, the Personality Inventory for DSM-5 (PID-5), which has been translated into several languages.

Configural Nonequivalence

Bagby et al. (2022) found evidence for a lack of configural invariance between White American (WA) and Black American (BA) groups in the United States. More specifically, they identified and subsequently confirmed on a replication sample the expected five-factor structure of the PID-5 for the WA group. However, the latent five-factor solution was not confirmed in the BA samples. For the BA group, a single-factor latent structure was identified in both samples. Bagby et al. (2022) argued that the single-factor solution for the BA group can be explained by the existence of large overlap amongst all the different pathological personality domains. The high degree of shared variance between the different domains could be a reflection of the relatively high degree of undifferentiated demoralization represented in the PID-5's item pool, a level of demoralization not surprising for a "racialized and prejudice-based living experience for many BAs in a predominantly non-Black society" (Bagby et al., 2022, p. 82). When a measure fails to meet the configural invariance standards across two or more groups, several practical implications emerge.

(1) Caution is warranted when interpreting or otherwise comparing scores obtained from participants belonging to the group for which the measure did not exhibit the same underlying latent structure – as the results observed by Bagby et al. (2022) suggest, the pattern of factor loadings might be indicative of a different factor structure for the BA group compared with the WA group, thus the interpretation of the measure's five-factor conventional structure is likely to be inadequate and biased for participants belonging to the BA group.
(2) Lack of configural invariance suggests that there might be differences in the way the focal constructs are conceptualized across the two groups, therefore any conclusions such as those based on incidence or prevalence rates derived from administering a nonequivalent measure might be biased.
(3) For practitioners and policymakers, the absence of configural invariance suggests that monitoring interventions or driving policies based on findings derived from the respective measure may not be equally effective or appropriate for the group on which the respective measure does not meet the configural invariance conditions.
(4) When a measure fails to meet the configural invariance conditions on a certain group it suggests that there is a need for a more comprehensive cultural adaptation process of the respective measurement instrument; researchers and psychometricians may need to extensively revise the respective instruments or develop a new one that optimally captures the focal constructs for the respective cultural group.
(5) The most serious implication is that the taxonomy that the measure intends to capture is inadequate for the respective group, thus the root problem is not one related to the measure, but rather to the entire taxonomy or conceptualization; in this case a reconceptualization of the entire taxonomy might be required to generate a culturally appropriate measure.

Metric Nonequivalence

Metric equivalence consists of imposing equality constraints on item loadings, ensuring that the relationship between indicators (items) and their corresponding latent factors are equivalent across groups from different cultures. An investigation estimating the PID-5 equivalence across US East Asian ($n = 321$), Southeast Asian ($n = 253$), and White participants ($n = 291$) identified that the measure exhibited item-level configural and metric invariance for 24 out of the 25 facet scales (Hricovec et al., 2023). One scale belonging to the Detachment domain, Suspiciousness, exhibited goodness-of-fit indices below the recommended thresholds, comparative fit index (CFI) = 0.886, root-mean-square error of approximation (RMSEA) = 0.071.

The lack of metric invariance informs the researcher(s) or practitioner(s) that the item loadings for the respective measure are not equivalent across groups. However, in this case, all of the participants spoke English fluently and had similar acculturation levels. Therefore, in this case, the lack of invariance could not have been caused by faulty or otherwise problematic item translation. In such cases, an inspection of item loadings across the investigated groups is recommended. As can be observed in Table 5.2, Item 131 ("People are basically trustworthy") and Item 177 ("I rarely feel that people I know are trying to take advantage of me") are the main culprits responsible for the lack of metric invariance. These items proved to be problematic across all three samples, their loadings being generally well below the .30 threshold.

Table 5.2 Factor loadings for Suspiciousness in three US cohorts, showing lack of metric invariance.

Item	White	East Asian	Southeast Asian
2	0.61	0.52	0.53
103	0.47	0.51	0.60
117	0.54	0.49	0.55
131	0.19	0.07	−0.04
133	0.63	0.53	0.70
177	0.04	0.08	0.27
190	0.73	0.65	0.78

Note. Values highlighted in gray indicate lack of metric invariance: Item 131 ("People are basically trustworthy") and Item 177 ("I rarely feel that people I know are trying to take advantage of me") are the main culprits responsible for the lack of metric invariance. Adapted from Hricovec et al. (2023).

To maximize the chances of replicability and to hone the precision of the instrument in estimating suspiciousness across the three groups, such items having nonsignificant loadings should be discarded. If they are not excluded, this could lead to biased conclusions – but that does not necessarily need to lead to such bias: Schmitt and Ali (2014) suggest that valid between-group comparisons may still be made if at least half of the items are invariant. Table 5.3 shows hypothetical problematic factor loadings, employing the same item set across three groups. As can be observed, although all the items have loadings higher than .30 for at least one of the groups, four out of the seven items have problematic loadings in Group 3. Consequently, in this case, meaningful between-group comparisons can only be made for Groups 1 and 2.

Table 5.3 Hypothetical pattern of loadings for Suspiciousness, showing lack of metric invariance.

Item	Group 1	Group 2	Group 3
2	0.55	0.52	0.31
103	0.47	0.45	0.06
117	0.54	0.49	0.55
131	0.59	0.61	0.07
133	0.50	0.53	0.09
177	0.04	0.08	0.33
190	0.73	0.65	0.08

Note. Values highlighted in gray indicate lack of metric invariance.

Scalar Nonequivalence

Scalar equivalence consists of the addition of supplementary equality constraints on item intercepts. To achieve scalar equivalence, a measure needs to have the same factor structure (configural invariance) and the same factor loadings (metric invariance) across groups, but also the item intercepts need to be equivalent across these groups. To further stress the necessity of identifying potential between-group differences for groups that do not necessarily belong to different cultures or to different sex- or age-based groups, we describe the results of a relatively recent investigation tapping into the equivalence of the PID-5 brief form (PID-5 BF) for sexual and gender minority groups (Asadi et al., 2024). In this specific investigation, Asadi et al. (2024) examined the various levels of invariance for PID-5 BF in both a clinical (n = 1,174) and a nonclinical sample (n = 1,456) that included, respectively in each sample, 254 and 151 individuals identifying as belonging to a sexual and gender minority group (SGM).

Such an investigation is not only timely with respect to this otherwise underresearched population, but it is also anchored in previous research reporting that there are notable differences in the way SGM individuals (gay, lesbian, bisexual, or otherwise nonheterosexual sexual orientation, and/or transgender, nonbinary, or otherwise gender diverse identities) experience psychiatric disparities when compared with heterosexual or cisgender individuals. For example, SGM individuals are more frequently diagnosed with borderline PD compared with cisgender individuals (e.g., Rodriguez-Seijas et al., 2021); the prevalence of mood disorders and substance abuse was also reported to be more prevalent within this group (e.g., Mahon et al., 2021; Ross et al., 2018).

In light of such findings, it would not be surprising to identify that the PID-5 exhibits differential functioning across the two groups – SGM and cisgender individuals. The results reported by Asadi et al. (2024) suggested that the PID-5 BF exhibited configural invariance across SGM and cisgender individuals in both the clinical and nonclinical samples. Progressively imposing more restrictive equality constraints on thresholds and loadings resulted in a decrease in the model fit, but the goodness-of-fit indices were still optimal.

A notable decrease in model fit was observed when equality constraints were imposed on item intercepts (Asadi et al., 2024). To detect the sources of invariance, the authors computed the modification indices and further removed the equality constraints on some of the items, thus attaining partial invariance. In the clinical sample, there were notable differences in the levels of endorsement for statements such as "I often feel like nothing I do really matters" (Item 4 – Detachment domain), "I crave attention" (Item 19, Antagonism domain), and "It's no big deal if I hurt other peoples' feelings" (Item 17, Antagonism domain). In the nonclinical sample, relaxing the equality constraints on Items 4 and 19 led to obtaining partial invariance (Asadi et al., 2024).

A direct consequence of nonequivalent item intercepts is that even if two individuals from different groups (SGM and cisgender, in this scenario) have the same level of the underlying constructs (e.g., detachment or antagonism domains), they might still have different expected scores on Items 4 and 19 due to this lack of intercept invariance. Lack of scalar invariance has several important implications. First, noninvariant item intercepts undermine the ability to compare directly latent construct means across groups. A second, indirect implication is that cutoff scores or recommended thresholds cannot be generalized across different groups for which scalar invariance cannot be established. Or, differently put, employing the same cutoff values would inevitably increase the frequency of Type I and Type II errors.

Third, the presence of noninvariant item intercepts often signals culture or group inappropriate or otherwise insensitive item contents, highlighting the influence of cultural, linguistic, or sociodemographic factors on how individuals perceive or respond to specific items. In this case, careful consideration of item content and wording is warranted.

Strict Invariance

Strict invariance, or residual invariance, imposes an additional set of equality constraints on the residual variances, testing the assumption that the amount of variance in manifest indicators that is not accounted for by the latent factors (i.e., residuals) remains the same across groups or test-taking conditions. If the equality constraints imposed on residual variances are not met, this suggests that the information provided by one or several items might be unreliable, as it leads to a greater variability in responses within one of the focal groups, variability which translates into differences in the residual variances of the respective items.

This level of invariance is oftentimes ignored, as it is sometimes considered too harsh – but it has important implications in high-stake testing contexts. For example, Hermes et al. (2019) tested several levels of invariance (including strict invariance) in groups of test takers who received different levels of exposure to computer-based training in tasks of cognitive ability. These training tasks were similar to the tasks featured in measures used for the selection of pilot trainees by various European airlines. The participants had access to similar cognitive ability training platforms and were subsequently tested with identical cognitive ability tests. Participants were divided into six different groups based on the number of computer-training trials that were completed. The authors tested gradually more restrictive models. By imposing equality constraints on residuals, Hermes et al. (2019) showed that the amount of variance in manifest indicators remained the same, irrespective of the number of training sessions. If this assumption would not have held, this would have reflected the fact that the overall variance of some items (and not others) was altered by exposure to the training sessions, thus altering the conclusions based on the respective items, and hampering the measure's consequential validity.

In the realm of personnel selection, various empirical investigations have estimated whether cognitive ability assessments exhibit invariance when delivered via mobile devices as opposed to PCs or laptops. King et al. (2015) collected data from 306 students who were randomly assigned to either PC or mobile-device groups and then completed various measures, including a cognitive ability assessment. While the measure demonstrated configural, metric, and scalar equivalence, it did not pass the test of strict invariance (King et al., 2015). This result showed that, for those specific tests, an individual had an increased chance of not answering correctly some items on which they would have responded correctly, provided that the respective items had been displayed on a different device (King et al., 2015). Such findings have important implications especially in those domains of applied psychology where scores are used to inform high-stake decisions.

Constraining Factor Means and Variances

In some specific instances, researchers and/or practitioners might choose to impose yet another set of equality constraints on factor variances and latent factor means. Before contrasting the actual factor means, homogeneity of variance must be attained. Consequently, a first step would be to impose equality constraints on factor variances. If variances across the two groups are not homogenous, systematic errors might be at play, and the subsequent comparisons made across the two groups are going to be biased. Conversely, if variances are equal, we can proceed to detect if the groups differ with respect to the latent means. Differences in latent means are estimated by fixing the latent mean to zero in one of the two or several groups and allowing the latent means in the other group(s) to be freely estimated.

Nowadays, job applicants are relying on smartphones or other mobile devices to complete the various online selection assessments. An empirical investigation compared the responses for large samples of applicants completing identical assessments of cognitive ability, biodata, work simulations and situational judgments tests, either in mobile format or on their PCs or laptops (Morelli et al., 2014). Complete invariance was attained for all of the measures employed in this specific investigation – and the study could proceed to investigate the latent means; incidentally, the latent mean in the group that completed the cognitive abilities via mobile devices was higher, although the magnitude of the difference was negligible. This implies that, generally, measures of cognitive ability (or at least those that were investigated in the study) can be confidently deployed on either mobile devices or PCs without any systematic biases altering the observed scores. In other words, the scores obtained via the two different methods are comparable.

Although this is not necessarily relevant for the illustration of approaches to invariance, we feel compelled to mention that the Morelli et al. (2014) findings contrast with the results obtained by King et al. (2015), and that the differences could be explained by several factors, such as test-taker motivation to complete the assessments correctly (one study recruited voluntary participants in exchange for exam credit, while the other involved real-life candidates).

Criteria for Rejecting Invariance

Analyses conducted in an SEM/CFA framework take advantage of the several goodness-of-fit indices that are habitually computed in these procedures. A detailed discussion of the assumptions on which the computation of each of these indices rests, far exceeds the scope of this chapter – but the various guidelines and recommendations that exist all share the idea that to reject invariance a considerable deterioration in goodness of fit must be observed (e.g., Cheung & Rensvold, 2002), with the notable exception of the chi-square test statistic (which is easily affected by sample size, so that this index is going to likely be significant irrespective of the differences in test functioning across the two groups). Various authors have proposed that decreases less than 0.01 in Tucker-Lewis Index (TLI) and CFI (Cheung & Rensvold, 2002), and increases of not more than 0.015 in RMSEA (Chen, 2007), from the progressively constrained model should be employed as benchmarks for detecting invariance.

Full Versus Partial Invariance

We draw attention here to the term "partial invariance." Partial invariance addresses situations where full equivalence between test versions for different groups cannot be achieved in any of the steps of the analysis. If invariance is not established in a certain step, researchers may focus on a subset of items that do show a good fit, proceeding with this reduced item set to assess partial equivalence. Essentially, partial equivalence suggests that while the entire item set does not demonstrate uniform equivalence across steps, a subset does exhibit invariance, offering a nuanced understanding of equivalence within the test. This approach is particularly common in test adaptations involving translations of larger tests (i.e., tests with a larger item set) or of tests that were developed not based on strong structural models but on more empirical approaches, where achieving full equivalence across languages is more challenging, in turn making partial invariance a practical solution for identifying and using items that are comparably effective across cultural or linguistic groups (Byrne et al., 1989).

Equivalence Across More Than Two Groups: Alignment

We finally mention one of the slightly more complicated problems (and current solution to it) that researchers may be confronted with: the impracticality of using the multigroup equivalence approach (irrespective of the statistical path taken, i.e., CFA or IRT) across more than two groups. Multigroup CFA compares two groups (e.g., two different language forms of the same test, or data coming from two groups of test takers who get the test administered with paper-and-pencil or online), but what is the correct approach when comparing, say, 50 or 100 groups? This is not a trivial question, but a practical and high-stakes one, because international comparative assessment programs such as the OECD Program for International Student Assessment (PISA) and Program for the International Assessment for Adult Competencies (PIAAC); or the IEA Trends in International Mathematics and Science Study (TIMSS), Progress in International Reading Literacy Study (PIRLS), International Civic and Citizenship Education Study (ICCS), and International Computer and Information Literacy Study (ICILS); and others are confronted with exactly this problem: How to ensure equivalence across a large number of groups?

Using the CFA approach in this case would require 2 × 2 comparisons of each of the various groups, which is impractical not only because of the large number of comparisons, but also because of the large number of modification indices that would have to be acknowledged in the end, and even that will still likely not lead to a good fit for the scalar model.

A solution to this problem was proposed by Asparouhov and Muthén (2014) and spearheaded by Byrne and van de Vijver (2017), among others. It is known as the *alignment method*. This method can estimate group-specific factor means and variances without requiring *downstream* measurement invariance – that is, without testing first for configural and metric invariance. The alignment method is based on the configural model and compares parameter stability for all of the parameters in every group, thus essentially running through all the consecutively more stringent steps in one go.

Conclusion

Conducting equivalence analyses should not be confined to the differences across cultures and/or test translations, or only to some measurement domains. However, establishing equivalence is warranted whenever there is a sufficiently strong theoretical and/or practical rationale suggesting that any given measure might function differently across groups of individuals (established by any criterion of interest). Equivalence should be investigated with respect to any potential variable on which a significant proportion of the target group or population might differ.

For example, even though the PID-5 facet scales were found to be invariant across sex (Suzuki et al., 2019), across various countries (Sorrel et al., 2021), or across clinical and nonclinical samples (Bach et al., 2018; Somma et al., 2019), some PID-5 scales exhibited nonequivalent functioning for groups in the US – namely, English-speaking Asian American participants compared with White Americans (Hricovec et al., 2023) or for groups of SGM compared with cisgender participants from the same culture (Asadi et al., 2024). Therefore, equivalence should not be confined to the usual comparisons between countries, cultures, or sex- or age-based groups.

A theoretical rationale that justifies cross-cultural investigations of equivalence is the conceptualization of cultural values formulated by Sagiv and Schwartz (2022), describing how and why Western and Eastern cultures emphasize different representations of desirable attitudes or behaviors, commonly referred to as values. Consequently, the frames of reference that people from different cultures might employ when reading, interpreting, and responding to particular items might be impacted by their different cultural values (Lvina et al., 2012). Differences in the way in which individuals view themselves, as being part of or independent of the broader social group (self-construal) have been shown to affect observed differences in measures of psychopathology (e.g., Maas et al., 2019).

In line with this theoretical rationale, equivalence analyses might be warranted to confidently use test-derived data when comparing people from, for example, Vietnam with those from the US. In contrast, a strong demonstration of equivalence might be less critical when people from similar countries are compared – for example, people from the Czech Republic and those from Slovakia.

One typical practical rationale for conducting equivalence analyses consists of comparing scores derived from administering identical measurements in different test-taking environments (paper-and-pencil vs. computer, or computer vs. mobile devices). For example, King et al. (2015) illustrated that while there are no considerable effects of administering situational judgment tests via mobile devices as compared with computers, the administration environment altered the way in which people responded to cognitive ability measures.

Equivalence analyses might be warranted when comparing individuals from different age groups, from different genders, or from other minority groups. Equivalence analyses might also be necessary when administering measures in different environments. At the same time, researchers and practitioners alike should carefully consider whether previous investigations suggest that the magnitude of such differences in test functioning will result in nonnegligible effect sizes. A detailed discussion of such aspects can be found in Somaraju et al. (2021).

Evidence for invariance should be interpreted as a continuum, and each individual empirical investigation cannot and should not be interpreted as definite and ultimate evidence either for or against equivalence. Conversely, a measure that shows invariance across a wide range of empirical investigations, groups, and settings is more likely to be universally applicable. Also, invariance should not be broadly evaluated, but instead, researchers and psychologists should weigh the evidence supporting the different forms of invariance. For example, there is considerable evidence suggesting that the PID-5 meets the thresholds for configural invariance across cultural and ethnic groups (Becker et al., 2023; Freilich et al., 2023; Thimm et al., 2016), across gender- or age-based groups (e.g., Suzuki et al., 2019, Vergauwe et al., 2023), and across clinical and nonclinical samples (e.g., Asadi et al., 2024). There is increasing evidence that the latent factor structure for the PID-5 replicates across different groups, informing about a robust measurement architecture on which the PID-5 rests. However, evidence supporting the measure's metric and especially scalar invariance is less consistent across the various investigated groups. This suggests that psychologists and researchers employing the PID-5 across different groups should dive into the item-level information. More specifically, a first step would consist of considering the item-factor loadings. As Schmitt and Ali (2014) have suggested, if more than half of the item loadings are equivalent, then between-group comparisons can be conducted, as the effects on observed scores are likely to be small in size and negligible. Conversely, if this requirement is not met, some items can and should not be included in scoring their respective scale, or scale scoring should not be done for the group plagued by invariant item loadings.

Equivalence is an important indicator of validity, one that is at the very heart of the assumptions on which we operate when interpreting test results: that similar scores mean similar things for different individuals, irrespective of the various groups they may be part of. The statistical techniques used for equivalence testing have evolved primarily in cross-cultural psychology to compare scores that were obtained with different language forms of a test, but our understanding of equivalence has evolved significantly since then. Investigating the invariant functioning of various psychological measures not only across cultures, but also across age, sex, or other demographics; across test-taking contexts (e.g., high vs. low stakes); or across the medium of administration (e.g., paper-and-pencil vs. digital) or across other modes, gives information about the potential biases that might be at play when comparing individuals from the respective groups.

We should, however, bear in mind that evidence of equivalence is only one of the many sources of evidence for validity and should not be regarded as the sole proof for a go-no-go decision in using a psychological measure in a specific context. Invariance becomes increasingly important in those situations where test scores are used to inform high-stakes decisions, especially when groups are compared or bias against a specific group is a possibility.

References

American Educational Research Association, American Psychological Association, & National Council on Measurement in Education. (2014). *Standards for educational and psychological testing*. The American Psychological Association (APA).

American Psychiatric Association. (2022). *Diagnostic and statistical manual of mental disorders* (5th ed., text rev.). https://doi.org/10.1176/appi.books.9780890425787

Asadi, S., Cunningham, T. J., Morgan, T. A., Zimmerman, M., & Rodriguez-Seijas, C. (2024). Examining measurement invariance in the Personality Inventory for DSM-5 Brief Form across sexual and gender minority status. *Assessment, 31*(3), 678–697. https://doi.org/10.1177/10731911231176449

Asparouhov, T., & Muthén, B. (2014). Multiple-group factor analysis alignment. *Structural Equation Modeling, 21*(4), 495–508. https://doi.org/10.1080/10705511.2014.919210

Bach, B., Sellbom, M., & Simonsen, E. (2018). Personality inventory for DSM-5 (PID-5) in clinical versus nonclinical individuals: Generalizability of psychometric features. *Assessment, 25*(7), 815–825. https://doi.org/10.1177/1073191117709070

Bagby, R. M., Keeley, J. W., Williams, C. C., Mortezaei, A., Ryder, A. G., & Sellbom, M. (2022). Evaluating the measurement invariance of the Personality Inventory for DSM-5 (PID-5) in Black Americans and White Americans. *Psychological Assessment, 34*(1), 82. https://doi.org/10.1037/pas0001085

Becker, L. G., Asadi, S., Zimmerman, M., Morgan, T. A., & Rodriguez-Seijas, C. (2023). Is there a bias in the diagnosis of borderline personality disorder among racially minoritized patients? *Personality Disorders: Theory, Research, and Treatment, 14*(3), 339–346. https://doi.org/10.1037/per0000579

Byrne, B. M. (2015). Adaptation of assessment scales in cross-national research: Issues, guidelines, and caveats. *International Perspectives in Psychology: Research, Practice, Consultation, 5*(1), 51–65. https://doi.org/10.1037/ipp0000042

Byrne, B. M., Shavelson, R. J., & Muthén, B. O. (1989). Testing for equivalence of factor covariance and mean structures: The issue of partial measurement invariance. *Psychological Bulletin, 105*(3), 456–466. https://doi.org/10.1037/0033-2909.105.3.456

Byrne, B. M., & van de Vijver, F. J. R. (2017). The maximum likelihood alignment approach to testing for approximate measurement invariance: A paradigmatic cross-cultural application. *Psicothema, 29*(4), 539–551. https://doi.org/10.7334/psicothema2017.178

Chen, F. F. (2007). Sensitivity of goodness of fit indexes to lack of measurement invariance. *Structural Equation Modeling, 14*(3), 464–504. https://doi.org/10.1080/10705510701301834

Cheung, G. W., & Rensvold, R. B. (2002). Evaluating goodness-of-fit indexes for testing measurement invariance. *Structural Equation Modeling, 9,* 233–255. https://doi.org/10.1207/S15328007SEM0902_5

Clauser, B. E., & Mazor, K. M. (1998). Using statistical procedures to identify differentially functioning test items. *Educational Measurement: Issues and Practice, 17,* 31–44. https://doi.org/10.1111/j.1745-3992.1998.tb00619.x

Freilich, C. D., Palumbo, I. M., Latzman, R. D., & Krueger, R. F. (2023). Assessing the measurement invariance of the Personality Inventory for DSM-5 across Black and White Americans. *Psychological Assessment, 35*(9), 721–728. https://doi.org/10.1037/pas0001255

Hermes, M., Albers, F., Böhnke, J. R., Huelmann, G., Maier, J., & Stelling, D. (2019). Measurement and structural invariance of cognitive ability tests after computer-based training. *Computers in Human Behavior, 93,* 370–378. https://doi.org/10.1016/j.chb.2018.11.040

Hricovec, M., Su, C., Bart, T., Marsh, K., Alsup, C. & Cicero, D. (2023). Measurement invariance of the Personality Inventory for the DSM-5 across U.S. East Asian, Southeast Asian, and White participants. *Personality Disorders: Theory, Research, and Treatment, 15*(1), 1–10. https://doi.org/10.1037/per0000647

Iliescu, D. (2017). *Adapting Tests in Linguistic and Cultural Situations.* Cambridge University Press. https://doi.org/10.1017/9781316273203

King, D. D., Ryan, A. M., Kantrowitz, T., Grelle, D., & Dainis, A. (2015). Mobile internet testing: An analysis of equivalence, individual differences, and reactions. *International Journal of Selection and Assessment, 23*(4), 382–394. https://doi.org/10.1111/ijsa.12122

Lvina, E., Johns, G., Treadway, D. C., Blickle, G., Liu, Y., Liu, J., Atay, S., Zettler, I., Solga, J., Noethen, D., & Ferris, G. R. (2012). Measure invariance of the Political Skill Inventory (PSI) across five cultures. *International Journal of Cross Cultural Management, 12*(2), 171–191. https://doi.org/10.1177/1470595812439870

Maas, J., Laceulle, O., & Bekker, M. (2019). The role of autonomy–connectedness in the relation between childhood stressful life events, current posttraumatic symptoms, and internalizing psychopathology in adulthood. *Psychological Trauma: Theory, Research, Practice, and Policy, 11*(3), 345. https://doi.org/10.1037/tra0000412

Mahon, C. P., Pachankis, J. E., Kiernan, G., & Gallagher, P. (2021). Risk and protective factors for social anxiety among sexual minority individuals. *Archives of Sexual Behavior, 50,* 1015–1032. https://doi.org/10.1007/s10508-020-01845-1

Mellenbergh, G. J. (1982). Contingency table models for assessing item bias. *Journal of Educational Statistics, 7,* 105–118. https://doi.org/10.3102/10769986007002105

Messick, S. (1990). Validity of test interpretation and use. *ETS Research Report Series, 1990*(1), 1487–1495. https://doi.org/10.1002/j.2333-8504.1990.tb01343.x

Messick, S. (1995). Validity of psychological assessment: Validation of inferences from persons' responses and performances as scientific inquiry into score meaning. *American Psychologist, 50*(9), 741–749. https://doi.org/10.1037/0003-066X.50.9.741

Morelli, N. A., Mahan, R. P., & Illingworth, A. J. (2014). Establishing the measurement equivalence of online selection assessments delivered on mobile versus nonmobile devices. *International Journal of Selection and Assessment, 22*(2), 124–138. https://doi.org/10.1111/ijsa.12063

Rodriguez-Seijas, C., Morgan, T. A., Zimmerman, M. (2021) Is there a bias in the diagnosis of borderline personality disorder among lesbian, gay, and bisexual patients? *Assessment, 28*(3), 724–738. https://doi.org/10.1177/1073191120961833

Ross, L. E., Salway, T., Tarasoff, L. A., MacKay, J. M., Hawkins, B. W., & Fehr, C. P. (2018). Prevalence of depression and anxiety among bisexual people compared to gay, lesbian, and heterosexual individuals: A systematic review and meta-analysis. *Journal of Sex Research, 55*(4–5), 435–456. https://doi.org/10.1080/00224499.2017.1387755

Sagiv, L., & Schwartz, S. H. (2022). Personal values across cultures. *Annual Review of Psychology, 73*, 517–546. https://doi.org/10.1146/annurev-psych-020821-125100

Schmitt, N., & Ali, A. A. (2014). The practical importance of measurement invariance. In C. E. Lance & R. J. Vandenberg (Eds.), *More statistical and methodological myths and urban legends: Doctrine, verity and fable in organizational and social sciences* (pp. 327–346). Routledge.

Schmitt, N., & Kuljanin, G. (2008). Measurement invariance: Review of practice and implications. *Human Resource Management Review, 18*, 210–222. https://doi.org/10.1016/j.hrmr.2008.03.003

Somaraju, A. V., Nye, C. D., & Olenick, J. (2021). A review of measurement equivalence in organizational research: What's old, what's new, what's next? *Organizational Research Methods, 25*(4), 741–785. https://doi.org/10.1177/10944281211056524

Somma, A., Krueger, R. F., Markon, K. E., & Fossati, A. (2019). The replicability of the personality inventory for DSM-5 domain scale factor structure in U.S. and non-U.S. samples: A quantitative review of the published literature. *Psychological Assessment, 31*(7), 861–877. https://doi.org/10.1037/pas0000711

Sorrel, M. A., García, L. F., Aluja, A., Rolland, J. P., Rossier, J., Roskam, I., & Abad, F. J. (2021). Cross-cultural measurement invariance in the Personality Inventory for DSM-5. *Psychiatry Research, 304*, 114134. https://doi.org/10.1016/j.psychres.2021.114134

Steenkamp, J.-B. E. M., & Baumgartner, H. (1998). Assessing measurement invariance in cross-national consumer research. *Journal of Consumer Research, 25*, 78–90. https://doi.org/10.1086/209528

Suzuki, T., South, S. C., Samuel, D. B., Wright, A. G. C., Yalch, M. M., Hopwood, C. J., & Thomas, K. M. (2019). Measurement invariance of the DSM-5 Section III pathological personality trait model across sex. *Personality Disorders: Theory, Research, and Treatment, 10*(2), 114–122. https://doi.org/10.1037/per0000291

Thimm, J. C., Jordan, S., & Bach, B. (2016). The Personality Inventory for DSM-5 Short Form (PID-5-SF): psychometric properties and association with Big Five traits and pathological beliefs in a Norwegian population. *BMC Psychology, 4*(1), 61. https://doi.org/10.1186/s40359-016-0169-5

Vandenberg, R. J. (2002). Toward a further understanding of an improvement in measurement invariance methods and procedures. *Organizational Research Methods, 5*(2), 139–158. https://doi.org/10.1177/1094428102005002001

Vandenberg, R. J., & Lance, C. E. (2000). A review and synthesis of the measurement invariance literature: Suggestions, practices, and recommendations for organizational research. *Organizational Research Methods, 3*(1), 4–69. https://doi.org/10.1177/109442810031002

van de Vijver, F. J. R. (2011). Bias and real differences in cross-cultural differences: neither friends not foes. In F. J. R. van de Vijver, A. Chasiotis & S. M. Breugelmans (Eds.), *Fundamental questions in cross-cultural psychology* (pp. 235–258). Cambridge. https://doi.org/10.1017/CBO9780511974090.011

van de Vijver, F. J. R., & Leung, K. (1997). Methods and data analysis of comparative research. In J. W. Berry, Y. H. Poortinga & J. Pandey (Eds.), *Handbook of cross-cultural psychology* (2nd ed.) (pp. 257–300). Allyn & Bacon.

van de Vijver, F. J. R., & Poortinga, Y. H. (1997). Towards an integrated analysis of bias in cross-cultural assessment. *European Journal of Psychological Assessment, 13*(1), 29–37. https://doi.org/10.1027/1015-5759.13.1.29

van de Vijver, F. J. R., & Poortinga, Y. (2005). Conceptual and methodological issues in adapting tests. In R. K. Hambleton, P. F. Merenda & C. D. Spielberger (Eds.), *Adapting educational and psychological tests for cross-cultural assessment* (pp. 39–64). Erlbaum.

Van de Vijver, F. J. R., & Tanzer, N. K. (1997). Bias and equivalence in cross-cultural assessment: An overview. *European Review of Applied Psychology, 47*, 263–279.

Vergauwe, J., Rouco, V., Franssens, R., Claes, L., Bastiaens, T., & De Clercq, B. (2023). Age and sex differences of the PID-5-100 maladaptive personality traits throughout adulthood. *Personality Disorders: Theory, Research, and Treatment, 14*(5), 512–526. https://doi.org/10.1037/per0000622

Widiger, T. A., & Trull, T. J. (2007). Plate tectonics in the classification of personality disorder: Shifting to a dimensional model. *American Psychologist, 62*(2), 71–83. https://doi.org/10.1037/0003-066X.62.2.71

Chapter 6

Instrumentation and Administration: Assuring Validity, Reliability, and Fairness

Tuulia M. Ortner, Sonja Breuer, and Natalie Badstuber

Abstract

This chapter explores the influence of *method effects* on psychological assessments, focusing on how test design and administration impact validity, reliability, and fairness. Method effects are examined through key dimensions such as item arrangement, response formats, and testing situations, all of which contribute to method variance by introducing unintended influences on test takers' performance. The chapter emphasizes how individual differences, such as sex, ethnicity, and personality traits, interact with situational dynamics, including examiner characteristics and environmental conditions, to shape test outcomes. Attention is further given to the biases and inequities that arise from these effects, such as stereotype threat, test anxiety, and differential perceptions of fairness. For instance, closed-ended response formats may favor individuals with high risk-taking tendencies, while open-ended tasks could disadvantage nonnative speakers or those with linguistic challenges. Similarly, item arrangement strategies like computerized adaptive testing (CAT) can enhance efficiency but may increase test anxiety and undermine metacognitive awareness. To address these challenges, the chapter proposes strategies for minimizing biases, such as refining test design, improving the testing environment, and tailoring administration to diverse populations. The importance of continuous education, empirical research, and practitioner collaboration is emphasized to ensure assessments remain valid, equitable, and reflective of the constructs they aim to measure. Ultimately, the chapter advocates for psychological measurement practices that better account for method effects and promote fairness in diverse contexts.

Introduction

When practitioners decide to administer a specific test, they usually choose the test on the basis of its evidenced validity, the expected duration of the test, and its appropriateness for the conditions under which it will be administered (e.g., Thielsch et al., 2012). Factors such as response formats, possible item sequences for presentation, or similar considerations are typically not, or only to a lesser extent, part of their deliberations. Researchers, too, are often not aware that common response formats and item presentation procedures do not necessarily provide the most valid option for all test takers. In fact, assessment tools' validity, reliability, and fairness hinge on not only *what* they aim to measure but also on *how* they are designed and administered.

The *method effects* addressed in this chapter refer to how error variance can cause unreliability, biases, or distortions in test scores and how such error variance can arise from the specific measurement methods and procedures employed, rather than from the underlying psychological constructs that researchers aim to measure (see Bagozzi & Yi, 1990; Schweizer, 2020). Test takers may therefore be affected by an unwanted and undesirable source of variance (van de Vijver & Poortinga, 2005), and general effects may lead to reduced reliability in the results for all test takers. However, the potential biases that may result – meaning systematic overestimations or underestimations of true performance caused by *method variance* (see Fiske, 1982) – may also lead to score inequivalence between groups of individuals and may systematically impact the scores of people who possess certain characteristics or are members of certain social or cultural groups. Van de Vijver and Poortinga (2005) have proposed two categories of method bias: *Instrument bias*, on the one hand, involves test properties that are not the target of assessment but which still induce differences in test scores. This kind of bias may be caused by aspects such as the wording, embedding, selection, and arrangement of items and response formats, scale length, and the mode of technical embedding (see Podsakoff et al., 2003). One possible source of instrument bias in testing occurs, for example, when certain test takers are more familiar with the stimuli or presentation procedures or when items or response formats are better matched with certain individuals' working style. *Administration bias*, on the other hand, refers to effects arising from the test situation, individuals' difficulties with the instructions, information given prior to testing, or communication problems (see also van de Vijver & Tanzer, 2004).

Each methodological aspect offers specific challenges and requires consideration, highlighting the need for a thorough understanding to minimize potential inequivalence. Method effects may impact performance through two paths: First, the demonstration of actual abilities in the test situation could be hindered because the specific method employed (e.g., instructions, task design, or task format) unjustifiably makes mental processing more difficult or easier for certain individuals, regardless of their actual abilities in the construct being assessed – for example, for reasons related to test-wiseness, interests, or cultural background.

Alternatively, the specific instructions, task design, test format, or situation may lead to different attitudes, feelings, or levels of motivation among test takers on the basis of prior experience or personality. In this case, the effect on test scores is mediated by intrapersonal processes. Especially for assessments of knowledge, skills, and abilities, test situations should allow all test takers to demonstrate their maximum performance (see Willingham & Cole, 1997; Helms, 2004).

Not only when considering the critical role of testing outcomes for individuals and organizations across various fields of practice (see also Leiner et al., 2018), but also for a better understanding of measurement procedures, it is important to address and understand method effects in research and their possible effects in application. This chapter aims to give an overview of current studies on selected method effects, including item selection and arrangement, response formats (e.g., closed- or open-ended required responses), and their effects on the resulting scores. We will furthermore shed light on a selection of possible aspects of the testing situation – for example, attitudes toward tests, *test administrator* (TA) characteristics, and different perceptions of test situations and their impact on test scores.

Item Arrangement Effects

Item arrangement effects refer to possible influences of the sequence and structure of item presentation (questions or tasks) on test takers' performances. We discuss three common arrangement designs: the *increasing scale approach*, *computerized adaptive testing* (CAT), and the *mixed scales approach.*

Traditionally, all test takers are given the same set of items in the same order, known as *fixed-item testing* (FIT; e.g., Ortner et al., 2013). This approach is mostly operationalized as the increasing scale approach, which means the items are arranged in order of increasing difficulty, which is typical of school exams. This strategy may be used to maintain or enhance test taker motivation, as individuals might find it encouraging to succeed on easier items before progressing to more challenging ones. Nevertheless, this effect may be reversed for individuals who already fail on the early items, leading to the double burden of deficient skills, deficient motivation, and additional, unwanted variance (Ortner et al., 2014).

CAT, a contemporary type of economical and informative assessment, often begins with an item of medium difficulty. Based on fixed item selection rules, each subsequent item is adjusted based on the test taker's estimated ability. The next item that is selected is often the most informative one available in the item pool, typically having around a 50% probability of being answered correctly, and is chosen from a large item bank on the basis of the test taker's previous responses (van der Linden & Glas, 2000; Wainer, 2002). As CAT requires real-time estimation of ability after each response, it relies on computerized administration.

CAT is closely associated with *item response theory* (IRT; Rasch, 1960), whereas FIT can be based on either IRT or *classical test theory* (CTT; e.g., Allen & Yen, 1979). When both FIT and CAT are based on IRT, CAT demonstrates clear psychometric advantages: It reduces individual error variance, even with fewer items, and requires less time for testing (e.g., Frey, 2023; Linacre, 2000; Wainer & Eignor, 2000). Furthermore, with each respondent receiving a unique set of questions, the risk of cheating may be reduced in group settings (Wise, 2019).

Nevertheless, research has also highlighted negative aspects of CAT in matrices tests, indicating method effects by comparing results from CAT with FIT scores from the same test in experimental settings. CAT revealed a motivational impact for higher ability test takers, putting them on the same level as lower ability test takers in terms of the number of solved items (e.g., Ortner et al., 2014). CAT was also revealed to undermine test takers' metacognitive competence by leading to feelings of overestimation in lower ability students and underestimation in higher ability students (Ortner et al., 2013). Furthermore, individuals with higher levels of test anxiety seem to perform worse on performance tests based on CAT as opposed to FIT (Akhtar et al., 2022; Ortner & Caspers, 2011).

Another comparative study on high school students who took an English test revealed that computer self-efficacy and the degree to which the students were satisfied with the training they received prior to taking the test positively influenced CAT attitude, whereas test anxiety negatively impacted CAT performance (Ling et al., 2017). Nevertheless, for a reading comprehension test, Brüggemann et al. (2024) did not find differences in state test anxiety between test modes in school children, but they did find higher cognitive loads in CAT (Brüggemann et al., 2023). The progression in item difficulty in FIT may help respondents gradually understand and engage with the material: For instance, in tests assessing numerical ability, items may progress from simple arithmetic to complex and combined mathematical problem-solving tasks. This progression may also lead to practice effects and dependency of solution probabilities between different items if respondents simply perform well as they become familiar with the task format rather than because their actual abilities are high. However, it makes sense that cognitive performance is presumed to increase with familiarity with the arrangement by reducing test takers' test anxiety (Sarnacki, 1979).

Another source of variance could be the ability to revisit previous items, which is inherently not feasible in CAT, by design. The opportunity to work on skipped items later may reduce negative attitudes and feelings (e.g., reactance), on the one hand, while also mitigating the effects of test-wiseness, on the other hand. For example, it prevents test takers from guessing answers for all remaining items when the test time runs out.

Although CAT today represents the standard approach in assessments of knowledge, skills, and abilities, especially for large-scale assessments, the practice of administering FIT remains widespread in the realm of personality questionnaires. Because personality items can often be rated in seconds, the economic advantage (i.e., shorter testings) offered by CAT is far less appealing than the potential loss of standardization. Altering the original item order has been revealed to significantly change item difficulties and outcomes in personality assessments (see Ortner, 2004, 2008). In mixed scale arrangements in personality assessments, items are typically distributed randomly across questionnaires so that response patterns cannot be influenced by item order. Mixed arrangements can reduce face validity and the occurrence of response biases such as anchoring, subtraction, and testlet effects, and in fact, the blocking of items of same scales has revealed different psychometric properties (e.g., Franke, 2019).

Effects of Response Format

Response formats can generally be categorized into two main types: *closed-ended* and *open-ended*. Closed-ended response formats, such as rating and Likert scales, forced-choice questions, or multiple-choice items, involve predefined response options, thereby facilitating quantitative analysis (see Box 6.1 for an item example). By contrast, open-ended formats allow respondents to provide more detailed and nuanced answers based on their own expression, as seen in essay questions or interviews (see Box 6.2 for an item example). It is widely recognized that variations in response formats may influence test takers' responses and may introduce method biases (e.g., Breuer et al., 2020, 2023b; Dykema et al., 2022; Krosnick & Presser, 2010; Reardon et al., 2018). In psychometric personality assessments, closed-ended response formats are predominantly utilized, whereas performance testing often employs both formats. Experimentally, method effects are more readily investigated in performance tests, which are characterized by unambiguous correct answers, compared with personality assessments. Thus, we address method effects related to response formats next.

Box 6.1 Example of a closed-ended response format item assessing psychological knowledge.

Which of the following best describes the concept of "cognitive dissonance"?

A) A state of mental discomfort arising from conflicting beliefs or behaviors.
B) The process of learning through reinforcement and punishment.
C) A condition where an individual exhibits excessive anxiety in social situations.
D) The tendency to attribute one's successes to internal factors and failures to external factors.

Box 6.2 Example of an open-ended response format item assessing psychological knowledge.

Explain the concept of "cognitive dissonance." Include an example from real life that illustrates how this phenomenon may affect an individual's behavior.

Open-ended formats in performance testing, also known as *constructed-response* or *free-response* formats, require test takers to generate their own responses without the constraints of predefined options. These include short-answer questions, fill-in-the-blanks, practical tasks, and essays. Open-ended items effectively reveal respondents' reasoning processes and capture a broader range of thought processes than closed-ended items do (e.g., Kastner & Stangl, 2011; Martinez, 1999).

Open-ended responses are particularly useful for assessing value judgments, idea generation (e.g., Haladyna & Rodriguez, 2013; Schult & Lindner, 2018), and free-recall knowledge, and from a test designers' view, they are often easier to create because no distractors are needed (e.g., Schult & Sparfeldt, 2018). However, their scoring is inherently bound to human raters' subjective evaluations, which can compromise objectivity. Definitions and applications of scoring procedures for open-ended items are also much more complex and time-consuming and effort-intensive than the scoring of closed-ended tasks (e.g., Downing, 2006; Kastner & Stangl, 2011).

Closed-ended response formats in performance testing typically include single-choice questions, where one out of several options is correct; multiple-choice items, where one or more alternatives may be correct; and true–false questions (i.e., marking an option as either correct or incorrect). These formats are highly efficient, objective, and precise in measurement, with economic administration and scoring procedures (e.g., Downing, 2006; Gierl et al., 2017; Kastner & Stangl, 2011; Martinez, 1999). Large numbers of items can be administered and automatically scored in a short time, facilitating broad coverage of topics (e.g., Linn, 2006). However, they may fail to assess or may oversimplify complex cognitive abilities (e.g., Wright et al., 2016) and can be challenging to create, especially when high-quality and plausible distractors need to be developed (e.g., Breuer et al., 2023b). It has been argued that the mere recognition of a correct response requires lower-level and different cognitive processes than recalling an answer in an open-ended format (Heyborne et al., 2011; Martinez, 1999).

Ideally, scores on a test designed to measure a specific ability, such as numerical understanding, would reflect only that ability. However, there is evidence that scores on tests designed to assess the same construct using different response formats often reflect characteristics of the measurement instrument that are not relevant to the ability being assessed (e.g., Kubinger, 2014). For instance, research has repeatedly demonstrated significant group differences in closed-ended tests based on individual characteristics such as sex, age, test anxiety, achievement motivation, or risk propensity (e.g., Alnabhan, 2002; Breuer et al., 2023a; Crocker & Schmitt, 1987; Irwing & Lynn, 2005; Rubio et al., 2010). By contrast, fewer method biases related to test takers' individual characteristics have been observed in open-ended assessments (e.g., DeMars, 1998; Reardon et al., 2018; Stanger-Hall, 2012).

Specifically, previous studies have indicated that men often outperform women on closed-ended tests, whereas women tend to perform equally or better on open-ended assessments (e.g., Reardon et al., 2018; Ryan & DeMark, 2002; Schwabe et al., 2015; Stanger-Hall, 2012). Individuals with higher levels of test anxiety, who were often women (e.g., Devine et al., 2012; Eman et al., 2012; Núñez-Peña et al., 2016; Putwain & Daly, 2014), tended to prefer and perform better on closed-ended assessments, as these formats were often perceived as less intimidating (Birenbaum & Feldman, 1998; Zeidner, 1998). Higher risk takers, who were more often men (e.g., Byrnes et al., 1999; Cobey et al., 2013; Riener & Wagner, 2018), were more likely to engage in guessing on closed-ended assessments, whereas lower risk takers tended to skip questions they were uncertain about (e.g., Alnabhan, 2002; Baldiga, 2013; Ben-Shakhar & Sinai, 1991; Rubio et al., 2010).

Furthermore, test takers with higher levels of achievement motivation, more frequently represented by women (e.g., DeMars et al., 2013; Schwabe et al., 2015; Spinath, 2014; Spinath et al., 2014), were often considered better test-taking strategists and achieved higher scores on closed-ended assessments (e.g., Bonner, 2013; Dodeen et al., 2014; Hayati & Ghojogh, 2008). These variations highlight the influence of method effects resulting only from the response format itself.

Tasks requiring open-ended responses often demand higher levels of cognitive effort and time compared with closed-ended tasks. This higher level of cognitive load can lead to varying levels of cognitive fatigue or disengagement, depending on test takers' levels of motivation or conscientiousness (e.g., Ackerman & Kanfer, 2009), potentially resulting in a decline in performance on open-ended items due to the response format used. Furthermore, responding to open-ended items sometimes requires a higher level of linguistic skills (e.g., Arthur & Everaert, 2012), raising further concerns about method bias stemming from response formats. For instance, non-native speakers or individuals with dyslexia might be systematically disadvantaged because their verbal skills impact their scores in domains such as mathematics or specific content areas (e.g., Collins et al., 2020).

Regarding closed-ended tasks too, recent research has indicated that performance can be influenced by method bias related to the response format itself (e.g., Breuer et al., 2023a, 2023b; Kubinger, 2014; Mingo et al., 2018). Closed-ended tests primarily assess the ability to recognize the correct response, rather than the ability to create it. This raises concerns about whether these tests truly measure the intended skills, as recognition might be a less important ability than independently applying knowledge, in many fields (Kubinger, 2014). For instance, test-taking strategies associated with test-wiseness, defined as "a subject's capacity to utilize the characteristics and formats of the test and/or test-taking situation to receive a high score" (Millman et al., 1965, p. 707), significantly enhanced performance on closed-ended items (e.g., Bonner, 2013; Heyborne et al., 2011). Utilizing such strategies (e.g., eliminating obviously incorrect distractors, selecting middle-positioned or more detailed answers, using trial-and-error, or making educated guesses) depends on test takers' personalities and the quality of the distractors, leading to these tests potentially not measuring abilities consistently. As these strategies exploit flaws in test construction, designing high-quality closed-ended items requires specific expertise, careful review, and training to minimize construction errors and method biases.

Lucky guessing has also been identified as a potential source of bias related to the method (e.g., Bonner, 2013; Kubinger & Gottschall, 2007). Depending on the number of response alternatives and the number of correct options, the probability of selecting the correct response just by chance can be as high as 50%. This probability is possibly even amplified by test-wiseness strategies, especially when distractors are of low quality, leading to further potential construct-irrelevant variance in test scores (Bonner, 2013). Chance factors can inflate scores on closed-ended assessments, particularly for those willing to guess rather than skip a question when uncertain about the correct answer. Such guessing, which is unrelated to the construct being measured, can therefore introduce method bias into the results. To mitigate these method effects, it is crucial to design response options in a way that reduces the effectiveness of test-wiseness strategies and to employ a large number of closed-ended items with lower chances of guessing – such as formats with multiple correct options and at least five high-quality alternatives (e.g., Kubinger, 2014; Lindner et al., 2021).

Effects of the Testing Situation

The context in which psychological assessments are conducted – encompassing factors such as the characteristics of the test examiner, the physical environment, and the method of administration – can introduce method variance, thereby influencing test takers' behaviors and perceptions and ultimately affecting the validity and reliability of the assessment outcomes. Recognizing assessment environments as stress-inducing contexts, Lazarus and Eriksen (1952) emphasized the need to consider situational influences in standardized testing to minimize bias. Lewin (1946) highlighted the interconnection between individuals and their environments, suggesting that people cannot be separated from their surroundings. Sarason (1978) further noted that individuals process situational cues differently, affecting their perceptions and responses. Kenrick and Funder (1988) proposed that testing situations can activate various personal traits, leading to diverse individual experiences despite standardized conditions. Factors such as sex, ethnicity, test anxiety, and self-perceived competencies contribute to this variability.

Although significant efforts are made to standardize testing environments to ensure fairness and objectivity, certain elements remain challenging to control. Still, the characteristics and behaviors of TAs can significantly impact the outcomes of psychological assessments. Early experiments by Rosenthal and Fode (1963) and Rosenthal and Jacobson (1968) demonstrated that examiners' expectations can systematically affect test takers' intellectual performance. This effect, known as *experimenter bias*, has been observed in studies where examiner attitudes influenced test outcomes, with positive or neutral examiners eliciting better performance than negative ones (Bookout & Hosford, 1969).

Although research on gender effects in test administration is limited, insights can be drawn from studies on ethnicity, such as *stereotype threat*. This phenomenon, identified by Steele and Aronson (1995), occurs when individuals perform worse due to perceived negative stereotypes about their group. For example, Marx and Goff (2005) found that Black students performed better when tested by Black test administrators, indicating that examiner identity can influence motivation and performance. Katz et al. (1965), too, suggested that Black test takers may be influenced by the ethnicity of the examiner, affecting their expectations and performance. *Social dominance theory* (Sidanius & Pratto, 1999), which suggests that dominant groups strive to maintain their status, may also apply to gender dynamics in testing. Men might outperform women when tested by female test administrators due to societal power dynamics, potentially leading men to exert more effort to maintain their perceived dominance (Carli, 2001; Carli & Eagly,

2001; Danso & Esses, 2001). In fact, experiments by Ortner and Vormittag (2011) revealed that male and female test takers tended to provide more positive self-assessments of their forthcoming performance when evaluated by a female TA. Additionally, women TAs were generally described stereotypically – that is, as more socially competent, respectful, and sensitive – making them preferred as TAs (Vormittag et al., 2015). Vormittag and Ortner (2014) also investigated the singular and combined effects of TA likability, TA sex, and test taker sex, on performance estimations and actual test performance. Their findings indicated that higher likability of the TA was associated with test takers' lower self-estimations of intellectual performance, suggesting that test takers may be more cautious in estimating their abilities when interacting with a likable TA, potentially perceived as attractive. Furthermore, both male and female test takers scored lower on knowledge tests when assessed by a likable same-sex TA compared with a likable opposite-sex TA or a nonlikable TA.

Regarding ethnicity, studies have shown that Black participants tend to score higher on assessments administered by Black TAs (e.g., Marx & Goff, 2005; Redding, 2019). TAs' age also appears to influence perceptions of expertise, with middle-aged TAs (older than 44 years) typically receiving higher expertise and preference ratings than younger TAs (under 35 years old; Vormittag et al., 2015). Desrichard et al. (2023) reported that older examiners elicited better performance from older participants. These effects suggest that even when TAs adhere strictly to given instructions and maintain objectivity with test takers, TAs' social position still exerts an independent effect that cannot be eliminated.

Sex differences in test takers' perceptions and responses to high-stakes testing scenarios exemplify how additional psychological characteristics influence testing outcomes. Research by Leiner et al. (2018) revealed that men often perceive high-stakes tests as opportunities for socialization, competition, and sometimes deceit, whereas women tend to experience these situations as high-pressure environments, leading to heightened test anxiety, perceptions of unfairness, and lower scores. Additionally, Ryan (2001) reported that perceptual differences related to ethnicity can influence test outcomes, with research indicating that Black test takers are more likely to attribute performance to luck and external factors (Helms, 1992), potentially leading to increased anxiety and decreased motivation, and therefore, lower validity of testing outcomes.

Several individual characteristics, such as personality traits, are significantly related to attitudes toward assessment methods. For example, extraversion was positively associated with a preference for oral examinations in university students, whereas neuroticism was negatively associated with a preference for both oral exams and continuous assessment (i.e., ongoing evaluations through quizzes, assignments, and participation throughout a course; Chamorro-Premuzic & Furnham, 2005). Sex differences also play a role, with men generally showing more positive attitudes toward written exams, whereas women are more prone to test anxiety, which impacts their perceptions of fairness and performance (Furnham & Chamorro-Premuzic, 2005). This also applies to computerized assessment methods (Terzis & Economides, 2011). Moreover, ethnicity-related differences suggest that expectations of test fairness and effectiveness can vary significantly, influencing motivation and performance outcomes (Oostrom et al., 2016). These attitudes toward assessment methods directly impact test performance, as they may enhance or hinder performance through expectations, particularly in high-stakes environments (Furnham & Chamorro-Premuzic, 2005; Neto et al., 2023). A summary of all of these effects is given in Table 6.1.

Table 6.1 Summary of effects.

	Source	Description	Impact
Item arrangement effects	Fixed-item testing (FIT)	Items are presented in a fixed order, often by increasing difficulty.	May motivate or demotivate test takers depending on initial success; introduces practice effects.
	Computerized adaptive testing (CAT)	Items adapt to the test taker's performance level based on responses.	Reduces testing time but may heighten test anxiety; can undermine metacognitive competence.
	Mixed-scale arrangements	Items are randomly distributed to avoid response biases.	Minimizes anchoring and testlet effects; may reduce face validity.
Response format effects	Closed-ended formats	Predefined response options (e.g., multiple-choice, true/false).	Prone to test-wiseness strategies, guessing, and recognition bias.
	Open-ended formats	Requires constructed responses (e.g., essays, short answers).	May disadvantage non-native speakers or individuals with dyslexia.
Test situation effects	Test anxiety	Emotional distress caused by high-stakes testing.	Disproportionately affects women and may lower cognitive performance.
	Stereotype threat	Performance is affected by awareness of negative group stereotypes.	Leads to reduced performance in ethnic minorities and women in specific domains.
	Examiner characteristics	Effects of examiner's sex, age, ethnicity, or likability.	Influences motivation, self-estimation, and actual performance.
Test takers' characteristics	Test-wiseness strategy use	Ability to exploit test format for higher scores (e.g., guessing, eliminating distractors).	Inflates scores unrelated to the construct being measured.
	Risk propensity	Tendency to guess or skip questions.	Men are more likely to guess, leading to higher scores in closed-ended formats.
	Achievement motivation	Effort and strategy use related to success orientation.	Women tend to score higher when motivation aligns with assessment format.

Conclusions and Outlook

Psychological assessments play a crucial role in various domains, but their accuracy hinges on careful consideration of test design and administration methods. It is important to emphasize that, despite the described biasing effects, assessment outcomes generally retain a strong foundation of validity and continue to play a crucial role in supporting valuable decisions and accurate diagnoses (see, e.g., Sackett et al., 2017). Nevertheless, understanding how item arrangement, response formats, and testing situations can influence assessment outcomes is essential for minimizing method biases. Addressing these effects is essential for ensuring that test scores accurately reflect the intended constructs and support valid inferences about test takers' abilities.

Arrangement effects refer to how the sequence and structure of item presentation influence test taker performance. These effects can be investigated through experimental studies comparing various arrangement designs and are inherently present in all forms of measurement, albeit in different ways. In practice, strategies aimed at reducing test anxiety may help decrease method variance, which could disproportionately affect women's scores (von der Embse et al., 2018). Test anxiety can directly impair cognitive performance on intelligence tests and may be further intensified by previous experiences with poor test outcomes (Hembree, 1988; Zeidner, 1998). To mitigate test design-related effects, it is beneficial to provide information and experience with test formats, offer practice tests that simulate the actual testing environment, minimize time pressure, and ensure a comfortable, distraction-free test setting.

Method effects in response formats are also evident in both closed-ended and open-ended assessment formats, with each influencing test taker performance and introducing potential biases. These effects can be investigated by comparing performance outcomes between closed-ended and open-ended formats, analyzing the influence of individual differences (e.g., test anxiety, risk propensity, achievement motivation) on performance, and examining the impact of test-wiseness strategies. Experimental designs allow for the investigation of variations, and their effects on the reliability of test scores.

Research findings underline the necessity of considering individual perceptions and situational dynamics to ensure the fairness and validity of standardized tests. A one-size-fits-all approach might be inadequate due to the diverse ways individuals perceive and interact with testing environments. Factors such as sex, ethnicity, test anxiety, and personal beliefs about ability can significantly affect how test takers respond to and perform in these situations, and these differences can lead to biases and disparities in test outcomes. By recognizing and addressing these variables, educators and TAs can create more equitable testing environments that reflect the diverse characteristics and needs of all test takers.

Also, the context in which psychological assessments are conducted, including factors such as the test administrator's characteristics, the physical environment, and previous experiences and information, can introduce method variance, which can affect test takers' behaviors and perceptions, ultimately impacting test performances. Research has demonstrated that examiners' expectations, sex, and ethnicity can influence test performance, with effects such as experimenter bias and stereotype threat, altering outcomes on the basis of test takers' characteristics, such as sex, ethnicity, and personality traits.

In assessment practice, we encourage practitioners to engage in continuous training and education on the latest research regarding method effects and strategies for minimizing their impact. Staying informed about advancements in the field enables practitioners to identify and mitigate method effects effectively. Understanding these effects in relation to test design and administration should inspire practitioners to implement and evaluate strategies to minimize them, ensuring that tests accurately measure the intended constructs rather than reflecting unintended biases. It is crucial to create testing environments that allow individuals with diverse experiences and personalities to demonstrate their knowledge, skills, and abilities. Additionally, practitioners should assess potential moderators or mediators of bias, and use statistical methods, such as IRT, to identify and control for method effects in their test data. Practitioners are also encouraged to update testing procedures on the basis of test taker feedback and empirical data, as well as collaborate with researchers to stay current with new findings on method effects.

References

Ackerman, P. L., & Kanfer, R. (2009). Test length and cognitive fatigue: An empirical examination of effects on performance and test-taker reactions. *Journal of Experimental Psychology: Applied, 15*(2), 163–181. https://doi.org/10.1037/a0015719

Akhtar, H., Silfiasari, Vekety, B., & Kovacs, K. (2022). The effect of computerized adaptive testing on motivation and anxiety: A systematic review and meta-analysis. *Assessment, 30*(5), 1379–1390. https://doi.org/10.1177/10731911221100995

Allen, M. J., & Yen, W. M. (1979). *Introduction to Measurement Theory*. Brooks/Cole.

Alnabhan, M. (2002). An empirical investigation of the effects of three methods of handling guessing and risk taking on the psychometric indices of a test. *Social Behavior and Personality, 30*(7), 645–652. https://doi.org/10.2224/sbp.2002.30.7.645

Arthur, N., & Everaert, P. (2012). Gender and performance in accounting examinations: Exploring the impact of examination format. *Accounting Education, 21*(5), 471–487. https://doi.org/10.1080/09639284.2011.650447

Bagozzi, R. P., & Yi, Y. (1990). Assessing method variance in multitrait-multimethod matrices: The case of self-reported affect and perceptions at work. *Journal of Applied Psychology, 75,* 547–560. https://doi.org/10.1037/0021-9010.75.5.547

Baldiga, K. (2013). Gender differences in willingness to guess. *Management Science, 60*(2), 434–448. https://doi.org/10.1287/mnsc.2013.1776

Ben-Shakhar, G., & Sinai, Y. (1991). Gender differences in multiple-choice tests: The role of differential guessing tendencies. *Journal of Educational Measurement, 28*(1), 23–35. https://doi.org/10.2307/1434682

Birenbaum, M., & Feldman, R. A. (1998). Relationships between learning patterns and attitudes towards two assessment formats. *Educational Research, 40*(1), 90–98. https://doi.org/10.1080/0013188980400109

Bonner, S. M. (2013). Mathematics strategy use in solving test items in varied formats. *Journal of Experimental Education, 81*(3), 409–428. https://doi.org/10.1080/00220973.2012.727886

Bookout, V., & Hosford, R. E. (1969). The effect of examiner status and examiner's expectations on achievement test performance. *Journal of Experimental Education, 38*(1), 69–74.

Breuer, S., Scherndl, T., & Ortner, T. M. (2020). Effects of response format on psychometric properties and fairness of a matrices test: Multiple-choice vs. free-response. *Frontiers in Education, 5*, Article 15. https://doi.org/10.3389/feduc.2020.00015

Breuer, S., Scherndl, T., & Ortner, T. M. (2023a). Effects of response format on achievement and aptitude assessment results: Multi-level random effects meta-analyses. *Royal Society Open Science, 10*, 220456. https://doi.org/10.1098/rsos.220456

Breuer, S., Scherndl, T., & Ortner, T. M. (2023b). Find the mistake! Psychometric properties of an innovative response format for figural matrices tasks. *Journal of Individual Differences, 44*(2), 83–96. https://doi.org/10.1027/1614-0001/a000386

Brüggemann, T., Ludewig, U., Lorenz, R., & McElvany, N. (2023). Effects of mode and medium in reading comprehension tests on cognitive load. *Computers & Education, 192*, 104649. https://doi.org/10.1016/j.compedu.2022.104649

Brüggemann, T., Ludewig, U., Lorenz, R., & McElvany, N. (2024). Effects of test mode and medium on elementary school students' test experience. *European Journal of Psychological Assessment, 40*(4), 282–289. https://doi.org/10.1027/1015-5759/a000767

Byrnes, J. P., Miller, D. C., & Schafer, W. D. (1999). Gender differences in risk taking: A meta-analysis. *Psychological Bulletin, 125*(3), 367–383. https://doi.org/10.1037//0033-2909.125.3.367

Carli, L. L. (2001). Gender and social influence. *Journal of Social Issues, 57*(4), 725–741. https://doi.org/10.1111/0022-4537.00238

Carli, L. L., & Eagly, A. H. (2001). Gender, hierarchy, and leadership: An introduction. *Journal of Social Issues, 57*(4), 629–636. https://doi.org/10.1111/0022-4537.00232

Chamorro-Premuzic, T., & Furnham, A. (2005). Personality and preference for academic assessment: A study with Australian university students. *Learning and Individual Differences, 15*(3), 247–256. https://doi.org/10.1016/j.lindif.2005.02.002

Cobey, K. D., Stulp, G., Laan, F., Buunk, A. P., & Pollet, T. V. (2013). Sex differences in risk taking behavior among Dutch cyclists. *Evolutionary Psychology, 11*(2), 350–364. https://doi.org/10.1177/147470491301100206

Collins, A. A., Compton, D. L., Lindstrom, E. R., & Gilbert, J. K. (2020). Performance variations across reading comprehension assessments: Examining the unique contributions of text, activity, and reader. *Reading and Writing: An Interdisciplinary Journal, 33*, 605–634. https://doi.org/10.1007/s11145-019-09972-5

Crocker, L., & Schmitt, A. (1987). Improving multiple-choice test performance for examinees with different levels of test anxiety. *Journal of Experimental Education, 55*(4), 201–205. https://doi.org/10.1080/00220973.1987.10806454

Danso, H. A., & Esses, V. M. (2001). Black experimenters and the intellectual test performance of White students: The tables are turned. *Journal of Experimental Social Psychology, 37*(2), 158–165. https://doi.org/10.1006/jesp.2000.1444

DeMars, C. E. (1998). Gender differences in mathematics and science on a high school proficiency exam: The role of response format. *Applied Measurement in Education, 11*(3), 279–299. https://doi.org/10.1207/s15324818ame1103_4

DeMars, C. E., Bashkov, B. M., & Socha, A. (2013). The role of gender in test-taking motivation under low-stakes conditions. *Research & Practice in Assessment, 8*, 69–82.

Desrichard, O., Heiser, N., Renaud, O., Zuber, S., Oris, M., & Kliegel, M. (2023). Contextual variation in cognitive performance of older adults: Demonstration of an age-of-examiner effect. *The Clinical Neuropsychologist, 37*(7), 1428–1440. https://doi.org/10.1080/13854046.2022.2150689

Devine, A., Fawcett, K., Szűcs, D., & Dowker, A. (2012). Gender differences in mathematics anxiety and the relation to mathematics performance while controlling for test anxiety. *Behavioral and Brain Functions, 8*, 33–33. https://doi.org/10.1186/1744-9081-8-33

Dodeen, H., Abdelfattah, F., & Alshumrani, S. (2014). Test-taking skills of secondary students: The relationship with motivation, attitudes, anxiety and attitudes towards tests. *South African Journal of Education, 34*(2), Article 866. https://doi.org/10.15700/201412071153

Downing, S. M. (2006). Twelve steps for effective test development. In S. M. Downing & T. M. Haladyna (Eds.), *Handbook of test development* (pp. 3–25). Lawrence Erlbaum.

Dykema, J., Schaefer, N. C., Garbarski, D., Assad, N., & Blixt, S. (2022). Towards a reconsideration of the use of agree-disagree questions in measuring subjective evaluations. *Research in Social and Administrative Pharmacy, 18*(2), 2335–2344. https://doi.org/10.1016/j.sapharm.2021.06.014

Eman, S., Dogar, I. A., Khalid, M., & Halder, N. (2012). Gender differences in test anxiety and examination stress. *Journal of Pakistan Psychiatric Society, 9*, 80–85.

Fiske, D. W. (1982). Convergent-discriminant validation in measurements and research strategies. In D. Brinbirg & L. H. Kidder (Eds.), *Forms of validity in research* (pp. 77–92). Jossey-Bass.

Franke, G. H. (2019). "The whole is more than the sum of its parts": The effects of grouping and randomizing items on the reliability and validity of questionnaires. *European Journal of Psychological Assessment, 35*(5), 717–726. https://psycnet.apa.org/doi/10.1027/1015-5759.13.2.67

Frey, A. (2023). Computerized adaptive testing and multistage testing. In R. J. Tierney, F. Rizvi, & K. Erkican (Eds.), *International encyclopedia of education* (4th ed., pp. 209–216). Elsevier. https://doi.org/10.1016/B978-0-12-818630-5.10028-4

Furnham, A., & Chamorro-Premuzic, T. (2005). Individual differences and beliefs concerning preference for university assessment methods. *Journal of Applied Social Psychology, 35(9)*, 1986–1994. https://doi.org/10.1111/j.1559-1816.2005.tb02205.x

Gierl, M. J., Bulut, O., Guo, Q., & Zhang, X. (2017). Developing, analyzing, and using distractors for multiple-choice tests in education: A comprehensive review. *Review of Educational Research, 87*, 1082–1116. https://doi.org/10.3102/0034654317726529

Haladyna, T. M., & Rodriguez, M. C. (2013). *Developing and validating test items.* Routledge. https://doi.org/10.4324/9780203850381

Hayati, A. M., & Ghojogh, A. N. (2008). Investigating the influence of proficiency and gender on the use of selected test-wiseness strategies in higher education. *English Language Teaching, 1*, 169–181. https://doi.org/10.5539/elt.v1n2p169

Helms, J. E. (1992). Why is there no study of cultural equivalence in standardized cognitive ability testing? *American Psychologist, 47*(9), 1083–1101. https://doi.org/10.1037/0003-066X.47.9.1083

Helms, J. E. (2004). Fair and valid use of educational testing in grades K-12. In J. E. Wall & G. R. Walz (Eds.), *Measuring up: Assessment issues for teachers, counselors, and administrators* (pp. 81–88). CAPS Press.

Hembree, R. (1988). Correlates, causes, effects, and treatment of test anxiety. *Review of Educational Research, 58*(1), 47–77. https://doi.org/10.3102/00346543058001047

Heyborne, W. H., Clarke, J. A., & Perrett, J. J. (2011). A Comparison of two forms of assessment in an introductory biology laboratory course. *Journal of College Science Teaching, 40*(5), 28–31. http://hdl.handle.net/1959.14/175225

Irwing, P., & Lynn, R. (2005). Sex differences in means and variability on the progressive matrices in university students: A meta-analysis. *British Journal of Psychology, 96*(4), 505–524. https://doi.org/10.1348/000712605X53542

Kastner, M., & Stangl, B. (2011). Multiple choice and constructed response tests: Do test format and scoring matter? *Procedia – Social and Behavioral Sciences, 12*, 263–273. https://doi.org/10.1016/j.sbspro.2011.02.035

Katz, I., Roberts, S. O., & Robinson, J. M. (1965). Effects of task difficulty, race of administrator, and instructions on digit-symbol performance of Negroes. *Journal of Personality and Social Psychology, 1*(4), 423–428. https://doi.org/10.1037/h0022080

Kenrick, D. T., & Funder, D. C. (1988). Profiting from controversy: Lessons from the person-situation debate. *American Psychologist, 43*(1), 23. https://doi.org/10.1037/0003-066x.43.1.23

Krosnick, J. A., & Presser, S. (2010). Question and questionnaire design. In P. V. Marsden & J. D. Wright (Eds.), *Handbook of survey research* (pp. 263–314). Emerald Group.

Kubinger, K. D. (2014). Gutachten zur Erstellung „gerichtsfester" Multiple-Choice-Prüfungsaufgaben [Expert report on the development of legally defensible multiple-choice examination items]. *Psychologische Rundschau, 65*(3), 169–178. https://doi.org/10.1026/0033-3042/a000218

Kubinger, K. D., & Gottschall, C. H. (2007). Item difficulty of multiple choice tests dependent on different item response formats – An experiment in fundamental research on psychological assessment. *Psychology Science, 49*(4), 361–374.

Lazarus, R. S., & Eriksen, C. W. (1952). Effects of failure stress upon skilled performance. *Journal of Experimental Psychology, 43*(2), 100–105. https://doi.org/10.1037/h0056614

Leiner, J. E. M., Scherndl, T., & Ortner, T. M. (2018). How do men and women perceive a high-stakes test situation? *Frontiers in Psychology, 9*, Article 2216. https://doi.org/10.3389/fpsyg.2018.02216

Lewin, K. (1946). Behavior and development as a function of the total situation. In L. Carmichael (Ed.), *Manual of child psychology* (pp. 791–844). Wiley. https://doi.org/10.1037/10756-016

Linacre, J. M. (2000). Computer-adaptive testing: A methodology whose time has come. In S. Chae, U. Kang, E. Jeon, & J. M. Linacre (Eds.), *Development of computerized middle school achievement test* (MESA Memorandum No. 69) (pp. 1–58). Komesa Press.

Lindner, M. A., Sparfeldt, J. R., Köller, O., Lukas, J., & Leutner, D. (2021). Ein Plädoyer zur Qualitätssicherung schriftlicher Prüfungen im Psychologiestudium. [A plea for quality assurance in written examinations in psychology degree programs]. *Psychologische Rundschau, 72*(2), 93–105. https://doi.org/10.1026/0033-3042/a000524

Ling, G., Attali, Y., Finn, B., & Stone, E. A. (2017). Is a computerized adaptive test more motivating than a fixed-item test? *Applied Psychological Measurement, 41*(7), 495–511. https://doi.org/10.1177/0146621617707556

Linn, R. L. (2006). The standards for educational and psychological testing: Guidance in test development. In S. M. Downing & T. M. Haladyna (Eds.), *Handbook of test development* (pp. 27–39). Lawrence Erlbaum.

Martinez, M. E. (1999). Cognition and the question of test item format. *Educational Psychologist, 34*(4), 207–218. https://doi.org/10.1207/s15326985ep3404_2

Marx, D. M., & Goff, P. A. (2005). Clearing the air: The effect of experimenter race on target's test performance and subjective experience. *British Journal of Social Psychology, 44*(4), 645–657. https://doi.org/10.1348/014466604X17948

Millman, J., Bishop, H., & Ebel, R. (1965). An analysis of test-wiseness. *Educational and Psychological Measurement, 25*, 707–726. https://doi.org/10.1177/001316446502500304

Mingo, M. A., Chang, H.-H., & Williams, R. L. (2018). Undergraduate students' preferences for constructed versus multiple-choice assessment of learning. *Innovative Higher Education, 43*, 143–152. https://doi.org/10.1007/s10755-017-9414-y

Neto, J., Neto, F., & Furnham, A. (2023). Predictors of students' preferences for assessment methods. *Assessment & Evaluation in Higher Education, 48*(4), 556–565. https://doi.org/10.1080/02602938.2022.2087860

Núñez-Peña, M. I., Suárez-Pellicioni, M., & Bono, R. (2016). Gender differences in test anxiety and their impact on higher education students' academic achievement. *Procedia - Social and Behavioral Sciences, 228*, 154–160. https://doi.org/10.1016/j.sbspro.2016.07.023

Oostrom, J. K., & De Soete, B. (2016). Ethnic differences in perceptions of cognitive ability tests: The explanatory role of self-serving attributions. *International Journal of Selection and Assessment, 24*(1), 14-23. https://doi.org/10.1111/ijsa.12125

Ortner, T. M. (2004). On changing the position of items in personality questionnaires: Analysing effects of item sequence using IRT. *Psychology Science, 46*(3), 336–351.

Ortner, T. (2008). Effects of changed item order: A cautionary note to practitioners on jumping to computerized adaptive testing for personality assessment. *International Journal of Selection and Assessment, 16*(3), 249–257. https://doi.org/10.1111/j.1468-2389.2008.00431.x

Ortner, T. M., & Caspers, J. (2011). Consequences of test anxiety on adaptive versus fixed item testing. *European Journal of Psychological Assessment, 27*(3), 157–163. https://doi.org/10.1027/1015-5759/a000062

Ortner, T. M., & Vormittag, I. (2011). Test administrator's gender affects female and male students' self-estimated verbal general knowledge. *Learning and Instruction, 21*(1), 14–21. https://doi.org/10.1016/j.learninstruc.2009.09.003

Ortner, T. M., Weisskopf, E., & Gerstenberg, F. X. R. (2013). Skilled but unaware of it: CAT undermines a test taker's metacognitive competence. *European Journal of Psychology of Education, 28*(1), 37–51. https://doi.org/10.1007/s10212-011-0100-7

Ortner, T. M., Weißkopf, E., & Koch, T. (2014). I will probably fail: Higher ability students' motivational experiences during adaptive achievement testing. *European Journal of Psychological Assessment, 30*(1), 48–56. https://doi.org/10.1027/1015-5759/a000168

Podsakoff, P. M., MacKenzie, S. B., Lee, J. Y., & Podsakoff, N. P. (2003). Common method biases in behavioral research: A critical review of the literature and recommended remedies. *Journal of Applied Psychology, 88*(5), 879–903. https://doi.org/10.1037/0021-9010.88.5.879

Putwain, D., & Daly, A. L. (2014). Test anxiety prevalence and gender differences in a sample of English secondary school students. *Educational Studies, 40*, 554–570. https://doi.org/10.1080/03055698.2014.953914

Rasch, G. (1960). *Probabilistic models for some intelligence and attainment tests.* University of Chicago Press.

Reardon, S. F., Kalogrides, D., Fahle, E. M., Podolsky, A., & Zárate, R. C. (2018). The relationship between test item format and gender achievement gaps on math and ELA tests in fourth and eighth grades. *Educational Researcher, 47*, 284–294. https://doi.org/10.3102/0013189X18762105

Redding, C. (2019). A teacher like me: A review of the effect of student-teacher racial/ethnic matching on teacher perceptions of students and student academic and behavioral outcomes. *Review of Educational Research, 89*(4), 499–535. https://doi.org/10.3102/0034654319853545

Riener, G., & Wagner, V. (2018). Gender differences in willingness to compete and answering multiple-choice questions: The role of age. *Economics Letters, 164*, 86–89. https://doi.org/10.1016/j.econlet.2018.01.012
Rosenthal, R., & Jacobson, L. (1968). Pygmalion in the classroom. *Urban Review, 3*(1), 16–20. https://doi.org/10.1007/BF02322211
Rosenthal, R., & Fode, K. L. (1963). The effect of experimenter bias on the performance of the albino rat. *Behavioral Science, 8*(3), 183–189. https://doi.org/10.1002/bs.3830080302
Rubio, V. J., Hernández, J. M., Zaldívar, F., Márquez, O., & Santacreu, J. (2010). Can we predict risk-taking behavior? Two behavioral tests for predicting guessing tendencies in a multiple-choice test. *European Journal of Psychological Assessment, 26*(2), 87–94. https://doi.org/10.1027/1015-5759/a000013
Ryan, A. M. (2001). Explaining the Black-White test score gap: The role of test perceptions. *Human Performance, 14*(1), 45–75. https://doi.org/10.1207/S15327043HUP1401_04
Ryan, J. M., & DeMark, S. (2002). Variation in achievement scores related to gender, item format, and content area tested. In G. Tindal & T. M. Haladyna (Eds.), *Large-scale assessment programs for all students: Validity, technical adequacy, and implementation* (pp. 67–88). Lawrence Erlbaum.
Sackett, P. R., Lievens, F., Van Iddekinge, C. H., & Kuncel, N. R. (2017). Individual differences and their measurement: A review of 100 years of research. *Journal of Applied Psychology, 102*, 254–273. https://doi.org/10.1037/apl0000151
Sarason, I. G. (1978). The test anxiety scale: Concept and research. In C. D. Spielberger & I. G. Sarason (Eds.), *Stress and anxiety* (Vol. 5, pp. 193–216). Hemisphere.
Sarnacki, R. E. (1979). An examination of test-wise in the cognitive test domain. *Review of Educational Research, 49*, 252–279. https://doi.org/10.3102/00346543049002252
Schult, J., & Lindner, M. A. (2018). Judgment accuracy of German elementary school teachers: A matter of response formats? *Zeitschrift für Pädagogische Psychologie, 32*, 75–87. https://doi.org/10.1024/1010-0652/a000216
Schult, J., & Sparfeldt, J. R. (2018). Reliability and validity of PIRLS and TIMSS: Does the response format matter? *European Journal of Psychological Assessment, 34*(4), 258–269. https://doi.org/10.1027/1015-5759/a000338
Schwabe, F., McElvany, N., & Trendtel, M. (2015). The school age gender gap in reading achievement: Examining the influences of item format and intrinsic reading motivation. *Reading Research Quarterly, 50*(2), 219–232. https://doi.org/10.1002/rrq.92
Schweizer, K. (2020). Method effects in psychological assessment. *Psychological Test and Assessment Modeling, 64*, 337–343.
Sidanius, J., & Pratto, F. (1999). *Social dominance: An intergroup theory of social hierarchy and oppression.* Cambridge University Press. https://doi.org/10.1017/CBO9781139175043
Spinath, B. (2014). The roles of intelligence, personality and motivation in girls' outperforming boys at school. *Personality and Individual Differences, 60*, 45. https://doi.org/10.1016/j.paid.2013.07.131
Spinath, B., Eckert, C., & Steinmayr, R. (2014). Gender differences in school success: what are the roles of students' intelligence, personality and motivation? *Educational Research, 56*, 230–243. https://doi.org/10.1080/00131881.2014.898917
Stanger-Hall, K. F. (2012). Multiple-Choice Exams: An Obstacle for Higher-Level Thinking in Introductory Science Classes. *CBE Life Sciences Education, 11*(3), 294–306. https://doi.org/10.1187/cbe.11-11-0100
Steele, C. M., & Aronson, J. (1995). Stereotype threat and the intellectual test performance of African Americans. *Journal of Personality and Social Psychology, 69*(5), 797–811. https://doi.org/10.1037/0022-3514.69.5.797
Terzis, V., & Economides, A. A. (2011). Computer based assessment: Gender differences in perceptions and acceptance. *Computers in Human Behavior, 27*(6), 2108–2122. https://doi.org/10.1016/j.chb.2011.06.005
Thielsch, M. T., Brandenburg, T., & Kanning, U. P. (2012). Diagnostische Verfahren im Praxiseinsatz [Psychological assessment in professional practice]. In R. Reinhardt (Ed.), *Wirtschaftspsychologie und Organisationserfolg* (pp. 57–64). Pabst.
van der Linden, W. J. & Glas, G. A. W (2000). *Computerized adaptive testing: Theory and practice.* Kluwer Academic Publishers.
van de Vijver, F. J. R., & Poortinga, Y. H. (2005). Conceptual and methodological issues in adapting tests. In R. K. Hambleton, P. F. Merenda, & C. D. Spielberger (Eds.), *Adapting educational and psychological tests for cross-cultural assessment* (pp. 39–63). Lawrence Erlbaum.

van de Vijver, F. J. R., & Tanzer, N. K. (2004). Bias and equivalence in cross-cultural assessment: An overview. *European Review of Applied Psychology, 54*(2), 119–135. https://doi.org/10.1016/j.erap.2003.12.004

von der Embse, N., Jester, D., Roy, D., & Post, J. (2018). Test anxiety effects, predictors, and correlates: A 30-year meta-analytic review. *Journal of Affective Disorders, 227*, 483–493. https://doi.org/10.1016/j.jad.2017.11.048

Vormittag, I., & Ortner, T. M. (2014). In the eye of the examinee: Likable examiners interfere with performance. *Social Psychology of Education, 17*(3), 401–417. https://doi.org/10.1007/s11218-014-9252-z

Vormittag, I., Ortner, T. M., & Koch, T. (2015). How test takers see test examiners. How they are perceived and who is preferred. *European Journal of Psychological Assessment, 31*(4), 254–262. https://doi.org/10.1027/1015-5759/a000232

Wainer, H. (2002). Introduction and history. In H. Wainer (Ed.), *Computerized adaptive testing: A primer* (pp. 1–21). Lawrence Erlbaum.

Wainer, H., & Eignor, D. (2000). Caveats, pitfalls, and unexpected consequences of implementing large scale computerized testing. In H. Wainer (Ed.), *Computerized adaptive testing: A primer* (pp. 271–299). Lawrence Erlbaum.

Wise, S. L. (2019). Controlling construct-irrelevant factors through computer-based testing: Disengagement, anxiety, and cheating. *Education Inquiry, 10*(1), 21–33. https://doi.org/10.1080/20004508.2018.1490127

Willingham, W. W., & Cole, N. S. (Eds.). (1997). *Gender and fair assessment*. Lawrence Erlbaum.

Wright, C. D., Eddy, S. L., Wenderoth, M. P., Abshire, E., Blankenbiller, M., & Brownell, S. E. (2016). Cognitive difficulty and format of exams predicts gender and socioeconomic gaps in exam performance of students in introductory biology courses. *CBE Life Sciences Education, 15*, 1–16. https://doi.org/10.1187/cbe.15-12-0246

Zeidner, M. (1998). *Test anxiety: The state of the art*. Springer.

Chapter 7

Item Response Format and Response Styles

Ana Hernández, Inés Tomás, and Clara Cuevas

Abstract

To ensure the validity of psychological assessments, it is necessary to understand and address different method effects and response styles. This chapter focuses on item response format features that mitigate the appearance of two specific response styles (extreme and midpoint), and it reviews the procedures that quantify and control for these response styles. The goal is to achieve more reliable and valid estimates of the traits of interest. By providing a comprehensive view of the interplay between item response formats and response styles, this chapter seeks to provide practical guidelines to accomplish this goal.

Method Effects and Item Response Format

Method effects refer to systematic unwanted variance linked to the way information is collected rather than to the construct being measured (Podsakoff et al., 2003). These effects are partly caused by the *item response format* (IRF; e.g., the number and labeling of options) used in surveys and questionnaires. The IRF, in turn, can strongly influence *response styles* (RSs), which reflect individuals' tendencies to respond in systematic ways regardless of the content of the item (van Vaerenbergh & Thomas, 2013). Statistically, RSs can be defined as the tendencies to use certain response categories that are not accounted for by the content trait. These RSs include agreeing with statements (acquiescence), selecting extreme options (*extreme response style* [ERS]), or choosing the middle option (*midpoint response style* [MRS]).

Although method effects are associated with the method itself, and RSs are related to personal tendencies, they overlap when the emergence of RSs depends on the IRF. Thus, RSs have two components: a *dispositional component* at the respondent level that is stable across traits and time (e.g., Austin et al., 2006; Kutscher & Eid, 2024; Weijters, Geuens et al., 2010) and a *contextual component* that is influenced by the IRF (Quirk & Kern, 2023; Weijters, Cabooter et al., 2010). These components can interact in complex ways, making their effects difficult to disentangle (Morren et al., 2011; Podsakoff et al., 2003).

Because IRF and RSs introduce unwanted variance when assessing the *trait of interest* (ToI), it is crucial to (a) minimize their effects through better questionnaire design and (b) use statistical methods to control for them. Other chapters (e.g., Chapter 8) discuss various method effects and RSs (e.g., negative wording and acquiescence). This chapter focuses on IRF, with special attention to graded response formats such as Likert scales, and two specific RSs: ERS and MRS, with an emphasis on strategies for prevention and correction.

ERS, MRS, and IRF

As mentioned above, ERS and MRS are especially prevalent on graded (i.e., Likert) scales. They are traditionally conceptualized as the tendency to select extreme responses (e.g., 1 or 5 on a 5-point scale) and, for an odd number of response options, the tendency to choose the middle category (e.g., 3 on a 5-point scale), respectively. They are typically understood as separate, negatively correlated styles, although this is not always the case. Some authors conceptualize ERS and MRS as degrees of person extremeness (Pargent, 2017). In this case, any item response (e.g., 4 on a 5-point scale) provides information about the extremeness tendency. From this perspective, avoiding extremes (Van Vaerenbergh & Thomas, 2013) falls between traditional MRS and ERS on this continuum. This view, however, is not the most common. Because both extreme and midpoint responses can occur together within the same sample (e.g., Weijters, Geuens et al., 2010) and ERS and MRS are not always negatively correlated, researchers have suggested that ERS and MRS involve distinct cognitive processes (Henninger & Plieninger, 2021), modeling them as separate dimensions in most cases.

Regardless of the way ERS and MRS are conceptualized, IRF influences the emergence of RSs because it shapes the salience and perceived meaning of the response categories, which affects the likelihood of choosing certain options (Weijters, Cabooter et al., 2010). Specifically, responding to survey items involves several cognitive stages - comprehension, retrieval, judgment, and response (Tourangeau et al., 2000), and MRS and ERS are particularly sensitive to the judgment phase, in which choices are mapped onto the IRF (Krosnick, 1991). Complex, lengthy, or ambiguous formats can increase the cognitive load and affect the judgment phase, leading to satisficing behaviors where respondents choose minimally acceptable responses to deal with cognitive overload (Krosnick, 1991). This strategy may result in the use of heuristic shortcuts, such as choosing extreme categories or the midpoint (e.g., Greenleaf, 1992). This practice is more likely in low-motivation scenarios (e.g., low-stakes assessments) or when respondents are not interested in the topic (Pokropek et al., 2023; Van Vaerenbergh & Thomas, 2013). However, research also suggests that MRS and ERS do not simply reflect satisficing and instead stem from more complex processes involving the relationship between the RS, the ToI, and the IRF (Henninger & Plieninger, 2021).

Whereas RSs are generally treated as systematic sources of error that confound the ToI measurement, some researchers argue that MRS and ERS reflect communication styles tied to personality and cultural factors such as collectivism (He, Bartram et al., 2014; He & van de Vijver, 2019). These styles act as communication filters linked to impression management and self-regulation processes, as in the promotion of a strong, unambiguous self-image, in the case of ERS, and prevention of potential negative judgments, by appearing more moderate, in the case of MRS (He, Van de Vijver et al., 2014). Given that these filters function as a tendency to use specific parts of the response scale - more extreme or moderate alternatives - the IRF (e.g., number of categories) also matters.

Consequences of ERS and MRS for ToI Inferences

Research shows strong evidence for the presence of ERS and MRS, especially on graded response scales (Kieruj & Moors, 2010; Morren et al., 2011; Wetzel & Carstensen, 2017). For instance, Wetzel and Carstensen (2017) estimated that 25% of the common variance in self-report questionnaires is due to ERS. This situation is concerning because ERS and MRS introduce irrelevant variance, distorting trait measurement and inferences. They can alter observed means and variances, biasing mean comparisons (e.g., Cheung & Rensvold, 2000) and distorting correlations between variables, which are the input for factor analysis and structural equation modeling, and the basis of psychometric indicators such as reliability, validity, and interrater agreement (Reynolds & Smith, 2010). Moreover, clusters of respondents with ERS or MRS might be mistakenly identified as content-based clusters (Takagishi et al., 2019), and conclusions about measurement invariance across groups can be misleading (Bolt & Johnson, 2009; Morren et al., 2011). At the individual level, decisions based on cutoff points, as in personnel selection, may also be biased (Hernández et al., 2004; Jin & Wang, 2014).

In general, ERS and MRS have been linked to intelligence and cognitive ability (Batchelor & Miao, 2016; Bolt & Johnson, 2009; Meisenberg & Williams, 2008) and, although not always consistently, to personality traits (Austin et al., 2006; Hernández et al., 2004), as well as sociodemographic variables such as sex, age, and education (Batchelor & Miao, 2016). Therefore, models and comparisons involving these variables should be interpreted with caution if response biases are not controlled for, given that RSs may offer alternative explanations for many findings. For example, Moors (2012) found that differences in passive leadership between men and women disappeared after controlling for ERS. Cultural differences in the use of extreme and midpoint categories also pose risks to cross-cultural comparisons if RSs are ignored (De Jong et al., 2008; Dibek & Cikrikci, 2021; Johnson et al., 2005; Lee et al., 2023).

Due to the negative effects of ERS and MRS, it is crucial to prevent them through careful questionnaire design. However, because fully preventing RS bias is difficult, diagnosing, controlling, and understanding their effects is the key to making sound conclusions about traits and their relationships. The following sections will focus on IRFs that mitigate ERS and MRS, and we discuss methods to quantify and control for these RSs. Although this chapter mostly adheres to the dominant perspective of considering ERS and MRS as unwanted sources of variance, it is acknowledged that quantifying and estimating RSs can contribute to our understanding of individual and cultural differences (He, Bartram et al., 2014; Böckenholt, 2017).

Preventing ERS and MRS Through IRF Design

The use of post hoc statistical methods to control ERS and MRS can be challenging for applied researchers. Because IRF can either increase or decrease extreme or midpoint responses, careful IRF design is a proactive way to reduce these RSs. However, it is unlikely that they will be eliminated entirely (Moors et al., 2014).

In terms of IRF, *graded response items* (GRI), such as Likert-type scales, are the most common formats used in psychology and the social sciences. They are used to measure constructs such as beliefs, attitudes, and personality. These scales typically ask respondents to indicate their level of agreement on a graded scale (e.g., *strongly disagree* to *strongly agree*). Other formats, such as frequency scales (e.g., *never* to *always*) or continuous formats (e.g., visual analogue scales), also influence ERS and MRS. This section focuses primarily on GRI, but also considers other formats.

Graded Response Items

In Likert's original proposal (1932), respondents rated their stance on a 5-point scale ranging from 1 (*strongly approve*) to 5 (*strongly disapprove*) with 3 (*undecided*) as the midpoint. This proposal assumes that responses reflect a single continuous latent construct with opposing feelings at the endpoints and neutrality at the midpoint. Likert acknowledged that the format could be adapted, but such changes have consequences. Key factors affecting ERS and MRS in GRI include the number of categories, the presence or absence of a midpoint, the labeling of the options, and the use of numbers with labels. These method effects can become more pronounced when uniform formats are used across constructs, increasing common method variance. Researchers and practitioners should note that altering the response format of existing standardized tests to reduce ERS and/or MRS precludes the use of existing norms and may affect key psychometric properties. See the International Test Commission guidelines for general test use: https://www.intestcom.org/files/guideline_test_use.pdf; and for research applications: https://www.intestcom.org/files/statement_using_tests_for_research.pdf.

Labeling All Response Categories Versus Endpoints

Some researchers argue that end labeling reduces cognitive load, simplifying the scale for respondents. However, the evidence suggests otherwise. Most studies indicate that end labeling increases ERS by making extreme categories more salient than the unlabeled options (Moors et al., 2014; Schaeffer & Dykema, 2020; Spratto et al., 2021; Weijters, Cabooter et al., 2010). This idea aligns with the satisficing theory, where the ambiguity of the unlabeled nonextreme categories leads to cognitive overload, promoting ERS.

In the case of MRS, research is scarce. However, adding a label to the midpoint may increase its salience, potentially increasing MRS and reducing ERS (Lau, 2008). Thus, full labeling seems more effective at minimizing both ERS and MRS and balancing category salience, although the effects may depend on the specific constructs being measured, whether the scales are bipolar or unipolar, and on the specific labels used (Steinberg & Rogers, 2022). Full labeling is also recommended to enhance reliability and validity, although with some exceptions (e.g., Weijters, Cabooter et al., 2010).

Number of Response Categories: Odd and Even Numbers

Although some research suggests that increasing the number of categories elevates the cognitive load, encouraging satisficing behaviors such as ERS and MRS (Kieruj & Moors, 2010), most of the evidence contradicts this proposal. When focusing on ERS, having fewer options (e.g., 3–5) makes the extremes more salient (Clarke, 2000; Harzing et al., 2009; de Rezende & de Madeiros, 2022). Conversely, providing a greater number of categories reduces ERS by increasing the psychological distance between the options, making extremes less appealing (Weijters et al., 2013). However, this effect is nonlinear. Adding more categories reduces ERS until reaching six or seven options, after which the gains diminish in terms of both reducing ERS and improving reliability and validity (Hamby & Peterson, 2016; Simms et al., 2019).

The interaction between labeling (full vs. endpoint) and the number of categories further complicates the relationship. For instance, when modeling ERS as latent classes and using end-labeled response formats, Kieruj and Moors (2010) found that ERS consistently emerged across different numbers of categories (from 4 to 11). In contrast, Weijters, Cabooter et al. (2010) modeled ERS as a quantitative latent factor and found that, although adding more categories reduced ERS, this effect was less pronounced on fully labeled scales, given that the intermediate options were more salient than the end-labeled options. This result suggests that full labeling reduces the need for more categories to mitigate ERS.

Focusing on MRS, research indicates that adding more response options also tends to reduce MRS. For example, Harzing et al. (2009) found that 7-point Likert scales led to lower MRS, compared with 5-point scales, because the additional intermediate categories decreased the salience of the midpoint. Similar results were observed across other types of scales, such as frequency scales (Weems & Onwuegbuzie, 2001). Although these results must be interpreted with caution because MRS was not quantified separately from the ToI, this evidence suggests that a 7-point scale is optimal for reducing MRS because adding more intermediate categories helps respondents to choose a more well-defined position.

In summary, although the relationship between the number of categories and the RS is complex, scales with 6 or 7 fully labeled response options are generally recommended to reduce ERS and MRS, and increase both reliability and validity.

Adequate Labeling of Response Categories

The benefits of full labeling depend on appropriate label selection. The psychological meaning and perceived equidistance of labels influence the way respondents interpret the options, affecting ERS, MRS, and the overall quality of the data. For example, ambiguous labels can lead respondents to gravitate toward extremes or the midpoint due to uncertainty or difficulty in discerning nuances between the options (Arce-Ferrer, 2006). Some labels foster equal-interval properties more than others. For instance, for a 5-point Likert scale, Casper et al. (2020) recommend labels that range from 1 (*disagree*) to 5 (*very much agree*), which, contrary to common practice, are not symmetric. In addition, absolute endpoints (e.g., *completely disagree*) tend to reduce extreme responses more than less absolute endpoints do (e.g., Wyatt & Meyers, 1987), although some studies offer conflicting results (Lau, 2008).

Tailored specific labels for constructs (e.g., importance, intensity) perform better than generic labels such as *agree–disagree* (Schaeffer & Dykema, 2020; Brown & Shulruf, 2023), because they encourage more careful cognitive processing (Gummer & Kunz, 2021). For the same reason, unambiguous frequency anchors (e.g., *once a week*) and behaviorally anchored rating scales reduce ERS more effectively than vague options such as *often* (Arce-Ferrer, 2006; Weijters et al., 2013).

The labeling of midpoints is especially critical for MRS. On bipolar scales (e.g., *strongly disagree* to *strongly agree*), the midpoint, typically labeled *neither agree nor disagree*, is assumed to represent neutrality (an absence of opinion), but respondents may choose it for reasons such as indifference or ambivalence, or because they do not want to show their true preferences

(Brown & Shulruf, 2023; Kulas & Stachowski, 2013). These responses can even reflect a moderate level of the ToI instead of neutrality. For instance, the response *neither agree nor disagree* to the item "I am satisfied with the feedback I receive" may indicate a moderate level of satisfaction or just a true and stable MRS (Leventhal et al., 2022). On unipolar scales (e.g., *not satisfied at all* to *very satisfied*), the midpoint theoretically corresponds to a moderate position in the ToI. However, in this case, the midpoint could be chosen for reasons other than "being in the middle" (Schaeffer & Dykema, 2020).

Thus, all of these reasons may increase the probability of choosing the midpoint, regardless of individuals' location on the latent trait (e.g., Hernández et al., 2004), but this depends on the specific labels used. For example, when comparing the midpoint labels *not sure*, *?*, and *in between*, using the Sixteen Personality Factor Questionnaire (16PF) data, only *in between* worked as intended (González-Romá & Espejo, 2003). The results of a study by Hernández et al. (2006) also suggested that using middle categories explicitly labeled to express an intermediate position on the latent continuum works better than using ambiguous labels.

Researchers might think of using an even number of options to avoid the problem of midpoint labels. However, this strategy may create issues for respondents who are genuinely neutral or in the middle, even if these issues are mitigated when the number of response categories is large enough (e.g., six; Hernández et al., 2004). In fact, the question of whether to include a midpoint remains unclear in terms of reliability, validity, and RSs (e.g., Chyung et al., 2017; Wang & Krosnick, 2020). If researchers opt to include a midpoint, additional options such as *don't know* or *not applicable* can prevent misuse of the middle category (e.g., Kulas & Stachowski, 2013), which is particularly important in online surveys where omissions are not allowed. However, these options could reduce the effective sample size if chosen frequently (Kulas et al., 2008).

Numbering and Visual Presentation of Response Options

Research on the impact of adding numerical labels to verbal-only scales has yielded mixed results. For example, Doe et al. (2023) found no significant differences, whereas Moors et al. (2014) observed that omitting numbers increases ERS, regardless of whether end or full labeling is used. However, researchers caution against using only numbers without verbal labels, a growing trend in smartphone surveys. Gummer and Kunz (2021) showed that this practice increases ERS and respondent burden. This effect was robust across other IRF characteristics such as generic versus specific labels or scale orientation.

When numbers are combined with verbal anchors, the choice of numbers is important. Bipolar scales with negative to positive ranges (e.g., –3 to +3) tend to encourage extreme responses more than unipolar formats with only positive numbers (e.g., 0 to 6), due to the dual activation of opposite poles (Moors et al., 2014). Some researchers also argue that the use of mixed positive and negative numbers on bipolar scales clarifies the meaning of the midpoint, which reduces the probability of choosing the middle category for reasons other than the expected ones, or as a satisficing shortcut, thus contributing to the prevention of MRS. These arguments have been supported empirically (Moors et al., 2014). Therefore, researchers must be aware that the recommendation to use positive numbers on unipolar scales and mixed numbers (positive and negative) on bipolar scales (Schaeffer & Dykema, 2020) may induce different levels of ERS and MRS.

The visual distance between response categories can also influence responses. For example, Weijters et al. (2021) provided evidence that vertical Likert-type formats tend to generate more ERS compared with horizontal formats. This effect is partly due to the compact nature of vertical scales, which decreases the perceived extremeness of endpoint responses. Thus, increasing the visual distance between categories could reduce ERS, although its effect on MRS has not yet been studied.

Other IRFs

Whereas GRI are dominant in social sciences, other formats may reduce systematic method variance and both ERS and MRS. Continuous response formats such as *visual analogue scales* (VAS) and sliders allow respondents to indicate their position along a continuum instead of choosing from discrete options (for a review, see Chyung et al., 2018). On VAS, respondents mark a spot on a line between two anchored endpoints. Sliders work similarly but involve dragging a marker, allowing for more dynamic interactions. Both of these types of scales can have additional numerical or verbal anchors.

Some studies suggest that continuous formats lead to higher reliability, but others argue that increased precision does not always improve measurement, because respondents may still coarsen their responses (e.g., Simms et al., 2019). For example, VAS (with endpoint labels) showed less ERS than 4-point full-labeled or 7-point end-labeled categories (de Rezende & de Medeiros, 2022). However, using different extensions of the *continuous response model*, Huang (2025) and Zopluoglu (2020) showed that continuous formats are not immune to ERS.

With regard to MRS, the limited existing research suggests that VAS can reduce MRS by making the midpoint less salient (de Rezende & de Medeiros, 2022). In any case, when using continuous formats, researchers should consider population characteristics – for example, sliders are difficult to use for individuals with low education levels (Funke et al., 2011), and VAS are not the best scales for individuals with stroke-related impairments (Price et al., 1999).

Forced-choice formats, especially multidimensional forced choice, have been shown to reduce MRS and ERS and other response biases such as social desirability, compared with Likert scales. These formats ask respondents to make relative judgments between items, limiting opportunities for middle or extreme response tendencies, even when a graded forced-choice format is used (Brown & Maydeu-Olivares, 2018). This format forces more deliberate decision making, thus reducing the likelihood of shortcut responses such as consistently choosing the middle or extreme options. Zhang, Luo, et al. (2024) found that the forced-choice format between two items that included five graded options (including the category "both statements are equally like me") demonstrated superior reliability and was less susceptible to ERS and MRS, while maintaining high levels of criterion validity and respondent satisfaction. However, in low-stake situations, forced-choice formats can lead to other biases and satisficing behaviors because they are more cognitively demanding. Additionally, traditional forced-choice formats produce ipsative data where scores are interdependent, hindering comparability across individuals. Quasi-ipsative formats and newer scoring models help to address this issue (e.g., Brown & Maydeu-Olivares, 2011, 2018).

Other response formats such as *funnel*, where respondents first indicate whether they agree or disagree with the statement and then specify the (dis)agreement intensity; or drag-and-drop, where respondents physically move items into response categories that best fit their answers, also show promise in reducing RSs (Böckenholt, 2017). However, the effectiveness of these formats needs further validation (Henninger et al., 2025). These formats require more cognitive effort and time, potentially leading to other biases such as nonresponse (Brown & Shulruf, 2023), especially in low-stake assessments.

Quantifying and Controlling for ERS and MRS

Although some features of IRF can alleviate ERS and MRS, no format is entirely immune to these RSs (Moors et al., 2014). Thus, to obtain better estimates of the ToI, researchers should control for these biases. This section reviews traditional and advanced modeling approaches, initially detailing methods to quantify ERS and MRS, and subsequently describing strategies to control for them.

Quantifying RS: ERS and MRS Indicators

When ERS and MRS are conceptualized as two different dimensions, one of the simplest and most common ways to obtain indicators of these RSs is by dichotomizing the items (e.g., for ERS, 1 for an extreme response and 0 otherwise) and subsequently counting or averaging the number of extreme or midpoint responses for ERS and MRS, respectively. Log-odds ratios have also been used to deal with different distributional shapes (see Weijters, Cabooter et al., 2010).

When ERS and MRS are conceptualized as two extremes of one dimension (degree of extremeness), a weighted score is used where more extreme categories have higher weights. In this case, the standard deviation of a respondent's item scores may also be used (e.g., Baumgartner & Steenkamp 2001).

Researchers can use the same items to capture both ToI and RSs simultaneously, using any of these strategies. However, while efficient, this practice may confound true respondent levels with RSs. To address this, the use of a set of heterogeneous items independent from the ToI is recommended (Weijters, Cabooter et al, 2010). For instance, Greenleaf (1992) developed a 16-item scale to quantify RSs, although other researchers chose their own set of independent items (as in Weijters, Cabooter et al., 2010). They also suggest using multiple indicators (testlets) of a specific RS to account for measurement error and residual correlations between items that share some variance. Table 7.1 shows scoring examples for the different RSs using an item with seven response options.

Table 7.1 Examples of scoring functions for ERS and MRS.

Conceptualization	Response style	Scoring function
ERS and MRS as two separate dimensions	ERS	1, 0, 0, 0, 0, 0, 1
	MRS	0, 0, 0, 1, 0, 0, 0
ERS and MRS as two extremes of a unique dimension	Extremeness degree (ERS–MRS)	3, 2, 1, 0, 1, 2, 3

Note. ERS = extreme response style; MRS = midpoint response style.

Anchoring vignettes can also help to address RSs. Respondents rate both themselves and hypothetical vignettes that exemplify various levels of the concept being measured on the same scale. Because the vignettes are standardized, the patterns and differences in the way respondents rate these vignettes can be used to assess RSs, including ERS and MRS (King et al., 2004). However, this approach assumes that all respondents perceive the vignettes similarly, and empirical evidence suggests that this is not always the case (Mõttus et al., 2012). Another less common method involves direct behavioral items, such as asking respondents how often they take extreme stances or prefer neutral opinions (He & Van de Vijver, 2019).

Controlling for ERS and MRS

After obtaining indicators of ERS and MRS, researchers have several strategies to control for their effects. Although the use of different items from the ones measuring the ToI is recommended, this approach lengthens questionnaires and increases model complexity. Alternatively, psychometric models that quantify and distinguish between the ToI and RSs without additional indicators provide a streamlined solution to addressing RS bias. Regardless of the approach, modeling RSs statistically can help to understand how different IRFs affect both ToI and RS estimates. In addition, controlling for ERS and MRS ensures a more precise and valid indicator of the ToI. Traditional approaches, such as factor analysis, reveal method effects such as acquiescence, but they are not suitable for ERS or MRS, because these styles display nonmonotonic relationships with item responses. Other models, mainly based on *item response theory* (IRT), are more appropriate. Although multinomial logistic factor models can model ERS and MRS (for example, the latent-class factor models proposed by Moors, 2003, where the RSs are modeled as qualitative differences or classes; see also Moors, 2012 – or those proposed by Johnson & Bolt, 2010, where RSs are operationalized as quantitative latent variables), this section will focus on IRT models, which are more common.

All models can be categorized based on their explanatory level, assumptions, and the way RSs are operationalized (Kutscher & Eid, 2024). Explanatory (ad hoc) models incorporate specific RSs directly into the model, often by adding RS indicators – for example, with Greenleaf's scale (Greenleaf, 1992), or modifying parameters to account for RSs. Exploratory (post hoc) models detect RSs during analysis without prior assumptions, making it possible to discover other RSs beyond ERS and MRS, such as acquiescence. These RSs can be operationalized as discrete (latent classes) or continuous variables, and RS dimensions can be modeled as separate traits (ERS and MRS) or as a single bipolar dimension with ERS and MRS at the extremes. This section outlines the main types of models and their key characteristics.

Regression-Based Approaches

The simplest method for controlling RS involves including ERS and MRS indicators as covariates in multiple regression or structural equation models. ToI scores are regressed on RS scores (e.g., ERS), and the residuals represent ToI scores adjusted for RS biases (e.g., Baumgartner & Steenkamp, 2001; Weijters et al., 2008). This approach always requires having indicators of MRS and ERS that ideally should be based on additional items different from those used to measure the ToI. Although simple, this explanatory approach has been criticized because it assumes that the effects of RSs are constant across the ToI levels (Bolt et al., 2014; Lu & Bolt,

2015). Despite these limitations, Wetzel et al. (2016) found that this approach performed reasonably well in controlling for ERS, when ERS and the content trait were independent.

IRT-Based Models

IRT models can simultaneously model ToIs and RS effects based on the content questionnaires alone, without including RS indicators (Wetzel & Carstensen, 2017), even though they can also be added. This section focuses on the most common IRT approaches employed to account for MRS and ERS.

1. Mixture distribution IRT models: *Mixed or mixture IRT models*, particularly Rasch models, have been used in an exploratory way to identify RSs such as ERS and MRS (e.g., Hernández et al., 2004; Wetzel et al., 2013). These models account for the possibility that different subgroups (i.e., latent classes) in a population may respond differently to items. These differences are represented by discrete classes of homogeneous respondents who show similar response patterns across items, such as extreme versus nonextreme respondents. Once the classes have been identified, item characteristics (e.g., thresholds) are examined to detect differences in RS behaviors across classes. Consequently, RSs such as ERS or MRS reflect qualitative differences between individuals, whereas the ToI is treated as a quantitative trait whose estimates, with some constraints, are comparable across subpopulations (Wetzel et al., 2013). Mixture IRT models do not require explicit ERS or MRS indicators or additional items other than those used to measure ToIs. However, these models assume no variability within each class, and they are incompatible with conceptualizing ERS and MRS as two continuous traits or one unidimensional trait that captures degrees of extremeness. Additionally, mixture models often face convergence issues when estimating more than one or two RSs (Böckenholt & Meiser, 2017).
2. Random item-specific parameters in (multidimensional) IRT models: In this case, certain item parameters, such as thresholds, are modeled as random coefficients that vary across individuals (Adams et al., 2019; see Henninger, 2021). These random item parameters capture variations in response behaviors due to RSs, allowing flexibility in the way different items are responded to across individuals. However, like mixture IRT models, these models are exploratory and do not estimate individual RS latent traits.
3. Multidimensional IRT models that include RS and ToI latent dimensions: The *multidimensional nominal response model* (MNRM) proposed by Bolt and Johnson (2009) stands out. This model incorporates two independent additive latent variables for the RS and the ToI, estimating intercepts and slopes for both. Because the category slopes determine how the likelihood of selecting each category changes in relation to the traits, the slope estimates of the additional factor can be interpreted post hoc to assess whether they fit a specific RS. For ERS, slopes should follow a curvilinear pattern where a higher ERS trait increases the likelihood of selecting extreme categories over intermediate ones (e.g., positive and large slopes for extreme categories and negative slopes for the other ones). The model is compensatory, which means that a RS can adjust responses to compensate for the ToI content. It can also be applied ad hoc by imposing category slope constraints to reflect specific RS patterns, making it possible to estimate the correlations between RS and ToI (Bolt & Newton, 2011). The adequacy of these constraints can be tested by fitting different models and comparing their goodness of fit (for recommendations on the use of statistical tests of overall model fit for multidimensional IRT models that incorporate RSs, see Starr et al., 2021).

In addition, by setting the ToI slope parameters at equally spaced intervals for all items (e.g., –2, –1, 0, 1, 2), it is possible to ensure that the greater the ToI, the greater the probability of endorsing the item (as in all cumulative models). This process turns the MNRM into the *multidimensional partial credit model* (MPCM). In this case, the ToI and RS traits are differentiated by multiplying each latent trait by indicator variables that highlight which response categories represent RS or ToI (Wetzel & Carstensen, 2017). For example, for the ToI, the indicator variable is 1 for all categories and items, whereas for RS, the indicator variable is 1, only for the extreme categories (ERS) or the midpoint (MRS).
These models often assume that RS effects are the same across items. Thus, Falk and Cai (2016) proposed a reparameterized version of the MNRM, allowing more flexibility by relaxing the assumption that RS effects are equally strong across items. This reparameterization facilitates simultaneous modeling of multiple ToIs and RS types such as ERS and MRS. Despite this improvement, disentangling the simultaneous effects of different ToIs and RSs can still make these models statistically challenging (Bolt et al., 2014). To address these issues, external RS indicators, such as anchoring vignettes, can be used to model RSs separately from ToIs (Bolt et al., 2014).
4. Person-specific adjustments in (multidimensional) IRT models: Instead of modeling RSs as latent variables, some IRT models incorporate person-specific parameters to adjust item characteristics, such as thresholds, based on individual RS tendencies. For example, the MNRM with anchoring vignettes proposed by Bolt et al. (2014) aligns with person-specific IRT models that change the item characteristics (i.e., intercepts) for each person to capture RSs, controlling for the ToI levels. Jin and Wang (2014) added a person-specific weighting parameter to the *generalized partial credit model* (GPCM), which acts as a moderator of item category thresholds. Jonas and Markon (2019) applied the same type of modification to Samejimas' (1969) *graded response model* using anchoring vignettes. Tutz et al. (2018) introduced a person parameter in the *partial credit model* (PCM), adjusting thresholds according to respondents' extremeness tendencies. In these models, RS is conceptualized as a single dimension of the degree of extremeness that expands or contracts the use of the response scale, thus altering the likelihood of selecting extreme or midpoint categories.
5. Hybrid IRT models: Based on traditional definitions of ERS and MRS, most multidimensional models assume that ERS and MRS effects are independent of item content and, thus, equally strong across all items. However, some researchers argue that items differ in their capacity to elicit extreme responses. By relaxing the assumption of uniform RS effects, hybrid models such as that of Huang (2016) incorporate both continuous RS and ToI factors and allow item parameters to vary by latent classes. This approach is based on the idea that the more an item is discriminative on the RS factor, the less informative it is on the ToI. It recognizes that items differ in the degree to which they trigger extreme responses, and that individuals vary in their tendency to respond at the extremes. Although this provides greater flexibility, the model is complex and may face application challenges due to sample size and convergence issues.
6. Item response tree (IRTree) models: Another emerging approach is the use of IRTree models, which are confirmatory multidimensional IRT models that treat RSs as continuous latent variables (e.g. Böckenholt, 2019; Thissen-Roe & Thissen, 2013). However, these models conceptualize the response process as a series of steps where RSs and ToIs influence different stages of response selection. Specifically, IRTrees decompose responses into pseudoitems or steps that reflect different cognitive processes involved in choosing a response (e.g., Ames

& Myers, 2021). Dichotomous or polytomous IRT models can be used in each step depending on whether the pseudo-items are binary or not. For example, in Figure 7.1 (Panel A), respondents first decide on the direction of their response (0 = *disagree*, 1 = *neutral*, or 3 = *agree*), which depends on the ToI, and then the intensity of their response, which reflects ERS (0 = *less extreme* or 1 = *more extreme*).

When modeling MRS, models were initially set up in such a way that selecting the midpoint reflected a lack of opinion (Böckenholt, 2017; Jeon & De Boeck, 2019), which may be adequate for "neutral" midpoint labels or based on the unrealistic assumption that the midpoint choice reflects a pure MRS and cannot reflect an intermediate or moderate ToI position (see Figure 7.1, Panel B). More recent proposals consider that midpoint selection may reflect systematic trait variance and an MRS that is part of the extremeness continuum, which seems more realistic (Leventhal et al., 2022) (see Figure 7.1, Panel C). In this case, there are multiple pathways leading to the selection of the midpoint. The branch probabilities are summed up in a multinomial processing tree (see Scharl & Gnambs, 2024). Despite the usefulness of IRTrees to model RSs, we still need to gain deeper insight into the cognitive processes underlying the responses, to decide which tree is appropriate.

Like other multidimensional IRT models, IRTrees do not require external RS indicators (e.g., Ames & Myers, 2021). However, researchers may choose to include external indicators such as anchoring vignettes or a set of heterogeneous items that are designed specifically to capture RSs and not to load on the ToI (e.g., Leventhal & Zigler, 2023). IRTree models offer flexibility to model ERS and MRS as two separate dimensions, allowing each RS to independently influence different stages of the decision-making process (e.g., Ames & Myers, 2021) or function as one bipolar dimension. For examples that involve modeling extremeness instead of merely restricting ERS to extreme categories, see Spratto et al. (2021) and Thissen-Roe and Thissen (2013). Other studies suggest that MRS correlates very highly with intermediate neighbors, suggesting that MRS may expand to several central categories and not just the midpoint (Zhang & Wang, 2020). Finally, when latent classes of respondents show different response processes leading to different RSs, mixed IRTree models can be useful for understanding the differences (e.g., Khorramdel et al., 2019).

All the models presented require specific constraints for statistical identification, and many can also accommodate a multiple group structure to facilitate comparisons across countries or other relevant groups (e.g., Bolt et al., 2014). However, they differ in the way ERS and MRS are conceptualized and modeled, and their level of flexibility. These are important aspects to consider when choosing a model. Several studies have compared the performance of different types of models and generally concluded that multidimensional IRT models and IRTrees work better than mixed IRT models (Böckenholt & Meiser, 2017; Wetzel et al, 2016; Zhang & Wang, 2020). In addition, the MNRM seems to perform better than IRTree models in the conditions analyzed by Zhang and Wang (2020).

When comparing the GPCM that includes a person-specific RS parameter, with both the MNRM and IRTrees, Leventhal (2019) found that the GPCM outperformed the other models across various survey lengths and formats. However, model efficacy may depend on the underlying data structure. Schoenmakers et al. (2024) compared IRTrees and the MNRM, and concluded that the IRTree tends to undercorrect ERS when the MNRM structure is more appropriate, and the MNRM tends to overcorrect ERS when the response process aligns more closely with an IRTree framework. The authors conclude that the right choice depends on whether RSs

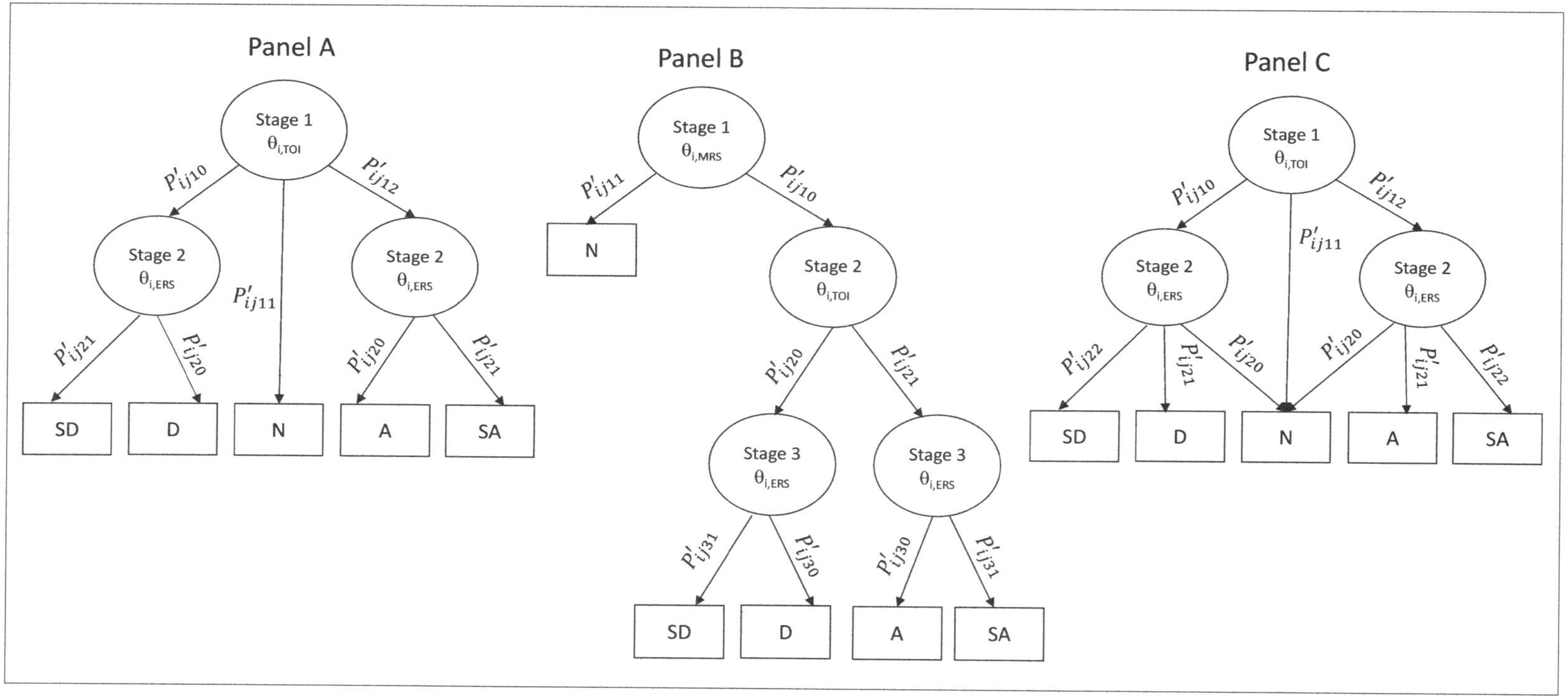

Figure 7.1 Three response processes for a 5-point Likert-type response scale. Panel A: Respondents first choose response direction (ToI) and then intensity (ERS). Panel B: Midpoint selection modeled as lack of opinion and pure MRS. Panel C: Midpoint selection modeled as arising from multiple pathways reflecting ToI and ERS on an extremeness continuum. SD = *strongly disagree*; D = *disagree*; N = *neutral*; A = *agree*, SA = *strongly agree*. Reproduced with permission of INFORMA UK, Ltd, through PLSclear from Leventhal et al., 2022.

affect both agreement and extremeness or just one of them. Certainly, more research is needed to guide model choice. Including additional items to capture RSs could allow the differences to emerge more clearly.

The models discussed so far are based on dominance processes, where the likelihood of endorsing an item increases as a respondent's trait level rises. However, in some cases, *ideal-point* (unfolding) models – where the probability of endorsement peaks when an item closely matches a respondent's "ideal point" on the trait – may better reflect response patterns (see Figure 7.2). According to the example depicted in Figure 7.2, if an item's location is close to zero on the latent continuum and a person's score on the continuum is also close to zero, the person would probably choose the middle (neutral) category under the dominance model. However, under the ideal-point model, the person would likely strongly agree with the item content. In the first case, a person with a high latent trait score would strongly agree with the item, regardless of the item's location. In contrast, under the ideal-point model, the person's agreement would depend on the item's location on the continuum.

Some limited research has examined the RS effects within ideal-point frameworks (e.g., Javaras & Ripley, 2007). For instance, Reimers et al. (2023) found that unfolding models are less susceptible to MRS (although some would argue that odd-numbered response scales do not fit the principles of ideal-point responding; Dalal et al., 2014), whereas dominance models are more affected by ERS, which suggests that model choice is essential in addressing RS bias. Liu and Wang (2019) introduced an IRT unfolding model with a dual latent trait structure where one trait represents the target construct and the other accounts for RSs. Their simulations revealed substantial estimation errors when RS was ignored, particularly when RS traits were highly correlated with the ToI. These results are consistent with those observed in dominance processes. Additionally, IRTrees have also shown potential in handling ERS and unfolding responses (He & Kern, 2024).

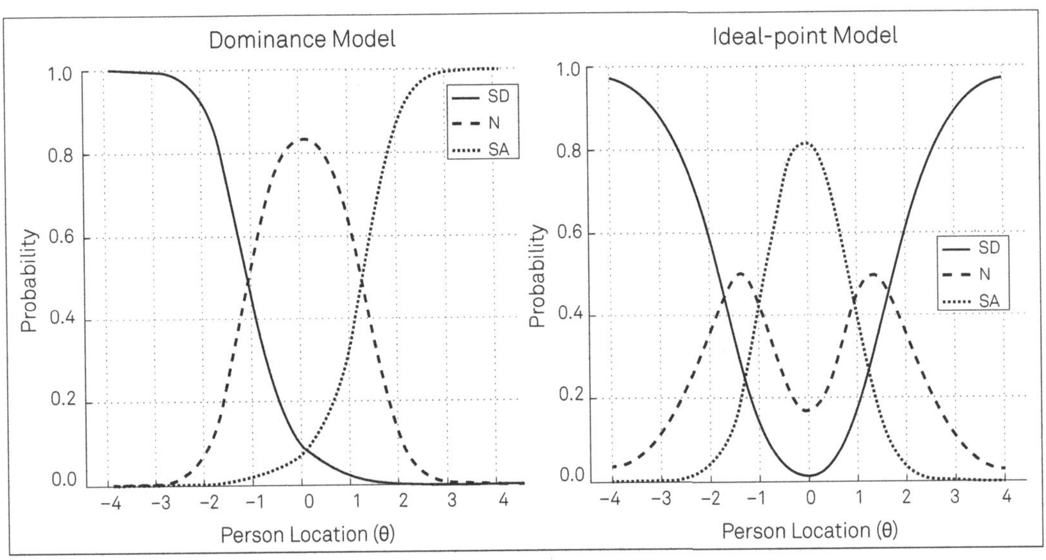

Figure 7.2 Dominance versus ideal-point modeling for an item with three response options. SD = *strongly disagree*; N = *neutral*; SA = *strongly agree*. Item location at zero.

Before incorporating RSs into modeling, researchers should assess whether the data align more with dominance or with unfolding response processes (e.g., Tay & Drasgow, 2012). Recent advancements, such as the mixture dominance-unfolding model of Zhang, Chalmers et al. (2024), even account for respondents potentially following different response processes within the same dataset.

Conclusion and Final Remarks

This chapter has examined how IRFs impact ERS and MRS, and has outlined strategies to mitigate these effects. Although item design, carefully choosing the labeling, and number of response categories can reduce RSs (de Rezende & de Medeiros, 2022; Weijters, Cabooter et al., 2010), these tendencies are also influenced by dispositional and cultural factors, which means they cannot be fully prevented. To safeguard the validity of inferences about ToIs, researchers should assess and control for RS effects when necessary, ideally combining item design and modeling techniques (Böckenholt, 2017).

Several examples of this integration can be found in the literature. Leventhal et al. (2022) use funnel response formats along with IRTree models to distinguish between mild opinions and the absence of an opinion within the "neutral" category, and to explore whether MRS lies on the ERS spectrum. Using item formats that guide respondents through a structured cognitive process allows researchers to better assess how participants interpret response options and model them. Mixture IRTrees could further assess individual variations in response processes across formats. Finally, Quirk and Kern (2023) underscore the practical advantages of using IRTree models early in experimental designs to optimize IRFs.

To control for ERS and MRS, a large number of options are available, mostly based on IRT modeling. Selecting the appropriate model depends on the researchers' understanding of the data and their conceptualization of RSs. The scant comparative research in this area highlights the advantages of multidimensional IRT models, particularly the MNRM and the GPCM with additional person parameters, as well as IRTree models.

When using ad hoc approaches, researchers must be aware that these approaches may fail to account for RS effects if the specific styles present are not explicitly included in the model (Schoenmakers et al., 2024). However, these models make it possible to conceptualize RSs as meaningful constructs, and not merely as sources of bias, as observed in personality research (He et al., 2014). The MNRM is particularly effective when additional indicators of RSs are included, especially when multiple ToIs are analyzed (Bolt & Newton, 2011; Weijters et al., 2008). IRTree models provide a nuanced analysis of the cognitive processes that lead to specific RSs, allowing researchers to examine how respondents interact with survey items. In this regard, cognitive interviewing is a valuable method for gaining greater insight into the response process, given that it can clarify whether ERS and MRS reflect genuine trait levels, satisficing behaviors, or communication styles (Morren et al., 2013; Tourangeau, 2018). Because the specific model used to adjust for RSs can affect the conclusions, Ulitzsch et al. (2023) recommend Bayesian model averaging as a means of accounting for model uncertainty, a recommendation that is endorsed here.

Although this chapter has focused on the most widely used methods for modeling ERS and MRS, other methods, such as person reliability and person-fit analyses, are valuable for detecting RS patterns (Adams et al., 2019; Wind & Ge, 2023). However, they do not directly control for RS effects when estimating ToIs.

Furthermore, there are interesting extensions of the models presented in this chapter, such as dynamic IRTree models (Merhof & Meiser, 2024), in which RSs fluctuate across items or survey conditions, enhancing our understanding of the interaction between the RS and the IRF. This area represents a critical direction for future research designed to disentangle stable dispositional tendencies from contextual influences linked to item characteristics (e.g., format and content), individual factors (e.g., mood), and assessment conditions (e.g., social desirability). Multilevel extensions of current models are also promising because they allow for the separation of an individual-level RS from group-based patterns influenced by cultural norms, as well as the analysis of intraindividual variability across items or over time (Deng et al., 2018; Hasselhorn et al., 2024; Lu & Bolt, 2015).

Challenges and Future Directions

Despite the progress made in modeling RSs with advanced approaches such as multidimensional IRT and IRTree models, significant challenges remain due to the complex parameters and substantial sample size requirements of these models. Future research should focus on developing and testing estimation methods that manage this complexity more effectively. Additionally, expanding these models to address other RSs, such as acquiescence and disacquiescence, and exploring their interactions with ERS and MRS, continue to be underdeveloped areas. Making these models more accessible through user-friendly software is also crucial for encouraging applied researchers to account for RSs in their work. Cross-validating findings using different methods for quantifying and controlling RSs, along with Bayesian model averaging to manage model uncertainty, will enhance the robustness of the conclusions (Ulitzsch et al., 2023). Adopting this comprehensive approach is expected to lead to more reliable and valid psychological assessments, thus improving the accuracy of inferences stemming from survey data.

References

Adams, D. J., Bolt, D. M., Deng, S., Smith, S. S., & Baker, T. B. (2019). Using multidimensional item response theory to evaluate how response styles impact measurement. *British Journal of Mathematical and Statistical Psychology, 72*(3), 466–485. https://doi.org/10.1111/bmsp.12169

Ames, A. J., & Myers, A. J. (2021). Explaining variability in response style traits: A covariate-adjusted IRTree. *Educational and Psychological Measurement, 81*(4), 756–780. https://doi.org/10.1177/0013164420969780

Arce-Ferrer, A. J. (2006). An investigation into the factors influencing extreme-response style: improving meaning of translated and culturally adapted rating scales. *Educational and Psychological Measurement, 66*(3), 374–392. https://doi.org/10.1177/0013164405278575

Austin, E. J., Deary, I. J., & Egan, V. (2006). Individual differences in response scale use: Mixed Rasch modelling of responses to NEO-FFI items. *Personality and Individual Differences, 40*(6), 1235–1245. https://doi.org/10.1016/j.paid.2005.10.018

Batchelor, J. H., & Miao, C. (2016). Extreme response style: A meta-analysis. *Journal of Organizational Psychology, 16*(2), 51–62.

Baumgartner, H., & Steenkamp, J. B. E. M. (2001). Response styles in marketing research: A cross-national investigation. *Journal of Marketing Research, 38*(2), 143–156. https://doi.org/10.1509/jmkr.38.2.143.18840

Böckenholt, U. (2017). Measuring response styles in Likert items. *Psychological Methods, 22*(1), 69–83. https://doi.org/10.1037/met0000106

Böckenholt, U. (2019). Assessing item-feature effects with item response tree models. *British Journal of Mathematical and Statistical Psychology, 72*(3), 486–500. https://doi.org/10.1111/bmsp.12163

Böckenholt, U., & Meiser, T. (2017). Response style analysis with threshold and multi-process IRT models: A review and tutorial. *British Journal of Mathematical and Statistical Psychology, 70*(1), 159–181. https://doi.org/10.1111/bmsp.12086

Bolt, D. M., & Johnson, T. R. (2009). Addressing score bias and differential item functioning due to individual differences in response style. *Applied Psychological Measurement, 33*(5), 335–352. https://doi.org/10.1177/0146621608329891

Bolt, D. M., Lu, Y., & Kim, J.-S. (2014). Measurement and control of response styles using anchoring vignettes: A model-based approach. *Psychological Methods, 19*(4), 528–541. https://doi.org/10.1037/met0000016

Bolt, D. M., & Newton, J. R. (2011). Multiscale measurement of extreme response style. *Educational and Psychological Measurement, 71*(5), 814–833. https://doi.org/10.1177/0013164410388411

Brown, A., & Maydeu-Olivares, A. (2011). Item response modeling of forced-choice questionnaires. *Educational and Psychological Measurement, 71*(3), 460–502. https://doi.org/10.1177/0013164410375112

Brown, A. & Maydeu-Olivares, A. (2018). Modelling forced-choice response formats. In P. Irwing, T. Booth, & D. J. Hughes (Eds.), *Wiley handbook of psychometric testing* (pp. 523–569). John Wiley & Sons Ltd. https://doi.org/10.1002/9781118489772.ch18

Brown, G., & Shulruf, B. (2023). Response option design in surveys. In L. R. Ford & T. A. Scandura (Eds.), *The SAGE handbook of survey development and application* (pp. 120–132). Sage. https://doi.org/10.4135/9781529617757

Casper, W. C., Edwards, B. D., Wallace, J. C., Landis, R. S., & Fife, D. A. (2020). Selecting response anchors with equal intervals for summated rating scales. *Journal of Applied Psychology, 105*(4), 390–409. https://doi.org/10.1037/apl0000444

Cheung, G. W., & Rensvold, R. B. (2000). Assessing extreme and acquiescence response sets in cross-cultural research using structural equations modeling. *Journal of Cross-Cultural Psychology, 31*(2), 187–212. https://doi.org/10.1177/0022022100031002003

Chyung, S. Y., Roberts, K., Swanson, I. & Hankinson, A. (2017). Evidence-based survey design: The use of a midpoint on the Likert scale. *Performance Improvement, 56,* 15–23. https://doi.org/10.1002/pfi.21727

Chyung, S. Y., Swanson, I., Roberts, K., & Hankinson, A. (2018). Evidence-based survey design: The use of continuous rating scales in surveys. *Performance Improvement, 57*(5), 38–48. https://doi.org/10.1002/pfi.21763

Clarke, I., III. (2000). Extreme response style in cross-cultural research: An empirical investigation. *Journal of Social Behavior & Personality, 15*(1), 137–152.

Dalal, D. K., Carter, N. T., & Lake, C. J. (2014). Middle response scale options are inappropriate for ideal point scales. *Journal of Business and Psychology, 29,* 463–478. https://doi.org/10.1007/s10869-013-9326-5

De Jong, M. G., Steenkamp, J.-B. E. M., Fox, J.-P., & Baumgartner, H. (2008). Using item response theory to measure extreme response style in marketing research: A global investigation. *Journal of Marketing Research, 45*(1), 104–115. https://doi.org/10.1509/jmkr.45.1.104

Deng, S., E. McCarthy, D., E. Piper, M., B. Baker, T., & Bolt, D. M. (2018). Extreme response style and the measurement of intra-individual variability in affect. *Multivariate Behavioral Research, 53*(2), 199–218. https://doi.org/10.1080/00273171.2017.1413636

de Rezende, N., & de Medeiros, D. (2022). How rating scales influence responses' reliability, extreme points, middle point and respondent's preferences. *Journal of Business Research, 138,* 266–274. https://doi.org/10.1016/j.jbusres.2021.09.031

Dibek, M. I., & Cikrikci, R. N. (2021). Modelling of the attitude-achievement paradox in TIMSS 2015 with respect to the extreme response style using multidimensional item response theory. *International Journal of Progressive Education, 17*(2), 194–209. https://doi.org/10.29329/ijpe.2021.332.12

Doe, R., Landrum, B. A., Lewis, K. M., Glenn, M. E., & Smith, J. D. (2023). Likert items: Should(n't) we really care? *International Journal of Social Science Studies, 11*(1), 32–38. https://doi.org/10.11114/ijsss.v11i1.5747

Falk, C. F., & Cai, L. (2016). A flexible full-information approach to the modeling of response styles. *Psychological Methods, 21*(3), 328–347. https://doi.org/10.1037/met0000059

Funke, F., Reips, U. D., Thomas, R. K. (2011). Sliders for the smart: Type of rating scale on the web interacts with educational level. *Social Science Computer Review, 29,* 221–231. https://doi.org/10.1177/0894439310376896

González-Romá, V., & Espejo, B. (2003). Testing the middle response categories "Not sure", "In between" and "?" in polytomous items. *Psicothema, 15*(2), 278–284.

Greenleaf, E. A. (1992). Measuring extreme response style. *Public Opinion Quarterly, 56*(3), 328–351. https://doi.org/10.1086/269326

Gummer, T., & Kunz, T. (2021). Using only numeric labels instead of verbal labels: Stripping rating scales to their bare minimum in web surveys. *Social Science Computer Review, 39*(5), 1003–1029. https://doi.org/10.1177/0894439320951765

Hamby, T. & Peterson, R. A. (2016). A meta-analytic investigation of the relationship between scale-item length, label format, and reliability. *Methodology, 12*(3), 89–98. https://doi.org/10.1027/1614-2241/a000112

Harzing, A. W., Baldueza, J., Barner-Rasmussen, W., Barzantny, C., Canabal, A., Davila, A., Espejo, A., Ferreira, R., Giroud, A., Koester, K., Liang, Y.-K., Mockaitis, A., Morley, M. J., Myloni, B., Odusanya, J. O. T., O'Sullivan, S. L.., Palaniappan, A. K.., Prochno, P., Choudhury, S. R., Saka-Helmhout, A., ... Zander, L. (2009). Rating versus ranking: What is the best way to reduce response and language bias in cross-national research? *International Business Review, 18*(4), 417–432. https://doi.org/10.1016/j.ibusrev.2009.03.001

Hasselhorn, K., Ottenstein, C., Meiser, T., & Lischetzke, T. (2024). The effects of questionnaire length on the relative impact of response styles in ambulatory assessment. *Multivariate Behavioral Research, 59*(5), 1043–1057. https://doi.org/10.1080/00273171.2024.2354233

He, J., Bartram, D., Inceoglu, I., & van de Vijver, F. J. R. (2014). Response styles and personality traits: A multilevel analysis. *Journal of Cross-Cultural Psychology, 45*(7), 1028–1045. https://doi.org/10.1177/0022022114534773

He, J., & van de Vijver, F. (2019). Assessment of the general response style: A cross-cultural validation. *Acta de Investigación Psicológica, 9*(3), 14–24. https://doi.org/10.22201/fpsi.20074719e.2019.3.320

He, J., Van de Vijver, F. J., Espinosa, A. D., & Mui, P. H. (2014). Toward a unification of acquiescent, extreme, and midpoint response styles: A multilevel study. *International Journal of Cross Cultural Management, 14*(3), 306–322. https://doi.org/10.1177/1470595814541424

He, S., & Kern, J. L. (2024). Investigating directional invariance in an item response tree model for extreme response style and trait-based unfolding responses. *Applied Psychological Measurement, 48*(4-5), 187–207. https://doi.org/10.1177/01466216241261705

Henninger, M. (2021). A novel partial credit extension using varying thresholds to account for response tendencies. *Journal of Educational Measurement, 58*(1), 104–129. https://doi.org/10.1111/jedm.12268

Henninger, M., & Plieninger, H. (2021). Different styles, different times: How response times can inform our knowledge about the response process in rating scale measurement. *Assessment, 28*(5), 1301–1319. https://doi.org/10.1177/1073191119900003

Henninger, M., Plieninger, H., & Meiser, T. (2025). The effect of response formats on response style strength: An experimental comparison. *European Journal of Psychological Assessment, 41*(1), 72–88. https://doi.org/10.1027/1015-5759/a000779

Hernández, A., Drasgow, F., & González-Romá, V. (2004). Investigating the functioning of a middle category by means of a mixed-measurement model. *Journal of Applied Psychology, 89*(4), 687–699. https://doi.org/10.1037/0021-9010.89.4.687

Hernández, A., Espejo, B., & González-Romá, V. (2006). The functioning of central categories Middle Level and Sometimes in graded response scales: Does the label matter? *Psicothema, 18*(2), 300–306.

Huang, H. Y. (2016). Mixture random-effect IRT models for controlling extreme response style on rating scales. *Frontiers in Psychology, 7,* Article 1706. https://doi.org/10.3389/fpsyg.2016.01706

Huang, H. Y. (2025). Exploring the influence of response styles on continuous scale assessments: Insights from a novel modeling approach. *Educational and Psychological Measurement, 85*(1), 178–214. https://doi.org/10.1177/00131644241242789

Javaras, K. N., & Ripley, B. D. (2007). An "unfolding" latent variable model for Likert attitude data: Drawing inferences adjusted for response style. *Journal of the American Statistical Association, 102*(478), 454–463. https://doi.org/10.1198/016214506000000960

Jeon, M., & De Boeck, P. (2019). Evaluation on types of invariance in studying extreme response bias with an IRTree approach. *British Journal of Mathematical and Statistical Psychology, 72*(3), 517–537. https://doi.org/10.1111/bmsp.12182

Jin, K.Y., & Wang, W.C. (2014). Generalized IRT models for extreme response style. *Educational and Psychological Measurement, 74*(1), 116–138. https://doi.org/10.1177/0013164413498876

Johnson, T. R., & Bolt, D. M. (2010). On the use of factor-analytic multinomial logit item response models to account for individual differences in response style. *Journal of Educational and Behavioral Statistics, 35*(1), 92–114. https://doi.org/10.3102/1076998609340529

Johnson, T., Kulesa, P., Cho, Y. I., & Shavitt, S. (2005). The relation between culture and response styles: Evidence from 19 countries. *Journal of Cross-Cultural Psychology, 36*(2), 264–277. https://doi.org/10.1177/0022022104272905

Jonas, K. G., & Markon, K. E. (2019). Modeling response style using vignettes and person-specific item response theory. *Applied Psychological Measurement, 43*(1), 3–17. https://doi.org/10.1177/0146621618798663

Khorramdel, L., von Davier, M., & Pokropek, A. (2019). Combining mixture distribution and multidimensional IRTree models for the measurement of extreme response styles. *British Journal of Mathematical and Statistical Psychology, 72*(3), 538–559. https://doi.org/10.1111/bmsp.12179

Kieruj, N. D., & Moors, G. (2010). Variations in response style behavior by response scale format in attitude research. *International Journal of Public Opinion Research, 22*(3), 320–342. https://doi.org/10.1093/ijpor/edq001

King, G., Murray, C. J., Salomon, J. A., & Tandon, A. (2004). Enhancing the validity and cross-cultural comparability of measurement in survey research. *American Political Science Review, 98*(1), 191–207. https://doi.org/10.1017/S000305540400108X

Krosnick, J. A. (1991). Response strategies for coping with the cognitive demands of attitude measures in surveys. *Applied Cognitive Psychology, 5*(3), 213–236. https://doi.org/10.1002/acp.2350050305

Kulas, J. T., & Stachowski, A. A. (2013). Respondent rationale for neither agreeing nor disagreeing: Person and item contributors to middle category endorsement intent on Likert personality indicators. *Journal of Research in Personality, 47*(4), 254–262. https://doi.org/10.1016/j.jrp.2013.01.014

Kulas, J. T., Stachowski, A. A., & Haynes, B. A. (2008). Middle response functioning in Likert-responses to personality items. *Journal of Business and Psychology, 22,* 251–259. https://doi.org/10.1007/s10869-008-9064-2

Kutscher, T., & Eid, M. (2024). Psychometric benefits of self-chosen rating scales over given rating scales. *Behavior Research Methods, 56*(7), 7440–7464. https://doi.org/10.3758/s13428-024-02429-w

Lau, M. Y. (2008). *Extreme response style: An empirical investigation of the effects of scale response format and fatigue* [Unpublished doctoral dissertation]. University of Notre Dame.

Lee, P., Joo, S., & Jia, Z. (2023). Cross-cultural differences in the use of the "?" Response category of the Job Descriptive Index: An application of the item response tree model. *International Journal of Selection and Assessment, 31,* 175–188. https://doi.org/10.1111/ijsa.12414

Leventhal, B. C. (2019). Extreme response style: A simulation study comparison of three multidimensional item response models. *Applied Psychological Measurement, 43*(4), 322–335. https://doi.org/10.1177/0146621618789392

Leventhal, B. C., Gregg, N., & Ames, A. J. (2022). Accounting for response styles: leveraging the benefits of combining response process data collection and response process analysis methods. *Measurement: Interdisciplinary Research and Perspectives, 20*(3), 151–174. https://doi.org/10.1080/15366367.2021.1953315

Leventhal, B. C., & Zigler, C. K. (2023). A tree-based approach to identifying response styles with anchoring vignettes. *Measurement: Interdisciplinary Research and Perspectives, 21*(2), 82–100. https://doi.org/10.1080/15366367.2022.2156219

Likert, R. (1932). A technique for the measurement of attitudes. *Archives of Psychology, 140,* 5–53.

Liu, C. W., & Wang, W. C. (2019). A general unfolding IRT model for multiple response styles. *Applied Psychological Measurement, 43*(3), 195–210. https://doi.org/10.1177/0146621618762743

Lu, Y., & Bolt, D. M. (2015). Examining the attitude-achievement paradox in PISA using a multilevel multidimensional IRT model for extreme response style. *Large-Scale Assessments in Education, 3,* 1–18. https://doi.org/10.1186/s40536-015-0012-0

Meisenberg, G., & Williams, A. (2008). Are acquiescent and extreme response styles related to low intelligence and education? *Personality and Individual Differences, 44*(7), 1539–1550. https://doi.org/10.1016/j.paid.2008.01.010

Merhof, V., & Meiser, T. (2024). Co-occurring dominance and ideal point processes: A general IRTree framework for multidimensional item responding. *Behavior Research Methods, 56*(7), 7005–7025. https://doi.org/10.3758/s13428-024-02405-4

Moors, G. (2003). Diagnosing response style behavior by means of a latent-class factor approach. Socio-demographic correlates of gender role attitudes and perceptions of ethnic discrimination reexamined. *Quality & Quantity, 37*, 277–302. https://doi.org/10.1023/A:1024472110002

Moors, G. (2012). The effect of response style bias on the measurement of transformational, transactional, and laissez-faire leadership. *European Journal of Work and Organizational Psychology, 21*(2), 271–298. https://doi.org/10.1080/1359432X.2010.550680

Moors, G., Kieruj, N., & Vermunt, J. (2014). The effect of labeling and numbering of response scales on the likelihood of response bias. *Sociological Methodology, 44*, 369–399. https://doi.org/10.1177/0081175013516114

Morren, M., Gelissen, J. P. T. M., & Vermunt, J. K. (2011). Dealing with extreme response style in cross-cultural research: A restricted latent class factor analysis approach. *Sociological Methodology, 41*, 13–47. https://doi.org/10.1111/j.1467-9531.2011.01238.x

Morren, M., Gelissen, J. P., & Vermunt, J. K. (2013). Exploring the response process of culturally differing survey respondents with a response style: A sequential mixed methods study. *Field Methods, 25*(2), 162–181. https://doi.org/10.1177/1525822X12453535

Mõttus, R., Allik, J., Realo, A., Rossier, J., Zecca, G., Ah-Kion, J., Amoussou-Yéyé, D., Bäckström, M., Barkauskiene, R., Barry, O., Bhowon, U., Björklund, F., Bochaver, A., Bochaver, K., de Bruin, G., Cabrera, H. F., Chen, S. X., Church, A. T., Cissé, D. D., ... Johnson, W. (2012). The effect of response style on self-reported conscientiousness across 20 countries. *Personality and Social Psychology Bulletin, 38*(11), 1423-1436. https://doi.org/10.1177/0146167212451275

Pargent, F. (2017). *Detection, avoidance, and compensation – three studies on extreme response style* [Unpublished doctoral dissertation]. Ludwig-Maximilians-Universität München.

Podsakoff, P. M., MacKenzie, S. B., Lee, J. Y., & Podsakoff, N. P. (2003). Common method biases in behavioral research: a critical review of the literature and recommended remedies. *Journal of Applied Psychology, 88*(5), 879–903. https://doi.org/10.1037/0021-9010.88.5.879

Pokropek, A., Khorramdel, L. & von Davier, M. (2023). Detecting and differentiating extreme and midpoint response styles in rating scales using tree-based item response models: Simulation study and empirical evidence. *Psychological Test and Assessment Modeling, 65*(2), 220–258.

Price, C. I. M., Curless, R. H., & Rodgers, H. (1999). Can stroke patients use visual analogue scales? *Stroke, 30*, 1357–1361. https://doi.org/10.1161/01.STR.30.7.1357

Quirk, V. L., & Kern, J. L. (2023). Using IRTree models to promote selection validity in the presence of extreme response styles. *Journal of Intelligence, 11*(11), 216. https://doi.org/10.3390/jintelligence11110216

Reimers, J., Turner, R. C., Tendeiro, J. N., Lo, W.-J., & Keiffer, E. (2023). The effects of aberrant responding on model-fit assuming different underlying response processes. *Applied Psychological Measurement, 47*(5–6), 420–437. https://doi.org/10.1177/01466216231201987

Reynolds, N., & Smith, A.M. (2010). Assessing the impact of response styles on cross-cultural service quality evaluation: A simplified approach to eliminating the problem. *Journal of Service Research, 13*, 230–243. https://doi.org/10.1177/1094670509360408

Samejima F. (1969) Estimation of latent ability using a response pattern of graded scores. *Psychometrika, 34* (S1), 1-97. https://doi.org/10.1007/BF03372160

Schaeffer, N. C., & Dykema, J. (2020). Advances in the science of asking questions. *Annual Review of Sociology, 46*, 37–60. https://doi.org/10.1146/annurev-soc-121919-054544

Scharl, A., & Gnambs, T. (2024). The impact of different methods to correct for response styles on the external validity of self-reports. *European Journal of Psychological Assessment, 40*(1), 13–21. https://doi.org/10.1027/1015-5759/a000731

Schoenmakers, M., Tijmstra, J., Vermunt, J., & Bolsinova, M. (2024). Correcting for extreme response style: Model choice matters. *Educational and Psychological Measurement, 84*(1), 145–170. https://doi.org/10.1177/00131644231155838

Simms, L. J., Zelazny, K., Williams, T. F., & Bernstein, L. (2019). Does the number of response options matter? Psychometric perspectives using personality questionnaire data. *Psychological Assessment, 31*(4), 557–566. https://doi.org/10.1037/pas0000648

Spratto, E. M., Leventhal, B. C., & Bandalos, D. L. (2021). Seeing the forest and the trees: Comparison of two IRTree models to investigate the impact of full versus endpoint-only response option labeling. *Educational and Psychological Measurement, 81*(1), 39–60. https://doi.org/10.1177/0013164420918655

Starr, J., Falk, C. F., Monroe, S. L., & Vachon, D. D. (2021). A comparison of limited-information test statistics for a response style MIRT model. *Multivariate Behavioral Research, 56*(4), 687–702. https://doi.org/10.1080/00273171.2020.1828024

Steinberg, L., & Rogers, A. (2022). Changing the scale: The effect of modifying response scale labels on the measurement of personality and affect. *Multivariate Behavioral Research, 57*(1), 79–93. https://doi.org/10.1080/00273171.2020.1807305

Takagishi, M., van de Velden, M., & Yadohisa, H. (2019), Clustering preference data in the presence of response-style bias. *British Journal of Mathematical and Statistical Psychology, 72,* 401–425. https://doi.org/10.1111/bmsp.12170

Tay, L., & Drasgow, F. (2012). Adjusting the adjusted χ^2/df ratio statistic for dichotomous item response theory analyses: Does the model fit? *Educational and Psychological Measurement, 72*(3), 510–528. https://doi.org/10.1177/0013164411416976

Thissen-Roe, A., & Thissen, D. (2013). A two-decision model for responses to Likert-type items. *Journal of Educational and Behavioral Statistics, 38*(5), 522–547. https://doi.org/10.3102/1076998613481500

Tourangeau, R. (2018). The survey response process from a cognitive viewpoint. *Quality Assurance in Education, 26*(2), 169–181. https://doi.org/10.1108/QAE-06-2017-0034

Tourangeau, R., Rips, L. J., & Rasinski, K. (Eds.). (2000). *The psychology of survey response.* Cambridge University Press. https://doi.org/10.1017/CBO9780511819322

Tutz, G., Schauberger, G., & Berger, M. (2018). Response styles in the partial credit model. *Applied Psychological Measurement, 42*(6), 407–427. https://doi.org/10.1177/0146621617748322

Ulitzsch, E., Lüdtke, O., & Robitzsch, A. (2023). The role of response style adjustments in cross-country comparisons: A case study using data from the PISA 2015 Questionnaire. *Educational Measurement: Issues and Practice, 42*(3), 65–79. https://doi.org/10.1111/emip.12552

Van Vaerenbergh, Y., & Thomas, T. D. (2013). Response styles in survey research: A literature review of antecedents, consequences, and remedies. *International Journal of Public Opinion Research, 25*(2), 195–217. https://doi.org/10.1093/ijpor/eds021

Wang, R., & Krosnick, J. A. (2020). Middle alternatives and measurement validity: a recommendation for survey researchers. *International Journal of Social Research Methodology, 23*(2), 169–184. https://doi.org/10.1080/13645579.2019.1645384

Weems, G. H., & Onwuegbuzie, A. J. (2001). The impact of midpoint responses and reverse coding on survey data. *Measurement and Evaluation in Counseling and Development, 34*(3), 166–176. https://doi.org/10.1080/07481756.2002.12069033

Weijters, B., Cabooter, E., & Schillewaert, N. (2010). The effect of rating scale format on response styles: The number of response categories and response category labels. *International Journal of Research in Marketing, 27*(3), 236–247. https://doi.org/10.1016/j.ijresmar.2010.02.004

Weijters, B., Geuens, M., & Baumgartner, H. (2013). The effect of familiarity with the response category labels on item response to likert. *Journal of Consumer Research, 40*(2), 368–381. https://doi.org/10.1086/670394

Weijters, B., Geuens, M., & Schillewaert, N. (2010). The stability of individual response styles. *Psychological Methods, 15*(1), 96–110. https://doi.org/10.1037/a0018721

Weijters, B., Millet, K., & Cabooter, E. (2021). Extremity in horizontal and vertical likert scale format responses. Some evidence on how visual distance between response categories influences extreme responding. *International Journal of Research in Marketing, 38*(1), 85–103. https://doi.org/10.1016/j.ijresmar.2020.04.002

Weijters, B., Schillewaert, N., & Geuens, M. (2008). Assessing response styles across modes of data collection. *Journal of the Academy of Marketing Science, 36*(3), 409–422. https://doi.org/10.1007/s11747-007-0077-6

Wetzel, E., Böhnke, J. R., & Rose, N. (2016). A simulation study on methods of correcting for the effects of extreme response style. *Educational and Psychological Measurement, 76*(2), 304–324. https://doi.org/10.1177/0013164415591848

Wetzel, E., & Carstensen, C. H. (2017). Multidimensional modeling of traits and response styles. *European Journal of Psychological Assessment, 33*(5), 352–364. https://doi.org/10.1027/1015-5759/a000291

Wetzel, E., Carstensen, C. H., & Böhnke, J. R. (2013). Consistency of extreme response style and non-extreme response style across traits. *Journal of Research in Personality, 47*(2), 178–189. https://doi.org/10.1016/j.jrp.2012.10.010

Wind, S. A., & Ge, Y. (2023). Identifying response styles using person fit analysis and response-styles models. *Measurement: Interdisciplinary Research and Perspectives, 21*(3), 147–166. https://doi.org/10.1080/15366367.2022.2104565

Wyatt, R. C., & Meyers, L. S. (1987). Psychometric properties of four 5-point Likert-type response scales. *Educational and Psychological Measurement, 47*(1), 27–35. https://doi.org/10.1177/0013164487471003

Zhang, B., Chalmers, R. P., Li, L., Sun, T., & Tay, L. (2024). One size does not fit all: Unraveling item response process heterogeneity using the mixture dominance-unfolding model (MixDUM). *Organizational Research Methods, 28*(4), 569-609. https://doi.org/10.1177/10944281241271323

Zhang, B., Luo, J., & Li, J. (2024). Moving beyond Likert and traditional forced-choice scales: A comprehensive investigation of the graded forced-choice format. *Multivariate Behavioral Research, 59*(3), 434–460. https://doi.org/10.1080/00273171.2023.2235682

Zhang, Y., & Wang, Y. (2020). Validity of Three IRT models for measuring and controlling extreme and midpoint response styles. *Frontiers in Psychology, 11*, Article 271. https://doi.org/10.3389/fpsyg.2020.00271

Zopluoglu, C. (2020). A finite mixture item response theory model for continuous measurement outcomes. *Educational and Psychological Measurement, 80*(2), 346–364. https://doi.org/10.1177/0013164419856663

Chapter 8

Using Negatively Phrased Items in Surveys

Christine DiStefano, Jungsun Go, and Geophrey Odero

Abstract

Acquiescence is the tendency for a respondent to agree to a survey question regardless of the content. To curb the potential for agreement bias, researchers often include both positively and negatively phrased items in the same survey. However, this practice has been debated as it may introduce construct-irrelevant variance, with bias more prominent for negatively phrased items. Confirmatory factor analysis (CFA) may be useful for accommodating biases associated with wording effects. This chapter evaluates various CFA strategies to wording effects associated with negatively phrased items and includes a discussion of the strengths and weaknesses of the various procedures. We include an empirical demonstration using the Rosenberg Self-Esteem scale to illustrate different CFA modeling techniques and to examine recommendations provided from the literature.

Introduction

In the social and behavioral sciences, self-report questionnaires are commonly used to measure unobservable constructs to provide insight regarding a subject's perceptions, behaviors, preferences, traits, attitudes, etc. Often, self-report instruments use a Likert response scale to collect data, prompting scale developers to make choices not only for item content, but also for related issues, such as the number of scale points to include and the choice (or absence) of anchor labels. Data resulting from a questionnaire are used to represent a respondent's placement on the latent variable(s) in question; however, variation associated with aspects related to the scale can confound responses (Fink, 2006; Hartley & Betts, 2010). When this construct-irrelevant variance is related to characteristics of the respondent and is systematic in nature, the variance may be considered a *response bias* (Baumgartner & Steenkamp, 2006).

With a self-report survey, characteristics of the Likert scale may contribute to a response bias. For example, an *extreme response bias* is defined as the tendency for a respondent to choose primarily category endpoints or extremes (i.e., only the highest or lowest response options) of a Likert scale. Recommendations to combat an extreme response style include ensuring that there are an adequate number of response categories to allow choice among categories, and thoughtfully choosing anchor labels during scale construction, so that respondents may utilize the full range of the scale (Fink, 2006).

Alternatively, a *midpoint response bias* may occur if there are an odd number of scale points. This bias is described as the tendency for a respondent to choose the neutral or midpoint of a Likert scale rather than committing to an "opinion." To discourage selecting a middle category, using an even number of scale points (e.g., four or six categories) and/or avoiding the use of noncommittal wording at the midpoint (e.g., *neutral* or *undecided*) are recommended (Baumgartner & Steenkamp, 2001; Fink, 2006; also see Chapter 7, "Item Response Format and Response Styles").

Besides scale choices, *question content* may contribute to a response bias. Two of the most studied item content response biases are *social desirability bias* and *acquiescence bias* (e.g., Baumgartner & Steenkamp, 2001; Weijters et al., 2008). *Social desirability* refers to the tendency for respondents to answer questions in such a way as to present themselves in socially acceptable terms (Edwards, 1957). Acquiescence bias refers to a respondent's tendency to respond positively or agree to the statements, regardless of how one feels (Krosnick, 1999). Other content-related response biases, such as *careless responding, satisficing* (i.e., lack of effort devoted to understanding question details), and *disacquiescence* (i.e., the tendency to provide negative responses regardless of content) have also been studied (e.g., Baumgartner & Steenkamp, 2001; Krosnick, 1999; Weijters et al., 2008; Wetzel et al., 2016). While systematic variance associated with any type of response bias may adversely affect survey data, this chapter will focus on acquiescence bias, as it is a commonly cited concern in social and behavioral survey research (Baumgartner & Steenkamp, 2001, 2006).

Defining Acquiescence

As a measurement phenomenon, acquiescence has had a long history in the social sciences literature (e.g., Lorge, 1937; Messick, 1966), with numerous studies investigating reasons acquiescence may occur. Acquiescence (sometimes also called a "yea-saying" or agreement response tendency) occurs when respondents agree with a statement without regard for the actual item content. When both positively and negatively worded items are included in a survey, the tendency can introduce measurement error, in which items containing positive wording have higher scores than negatively phrased items; this may lend itself to negative bias observed with items which are negatively phrased (Hutton, 2017).

Acquiescence may be confused with, or even confounded with, careless responding and/or socially desirable responding (Ross & Mirowsky, 1984). Socially desirable responding occurs when a question may be thought to have a "right" or norm-conforming answer and the respondent wishes to project an image that is positive and "proper" when viewed by outsiders (Mirowsky & Ross, 1983; Ross & Mirowsky, 1984). This type of responding results in self-report data that will be (in the mind of the examinee) pleasing to others' point of view. Related to acquiescence, agreeing with statements, regardless of content, may be thought of as a type of "nonresistant" or *submissive response bias* (Carr, 1971) where a respondent may wish to appear agreeable to persons administering the survey. Comparing between the two effects, acquiescence could be thought of as a deferential response to items which do not have a socially or morally "correct" answer (i.e., neutral items; Ross & Mirowsky, 1984).

When respondents do not fully attend to or fully process question content, careless responding occurs (e.g., Kam & Meyer, 2015; Meade & Craig, 2012). An acquiescence response bias may resemble careless responding; however, researchers have hypothesized that acquiescent responders do pay more attention to the item content than careless responders. When contrasting the two types of effects, acquiescent responders provide biased responses when evaluating statements of different wording direction (i.e., positively worded items have different scores than negatively worded items, even when the item content is similar) and careless responders provide similar data, irrespective of item content or direction (Kam & Meyer, 2015).

Avoiding Acquiescence: Items and Surveys

The most popular (and long-standing) recommendation to combat acquiescence has been to include items on the same survey which vary in wording direction (Schriesheim & Hill, 1981; Spector, 1992). Positively or directly phrased statements are statements aligned in the same direction as the construct, while negatively phrased statements are phrased in the opposite direction as the construct (Colston, 1999). These wording directions are sometimes termed *clear* (referring to direct phrasing) and *unclear* (opposite phrasing; e.g., Colston, 1999; Chyung et al., 2018). It is typically considered that positive items are those in which higher levels of endorsement also relate to a higher amount of the construct. However, what constitutes positive or negative depends on the operational definition of the construct under study.

Negatively phrased statements may include negated wording, such as "no" or "not" in the statement (Barnette, 2000; Chyung et al., 2018). Items can, however, also be constructed to change the direction of a statement by including a prefix or suffix (e.g., un-, dis-, -less) to reverse meaning or wording to a statement thought to be opposite (Chyung et al., 2018; Colston, 1999). An example of wording direction and wording choices can be seen with the Rosenberg Self-Esteem (RSE) scale (Rosenberg, 1965). This 10-item unidimensional scale measuring global self-worth is often used with studies of negative wording, due to the long-standing prevalence of a response bias observed over administrations with many different populations and research situations. The RSE scale includes five positively worded items; these items are aligned in the same direction as the focal construct, self-worth (e.g., "I feel I have a number of good qualities"). The RSE scale also includes five negatively worded items. Two items include negated words (e.g., "I feel I do not have much to be proud of") and three are negatively phrased relative to the construct, but do not use negated words (e.g., "I certainly feel useless at times").

Researchers have suggested that negatively worded items which refrain from including "no" or "not" tend to be easier for respondents to understand (e.g., Barnette, 2000; Colston, 1999). This is because a respondent must first understand what is asked and then negate the statement, translating the intent to the opposite of what is asked. Despite caveats related to mixing wording direction on the same form, many survey developers currently create scales that include both positive and negative phrasing. This practice is done for a variety of reasons, such as to make the scale more engaging to respondents, to heighten interest when reading items, and to ensure that respondents are attentive to the survey's content (Fink, 2006).

Regarding the creation of a survey, researchers have provided conflicting advice about whether or not to include negatively worded items on the same scale, and if so, how many items of each direction to include (e.g., Nunnally, 1978; Chyung et al., 2018). To counteract acquiescence, survey researchers originally suggested creating a balanced scale, which includes equal numbers of positive and negative worded items (e.g., Cloud & Vaughan, 1970; Martin, 1964;

McClendon, 1992; Nunnally, 1967, 1978; Paulhus, 1991; Ray, 1979; Spector, 1992). The thought was that while bias may be apparent in one *set* of wording (e.g., negatively worded), the presence of equal numbers of items in the opposite direction (e.g., positively worded) would *balance* the effects due to bias. Including only a few items in a different direction than the remainder of the items on a scale may be interpreted as confusing or ambiguous (Ibrahim, 2001; Roszkowski & Soven, 2010).

Most survey researchers recommend constructing a survey with items in only one direction, rather than creating a scale with mixed phrasing. Typically, the suggestion is to use items phrased in the same direction as the construct, which generally refers to use of positive or direct wording (e.g., Barnette, 2000; DeVellis, 2003; Greenberger et al., 2003; Ibrahim, 2001; Salazar, 2015; Schriesheim & Hill, 1981; Suárez-Alvarez et al., 2018; Vigil-Colet, Navarro-González, & Morales-Vives, 2020).

Other researchers, however, suggest that items of mixed wording may be included on the same scale if researchers are attentive to issues related to item construction, placement, and the reporting of results, to lessen the effects of a (potential) response bias (e.g., Ferrando & Lorenzo-Seva, 2010; Podsakoff et al., 2003; Weijters et al., 2013; Weijters & Baumgartner, 2012). Recommendations to reduce response biases include grouping items by wording type and alerting respondents to format changes (Roszkowski & Soven, 2010); using a symmetric response scale with equal numbers of positive and negative scale points (Locker et al., 2007); using negative phrasing but refraining from introducing statements that include the word "not" or "never" (Barnette, 2000; Johnson et al., 2004; Schriesheim et al., 1991); putting negatively worded items early in a survey (Merritt, 2012); and summarizing results separately, by wording type (Weems et al., 2003; Hartley, 2014).

Differing Responses to Negatively Worded Items

If items are of mixed direction, researchers should observe differences in the data. For a positively worded item, if a respondent endorses a (numerically) higher Likert category (i.e., higher observed item score), the corresponding score on the latent variable is also high. Negatively worded items result in lower Likert score endorsement, relating to higher scores on the construct. When both positively and negatively worded items are included, negatively worded items are typically reverse coded prior to analysis, as items in different directions may provide erroneous results when creating factor scores or reliability estimates (Bandalos, 2018). However, beyond reverse coding, researchers have suggested reasons for why negatively worded items may be answered differently from positively worded items, such as difficulties due to wording interpretation, as well as characteristics of the respondents.

Interpretation Difficulties With Negatively Worded Items

When including items of mixed wording to measure the same construct, an important assumption is that both positively and negatively worded items measure the same construct in the same manner, meaning that respondents should provide equivalent responses (after item reversal) regardless of the item direction (Marsh, 1996). However, even after negatively phrased items are reverse coded for analyses, systematic variation may remain due to the wording direction, outside of measuring a construct (Barnette, 2000; DiStefano & Motl, 2006; Horan et al., 2003; Lee et al., 2016). Negatively worded items may result in items that are interpreted differently by respondents (Colston, 1999; Johnson et al., 2004) and thus, do not provide equivalent measurement. For example, a positive word (e.g., "supportive") may not hold the same meaning to respondents if a negated phrase is used (e.g., "not supportive") or a direct negative word (e.g., "unsupportive").

Additionally, negative items are thought to require an increased cognitive load, due to the additional mental effort required to understand what is being asked. This increase is due to the mental time needed for reversing the statement prior to responding (Chyung et al., 2018; Knowles & Condon, 1999). Related to increased cognitive difficulty, acquiescence may arise from confusion deciphering what is being asked and with unfamiliar wording or convoluted phrasing. Problems related to question comprehension may be attributed to acquiescence as these items require increased comprehension and response times, leading to an increased possibility for errors (Lee et al., 2016). A scale with mixed wording is thought to introduce cognitive "bumps" and to encourage respondents to read each survey item more carefully; however, items in different directions tend to make a scale more difficult for respondents to understand, leading to confusion (Peterson, 2000; Podsakoff et al., 2003; Sonderen et al., 2013).

Related to this are issues such as scale length (Kieruj & Moors, 2013; Soto & John, 2017), number of response points (Kutscher & Eid, 2020), and item length (e.g., Davis et al., 2020), which can influence acquiescence (and promote satisficing rather than the respondent's attending to the content of the item).

Respondents Responding Differently to Negatively Worded Items

Prior studies have investigated the relationship between response styles associated with negative item phrasing and characteristics of the individual. Two areas that have received attention are individuals' demographic characteristics and personality traits. For respondents with low levels of life satisfaction, concern over a possible negative evaluation by others is related to a method effect for negative items (e.g., DiStefano & Motl, 2006). In support of this hypothesis, de Jonge and Slates (2005) found neurotic individuals were less likely to exhibit an effect associated with negative item phrasing, whereas extraversion was positively related to the presence of a response bias. Individuals with higher levels of self-consciousness (DiStefano & Motl, 2006; Quilty et al., 2006) or higher levels of self-esteem (Quilty et al., 2006) were also less likely to endorse negatively worded items, as were respondents with higher levels of life satisfaction (Lindwall et al., 2012). In general, subjects with a greater fear of negative evaluations or who are more "in tune" with their sense of self may be more likely to reflect on their behavior more accurately and, as such, are not as sensitive to an item's wording direction.

Researchers have also examined demographic characteristics of the respondents, such as race and/or culture, sex, and age to determine how these aspects may relate to a wording effect due to negative phrasing. Generally, investigations of sex of respondent have not yielded significant differences regarding a response bias due to negative wording (Borgers et al., 2004; Chen et al., 2010; DiStefano & Motl, 2006, 2009; Greenberger et al., 2003; Lindwall et al., 2012; Michaelides et al., 2016).

Findings for race and ethnicity, however, have yielded confounding results. Some studies have found race and culture were not significantly related to negative wording bias (Greenberger et al., 2003; Xin & Chi, 2010), with groups responding similarly. However, other studies have shown different results according to race and culture, with differential effects, primarily with nonnative speakers (e.g., non-English-speaking groups) relative to the language of the survey (Davis et al., 2020; Yang et al., 2012).

Other demographic characteristics have been found to be related to negative wording bias. Children have been found to illustrate a greater tendency for a response bias related to negative wording (Borgers et al., 2004; Chen et al., 2010) as have older respondents (Fox et al., 2007). Negative wording bias has been found to relate to the cognitive ability of the respondents, with persons having lower levels of cognitive ability or lower levels of education, demonstrating higher bias (Gnambs & Schroeders, 2020; Narayan & Krosnick, 1996).

Finally, it is recognized that there may be an interaction between personality and demographic characteristics that affects responses to negatively worded items. For example, among women, acquiescence was correlated with personality measures measuring perceptions by others, whereas acquiescence among men was related to extraverted behaviors (DiStefano et al., 2012a).

As another example, older individuals with depression were more likely to endorse negatively worded items (Lindwall et al., 2012). Thus, instead of avoiding acquiescence, negative wording may intensify response bias depending on the characteristics of the population under study.

Including Negative Wording: Effects on Results

With items of mixed direction, systematic variance related to the mechanism used to collect the data, but irrelevant to the construct, is often present (Marsh, 1989; Marsh & Grayson, 1995). This bias may impact the descriptive information and psychometric indices calculated from the data. For example, negatively worded items tend to produce lower mean values and lower reliability estimates than do responses to positively worded items (e.g., Chang, 1995; Finney, 2001; Lin et al., 2013; Schriesheim & Hill, 1981; Weems et al., 2003), as well as reduced item discrimination values (Carlson et al., 2011; Chiavaroli, 2017; Suárez-Alvarez et al., 2018).

More importantly, response bias due to wording may influence interpretations about the construct under study. When scales (or subscales) are considered unidimensional, response bias due to negatively worded items may affect the underlying structure of the scale. Instead of one factor, multiple factors will emerge from the data, where factors are created due to items differing in item wording direction, rather than in content (e.g., Carmines & Zeller, 1979). Treating a unidimensional scale as a multidimensional structure may provide problematic results. Interpretation of factor scores may be problematic, as an unnecessarily complex factor structure coupled with weak factor loadings can produce inaccurate factor score estimates (Ferrando & Navarro-González, 2018). Instead of creating factors that result from item wording direction, the variance related to wording effect biases can be integrated into analyses through structural equation modeling techniques.

Using CFA to Accommodate Negative Wording

Studies which investigate response biases due to negative wording typically use a *confirmatory factor analysis* (CFA; Jöreskog, 1974) latent framework to disentangle the variability related to negative phrasing. These models may be useful when both positively and negatively phrased items are included to measure a trait of interest. While the methods may be used with multidimensional models, for clarity of the nuances associated with different CFA approaches, the discussion here is restricted to surveys that measure a single construct. Furthermore, many previous studies have reported the factor structure of a unidimensional instruments as multidimensional, yet this situation has often resulted from neglecting wording effects (Abubakar & Fischer, 2012; Hankins, 2008; Lima & de Souza, 2019; Smith et al., 2013). Here, we describe selected models often used to accommodate negative items; model strengths and considerations are discussed.

Using MTMM Modeling Strategies With Negatively Worded Items

Many researchers have linked a *multitrait-multimethod* (MTMM) conceptual framework (Campbell & Fiske, 1959) with CFA techniques to assist in the separation and empirical estimation of substantive content and method effects (e.g., Horan et al., 2003; Marsh, 1989; Marsh & Grayson, 1995). Various conceptualizations for handling method effects within the MTMM framework exist (for additional details, see Marsh & Grayson, 1995); however, two of the most popular models for accommodating negatively worded items within a survey are the *correlated trait-correlated uniqueness* (CT-CU) and *correlated trait-correlated method* (CT-CM) models (e.g., Marsh & Grayson, 1995).

CT-CU Model

The CT-CU framework attempts to resolve wording effects by introducing correlations between uniqueness terms of items with similar phrasing, where correlations are typically included among negatively worded items. The CT-CU model is illustrated in Figure 8.1. Under this framework, systematic variability related to wording used with the items is captured in the error terms. The variance is separate from an item's relationship with the construct but is related to other items (irrespective of content) worded in the same direction, relative to the construct. Thus, the CT-CU model separates variance attributed to the wording effects from the substantive content by treating residual variance between items worded in the same direction as error, which should be removed from interpretations. This viewpoint means that a potential response effect related to negative wording cannot be considered as a distinct entity that could have meaningful relations with other latent factors or observed variables (Marsh, 1989).

In terms of strengths, the CT-CU model is easy to construct and does not yield estimation problems, almost always converging to a proper solution (Abubakar & Fischer, 2012; Smith et al., 2013). Also, correlating residual terms tends to yield good fitting models. Thus, CT-CU may yield exceptionally favorable model-data fit results as compared with other CFA models used to accommodate wording effects, especially if many negatively worded items are included in a scale.

However, drawbacks may be noted. The CT-CU model results may make it difficult for researchers to determine the strength of wording effects as compared with the strength of the relationship of an item to the focal trait, because wording effects are represented as correlated uniqueness terms. Furthermore, as the method effects are not included as a latent variable, the variance attributed to negative wording may relate to multiple sources (e.g., Eid et al., 2003).

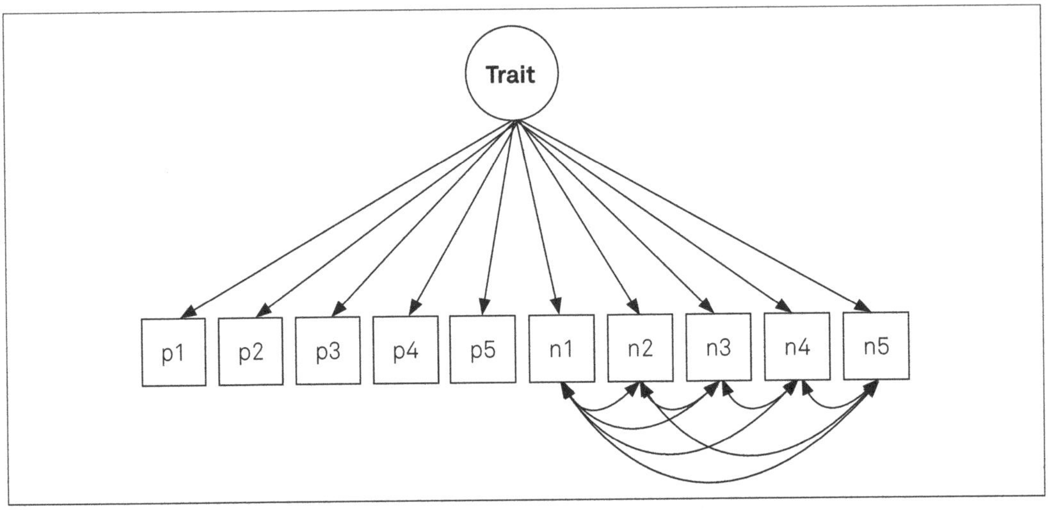

Figure 8.1 Correlated trait–correlated uniqueness model. p = positively worded items; n = negatively worded items.

In other words, by allowing the residual terms to correlate, the CT-CU model captures the systematic variation associated with the wording effects and other unknown causes (Wu et al., 2017). Finally, CT-CU models generally yield a good fit, including correlations among error terms which may provide an overly optimistic view of model–data fit. And if many uniqueness terms are included, improvements in global fit may be due to capitalization on chance occurrences within a set of data.

CT-CM Model

The CT-CM model considers a response style associated with negative wording effects as a separate latent variable. Thus, the approach typically includes a latent variable in the CFA for the focal trait along with factors that relate to wording direction (e.g., one factor related to positive wording and one related to negative item wording). Under this framework, wording effect factors are allowed to correlate (NB: the traditional bifactor model is similar to the CT-CM, without correlations among method factors. This is also referred to as the *correlated trait–uncorrelated method* model by Marsh and Grayson, 1995). However, covariance terms between the construct(s) and wording effect factor(s) are constrained to zero (Figure 8.2). This allows variance associated with the wording effects to be removed from the variance related to the construct of interest.

The CT-CM model may be useful for examination of characteristics which may influence responses (e.g., personality characteristics) as well as examination of empirical relations between the wording effect factor and other factors or characteristics of respondents (Bollen & Paxton, 1998; Jackson & Messick, 1961). One caveat, however, is that the CT-CM framework often yields nonconvergent solutions or solutions with unreasonable parameter estimates (i.e., standardized loading values above 1.0, negative variance estimates; Marsh, 1989; Marsh & Grayson, 1995). Marsh and Grayson (1995) noted that the difficulties in estimation arise from the assumption of orthogonality between the construct and the wording effect factors. The authors also

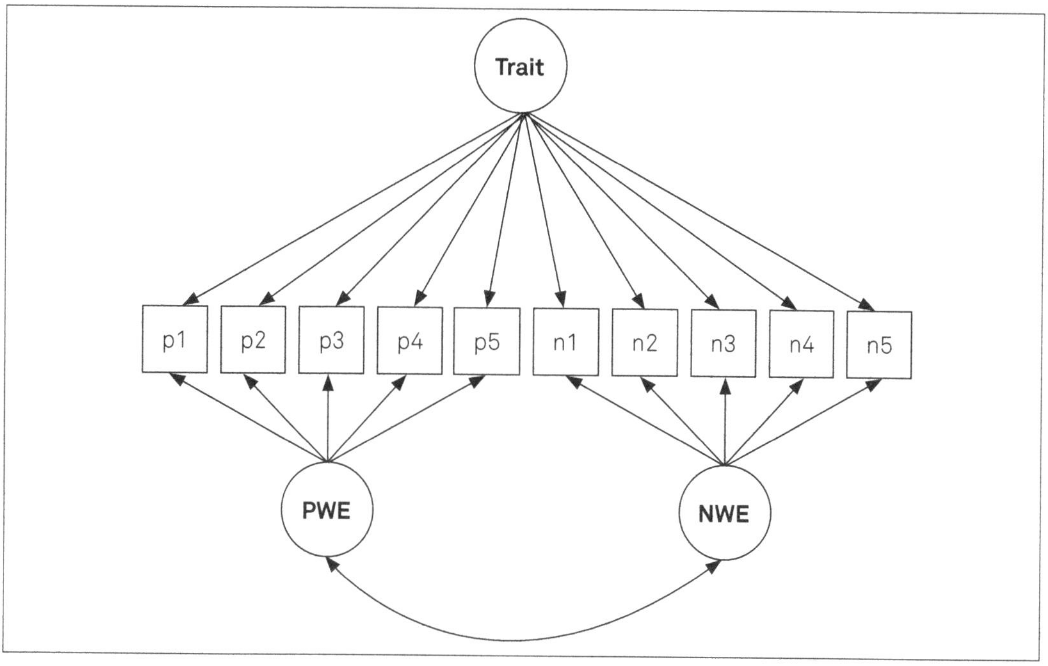

Figure 8.2 A correlated trait–correlated method model. p = positively worded items; n = negatively worded items; PWE = positive wording effect; NWE = negative wording effect. Item uniqueness terms are omitted for clarity.

noted that the reason for the trait factor and the wording effect factors being uncorrelated in the CT-CM model is to avoid technical problems, or it may be for making the decomposition of variance into distinct sources possible, rather than based on a substantive likelihood or empirical rationale (Marsh & Grayson, 1995). An additional concern with the CT-CM model is that it allows for correlations among different method factors (i.e., effects due to positive and negative phrasing), which may not be overly realistic in practice (Wang et al., 2016).

While the CT-CM has been used in many investigations of method effects due to wording direction, including both positive and negative method factors, the approach is not often selected as producing the optimal model. Also, method factors may be difficult to interpret conceptually, as there may be additional considerations (i.e., *ancillary traits*; Maul, 2013) that influence how a person responds to the item, and both the trait and ancillary factors unique to the method used to collect the data, influence a response. Thus, interpreting two method factors (and consideration of multiple ancillary traits) may be exceptionally difficult. On the other hand, studies that have compared both the CT-CM and the CT-CU models have found similar results in terms of model fit (Tomás & Oliver, 1999; Horan et al., 2003; Lima & de Souza, 2019). These studies have largely used unidimensional investigations with the RSE scale; thus, similarity in the results may be due to the equal number of positive and negative worded items in the measure.

CT-C(M-1)

As noted, researchers who include both positive and negative wording effects may encounter estimation and interpretation difficulties when using CT-CM. An alternative method for accommodating negative wording effects is to use the *correlated trait-correlated method minus one* (CT-C[M-1]) model (Eid, 2000). This model is similar to the CT-CM, but includes one fewer method factor than the number of (data collection) methods studied. The method not modeled as a method factor is chosen as the comparison standard. Typically, researchers using the CT-C(M-1) use positive phrasing as the comparison method, and an effect due to negative phrasing is modeled with a method factor (Motl & DiStefano, 2002). Figure 8.3 depicts the CT-C(M-1) framework. Note that there is only one trait in Figure 8.3; however, this may be easily extended to include other traits (for additional information, see Eid, 2000).

When considering between the CT-CM and the CT-C(M-1) model, researchers should recognize that the interpretation of the items which associate with the negative wording factor differs between the two models. The wording effects in the CT-C(M-1) model represent the level of deviation of negatively worded indicators from the true score of the indicator measured with the comparison method (Eid et al., 2003). In other words, the wording effect is a residual factor, representing the percentage of variance accounted for by use of negatively worded items as compared with using positively worded items (i.e., the standard method) to measure the trait. Thus, the CT-C(M-1) explains the negative wording effects in terms of convergent validity (Maydeu-Olivares & Coffman, 2006).

The CT-CM model represents wording effects more along the lines of a traditional MTMM framework, where the variance associated with an item is decomposed to account for the relation of an item to the substantive factor and remaining variance related to the method used to collect the data (Eid et al., 2003). In this sense, the trait and wording factors (i.e., positive and negative wording) contribute independently to an observed response. However, when a correlation is included among the wording effect factors, part of the shared variability in the items could be due to the common trait being measured by the set of items and not related to the specific method used to obtain the data (Marsh & Grayson, 1995).

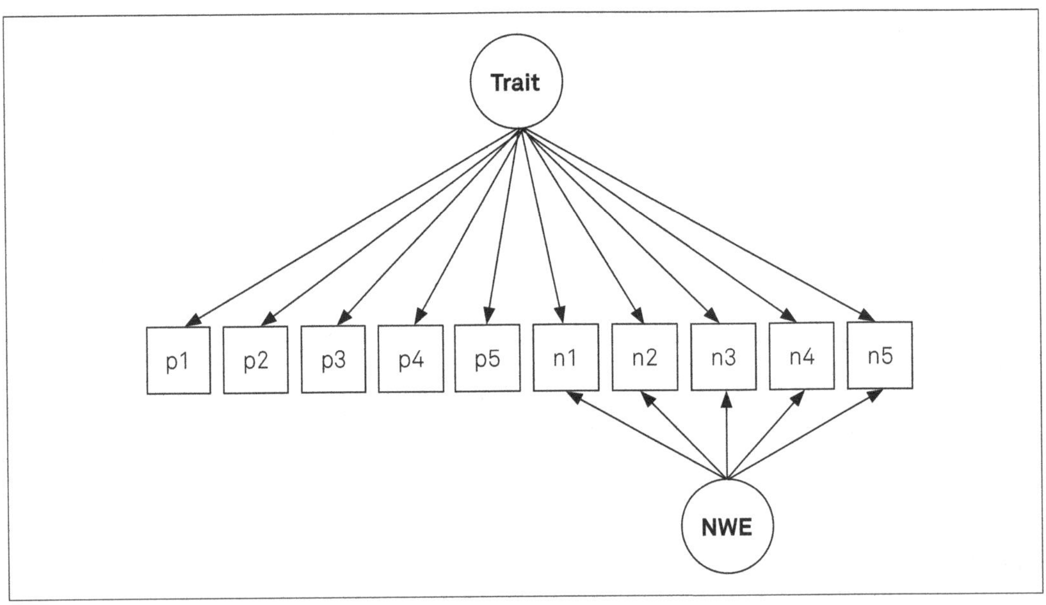

Figure 8.3 A correlated trait–correlated method minus one model. p = positively worded items; n = negatively worded items, NWE = negative wording effect. Item uniqueness terms are omitted for clarity.

As a strategy to deal with negative wording, CT-C(M-1) has both strengths and shortcomings. A major strength is that the framework overcomes the identification problems and/or improper solutions that often occur with the CT-CM model. Also, as one method is used as the point of reference, not all method factors can be correlated. This combination of measuring a trait by a standard method (e.g., positive phrasing) that is not correlated with other method factors, resolves the ambiguity that arises with the interpretation of the trait factor and the wording effect factors when methods are correlated (Eid et al., 2003). Furthermore, the CT-C(M-1) model may provide a more realistic view of measurement, as it recognizes that the traits and the methods used to measure latent variables are intertwined. Shortcomings in use of the CT-C(M-1) model relate to the difficulty in the interpretation of the results obtained, as the loading values represent the deviation of the nonstandard method (e.g., negative wording) from the reference method. Another challenge noted in interpretation is the inconsistency with model fit, as the fit results differ depending upon which set of items (i.e., negatively worded or positively worded) is used as the reference method (Maydeu-Olivares & Coffman, 2006).

Random Intercept Model

Maydeu-Olivares and Coffman (2006) suggest the use of the *random intercept* (RI) model as an alternative model to accommodate wording effects. The RI model decomposes the item intercept that is inherent (but not often estimated) with an underlying CFA model into two parts: a fixed intercept and an RI. The fixed portion of the intercept is similar to the intercept value included in the underlying CFA formula – that is, the item intercept is the mean (average) item value, common to all respondents for a given item, and a random component is included (variance of intercept term) to capture individual differences in responding. Thus, variance of the responses can be decomposed into three parts: trait variance, an RI, and measurement error. Figure 8.4 displays the RI model.

Under this framework, the RI factor is assumed to represent differences in response style among respondents (i.e., differences in how an individual uses the scale). Here, the variance of the intercept factor estimates the variability among respondents due to differences in wording

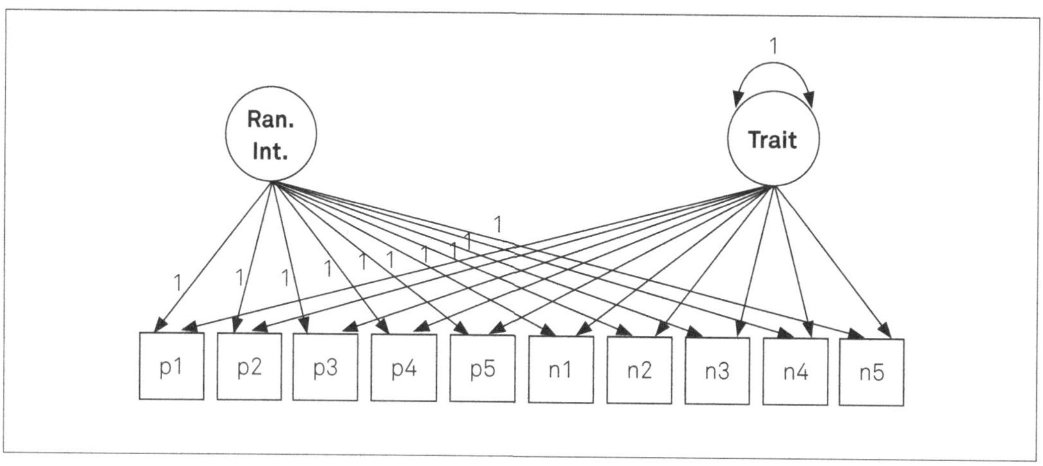

Figure 8.4 Random intercept model. p = positively worded items; n = negatively worded items, Ran. Int. = random intercept factor. Item uniqueness terms are omitted for clarity.

direction. The larger the variance of the intercept factor, the more the variability in responses – in other words, the greater the discrepancies in the use of the scale. When the variance associated with the intercept factor is small, the RI model does not show differences due to use of the scale, and no correction for wording is needed (i.e., the intercept factor may be removed). If a researcher is interested in using the RI model, the variance associated with the intercept factor should be significant (and meaningful), and the loading estimates relating items to their focal construct should be significant.

The RI is not as widely known compared with other strategies commonly employed to correct for with negative wording – for example, CT-CM, CT-C(M-1), and CT-CU – however, the model may have some benefits. The RI framework is parsimonious, providing a view of the construct without overparameterization or interpretation problems. Also, while the intercept factor could be interpreted as a substantive factor, this is not the typical case. Apart from the factor variance, the intercept factor is included to account for individual differences in responding (Maydeu-Olivares & Coffman, 2006).

There are limitations with the RI framework for dealing with method effects. First, the relation between the intercept factor and the trait factor is fixed to zero; this assumption (as made with other models) is made to avoid estimation problems (Maydeu-Olivares & Coffman, 2006). Further, all factor loadings on the intercept factor are fixed across individuals and at the same value, typically fixed to 1. Even if a different value is used, the loadings must be set to the same value (i.e., invariant) across individuals. This is a strong assumption, suggesting that there is one response style factor that applies in the same way to all items, regardless of item wording direction (Geiser et al., 2008). In other words, an acquiescent response style would have the same influence on both positively and negatively worded items. This assumption may not be reasonable in practice. Thus, the RI model may be appropriate if there is good reason to assume that a consistent response style impacts all items in the same way (Geiser et al., 2008).

Another caveat when using the RI model concerns the interpretation of the RI factor, as this framework includes item mean values in the estimation process (i.e., mean structure model). In other words, even though the values are fixed to 1 with the RI factor, each item includes the item average as the fixed component and individuals' deviations from the item mean value are collected in the variability of the respective latent factor (Maydeu-Olivares & Coffman, 2006). This interpretation is correct if the item-level data are (or appropriate for analysis as) continuous variables and are analyzed with an appropriate estimator (e.g., *maximum likelihood-based techniques*). Data that are categorical and treated as such within CFA do not have item mean values; instead, item threshold values are estimated (Finney & DiStefano, 2013). While the RI factor with fixed item values may be estimated with items treated as categorical, the interpretation of the latent intercept factor variability may not hold the same meaning as defined originally. Thus, the RI framework seems to be best suited for controlling wording effects when used with continuous item-level data.

Deciding Among Prospective Models

Evaluating which model to use to accommodate effects due to negative wording may be based on several considerations. For example, model choice may relate to theory or a researcher's perspective to deal with wording effects (e.g., incorporation of a wording effect factor into a broader model). Other researchers may evaluate and compare different ways of treating method effects, comparing different models in terms of global and local model fit (DiStefano, 2016). Commonly used global fit indices include: chi-squared, root-mean-square error of approximation (RMSEA), standardized root mean square residual (SRMR), comparative fit index (CFI), Tucker-Lewis Index (TLI), and, depending on the estimation method used, the Akaike information criterion (AIC) and the Bayesian information criterion (BIC) or the weighted root mean square residual. Using the global fit indices, researchers can evaluate how well the tested model reproduces the relations underlying the input data. One difficulty arising from relying on global fit is that these indices evaluate the whole model and do not necessarily identify if model misspecification is occurring. In other words, some parts of the model may fit better than other parts, but it is not straightforward to identify which areas are misfitting.

Measures of local fit may help to pinpoint the source of misfit. Some local fit measures include examining the direction and the magnitude of parameter estimates to ensure they match theory or prior studies, squared multiple correlation values to determine the amount of indicators' variances explained by the latent factor, Z-values/Wald tests to investigate if the relationship of the indicator to the latent factor is statistically significant, and the size of standard errors to check whether an indicator has measurement problems or a construct is not precisely measured by the indicators in the model (DiStefano, 2016).

Even though global and local fit information may indicate an acceptable model, Marsh et al. (2004) have noted that many empirical research conditions would result in a good model fit, even under misspecified conditions. Said another way, under most empirical research situations, researchers are likely to misspecify a model if a decision is made only based on fit information; thus, investigations of local and global fit among alternative perspectives, theory, and interpretability are also important. Beyond "internal" investigations of how to deal with a method effect, researchers may consider how the wording effects could impact the criterion-validity estimates, by considering relations to an external measure. For example, researchers may want to examine how alternative representations of wording effects impact the estimated relationships between the instrument being studied and an outside criterion, to ensure that the relations between outcome variables and a method factor exhibit meaningful patterns.

Empirical Example

As scales including negative wording are often used to control acquiescence, we provide an illustration of different modeling strategies for a scale with positively and negatively worded items on the same scale. Data were collected from 362 college students, 62 (17.2%) male and 295 (82.2%) female, in undergraduate courses of psychology, statistics, and education (four students did not report gender and one reported neither male nor female). The population was one of convenience, but also allowed examination of wording effects in a sample of examinees that largely avoided problems seen with previous samples of elderly participants, children, non-native-language speakers, and respondents with low cognitive ability (Borgers et al., 2004; Chen et al., 2010; Fox et al., 2007; Gnambs & Schroeders, 2020; Narayan & Krosnick, 1996). Respondents were recruited from classes taken by students in the general college population rather than a course required by a specific major. For the sample, average student age was 19.3 years (SD ± 1.7 years) with a range of 17 to 36 years. The sample of students was primarily White

(74.7%) with 11.1% of students identifying as African American; while remaining groups (Asian, Hispanic, Native American, Pacific Islander, and Mixed) made up roughly 14% of the sample. In terms of rank, 26.9% of the sample were first-year students, 49.9% second-year, 18.9% third-year students, and 6.4% in their fourth year; three students (0.8%) did not report their year in school. Students' self-reported GPAs were high, with 62.5% of the sample reporting a GPA between 4.0 and 3.6; 28.3% between 3.1 and 3.5, 7.2% between 2.6 and 3.0, and 1.9% in the range of 2.1 to 2.5.

Instrumentation

The RSE was used for this example because it has revealed the presence of method effects due to negatively worded items with previous studies (Horan et al., 2003; Motl & DiStefano, 2002; Tomás & Oliver, 1999). The scale measures a subject's global self-esteem (Rosenberg, 1965), where higher scores illustrate higher self-esteem. It consists of 10 items, five positively worded and five negatively worded. All items on the RSE were rated on a 4-point Likert scale with verbal anchors of *strongly disagree* (1), *disagree* (2), *agree* (3), and *strongly agree* (4). Items are taken from the scale and listed in Table 8.1; bolding is included to emphasize negative phrasing.

Table 8.1 Rosenberg Self-Esteem scale

Item	Rosenberg Self-Esteem scale
1	On the whole, I am satisfied with myself.
2	**At times, I think I am no good at all.**
3	I feel that I have a number of good qualities.
4	I am able to do things as well as most other people.
5	**I feel I do not have much to be proud of.**
6	**I certainly feel useless at times.**
7	I feel that I'm a person of worth, at least on an equal plane with others.
8	**I wish I could have more respect for myself.**
9	**All in all, I am inclined to feel that I am a failure.**
10	I take a positive attitude toward myself.

Note. Negatively worded items in bold.

Respondents completed the RSE via an online survey. In addition, two small two-item scales measuring anxiety and depression were administered. The Generalized Anxiety Disorder 2-item (GAD-2) scale (Kroenke et al., 2007) provides an overview of a respondents' level of anxiety. The two items refer to the frequency of anxious feelings (e.g., nervousness and uncontrolled worry) experienced during the past 2 weeks. The GAD-2 has shown acceptable levels of reliability (α = .77–.81, test-retest reliability = .81; Hughes et al., 2018; Sapra et al., 2020; Staples et al., 2019). A GAD-2 total score above 3 showed adequate levels of sensitivity (.65–.76) and specificity (.81–.88) to detect general anxiety disorder (Plummer et al., 2016; Sapra et al., 2020).

The Patient Health Questionnaire-2 (PHQ-2; Kroenke et al., 2003) is a two-item screener measuring the frequency of a depressed mood or lack of pleasure in typical activities over the past 2 weeks. The PHQ-2 showed acceptable reliability (α = .82–.85, test-retest reliability = .79–.81; Sapra et al., 2020; Staples et al., 2019; Silverberg et al., 2021). A PHQ-2 score above 3 yielded a sensitivity of .83 and a specificity of .92 for major depression (Kroenke et al., 2003). Both the GAD-2 and the PHQ-2 use a 4-point Likert scale for measurement, with anchors of *not at all* (0), *several days* (1), *more than half the days* (2), and *almost every day* (3). These two scales were used as external criteria to compare different methods of accommodating negatively worded items with selected outcomes.

Analyses

To illustrate the effects of negative wording on psychometric criteria, a series of tests were conducted. With all analyses, negative items on the RSE scale were reverse coded to match the direction of the self-esteem factor (i.e., reporting a positive view of oneself). First, it was of interest to examine how including negatively worded items to control acquiescence may affect descriptive statistics and reliability estimates. Descriptive statistics (e.g., mean values, standard deviation) and Cronbach's α estimates were computed for the RSE items separately by wording and for the total scale.

Second, it was of interest to examine different CFA models, with a focus on the CT-CM, CT-CU, CT-C(M-1), and RI. Each model was estimated with Mplus (v. 8.10; Muthén & Muthén, 2017) treating item-level data as continuous, and using the maximum likelihood mean- and variance- (MLMV) adjustment to correct for nonnormality in the observed data. While four category data may be better considered as ordinal, MLMV was used to provide an appropriate examination of the RI model. Each modeling strategy was evaluated using global and local fit information. Models were evaluated using indices often used with CFA and with commonly used recommendations for fit (Hu & Bentler, 1999; Tanaka, 1993) the: chi-square statistic, nonnormed fit index (NNFI; or TLI), CFI, RMSEA with associated 90% confidence interval, and SRMR. In addition, the AIC and BIC were included to compare values across nonnested models.

For interpreting global fit indices, chi-square fit indices often show significance; thus, the normed chi-square (χ^2/df) was also used to compare across models with differing numbers of paths estimated; here, large normed chi-square values tend to show (as a general principle) poor model–data fit, with values around 2.0 generally indicating acceptable fit (DiStefano, 2016). NNFI and CFI values of 0.95 or greater are largely indicative of acceptable model–data fit, and SRMR values less than 0.08 are indicative of an acceptable model (Hu & Bentler, 1999; Browne & Cudeck, 1992). RMSEA values lower than 0.08 indicate acceptable fit and values 0.05 or lower illustrate good fit. Finally, lower AIC and BIC were indicative of better fit. Parameter estimates, standard errors, residual values, and modification indices were examined for local fit evidence.

Lastly, for each model tested, a small structural equation model was run. The GAD-2 and PHQ-2 scales were used as outcome variables, with each latent variable defined by their scales' two observed items. These factors were regressed on the method effect variable (when included) and the self-esteem trait, respectively. Parameter estimates for the structural components can demonstrate how values vary among models commonly used for treating wording effects.

The data and the Mplus code (as well as the RStudio code as an alternative) can be accessed via the Center for Open Science website (https://osf.io/vempx). We hope that this will facilitate conducting similar analyses of the readers' own data.

Results

After negatively worded items were reverse coded, descriptive information was investigated for each set of items by wording style and the total self-esteem scale. Table 8.2 provides descriptive information and Cronbach's α estimates for items of different wording type. Overall mean values for the set of items showed a lower overall mean value for negatively worded items with a higher level of variability among ratings. RSE item agreement ratings ranged between *disagree* to *agree* (item means from 2.27–3.17) while positively worded item means were all within an agreement level (item mean range 3.04–3.30). There were no differences observed in overall reliability estimates, with both positively and negatively worded items yielding α = .826. Values for the entire RSE scale masked some of the differences in positive and negative item responses and reported a high level of reliability when the set of 10 RSE items was considered together.

Table 8.2 Descriptive statistics for Rosenberg Self-Esteem scale

	Positive RSE items	Negative RSE items	Total RSE scale
Mean (*SD*)	3.16 (0.45)	2.77 (0.61)	2.96 (0.47)
Cronbach's α	.826	.826	.870

Note. *N* = 362. RSE = Rosenberg Self-Esteem scale.

Turning to the use of CFA to accommodate negative wording, CT-CM, CT-CU, CT-C(M-1), and RI were estimated using the RSE data, and indices of global and local fit compared. In addition, the unidimensional model of self-esteem was included as a comparison, as many scales including mixed wording items may measure one construct. With the analyses, the CT-CM model did not converge, even after using suggested starting values and increasing the number of iterations. As stated earlier in the "Using MTMM Modeling Strategies with Negatively Worded Items" section, convergence problems related to the CT-CM have been noted in prior research; thus, this model will not be considered further.

The remaining models converged to proper solutions; fit information for these models is included in Table 8.3. Viewing the different models, the unidimensional model did not demonstrate acceptable fit across the set of global indices. The other three models yielded adequate fit, with CFI and SRMR values approximating or exceeding their respective cutoff values. TLI values were under the .95 cutoff, but closest to the cutoff for the RI model and slightly lower for the CT-CU and CT-C(M-1) models. RMSEA values were lowest for the RI model; however, confidence intervals overlapped for all models, showing that the models were very similar in reproducing relationships in the input matrix. Thus, the models CT-CU, CT-C(M-1), and RI yielded roughly equivalent fit to the data.

Table 8.3 Global fit of models to accommodate negative wording

Models	Unidimensional	CT-CU	CT-C(M-1)	Random intercept
Chi-square (*df*), *p* value	194.21 (35) *p* < .0001	68.52 (25) *p* < .0001	89.15 (30) *p* < .0001	92.84 (34) *p* = .001
Normed chi-square	5.55	2.74	2.97	2.73
Akaike information criterion	6280.84	6086.38	6107.55	6102.86
Bayesian information criterion	6397.51	6241.94	6243.66	6223.42
Comparative fit index	0.832	0.954	0.937	0.938
Tucker-Lewis Index	0.783	0.917	0.906	0.918
RMSEA (90% CI) *p* value	0.112 (0.097–0.128) *p* < .0001	0.069 (0.050–0.089) *p* = .049	0.074 (0.056–0.092) *p* = .013	0.069 (0.053–0.086) *p* = .030
SRMR	0.072	0.034	0.039	0.038

Note. CT-CM model is not included due to non-convergence. CT-CU = correlated trait–correlated uniqueness; CT-C(M-1) = correlated trait–correlated method minus 1; RMSEA = root-mean-square error of approximation, SRMR = standardized root mean square residual.

For the evaluation of local fit indices, loading parameter estimates were significant across all tested models. As our goal here is to illustrate how to interpret parameters with alternative models for countering acquiescence, we focus on local fit for the CT-CU, CT-C(M-1), and RI models. Parameter values for these three models are included in Table 8.4, where item numbers refer to a specific RSE item as noted in Table 8.1.

First, considering the CT-CU, this modeling procedure removes the variability associated with negatively worded items from further consideration. This process resulted in higher completely standardized item loadings for positively worded items (average standardized loading value = .71) as compared with a moderate value for negatively worded items (average = .49). This pattern was partly due to the variance attributed to the loading parameter shared with the uniqueness term. Also, higher error term values result in lower loading values, as a finite amount of item variance was split between the two sources. As noted by Bandalos (2021), correlated error terms were found to be related to similarity of wording. For example, the highest standardized error term (.51) was between Item 2 ("At times, I think I am no good at all") and Item 6 ("I certainly feel useless at times"). Negatively worded items on the RSE scale are similar in wording.

Bandalos (2021) found that correlated error terms were higher when items were in proximity on a questionnaire. As the RSE is very short, there is not much room to randomly distribute items of varying wording across the scale; however, this recommendation may be considered if negatively worded items are included on a longer questionnaire, to help reduce the amount of relationship shared due to wording direction.

Table 8.4 Standardized parameter estimates for selected models used to account for negative method effects.

Correlated trait–correlated uniqueness (CT-CU)						Correlated trait–correlated method minus one (CT-C(M−1))			Random intercept (RI)	
	Trait	Uniqueness					Trait	ME		Trait
Item 1	0.66					Item 1	0.66		Item 1	0.61
Item 3	0.77					Item 3	0.77		Item 3	0.66
Item 4	0.71					Item 4	0.71		Item 4	0.63
Item 7	0.64					Item 7	0.64		Item 7	0.57
Item 10	0.75					Item 10	0.75		Item 10	0.69
Item 2	0.48					**Item 2**	0.47	0.59	**Item 2**	−0.69
Item 5	0.49	0.31				**Item 5**	0.50	0.47	**Item 5**	−0.66
Item 6	0.51	0.51	0.34			**Item 6**	0.50	0.60	**Item 6**	−0.72
Item 8	0.42	0.28	0.22	0.31		**Item 8**	0.42	0.37	**Item 8**	−0.53
Item 9	0.57	0.37	0.48	0.38	0.18	**Item 9**	0.57	0.49	**Item 9**	−0.73
		Item 2	**Item 5**	**Item 6**	**Item 8**					

Note. Negatively worded items are bolded; Variance of random intercept (RI) factor under RI model = 0.034 (standard error = .009), $p < .0001$. Negative items are recorded in correlated trait–correlated uniqueness and correlated trait–correlated method minus one. For the RI model, nonrecoded data were used. Standardized values for the intercept terms under the RI model do not equal 1, due to calculation of standardized parameters: (loading value × standard deviation of factor) divided by the standard deviation of the observed item in question (see Brown, 2015, for more information). ME = Method Effect.

As shown in Table 8.4, all parameter estimates under the CT-C(M-1) related to the trait factor, with positively worded items considered as the standard method, and therefore, not included on the method factor. Negatively worded items were compared to the standard method to measure self-esteem, with the item variability decomposed into components that relate to the trait, measurement method, and residual (Eid et al., 2003).

Considering negatively worded items, if the amount of shared variance between the item and self-esteem (trait) factor is larger than the variance attributed to the method factor, the two phrasing directions are comparable. However, if the variance shared between an item and the method factor is consistently larger than the variance associated with the trait, then the negative phrasing is clouding measurement of the construct (self-esteem).

Viewing the standardized parameter estimates, the five positive items yielded larger standardized loading values, with an average standardized value of .71 across the set of positively worded items. This shows that a typical item phrased using the standard method of measuring self-esteem shares roughly 50% of the variance with the construct. Negatively worded items loaded moderately (.42–.57) on the self-esteem factor, with corresponding loadings on the method effect factor at a similar level (.37–.60). With this set of items, the observed score variance shared with the method effect factor was higher (or approximately equal) to the observed score variance shared with the trait factor for all but one item (Item 10) on the RSE scale. This suggests that the two methods used to measure self-esteem (i.e., positively worded and negatively worded items) provided inconsistent measurement of the trait (e.g., Eid, 2000; Yang et al., 2012).

With negatively worded items, the method-specificity coefficient denotes the part of the variance of the negatively worded items that is not shared with the standard method (e.g., Eid et al., 2003). Squaring the standardized loading values for negatively worded items shows that between 14% and 35% of the variance of negatively worded items is attributed to using a measurement method (negative phrasing) that differs from the standard (positive phrasing). Dividing an item's squared standardized loading on the method factor by the total variance accounted for by a negatively worded item (i.e., reliability coefficient, R^2) showed that between 42% and 61% of the total variability accounted for by negatively worded items was related to the wording direction (i.e., method of measuring) rather than shared with the trait.

When analyzing questionnaire data that includes both positively and negatively worded items, typical practice is to recode negatively worded items so that all items are in the same direction relative to the trait (e.g., Marsh & Grayson, 1995). However, under the RI model, if recoded data are used, standardized loading values for positively worded items will be low, nonsignificant, and of mixed direction, while parameter estimates for negatively worded items report moderate (.29–.51), significant and positive estimates. In other words, if recoded data are not correctly represented, researchers may encounter confusing results, leading to a disregard of the RI model as a viable analysis strategy (e.g., Gu et al., 2015). To create meaningful results with the RI model, RSE data were used in their *original* (i.e., nonrecoded) format. Alternatively, recoded data may be used and values on the RI factor set to 1.0 for positively worded items and -1.0 for negatively phrased items (e.g., Schmalbach et al., 2021).

Table 8.4 shows that standardized parameter estimates under the RI model demonstrated large, significant values for both positively and negatively worded items, where negative signs were included with negatively phrased items. The negative parameter is in line with the nonrecoded format, as these items are written opposite to the construct of (positive) self-esteem. The RI factor variance was small in magnitude, .034, but significant, illustrating that there may have been some RSE respondents with consistent response tendencies. Following Maydeu-Olivares and Coffman (2006) and their notation (p. 353), the amount of variation in an observed item (y_i) can be divided to illustrate the amount of variance that relates to the RI (ϕ/y_i), where ϕ is the variance of the RI factor (for the set of RSE items, observed variances values for Items 1 to 10 were 0.381, 0.623, 0.252, 0.365, 0.526, 0.696, 0.325, 0.778, 0.548, and 0.365, respectively).

Using the observed item variances, the RI accounted for roughly 4%–6% of the variance for negatively worded items and roughly 8%–12% of the variance for positively worded items. As the negatively worded items had higher observed variances and the RI accounted for a small amount of variance, there was a higher portion of the variability for an observed item that was due to the RI. Said another way, the responses for individuals were more distinct for the positively worded items than for the negatively worded items on the RSE scale. As items are typically not examined by wording, this may suggest that there is greater *nonuniformity* in responding to the negatively worded items for individuals.

The RI model may be appropriate to use if a researcher can consider a consistent response style, but as responses to the RSE scale may be confounded with other response styles (e.g., social desirability, careless responding, etc.), the different response styles may impose differing influences on the scale items, and the interpretation be difficult to untangle (e.g., Geiser et al., 2008).

Relations With External Variables

To illustrate how different conceptualizations of method effects may relate to outcome variables, a small structural equation model was conducted. Latent variables of depression and anxiety were created and related to the self-esteem factor (i.e., RSE) and, where relevant, method effects factors. For interpretation, we note that the trait of self-esteem is in a positive direction (i.e., higher RSE scores indicate higher self-esteem) and depression and anxiety are in the opposite direction (i.e., higher scores indicate higher levels of problematic behaviors). Standardized structural paths are provided in Table 8.5.

Table 8.5 Standardized structural coefficients, by RSE model type

Model	Factor(s)	Depression	Anxiety
Unidimensional	RSE	−0.635	−0.459
CT-CU	RSE	−0.583	−0.421
CT-C(M-1)	RSE	−0.522	−0.372
	Negative method effect	−0.358	−0.280
Random intercept	RSE	−0.628	−0.456
	Intercept	0.074^{ns}	0.057^{ns}

Note. CT-CU = correlated trait-correlated uniqueness; CT-C(M-1) = correlated trait-correlated method minus one; ns = nonsignificant parameter; RSE = Rosenberg Self-Esteem scale.

Across all models, self-esteem yielded significant large relationships with depression and moderate, significant relationships with anxiety. The unidimensional model provided the highest structural estimates between RSE and outcome variables, depression and anxiety. However, parameter estimates under the RI were very close to the values of the unidimensional model, while also allowing response variation for negative wording. The results were in line with results demonstrated by Maydeu-Olivares and Coffman (2006), who found factor scores under the RI model provided estimates roughly equivalent to sum score values. Structural paths also demonstrated no significant relationship between the intercept factor and outcome variables, showing no relationship between idiosyncratic responses of one's level of depression or anxiety. Similar results between external criteria and a RI factor were noted by Maydeu-Olivares and Coffman (2006).

The CT-CU and CT-C(M-1) models yielded lower parameter estimates with outcome variables than those observed with the RI model; however, both allowed parameter estimates associated with negatively worded items to be freely estimated.

Considering the CT-CU, the relations with outcome variables were at slightly lower levels due to variability attributed to uniqueness terms of negatively worded items. Researchers selecting this framework remove variability for items of opposite direction with the latent variable, and thus achieve not only a good fitting model, but demonstrate relations with outcome variables that are of similar magnitude with other modeling strategies. The amount of variability associated with uniqueness terms does lower the parameter relations with outcome variables. If there are a high number of items in the opposite direction from the construct, the amount of variability removed could adversely impact the relations with outcome variables and provide an overinflated view of model fit.

The CT-C(M-1) model showed the lowest associations between the self-esteem trait and outcome factors of depression and anxiety. The method effect related to negative wording yielded significant, low to moderate relations with the outcome variables. In other words, a greater tendency to exhibit a response style associated with negatively worded items was related to lower levels of both depression and anxiety. Although values were significant, parameter estimates were of a relatively low magnitude. While not included in this example, personality characteristics have been found to relate to observing a method effect to negatively worded items (e.g., DiStefano & Motl, 2006; Quilty et al., 2006) and could contribute to the presence of method effects as well as the influence of method effects for negatively worded items on outcomes.

Suggestions for Future Research

Questionnaires in the social sciences commonly include negatively worded items for a variety of reasons; however, the most often noted reason is to counter acquiescence bias (Schriesheim & Hill, 1981; Spector, 1992). Given the prominence of such scales in the social sciences, researchers can benefit from recognizing that the responses obtained are likely confounded with variation related to item phrasing (e.g., Fink, 2006; Hartley & Betts, 2010).

Mixed wording may impact psychometric properties (e.g., reliability and validity estimates), which are frequently examined to confirm the survey results' validity. For instance, utilizing a mixed-worded scale as opposed to one with all items positively worded has been shown to reduce internal consistency reliability estimates (e.g., Barnette, 2000). Test-retest reliability has also been shown to be negatively impacted by the inclusion of negatively worded items with positively worded items on the same scale (e.g., Jiang et al., 2017). Research has also revealed that the inclusion of negatively phrased items may compromise an instrument's validity by altering the scale's factor structure (e.g., Wu et al., 2017). Thus, while researchers often include negatively worded items, knowledge of the impact of mixed wording can be weighed against the need to control for acquiescence.

Researchers may accommodate these method effects into their structural model, allowing for a better view of the focal construct(s) and avoiding the chance that the wording direction adversely affects the dimensional structure of the scale. This chapter discussed four commonly used CFA techniques to control wording effects associated with negatively worded items: CT-CM, CT-CU, CT-C(M-1), and RI. Each model has areas for researchers to consider when choosing a CFA framework. Table 8.6 summarizes the main characteristics regarding each model's interpretation and major advantages and considerations of these commonly used techniques for accommodating negatively worded items.

While this chapter has served as an introduction to accommodating acquiescence with wording effects, we recognize that there are limitations to the discussion here. For example, the chapter has discussed commonly used techniques to deal with acquiescence; however, there are additional strategies that researchers may choose to investigate. For example, use of different labeling options may be a consideration. Some researchers recommend refraining from using anchors from an *agree–disagree* scale (including "yes/no" and "true (of me) – false (of me)" variations) and advocate for the use of alternative question types, less prone to acquiescence bias (e.g., Kuru & Pasek, 2016). Use of item-specific questions is one alternative. In other words, rather than including a statement with an "agree" or "disagree" option (e.g., "I like the color red"), the statement could be changed to a direct question, with response options that represent a range that reflects the extremes of an attitude or behavior (e.g., "Do you like the color red?") with response options ranging from *not at all* to *very much* (e.g., Kuru & Pasek, 2016).

Table 8.6 Summary of select CFA models commonly used to account for negative wording

Model	Interpretation	Advantages	Considerations
CT-CU	Correlations between uniqueness terms among the negatively worded items (treated as error)	• Easy to construct • No estimation problems • Almost always converged to a proper solution • Tends to produce good fitting models	• Difficult to determine the strength of wording effects as compared with the strength of the relationship of an item to the focal trait
CT-CM	Latent factors that relate to wording direction (one factor related to positive wording and one factor related to negative wording)	• Variance associated with the wording effects can be removed from the variance related to focal trait • Including method factors may allow for examination with other latent variables or respondent characteristics	• May have difficulty converging or provide a solution with unreasonable parameter • Difficulties in estimation due to the assumption of orthogonality between the construct and wording effect factors

Table 8.6 Continued

Model	Interpretation	Advantages	Considerations
CT-C(M-1)	A latent factor related to the "nonstandard" method of measurement (typically for negatively worded items)	• Overcomes identification problems or improper solutions that often occur with the CT-CM model • The ambiguity in interpretation of the trait and wording effect factor is resolved by only including one method factor • Provides a more realistic view of measurement by recognizing that the trait and methods are intertwined	• Wording effect is a residual factor, representing the level of deviation of negatively worded items form the true score of the items measured with the reference method (i.e., positive wording) • Wording effect – percentage of variance accounted for by using negative wording as compared with the reference method (i.e., positive wording) • Inconsistency with model fit depending on which set of items (i.e., either positively or negatively worded items) is used as the reference method
Random intercept	The variance of the random intercept factor estimates the variability among the respondents due to different wording direction	• Parsimonious – providing a view of the construct without over-parameterization or interpretation problems • Allows for individual differences in method responses	• Variance associated with the random intercept factor and loadings relating items to their focal construct should be significant • All factor loadings on the intercept factor are fixed to the same value, meaning a homogenous response style • Appropriate if there is a reason to consider a consistent response style across all items • Data must be in nonrecoded format (or intercept terms varied) to provide meaningful responses

Note. CFA = confirmatory factor analysis; CT-CM = correlated trait–correlated method; CT-C(M-1) = correlated trait–correlated method minus one; CT-CU = correlated trait–correlated uniqueness;

Future Areas of Research

When considering controlling acquiescence by including negatively worded items, there are many avenues that might benefit from additional research. Fit indices are one area that might be of interest. For example, many scales measuring one dimension include negatively worded items, which may result in a multidimensional structure being identified. Two newer indices have been created to examine if a structure is "essentially unidimensional." The *Explained Common Variance Index* (ECV; Bentler, 2009; Reise et al., 2010) assesses the strength of the trait factor relative to the strength of the wording effect factors. Higher values of the ECV suggest that the item variances are mostly attributable to the trait factor, and that wording effects do not exhibit a great effect on the data. The *percentage of uncontaminated correlations* (PUC) is another fit index which may be examined. This index is defined as the percentage of item correlations that are explained only by the trait factor (Reise et al., 2013). High values of the PUC suggest a larger effect of the trait factor and a lower impact of the wording effect factors. Both the ECV and the PUC can be calculated by information (i.e., correlations or variance terms) that are readily available as part of analyses. These indices may help researchers decide whether the effects of the wording effect can be avoided – thus allowing fit and use of a unidimensional model. However, there has been relatively little systematic research of the ECV and PUC indices, and conditions under which these indices may provide trustworthy information. This area may be of interest to examine in future methodological studies.

Second, the unidimensional RSE scale was used as an empirical example; however, some survey instruments use mixed item wordings and are intended to measure multiple constructs while also including negatively worded items (e.g., Big Five Personality Test, Goldberg, 1993; Behavioral and Emotional Screening System, Teacher Rating Scales, Kamphaus & Reynolds, 2015; General Health Questionnaire-28, Goldberg & Hillier, 1979). With multidimensional scales, the tripartite model may be an option (e.g., Clark & Watson, 1991; Dunbar et al., 2000; Schönberger & Ponsford, 2010). The tripartite model specifies a higher order conceptualization of wording effects. The content domains are represented as first-order factors by their respective items; however, items that are negatively worded are modeled as a second-order factor influencing the subdomain factors. Thus, the influence of wording is modeled to have a direct influence on each set of items that are phrased in the same direction.

As another avenue for future research, alternative indices, as opposed to more traditional fit indices, may be useful when comparing different methods to accommodate negatively worded items. For instance, the *construct replicability* (H index) and *average variance extracted* (AVE) index can be investigated with wording effects. As an index of replicability, H suggests whether the tested model is more likely to be stable and replicable across studies. A latent variable that produces an H index value of .8 and above is considered well-defined by the tested model (Rodriguez et al., 2016). The AVE for a latent variable indicates how much variation in the observed measures can be explained on average by the latent variables. An AVE of at least .5 is highly recommended (Fornell & Larcker, 1981). Studies of these indices in the presence of wording effects have not yet been conducted.

When comparing multiple models to accommodate negative wording, more than one model may meet suggested index cutoff values, making it difficult to defend selection of one model over another. Yuan et al. (2016) proposed a method for examining model fit. Equivalence testing fit indices recognize that some level of misspecification may be tolerable, referred to as the *T*-size. This tolerable (i.e., *T*) amount of misspecification can be applied to traditional fit statistics, producing an adjusted value (e.g., CFI_T, $RMSEA_T$). With equivalence testing, a confidence level (e.g., $1 - \alpha$) is selected, and population values based on the current model are created at various confidence levels. The adjusted index can be compared with population cutoff boundaries for fit (e.g., excellent, close, fair, and mediocre or poor; Marcoulides & Yuan, 2017). Equivalence fit indices may be an option for researchers to examine additional fit information when different frameworks used to accommodate negative wording produce similar fit.

Besides choosing a model that is in line with theory and useful to describe the situation at hand, Maydeu-Olivares and Coffman (2006) recommended analyzing the connection between the factor scores derived from each model and outside standards that are known to predict or be predicted by the focal trait, to see if these correlations perform as expected. Thus, looking beyond the relations modeled within one set of data can help extend the measurement model findings to develop validity, by including the model in a larger nomological network of relations.

In line with the consideration that systematic variance associated with responses to negatively worded items represents a response style (e.g., Horan et al., 2003), researchers have investigated latent modeling techniques which consider subgroups of respondents that share similar response tendencies. A mixture modeling framework may be useful to identify such subgroups. This framework combines identification of underlying latent classes, with CFA, allowing the specification of relations between items and trait(s) that are unique to classes (for additional details, see Lubke & Muthén, 2005). The mixture modeling framework has been used with the study of response tendencies such as careless responding (e.g., Arias et al., 2020; Meade & Craig, 2012), neutral response tendencies (e.g. Colombi et al., 2021) and extreme response tendencies (e.g., Colombi et al., 2021; Elliott et al., 2009).

These methods have also been used to identify acquiescent responding and allow for differences in estimated relations between items and a latent trait or traits (e.g., DiStefano et al., 2012b; Kam & Fan, 2020). One benefit of these models is that the methods recognize heterogeneity in the distribution of responses and allow for class-specific parameter estimates; this method may provide unique estimates by class, illuminating differences in response patterns due to "other" characteristics, thus providing more accurate measurement. Future investigations may examine the use of factor mixture modeling as compared with models in the CFA framework, to determine how these methods accommodate acquiescence and/or negative wording, and the impact on outcome variables.

In conclusion, many researchers choose to include items of varying wording direction on scales in the hope of limiting the tendency for acquiescence; however, as discussed, including both positively and negatively worded items on the same scale is not without controversy. The information presented here should help researchers to consider if negatively and positively worded items are to be used in the same survey. A greater understanding of nuances inherent with this choice can assist with the overarching goal of producing sound measurement of the focal construct(s).

References

Abubakar, A., & Fischer, R. (2012). The factor structure of the 12-item General Health Questionnaire in a literate Kenyan population. *Stress and Health, 28*(3), 248–254. https://doi.org/10.1002/smi.1420

Arias, V. B., Garrido, L. E., Jenarol, C. Martínez-Molina, A., & Arias, B. (2020). A little garbage in, lots of garbage out: Assessing the impact of careless responding in personality survey data. *Behavior Research Methods, 52*, 2489–2505. https://doi.org/10.3758/s13428-020-01401-8.

Bandalos, D. L. (2018). *Measurement theory and applications for the social sciences*. Guilford Press.

Bandalos, D. L. (2021). Item meaning and order as causes of correlated residuals in confirmatory factor analysis. *Structural Equation Modeling, 28*(6), 903–913. https://doi.org/10.1080/10705511.2021.1916395

Barnette, J. J. (2000). Effects of stem and Likert response option reversals on survey internal consistency: If you feel the need, there is a better alternative to using those negatively worded stems. *Educational and Psychological Measurement, 60*(3), 361–370. https://doi.org/10.1177/00131640021970592

Baumgartner, H., & Steenkamp, J.-B. E. M. (2001). Response styles in marketing research: A cross-national investigation. *Journal of Marketing Research, 38*(2), 143–156. http://www.jstor.org/stable/1558620 https://doi.org/10.1509/jmkr.38.2.143.18840

Baumgartner, H., & Steenkamp, J. (2006). Response biases in marketing research. In R. Grover & M. Vriens (Eds.), *The handbook of marketing research: Uses, misuses, and future advances* (pp. 95–109). Sage. https://doi.org/10.4135/9781412973380

Bentler, P. M. (2009). Alpha, dimension-free, and model-based internal consistency reliability. *Psychometrika, 74*(1), 137–143. https://doi.org/10.1007/s11336-008-9100-1

Bollen, K. A., & Paxton, P. (1998). Detection and determinants of bias in subjective measures. *American Sociological Review*, 465–478. https://doi.org/10.2307/2657559

Borgers, N., Sikkel, D., & Hox, J. (2004). Response effects in surveys on children and adolescents: The effect of number of response options, negative wording, and neutral mid-point. *Quality and Quantity, 38*, 17–33. https://doi.org/10.1023/B:QUQU.0000013236.29205.a6

Brown, T. A. (2015). *Confirmatory factor analysis for applied research* (2nd ed.). Guilford Press.

Browne, M. W., & Cudeck, R. (1992). Alternative ways of assessing model fit. *Sociological Methods & Research, 21*(2), 230–258. https://doi.org/10.1177/0049124192021002005

Campbell, D. T., & Fiske, D. W. (1959). Convergent and discriminant validation by the multitrait-multimethod matrix. *Psychological Bulletin, 56*(2), 81–105. https://doi.org/10.1037/h0046016

Carlson, M., Wilcox, R., Chou, C. P., Chang, M., Yang, F., Blanchard, J., Marterella, A., Kuo, A. & Clark, F. (2011). Psychometric properties of reverse-scored items on the CES-D in a sample of ethnically diverse older adults. *Psychological Assessment, 23*(2), 558–562. https://doi.org/10.1037/a0022484

Carmines, E. G., & Zeller, R. A. (1979). *Reliability and validity assessment*. Quantitative Applications in the Social Sciences. Sage. https://doi.org/10.4135/9781412985642

Carr, L. G. (1971). The Srole items and acquiescence. *American Sociological Review, 36*(2), 287–293. https://doi.org/10.2307/2094045

Chang, L. (1995). Connotatively consistent and reversed connotatively inconsistent items are not fully equivalent: Generalizability study. *Educational and Psychological Measurement, 55*(6), 991–997. https://doi.org/10.1177/0013164495055006007

Chen, Y. H., Rendina-Gobioff, G., & Dedrick, R. F. (2010). Factorial invariance of a Chinese self-esteem scale for third and sixth grade students: Evaluating method effects associated with positively and negatively worded items. *International Journal of Educational Psychological Assessment, 6*, 21–35.

Chiavaroli, N., (2017). Negatively-worded multiple choice questions: An avoidable threat to validity. *Practical Assessment, Research, and Evaluation, 22*(1), 3. https://doi.org/10.7275/ca7y-mm27

Chyung, S. Y., Barkin, J. R., & Shamsy, J. A. (2018). Evidence-based survey design: The use of negatively worded items in surveys. *Performance Improvement, 57*(3), 16–25. https://doi.org/10.1002/pfi.21749

Clark, L. A., & Watson, D. (1991). Tripartite model of anxiety and depression: Psychometric evidence and taxonomic implications. *Journal of Abnormal Psychology, 100*(3), 316–336. https://doi.org/10.1037/0021-843X.100.3.316

Cloud, J., & Vaughan, G. M. (1970). Using balanced scales to control acquiescence. *Sociometry, 33*(2), 193–202. https://doi.org/10.2307/2786329

Colombi, R., Giordano, S., & Tutz, G. (2021). A rating scale mixture model to account for the tendency to middle and extreme categories. *Journal of Educational and Behavioral Statistics, 46*(6), 682–716. https://doi.org/10.3102/1076998621992554

Colston, H. L. (1999). "Not good" is "bad," but "not bad" is not "good": An analysis of three accounts of negation asymmetry. *Discourse Processes, 28*(3), 237–256. https://doi.org/10.1080/01638539909545083

Davis, R. E., Lee, S., Johnson, T. P., Conrad, F., Resnicow, K., Thrasher, J. F.,Mesa, A. & Peterson, K. E. (2020). The influence of item characteristics on acquiescence among Latino survey respondents. *Field Methods, 32*(1), 3–22. https://doi.org/10.1177/1525822X19873272

de Jonge, P. & Slates, J. P. J. (2005). Response sets in self-report data and their associations with personality traits. *European Journal of Psychiatry, 19*(4), 209–214. https://doi.org/10.4321/S0213-61632005000400002

DeVellis, R. F. (2003). *Scale development: Theory and applications* (2nd ed.). Sage.

DiStefano, C. (2016). Examining fit with structural equation models. In K. Schweizer & C. DiStefano (Eds.), *Principles and methods of test construction: Standards and recent advances* (pp. 166–193). Hogrefe.

DiStefano, C., Morgan, G. B., & Motl, R. W. (2012a). An examination of personality characteristics related to acquiescence. *Journal of Applied Measurement, 13*(1), 41–56.

DiStefano, C., Morgan, G. B., & Motl, R. W. (2012b). Detecting acquiescence underlying Rosenberg's self-esteem scale using the Rasch partial credit model. In S. De Wals & K. Meszaros (Eds.) *Handbook on psychology of self-esteem* (pp. 195–210). Nova Science.

DiStefano, C., & Motl, R. W. (2006). Further investigating method effects associated with negatively worded items on self-report surveys. *Structural Equation Modeling: A Multidisciplinary Journal, 13*(3), 440–464. https://doi.org/10.1207/s15328007sem1303_6

DiStefano, C., & Motl, R. W. (2009). Personality correlates of method effects due to negatively worded items on the Rosenberg Self-Esteem Scale. *Personality and Individual Differences, 46*(3), 309–313. https://doi.org/10.1016/j.paid.2008.10.020

Dunbar, M., Ford, G., Hunt, K., & Der, G. (2000). A confirmatory factor analysis of the Hospital Anxiety and Depression scale: comparing empirically and theoretically derived structures. *British Journal of Clinical Psychology, 39*(1), 79–94. https://doi.org/10.1348/014466500163121

Edwards, A. L. (1957). *The social desirability variable in personality assessment and research.* Dryden Press.

Eid, M. (2000). A multitrait-multimethod model with minimal assumptions. *Psychometrika, 65*(2), 241–261. https://doi.org/10.1007/BF02294377

Eid, M., Lischetzke, T., Nussbeck, F. W., & Trierweiler, L. I. (2003). Separating trait effects from trait-specific method effects in multitrait-multimethod models: A multiple-indicator CT-C (M-1) model. *Psychological Methods, 8*(1), 38–60. https://doi.org/10.1037/1082-989X.8.1.38

Elliott, M. N., Haviland, A. M., Kanouse, D. E., Hambarsoomian, K., & Hays, R. D. (2009). Adjusting for subgroup differences in extreme response tendency in ratings of health care: impact on disparity estimates. *Health Services Research, 44*, 542–561. https://doi.org/10.1111/j.1475-6773.2008.00922.x

Ferrando, P. J., & Lorenzo-Seva, U. (2010). Acquiescence as a source of bias and model and person misfit: A theoretical and empirical analysis. *British Journal of Mathematical and Statistical Psychology, 63*(2), 427–448. https://doi.org/10.1348/000711009X470740

Ferrando, P. J., & Navarro-González, D. (2018). Assessing the quality and usefulness of factor-analytic applications to personality measures: A study with the statistical anxiety scale. *Personality and Individual Differences, 123*, 81–86. https://doi.org/10.1016/j.paid.2017.11.014

Fink, A. (2006). *How to ask survey questions* (3rd ed.). Sage.

Finney, S. J. (2001). *A comparison of the psychometric properties of negatively and positively worded questionnaire items.* ProQuest Dissertations Publishing.

Finney, S. J., & DiStefano, C. (2013). Nonnormal and categorical data in structural equation modeling. In G. R. Hancock & R. O. Mueller (Eds.), *Structural equation modeling: A second course* (2nd ed., pp. 439–492). IAP Information Age.

Fornell, C., & Larcker, D. F. (1981). Evaluating structural equation models with unobservable variables and measurement error. *Journal of Marketing Research, 18*(1), 39–50. https://doi.org/10.1177/002224378101800104

Fox, M. T., Sidani, S., & Streiner, D. (2007). Using standardized survey items with older adults hospitalized for chronic illness. *Research in Nursing & Health, 30*(4), 468–481. https://doi.org/10.1002/nur.20201

Geiser, C., Eid, M., & Nussbeck, F. W. (2008). On the meaning of the latent variables in the CT-C (M-1) model: A comment on Maydeu-Olivares and Coffman (2006). *Psychological Methods, 13*(1), 49–57. https://doi.org/10.1037/1082-989X.13.1.49

Gnambs, T., & Schroeders, U. (2020). Cognitive abilities explain wording effects in the Rosenberg Self-Esteem Scale. *Assessment, 27*(2), 404–418. https://doi.org/10.1177/1073191117746503

Goldberg, L. R. (1993). The structure of phenotypic personality traits. *American Psychologist, 48*(1), 26–34. https://doi.org/10.1037/0003-066X.48.1.26

Goldberg, D. P. & Hillier, V. F. (1979). A scaled version of the General Health Questionnaire. *Psychological Medicine, 9*, 139–145. https://doi.org/10.1017/S0033291700021644

Greenberger, E., Chen, C., Dmitrieva, J., & Farruggia, S. P. (2003). Item-wording and the dimensionality of the Rosenberg Self-Esteem Scale: Do they matter? *Personality and Individual Differences, 35*(6), 1241–1254. https://doi.org/10.1016/S0191-8869(02)00331-8

Gu, H., Wen, Z., & Fan, X. (2015). The impact of wording effect on reliability and validity of the Core Self-Evaluation Scale (CSES): A bi-factor perspective. *Personality and Individual Differences, 83*, 142–147. https://doi.org/10.1016/j.paid.2015.04.006

Hankins, M. (2008). The factor structure of the twelve item General Health Questionnaire (GHQ-12): the result of negative phrasing? *Clinical Practice and Epidemiology in Mental Health, 4*, 1–8. https://link.springer.com/article/10.1186/1745-0179-4-10

Hartley, J. (2014). Some thoughts on Likert-type scales. *International Journal of Clinical and Health Psychology, 14*(1), 83–86. https://doi.org/10.1016/S1697-2600(14)70040-7

Hartley, J., & Betts, L. (2010). Four layouts and a finding: The effects of changes in the order of the verbal labels and numerical values on Likert-type scales. *International Journal of Social Research Methodology, 13*(1), 17–27. https://doi.org/10.1080/13645570802648077

Horan, P. M., DiStefano, C., & Motl, R. W. (2003). Wording effects in self-esteem scales: Methodological artifact or response style? *Structural Equation Modeling, 10*(3), 435–455. https://doi.org/10.1207/S15328007SEM1003_6

Hu, L. T., & Bentler, P. M. (1999). Cutoff criteria for fit indexes in covariance structure analysis: Conventional criteria versus new alternatives. *Structural Equation Modeling, 6*(1), 1–55. https://doi.org/10.1080/10705519909540118

Hughes, A. J., Dunn, K. M., Chaffee, T., Bhattarai, J., & Beyer, M. (2018). Diagnostic and clinical utility of the GAD-2 for screening anxiety symptoms in individuals with multiple sclerosis. *Archives of Physical Medicine and Rehabilitation, 99*(10), 2045–2049. https://doi.org/10.1016/j.apmr.2018.05.029

Hutton, A. C. (2017). *Assessing acquiescence in surveys using positively and negatively worded questions* [Unpublished doctoral dissertation]. Virginia Commonwealth University.

Ibrahim, A. M. (2001). Differential responding to positive and negative items: The case of a negative item in a questionnaire for course and faculty evaluation. *Psychological Reports, 88*(2), 497–500. https://doi.org/10.2466/pr0.2001.88.2.497

Jackson, D. N., & Messick, S. (1961). Response styles on the MMPI: Comparison of clinical and normal samples. *Research Bulletin (Educational Testing Service), 1961*(2), i–44. https://doi.org/10.1002/j.2333-8504.1961.tb00948.x

Jiang, J. M., Seng, E. K., Zimmerman, M. E., Sliwinski, M., Kim, M., & Lipton, R. B. (2017). Evaluation of the reliability, validity, and predictive validity of the subscales of the perceived stress scale in older adults. *Journal of Alzheimer's Disease, 59*(3), 987–996. https://doi.org/10.3233/JAD-170289

Johnson, J. M., Bristow, D. N., & Schneider, K. C. (2004). Did you not understand the question or not? An investigation of negatively worded questions in survey research. *Journal of Applied Business Research, 20*(1), 75–86.

Jöreskog, K. G. (1974). Analyzing psychological data by structural analysis of covariance Matrices. *Psychometrika, 43*, 443–477. https://doi.org/10.1007/BF02293808

Kam, C. C. S., & Fan, X. (2020). Investigating response heterogeneity in the context of positively and negatively worded items by using factor mixture modeling. *Organizational Research Methods, 23*(2), 322–341. https://doi.org/10.1177/1094428118790371

Kam, C. C. S., & Meyer, J. P. (2015). How careless responding and acquiescence response bias can influence construct dimensionality: The case of job satisfaction. *Organizational Research Methods, 18*(3), 512–541. https://doi.org/10.1177/1094428115571894

Kamphaus, R. W., & Reynolds, C. R. (2015). *Behavior Assessment System for Children* (3rd ed.). Pearson.

Kieruj, N. D., & Moors, G. (2013). Response style behavior: Question format dependent or personal style? *Quality & Quantity, 47*(1), 193–211. https://doi.org/10.1007/s11135-011-9511-4

Knowles, E. S., & Condon, C. A. (1999). Why people say "yes": A dual-process theory of acquiescence. *Journal of Personality and Social Psychology, 77*(2), 379. https://doi.org/10.1037/0022-3514.77.2.379

Kroenke, K., Spitzer, R. L., & Williams, J. B. (2003). The Patient Health Questionnaire-2: validity of a two-item depression screener. *Medical Care,* 1284–1292. https://doi.org/10.1097/01.MLR.0000093487.78664.3C

Kroenke, K., Spitzer, R. L., Williams, J. B., Monahan, P. O., & Löwe, B. (2007). Anxiety disorders in primary care: prevalence, impairment, comorbidity, and detection. *Annals of Internal Medicine, 146*(5), 317–325. https://doi.org/10.7326/0003-4819-146-5-200703060-00004

Krosnick J. A. (1999). Survey research. *Annual Review of Psychology, 50*, 537–567. https://doi.org/10.1146/annurev.psych.50.1.537

Kuru, O., & Pasek, J. (2016). Improving social media measurement in surveys: Avoiding acquiescence bias in Facebook research. *Computers in Human Behavior, 57*, 82–92. https://doi.org/10.1016/j.chb.2015.12.008

Kutscher, T., & Eid, M. (2020). The effect of rating scale length on the occurrence of inappropriate category use for the assessment of job satisfaction: An experimental online study. *Journal of Well-Being Assessment, 4*, 1–35. https://doi.org/10.1007/s41543-020-00024-2

Lee, C. T., Lin, C. Y., Tsai, M. C., Strong, C., & Lin, Y. C. (2016). Psychometric evaluation and wording effects on the Chinese version of the parent-proxy Kid-KINDL. *Health and Quality of Life Outcomes, 14*(1), 1–10. https://doi.org/10.1186/s12955-016-0526-3

Lima, T. J. S. D., & de Souza, L. E. C. (2019). Rosenberg self-esteem scale: Method effect and gender invariance. *Psico-USF, 24*, 517–528. https://doi.org/10.1590/1413-82712019240309

Lin, C. Y., Luh, W. M., Cheng, C. P., Yang, A. L., Su, C. T., & Ma, H. I. (2013). Measurement equivalence across child self-reports and parent-proxy reports in the Chinese version of the pediatric quality of life inventory version 4.0. *Child Psychiatry & Human Development, 44*, 583–590.

Lindwall, M., Barkoukis, V., Grano, C., Lucidi, F., Raudsepp, L., Liukkonen, J., & Thøgersen-Ntoumani, C. (2012). Method effects: The problem with negatively versus positively keyed items. *Journal of Personality Assessment, 94*(2), 196–204. https://doi.org/10.1080/00223891.2011.645936

Locker, D., Jokovic, A., & Allison, P. (2007). Direction of wording and responses to items in oral health-related quality of life questionnaires for children and their parents. *Community Dentistry and Oral Epidemiology, 35*(4), 255–262. https://doi.org/10.1111/j.1600-0528.2007.00320.x

Lorge, I. (1937). Gen-like: Halo or reality. *Psychological Bulletin, 34*, 545–546.

Lubke, G. H., & Muthén, B. (2005). Investigating population heterogeneity with factor mixture models. *Psychological Methods, 10*, 21–39. https://doi.org/10.1037/1082-989X.10.1.21

Marcoulides, K. M., & Yuan, K. H. (2017). New ways to evaluate goodness of fit: A note on using equivalence testing to assess structural equation models. *Structural Equation Modeling, 24*(1), 148–153. https://doi.org/10.1080/10705511.2016.1225260

Marsh H. W. (1989). Confirmatory factor analysis of multitrait-multimethod data: Many problems and a few solutions. *Applied Psychological Measurement, 13*, 335–361. https://doi.org/10.1177/014662168901300402

Marsh, H. W. (1996). Positive and negative global self-esteem: A substantively meaningful distinction or artifactors? *Journal of Personality and Social Psychology, 70*(4), 810. https://doi.org/10.1037/0022-3514.70.4.810

Marsh, H. W., & Grayson, D. (1995). Latent variable models of multitrait-multimethod data. In R. H. Hoyle (Ed.), *Structural equation modeling: Concepts, issues, and applications* (pp. 177–198). Sage.

Marsh, H. W., Wen, Z., & Hau, K. T. (2004). Structural equation models of latent interactions: evaluation of alternative estimation strategies and indicator construction. *Psychological Methods, 9*(3), 275–300. https://doi.org/10.1037/1082-989X.9.3.275

Martin, J. (1964). Acquiescence–Measurement and theory. *British Journal of Social & Clinical Psychology, 3*(3), 216–225. https://doi.org/10.1111/j.2044-8260.1964.tb00430.x

Maul, A. (2013). Method effects and the meaning of measurement. *Frontiers in Psychology, 4*, 1–13. https://doi.org/10.3389/fpsyg.2013.00169

Maydeu-Olivares, A., & Coffman, D. L. (2006). Random intercept item factor analysis. *Psychological Methods, 11*(4), 344–362. https://doi.org/10.1037/1082-989X.11.4.344

McClendon, M. J. (1992). *On the measurement and control of acquiescence in latent variable models* [Paper presentation]. Annual meeting of the American Sociological Association, Pittsburgh, PA, USA.

Meade, A. W., & Craig, S. B. (2012). Identifying careless responses in survey data. *Psychological Methods, 17*(3), 437–455. https://doi.org/10.1037/a0028085

Merritt, S. M. (2012). The two-factor solution to Allen and Meyer's (1990) affective commitment scale: Effects of negatively worded items. *Journal of Business and Psychology, 27*, 421–436. https://doi.org/10.1007/s10869-011-9252-3

Messick, S. (1966). The psychology of acquiescence: An interpretation of research evidence. *Research Bulletin (Educational Testing Service.), 1966*(1), i–44. https://doi.org/10.1002/j.2333-8504.1966.tb00357.x

Michaelides, M. P., Zenger, M., Koutsogiorgi, C., Brähler, E., Stöbel-Richter, Y., & Berth, H. (2016). Personality correlates and gender invariance of wording effects in the German version of the Rosenberg Self-Esteem Scale. *Personality and Individual Differences, 97*, 13–18. https://doi.org/10.1016/j.paid.2016.03.011

Mirowsky, J., & Ross, C. E. (1983). Paranoia and the structure of powerlessness. *American Sociological Review*, 228–239. https://doi.org/10.2307/2095107

Motl, R. W., & DiStefano, C. (2002). Longitudinal invariance of self-esteem and method effects associated with negatively worded items. *Structural Equation Modeling, 9*(4), 562–578. https://doi.org/10.1207/S15328007SEM0904_6

Muthén, L. K., & Muthén, B. O. (2017). *Mplus statistical analysis with latent variables user's guide (Version 8.10)*. References-Scientific Research.

Narayan, S., & Krosnick, J. A. (1996). Education moderates some response effects in attitude measurement. *Public Opinion Quarterly, 60*(1), 58–88. https://doi.org/10.1086/297739

Nunnally, J.C. (1967). *Psychometric theory* (1st ed.). McGraw-Hill.

Nunnally, J. C. (1978). An overview of psychological measurement. In B.B. Wolman (Ed.), *Clinical diagnosis of mental disorders: A handbook* (pp. 97–146). Springer.

Paulhus, D. (1991). Measurement and control of response bias. In J. Robinson, P. Shaver, & L. Wrightsman (Eds.), *Measures of personality and social psychological attitudes* (pp. 17–59). Academic Press. https://doi.org/10.1016/B978-0-12-590241-0.50006-X

Peterson, R. A. (2000). *Constructing effective questionnaires*. Sage. https://doi.org/10.4135/9781483349022

Plummer, F., Manea, L., Trepel, D., & McMillan, D. (2016). Screening for anxiety disorders with the GAD-7 and GAD-2: A systematic review and diagnostic metaanalysis. *General Hospital Psychiatry, 39*, 24–31. https://doi.org/10.1016/j.genhosppsych.2015.11.005

Podsakoff, P. M., MacKenzie, S. B., Lee, J.-Y., & Podsakoff, N. P. (2003). Common method biases in behavioral research: A critical review of the literature and recommended remedies. *Journal of Applied Psychology, 88*(5), 879–903. https://doi.org/10.1037/0021-9010.88.5.879

Quilty, L. C., Oakman, J. M., & Risko, E. (2006). Correlates of the Rosenberg self-esteem scale method effects. *Structural Equation Modeling, 13*(1), 99–117. https://doi.org/10.1207/s15328007sem1301_5

Ray, J. J. (1979). A quick measure of achievement motivation: Validated in Australia and reliable in Britain and South Africa. *Australian Psychologist, 14*(3), 337–344. https://doi.org/10.1080/00050067908254361

Reise, S. P., Bonifay, W. E., & Haviland, M. G. (2013). Scoring and modeling psychological measures in the presence of multidimensionality. *Journal of Personality Assessment, 95*(2), 129–140. https://doi.org/10.1080/00223891.2012.725437

Reise, S. P., Moore, T. M., & Haviland, M. G. (2010). Bifactor models and rotations: Exploring the extent to which multidimensional data yield univocal scale scores. *Journal of Personality Assessment, 92*(6), 544–559. https://doi.org/10.1080/00223891.2010.496477

Rodriguez, A., Reise, S. P., & Haviland, M. G. (2016). Evaluating bifactor models: Calculating and interpreting statistical indices. *Psychological Methods, 21*(2), 137–150. https://doi.org/10.1037/met0000045

Rosenberg, M. (1965). The Measurement of Self-Esteem. In M. Rosenberg (Ed.), *Society and the Adolescent Self-Image* (pp. 16–36). Princeton University Press. https://doi.org/10.1515/9781400876136-003

Ross, C. E., & Mirowsky, J. (1984). Socially-desirable response and acquiescence in a cross-cultural survey of mental health. *Journal of Health and Social Behavior, 25*, 189–197. https://doi.org/10.2307/2136668

Roszkowski, M. J., & Soven, M. (2010). Shifting gears: Consequences of including two negatively worded items in the middle of a positively worded questionnaire. *Assessment & Evaluation in Higher Education, 35*(1), 113–130. https://doi.org/10.1080/02602930802618344

Salazar, M. S. (2015). The dilemma of combining positive and negative items in scales. *Psicothema, 27*(2), 192–199. https://doi.org/10.7334/psicothema2014.266

Sapra, A., Bhandari, P., Sharma, S., Chanpura, T., & Lopp, L. (2020). Using Generalized Anxiety Disorder-2 (GAD-2) and GAD-7 in a primary care setting. *Curēus (Palo Alto, CA), 12*(5), e8224–e8224. https://doi.org/10.7759/cureus.8224

Schmalbach, B., Zenger, M., Michaelides, M. P., Schermelleh-Engel, K., Hinz, A., Körner, A., Beutel, M. E., Decker, O., Kliem, S., & Brähler, E. (2021). From bi-dimensionality to uni-dimensionality in self-report questionnaires: Applying the random intercept factor analysis model to six psychological tests. *European Journal of Psychological Assessment, 37*(2), 135–148. https://doi.org/10.1027/1015-5759/a000583

Schönberger, M., & Ponsford, J. (2010). The factor structure of the Hospital Anxiety and Depression Scale in individuals with traumatic brain injury. *Psychiatry Research, 179*(3), 342–349. https://doi.org/10.1016/j.psychres.2009.07.003

Schriesheim, C. A., Eisenbach, R. J., & Hill, K. D. (1991). The effect of negation and polar opposite item reversals on questionnaire reliability and validity: An experimental investigation. *Educational and Psychological Measurement, 51*(1), 67–78. https://doi.org/10.1177/0013164491511005

Schriesheim, C. A., & Hill, K. D. (1981). Controlling acquiescence response bias by item reversals: The effect on questionnaire validity. *Educational and Psychological Measurement, 41*(4), 1101–1114. https://doi.org/10.1177/001316448104100420

Silverberg, J. I., Lee, B., Lei, D., Yousaf, M., Janmohamed, S. R., Vakharia, P. P., Chopra, R., Chavda, R., Gabriel, S., Patel, K. R., Singam, V., Kantor, R., & Hsu, D. Y. (2021). Measurement properties of Patient Health Questionnaire 9 and Patient Health Questionnaire 2 in adult patients with atopic dermatitis. *Dermatitis, 32*(4), 225–231. https://doi.org/10.1097/DER.0000000000000653

Smith, A. B., Oluboyede, Y., West, R., Hewison, J., & House, A. O. (2013). The factor structure of the GHQ-12: The interaction between item phrasing, variance and levels of distress. *Quality of Life Research, 22*, 145–152. https://doi.org/10.1007/s11136-012-0133-7

Soto, C. J., & John, O. P. (2017). Short and extra-short forms of the Big Five Inventory–2: The BFI-2-S and BFI-2-XS. *Journal of Research in Personality, 68*, 69–81. https://doi.org/10.1016/j.jrp.2017.02.004

Spector, P. (1992). *Summated rating scale construction: An introduction.* Sage.

Staples, L. G., Dear, B. F., Gandy, M., Fogliati, V., Fogliati, R., Karin, E., Nielssen, O., & Titov, N. (2019). Psychometric properties and clinical utility of brief measures of depression, anxiety, and general distress: The PHQ-2, GAD-2, and K-6. *General Hospital Psychiatry, 56*, 13–18. https://doi.org/10.1016/j.genhosppsych.2018.11.003

Suárez Álvarez, J., Pedrosa, I., Lozano, L. M., García Cueto, E., Cuesta Izquierdo, M., & Muñiz Fernández, J. (2018). Using reversed items in Likert scales: A questionable practice. *Psicothema, 30*(2), 149–158. https://doi.org/10.7334/psicothema2018.33

Tanaka, J. S. (1993). Multifaceted Conceptions of Fit in Structural Equation Models. In K. A. Bollen, & J. S. Long (Eds.), *Testing Structural Equation Models* (pp. 10-39). Sage.

Tomás, J. M., & Oliver, A. (1999). Rosenberg's self-esteem scale: Two factors or method effects. *Structural Equation Modeling, 6*(1), 84–98. https://doi.org/10.1080/10705519909540120

Vigil Colet, A., Navarro González, D., & Morales Vives, F. (2020). To reverse or to not reverse Likert-type items: That is the question. *Psicothema, 32*(1), 108–114. https://doi.org/10.7334/psicothema2019.286

van Sonderen, E., Sanderman, R., Coyne, J. C. (2013). Ineffectiveness of reverse wording of questionnaire items: Let's learn from cows in the rain. *PLoS ONE, 8*(7), e68967. https://doi.org/10.1371/journal.pone.0068967

Wang, Y., Kong, F., Huang, L., & Liu, J. (2016). Neural correlates of biased responses: The negative method effect in the Rosenberg Self-Esteem Scale is associated with right amygdala volume. *Journal of Personality, 84*(5), 623–632. https://doi.org/10.1111/jopy.12185

Weems, G. H., Onwuegbuzie, A. J., & Lustig, D. (2003). Profiles of respondents who respond inconsistently to positively-and negatively-worded items on rating scales. *Evaluation & Research in Education, 17*(1), 45–60. https://doi.org/10.1080/14664200308668290

Weijters, B., & Baumgartner, H. (2012). Misresponse to reversed and negated items in surveys: A review. *Journal of Marketing Research, 49*(5), 737–747. https://doi.org/10.1509/jmr.11.0368

Weijters, B., Geuens, M., & Baumgartner, H. (2013). The effect of familiarity with the response category labels on item response to Likert scales. *Journal of Consumer Research, 40*(2), 368–381. https://doi.org/10.1086/670394

Weijters, B., Schillewaert, N., & Geuens, M. (2008). Assessing response styles across modes of data collection. *Journal of the Academy of Marketing Science, 36*, 409–422. https://doi.org/10.1007/s11747-007-0077-6

Wetzel, E., Böhnke, J. R., & Brown, A. (2016). Response biases. In F. T. L. Leong, D. Bartram, F. M. Cheung, K. F. Geisinger, & D. Iliescu (Eds.), *The ITC international handbook of testing and assessment* (pp. 349–363). Oxford University Press. https://doi.org/10.1093/med:psych/9780199356942.003.0024

Wu, Y., Zuo, B., Wen, F., & Yan, L. (2017). Rosenberg Self-Esteem Scale: Method effects, factorial structure and scale invariance across migrant child and urban child populations in China. *Journal of Personality Assessment, 99*(1), 83–93. https://doi.org/10.1080/00223891.2016.1217420

Xin, Z., & Chi, L. (2010). Wording effect leads to a controversy over the construct of the social dominance orientation scale. *The Journal of Psychology, 144*(5), 473–488. https://doi.org/10.1080/00223980.2010.496672

Yang, Y., Chen, Y.-H., Lo, W.-J., & Turner, J. E. (2012). Cross-cultural evaluation of item wording effects on an attitudinal scale. *Journal of Psychoeducational Assessment, 30*(5), 509–519. https://doi.org/10.1177/0734282911435461

Yuan, K. H., Chan, W., Marcoulides, G. A., & Bentler, P. M. (2016). Assessing structural equation models by equivalence testing with adjusted fit indexes. *Structural Equation Modeling, 23*(3), 319–330. https://doi.org/10.1080/10705511.2015.1065414

Chapter 9

Missing Data: How to Handle Incomplete Data

Norman Rose

Abstract

Missing values are a common problem in psychological and social science data and are often difficult to avoid. Since the introduction of a comprehensive statistical theory of missingness in the 1970s by Donald B. Rubin, many approaches have been developed to deal with missing data, whereby a fundamental distinction can be made between model-based and imputation-based methods. Model-based methods, such as *full information maximum likelihood* (FIML), take the missing values directly into account at the stage of parameter estimation. Imputation-based methods are stepwise procedures, in which the missing values are replaced in a first step using suitable imputation models. The filled-in datasets are used for parameter estimation with standard estimation methods in a second step. *Multiple imputation* (MI) with repeated imputation of missing values from a set of plausible values is the method of choice among those using the imputation-based methods but requires more complex statistical inference procedures. In this chapter, FIML and MI are explained as current state-of-the-art procedures, particularly regarding their application in psychometric models (i.e., structural equation models and item-response theoretical models). However, FIML and MI are no panacea. The assumptions and conditions under which FIML and MI lead to unbiased estimates are explained with reference to Rubin's theory of missing values. The challenges and pitfalls of handling missing values are illustrated. In particular, the adequate consideration of missing relevant covariates as auxiliary variables using FIML or MI is outlined in detail. Software options for missing values and the handling of missing values in the free software *R* are illustrated.

Introduction

Missing data are common in psychological and educational assessments for many different reasons. Unit nonresponses occur when individuals refuse to participate in assessments, which can lead to selected and unrepresentative samples. Participants of a survey are often not able or not willing to answer all items, resulting in incomplete datasets. These item nonresponses can be due to omissions of items during the assessment or not-reached items in time (e.g., under time limitations). Illegibility of item responses to test items, which are not codable in the final data, also results in missing values. Omitted, not-reached, and not-codable item responses are typical examples of *unintended missing data*, which need to be distinguished from what are referred to as *planned missing data* (i.e., missing data by design). The latter are accepted in order to reduce the burden on test takers. Especially in assessments that include many different tests or long questionnaires with many items, participants may become fatigued during the assessment. This poses a threat to the quality of resulting data.

Planned missing data are under researchers' control through the testing design, whereas unintended missing data are a nuisance and may threaten statistical inference. However, both planned and unintended missing data require decisions by the statistician or psychometrician on how to handle them in the analysis and in the psychometric modeling of the data.

Most statistical software packages come with default settings for handling incomplete data, but that should not be carelessly relied upon. Not thinking about the problem of missing data means relying on such default settings, which can be detrimental, even in cases of planned missing data. For example, *complete-case analysis* (i.e., listwise deletion of cases with incomplete data) is the most common default setting for handling missing values to this day. However, is this approach justifiable from a statistical point of view? Unfortunately, there is no general answer to that question. If the occurrence of missing data is purely random (e.g., missingness is independent of persons and variables in the dataset), then listwise deletion leads to a reduced but still representative sample. Therefore, no systematic bias of parameter estimates is introduced. This may not be the case, when *missingness* stochastically depends on persons and variables in the data. What can be done in such a situation? Again, there is no general answer, because different stochastic dependencies between missingness and observed and unobserved variables can be distinguished, with different implications regarding the handling of missing data.

In his general statistical theory of missing data, Rubin (1976) distinguishes among *missing completely at random* (MCAR), *missing at random* (MAR), and *not missing at random* (NMAR). Assume that X and Z were two variables in a questionnaire. X denotes the participants' income and Z their highest completed level of education. Income is known to be sensitive information that is often not provided by survey participants. MCAR means that the occurrence of missing values of X is stochastically independent of income and education (e.g., X and Z). If missingness in X depends on both income and the educational level, then the missing data are MAR if and only if missingness of X is *conditionally* stochastically independent of the income *given* the educational level Z. However, if the occurrence of missing data in X also stochastically depends on income itself over and above Z, then the missing data are NMAR.

This very simple introductory example illustrates that the terminology is anything but self-explanatory and can be even misleading (Schafer & Graham, 2002). For example, the occurrence of missing values is formally considered a random variable, even if the missing data are denoted as *not* missing at random. The definitions of MCAR, MAR, and NMAR are based on unconditional and conditional stochastic (in)dependencies of observed and unobserved variables including the variable *missingness*.

Due to the important implications of Rubin's taxonomy regarding the appropriate handling of missing data, the present chapter starts with a detailed description of missing data theory, which consists of three parts: The first subsection introduces the taxonomy of missing data with the general definitions of MCAR, MAR, and NMAR. The second subsection ("Statistical Inference Based on Incomplete Data") explains the likelihood-based and Bayesian inference in the presence of missing data under MCAR, MAR, and NMAR. The first two parts are summarized and integrated with respect to the implications for the handling of missing data in the third subsection. Note that the second part is mathematically more demanding and is aimed primarily at interested readers who want to gain a deeper understanding.

The problem of missing data is not specific for psychological and educational measurement. Therefore, the introductory part in the section on missing data theory is quite general. However, the use of missing data approaches, such as *full information maximum likelihood* (FIML) *estimation* or *multiple imputation* (MI) will be explained regarding psychometric models and latent variable models – that is, *item response theory* (IRT) and *confirmatory factor analysis* (CFA) models. Despite many alternative methods for handling missing data, this chapter focuses on FIML and MI as current state-of-the-art methods for handling missing data (Schafer & Graham, 2002). An overview of traditional approaches for missing data can be found elsewhere (Enders, 2010, pp. 37–55; Little & Rubin, 2019, pp. 47–84).

FIML is a model-based approach that allows parameter estimation based on incomplete data, whereas imputation-based approaches are two-step procedures. The missing values are filled in with plausible values in a first step based on the *imputation model*. The filled-in data are then used for parameter estimation with standard estimation procedures for complete data in a second step.

Both methods have different advantages and disadvantages. FIML requires correct specification of the substantive model (i.e., the model of researchers' interest, such as an IRT model or a CFA) taking the type of missing data into account. Imputation-based approaches require the appropriate specification of an imputation model considering (a) the type of missing data, and (b) the substantive model, which is applied subsequently to the filled-in datasets.

The major challenge for FIML as well as MI is the correct inclusion of *missing-relevant covariates* in the estimation procedure or the imputation model. These covariates are auxiliary variables, which are not of interest in the substantive model. Ignoring missing-relevant covariates can result in severely biased parameter estimates. However, the substantive model needs to remain unaltered when missing-relevant covariates are included for unbiased parameter estimation with FIML. Hypothetical examples are used in this chapter to illustrate challenges and pitfalls in model specification using FIML and the specification of the imputation model using MI with missing-relevant covariates. In addition, a real data example from a study by Richter et al. (2022) with a commented R script is provided in the supplementary material to this chapter (available at https://osf.io/kt8e5/).

Missing data that are NMAR are also called *nonignorable*, which means that the missing data mechanism must be taken into account for parameter estimation or the imputation of missing values. An outline of approaches for handling nonignorable missing values as the most challenging type of missing data is presented. Finally, an overview of existing computer programs and software packages for handling missing data is given in a separate section at the end of this chapter (see "Statistical Software for Missing Data Problems").

Missing Data Theory

Applications of psychometric models in the frameworks of *classical test theory* (CTT) and IRT aim at inferring characteristics of persons (e.g., personality traits, attitudes, competences) and tests (e.g., item parameters) from observed response behavior of the test takers. In the presence of missing data, the essential question is whether statistical inference based on incomplete observed data systematically differs from inference based on complete data. If not, then the parameter estimation based on incomplete data is unbiased. Unfortunately, this question is purely theoretical, as the complete data are never available. Nevertheless, the question under which conditions statistical inference with incomplete data is unbiased can be answered theoretically. Rubin (1976) introduced a general framework for missing data with a taxonomy of missing data, which has implications for handling missing data in statistical analyses.

Taxonomy of Missing Data

Rubin (1976) introduced a classification system of missing data based on probability theory, as commonly used in statistics. In this theory, the occurrence of missing data is considered as a probabilistic event. Thus, missingness can be represented by random variables that have a probability distribution as well as a joint distribution with other random variables (e.g., manifest variables of the psychometric models and covariates). The stochastic relationship between the variables of the substantive model of interest (e.g., the psychometric model) and the occurrence of missing data serves for defining the types of missingness, according to Rubin (1976). Three sets of random variables are distinguished here. Let $\boldsymbol{X} = X_1, ..., X_I$ be the manifest variables in the measurement model with the potentially multidimensional latent variable θ. Therefore, $X_1, ..., X_I$ codes the item responses of the I items $i = 1, ..., I$ of the test. Missingness in $\mathbf{X}$ is represented by the set of missing indicator variables $\boldsymbol{M} = M_1, ..., M_I$. A nonresponse to item i is indicated by $M_i = 1$, whereas $M_i = 0$ indicates an observed response to item i. Potentially missing-relevant covariates $\boldsymbol{Z} = Z_1, ..., Z_J$ are other variables that were assessed in a study, but which are not part of the measurement model based on $\mathbf{X}$ and are denoted as covariates. Examples are age, sex, socioeconomic status, and scores of other tests or questionnaires.

A covariate Z_j is missing-relevant if missingness $\mathbf{M}$ is stochastically dependent on Z_j. For example, age is a missing-relevant covariate if the number of not-reached items in a time-limited test increases with test takers' age. X can be partitioned $\mathbf{X} = (\mathbf{X}_{obs}, \mathbf{X}_{mis})$ into the observed part $\mathbf{X}_{obs}$ and the missing part $\boldsymbol{X}_{mis}$. All variables X_i with $M_i = 1$ are included in the missing part $\boldsymbol{X}_{mis}$, and $\boldsymbol{X}_{obs}$ consists of all variables X_i with $M_i = 0$. Basically, three different types of missingness – the *missing data mechanisms* – are defined based on the joint distribution of $\boldsymbol{M}, \boldsymbol{X}_{obs}, \boldsymbol{X}_{mis}$, and $\boldsymbol{Z}$: (a) MCAR, (b) MAR, and (c) NMAR.

MCAR is defined as the stochastic independence of the missing indicators from the variables in the assessment, as shown in Equation 1.

$$Pr(\boldsymbol{M} \mid \boldsymbol{X}) = Pr(\boldsymbol{M}). \tag{1}$$

Therefore, the probability of item nonresponses does not depend on the items. Due to the distinction between the manifest variables $\boldsymbol{X}$ of the measurement model of $\boldsymbol{\theta}$ and the covariates $\boldsymbol{Z}$, two MAR definitions can be differentiated. First, ($\boldsymbol{X}_{obs}$)-conditional MAR, which is defined as conditional stochastic independence of missingness from the unobserved variables $\boldsymbol{X}_{mis}$ and the covariates $\boldsymbol{Z}$ given the observed variables $\boldsymbol{X}_{obs}$.

$$Pr(\boldsymbol{M} \mid \boldsymbol{X}_{obs}, \boldsymbol{X}_{mis}, \boldsymbol{Z}) = Pr(\boldsymbol{M} \mid \boldsymbol{X}_{obs}). \tag{2}$$

Therefore, the probability of item nonresponses only depends on observable manifest variables of the measurement model of $\boldsymbol{\theta}$. Second, there is ($\boldsymbol{X}_{obs}$, $\boldsymbol{Z}$)-conditional MAR where missingness is conditionally stochastically independent of the unobserved variables X_{mis} given the observed variables X_{obs} and the covariates Z.

$$Pr(M \mid X_{obs}, X_{mis}, Z) = Pr(M \mid X_{obs}, Z). \tag{3}$$

If missingness in X also depends on the unobserved variables X_{mis}, then the missing data mechanism is NMAR.

$$Pr(M \mid X_{obs}, X_{mis}, Z) \neq Pr(M \mid X_{obs}, Z). \tag{4}$$

Therefore, there remains a conditional stochastic dependence of the missing indicators M and the unobserved part after accounting for the observable variables X_{obs} and Z (Schafer & Graham, 2002).

A note is needed here about the term "missing data mechanism," which is potentially misleading and inconsistently used in the literature (Enders, 2010, p. 5). It is important to recognize that neither a real-world process is meant nor causal relations between the variables M, X_{obs}, X_{mis}, and Z (Schafer & Graham, 2002). Rather, the stochastic relationships among these variables are the defining feature of the missing data mechanisms.

Statistical Inference Based on Incomplete Data

In principle, the problem of missing data cannot be ignored in statistical analyses. Even complete-case analysis is an approach to handle missing values by estimating parameters of substantive models of interest, based on a subsample of cases with complete data. Complete-case analysis does not necessarily lead to biased parameter estimates, but unbiasedness depends on certain assumptions. In other words, the adequacy of complete-case analysis or any other approach for handling missing data depends on the type of missingness (i.e., the missing data mechanism). Rubin (Little & Rubin, 2002; Rubin, 1976) and his colleagues explicated the necessary conditions for unbiased sample-based inference with incomplete data when using *maximum likelihood* (ML) inference as well as Bayesian inference.

To spell out these conditions a bit, more notation is required. There are two parameter vectors – ι_X and ι_M. The vector ι_X refers to the parameters of the substantive model regarding the manifest variables X (e.g., the item and person parameters of an IRT model or a CFA, etc.), while ι_M consists of the parameters of the conditional distribution $Pr(M \mid X_{obs}, X_{mis}, Z)$, which has been used for the definition of the missing data mechanisms (see Equation 1, Equation 2, Equation 3, and Equation 4). Note that the parameters in ι_M of the missingness model are typically nuisance parameters, which are not of interest. For example, a psychometrician who aims at estimating item and person parameters (ι_X) of the Rasch model (Rasch, 1960) is rarely interested in conditional and marginal probabilities of missing patterns (M) due to omitted or not-reached items. However, the psychometrician needs to know whether parameters of the Rasch model can be estimated, using the incomplete data X_{obs} only. If not, the question arises as to whether the inclusion of the covariates Z or even a complex joint model of X_{obs}, Z, and M is required to ensure unbiased parameter estimation of the Rasch model.

Examples of the specification of joint models that include M in addition to X_{obs} and potential missing-relevant covariates Z are outlined in the section "Approaches for Nonignorable Item

Nonresponses," below. The following two sections on likelihood inference and Bayesian inference with missing data are a bit more mathematical and involve calculation rules for unconditional and conditional densities, and the factorization of joint probability density functions. Interested readers can find more information in Kenward and Molenberghs (1998), Kim and Shao (2014), Little and Rubin (2019), Rose (2013), and Schafer (1997).

Likelihood Inference With Missing Data

As noted previously, missingness in $\boldsymbol{X}$ is considered to be a random variable, represented by $\boldsymbol{M}$, which has a joint distribution $f(\boldsymbol{M}, \boldsymbol{X}_{obs}, \boldsymbol{X}_{mis}, \boldsymbol{Z}; \boldsymbol{\iota}_X, \boldsymbol{\iota}_M)$ with observed and missing variables $\boldsymbol{X}_{\text{obs}}$, $\boldsymbol{X}_{\text{mis}}$, and $\boldsymbol{Z}$. In general, a likelihood function $\mathcal{L}(\boldsymbol{X}; \boldsymbol{\iota})$ of any random variable $\boldsymbol{X}$ is defined as the function that is proportional to the probability or density function $f(\boldsymbol{X}; \boldsymbol{\iota})$ of $\boldsymbol{X}$ with the parameter vector $\boldsymbol{\iota}$ (Etz, 2018). Accordingly, ML estimation with missing data and missing-relevant covariates is based on a joint model of $\boldsymbol{M}$, $\boldsymbol{X}_{\text{obs}}$, $\boldsymbol{X}_{\text{mis}}$, and $\boldsymbol{Z}$. The complete data likelihood function $\mathcal{L}(\boldsymbol{M}, \boldsymbol{X}_{obs}, \boldsymbol{X}_{mis}, \boldsymbol{Z}; \boldsymbol{\iota}_X, \boldsymbol{\iota}_M)$, which includes the missing part $\boldsymbol{X}_{\text{mis}}$, is proportional to the joint distribution (Equation 5):

$$\mathcal{L}(\boldsymbol{M}, \boldsymbol{X}_{obs}, \boldsymbol{X}_{mis}, \boldsymbol{Z}; \boldsymbol{\iota}_X, \boldsymbol{\iota}_M) \propto f(\boldsymbol{M}, \boldsymbol{X}_{obs}, \boldsymbol{X}_{mis}, \boldsymbol{Z}; \boldsymbol{\iota}_X, \boldsymbol{\iota}_M). \tag{5}$$

The complete data likelihood is purely theoretical and cannot be directly maximized to estimate parameters $\boldsymbol{\iota}_X$ and $\boldsymbol{\iota}_M$ because of the missing variables $\boldsymbol{X}_{\text{mis}}$. However, Equation 5 is essential for investigating ML estimation in the presence of missing data. The following derivations of likelihood functions in presence of missing data (Equation 6, Equation 7, Equation 8, and Equation 9) are based on general calculation rules for conditional and joint density functions as described in standard text books (e.g., Blitzstein & Hwang, 2019, pp. 312–322). For further information on likelihood-based inference and deriving likelihood functions under different missing data mechanisms, see Kim and Shao (2014), Little and Rubin (2019), Mislevy (2016), Mislevy and Wu (1996), and Seaman et al. (2013).

ML estimation with real data is based on the observed data likelihood function, which is proportional to the integral of complete data likelihood function over the missing part $\boldsymbol{X}_{\text{mis}}$.

$$\mathcal{L}(\boldsymbol{M}, \boldsymbol{X}_{obs}, \boldsymbol{Z}; \boldsymbol{\iota}_X, \boldsymbol{\iota}_M) \propto \int f(\boldsymbol{M}, \boldsymbol{X}_{obs}, \boldsymbol{X}_{mis}, \boldsymbol{Z}; \boldsymbol{\iota}_X, \boldsymbol{\iota}_M) d\boldsymbol{X}_{mis}. \tag{6}$$

The crucial question is under what conditions the ML estimate obtained from maximizing the observed data likelihood is unbiased. To answer this question, the joint distribution in Equation 6 can be factorized, so that

$$\mathcal{L}(\boldsymbol{M}, \boldsymbol{X}_{obs}, \boldsymbol{Z}; \boldsymbol{\iota}_X, \boldsymbol{\iota}_M) \propto \int f(\boldsymbol{X}_{obs}, \boldsymbol{X}_{mis}, \boldsymbol{Z}; \boldsymbol{\iota}_X) Pr(\boldsymbol{M} \mid \boldsymbol{X}_{obs}, \boldsymbol{X}_{mis}, \boldsymbol{Z}; \boldsymbol{\iota}_M) d\boldsymbol{X}_{mis}. \tag{7}$$

The second factor in the integral is the conditional distribution of missingness that served for defining the missing data mechanisms. Inserting the conditional distribution of $\boldsymbol{M}$ under the different missing data mechanisms allows for studying the implications regarding the observed data likelihood. If the missing data is $(\boldsymbol{X}_{\text{obs}}, \boldsymbol{Z})$-conditional MAR, then it follows from Equation 3 that:

$$\mathcal{L}(\boldsymbol{M}, \boldsymbol{X}_{obs}, \boldsymbol{Z}; \iota_X, \iota_M) \propto \int f(\boldsymbol{X}_{obs}, \boldsymbol{X}_{mis}, \boldsymbol{Z}; \iota_X) Pr(\boldsymbol{M} \mid \boldsymbol{X}_{obs}, \boldsymbol{X}_{mis}, \boldsymbol{Z}; \iota_M) d\boldsymbol{X}_{mis}$$

$$\propto Pr(\boldsymbol{M} \mid \boldsymbol{X}_{obs}, \boldsymbol{Z}; \iota_M) \int f(\boldsymbol{X}_{obs}, \boldsymbol{X}_{mis}, \boldsymbol{Z}; \iota_X)\, d\boldsymbol{X}_{mis}. \tag{8}$$

As can be moved out of the integral over the missing part, the likelihood consists of two independent factors with different sets of parameters, which can be maximized independently. Therefore, the parameters ι_X of the psychometric model can be estimated without bias by maximizing the observed data likelihood of $\boldsymbol{X}_{\text{obs}}$ and $\boldsymbol{Z}$ only, which is proportional to the second factor in Equation 8.

$$\mathcal{L}(\boldsymbol{X}_{obs}, \boldsymbol{Z}; \iota_X) \propto \int f(\boldsymbol{X}_{obs}, \boldsymbol{X}_{mis}, \boldsymbol{Z}; \iota_X) d\boldsymbol{X}_{mis}. \tag{9}$$

Therefore, likelihood-based estimation of ι_X based on a model of the observed variables $\boldsymbol{X}_{\text{obs}}$ and $\boldsymbol{Z}$ is unbiased if the missing data mechanism is $(\boldsymbol{X}_{\text{obs}}, \boldsymbol{Z})$-conditional MAR. No joint model for missingness $\boldsymbol{M}$ and $(\boldsymbol{X}_{\text{obs}}, \boldsymbol{Z})$ is required. The same is true if the item nonresponses are $(\boldsymbol{X}_{\text{obs}})$-conditional MAR or MCAR because the factorization of the observed data likelihood according to Equation 9 also works. Moreover, as missingness is stochastically independent of $\boldsymbol{Z}$ given $\boldsymbol{X}_{\text{obs}}$, unbiased estimation of ι_X is even valid when missing-relevant covariates $\boldsymbol{Z}$ are not taken into account. Therefore, maximizing the observed data likelihood $\mathcal{L}(\boldsymbol{X}_{\text{obs}}; \iota_X)$ of the manifest variables $\boldsymbol{X}_{\text{obs}}$ of the substantive model allows for an unbiased ML estimation.

Bayesian Inference With Missing Data

A general introduction to Bayesian statistics is far beyond the scope of this chapter. Interested readers are referred to Gelman et al. (2013), Jackman (2009), and Levy and Mislevy (2017). At this point, it is only important to know that (a) unknown parameters are considered random variables in Bayesian statistics, and (b) all statistical inference about the unknown parameters rests upon the *posterior distribution* $f(\iota_X \mid \boldsymbol{M}, \boldsymbol{X}_{\text{obs}}, \boldsymbol{Z})$ of the unknown parameters given the observed variables. The expected values, medians or modes of posterior distributions (i.e., expected a posteriori, median a posteriori, or maximum a posteriori) serve as point estimates in Bayesian analyses. Standard deviations, credibility intervals, or highest density regions of posterior distributions quantify the uncertainty of the statistical inference given the data and the prior knowledge or beliefs. All Bayesian analyses require such prior information, which needs to be formally represented by the *prior distributions* of the model parameters. Prior distributions specify what values or ranges of values in the parameter space are assumed more or less likely before the data analysis. The prior beliefs or knowledge can impact the posterior distribution and the statistical inference more or less strongly, depending on the specification of the prior distribution by the statistician (i.e., strongly vs. weakly informative prior distributions). It should be noted that the appropriate choice of prior distributions for different parameters in different models is one of the arts in Bayesian data analysis. Fortunately, there is a lot of guidance on that issue in the literature (Gelman et al., 2013; Jackman, 2009).

In multiparameter models, a joint prior distribution for all model parameters needs to be specified. In Bayesian inference with missing values, missingness represented by $\boldsymbol{M}$ must be taken into account, just as with likelihood inference. A fully Bayesian psychometric model of

$\boldsymbol{X}_{\text{obs}}$, $\boldsymbol{Z}$, and $\boldsymbol{M}$ with incomplete data requires a joint prior distribution $f(\iota_X, \iota_M)$, which is part of the joint posterior distribution $f(\iota_X, \iota_M \mid \boldsymbol{M}, \boldsymbol{X}_{\text{obs}}, \boldsymbol{Z})$ given by Equation 10:

$$f(\iota_X, \iota_M \mid \boldsymbol{M}, \boldsymbol{X}_{obs}, \boldsymbol{Z}) = \frac{\int f(\boldsymbol{M}, \boldsymbol{X}_{obs}, \boldsymbol{X}_{mis}, \boldsymbol{Z}; \iota_X, \iota_M) f(\iota_X, \iota_M) d\boldsymbol{X}_{mis}}{\iiint f(\boldsymbol{M}, \boldsymbol{X}_{obs}, \boldsymbol{X}_{mis}, \boldsymbol{Z}; \iota_X, \iota_M) f(\iota_X, \iota_M) d\boldsymbol{X}_{mis} d\iota_M d\iota_X}$$

$$= \frac{\int f(\boldsymbol{X}_{obs}, \boldsymbol{X}_{mis}, \boldsymbol{Z}; \iota_X) Pr(\boldsymbol{M} \mid \boldsymbol{X}_{obs}, \boldsymbol{X}_{mis}, \boldsymbol{Z}; \iota_M) f(\iota_X, \iota_M) d\boldsymbol{X}_{mis}}{\iiint f(\boldsymbol{X}_{obs}, \boldsymbol{X}_{mis}, \boldsymbol{Z}; \iota_X) Pr(\boldsymbol{M} \mid \boldsymbol{X}_{obs}, \boldsymbol{X}_{mis}, \boldsymbol{Z}; \iota_M) f(\iota_X, \iota_M) d\boldsymbol{X}_{mis} d\iota_X d\iota_M}. \tag{10}$$

As in the case of ML inference, the question is which conditions allow for a less complex model based on ($\boldsymbol{X}_{\text{obs}}$, $\boldsymbol{Z}$) or $\boldsymbol{X}_{\text{obs}}$ without $\boldsymbol{M}$ to yield unbiased Bayesian inference regarding ι_X. In other words, when is the posterior distribution $f(\iota_X \mid \boldsymbol{X}_{\text{obs}}, \boldsymbol{Z})$ sufficient for Bayesian parameter estimation of the substantive model?

The following derivations of Equation 11 and Equation 12 are based on the proof of Theorem 2 given by Seaman et al. (2013, p. 297). The posterior distribution $f(\iota_X \mid \boldsymbol{X}_{\text{obs}}, \boldsymbol{Z})$ can be derived from Equation 10 by averaging over the missing part $\boldsymbol{X}_{\text{mis}}$ and the parameters ι_M of missingness. If the missing data mechanism is ($\boldsymbol{X}_{\text{obs}}$, $\boldsymbol{Z}$)-conditional MAR, then

$$f(\iota_X \mid \boldsymbol{M}, \boldsymbol{X}_{obs}, \boldsymbol{Z}) = \frac{\iint f(\boldsymbol{M}, \boldsymbol{X}_{obs}, \boldsymbol{X}_{mis}\, \boldsymbol{Z}; \iota_X, \iota_M) f(\iota_X, \iota_M) d\boldsymbol{X}_{mis} d\iota_M}{\iiint f(\boldsymbol{M}, \boldsymbol{X}_{obs}, \boldsymbol{X}_{mis}\, \boldsymbol{Z}; \iota_X, \iota_M) f(\iota_X, \iota_M) d\boldsymbol{X}_{mis} d\iota_M d\iota_X}$$

$$= \frac{\iint f(\boldsymbol{X}_{obs}, \boldsymbol{X}_{mis}, \boldsymbol{Z}; \iota_X) Pr(\boldsymbol{M} \mid \boldsymbol{X}_{obs}, \boldsymbol{X}_{mis}, \boldsymbol{Z}; \iota_M) f(\iota_X, \iota_M) d\boldsymbol{X}_{mis} d\iota_M}{\iiint f(\boldsymbol{X}_{obs}, \boldsymbol{X}_{mis}, \boldsymbol{Z}; \iota_X) Pr(\boldsymbol{M} \mid \boldsymbol{X}_{obs}, \boldsymbol{X}_{mis}, \boldsymbol{Z}; \iota_M) f(\iota_X, \iota_M) d\boldsymbol{X}_{mis} d\iota_X d\iota_M}. \tag{11}$$

If and only if the parameter vectors ι_X and ι_M are a priori independent, then the joint prior distribution $f(\iota_X, \iota_M)$ can be written as simple product $f(\iota_X)f(\iota_M)$. In this case the parameter spaces of ι_X and ι_M are a Cartesian product, and there are no a priori ties between both sets of parameters. Under this condition Equation 11 can be simplified:

$$f(\iota_X \mid \boldsymbol{M}, \boldsymbol{X}_{obs}, \boldsymbol{Z}) = \frac{\int Pr(\boldsymbol{M} \mid \boldsymbol{X}_{obs}, \boldsymbol{Z}; \iota_M) f(\iota_M) d\iota_M \int f(\boldsymbol{X}_{obs}, \boldsymbol{X}_{mis}, \boldsymbol{Z}; \iota_X) f(\iota_X) d\boldsymbol{X}_{mis}}{\int Pr(\boldsymbol{M} \mid \boldsymbol{X}_{obs}, \boldsymbol{Z}; \iota_M) f(\iota_M)\, d\iota_M \iint f(\boldsymbol{X}_{obs}, \boldsymbol{X}_{mis}, \boldsymbol{Z}; \iota_X) f(\iota_X) d\boldsymbol{X}_{mis} d\iota_X}$$

$$= \frac{\int f(\boldsymbol{X}_{obs}, \boldsymbol{X}_{mis}, \boldsymbol{Z}; \iota_X) f(\iota_X) d\boldsymbol{X}_{mis}}{\iint f(\boldsymbol{X}_{obs}, \boldsymbol{X}_{mis}, \boldsymbol{Z}; \iota_X) f(\iota_X) d\boldsymbol{X}_{mis} d\iota_X}$$

$$= \frac{\mathcal{L}(\boldsymbol{X}_{obs}, \boldsymbol{Z}; \iota_X) f(\iota_X)}{f(\boldsymbol{X}_{obs}, \boldsymbol{Z})}. \tag{12}$$

The numerator of Equation 12 is simply the observed data likelihood weighted by the prior distribution $f(\iota_X)$ of ι_X. The denominator of Equation 12 is the marginal distribution $f(\boldsymbol{X}_{\text{obs}}, \boldsymbol{Z})$ of the observed variables. For any realized data ($\boldsymbol{X}_{\text{obs}} = \boldsymbol{x}_{\text{obs}}$, $\boldsymbol{Z} = \boldsymbol{z}$) the denominator $f(\boldsymbol{X}_{\text{obs}} = \boldsymbol{x}_{\text{obs}}, \boldsymbol{Z} = \boldsymbol{z})$ is a normalizing constant which ensures that $f(\iota_X \mid \boldsymbol{M}, \boldsymbol{X}_{\text{obs}}, \boldsymbol{Z})$ is a proper probability density or probability mass function. The key message of Equation 12 is that the posterior distribution of the model parameters ι_X given the observed data $\boldsymbol{X}_{\text{obs}}$ and $\boldsymbol{Z}$ is independent of $\boldsymbol{M}$. Therefore, if (a) the missing data mechanism is ($\boldsymbol{X}_{\text{obs}}$, $\boldsymbol{Z}$)-conditional MAR, and (b) the parameters ι_X and ι_M are a priori independent, then $f(\iota_X \mid \boldsymbol{M}, \boldsymbol{X}_{\text{obs}}, \boldsymbol{Z}) = f(\iota_X \mid \boldsymbol{X}_{\text{obs}}, \boldsymbol{Z})$, and unbiased Bayesian inference does not require a complex model including $\boldsymbol{M}$.

Theoretical Implications for Handling Missing Data

The essential message of the derivations shown by Equations 8–12 is that the different missing data mechanisms have different implications regarding how to handle missing values to ensure valid statistical inference. In summary, if the missing data mechanism is MCAR or MAR – for example, ($\boldsymbol{X}_{\text{obs}}$, $\boldsymbol{Z}$)-conditional or ($\boldsymbol{X}_{\text{obs}}$)-conditional MAR, then the missing data are *ignorable*, which means $\boldsymbol{M}$ can be ignored for parameter estimation of $\iota_{\boldsymbol{X}}$ of the substantive model. If the missing data mechanism is ($\boldsymbol{X}_{\text{obs}}$, $\boldsymbol{Z}$)-conditional MAR, then the missingness depends on the covariates $\boldsymbol{Z}$ over and above the observed part $\boldsymbol{X}_{\text{obs}}$. Therefore, the covariate $\boldsymbol{Z}$ is missing-relevant and cannot be ignored when estimating $\iota_{\boldsymbol{X}}$ even if $\boldsymbol{Z}$ is not of interest in the substantive model. The covariates in $\boldsymbol{Z}$ are then *missing-relevant auxiliary variables.*

How to take auxiliary variables into account in likelihood-based inference and in *imputation methods* (IMs) will be discussed in the remainder of this chapter. If the missing data are ($\boldsymbol{X}_{\text{obs}}$)-conditional MAR, then $\boldsymbol{M}$ and $\boldsymbol{Z}$ can be ignored for estimation of $\iota_{\boldsymbol{X}}$ of the substantive model. Finally, missing data that are MCAR imply that missingness is stochastically independent of all variables $\boldsymbol{X}$. This implies that the realized observed data within each missing pattern $\boldsymbol{M} = \boldsymbol{m}$ are random draws from the distribution of $\boldsymbol{X}$. This holds also true for the cases with complete data (i.e., $\boldsymbol{M} = \boldsymbol{0}$), implying that a *complete-case analysis* (i.e., *listwise deletion*) is sufficient for unbiased parameter estimation. Note the difference to missing data that are ($\boldsymbol{X}_{\text{obs}}$)-conditional MAR instead of MCAR. Listwise deletion can lead to severely biased parameter estimates if the missing data mechanism is ($\boldsymbol{X}_{\text{obs}}$)-conditional or ($\boldsymbol{X}_{\text{obs}}$, $\boldsymbol{Z}$)-conditional MAR.

Unbiased statistical inference under both MAR conditions requires the use of the full information of $\boldsymbol{X}_{\text{obs}}$ or ($\boldsymbol{X}_{\text{obs}}$, $\boldsymbol{Z}$) for parameter estimation, instead of using only limited information of complete cases only. Again, listwise deletion is often the only option for many standard estimation techniques, such as OLS regressions, principal component or principal axis analysis, etc., which require that the missing data mechanism is MCAR. Whenever this strict assumption does not hold true, appropriate statistical methods such as FIML or IMs are required for unbiased parameter estimation.

Study Design and Missing Data

Missing data theory implies that the missing data mechanism needs to be known to decide how to manage item nonresponses. Unfortunately, the missing data mechanism is often unknown and could only be verified if the missing part $\boldsymbol{X}_{\text{mis}}$ was available. That is never the case! However, there are study designs where the missing data are under the researchers' control. What is referred to as *planned missing data* by design needs to be distinguished from unintentional missing data due to omitted, not-reached, or not-codable item responses. The missing data mechanism of planned missing data due to design is known before any data are collected. Either the study design ensures that the planned missing data are MCAR, or the conditions and variables that are associated with missing data are known, and can be taken into account in the later statistical analysis.

Planned Missing Data

Planned missing data are a viable choice in extensive assessments using many measurement instruments (e.g., test and questionnaires) to reduce individual burden of study participants (Rhemtulla & Hancock, 2016). Examples are cross-sectional and longitudinal *three-form designs* (Graham et al., 2001, 2006), *matrix designs* (Kaplan & Su, 2016; Mislevy et al., 1992), and *cohort sequential designs* (Prinzie & Onghena, 2005). In three-form designs and matrix sampling designs, there are different test forms with only subsets of items, which are randomly assigned to participants. The missing data mechanism is MCAR due to randomization.

If the assignment of test forms depends on known variables $\boldsymbol{Z}$, the missing data mechanism is ($\boldsymbol{Z}$)-conditional MAR. For example, let there be three forms of a scholastic achievement test of different difficulty (e.g., basic, intermediate, and advanced). Each test form consists of a different but overlapping subset of items. The students' stratified average grade (Z) is used for assigning the test forms to students. The basic test is assigned to the lower stratum, the intermediate test to the middle stratum, and the difficult test is assigned to the upper stratum. The resulting missing data due to not-administered items in the different test forms only depend on the stratified averaged grade. Therefore, an appropriate psychometric analysis of the scholastic school test requires inclusion of the stratified average grade as a missing-relevant auxiliary variable.

The missing data mechanism is ($\boldsymbol{X}_{\text{obs}}$)-conditional MAR, if the occurrence of missing data only depends on the observed variables that constitute the measurement model. This is the case in *computerized adaptive testing* (CAT) procedures based on IRT models (Mislevy & Wu, 1996). In CAT, the test taker's value on the latent variable is repeatedly reestimated after each item response. The test starts with a fixed or randomly selected item from the item pool. The subsequent items $i + 1$ are selected based on the response to the previous items 1 to i, in order to maximize the test information function (i.e., to minimize the standard error). Therefore, the selection of items and the missing pattern only depends on the test taker's response behavior.

Branched tests and multistage tests are further test designs with missing data that are ($\boldsymbol{X}_{\text{obs}}$)-conditional MAR. Psychometric analysis of $\boldsymbol{X}_{\text{obs}}$ is sufficient for unbiased parameter estimation in this case. For example, reestimation of item parameters of an item pool based on the item responses obtained from CAT using FIML is unbiased, even if the proportion of missing values is quite large. However, sometimes the starting item in CAT or multistage tests is not randomly selected but depends on prior information such as age, educational achievement, and other demographic variables. The latter are then also missing-relevant auxiliary variables $\boldsymbol{Z}$ and the missing data mechanism is ($\boldsymbol{Z}$, $\boldsymbol{X}_{\text{obs}}$)-conditional MAR, implying that $\boldsymbol{Z}$ needs to be considered in reestimating the item parameters of the item pool.

Unintentional Missing Data

Planned missing data by design are under the researcher's control, whereas unintentional or unplanned missing data are not. Any assumption of an ignorable missing data mechanism underlying unintentional missing data is an assumption that cannot be verified. At least there is a test of the null hypothesis that missing data are MCAR, which allows for empirical falsification (not verification!) of the MCAR assumption (Little, 1988). However, the missing data mechanism may or may not be ignorable when the MCAR assumption does not hold true. Therefore, the value of the MCAR test is limited. The assumption of an ignorable missing data mechanism is tempting, as the statistical modeling of nonignorable missing data is much more challenging. However, its plausibility and tenability should be critically considered. For example, if test takers of an intelligence test omit items they cannot solve, the item nonresponses are potentially nonignorable. This is also the case if unmeasured variables exist that are stochastically related to missingness as well as to the variables $\boldsymbol{X}$.

Statistical inference with missing data that are NMAR requires a joint model of $\boldsymbol{X}_{obs}$ and $\boldsymbol{M}$. These models allow for parameter estimation without the MCAR or MAR assumptions, but they have the disadvantage of relying on other relatively strict assumptions. Therefore, it is often recommended to use an *inclusive analysis strategy,* where as many potentially missing-relevant auxiliary variables as possible are included to make the MAR assumption tenable (Collins et al., 2001; Schafer & Graham, 2002). Using the inclusive analysis strategy, in conjunction with models for ignorable missing data, should be preferred to more complex models for nonignorable missing data, even if the MAR assumption is questionable. Indeed, the bias due to violation of the MAR assumptions can be smaller than the bias due to the violated assumptions of models for nonignorable missing data.

However, models for nonignorable missing data should always be considered as alternatives and play an important role for sensitivity analysis. A short review of statistical methods for nonignorable missing data is given below in the section "Approaches for Nonignorable Item Nonresponses" FIML and MI are the most popular methods for handling missing data. There is a growing number of statistical software programs with user friendly implementations for these methods. Therefore, both approaches will be explained in more detail in the following two sections.

FIML Estimation

ML estimation is a very general approach for estimating parameters of a wide range of statistical models, including latent variable models of CTT and IRT models and their extensions. In a nutshell, ML estimation of a parameter vector $\boldsymbol{\iota}_X$ of a statistical model of the variables $\boldsymbol{X} = X_1, ..., X_I$ (i.e., the substantive model) requires maximization of the likelihood function $L(\boldsymbol{X}; \boldsymbol{\iota}_X)$, which is the product shown in Equation 13

$$\mathcal{L}(\boldsymbol{X}; \boldsymbol{\iota}_X) = \prod_{n=1}^{N} f(\boldsymbol{X}_n; \boldsymbol{\iota}_X), \tag{13}$$

with $f(\boldsymbol{X}_n; \boldsymbol{\iota}_X)$ as the parametric density function of the variables $\boldsymbol{X}$ of the n-th observation under the statistical model indexed by $\boldsymbol{\iota}_X$. The ML estimator $\hat{\boldsymbol{\iota}}_X$ is the value of the parameter space that maximizes the likelihood function. Note that the log-likelihood function $\ell(\boldsymbol{X}; \boldsymbol{\iota}_X) = \ln \mathcal{L}(\boldsymbol{X}; \boldsymbol{\iota}_X)$ is maximized instead of $\mathcal{L}(\boldsymbol{X}; \boldsymbol{\iota}_X)$, due to better mathematical properties. In the case of ignorable missing data, either the observed log-likelihood $\ell(\boldsymbol{X}_{obs}; \boldsymbol{\iota}_X)$ can be maximized if the missing data mechanism is ($\boldsymbol{X}_{obs}$)-conditional MAR, or $\ell(\boldsymbol{X}_{obs}, \boldsymbol{Z}; \boldsymbol{\iota}_X)$ of a joint model of $\boldsymbol{X}_{obs}$ and $\boldsymbol{Z}$ needs to be maximized if the missing data mechanism is ($\boldsymbol{Z}, \boldsymbol{X}_{obs}$)-conditional MAR (see the section "Likelihood Inference With Missing Data"). The specific mathematical formulation of the log-likelihood functions $\ell(\boldsymbol{X}; \iota_X)$ or $\ell(\boldsymbol{X_{obs}}; \iota_X)$ depends on the respective statistical model and looks quite different for *structural equation model* (SEM) versus IRT models.

SEM-based psychometric models are based on variance-covariance matrices and mean vectors of manifest variables. IRT models are based on response pattern probabilities. Consequently, the inclusion of missing-relevant auxiliary variables $\boldsymbol{Z}$ in a joint model of $\boldsymbol{X_{obs}}$ and $\boldsymbol{Z}$ for parameter estimation based on $\ell(\boldsymbol{X_{obs}}, \boldsymbol{Z}; \iota_X)$ is also different for SEM and IRT models.

Estimating Parameters of SEM With FIML

Let there be the variance-covariance matrix $\boldsymbol{\Sigma_X}$ and the mean vector $\boldsymbol{\mu_X}$ of continuous manifest variables $\boldsymbol{X} = X_1, ..., X_I$ of the substantive model. In absence of any missing data, the log-likelihood function of observed variables $\boldsymbol{X}$ in SEM is shown in Equation 14:

$$\ell(\boldsymbol{X}; \iota_X) = -\frac{N}{2}\Big(c\ln(2\pi) + \ln|\boldsymbol{\Sigma}(\iota_X)| + tr\big[\boldsymbol{\Sigma_X}\boldsymbol{\Sigma}^{-1}(\iota_X)\big] + [\boldsymbol{\mu_X} - \boldsymbol{\mu}(\iota_X)]^T\boldsymbol{\Sigma}^{-1}(\iota_X)[\boldsymbol{\mu_X} - \boldsymbol{\mu}(\iota_X)]\Big), \quad (14)$$

with $\boldsymbol{\Sigma}(\iota_X)$ and $\boldsymbol{\mu}(\iota_X)$ as model-implied variance-covariance matrix and mean vector of $\boldsymbol{X}$ (Rosseel, 2021). The constant c is the number of variables $X_1, ..., X_I$ in the model.

However, if there are missing data, the observed data likelihood is the sum of the individual likelihood functions of each case $n = 1, ..., N$ (Enders, 2001; Peters & Enders, 2002; Equation 15):

$$\ell(\boldsymbol{X_{obs}}; \iota_X) = \sum_{n=1}^{N} \underbrace{c_n - \frac{1}{2}\Big(\ln|\boldsymbol{\Sigma}_n(\iota_X)| + \big[\boldsymbol{X}_{n,obs} - \boldsymbol{\mu}_n(\iota_X)\big]\boldsymbol{\Sigma}_n^{-1}(\iota_X)\big[\boldsymbol{X}_{n,obs} - \boldsymbol{\mu}_n(\iota_X)\big]\Big)}_{\ell_n(\boldsymbol{X}_{n,obs};\iota_X)}, \quad (15)$$

Note that the length of the vectors $\boldsymbol{X}_{n,obs}$ and and $\boldsymbol{\mu}_n(\iota_X)$ the dimensions of $\boldsymbol{\Sigma}_n(\iota_X)$ in the individual likelihood functions $\ell_n(\boldsymbol{X}_{n,obs}; \iota_X)$ depend on the number of missing values. The matrix- and vector-elements of that refer to missing variables that are omitted. If case n has r missing values, then $\boldsymbol{X}_{n,obs}$ and $\boldsymbol{\mu}_n(\iota_X)$ are $(I - r) \times 1$ vectors $\boldsymbol{\Sigma}_n(\iota_X)$ and is a $(I - r) \times (I - r)$ matrix. The term c_n is a constant, which depends on the number of observed variables of case n. Fortunately, FIML estimation based on the observed data log-likelihood $\ell(\boldsymbol{X_{obs}}; \iota_X)$ is unbiased when the missing data mechanism is MCAR or ($\boldsymbol{X}_{obs}$)-conditional MAR. The model specification of SEM is identical to the case of complete data. However, if the missing data mechanism is ($\boldsymbol{Z}$, $\boldsymbol{X}_{obs}$)-conditional MAR, the auxiliary variables $\boldsymbol{Z}$ need to be included in a joint model of $\boldsymbol{X_{obs}}$ and $\boldsymbol{Z}$. In this case, parameter estimation is based on maximizing the log-likelihood function $\ell(\boldsymbol{X_{obs}}, \boldsymbol{Z}; \iota_X)$, which is

$$\ell(\boldsymbol{X}_{obs,Z}; \iota_{XZ}) = \sum_{n=1}^{N} \underbrace{c_n - \frac{1}{2}\Big(\ln|\boldsymbol{\Sigma}_n(\iota_{XZ})| + [(\boldsymbol{X}_{obs}, \boldsymbol{Z})_n - \boldsymbol{\mu}_n(\iota_{XZ})]\boldsymbol{\Sigma}_n^{-1}(\iota_{XZ})[(\boldsymbol{X}_{obs}, \boldsymbol{Z})_n - \boldsymbol{\mu}_n(\iota_{XZ})]\Big)}_{\ell_n(\boldsymbol{X}_{n,obs}, \boldsymbol{Z}; \iota_{XZ})}. \quad (16)$$

Note that Equation 16 is basically identical to Equation 15. The only difference is that observed variables of observation n also includes the auxiliary variables $\boldsymbol{Z}$, whose information regarding variables $\boldsymbol{X}$ of the substantive model is incorporated by the joint model-implied variance-covariance matrices $\boldsymbol{\Sigma}_n(\boldsymbol{\iota}_{XZ})$.

However, the specification of a joint model of $\boldsymbol{X}_{obs}$ and the auxiliary $\boldsymbol{Z}$ needs to be done cautiously, because the substantive model must not be altered by the inclusion of $\boldsymbol{Z}$. The substantive model needs to be preserved as a part of the joint model. Two approaches are commonly used. First, the auxiliary variables are included as additional dependent variables in the *extra dependent variable* (extra DV) model. Second, all auxiliary variables are allowed to correlate with all manifest variables or their residuals in the *saturated correlates model* (Enders, 2008; Graham, 2003). In the extra DV model (see Figure 9.1, Joint Model A), all auxiliary variables are (a) regressed on all manifest exogenous variables (i.e., variables that are not predicted by other variables in the model), (b) correlated with the residuals of all manifest endogenous variables (i.e., variables that are predicted by other variables in the model), and (c) correlated among each other. This specification ensures that no unintended restrictions regarding the substantive model are introduced by incorporating $\boldsymbol{Z}$ in the joint model.

In latent variable models, such a CFA models (see Figure 9.1, Joint Model B), missing-relevant covariates $\boldsymbol{Z}$ can be easily included with the saturated correlates model. In this model, all auxiliary variables are (a) correlated with all residuals of all manifest endogenous variables in the measurement model and (b) correlated among each other. Note that the degrees of freedom remain equal to that of the substantive model. However, evaluation of model fit must be done with some caution. Incremental fit indices, such as the comparative fit index (CFI), the normed fit index (NFI), and the Tucker-Lewis Index (TLI), are based on model comparisons of the fitted model with the baseline model. However, the baseline model of the joint model with the auxiliary variables is inappropriate for evaluating model fit of the substantive model only. An alternative baseline model must be calculated instead, which remains saturated regarding the auxiliary variables (Graham, 2003; Graham & Coffman, 2012). The R package *semTools* (Jorgensen et al., 2022) provides functions that automate the specification of a joint model of auxiliary variables and target variables of the substantive model and that compute correct incremental fit measures.

It is important to note that the described models are linear models for continuous manifest variables. In recent years, SEM for dichotomous and ordered categorical variables has become

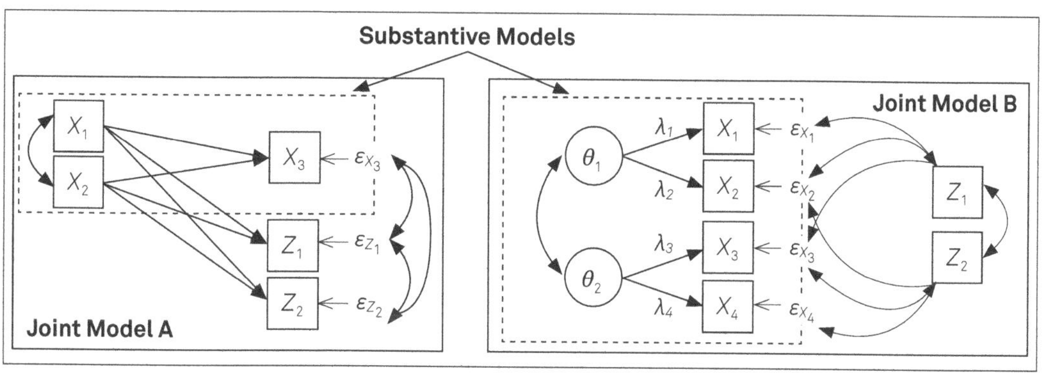

Figure 9.1 Including missing-relevant auxiliary variables into structural equation modeling (SEM). According to the extra dependent variable (DV) model (Joint Model A, left) and the saturated correlates model (Joint Model B, right).

popular for estimating latent variable models with dichotomous or ordinal indicator variables. Unweighted and weighted least square estimators instead of ML estimators are commonly used for parameter estimation based on tetrachoric, polychoric, and polyserial correlations. At the time of writing, there is no FIML-equivalent (un)weighted least square estimator for SEM with categorical variables. The only estimator which is promising for SEM with categorical variables under ignorable missingness is pairwise maximum likelihood estimation (PML estimation; Katsikatsou et al., 2012). PML estimation is implemented in the R package *lavaan* (Rosseel, 2012). However, the current implementation only allows for including categorical variables.

Continuous missing-relevant auxiliary variables need to be categorized before they can be considered in a joint model using PML. Alternatively, the item nonresponses can be handled with MI. (Un)weighted least square estimators for SEM with categorical variables can then be used for parameter estimation with the multiply imputed datasets.

Estimating Parameters of IRT Models

Different ML estimators have been developed for estimating item and person parameters of unidimensional and multidimensional, one, two, and more parameter IRT models. *Joint maximum likelihood* (JML) estimation is used for simultaneous item and person parameter estimation (Birnbaum, 1968). *Conditional maximum likelihood* (CML) estimation serves for item parameter estimation of dichotomous and ordinal Rasch models (Birnbaum, 1968). *Marginal ML* (MML) estimation allows for concurrent estimation of item parameters and parameters of the distribution of the unidimensional or multidimensional latent variable $\boldsymbol{\theta}$ (Bock & Aitkin, 1981). Furthermore, MML can be extended by including missing-relevant covariates $\boldsymbol{Z}$.

The observed data likelihood of item responses to a measurement instrument with I categorical items X_i with $i = 1, ..., I$ is the product of the N observed response patterns (Baker & Kim, 2004; De Ayala, 2013; Equation 17):

$$\mathcal{L}(\boldsymbol{X}_{\boldsymbol{obs}}; \boldsymbol{\iota}_{\boldsymbol{X}}) = \prod_{n=1}^{N} P\left(\boldsymbol{X}_{\boldsymbol{n,obs}} = \boldsymbol{x}_{\boldsymbol{n,obs}} \mid \boldsymbol{\theta}_n; \boldsymbol{\iota}_{\boldsymbol{X}}\right). \tag{17}$$

$\boldsymbol{X}_{\boldsymbol{n,obs}} = \boldsymbol{x}_{\boldsymbol{n,obs}}$ is the observed response pattern of case n. Under the assumption of local stochastic independence (e.g., $P(X_i = x_i \mid X_1, ..., X_{i-1}, X_{i+1}, ..., X_I, \boldsymbol{\theta}) = P(X_i = x_i \mid \boldsymbol{\theta})$) for all items $i = 1,..., I$, Equation 17 can be rewritten as (Rose, 2013, p. 166):

$$\mathcal{L}(\boldsymbol{X}_{\boldsymbol{obs}}; \boldsymbol{\iota}_{\boldsymbol{X}}) = \prod_{n=1}^{N} \prod_{i=1}^{I} P(X_{ni} = x_{ni} \mid \boldsymbol{\theta}_n; \boldsymbol{\iota}_{\boldsymbol{X}})^{1-m_{ni}}. \tag{18}$$

The term $P(X_{ni} = x_{ni} \mid \boldsymbol{\theta}_n; \boldsymbol{\iota}_{\boldsymbol{X}})$ refers to the model-based conditional probability that case n answers to item i in the response category x_{ni}. Due to the exponent $(1 - m_{ni})$ in Equation 18, only the observed item responses ($m_{ni} = 0$) are included, whereas item nonresponses ($m_{ni} = 1$) do not contribute to $\mathcal{L}(\boldsymbol{X}_{\boldsymbol{obs}}, \boldsymbol{\iota}_{\boldsymbol{X}})$. Item and person parameters (i.e., $\boldsymbol{\iota}_{\boldsymbol{X}}$ and $\boldsymbol{\theta}_n$) can be estimated simultaneously by maximizing the observed data likelihood with respect to the unknown parameters (i.e., JML). No missing-related bias is introduced with JML estimation in the case of missing data that are MCAR or ($\boldsymbol{X_{obs}}$)-conditional MAR.

CML estimation is used for item parameter estimation in the family of Rasch models for dichotomous and ordinal variables (Andersen, 1972). In these models, the sum score $T = \sum_{i=1}^{I} X_i$ is a sufficient statistic with respect to the latent variable $\boldsymbol{\theta}$. Therefore, the person parameters (e.g., the individual values of $\boldsymbol{\theta}$) do not need to be estimated jointly with the item parameters. However, the sufficiency of the sum score holds only true for a fixed set of items. In the case of item nonresponses, test takers answer to a different set of items defined by the missing pattern $\boldsymbol{M} = \boldsymbol{m}$. Therefore, the sum score is only a sufficient statistic within each missing pattern $\boldsymbol{m}$. Therefore, the conditional observed data likelihood must be written as the product of the conditional likelihood functions $\mathcal{L}_{CML}(\boldsymbol{X_{obs}} | \boldsymbol{M} = \boldsymbol{m}; \iota_X)$ for each observed missing pattern $\boldsymbol{M}=\boldsymbol{m}$ (Mair & Hatzinger, 2007):

$$\mathcal{L}_{CML}(\boldsymbol{X_{obs}}; \iota_X) = \prod_{m} \underbrace{\frac{\exp\left[\sum_i\left(\beta_i \sum_{n=1}^{N_m} x_{xi}\right)\right]}{\prod_T \gamma_{Tm}{}^{N_{Tm}}}}_{\mathcal{L}_{CML}(\boldsymbol{X_{obs}}|\boldsymbol{M}=\boldsymbol{m};\iota_X)}. \tag{19}$$

N_m is the number of cases with missing pattern $\boldsymbol{m}$, and γ_{Tm} denotes the elementary symmetric function for a given total score T under the missing pattern $\boldsymbol{m}$. CML-based item parameter estimates obtained by maximizing Equation 19 are unbiased if the missing data are ($\boldsymbol{X_{obs}}$)-conditional MAR.

Neither JML nor CML allows one to consider missing-relevant covariates $\boldsymbol{Z}$. Therefore, parameter estimates are potentially biased if the item nonresponses are ($\boldsymbol{Z}, \boldsymbol{X_{obs}}$)-conditional MAR. MML estimation can be used alternatively in this situation (Bock & Aitkin, 1981). In general, MML estimation allows for estimating item parameters and parameters of a structural model (i.e., parameters of the distribution of $\boldsymbol{\theta}$, or a joint distribution of $\boldsymbol{\theta}$ and covariates $\boldsymbol{Z}$). The estimation requires numerical integration over the unconditional or $\boldsymbol{Z}$-conditional distribution of latent variables $\boldsymbol{\theta}$. The observed data likelihood of the MML estimator with missing-relevant covariates $\boldsymbol{Z}$ can be written as (Rose, 2013, p. 168):

$$\mathcal{L}(\boldsymbol{X_{obs}} \mid \boldsymbol{Z}; \iota_X) = \prod_{n=1}^{N} \int \prod_{i=1}^{I} P(X_{ni} = x_{ni} \mid \boldsymbol{\theta}_n; \iota_X)^{1-m_{ni}} f(\boldsymbol{\theta}_n \mid \boldsymbol{Z}) d\boldsymbol{\theta}_n. \tag{20}$$

The missing-related information is considered in the underlying model of Equation 20 by allowing distributional differences of the latent variable $\boldsymbol{\theta}$ depending on the auxiliary variables $\boldsymbol{Z}$. Note that the measurement model of $\boldsymbol{\theta}$ (i.e., substantive model) is preserved in the joint model of $\boldsymbol{Z}$ and $\boldsymbol{X_{obs}}$.

A typical example of using this kind of IRT model has been described in this chapter in the section "Planned Missing Data," using a scholastic achievement test with three different but partially overlapping sets of items, which differ in difficulty (e.g., basic, intermediate, and advanced). When test forms are assigned to students based on their stratified average grade (Z; low ($Z = 0$); intermediate ($Z = 1$), and high ($Z = 2$) achievers), then the item nonresponses are ($\boldsymbol{Z}, \boldsymbol{X}_{\text{obs}}$)-conditional MAR. As missingness depends on Z, the stratified average grade needs to be included in the model. This can be done by specifying a unidimensional or multidimensional latent regression $E(\boldsymbol{\theta} \mid Z) = \boldsymbol{\beta}_0 + \boldsymbol{\beta}_1 I_{Z=1} + \boldsymbol{\beta}_2 I_{Z=2}$. In this equation, $I_{Z=1}$ and $I_{Z=2}$ are indicator variables for intermediate and high achievers. The low achievers are the reference group. *Multiple-group IRT* (MG-IRT) models are a less restrictive alternative for latent regression models in cases of categorical auxiliary variables $\boldsymbol{Z}$. The groups are defined by the observed values $\boldsymbol{Z} = \boldsymbol{z}$. MML estimation can also be used for estimating item parameters as well as the group-specific distributions of $\boldsymbol{\theta}$ for each group $\boldsymbol{Z} = \boldsymbol{z}$. Of course, MG-IRT models and latent regression models can also be combined to take categorical and metric auxiliary variables into account.

Multiple Imputation

The general idea of all IMs is (a) to replace the missing values in the incomplete dataset (imputation phase) and (b) to analyze the filled-in data subsequently with common methods for complete data (analysis phase). Unbiased sample-based inference of filled-in datasets requires (a) that the imputed values are appropriate or plausible and (b) that the uncertainty of the imputation method regarding the missing values is properly taken into account. The latter is important because imputed values must not be confused with observed values. It is possible and even very likely that the imputed values differ more or less from the true but missing values. This needs to be considered in statistical inference.

Many different imputation methods have been proposed that range from simple and naive univariate replacement of missing values, to imputations by means of complex multivariate parametric imputation models. An overview of all of these methods is far beyond the scope of this chapter. Interested readers are referred to Durrant (2009) and Schafer and Graham (2002).

MI has proved to be the imputation method of choice in most applications (Little & Rubin, 2019; Schafer & Graham, 2002). Therefore, we confine ourselves in this chapter to MI of item nonresponses.

The MI approach is far more than the mere repeated imputation of missing values. It also includes the entire statistical methodology for analyzing the multiply imputed datasets, which can largely be traced back to Rubin's work in the 1970s and 1980s (Little & Rubin, 2019; Rubin, 1987, 1996; Rubin & Schenker, 1986). Therefore, the computational steps that lead to final point estimates (and their variances) as well as to test statistics are called *Rubin's rules* (Enders, 2010; Schafer, 1997, 1999).

Predictive Distribution and the Imputation Model

As the name suggests, multiple filled-in datasets are generated with multiple imputations instead of a single one as in the case of single imputation methods. In order to explain why this is useful and how MI works, the joint distribution $f(\boldsymbol{M}, \boldsymbol{X}_{obs}, \boldsymbol{X}_{mis}, \boldsymbol{Z})$ is considered once more but with a different factorization compared with that in Equation 7:

$$f(\boldsymbol{M}, \boldsymbol{X}_{obs}, \boldsymbol{X}_{mis}, \boldsymbol{Z}) = \underbrace{f(\boldsymbol{X}_{mis} \mid \boldsymbol{M}, \boldsymbol{X}_{obs}, \boldsymbol{Z})}_{\text{Predictive distribution}} f(\boldsymbol{M}, \boldsymbol{X}_{obs}, \boldsymbol{Z}). \tag{21}$$

This first factor in Equation 21 is the *predictive distribution* of $\boldsymbol{X}_{mis}$, which is of crucial interest for MI. The predictive distribution is the conditional distribution of the unobserved variables

$\boldsymbol{X}_{mis}$ given the observed part $\boldsymbol{X}_{obs}$, the covariates $\boldsymbol{Z}$, and missing indicators $\boldsymbol{M}$. Thus, different values or ranges of values of $\boldsymbol{X}_{mis}$ are more or less likely, given the observed variables ($\boldsymbol{X}_{obs}$, $\boldsymbol{Z}$, $\boldsymbol{M}$). The predictive distribution represents the uncertainty of the imputed values regarding the unobserved variables $\boldsymbol{X}_{mis}$. This uncertainty is a nuisance and a source of variance of the parameter estimates, and needs to be considered in the estimation of standard errors. MI is a stochastic imputation method where item nonresponses are replaced by random draws from the predictive distribution.

If the incomplete data are imputed Q times with random numbers from the predictive distribution, then Q imputed datasets are generated, which vary more or less regarding the imputed values. The variation in the parameter estimates across the filled-in datasets due to different imputed values is used in the following statistical analyses to obtain correct standard errors and test statistics (see the section "Parameter Estimation and Statistical Inference Using MI," below).

However, the first challenge is to obtain random draws from the predictive distribution. This requires specification of an appropriate imputation model with the parameter vector $\boldsymbol{\iota}_{imp}$, depending (a) on the missing data mechanism, (b) on the characteristics of the variables X_1, ..., X_I, Z_1, ..., Z_J (e.g., the scale level), and (c) their joint multivariate distribution. The missing data mechanism must be considered for selecting the variables that need to be included in the imputation model. If the missing data are nonignorable (i.e., NMAR), then the predictive distribution of $\boldsymbol{X}_{mis}$ depends on the missing indicator variables M_1, ..., M_Q, which need to be included in the imputation model as predictor variables. However, the inclusion of $\boldsymbol{M}$ complicates parameter estimation and, therefore, proper random draws from the predictive distribution as the extended imputation models are typically not identified. If the item nonresponses are ignorable (e.g., MCAR or MAR), then $\boldsymbol{M}$ and $\boldsymbol{X}_{mis}$ are conditionally stochastically independent by definition, given ($\boldsymbol{X}_{obs}$, $\boldsymbol{Z}$; see Equation 3). Therefore, the predictive distribution is shown in Equation 22:

$$f(\boldsymbol{X}_{mis} \mid \boldsymbol{M}, \boldsymbol{X}_{obs}, \boldsymbol{Z}) = f(\boldsymbol{X}_{mis} \mid \boldsymbol{X}_{obs}, \boldsymbol{Z}). \tag{22}$$

This means that $\boldsymbol{M}$ can be left out of the imputation model.

Different methods have been developed and implemented to obtain random draws from the posterior predictive distribution. We only discuss two commonly used approaches in this chapter, which are available in many statistical software packages: (1) MI from the joint multivariate distribution and (2) MI by *chained equations.*

MI From the Joint Multivariate Distribution

The imputation model rests upon the assumption that $\boldsymbol{X}$ is multivariate normally distributed $\boldsymbol{X} \sim N(\boldsymbol{\mu}, \boldsymbol{\Sigma})$. Under that assumption, all variables X_i can be written as linear regressions plus a normally distributed residual $\varepsilon_i \sim N(0, \sigma_{\varepsilon i})$.

$$\begin{aligned} X_i &= E(X_i \mid \boldsymbol{X}_{-i}, \boldsymbol{Z}) + \varepsilon_i \\ &= \sum\nolimits_{j \neq i} \beta_j X_j + \sum\nolimits_{h} Z_h + \varepsilon_i. \end{aligned} \tag{23}$$

Note that the variables without missing values (e.g., $Z_1, ..., Z_m$) do not need to be normally distributed. However, the assumption of conditional linearity of all Y_i regarding the completely observed covariates $Z_1, ..., Z_m$ must hold true. The parameter vector $\boldsymbol{\iota}_{imp}$ consists of the unknown mean vector $\boldsymbol{\mu}$ and the variance-covariance matrix $\boldsymbol{\Sigma}$. The regression coefficients in Equation 23 as well as the residual variances $\sigma_{\varepsilon i}$ are simply functions of ($\boldsymbol{\mu}$, $\boldsymbol{\Sigma}$) and vice versa. Random draws from a multivariate normal distribution can easily be generated if $\boldsymbol{\mu}$ and $\boldsymbol{\Sigma}$ are known. However, in the case of item nonresponses, $\boldsymbol{\mu}$ and $\boldsymbol{\Sigma}$ must be estimated from the observed incomplete data. In order to get proper multiple imputations, the uncertainty of the estimates $\hat{\boldsymbol{\mu}}$ and $\hat{\boldsymbol{\Sigma}}$ of the imputation models needs to be taken into account (Schafer, 1997, pp. 147–192). This can be achieved by random draws from the Bayesian posterior predictive distribution of $\boldsymbol{X}_{mis}$ given the observed variables and the multivariate normal model indexed by $\boldsymbol{\iota}_{imp}$, which is

$$f(\boldsymbol{X}_{mis} \mid \boldsymbol{M}, \boldsymbol{X}_{obs}, \boldsymbol{Z}) = \int f(\boldsymbol{X}_{mis} \mid \boldsymbol{X}_{obs}, \boldsymbol{Z}; \boldsymbol{\iota}_{imp})\, f(\boldsymbol{\iota}_{imp} \mid \boldsymbol{X}_{obs}, \boldsymbol{Z})\, d\boldsymbol{\iota}_{imp}. \tag{24}$$

In Equation 24, $f(\boldsymbol{\iota}_{imp} \mid \boldsymbol{X}_{obs}, \boldsymbol{Z})$ is the posterior distribution of the parameter of the imputation model given the observed variables ($\boldsymbol{X}_{obs}$, $\boldsymbol{Z}$). Random draws from the posterior predictive distribution are not conditional on the point estimates $\hat{\boldsymbol{\mu}}$ and $\hat{\boldsymbol{\Sigma}}$, but they take the complete joint parameter space of $\boldsymbol{\mu}$ and $\boldsymbol{\Sigma}$ into account (i.e., by integration over $f(\boldsymbol{\iota}_{imp} \mid \boldsymbol{X}_{obs}, \boldsymbol{Z})$).

An application of *Markov chain Monte Carlo* sampling can be used to generate realizations of the posterior predictive distribution. This is an iterative, simulation-based algorithm. In the cases of MI, it is a kind of back-and-forth algorithm. First, the parameters $\hat{\boldsymbol{\iota}}_{imp}^{(t)}$ of the imputation model are estimated in iteration step t. Second, the random draws from $f\left(\boldsymbol{X}_{mis} \mid \boldsymbol{X}_{obs}, \boldsymbol{Z}; \hat{\boldsymbol{\iota}}_{imp}^{(t)}\right)$ are used to fill in the missing values. The filled-in dataset $\boldsymbol{X}^{*(t)}$ is then used to reestimate $\hat{\boldsymbol{\iota}}_{imp}^{(t+1)}$ in the subsequent iteration step $t + 1$, and so on, until a stop criterion is reached. The algorithm starts with plausible initial estimates $\hat{\boldsymbol{\iota}}_{imp}^{(0)}$ (i.e., starting values). After a certain number t_B of iterations (i.e., the burn-in period) the algorithm converges to the stationary posterior predictive distribution. The filled-in datasets $\boldsymbol{X}^{*(t)}$ starting from iteration $t = t_B + 1$ can be used for further statistical analyses.

MI by Chained Equations

The multivariate normal model is a joint model for all variables with missing data. However, a joint density of random variables can be fully described by the conditional densities of the single component variables X_1 to X_I. This is the theoretical basis of a sequential procedure where missing values are imputed variable-by-variable based on separate models for each variable X_i conditional on the observed information of variable i (e.g., $X_{i;obs}$), all other variables $\boldsymbol{X}_{-i}$, $= X_1, ..., X_{i-1}, X_{i+1}, ..., X_I$, and $\boldsymbol{Z}$. The imputed values of a variable X_i are random draws from the predictive distributions $f(X_{i;mis} \mid X_{i;obs}, \boldsymbol{X}_{-i}, \boldsymbol{Z}; \boldsymbol{\iota}_i)$. No parametric assumption regarding the joint multivariate distribution is needed. The parameter vector $\boldsymbol{\iota}_{imp} = (\boldsymbol{\iota}_1, \dots, \boldsymbol{\iota}_i, \dots, \boldsymbol{\iota}_I)$ consists of variable-specific parameter vectors of i predictive distributions of the variable $X_1, ..., X_I$. The major advantage of the sequential approach is its flexibility to handle continuous, dichotomous, unordered and ordered categorical variables as well as count data. For each variable an appropriate regression model $X_i = E(X_i \mid \boldsymbol{X}_{-i}, \boldsymbol{Z}) + \varepsilon_i$ is specified. The parametric models of the regressions $E(X_i \mid \boldsymbol{X}_{-i}, \boldsymbol{Z})$ are chosen according to the scale level of X_i. Linear models are commonly used for continuous variables. Binary, ordinal, and multinomial logistic regressions are used for dichotomous, ordinal, and unordered categorical variables, respectively. Poisson or negative-binomial regressions can be used for count data.

As a sequence of regression models is employed, the method is also called *multiple imputation by chained equations* (MICE). The set of predictor variables for the variables X_i can differ, which allows for more parsimonious imputation models if the number of variables is large. A variant of a *Gibbs sampler* can be used to generate random draws from posterior predictive distributions using MICE. The Gibbs sampler is another instance of iterative MCMC algorithms (Gelfand, 2000). The algorithm for generating multiple imputations in the R package *mice* works as follows (Van Buuren & Groothuis-Oudshoorn, 2011):

1. Generate an initial filled-in dataset $\boldsymbol{X}^{*(0)}$ by imputing missing values of each variable X_i by simple random draws from the observed marginal distributions of each $X_{i;obs}$
2. for $t = 1, ..., T$

$$\text{sample } \hat{\boldsymbol{\iota}}_1^{(t)} \text{ from } f\left(\boldsymbol{\iota}_1 \mid X_{1;obs}, X_2^{*(t-1)}, \ldots, X_I^{*(t-1)}, \boldsymbol{Z}\right)$$

$$\text{sample } X_1^{*(t)} \text{ from } f\left(X_1 \mid X_{1;obs}, X_2^{*(t-1)}, \ldots, X_I^{*(t-1)}, \boldsymbol{Z}; \hat{\boldsymbol{\iota}}_1^{(t)}\right)$$

$$\text{sample } \hat{\boldsymbol{\iota}}_2^{(t)} \text{ from } f\left(\boldsymbol{\iota}_2 \mid X_{2;obs}, X_1^{*(t)}, \boldsymbol{X}_{-1}^{*(t-1)}, \boldsymbol{Z}\right)$$

$$\text{sample } X_2^{*(t)} \text{ from } f\left(X_2 \mid X_{2;obs}, X_1^{*(t)}, X_3^{*(t-1)}, \ldots, X_I^{*(t-1)}, \boldsymbol{Z}; \hat{\boldsymbol{\iota}}_2^{(t)}\right)$$

$$\vdots$$

$$\text{sample } \hat{\boldsymbol{\iota}}_I^{(t)} \text{ from } f\left(\boldsymbol{\iota}_I \mid X_{I;obs}, \boldsymbol{X}_{-I}^{*(t)}, \boldsymbol{Z}\right)$$

$$\text{sample } X_I^{*(t)} \text{ from } f\left(X_I \mid X_{I;obs}, \boldsymbol{X}_{-I}^{*(t)}, \boldsymbol{Z}; \hat{\boldsymbol{\iota}}_I^{(t)}\right)$$

3. Stop when the number of iterations T is reached.

Thus, the second step involves sampling from the posterior distributions $f\left(\boldsymbol{\iota}_i \mid X_{i;obs}, \boldsymbol{X}_{-i}^{*(t)}, \boldsymbol{Z}\right)$ of the parameters $\boldsymbol{\iota}_i$ of the variable-specific regression models, followed by sampling from the posterior predictive distributions $f\left(X_i \mid X_{i;obs}, \boldsymbol{X}_{-i}^{*(t)}, \boldsymbol{Z}; \hat{\boldsymbol{\iota}}_i^{(t)}\right)$. The filled-in datasets $\boldsymbol{X}^{*(t)}$ with $t < T$ are preliminary within the imputation algorithm. The filled-in datasets that are generated after the final iteration T (e.g., $t \geq T$) can be used for further statistical analyses, if convergence has been reached. Following Van Buuren and Groothuis-Oudshoorn (2011) a fairly small number of 10 to 20 iterations are typically sufficient for convergence of the MICE algorithm.

Parameter Estimation and Statistical Inference Using MI

After having generated the imputed values, each filled-in dataset can be analyzed with commonly used parameter estimation methods for complete data in the analysis phase. The parameter vector $\boldsymbol{\iota}_X$ of the substantive models of interest is separately estimated for each filled-in dataset. If there are Q imputed datasets $q = 1, ..., Q$, then Q sample estimates $\hat{\boldsymbol{\iota}}_X^{(1)}, ..., \hat{\boldsymbol{\iota}}_X^{(Q)}, ...,$ are obtained, which need to be combined into the final point estimate $\hat{\boldsymbol{\iota}}_X$ in the *pooling phase*. The point estimate is simply the average $\hat{\boldsymbol{\iota}}_X = Q^{-1} \sum_{q=1}^{Q} \hat{\boldsymbol{\iota}}_X^{(q)}$ of the single point estimates $\hat{\boldsymbol{\iota}}_X^{(q)}$ from the Q filled-in datasets.

The estimation of the variance-covariance matrix of $\hat{\boldsymbol{\iota}}_X$ and the standard errors is more complex. Let be $\boldsymbol{V}_T$ the total variance-covariance matrix of the final vector estimate $\hat{\boldsymbol{\iota}}_X$, which consists of two components (Rubin, 1987; Rubin & Schenker, 1986) as shown in Equation 25:

$$\boldsymbol{V}_T = \boldsymbol{V}_W + \boldsymbol{V}_B + \frac{\boldsymbol{V}_B}{Q}. \tag{2.5}$$

$\boldsymbol{V}_B$ refers to the between-imputation variance and $\boldsymbol{V}_W$ denotes the within-imputation variance, which are defined as:

$$\boldsymbol{V}_B = \frac{1}{Q-1}\sum_{q=1}^{Q}\left(\hat{\boldsymbol{\iota}}_X^{(q)} - \hat{\boldsymbol{\iota}}_X\right)\left(\hat{\boldsymbol{\iota}}_X^{(q)} - \hat{\boldsymbol{\iota}}_X\right)^T$$

$$\boldsymbol{V}_W = \frac{1}{Q}\sum_{q=1}^{Q} vcov\left(\hat{\boldsymbol{\iota}}_X^{(q)}\right). \tag{26}$$

In Equation 26, $vcov\left(\hat{\boldsymbol{\iota}}_X^{(q)}\right)$ is the variance-covariance matrix of the estimated parameter vector obtained from the q-th filled-in dataset.

Enders (2010, pp. 223–224) used an ANOVA analogy for explaining the two variance partitions: The between-imputation variance $\boldsymbol{V}_B$ is the part of the total sampling variation of $\hat{\boldsymbol{\iota}}_X$ due to missing data, where missingness is considered as a predictor for explaining the sampling variance of estimate $\hat{\boldsymbol{\iota}}_X$.Therefore, the within-imputation variance is the residual sampling variation of $\hat{\boldsymbol{\iota}}_X$, which is not attributable to missingness. The between-imputation variance accounts for the fact that imputed values are not observed values but random draws from a posterior distribution given the observed part $\boldsymbol{X}_{obs}$ and the covariates $\boldsymbol{Z}$ under the model assumptions of the imputation model. Thus, the imputed values are simply a set of plausible values for $\boldsymbol{X}_{mis}$, which differ to an unknown degree from the true but unobserved values. This uncertainty is a source of variance that contributes to the total sampling variance of $\hat{\boldsymbol{\iota}}_X$. The variance-covariance matrix and the standard errors of the parameter estimates are essential for single-parameter and multiparameter tests with multiply imputed data.

Single Parameter *t* Test With Multiply Imputed Data

Testing single parameters by a t test with multiply imputed data requires some calculations according to Rubin's rules. In general, the t test requires the t value and the degrees of freedom (abbr. *df*). The t value of the single point estimate $\hat{\boldsymbol{\iota}}_X$ is the ratio $\hat{\iota}_X = (\hat{\iota}_X - \iota_0)/SE(\hat{\iota}_X)$, with ι_0 the value of ι_X under the null hypothesis H_0: $\iota_X = \iota_0$. The standard error is $SE(\hat{\iota}_X) = \sqrt{V_W + V_B + Q^{-1}V_B}$, with $V_B = (Q-1)^{-1}\sum_{q=1}^{Q}\left(\hat{\iota}_X^{(q)} - \hat{\iota}_X\right)^2$ and $V_W = Q^{-1}\sum_{q=1}^{Q} SE\left(\hat{\iota}_X^{(q)}\right)^2$, which is equal to the square root of the diagonal elements of $\boldsymbol{V}_T$ in multiparameter models (see Equation 25). The t reference distribution depends on the degrees of freedom df_{MI}, which depend on the number of imputations (Q) and both variance components V_B and V_W as shown in Equation 27:

$$df_{MI} = (Q-1)\left(1 + \frac{V_W}{V_B(1+Q^{-1})}\right). \tag{27}$$

Alternative *df* formulas are recommended for small samples (Barnard & Rubin, 1999), as in Equation 28:

$$\widetilde{df}_{MI} = \left(\frac{1}{df_{MI}} + \frac{1}{u}\right)^{-1}, \tag{28}$$

with the correction factor as shown in Equation 29:

$$u = (1 - FMI)df_c\left(\frac{df_c + 1}{df_c + 3}\right). \tag{29}$$

Here df_c represents the nominal degrees of freedom of the complete dataset (i.e., as if there were no missing values). The *fraction of missing information* (FMI) is essentially the proportion of between-variance on the total sampling variance of $\hat{\iota}_X$. Therefore, the FMI multiplied by 100 can be interpreted as the percentage of the sampling variance of $\hat{\iota}_X$ due to missingness in the data (Enders, 2010, p. 225).

Multiparameter Tests With Multiply Imputed Data

Different test statistics have been developed for testing *omnibus hypotheses* that involve multiple parameters of the parameter vector $\boldsymbol{\iota}_X$. Multiparameter tests are widely used in psychometric modeling. Many substantial research questions can be translated into testable omnibus hypotheses. For example, let there be a measurement model of θ based on the manifest variables X_1, ... X_w and a set of predictor variables X_{w+1}, ..., X_l to explain variance in the latent variable θ. All regression coefficients in a multiple regression $E(\theta \mid X_{w+1}, ..., X_l)$ are tested, with the null hypothesis H_0: $\boldsymbol{\beta} = \mathbf{0}$, where $\boldsymbol{\beta}$ and $\mathbf{0}$ are vectors of equal length. This omnibus hypothesis with a latent outcome in SEM is the counterpart of the F test with H_0: $R^2 = 0$ in ordinary least square regression models.

The Wald test can be used to test omnibus hypotheses. Statistical comparisons of nested models are further instances of multiparameter tests. For example, the assumption of strong measurement invariance across groups can be tested by comparing two nested multiple-group SEM M_0 and M_1. M_0 is the restrictive model of the null hypothesis with equally constrained factor loadings and measurement intercepts across groups. M_1 is the less restrictive model without the equality constraints.

The *likelihood ratio* (LR) test is commonly used for statistical model comparisons. Both testing approaches, the Wald test and the LR test, have also been adapted for the statistical tests with multiply imputed data. Three statistics, denoted by D_1 to D_3 are widely used. D_1 and D_2 refer to Wald-like tests, and the D_3 statistic serves for model comparisons based on LRs.

The computational details for the three test statistics and their degrees of freedom are not presented here. Interested readers are referred to Enders (2010, pp. 233–242). Note that the different test statistics have different small sample properties and may differ in empirical Type I error rates and power (Grund et al., 2016; Liu & Enders, 2017). Neither the calculations according to Rubin's rules for single parameter t tests nor the multiparameter tests must be done by hand. Fortunately, many statistical software programs, such as Mplus and R, can handle multiply imputed data and have implementations of the described statistical testing procedures (see supplementary material: https://osf.io/kt8e5/).

How Many Imputations?

Not so long ago, five imputed filled-in datasets were regarded as sufficient for statistical inference based on multiply imputed data. However, it has been shown that the standard error of a single parameter estimate $\hat{\iota}_X$ is $SE(\hat{\iota}_X) = \sqrt{V_W + V_B + Q^{-1}V_B}$, where the between-imputation variance component V_B is weighted by $(1 + Q^{-1})$ (see also Equation 25 for variance-covariance matrix $\boldsymbol{V_T}$). Therefore, the sampling variance decreases with increasing imputations so that the power of single-parameter and multiparameter tests increases. Currently, a minimum number of 20 imputed datasets is recommended (Enders, 2010, p. 212). Especially if only small effect sizes are expected, larger numbers of imputations can be useful (Graham et al., 2007).

Specification of the Imputation Model

Variable Selection

There are three aspects which need to be considered to select variables for the imputation model: (a) bias, (b) power, and (c) model complexity. In general, all variables of the substantive model – with or without missing values – need to be part of the imputation model. Otherwise, the parameter estimates of the substantive model are potentially biased. As outlined in the section "Implications of Missing Data Mechanism for Handling of Missing Data," unbiased statistical inference with multiply imputed data requires the inclusion of all variables in the imputation model to satisfy the MAR assumption (i.e., $\boldsymbol{M}$ is conditionally stochastically independent of $\boldsymbol{X_{mis}}$, given the observed variables $\boldsymbol{X_{obs}}$ and $\boldsymbol{Z}$, see Equation 1, Equation 2, and Equation 3). Therefore, all variables of the substantive model and all missing-relevant auxiliary variables need to be included in the imputation model. As outlined in the section "Study Design and Missing Data," only in the case of planned missing data by design are all missing-relevant auxiliary variables known design variables.

In the case of unintentional missing data, the missing-related factors are typically unknown. The inclusion strategy is recommended in this situation (Collins et al., 2001). Therefore, a large number of potentially missing-relevant variables are included, which are likely predictive for missingness ($\boldsymbol{M}$) as well as the missing variables ($\boldsymbol{X_{mis}}$). The MAR assumption becomes more and more plausible with an increasing number of covariates in the imputation model (Collins et al., 2001).

Another reason for adding more auxiliary variables is the accuracy of parameter estimation and statistical power. As shown in the section "Parameter Estimation and Statistical Inference Using MI," the between-imputation variance $\boldsymbol{V_B}$ contributes to the total sampling variance $\boldsymbol{V_T}$ of parameter estimates (see Equation 25 and Equation 26). If there are strong predictors of missing variables in $\boldsymbol{X_{mis}}$, then accurate imputations can be generated and the between-variance decreases. This leads to lower standard errors and a higher statistical power in uniparameter and multiparameter tests. For that reason, the inclusion of covariates $\boldsymbol{Z}$ in the imputation model can be valuable even if the missing data mechanism is MCAR or ($\boldsymbol{X_{obs}}$)-conditional MAR.

An unbiased parameter estimation requires not only the consideration of all missing-relevant variables but also the correct specification of the imputation model with regard to the substantive model. Therefore, potential nonlinear relationships, interaction between variables, and nested data structures may need to be considered. Therefore, the imputation model can quickly become very complex, especially with a large number of variables. For example, if MICE is used for MI in a dataset with 100 variables, then each incomplete variable X_i is regressed on all 99 other variables $X_{j \neq i}$.

In cases of additional interactions and nonlinearities, the number of predictors in the regression models further increases. The imputation algorithm most likely ends up in computational problems and nonconvergence. In general, the number of variables should not exceed the number of cases (Enders, 2010, p. 255). Therefore, the inclusive strategy becomes necessarily impracticable with many variables.

Real data analysis of high-dimensional multivariate incomplete data with MI requires far more than just listing as many variables as possible in an imputation software program. A thorough selection of covariates from a potentially large set of missing-relevant auxiliary variables is required. Covariates of the imputation model should be (a) associated with the occurrence of missing data and (b) predictive for the missing variables. Covariates that (a) are not related to missingness, (b) turn out to be uncorrelated with incomplete variables, (c) induce multicollinearity, or (d) lead to "perfect" predictions, should be left out of the imputation model. Perfect predictions typically occur if the response categories of the incomplete categorical variable are perfectly separated by the covariates, which leads to infinite ML estimates and invalid improper imputations (Nguyen et al., 2021; White et al., 2010).

Some of the implemented MICE algorithms allow for the selection of only the most predictive variables for each incomplete variable and provide further functionality for automatic predictor selection and for resolving the problem of multicollinearity (i.e., the R package *mice*). Further guidelines and recommendations for selecting variables in the imputation model can be found in Van Buuren (2018, pp. 127–129). Nevertheless, convergence diagnostics should always be used to rule out computational problems, feedback loops, breakdowns, and failures of the imputation (Nguyen et al., 2021). Comparisons of the distributions of incomplete and multiply imputed data, as well as trace plots of distributional parameters (e.g., means and standard deviations) of the imputed variables across the iteration process are commonly used for graphical inspection of convergence (Van Buuren, 2018, pp. 142–151). A complete guide on convergence diagnostics is far beyond the scope of this chapter. However, readers are strongly advised to learn more about convergence diagnostics before starting with MI of real data (Abayomi et al., 2008; Nguyen et al., 2017).

Challenges and Pitfalls in Model Specification

If the imputation of missing values were generated from a comprehensive model that includes all underlying causes and contributing factors of the participants' response behavior, the true data generating process would be represented, and all complexities of the complete data will have been preserved in the filled-in datasets. Unfortunately, this is impossible in almost all real world applied psychometric data analyses. The illustrated imputation methods in this chapter rely on regression models, which (a) merely include the observed variables $\boldsymbol{X}_{obs}$ and $\boldsymbol{Z}$ and (b) rest upon certain assumptions (e.g., distributional assumptions, homoscedasticity of the residuals, linearity, etc.). In other words, the imputed values always result from simplified statistical models (i.e., the imputation model). The key question is how simple the imputation model can be without producing biased estimates of the substantive model. This question cannot be answered in general terms, but only with regard to a specific substantive model.

For example, let there be an incomplete dataset with three continuous variables X_1, X_2, and X_3. Let there be two different substantive models A and B. Model A is the linear regression $E(X_1 \mid X_2, X_3) = \beta_0 + \beta_1 X_2 + \beta_2 X_3$, and Model B is the nonlinear regression $E(X_1 \mid X_2, X_3) = \beta_0 + \beta_1 X_1 + \beta_2 X_1^2 + \beta_3 X_1^3 + \beta_4 X_2 + \beta_5 X_3$. Suppose that MICE was used with an imputation model consisting of three linear regressions $E(X_l \mid X_m, X_n) = \beta_l + \beta_{lm} X_m + \beta_{ln} X_n$ for each variable X_1 to X_3. Using the very same filled-in datasets for further statistical analyses would yield unbiased parameter estimates of Model A but fairly biased estimates of Model B, depending on the degree of nonlinearity and the proportion and distribution of missing data. The reason is that the imputation model does not account for the complex nonlinear relationships between the variables in Model B. The imputation model and Model B are said to be *uncongenial* (Xie & Meng, 2017), whereas Model A and the imputation model are *congenial,* as they correspond to each other. This is easy to see because Model A equals the imputation model of the variable X_1. However, a linear CFA of the three variables X_1, X_2, and X_3 is also congenial with the linear imputation model, which is not obvious. The reason is that model estimation of the linear CFA rests upon the variance-covariance matrix and the mean vector of the three variables, which have a one-to-one correspondence to the parameters of the linear regressions in the imputation model.

The concept of (un-)congeniality is not trivial, and the question of whether an imputation model is congenial with regard to a specific substantive model is sometimes difficult to answer in real data analyses. However, the most important implication is that the imputation model must be at least as saturated or complex as the substantive model, to avoid biased parameter estimates in the analysis phase. To illustrate this key concept, the following three examples demonstrate how to perserve the complexity of the substantive model in the imputation model: Example A: explanatory SEM with nonlinear regressions of latent variables; Example B: multiple-group CFA; and Example C: multilevel SEM. Readers are also referred to the supplementary material to this chapter, where the issue of congeniality is illustrated using single- and multiple-group SEM for continuous and ordinal variables (see supplementary material to this chapter available at https://osf.io/kt8e5/).

In Example A, an explanatory SEM with a nonlinear regression $E(\theta \mid X_4, X_5) = \beta_0 + \beta_1 X_4 + \beta_2 X_5 + \beta_3 X_4^2 + \beta_4 X_4 X_5$ is considered. The latent variable θ is measured by three manifest variables X_1, X_2, and X_3. The model equations of the measurement model are given

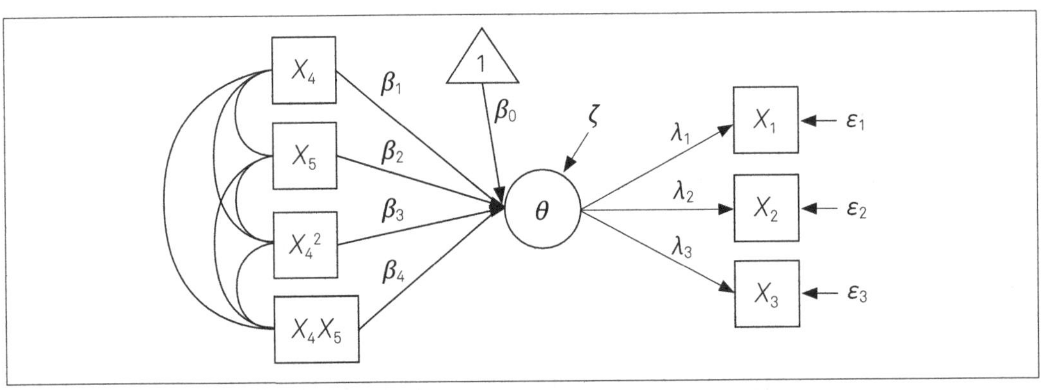

Figure 9.2 Explanatory structural equation model (SEM) with a nonlinear regression of the latent variable θ on the manifest variables X_4 and X_5 (Example A).

by $X_i = \nu_i + \lambda_i\theta + \varepsilon_i$, with $i = 1, ..., 3$. The path diagram of the model is shown in Figure 9.2. All five manifest variables X_1 to X_5 have missing values. What is the appropriate imputation model in this case? To answer this question, the implication of the substantive model regarding the stochastic relationships between the manifest variables X_1 to X_5 must be considered. First, the measurement model of θ implies pairwise linear relationships between the manifest variables X_1, X_2, and X_3. Second, the nonlinear relationships between the predictors X_4 and X_5 and the latent variable θ imply nonlinear relations between X_4 and X_5 and the indicators of θ (i.e., X_1 to X_3). Therefore, a congenial imputation model of X_1, X_2, and X_3 requires the inclusion of the squared variable and the product term as predictors.

It is important to note that the functions X_4^2, and X_4X_5 are variables, which also have missing values that need to be handled. Two approaches for the imputation of functions (e.g., polynomial functions, exponential functions, logarithm, interaction terms, etc.) of incomplete variables can be distinguished (Von Hippel, 2009): (a) the *impute-then-transform* approach and (b) the *transform-then-impute* approach.

The impute-then-transform approach starts with imputing missing values of the manifest variables $X_1, ..., X_I$. The transformations or functions of $X_1, ..., X_I$ are computed in the second step within each filled-in dataset using the imputed variables. In contrast, the functions or transformations of $X_1, ..., X_I$ in the incomplete dataset are computed first, when the impute-then-transform approach is used. The resulting missing values in these functions or transformations are then imputed, just like missing values of any other variable. Although it may seem counter-intuitive at first, the transform-then-impute approach has proved superior to the impute-then-transform approach for MI of continuous variables from the joint multivariate distribution (Von Hippel, 2009). Therefore, to account for the missing values and the nonlinearities in the substantive model of Example A, it is recommended to compute the functions X_4^2 and X_4X_5 in the incomplete dataset in a first step. Subsequently, an imputation model is specified including all variables $X_1, ..., X_5$ and the functions X_4^2, and X_4X_5.

Unfortunately, the transform-then-impute approach is not always the optimal choice for MI of functions of incomplete variables. There can be convergence problems due to linear dependencies and feedback loops, especially when using MICE. Passive imputation of functions of incomplete variables is recommended as an alternative (Van Buuren, 2018, pp. 129–142). The incomplete variables are imputed and the functions of the incomplete variables (i.e., interaction terms, squares etc.) are then computed *on-the-fly* (i.e., within each iteration step) based on the imputed values. Therefore, these functions can serve as predictors for other incomplete variables in the imputation model. This is the distinctive feature of passive imputation using MICE compared with the impute-then-transform approach using MI from the joint multivariate normal distribution.

Therefore, in Example A the variables $X_1, ..., X_5$ were imputed and so were the functions X_4^2 and X_4X_5 in each iteration step. However, the sets of predictors are different for the single variables. The functions X_4^2, and X_4X_5 serve only as additional predictors for X_1, X_2, and X_3 but not for the incomplete variables X_4 and X_5. This breaks potential feedback loops without neglecting nonlinearities. The disadvantage of the passive imputation strategy is that the imputation models of single variables must be adapted, which can be challenging in cases of large imputation models.

In Example B, a hypothetical multiple-group SEM is considered with 10 manifest variables $X_1, ..., X_{10}$ from a questionnaire assessing romantic jealousy (Bauer, 1988; Richter et al., 2022). Let there be a number of fully observed and potentially missing-relevant covariates including the grouping variable *sex* denoted by Z. A psychometrician was interested in the question whether a common metric of the latent variable θ across the gender groups can be established, which is a prerequisite for meaningful group comparisons of means and variances of θ across the sex groups. A common metric requires *strong factorial invariance* across groups, which is defined by group-invariant factor loadings and measurement intercepts in a linear CFA (Meredith, 1993). The substantive model is a *multiple-group CFA* (MG-CFA) that can be used for parameter estimation and to test the hypothesis of strong factorial invariance. The question is whether and if so, how, the grouping variable *sex* must be considered in the imputation model.

The answer is yes, *sex* is part of the substantive model and must be taken into account in the imputation phase, even if the missing data mechanism is MCAR. A common imputation model for the whole sample that ignores participants' sex rests upon the implicit assumption of identical model-implied variance-covariance matrices and mean vectors for both groups. Therefore, possible differences in the true variances-covariance structure and means between the groups are leveled due to the group-invariant imputation model. The parameters of the MG-CFA are then potentially biased, and the test of strong factorial invariance is not valid. Enders and Gottschall (2011) demonstrated that separate group imputation is appropriate to preserve the multiple-group data structure. Therefore, the imputed values are generated separately for each group using MICE or the multivariate normal model. The resulting group-specific filled-in datasets are then recombined for further statistical analyses. Note that the real data example of the study of Richter et al. (2022) with a single- and multiple-group SEM is continued in the supplementary material of this chapter (see supplementary material: https://osf.io/kt8e5/).

Example C is a *multilevel SEM* (MSEM) that takes nested data structures into account. In cases when individuals are nested within groups, such as students within classes and classes within schools, dependencies in the data can result that need to be considered in psychometric analyses too (Hox, 2013; Muthén & Asparouhov, 2011). In MSEM, the manifest variables are disaggregated into level-specific components. For example, in a two-level SEM, the manifest variables are a sum $X_i = X_i^{(w)} + X_i^{(b)}$, with the between-part $X_i^{(b)} = E(X_i \mid C)$ and the within-part $X_i^{(w)} = X_i - E(X_i \mid C)$. $E\,(X_i \mid C)$ denotes the regression of X_i on the cluster variable C whose values are the conditional expected values $E\,(X_i \mid C = c)$ – that is, the true cluster means. The within-part $X_i^{(w)}$ is the difference of the individual variable X_i from the true cluster means. Accordingly, the variance-covariance matrix is additively composed $\Sigma = \Sigma^{(w)} + \Sigma^{(b)}$ by the variance-covariance matrix $\Sigma^{(w)}$ of the within-parts $X_i^{(w)}$, and the variance-covariance matrix $\Sigma^{(b)}$ of the between-parts $X_i^{(b)}$.

MSEM allows us to analyze variance-covariance structures at different levels (e.g., student level and class level) in a joint model. For example, level-specific measurement models can be specified in a multilevel CFA with potentially different factor structures at different levels. Such models can easily be extended to explanatory MSEM with predictors or outcomes of the latent variables. The model of the hypothetical Example C is shown in Figure 9.3. The latent variable θ is measured by the manifest variables X_1, X_2, and X_3.

Note that the factor loadings are invariant across the two levels, implying that the latent variable θ can also be written as the sum $\theta = \theta^{(w)} + \theta^{(b)}$ of the between-part $\theta^{(b)}$ and the within-part $\theta^{(w)}$. There are two predictors: first, the level-1 predictor X_4 in the regression $E\left(\theta^{(w)} \mid X_4\right) = \beta_1^{(r)} X_4$, with a random-slope $\beta_1^{(r)}$, and second, the level-2 predictor X_5 in the regression $E\,(\theta^{(b)} \mid X_5) = \gamma_2 X_5$. Formally, the random slope $\beta_1^{(r)}$ is also a latent level-2 variable in a two-level SEM, which is specified as an outcome in Example C, with the model equation

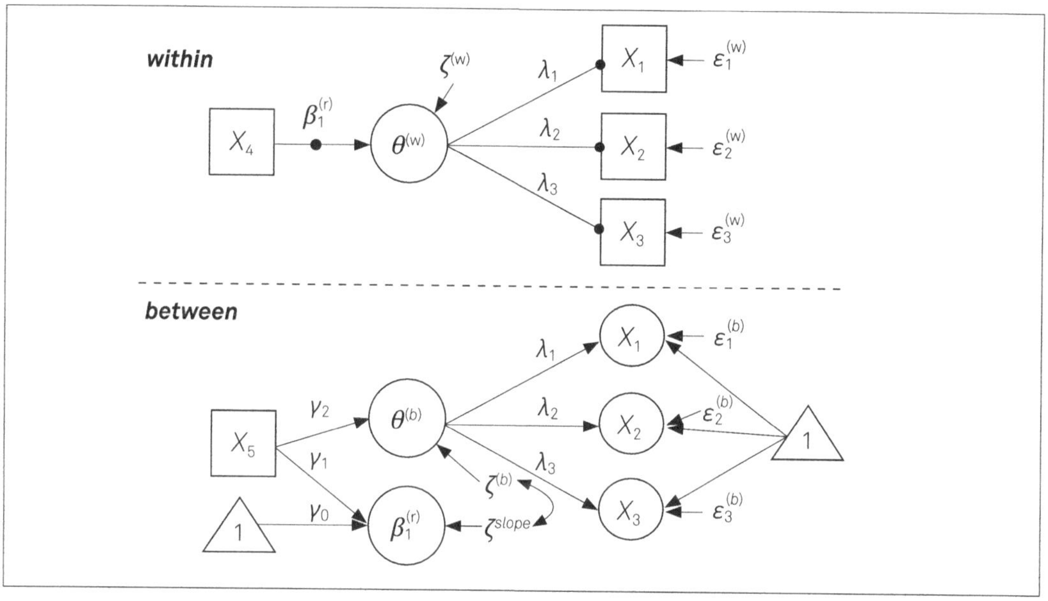

Figure 9.3 Two-level structural equation model (SEM) with the latent variable θ as the dependent variable in regression on the Level 1 predictor X_4 and the Level 2 predictor X_5. The cross-level interaction due to the regression of the random slope $\beta_1^{(r)}$ on X_5 (Example C). The solid circles indicate random coefficients.

$\beta_1^{(r)} = \gamma_0 + \gamma_1 X_5 + \zeta_{slope}$. Inserting this equation into the regression $E(\theta^{(w)} \mid X_4)$ yields, as shown in Equation 30,

$$\begin{aligned} E(\theta^{(w)} \mid X_4) &= (\gamma_0 + \gamma_1 X_5 + \zeta_{slope})X_4 + \zeta^{(w)} \\ &= \gamma_0 X_4 + \gamma_1 X_5 X_4 + \zeta_{slope} X_4 + \zeta^{(w)}. \end{aligned} \tag{30}$$

Therefore, the slopes-as-outcome model implies a cross-level interaction between X_4 and X_5 regarding the latent variable θ. Inserting the model equations of the latent variables in model equations of the variables X_i, with $i = 1, \ldots, 3$, yields Equation 31:

$$\begin{aligned} X_i &= X_i^{(b)} + X_i^{(w)} \\ &= \lambda_i \theta^{(b)} + \varepsilon_i^{(b)} + \lambda_i \theta^{(w)} + \varepsilon_i^{(w)} \\ &= \lambda_i \gamma_0 X_4 + \lambda_i \gamma_1 X_5 X_4 + \lambda_i \zeta_{slope} X_4 + \lambda_i \gamma_2 X_5 + \lambda_i \zeta^{(w)} + \lambda_i \zeta^{(b)} + \varepsilon_i^{(b)} + \varepsilon_i^{(w)}. \end{aligned} \tag{31}$$

There are two important terms $\lambda_i \gamma_1 X_5 X_4$ and $\lambda_i \zeta_{slope} X_4$ here that imply that a congenial imputation model of the variables X_1 to X_3 requires the inclusion of the interaction between X_4 and X_5 as well as a random-slope of the variable X_4. Furthermore, random-intercepts need to be included in the imputation models of each manifest variable X_1 to X_5 to preserve the intraclass correlations. Due to its flexibility, the MICE algorithm is a good choice for imputing such multilevel data with random-slopes and interactions.

Example C illustrates that imputation models can quickly become very complex even if the number of manifest variables is small. Furthermore, the example shows that implications of the substantive model regarding the congenial imputation model might not always be obvious. Following the inclusive strategy, it is tempting to simply include as many variables as possible in an imputation model, which is as complex as possible. Unfortunately, the complexity of the imputation model is limited. It is just impossible to take all possible nonlinear relationships, interactions, and nested data structures into account. Overly complex imputation models with a large number of parameters tend to become unstable and they often suffer from convergence problems. Therefore, there is a tradeoff between the complexity of the imputation model, on the one hand, and the estimation, convergence, and stability of the imputation model, on the other hand. Finding a good compromise is certainly the art of using multiple imputation. Especially, in cases of datasets with a large number of incomplete variables and complex relationships, the simultaneous imputation of all variables may not work. MI of subsets of variables that are selected with respect to particular substantive models can be a viable choice in such situations. The deliberate selection of additional missing-relevant auxiliary variables should be tailored to the respective substantive models. Especially in cases of complex substantive models, which imply complex imputation models, FIML estimation should be considered as an alternative for MI.

Approaches for Nonignorable Item Nonresponses

In the section "Statistical Inference Based on Incomplete Data," it was shown that missingness, which is represented by $\boldsymbol{M}$, can be ignored for unbiased statistical inference regarding the parameter vector ι_X of a substantive model, if the missing data mechanism is MCAR or MAR. Therefore, these missing data mechanisms are called *ignorable*. Parameter estimates obtained by FIML or multiply imputed data using only the observed variables $\boldsymbol{X}_{obs}$ or $(\boldsymbol{X}_{obs}, \boldsymbol{Z})$ are unbiased. Accordingly, it is tempting to assume ignorable missingness. However, there are many situations where item nonresponses are likely NMAR – for example, omitted and not-reached items in intelligence or achievement tests. A positive correlation between item difficulty and the proportion of item nonresponses may indicate that test takers tend to omit items they cannot solve (Rose et al., 2010). In this case, the probability of answering the items depends on the item response itself, and the missing data mechanism is most likely nonignorable. In other words, $\boldsymbol{M}$ cannot be ignored for estimating the parameter vector ι_X of a substantive model. Unbiased parameter estimation requires a joint model of $(\boldsymbol{M}, \boldsymbol{X}_{obs})$. The covariate $\boldsymbol{Z}$ is left out in this section as it is not part of the substantive model. However, this is just for the sake of simplicity. Missing-relevant covariates are also routinely used as additional sources of information regarding the missing part $\boldsymbol{Y}_{mis}$ in model-based and imputation-based approaches for handling nonignorable item nonresponses.

Selection Models and Pattern Mixture Models

Two major classes of models have been developed for nonignorable missing data (Glynn et al., 1986; Little, 2008): *selection models* and *pattern mixture models*. These two models refer to two alternative factorizations of the joint distribution of the complete data $f(\boldsymbol{M}, \boldsymbol{X})$, with $\boldsymbol{X} = (\boldsymbol{X}_{obs}, \boldsymbol{X}_{mis})$.

The selection models (Heckman, 1976, 1979) are based on the factorization as shown in Equation 32:

$$f(\boldsymbol{M}, \boldsymbol{X}; \iota_X, \iota_M) = f(\boldsymbol{M} \mid \boldsymbol{X}; \iota_M) f(\boldsymbol{X}; \iota_X). \tag{32}$$

The unconditional parametric distribution $f(\boldsymbol{X}; \iota_X)$ represents the substantive model. The conditional distribution $f(\boldsymbol{M} \mid \boldsymbol{X}; \iota_X)$ refers to the stochastic model of missingness depending on $\boldsymbol{X}$. For example, a selection model for an item i with nonignorable missing data includes not only the substantive model of X_i, but also a binomial regression model $P(M_i = 0 \mid \boldsymbol{X})$. The latter takes account of the conditional probability that X_i is observed given the variables $\boldsymbol{X}$ of the substantive model. As X_i can never be observed if $M_i = 1$, any information regarding the joint distribution of X_i and M_i can only be inferred from the observed data under very strong and often untestable assumptions (e.g., distributional assumptions, such as latent normality). Typically, selection models are highly sensitive to violations of model assumptions. This is the major drawback of this class of models.

Pattern mixture models (Little, 1993; Molenberghs et al., 2004) refer to the alternative factorization of the joint distribution of $\boldsymbol{M}$ and $\boldsymbol{X}$, which is, as shown in Equation 33

$$f(\boldsymbol{M}, \boldsymbol{X}; \iota_X, \iota_M) = f(\boldsymbol{M}; \iota_M)\, f(\boldsymbol{X} \mid \boldsymbol{M}; \iota_X). \tag{33}$$

In Equation 33, $f(\boldsymbol{M}; \iota_M)$ is the marginal distribution of missingness (i.e., the probabilities of all possible missing patterns). The conditional distribution $f(\boldsymbol{X} \mid \boldsymbol{M}; \iota_X)$ refers to the substantive model of $\boldsymbol{X}$ for each missing pattern $\boldsymbol{M} = \boldsymbol{m}$. Therefore, pattern mixture models can be considered as multiple group models with the missing patterns as the grouping variable. The final parameter estimates $\hat{\iota}_X$ are obtained by averaging the pattern-specific parameter estimates $\hat{\iota}_X^{(m)}$ over the marginal distribution of $\boldsymbol{M}$. However, with the exception of cases with complete data ($\boldsymbol{M} = \boldsymbol{1}$), there are always one or more parameters in the vector ι_X that cannot be estimated due to the missing values. Therefore, pattern mixture models are inherently underidentified, and parameter estimation requires additional assumptions or restrictions.

For example, the inestimable parameters for cases with the missing pattern $\boldsymbol{M} = \boldsymbol{m}$ can be constrained to be equal to the estimates in the subgroup of cases without missing data (Little, 1993, 1994). Other identifying restrictions are discussed in the literature (Molenberghs et al., 2004; Thijs et al., 2002). However, the validity or tenability of these inevitable identifying restrictions cannot be proved or tested. These are the major limitations of the pattern mixture models.

The MCAR or MAR assumption is critical when using missing data methods that ignore the missing data mechanism. However, abandoning the ignorability assumptions may not resolve the missing data problem, due to the quite strict and untestable assumptions and restrictions of selection models as well as pattern mixture models. This might be one of the reasons for the limited use of these models in applied empirical research. Due to the possibility of trying different identifying restrictions to the same incomplete data, pattern mixture models are often recommended as a part of sensitivity analysis to compare different approaches to handle item nonresponses (Enders, 2010).

Psychometric Models for Nonignorable Item Nonresponses

Based on the idea of addressing nonignorable item nonresponses by a joint model of ($\boldsymbol{M}$, $\boldsymbol{X}_{obs}$), several model-based approaches have been developed in psychometrics. The basic idea is to combine the measurement model based on the observed item responses $\boldsymbol{X}_{obs}$ (i.e., the substantive model) with a psychometric model of the binary missing indicators $\boldsymbol{M} = M_1, ..., M_I$. It is assumed that the missing indicator variables are the manifest variables in a measurement model of a one-dimensional or multidimensional latent missing propensity $\boldsymbol{\theta}_M$ (Glas & Pimentel, 2008; Holman & Glas, 2005; Korobko et al., 2008; Moustaki & Knott, 2000; O'Muircheartaigh & Moustaki, 1999). A simple example of this class of models is the two-dimensional IRT model shown in Figure 9.4 (left), which includes the measurement model of the latent missing propensity θ_M. The model equation of a single missing indicator M_i, with $i = 1, ..., I$ is, shown in Equation 34:

$$Pr(M_i = 1|\theta_M; \iota_M) = \frac{exp[\alpha_i(\theta_M - \beta_i)]}{1 + exp[\alpha_i(\theta_M - \beta_i)]}. \tag{34}$$

The substantive model is a measurement model of the latent variable θ based on the observed part $\boldsymbol{X}_{obs}$, which is preserved as a submodel within the joint model of $\boldsymbol{M}$ and $\boldsymbol{X}_{obs}$.

The model can be simplified by using functions $f(\boldsymbol{M})$ of the missing indicators as predictors in a latent regression model $E(\theta \mid f(\boldsymbol{M}))$ as shown in Figure 9.4 (right; Rose, 2013, 2015; Rose et al., 2016). The sum of missing items $f(\boldsymbol{M}) = \sum_{i=1}^{I} M_i$ is a function that can be used in the latent regression model.

The underlying rationale of these models is that the information in $\boldsymbol{M}$ regarding $\boldsymbol{X}_{mis}$ is summarized in the latent missing propensity $\boldsymbol{\theta}_M$ or the functions $f(\boldsymbol{M})$. This information is then used for the estimation of the parameter vector $\boldsymbol{\iota}_X$ in the joint model of $\boldsymbol{M}$ and $\boldsymbol{X}_{obs}$. Although these models have been repeatedly applied, especially in educational assessments (Sinharay, 2021), they are not routinely used and are still disputed (Robitzsch, 2021). The reason is that these models also rest upon critical assumptions, such as conditional stochastic independence of the missing indicators of all manifest items $X_i, ..., X_I$ of the measurement model (e.g., $\boldsymbol{X}$) given (a) the latent variables ($\boldsymbol{\theta}$, $\boldsymbol{\theta}_M$) in the multidimensional IRT model, or (b) given the latent variable $\boldsymbol{\theta}$ and the functions $f(\boldsymbol{M})$ in the latent regression model.

It should be noted that less restrictive but more complex versions of these models have been proposed that allow for conditional stochastic dependencies between items and their missing indicators (Mislevy & Wu, 1996; Robitzsch, 2021). However, at the time of writing, these models are still subject to methodological research and are far from being routinely used in applied psychometrics.

Speeded tests also produce item nonresponses due to not-reached items, which should not be confused with missing values due to omitted items. In fact, missingness due to omitted versus not-reached items can have quite different missing data mechanisms (Pohl et al., 2014; Rose et al., 2016). In speeded tests, the response behavior depends not only on the theoretical construct of interest but also on processing speed. Specialized psychometric IRT models (Doebler & Holling, 2016; Glas & Pimentel, 2008) as well as CFA/SEM models (Schweizer, Gold, & Krampen, 2020; Schweizer, Gold, Krampen, & Wang, 2020; Schweizer et al., 2019) have been developed to handle nonignorable item nonresponses and to model processing speed as an additional factor underlying test takers' response behavior. Speeded tests are widely used and of particular interest in psychometrics. Therefore, modeling of data from speeded tests within the CFA framework is explained in more detail in Chapter 10.

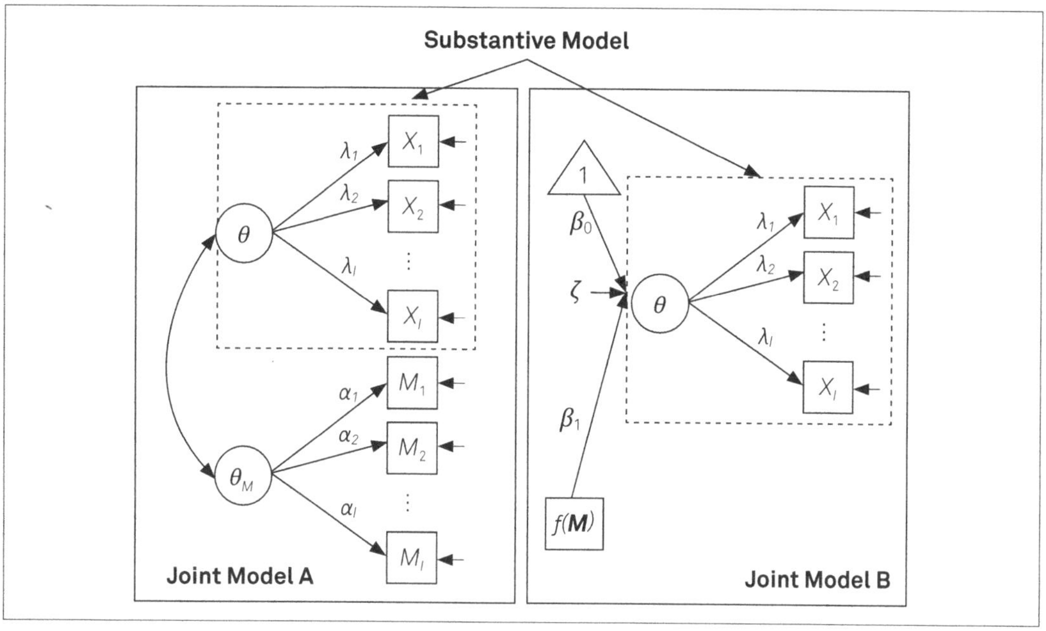

Figure 9.4 Joint models of $\boldsymbol{X}_{obs}$ and $\boldsymbol{M}$ for nonignorable item nonresponses. Joint Model A: The multidimensional IRT models with a latent missing propensity (left); and Joint Model B: the latent regression model with the function $f(\boldsymbol{M})$ of the missing indicators as a predictor in the latent regression $E(\theta \mid f(\boldsymbol{M}))$, as shown on the right.

Imputation of Nonignorable Item Nonresponses

Nonignorable item nonresponses mean that the predictive distribution (see Equation 13) of the missing item responses differ from the observed item responses. Therefore, conditional stochastic independence of $\boldsymbol{X}$ and $\boldsymbol{M}$ does not hold true (i.e., Equation 14 is not valid), which implies that missingness (i.e., $\boldsymbol{M}$) cannot be left out of the imputation model. However, the imputation model with the missing indicators $M_1, \ldots M_I$ as predictors for the incomplete variables $X_1, \ldots X_I$ is not identified without additional restrictions. The *delta-adjustment* has been proposed, where the conditional mean differences in X_i for cases with an observed response ($M_i = 1$) and cases with missing values ($M_i = 0$) are expressed by a parameter δ (Rubin, 1987, p. 203). Different fixed values of δ can be used for sensitivity analysis to check sensitivity of the results regarding the assumption of an ignorable missing data mechanism (Leacy et al., 2017; Tompsett et al., 2018). The random-indicator approach is a promising iterative imputation procedure that allows for estimating δ from the observed data (Jolani, 2012).

Statistical Software for Missing Data Problems

Many statistical software packages provide methods for handling missing data. R (Version 4.5.2), Mplus (Version 8.9), SPSS (Version 27.0), STATA (Release 18), and SAS (Version 9.4) can be used for imputing incomplete data by MI.

There are different implementations of MI in a number of R packages. The R packages *Amelia* (Honaker et al., 2011) and *norm* (Novo & Schafer, 2023) allow for MI based on the joint multivariate normal distribution. The *mice* package is a very popular and quite flexible R package for MI by chained equations for single and multilevel data (Van Buuren & Groothuis-Oudshoorn, 2011). The random-indicator approach of Jolani (2012) to impute nonignorable missing data is also implemented in the *mice* package. The R package *miceadds* extends the functionality of the *mice* package in many ways (Robitzsch & Grund, 2023). For example, *miceadds* allows for (a) MI of hierarchical and nonhierarchical multilevel data with two or more levels, (b) MI based on partial least squares, or (c) drawing plausible values of latent variables, which are MI of the latent variables taking the measurement error into account. The two R packages *jomo* (Quartagno & Carpenter, 2022) and *mitml* (Grund & Robitzsch, 2021) are two alternative packages for MI of single and multilevel data with user-friendly functionality for the subsequent analysis of multiply imputed data. The R package *semTools* is very useful for structural equation modeling with multiply imputed values (Jorgensen et al., 2022). The *sem.mi()* and *cfa.mi()* functions are wrapper functions for the *lavaan* package (Rosseel, 2012), which automates the analysis phase and the pooling phase using SEM in R.

FIML is implemented in many software packages for parameter estimation of SEM based on incomplete data. Mplus allows for FIML estimation of a broad range of linear, nonlinear single, and multilevel models. The R package *lavaan* allows for FIML in single and multiple group SEM. Furthermore, the pairwise ML estimation for SEM with binary and ordinal manifest variables is implemented in *lavaan*. The *semTools* R package provides functions that facilitate the inclusion of missing-relevant covariates in SEM. The *auxiliary()* function requires the model specification of the substantive model in *lavaan* and the list of missing-relevant covariates. The saturated correlates model is then specified internally and *lavaan* is called for parameter estimation. The function also returns the correct incremental model fit indices of the substantive model by internally fitting an adequate baseline model.

Mplus is currently the most flexible software for FIML estimation of a wide range of unidimensional and multidimensional, single and multiple group IRT models, and allows for including missing-relevant covariates in latent regression models. FIML as well as fully Bayesian estimation procedures are available in Mplus. Unidimensional IRT models with incomplete data can be fitted in R with the *ltm* package (Rizopoulos, 2006). However, unbiased parameter estimation requires that the missing data mechanism is ($\boldsymbol{X}_{obs}$)-conditional MAR, because no missing-relevant covariates can be included. The R package *TAM* allows to fit unidimensional and multidimensional IRT models, and it allows for the inclusion of missing-relevant covariates in a latent regression model (Robitzsch et al., 2021). The *mirt* R package can be used to fit unidimensional and multidimensional IRT models and multiple group IRT models in R but does not allow for simultaneous estimation of a latent regression model (Chalmers, 2012). Therefore, only categorical missing-relevant covariates can be considered as grouping variables.

It is impossible to provide a complete list of statistical software with a comprehensive overview of their respective capacities to handle missing data in this chapter. However, missing data are a common problem, and the information about the options for handling missing data can be found in the documentation of the respective software packages. A valuable resource is also the consultation of many user forums for statistical software where questions about handling missing values are discussed.

Summary

Item nonresponses are nearly inevitable in psychological assessments. In most cases item nonresponses are a nuisance, but sometimes they are intended (i.e., planned missing data by design). Therefore, missing data is an everyday problem for psychometricians and data analysts, but it is unfortunately not a trivial problem. There is no one-size-fits-all approach for item nonresponses. Even the handling of planned missing values requires deliberate methodological decisions taking into consideration the study design, the amount of missing data, and the intended analyses (i.e., the substantive models in later psychometric analyses). Unintended missing data due to omitted, not-reached, and not-codable items are not under the researchers' control. They are even more challenging, as the missing data mechanism is unknown. Further statistical analyses and psychometric modeling rest upon untestable assumptions regarding the missing data mechanism. Therefore, the data analyst is required to make well-considered decisions under uncertainty, but based on the best of their knowledge. The guiding questions in the decision process on handling missing data are shown in Figure 9.5.

FIML and standard implementations of MI require that the missing data mechanism is ignorable (i.e., MCAR or MAR). FIML and MI are commonly used state-of-the-art methods for item nonresponses, which implies that an ignorable nonresponse mechanism is explicitly or implicitly assumed. Usually, statistical methods that rely on strict and untestable assumptions are avoided. However, the less restrictive assumption of a nonignorable missing data mechanism is critical as well. All currently existing methods for handling nonignorable item nonresponses rest upon other, but also quite strict and often untestable assumptions. Therefore, the superiority of these methods to FIML and MI is questionable even if the assumption of an ignorable missing data mechanism does not hold true. The handling of nonignorable missing data is a perennial issue in methodological research. The development of more advanced and probably less restrictive approaches can be expected. At the time of writing, the approaches for nonignorable missing values are mainly used in the context of sensitivity analyses.

It is recommended to increase the plausibility of the ignorability assumption by selecting missing-relevant covariates when FIML or MI is used for unintended missing data (e.g., inclusive strategy). Ideally, the potentially missing-relevant covariates need to already be considered in the planning phase of psychological assessments. Unbiased parameter estimation using FIML is sometimes challenging, as the substantive models must be preserved in the joint model with the missing-relevant covariates. The extra DV model and the saturated correlates model can be used for SEM of incomplete data with missing-relevant covariates. The latter can also be included in latent regression models or multiple group models for parameter estimation of IRT models with incomplete data.

MI is a general approach to handle ignorable missing data. However, the adequacy of the imputation model regarding the substantive model must be ensured. The imputation model and the substantive model must be *congenial*, which means that the complexities of the substantive models (e.g., nonlinear dependencies, interactions, hierarchical data structures, etc.) must be considered in the imputation model. Otherwise, parameter estimation can be severely biased. Therefore, the deliberate specification of the imputation model is of utmost importance. The statistical analysis of multiply imputed data requires separate parameter estimation with each filled-in dataset (analysis phase), and the subsequent combination of the resulting point estimates and statistics (pooling phase). Fortunately, this procedure as well as the single-parameter and multiparameter tests are fully automated in many statistical software packages.

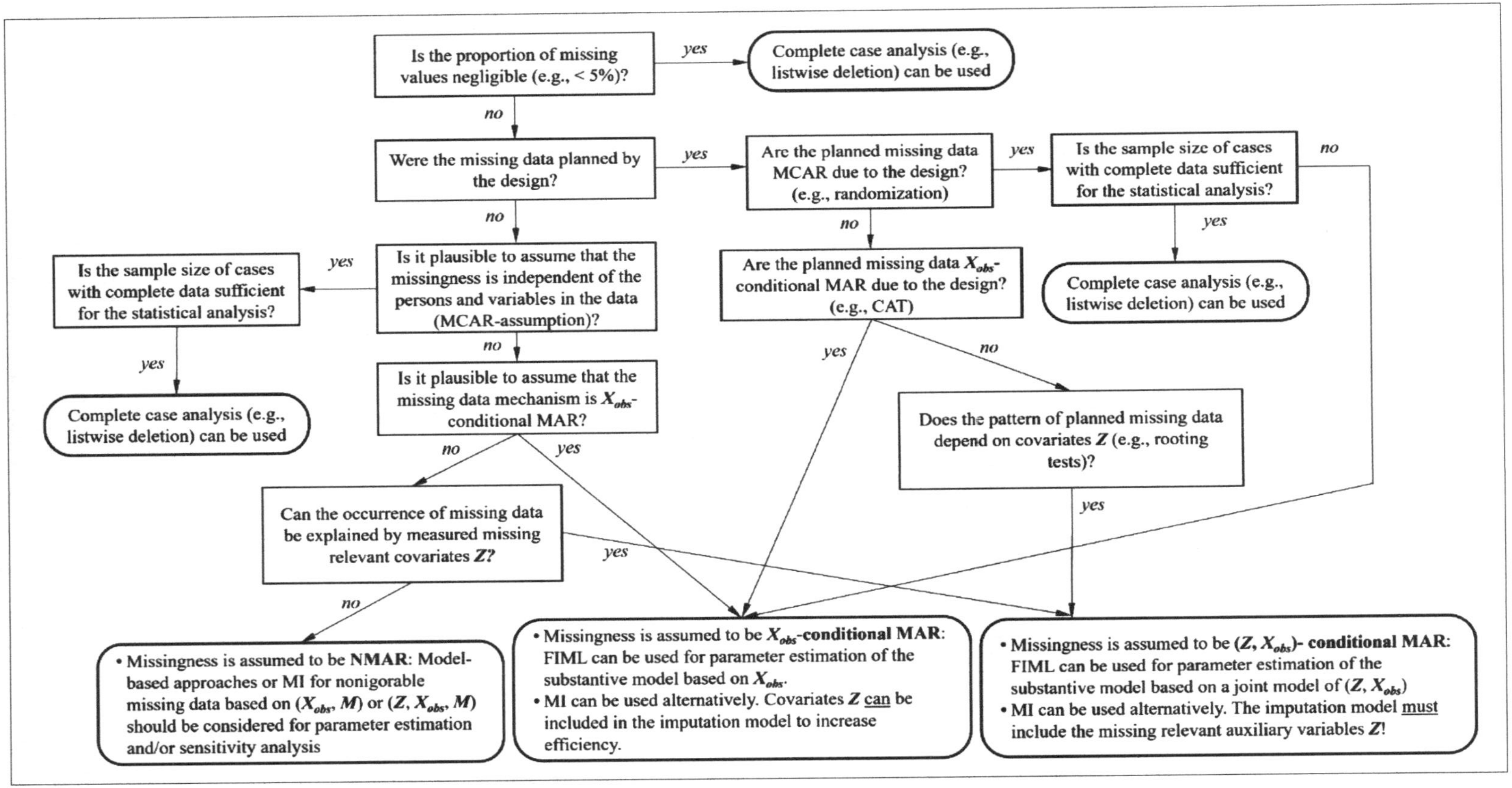

Figure 9.5 Guiding questions in considerations of how to handle missing data. CAT = computerized adaptive testing; FIML = full information maximum likelihood; MAR = missing at random; MCAR = missing completely at random; MI = multiple imputation; NMAR = not missing at random.

Of course, it is impossible to fully cover all currently used approaches to handle missing data in a single book chapter. For example, many different single imputation methods have been proposed, ranging from naive to elaborate (Huisman, 2000; Rubin & Little, 2002). The expectation-maximization (EM) algorithm has not been addressed in this chapter, but it is widely used to handle many different missing data problems including latent variables models (Dempster et al., 1977; McLachlan & Krishnan, 2007). In fact, latent variables are a form of inherently missing data. The MML estimator used for parameter estimation of IRT models is an example of the application of the EM algorithm (Bock & Aitkin, 1981; Hsu, 2000).

Fully Bayesian methods and models for missing data are a huge topic that deserves its own chapter. An overview is given by Das et al. (2008) and Ma and Chen (2018). There are also recent developments for handling item nonresponses, such as the factored regression modeling approach for missing data (Keller, 2022; Keller & Enders, 2022; Lüdtke et al., 2020a, 2020b), which relies on the fact that a joint distribution can be fully described as a product of conditional densities (see the section "MI by Chained Equations"). A set of regression equations including the substantive model of interest is specified in a joint multivariate model with the missing relevant covariates. A good overview of the current state of research on missing data is given by Enders (2023).

It is worth concluding this chapter by noting that the best way to handle (unintended) missing data is to avoid them – by optimizing the survey, the instruments, and the data collection design (de Leeuw, 2001).

References

Abayomi, K., Gelman, A., & Levy, M. (2008). Diagnostics for multivariate imputations. *Journal of the Royal Statistical Society Series C: Applied Statistics, 57*(3), 273–291. https://doi.org/10.1111/j.1467-9876.2007.00613.x

Andersen, E. B. (1972). The numerical solution of a set of conditional estimation equations. *Journal of the Royal Statistical Society: Series B (Methodological), 34*(1), 42–54. https://doi.org/10.1111/j.2517-6161.1972.tb00887.x

Baker, F. B., & Kim, S.-H. (2004). *Item response theory: Parameter estimation techniques*. CRC Press.

Barnard, J., & Rubin, D. B. (1999). Miscellanea: Small-sample degrees of freedom with multiple imputation. *Biometrika, 86*(4), 948–955. https://doi.org/10.1093/biomet/86.4.948

Bauer, B. (1988). *Eifersucht in Partnerschaften: Zusammenhang der Eifersuchtsdisposition mit ausgewählten Persönlichkeitsmerkmalen und demographischen Variablen* [Jealousy in relationships: Relationship between jealousy disposition and selected personality traits and demographic variables] [Unpublished Master's thesis]. University of Trier.

Birnbaum, A. (1968). Some latent trait models and their use in inferring an examinee's ability. In F. M. Lord & M. R. Novick (Eds.), *Statistical theories of mental test scores* (pp. 397–479). Addison-Wesley.

Blitzstein, J. K., & Hwang, J. (2019). *Introduction to probability*. CRC Press. https://doi.org/10.1201/9780429428357

Bock, R. D., & Aitkin, M. (1981). Marginal maximum likelihood estimation of item parameters: Application of an EM algorithm. *Psychometrika, 46*(4), 443–459. https://doi.org/10.1007/BF02293801

Chalmers, P. R. (2012). mirt: A multidimensional item response theory package for the R environment. *Journal of Statistical Software, 48*(2), 1–29. https://doi.org/10.18637/jss.v048.i06

Collins, L. M., Schafer, J. L., & Kam, C.-M. (2001). A comparison of inclusive and restrictive strategies in modern missing data procedures. *Psychological Methods, 6*(4), 330. https://doi.org/10.1037/1082-989X.6.4.330

Das, S., Chen, M.-H., Kim, S., & Warren, N. (2008). A Bayesian structural equations model for multilevel data with missing responses and missing covariates. *Bayesian Analysis, 3*(1), 197–224.

De Ayala, R. J. (2013). *The theory and practice of item response theory*. Guilford Press.

de Leeuw, E. D. (2001). Reducing missing data in surveys: An overview of methods. *Quality and Quantity, 35*(2), 147–160. https://doi.org/10.1023/A:1010395805406

Dempster, A. P., Laird, N. M., & Rubin, D. B. (1977). Maximum likelihood from incomplete data via the EM algorithm. *Journal of the Royal Statistical Society: Series B (Methodological), 39*(1), 1–22. https://doi.org/10.1111/j.2517-6161.1977.tb01600.x

Doebler, A., & Holling, H. (2016). A processing speed test based on rule-based item generation: An analysis with the Rasch Poisson Counts model. *Learning and Individual Differences, 52*, 121–128. https://doi.org/10.1016/j.lindif.2015.01.013

Durrant, G. B. (2009). Imputation methods for handling item-nonresponse in practice: Methodological issues and recent debates. *International Journal of Social Research Methodology, 12*(4), 293–304. https://doi.org/10.1080/13645570802394003

Enders, C. K. (2001). A primer on maximum likelihood algorithms available for use with missing data. *Structural Equation Modeling, 8*(1), 128–141. https://doi.org/10.1207/S15328007SEM0801_7

Enders, C. K. (2008). A note on the use of missing auxiliary variables in full information maximum likelihood-based structural equation models. *Structural Equation Modeling, 15*(3), 434–448. https://doi.org/10.1080/10705510802154307

Enders, C. K. (2010). *Applied missing data analysis*. Guilford Press.

Enders, C. K. (2023). Missing data: An update on the state of the art. *Psychological Methods, 30*(2), 322–339. https://doi.org/10.1037/met0000563

Enders, C. K., & Gottschall, A. C. (2011). Multiple imputation strategies for multiple group structural equation models. *Structural Equation Modeling, 18*(1), 35–54. https://doi.org/10.1080/10705511.2011.532695

Etz, A. (2018). Introduction to the concept of likelihood and its applications. *Advances in Methods and Practices in Psychological Science, 1*(1), 60–69. https://doi.org/10.1177/2515245917744314

Gelfand, A. E. (2000). Gibbs sampling. *Journal of the American Statistical Association, 95*(452), 1300–1304. https://doi.org/10.1080/01621459.2000.10474335

Gelman, A., Carlin, J. B., Stern, H. S., Dunson, D. B., Vehtari, A., & Rubin, D. B. (2013). *Bayesian data analysis* (3rd ed.). Chapman and Hall; CRC Press. https://doi.org/10.1201/b16018

Glas, C. A. W., & Pimentel, J. L. (2008). Modeling nonignorable missing data in speeded tests. *Educational and Psychological Measurement, 68*(6), 907–922. https://doi.org/10.1177/0013164408315262

Glynn, R. J., Laird, N. M., & Rubin, D. B. (1986). Selection modelling versus mixture modelling with nonignorable nonresponse. In H. Wainer (Ed.), *Drawing inferences from self-selected samples* (pp. 115–142). Springer. https://doi.org/10.1007/978-1-4612-4976-4_10

Graham, J. W. (2003). Adding missing-data-relevant variables to FIML-based structural equation models. *Structural Equation Modeling, 10*(1), 80–100. https://doi.org/10.1207/S15328007SEM1001_4

Graham, J. W., & Coffman, D. L. (2012). Structural equation modeling with missing data. In R. H. Hoyle (Ed.), *Handbook of structural equation modeling* (pp. 277–297). Guilford Press.

Graham, J. W., Olchowski, A. E., & Gilreath, T. D. (2007). How many imputations are really needed? Some practical clarifications of multiple imputation theory. *Prevention Science, 8*(3), 206–213. https://doi.org/10.1007/s11121-007-0070-9

Graham, J., Taylor, B., & Cumsille, P. (2001). New methods for the analysis of change. In L. Collins & A. Sayer (Eds.), *New methods for the analysis of change* (pp. 335–353). American Psychological Association.

Graham, J. W., Taylor, B. J., Olchowski, A. E., & Cumsille, P. E. (2006). Planned missing data designs in psychological research. *Psychological Methods, 11*, 323–343. https://doi.org/10.1037/1082-989X.11.4.323

Grund, S., Lüdtke, O., & Robitzsch, A. (2016). Pooling ANOVA results from multiply imputed datasets. *Methodology, 12*(3), 75–88. https://doi.org/10.1027/1614-2241/a000111

Grund, S., & Robitzsch, A. (2021). *mitml: Tools for multiple imputation in multilevel modeling* (Version R package version 0.4-3). https://CRAN.R-project.org/package=mitml

Heckman, J. (1976). The common structure of statistical models of truncation, sample selection and limited dependent variables and a simple estimator for such models. *Annals of Economic and Social Measurement, 5*(4), 475–492.

Heckman, J. (1979). Sample selection bias as a specification error. *Econometrica, 47*(1), 153–161. https://doi.org/10.2307/1912352

Holman, R., & Glas, C. A. W. (2005). Modelling non-ignorable missing-data mechanisms with item response theory models. *British Journal of Mathematical and Statistical Psychology, 58*(1), 1–17. https://doi.org/10.1111/j.2044-8317.2005.tb00312.x

Honaker, J., King, G., & Blackwell, M. (2011). Amelia II: A program for missing data. *Journal of Statistical Software, 45*(7), 1–47. https://doi.org/10.18637/jss.v045.i07

Hox, J. (2013). Multilevel regression and multilevel structural equation modeling. In T. D. Little (Ed.), *The Oxford handbook of quantitative methods* (Vol. 2, pp. 281–294). Oxford University Press. https://doi.org/10.1093/oxfordhb/9780199934898.013.0014

Hsu, Y. (2000). On the Bock-Aitkin procedure – From an EM algorithm perspective. *Psychometrika, 65*(4), 547–549. https://doi.org/10.1007/BF02296345

Huisman, M. (2000). Imputation of missing item responses: Some simple techniques. *Quality and Quantity, 34*, 331–351. https://doi.org/10.1023/A:1004782230065

Jackman, S. (2009). *Bayesian analysis for the social sciences*. Wiley. https://doi.org/10.1002/9780470686621

Jolani, S. (2012). *Dual imputation strategies for analyzing incomplete data* [Doctoral dissertation]. Utrecht University. https://dspace.library.uu.nl/handle/1874/257547

Jorgensen, T. D., Pornprasertmanit, S., Schoemann, A. M., & Rosseel, Y. (2022). *semTools: Useful tools for structural equation modeling* (Version R package version 0.5-6). https://CRAN.R-project.org/package=semTools

Kaplan, D., & Su, D. (2016). On matrix sampling and imputation of context questionnaires with implications for the generation of plausible values in large-scale assessments. *Journal of Educational and Behavioral Statistics, 41*(1), 57–80. https://doi.org/10.3102/1076998615622221

Katsikatsou, M., Moustaki, I., Yang-Wallentin, F., & Jöreskog, K. G. (2012). Pairwise likelihood estimation for factor analysis models with ordinal data. *Computational Statistics & Data Analysis, 56*(12), 4243–4258. https://doi.org/10.1016/j.csda.2012.04.010

Keller, B. T. (2022). An introduction to factored regression models with Blimp. *Psych, 4*(1), 10–37. https://doi.org/10.3390/psych4010002

Keller, B. T., & Enders, C. K. (2022). An investigation of factored regression missing data methods for multilevel models with cross-level interactions. *Multivariate Behavioral Research, 58*(5), 1–26.

Kenward, M. G., & Molenberghs, G. (1998). Likelihood based frequentist inference when data are missing at random. *Statistical Science, 13*(3), 236–247. http://www.jstor.org/stable/2676702 https://doi.org/10.1214/ss/1028905886

Kim, J. K., & Shao, J. (2014). *Statistical methods for handling incomplete data*. CRC Press.

Korobko, O. K., Glas, C. A. W., Bosker, R. J., & Luyten, J. W. (2008). Comparing the difficulty of examination subjects with item response theory. *Journal of Educational Measurement, 45*, 139-157. https://doi.org/10.1111/j.1745-3984.2007.00057.x

Leacy, F. P., Floyd, S., Yates, T. A., & White, I. R. (2017). Analyses of sensitivity to the missing-at-random assumption using multiple imputation with delta adjustment: Application to a tuberculosis/HIV prevalence survey with incomplete HIV-status data. *American Journal of Epidemiology, 185*(4), 304–315. https://doi.org/10.1093/aje/kww107

Levy, R., & Mislevy, R. J. (2017). *Bayesian psychometric modeling*. Chapman and Hall; CRC Press. https://doi.org/10.1201/9781315374604

Little, R. J. A. (1988). A test of missing completely at random for multivariate data with missing values. *Journal of the American Statistical Association, 83*(404), 1198–1202. https://doi.org/10.1080/01621459.1988.10478722

Little, R. J. A. (1993). Pattern-mixture models for multivariate incomplete data. *Journal of the American Statistical Association, 88*(421), 125–134. https://doi.org/10.1080/01621459.1993.10594302

Little, R. J. A. (1994). A class of pattern-mixture models for normal incomplete data. *Biometrika, 81*(3), 471–483. https://doi.org/10.1093/biomet/81.3.471

Little, R. J. A. (2008). Selection and pattern-mixture models. In G. Fitzmaurice, M. Davidian, G. Verbeke, & G. Molenberghs (Eds.), *Longitudinal data analysis* (pp. 409-432). Chapman and Hall; CRC Press. https://doi.org/10.1201/9781420011579.ch18

Little, R. J., & Rubin, D. B. (2019). *Statistical analysis with missing data* (3rd ed.). Wiley.

Liu, Y., & Enders, C. K. (2017). Evaluation of multi-parameter test statistics for multiple imputation. *Multivariate Behavioral Research, 52*(3), 371–390. https://doi.org/10.1080/00273171.2017.1298432

Lüdtke, O., Robitzsch, A., & West, S. G. (2020a). Analysis of interactions and nonlinear effects with missing data: A factored regression modeling approach using maximum likelihood estimation. *Multivariate Behavioral Research, 55*(3), 361–381. https://doi.org/10.1080/00273171.2019.1640104

Lüdtke, O., Robitzsch, A., & West, S. G. (2020b). Regression models involving nonlinear effects with missing data: A sequential modeling approach using Bayesian estimation. *Psychological Methods, 25*, 157–181. https://doi.org/10.1037/met0000233

Ma, Z., & Chen, G. (2018). Bayesian methods for dealing with missing data problems. *Journal of the Korean Statistical Society, 47*(3), 297–313. https://doi.org/10.1016/j.jkss.2018.03.002

Mair, P., & Hatzinger, R. (2007). CML based estimation of extended Rasch models with the eRm package in R. *Psychology Science, 49*(1), 26–43.

McLachlan, G. J., & Krishnan, T. (2007). *The EM algorithm and extensions*. Wiley.

Meredith, W. (1993). Measurement invariance, factor analysis and factorial invariance. *Psychometrika, 58*(4), 525–543. https://doi.org/10.1007/BF02294825

Mislevy, R. J. (2016). Missing responses in item response modeling. In W. J. van der Linden (Ed.), *Handbook of item response theory, Volume 1: Statistical tools* (1st ed., Vol. 2, pp. 171–194). Chapman and Hall; CRC Press.

Mislevy, R. J., Beaton, A. E., Kaplan, B., & Sheehan, K. M. (1992). Estimating population characteristics from sparse matrix samples of item responses. *Journal of Educational Measurement, 29*(2), 133–161. https://doi.org/10.1111/j.1745-3984.1992.tb00371.x

Mislevy, R. J., & Wu, P. K. (1996). Missing responses and IRT ability estimation: Omits, choice, time limits, and adaptive testing. *ETS Research Report Series, 1996*(2), 1–36. https://doi.org/10.1002/j.2333-8504.1996.tb01708.x

Molenberghs, G., Thijs, H., Michiels, B., Verbeke, G., & Kenward, M. G. (2004). Pattern-mixture models. *Journal de la Société française de Statistique, 145*(2), 49–77.

Moustaki, I., & Knott, M. (2000). Weighting for item non-response in attitude scales by using latent variable models with covariates. *Journal of the Royal Statistical Society, Series A*, 163. https://doi.org/10.1111/1467-985X.00177

Muthén, B., & Asparouhov, T. (2011). Beyond multilevel regression modeling: Multilevel analysis in a general latent variable framework. In J. Hox & J. K. Roberts (Eds.), *Handbook of advanced multilevel analysis* (pp. 15–40). Taylor and Francis.

Nguyen, C. D., Carlin, J. B., & Lee, K. J. (2017). Model checking in multiple imputation: An overview and case study. *Emerging Themes in Epidemiology, 14*(1), 8. https://doi.org/10.1186/s12982-017-0062-6

Nguyen, C. D., Carlin, J. B., & Lee, K. J. (2021). Practical strategies for handling breakdown of multiple imputation procedures. *Emerging Themes in Epidemiology, 18*(5). https://doi.org/10.1186/s12982-021-00095-3

Novo, A. A., & Schafer, J. L. (2023). *norm: Analysis of multivariate normal datasets with missing values* (R package version 1.0-11.0). https://CRAN.R-project.org/package=norm

O'Muircheartaigh, C., & Moustaki, I. (1999). Symmetric pattern models: A latent variable approach to item non-response in attitude scales. *Journal of the Royal Statistical Society: Series A (Statistics in Society), 162*(2), 177–194. https://doi.org/10.1111/1467-985X.00129

Peters, C. L. O., & Enders, C. (2002). A primer for the estimation of structural equation models in the presence of missing data: Maximum likelihood algorithms. *Journal of Targeting, Measurement and Analysis for Marketing, 11*(1), 81–95. https://doi.org/10.1057/palgrave.jt.5740069

Pohl, S., Gräfe, L., & Rose, N. (2014). Dealing with omitted and not-reached items in competence tests: Evaluating approaches accounting for missing responses in item response theory models. *Educational and Psychological Measurement*, 74. https://doi.org/10.1177/0013164413504926

Prinzie, P., & Onghena, P. (2005). Cohort sequential design. In B. S. Everitt & D. C. Howell (Eds.), *Encyclopedia of statistics in behavioral science* (Vol. 2, pp. 319–322). Wiley. https://doi.org/10.1002/0470013192.bsa110

Quartagno, M., & Carpenter, J. (2022). *jomo: A package for multilevel joint modelling multiple imputation* (R package version 2.7-3). https://CRAN.R-project.org/package=jomo

Rasch, G. (1960). *Probabilistic models for some intelligence and attainment tests*. Danmarks Paedogogiske Institut.

Rhemtulla, M., & Hancock, G. R. (2016). Planned missing data designs in educational psychology research. *Educational Psychology, 51*, 305–316. https://doi.org/10.1080/00461520.2016.1208094

Richter, M., Schlegel, K., Thomas, P., & Troche, S. J. (2022). Adult attachment and personality as predictors of jealousy in romantic relationships. *Frontiers in Psychology*, 13. https://doi.org/10.3389/fpsyg.2022.861481

Rizopoulos, D. (2006). ltm: An R package for latent variable modelling and item response theory analysis. *Journal of Statistical Software, 17*(5), 1–25. https://doi.org/10.18637/jss.v017.i05

Robitzsch, A. (2021). On the treatment of missing item responses in educational large-scale assessment data: An illustrative simulation study and a case study using PISA 2018 mathematics data. *European Journal of Investigation in Health, Psychology and Education, 11*(4), 1653–1687. https://doi.org/10.3390/ejihpe11040117

Robitzsch, A., & Grund, S. (2023). *miceadds: Some additional multiple imputation functions, especially for 'mice'* (R package version 3.16-18). https://CRAN.R-project.org/package=miceadds

Robitzsch, A., Kiefer, T., & Wu, M. (2021). *TAM: Test analysis modules* (R package version 3.7-16). https://CRAN.R-project.org/package=TAM

Rose, N. (2013). *Item nonresponses in educational and psychological measurement* [Unpublished doctoral dissertation]. Friedrich-Schiller-University Jena.. http://d-nb.info/1036873145/34

Rose, N. (2015). Commonalities and differences in IRT-based methods for nonignorable item-nonresponses. *Psychological Test and Assessment Modeling, 57*(4). 472–498.

Rose, N., von Davier, M., & Nagengast, B. (2016). Modeling omitted and not-reached items in IRT models. *Psychometrika, 82*(3), 795-819. https://doi.org/10.1007/s11336-016-9544-7

Rose, N., Von Davier, M., & Xu, X. (2010). *Modeling nonignorable missing data with item response theory (IRT).* (ETS Research Report: ETS RR-10-11). E. T. Service. https://doi.org/10.1002/j.2333-8504.2010.tb02218.x

Rosseel, Y. (2012). lavaan: An R package for structural equation modeling. *Journal of Statistical Software, 48*(2), 1–36. https://doi.org/10.18637/jss.v048.i02

Rosseel, Y. (2021). Evaluating the observed log-likelihood function in two-level structural equation modeling with missing data: From formulas to R code. *Psych, 3*(2), 197–232. https://doi.org/10.3390/psych3020017

Rubin, D. B. (1976). Inference and missing data. *Biometrika, 63*(3), 581–592. https://doi.org/10.1093/biomet/63.3.581

Rubin, D. B. (1987). *Multiple imputation for nonresponse in surveys.* Wiley. https://doi.org/10.1002/9780470316696

Rubin, D. B. (1996). Multiple imputation after 18+ years. *Journal of the American Statistical Association, 91*(434), 473–489. https://doi.org/10.2307/2291635

Rubin, D. B., & Little, R. J. A. (2002). Single imputation methods. In R. J. A. Little & D. B. Rubin (Eds.), *Statistical analysis with missing data* (2nd ed., pp. 59–74). Wiley.

Rubin, D. B., & Schenker, N. (1986). Multiple imputation for interval estimation from simple random samples with ignorable nonresponse. *Journal of the American Statistical Association, 81*(394), 366–374. https://doi.org/10.1080/01621459.1986.10478280

Schafer, J. L. (1997). *Analysis of incomplete multivariate data.* Chapman and Hall; CRC Press. https://doi.org/10.1201/9781439821862

Schafer, J. L. (1999). Multiple imputation: a primer. *Statistical Methods in Medical Research, 8*(1), 3–15. https://doi.org/10.1177/096228029900800102

Schafer, J. L., & Graham, J. W. (2002). Missing data: Our view of the state of the art. *Psychological Methods, 7*(2), 147–177. https://doi.org/10.1037/1082-989X.7.2.147

Schweizer, K., Gold, A., & Krampen, D. (2020). A semi-hierarchical confirmatory factor model for speeded data. *Structural Equation Modeling, 27*(5), 773–780. https://doi.org/10.1080/10705511.2019.1707083

Schweizer, K., Gold, A., Krampen, D., & Wang, T. (2020). On modeling missing data of an incomplete design in the CFA framework [Methods]. *Frontiers in Psychology*, 11. https://doi.org/10.3389/fpsyg.2020.581709

Schweizer, K., Reiß, S., Ren, X., Wang, T., & Troche, S. J. (2019). Speed effect analysis using the CFA framework. *Frontiers in Psychology*, 10. https://doi.org/10.3389/fpsyg.2019.00239

Seaman, S., Galati, J., Jackson, D., & Carlin, J. (2013). What is meant by "missing at random"? *Statistical Science, 28*(2), 257–268. https://doi.org/10.1214/13-STS415

Sinharay, S. (2021). Reporting proficiency levels for examinees with incomplete data. *Journal of Educational and Behavioral Statistics, 47*(3), 263–296. https://doi.org/10.3102/10769986211051379

Thijs, H., Molenberghs, G., Michiels, B., Verbeke, G., & Curran, D. (2002). Strategies to fit pattern-mixture models. *Biostatistics, 3*(2), 245–265. https://doi.org/10.1093/biostatistics/3.2.245

Tompsett, D. M., Leacy, F., Moreno-Betancur, M., Heron, J., & White, I. R. (2018). On the use of the not-at-random fully conditional specification (NARFCS) procedure in practice. *Statistics in Medicine, 37*(15), 2338–2353. https://doi.org/https://doi.org/10.1002/sim.7643

Van Buuren, S. (2018). *Flexible imputation of missing data.* CRC Press.

Van Buuren, S., & Groothuis-Oudshoorn, K. (2011). mice: Multivariate imputation by chained equations in R. *Journal of Statistical Software, 45*, 1–67. https://doi.org/10.18637/jss.v045.i03

Von Hippel, P. T. (2009). How to impute interactions, squares, and other transformed variables. *Sociological Methodology, 39*(1), 265–291. https://doi.org/10.1111/j.1467-9531.2009.01215.x

White, I. R., Daniel, R., & Royston, P. (2010). Avoiding bias due to perfect prediction in multiple imputation of incomplete categorical variables. *Computational Statistics & Data Analysis, 54*(10), 2267–2275. https://doi.org/10.1016/j.csda.2010.04.005

Xie, X., & Meng, X.-L. (2017). Dissecting multiple imputation from a multi-phase inference perspective: What happens when God's, imputer's and analyst's models are uncongenial? *Statistica Sinica, 27*(4), 1485–1545. https://doi.org/10.5705/ss.2014.067

Chapter 10

The Effect of Speededness

Karl Schweizer, Xuezhu Ren, and Tengfei Wang

Abstract

A speed effect is a method effect observable in data collected with a time limit in testing. It implies incompleteness, since the time limit prevents participants from completing all items. Besides the time limit, cognitive speed determines how many items each individual completes. A method for describing the frequency distribution of missing responses in a sample is outlined. This method makes use of the logistic function and can be employed in confirmatory factor analysis for capturing systematic variation associated with the speed effect. It enables investigations of the structural validity of data, showing a speed effect without replacement.

Introduction

Not enough time for completing all items of a scale or questionnaire is an everyday situation that endangers the quality of psychological research, and therefore, requires treatment in a book on method effects in psychological assessment. Accordingly, this chapter introduces missing data due to the lack of enough testing time, and its formal representation and control in structural investigations, using *confirmatory factor analysis* (CFA).

The term *speed effect* (or *speededness*) refers to the incompleteness of data because of a time limit in testing (Oshima, 1994). Considered in more detail, the incompleteness of data originates from participants who are unable to complete all items of the administered test within the allotted time span. Usually there are individual differences in the number of uncompleted items. For some participants, this number is large, whereas for others it is small, or even zero. Since responses are the precondition for assigning values to the corresponding spots of the data matrix serving as the input to data analysis for investigating experimental effects, or for structural investigations as examples, missing responses are detrimental in a number of ways. Following established conventions, such missing values are referred to here as *missing data* or simply *missings* (see also Chapter 9: "Missing Data: How to Handle Incomplete Data").

Many perspectives have been taken in research on missing data. One major perspective is guided by the aim to identify types of missing data, and to use this knowledge to prevent possible impairments in the data analysis by imputation (Rubin, 1976; see also Chapter 9 in this present book). Another major perspective aims at developing measurement models in the framework of item response theory, for dealing with missing data by considering a number of special structural features including latent classes and external variables (for an overview, see Cintron, 2021). Such models are employed for generating replacements for missings. The perspective taken in writing this chapter focuses on the missing data problem in the framework of CFA and differs from the other approaches by making structural investigations possible without the replacement of missing data.

This chapter provides general information on missing data, and the speed effect (see the sections "Speed Effect as Source of Missing Data," and "Speed Effect as a Characteristic of a Sample"), introduces the formal representation of the speed effect that prepares for a statistical investigation in the framework of CFA (see sections "Speed-Effect Measurement Model," "Characteristic Course of the Speed Effect," and "Formal Representation of Missings"), and describes how to conduct that investigation with real data (see the section "An Example"). The Appendix includes the program code used in investigating the data serving as an example.

Speed Effect as Source of Missing Data

According to the categorical scheme of missing data of Little and Rubin (2002), missing data due to a time limit are *missing data that are not at random* (MNAR). While in the other categories, such as *missing data that are completely at random* (MCAR) and *missing data that are at random* (MAR), random influences are considered major reasons for missings, such influences do not play a role in MNAR. Missing data because of a speed effect can be considered as MNAR for two reasons: First, the presence of a time limit in testing is a fundamental aspect of collecting performance data (Gulliksen, 1950). Without the time limit, virtually each participant can be expected to complete all items in whatever way. Second, participants differ in their speed of cognitive processing (Oshima, 1994; Partchev et al., 2013). This implies that each participant needs a specific time span for completing each item and that these time spans determine whether the participants can complete all items before the time runs out. We like to add that the MNAR category of Little and Rubin (2002) is not restricted to missing data in the sense of the speed effect. It also includes missing data due to a planned missing data design (Rhemtulla & Hancock, 2016; Rioux et al., 2020) and incompleteness because of ethical issues preventing data collection (Oommen, 2023).

The speed effect in psychological assessment is a *method effect* (Maul, 2013; Podsakoff et al., 2003; Schweizer, 2020) since it is mainly due to a characteristic of the measurement procedure – that is, the time limit in testing. Without this time limit it would be exclusively the latent ability stimulated by the test items, that would determine the participants' performance, and there would be no speed effect. But, under the condition of a time limit in testing there are in fact two latent sources of performance: the stimulated latent ability and speed of cognitive processing (Oshima, 1994; Partchev et al., 2013). This contradicts a basic assumption of psychological testing: the stimulated latent ability is the only systematic source of responding to a test item, while all other influences are random. If there is another systematic source of responding, this assumption of the theory of psychological testing is called into question. As a consequence, the validity of measurement is compromised (Lu & Sireci, 2007). If such a characteristic of the measurement procedure results in validity impairment, it is referred to as a method effect, unless missingness is selected as performance indicator.

The speed effect has found its way into psychological assessment through the search for the best way of measuring performance by asking participants to complete psychological tests. Such tests were expected to enable the prediction of academic success (e.g., the prediction of course grades), and they were thought to serve selection and placement purposes. Out of these considerations, two assessment approaches have emerged: assessment via speed tests, on one hand, and via *power tests*, on the other (Gulliksen, 1950).

A major characteristic of assessment using speed tests is the limitation of the time for completing the items of the test in the same way for each participant. Such a limitation is favorable regarding the economy of testing and the standardization of the testing condition, which is a property thought to boost the internal validity of measurement (Campbell & Stanley, 1966). Furthermore, such time limits seem to be similar to the concept of efficiency in physics, which is defined as the ratio of the completed work to processing time (Wilhelm & Schulze, 2002).

In contrast, assessment using power tests is expected to ensure that all participants have the same chance to tackle and complete each item of the test – although actual cases of unlimited testing time have been rare. This approach focuses on performance in light of items that show different degrees of difficulty, with the expectation that all participants would complete all items, but differ in the number of their correct answers.

For a while there was the opinion that both approaches reflected participants' performance equally well, until the fundamental differences of the approaches became apparent (Rindler, 1979). The original opinion – equivalence of approaches (speed and power) – implied that individual differences in speed of responding could perfectly predict individual differences in correctness of responding. However, this assumption has been contradicted by a host of studies on the cognitive basis of intelligence, showing that measures of speed and measures of capacity based on correctness of answers are not equivalent (Stankov, 2010).

Furthermore, the autonomy of the two approaches is to be called into question. For example, a pure speed test requires "items so easy that they never give a wrong answer to any of them" (Gulliksen, 1950, p. 230). This requirement is unlikely to ever be met, because extremely easy items may lead to careless responding and thus to incorrect responses, although participants are able to do better. Such behavior can be avoided by including some more demanding items into a sequence of otherwise very easy items. Thus, this argument appears to favor power testing over speed testing.

Yet, power testing shows a downside of its own. Participants do not just complete one item after the other. Instead, they evaluate the outcome of their cognitive processing and are frequently well aware of the low quality of the response. If there is ample time for completing the items, they may stop and wait for inspiration and all kinds of helpful cues. The more time is available, the greater the possibility that participants will resort to unauthorized means for completing the test items correctly.

As a consequence of such complications, nowadays most tests include features of both speed and power testing, although the discrimination is still in use: Tests are referred to as power tests if they include items from a broad range of difficulty levels, together with a liberal time allotment, while tests are characterized as speed tests if the items are from a low-difficulty range and the time limit is demanding.

Speed Effect as a Characteristic of a Sample

In the case of testing without a time limit, each participant will eventually complete all items and reach the highest possible score. But, if there is a time limit, only a subset of participants will complete all items. For such participants, performance depends solely on the latent attribute that is stimulated by the test items and on random influences (and eventually on their testing strategy). In the other participants, performance not only depends on the latent source stimulated by the items but also on (lack of enough) speed, and on random influences (Oshima, 1994; Partchev et al., 2013). This means that participants can be subdivided into two groups, because they differ according to the main sources of performance, with consequences for measurement validity: In one group, the results of measurement reflect individual differences in the measured attribute, whereas in the other group the results not only reflect individual differences in the measured attribute but also in speed of cognitive processing. It is obvious that the scale in some participants does not exclusively measure what it is expected to measure, because of the time limit in testing. This means validity impairment.

The theoretical analysis not only reveals the validity impairment because of the time limit, but also suggests adaptation of structural investigations by factor-analytic methods to this situation. Factor analysis already shows a long tradition of investigating method effects. Starting from the multitrait-multimethod design proposed for the detection of method effects (Campbell, & Fiske, 1959), a number of multitrait-multimethod models have been developed and employed for separating the effects that are due to trait sources and observational methods (Byrne, 2016). Different observational sources of method effects have been identified by such models (see also Chapter 2).

In addition, a special branch of factor analysis has turned out to fit especially well with examining the characteristics of a speed effect: CFA with fixed factor loadings reflecting characteristics of such an effect (Ren et al., 2017; Schweizer & Ren, 2013; Schweizer, Reiß et al., 2019). Such a CFA model assumes two latent variables: one of them representing the measured attribute and the other, speed of cognitive processing. Since such a model has the status of a hypothesis, its appropriateness must be checked by empirical investigation. In empirical studies, it was demonstrated that the speed latent variable actually correlated with an external measure of mental speed, while it was unrelated to an attribute latent variable that was based on unspeeded data (data collected with a very liberal time limit; Borter et al., 2023; Zeller et al., 2020).

Speed-Effect Measurement Model

The measurement model for *speed-effect analysis* can be considered as an enlargement of the customary one-factor confirmatory factor analysis (CFA) model (Graham, 2006) by an additional latent variable. Such a model is also referred to as a *bifactor model* (Reise, 2012). It includes two latent variables for representing the attribute measured by the scale, on the one hand, and cognitive speed, on the other hand, $\xi_{\text{attribute}}$ and ξ_{speed}, respectively. The equation of the measurement model sets the manifest variables reflecting the centered observations ($\mathbf{x}$) equal to the sum composed of three components, one reflecting the attribute contribution, another one the speed contribution and a further one reflecting uniqueness. This model is defined in Equation 1:

$$\mathbf{x} = \boldsymbol{\lambda}_{\text{attribute}}\, \xi_{\text{attribute}} + \boldsymbol{\lambda}_{\text{speed}}\, \xi_{\text{speed}} + \boldsymbol{\delta}, \qquad (1)$$

where $\mathbf{x}$ is the $p \times 1$ vector of manifest variables, $\boldsymbol{\lambda}_{\text{attribute}}$ and $\boldsymbol{\lambda}_{\text{speed}}$ the $p \times 1$ vectors of factor loadings, and $\boldsymbol{\delta}$ the $p \times 1$ vector of residuals. The first component of the sum is expected to account for systematic variation of data due to the attribute measured by the scale, and the second component for systematic variation due to cognitive speed. This model and multitrait-multimethod models (Byrne, 2016) share the feature that the manifest variables load on both method (i.e., speed) and attribute latent variables.

The customary way of conducting factor analysis is estimating factor loadings. The corresponding measurement model (Equation 1) includes latent variables with free factor loadings. Figure 10.1 provides an illustration of such a model. The application of such a model to data means estimation of all factor loadings on the attribute latent variable and of those of items i to p on the cognitive speed latent variable. Furthermore, the residual variances (δs) are estimated. The model with free factor loadings is likely to yield valid results if item i is known, and there are no other systematic influences.

However, there is another method effect showing a course along the sequence of items of a scale that is similar to the speed effect: the *item position effect* (see also Chapter 11), which reflects sources unrelated to the speed effect (Hartig et al., 2007; Knowles, 1988; Schweizer, 2012). This means that using free factor loadings can lead to confusion of different effects – namely, the speed effect and the item position effect. Such confusion can be avoided by using fixed instead of free factor loadings for the cognitive speed latent variable. This can be done as part of a hybrid measurement model, including one latent variable with fixed factor loadings and another one with free factor loadings (Figure 10.2A), or as a measurement model with fully fixed factor loading (Figure 10.2B).

In measurement models with free factor loadings (Figure 10.1), it is necessary to assure that this model is identified and can be estimated. This can be achieved by setting the variance parameters of the matrix of variance parameters and covariance parameters – that is, the variance

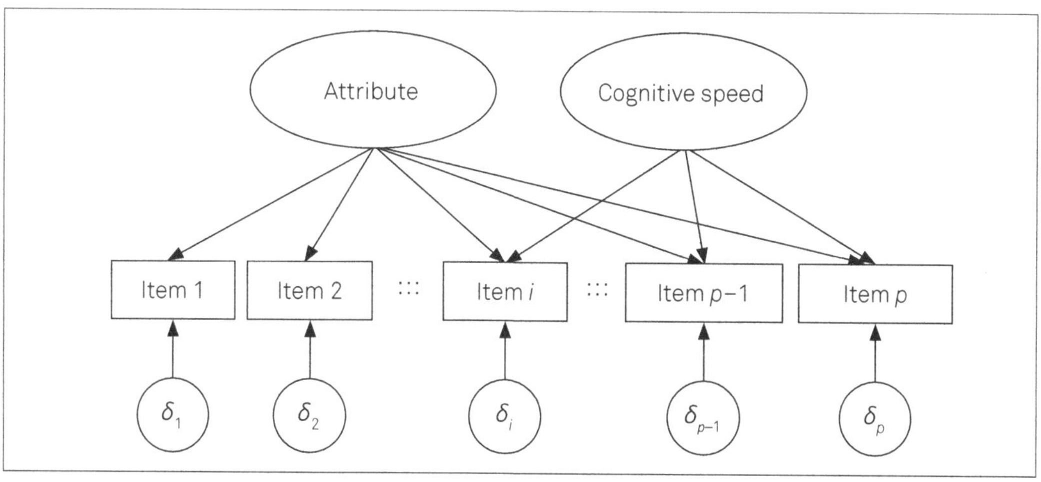

Figure 10.1 Illustration of a confirmatory factor analysis model with free factor loadings. For investigating data showing a speed effect (arrows with solid shaft signify parameters that are estimated). The data collected by items i to p are assumed to show a speed effect.

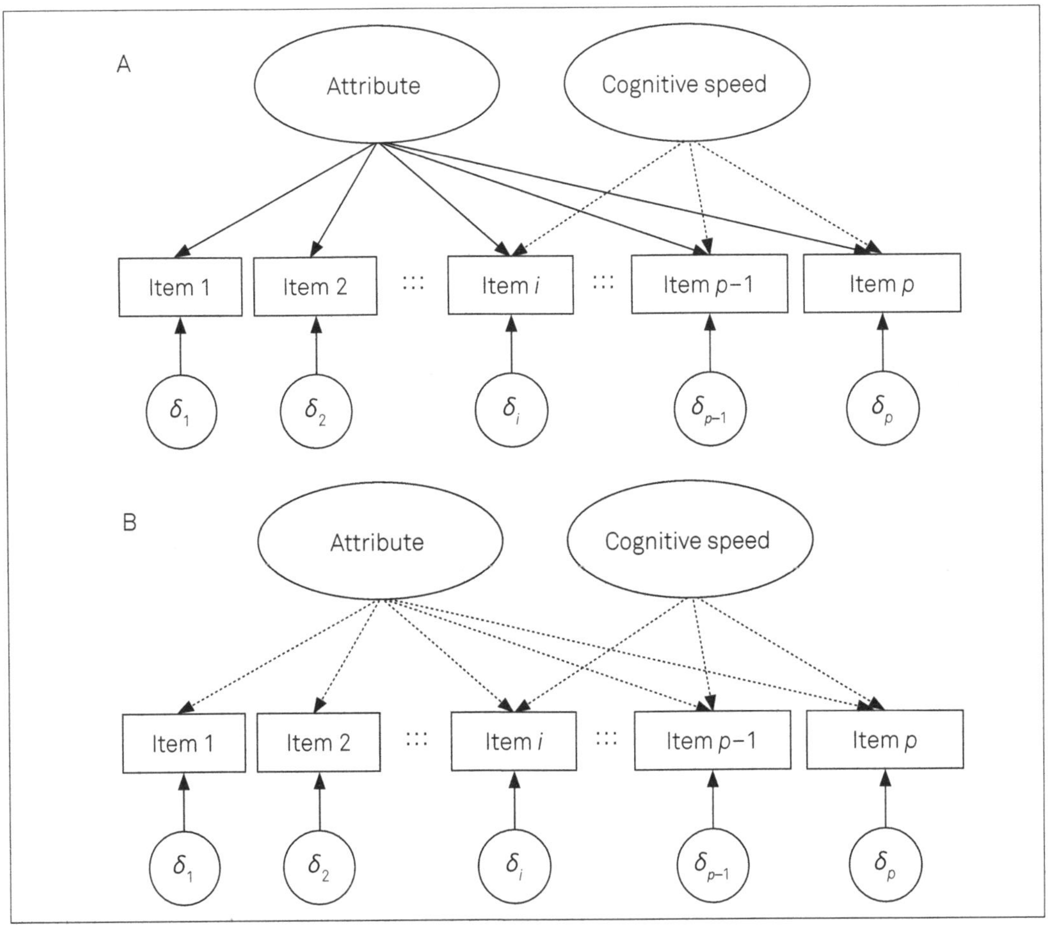

Figure 10.2 Illustration of speed effect models including a cognitive speed latent variable with fixed factor loadings (A, B). Arrows with solid shaft signify parameters that are estimated, and arrows with dashed shafts fixed parameters.

parameters of the attribute and speed latent variables – equal to one (Schweizer et al., 2019). These parameters are ingredients of the model-implied covariance matrix, $\mathbf{\Sigma}$, that is a $p \times p$ matrix designed to reproduce the $p \times p$ empirical matrix, **S** (Jöreskog, 1970). It includes the $q \times q$ matrix of variances and covariances of latent variables, $\mathbf{\Phi}$, with the variance parameters as components:

$$\mathbf{\Sigma} = \mathbf{\Lambda\Phi\Lambda}' + \mathbf{\Theta} \tag{2}$$

where $\mathbf{\Lambda}$ is the $p \times q$ matrix of factor loadings and $\mathbf{\Theta}$ the $p \times p$ diagonal matrix of residual components.

In contrast, in measurement models with fixed factor loadings (Figure 10.2B), adaptation of the model-implied covariance matrix to the empirical covariance matrix is achieved by estimating the variance parameters, $\phi_{\text{attribute}}$ and ϕ_{speed}, so that the difference between $\mathbf{\Sigma}$ and **S** according to the fitting function, is minimum. The hybrid model illustrated by Figure 10.2A includes both ways of assuring that the model is identified and can be estimated.

Characteristic Course of the Speed Effect

In CFA models with free factor loadings, the separation of the method effect from the effect due to the attribute is guided by the multitrait-multimethod design. This method is not suitable if the effect that is to be represented by a latent variable unfolds in a characteristic way along a series of items like the speed effect, the item position effect, or the difficulty effect. It is not suitable, because estimation of factor loadings is rather blind for the origin of the common systematic variation that is to be accounted.

In contrast, theory-guided decomposition of common systematic variation, which means using fixed factor loadings, is the method that can assure that the latent variable accounts for what it is expected to account for. In the case of the speed effect, it is the distribution of the omissions that characterizes the effect. In the estimation of parameters, the amount of the observed variation that is in line with the quantified expectations across the series of items based on the assumed distribution is determined. This assures that the latent variable represents this effect while not being influenced by another effect.

Accordingly, in CFA models for the separation of the effect of cognitive speed from the effect due to the attribute, decomposition of common systematic variation in accordance with the characteristic course of the speed effect, is accomplished. This course reflects the increasing number of participants in a sample, who are unable to complete items along the sequence of items of the scale. This course is assumed to unfold as a function of the distribution of the participants' characteristic speed of cognitive processing. A participant's cognitive processing stimulated by an item is assumed to extend to a larger number of neurological subprocesses, and the temporal characteristics of these subprocesses determine the participant's characteristic speed of cognitive processing. Under this condition, the *central limit theorem* (Fischer, 2011) suggests that speed of cognitive processing follows a normal distribution $N(\mu,\sigma)$ in the population.

Therefore, the normal distribution is selected as outset for determining the distribution of missing data along the sequence of items of the scale in a given sample with a limited number of participants, which we consider as the characteristic course of the speed effect. In a sample this is in fact a frequency distribution that is similar to the normal distribution, which is obtained by identifying the first item that is not completed by each participant, and by accumulating these observations (see Figure 10.3). Figure 10.3 assumes that all participants are able to complete items 1 to item $i + 1$ and that no one is able to reach item $i + 13$. Furthermore, for the largest number of participants, it is item $i + 7$ that was the first omitted item.

To arrive at the expected frequency distribution of missing data, the counts of Figure 10.3 need to be accumulated in the sense of creating a cumulative distribution: This starts with the second item, which means combining the count of the first item and that of the second item, and using the result for replacing the count to the second item. Next, the new count of the second item and the original count of the third item are combined to give the new count of the third item, and so on. Proceeding in this way transforms the frequency distribution similar to the normal distribution in a cumulative frequency distribution, similar to a cumulative normal distribution. It represents the idea of the characteristic course of the speed effect. Figure 10.4 provides an illustration of the cumulative frequency distribution together with the original frequency distribution.

The cumulative frequency distribution shows a monotonic increase from item $i + 1$ to item $i + 13$. In reasoning data with a time limit in testing, free factor loadings were employed for estimating the speed effect along the sequence of items and subsequently compared with factor

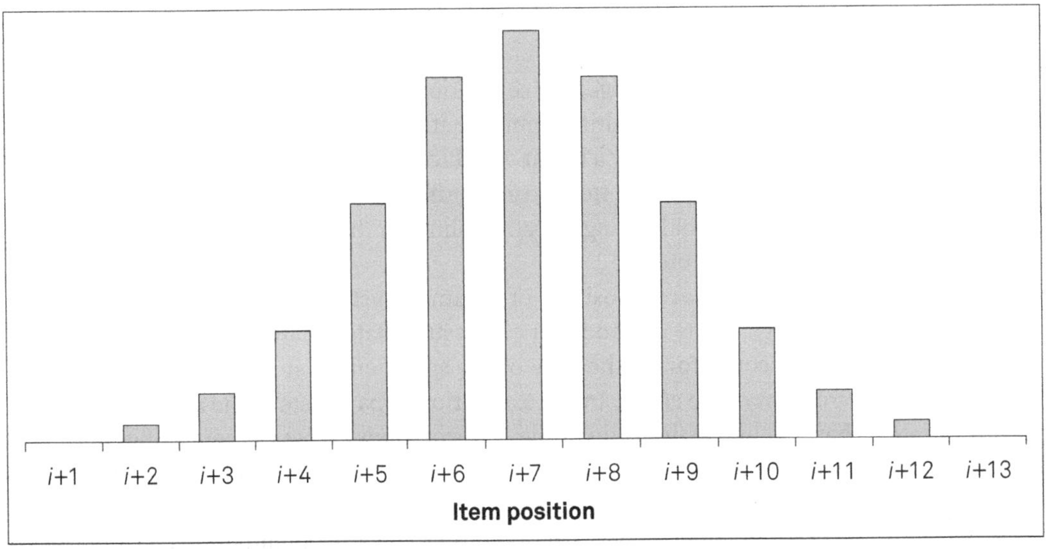

Figure 10.3 Expected frequency distribution of the first not-completed items as a bar graph.

loadings that were fixed according to the cumulative normal distribution. They showed a considerable degree of agreement (Schweizer et al., 2019). Exact agreement should not be expected, since the actual course of the curve may also be influenced by differences in item difficulties and by participants' test-taking strategies, such as selective responding (Stenlund et al., 2018) and rapid guessing (Wise, 2017). Furthermore, random influences may lead to deviation (e.g., carelessness, fatigue, postponement of responding combined with obliviousness, insecurity about the correctness of a possible response).

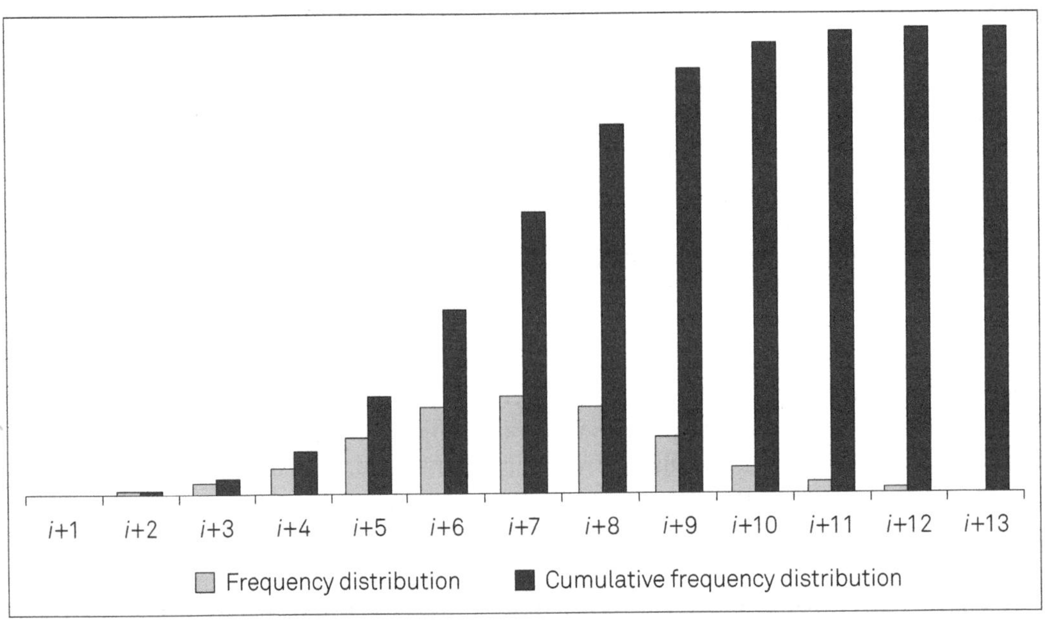

Figure 10.4 Illustration of an original expected frequency distribution of the first not-complete items together with the corresponding expected cumulative frequency distribution.

The cumulative frequency distribution and the cumulative normal distribution are assumed to show asymptotic convergence. Therefore, the cumulative normal distribution can be considered for obtaining expected values regarding the characteristic course of the speed effect as it is obvious in the frequency of missing data. In order to make use of the characteristic course for separating effects due to the measured attribute and cognitive speed, expected values must be made available. Such values can be achieved by the logistic function since this function approximates the cumulative normal distribution (Lord, 1965) – that is, the logistic function $g_{\text{logistic}}()$ provides for item i ($i = i_{\text{onset}}, \ldots, p$; in Figure 10.3: $i_{\text{onset}} = i + 2$) an estimate of the ratio of the number of participants who do not reach this item, N_i, and the number of all participants, N:

$$g_{\text{logistic}}(i) \approx \frac{N_i}{N}. \tag{3}$$

The reasons for deviations mentioned in the previous paragraph are likely to prevent exact correspondence of $g_{\text{logistic}}()$ and the ratio. Item i_{onset} denotes the first item showing a noticeable speed effect.

Logistic function $g_{\text{logistic}}()$ is defined in considering the exponential function, $e^{()}$:

$$g_{\text{logistic}}(i) = \frac{e^{i}}{1+e^{i}} \tag{4}$$

for item i ($i = i_{\text{onset}}, \ldots, p$). This basic version of the logistic function does not take the specific time limit in testing into consideration and, therefore, is often inappropriate for directly representing the speed effect. This is apparent when the same test is administered with different time limits.

For example, a time limit of 10 minutes may cause 50% of participants to omit Item 20 and the following items, whereas a time limit of 15 minutes enables 50% of participants to complete all items up to Item 25. This example reveals that the logistic function needs to be modified to allow for an adaptation of the cumulative frequency distribution – for example, the distribution of missing data. Such adaptation can be achieved by adding the turning point of the curve representing the cumulative normal distribution as another parameter to the equation (Schweizer et al., 2019). We refer to this as the *tp* parameter. The revised logistic function including this parameter is given by Equation 5:

$$g_{\text{logistic}}(i) = \frac{e^{i-tp}}{1+e^{i-tp}}. \tag{5}$$

A modification of *tp* means a shift of the curve depicting the cumulative normal distribution on the horizontal axis. Using expected values for the separation of the effects of the measured attribute and cognitive speed requires the adaptation of Equation 5, so that it shows the best degree of fit with the distribution of missing data. This can be accomplished by comparing the fit results for different *tp*s. Figure 10.5 illustrates how modifying the turning point changes the course of the curve representing the cumulative normal distribution.

The curves for the four turning points in Figure 10.5 make obvious that finding the turning point providing the best fit of observed and expected frequencies of missing data is essential for investigations using expected values as fixed factor loadings. Since so far, an automatic procedure for determining the most appropriate *tp* is not available, it is up to the researcher to identify it by comparing the fit results observed with different *tp*s or by locating the item with 50% missing data.

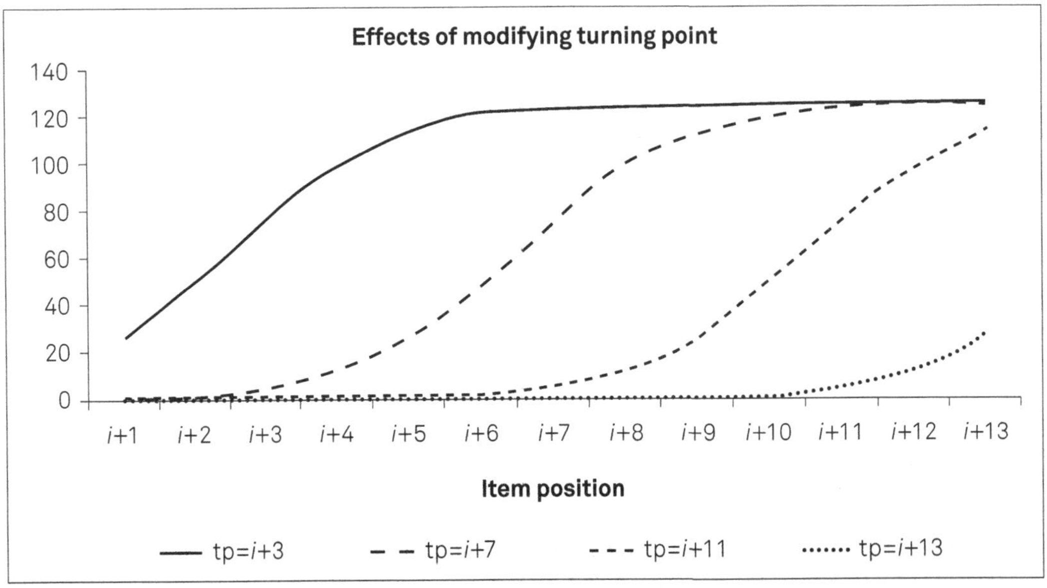

Figure 10.5 Illustration of the curves representing cumulative normal distributions with different turning points. Horizontal axis: arrangement of items; vertical axis: number of participants; tp = turning point.

Although in most cases it is sufficient to find the appropriate *tp*, there may be the need to adjust the degree of steepness of the curve at the turning point in order to get an agreeable degree of correspondence between observed and expected values describing missing data. This is because in large time spans necessary for completing individual items, the shift from no missings to no responses is likely to be restricted to a few items only, whereas in small time spans it involves a larger number of items. This can be achieved by including a weight parameter, a ($a > 0$), in the logistic function (Schweizer et al., 2019):

$$g_{\text{logistic}}(i) = \frac{e^{a(i-tp)}}{1+e^{a(i-tp)}}. \tag{6}$$

Finding the value for a that provides the best fit of observed and expected values describing missing data can contribute to the optimal separation of the effect of the measured attribute and cognitive speed. Yet, its impact on results appears to be smaller than the impact of adapting the *tp* parameter.

Although the customary CFA model that includes free factor loadings is most frequently used in investigating data, the use of fixed factor loadings is also well-established. Fixed factor loadings are employed in longitudinal data (McArdle, 2009) and invariance analysis (Schmitt & Kuljanin, 2008). If fixed factor loadings are selected for the attribute component of the measurement model (Equation 1), it is mostly done on the assumption of equal contributions of the latent source to all responses. This means that the factor loadings are fixed to equal values. This gives rise to a configuration of factor loadings that is known as the *tau-equivalent measurement model* (Graham, 2006).

In contrast, fixation for factor loadings on the cognitive speed latent variable must be in line with what is expected because of the course of missing data. Values for the fixation of entries of the vector of factor loadings, $\boldsymbol{\lambda}_{\text{speed}}$ (i.e., the speed component of Equation 1), can be obtained by Equation 4 to Equation 6. The vector of factor loadings $\boldsymbol{\lambda}_{\text{speed}}$ has to be specified in the following way:

$$\boldsymbol{\lambda}_{\text{speed}} = \begin{bmatrix} 0 \\ . \\ . \\ 0 \\ g_{\text{logistic}}(i_{\text{onset}}) \\ . \\ . \\ g_{\text{logistic}}(i_{\text{onset}} + j) \\ . \\ . \\ g_{\text{logistic}}(p) \end{bmatrix}. \qquad (7)$$

Experiences with real and simulated data have shown that it is important to start with i_{onset}. All entries preceding the item i_{onset} must be set to zero.

Finally, the question regarding the relationship of the attribute and speed latent variables needs to be addressed. We assume that these latent variables are independent of each other – that is, the corresponding parameter of the matrix of variances and covariances is set to zero. A recent investigation of the effect of setting free the covariance parameter suggests that valid results can only be expected in the case of a positive estimate, whereas in the other case, it is likely that overly large estimates will be observed (Schweizer et al., 2024).

Formal Representation of Missings

An important problem that needs to be addressed before presenting an example is the representation of missing data in the data matrix that is investigated. As with most statistical procedures, CFA requires complete data. But, when dealing with data affected by a speed effect, meaning a data matrix with MNAR (Little & Rubin, 2002), this requirement is not met. Therefore, it is necessary to work out a way of representing missing data so that the data matrix is complete and yields systematic variation that is due to missing data because of a lack of cognitive speed. Such systematic variation must be distinguishable from systematic variation associated with the measured attribute. Furthermore, a sufficiently good account of this systematic variation by the cognitive speed latent variable must be achievable.

A solution to the problem of representing missings has opened up for binary data (work regarding interval-level data is in progress). In binary data, there are two options: missings can be represented by the code of a correct response (mostly "1") or into the code of an incorrect response (mostly "0"); otherwise, the data are no longer binary. It is recommended to represent an item of missing data as an incorrect response. This recommendation may be considered as unreasonable unless it can be demonstrated that in this way unique systematic variation is created, associated with missing data. Such a demonstration is possible on the basis of covariance coefficients (respectively, specific correlation coefficients). In both cases, the information on the participants' responses is transformed into probability information. This means binary information on the individual participants is transformed into continuous information that refers to the sample.

One coefficient considered for the purpose of demonstrating the speed effect was the tetrachoric correlation applied to reasoning data (Ren et al., 2017; Schweizer et al., 2023). The computation of this correlation includes the estimation of latent thresholds, τ (Tallis, 1962). A threshold brings about the transformation of the binary random variable X_i ($i = 1, ..., p$) into a continuous random variable V_i ($i = 1, ..., p$) that follows the normal distribution. This transformation is based on probabilities such that:

$$Pr(X_i = 1) = Pr(V_i > \tau). \tag{8}$$

After this transformation, the correlation of variables V_i and V_j ($i, j = 1, ..., p, i \neq j$), which is referred to as the tetrachoric correlation of V_i and V_j, is estimated.

Another coefficient considered is the probability-based covariance that is applied for investigating reasoning data and simulated data (Schweizer et al., 2020; Schweizer, Troche et al., 2019). A major characteristic of this coefficient also is that it is based on probabilities. The probability-based covariance of random variables X_i and X_j ($i,j = 1, ..., p$) of binary responses with 1 as code for correct responses is defined as

$$cov(X_i, X_j) = Pr(X_i = 1 \wedge X_j = 1) - Pr(X_i = 1)\ Pr(X_j = 1). \tag{9}$$

What both coefficients have in common is the focus on correct responses. Therefore, it is not necessary to distinguish between incorrect responses and missing data. Nevertheless, missing data exert a systematic influence on the result of computing tetrachoric correlations and probability-based covariances. This influence can be demonstrated with respect to the probability of a correct response in the random variable X_i, $\Pr(X_i = 1)$. If the data matrix is complete and the only systematic source of responding is the latent attribute, $\xi_{attribute}$, then the following relationship holds:

$$Pr(X_i = 1)_{complete\_data\_matrix} = Pr(X_i = 1|\xi_{attribute})_{complete\_data\_matrix}. \tag{10}$$

However, if the data matrix is incomplete in X_i because of a time limit, the count of correct responses is likely to be reduced. This means that in incomplete data, Equation 10 is unlikely to hold. Assuming independence of the measured attribute and cognitive speed, it is even possible to predict the decreased probability by taking the probability of missing data into consideration:

$$Pr(X_i = 1)_{complete\_data\_matrix} = Pr(X_i = 1|\xi_{attribute})_{complete\_data\_matrix} \times$$

$$[1 - Pr(X_i \text{ is missing})]. \tag{11}$$

Note a multiplicative relationship is selected to relate the two terms. This means that the probabilities, which are basic to the computation of the tetrachoric correlation and the probability-based covariance, are subjected to a systematic influence by missing data. This systematic influence is transformed into variation of the sizes of correlations and covariances. The cognitive speed latent variable of the CFA measurement model is expected to account for the systematic variation due to missing data. If it does not, the result of an investigation will be a model misfit.

An Example

The next section presents a hands-on example of the procedure described in the previous sections. In this example, data were a randomly selected subset of a large dataset (Schweizer et al., 2019). This subset included the data collected using an easy cognitive performance test in 120 university students. This test included 40 items with a low degree of difficulty, and was administered under a time constraint of 8 minutes. The items required the detection of error in sequences of numbers and letters. This means that it largely corresponded to the concept of a speed test. The code for correct responses was "1," for incorrect responses "0," and for missing responses "9." The data collected for the 20 odd-numbered items were selected for this demonstration.

For the first step, Figure 10.6 provides a graphical representation of the course of the missing data (item labels are revised). As is apparent, up to Item 13, there were no, or only a very few, missing data. In the following items, there was a nonmonotonic increase of missing data. Fifty-two percent of the participants did not provide a response to Item 20. The deviations from the expected smoothly increasing curve, suggest that the items showed some variation in item difficulty – that is, the course of the curve was not only due to cognitive speed, but presumably also due to varying difficulties of items.

In the second step, the logistic function (see Equation 4) was adapted to the frequency distribution. This means that turning point tp (Equation 5) and weight a (Equation 6) had to be selected appropriately. Since the percentage of missing data in Item 20 was close to 50, tp was set to 20 (otherwise it could be determined by fitting the logistic curve). Furthermore, curves for different as were computed, and the a associated with the smallest deviation from the frequency distribution of missing data was determined. Figure 10.7 shows the courses of curves for

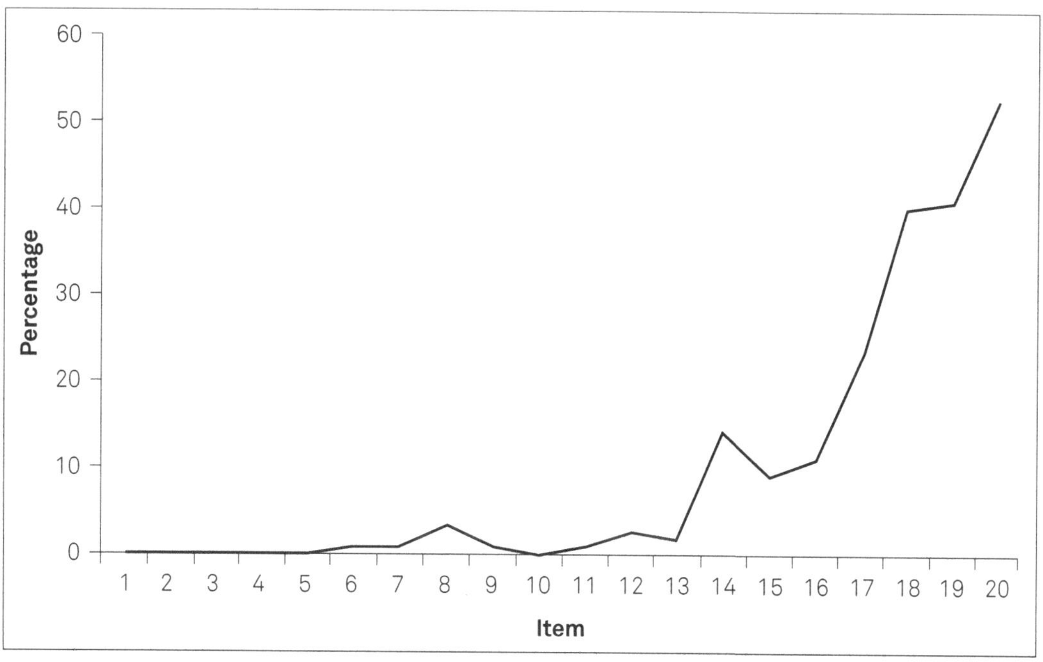

Figure 10.6 Graphical representation of the percentages of missing data as continuous curve.

$a = 1, 2, 2.5$, and 3. It is apparent that the standard curve ($a = 1$) is inappropriate here, whereas the other curves show intersections with the curve based on the frequency distribution of missing data. According to the sum of squared deviations, $a = 2.5$ leads to the best degree of agreement with the observed frequency distribution. Yet, since the course based on the observed frequency distribution of missing data also shows the influence of difficult items, the sum of squared deviations does eventually not reflect the course representing cognitive speed well. Also noteworthy is that these are considerations based on figural features, whereas in CFA, the explained common systematic variation counts. This means that a post hoc adjustment may be necessary.

The structural investigation of the described data was conducted to provide evidence of one underlying dimension associated with the measured attribute, while also taking the effect of cognitive speed into consideration. Such an investigation starts with the demonstration that a one-factor model is insufficient to account for all systematic variation of the data. Afterwards a bifactor model with one additional latent variable representing cognitive speed is used (1) to reach good (or at least acceptable) model fit and (2) to demonstrate an improvement in model fit over what is observed for the one-factor model. In the present investigation, two bifactor models with the latent variable specified as attribute latent variable were considered: one with free factor loadings and one with fixed factor loadings. The two bifactor models additionally included the cognitive speed latent variable that is specified as latent variable with fixed factor loadings, fixed to reflect the adapted course of the logistic function.

A more detailed description of the provisions would include several steps. Firstly, since the columns of the data matrix must show a minimum degree of variance for covariance analysis, columns associated with very easy items have to be excluded from the computations. In the example, the first nine columns/items have to be omitted. Secondly, a specification of the logistic curve has to be selected. In the first attempt, tp is set to 20 and a to 2.5. Since higher item

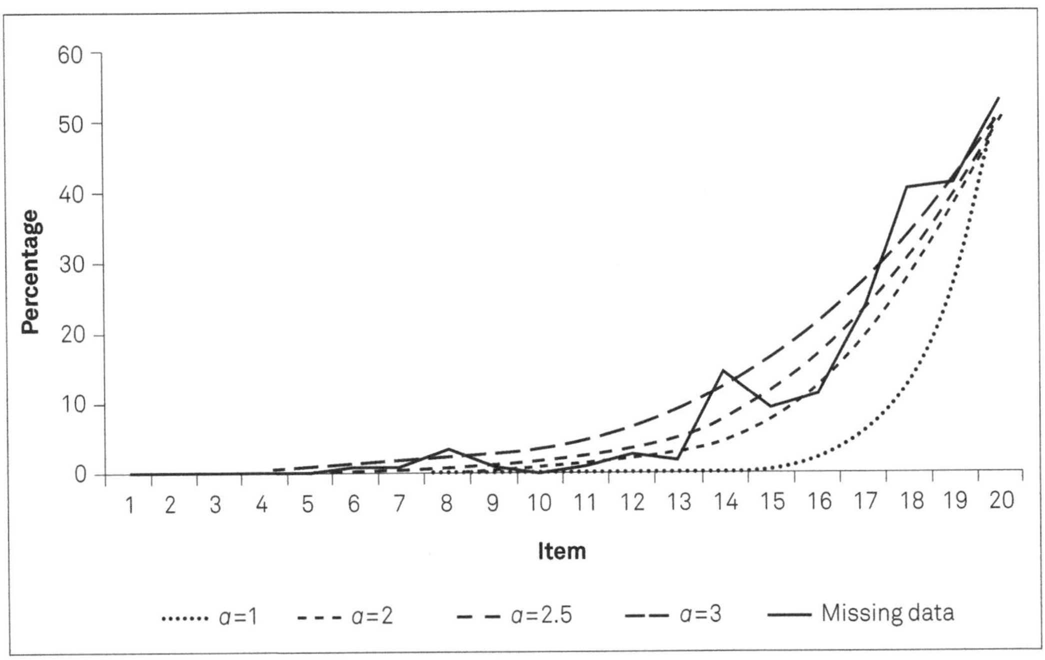

Figure 10.7 Graphical representation of variants of the logistic function due to different selections of weight a, and of the curve based on missing data.

difficulties may have caused a deviation from the true course, in a second attempt a is set to 2. Thirdly, the fixations for the factor loadings have to be specified. If the input to CFA are tetrachoric correlations, the factor loadings on the attribute latent variables simply need to be set to 1 (in the case of no scaling of the variance parameter) and the factor loadings on the cognitive speed latent variable to what is expected according to Equation 7. If the input are probability-based covariances, an additional transformation is necessary that links the binomial distribution of binary data to the normal distribution (Note: In tetrachoric correlation, this transformation is accomplished as part of computing these correlations; McCullagh & Nelder, 1985; Nelder & Wedderburn, 1972). This transformation is realized by the multiplication of the course-reflecting fixation with weight v_i ($i = 1, ..., p$) that is defined as a function of the probability (Pr) of the response to item i ($i = 1, ..., p$), X_i ($X_i \in [0,1]$), such that

$$v_i = \sqrt{Pr(X_i = 1) \times [1 - Pr(X_i = 1)]} \tag{12}$$

(Zeller et al., 2017). This is a weight that varies between its maximum value for $p = 0.5$ and zero for $p = 0$ and $p = 1$. This means for the fixed factor loadings of X_i on the attribute latent variable, $\lambda_{\text{attribute\_}i}$, with fixation 1:

$$\lambda_{\text{attribute\_}i} = v_i \times 1 \tag{13}$$

and on the cognitive speed latent variable:

$$\lambda_{\text{speed\_}i} = v_i \times g_{\text{logistic}}(i). \tag{14}$$

Parameters are estimated by the maximum likelihood estimation method of LISREL (Jöreskog & Sörbom, 2006). Table 10.1 provides the results of investigating model fit. We used the following fit indices and established criteria (in parentheses: good fit; acceptable fit) for the evaluation of the quality of the model: χ^2, root-mean-square error of approximation (RMSEA; ≤ 0.06; ≤ 0.08), standardized root mean square residual (SRMR; ≤ 0.08; ≤ 1.00), nonnormed fit index (NNFI; ≥ 0.95; ≥ 0.90), and comparative fit index (CFI; ≥ 0.95; ≥ 0.90). For details, see DiStefano (2016) and Hu and Bentler (1999). For comparing different models, we used CFI difference (0.01) and RMSEA difference (0.015) with criteria (in parentheses) according to Cheung and Rensvold (2002).

Table 10.1 Results of investigating model fit

Model type	n^a	a^b	χ^2	*df*	RMSEA	SRMR	CFI	NNFI	AIC
Congeneric	1		94.6	44	0.098	0.096	0.770	0.713	138.6
Fully fixed	1		190.5	54	0.146	0.159	0.440	0.430	214.5
Hybrid	2	2.50	57.2	43	0.053	0.075	0.920	0.897	103.2
Fully fixed	2	2.50	77.8	53	0.063	0.101	0.864	0.859	103.8
Hybrid	2	2	55.3	43	0.049	0.071	0.928	0.908	101.3
Fully fixed	2	2	73.2	53	0.057	0.099	0.885	0.880	99.2

Note. AIC = Akaike information criterion; CFI = comparative fit index; *df* = degrees of freedom; NNFI = nonnormed fit index; RMSEA = root-mean-square error of approximation; SRMR = standardized root mean square residual. [a]Number of latent variables included in the confirmatory factor analysis model. [b]Weight selected for adjusting the logistic function (Equation 6).

The fit results for the congeneric and hybrid (factor loadings on attribute latent variable are estimated) and fully fixed models (all factor loadings are fixed) are included in Table 10.1. The first and second rows of this table include the results for the one-factor models. None of the fit indices with a cutoff (RMSEA, SRMR, CFI, and NNFI) indicate good model fit. The third and fourth rows comprise the fit results for the bifactor models when weight *a* is set to 2.5. All fit indices for these models indicate considerably better fit than what is observed for the one-factor models. In the hybrid model, two fit indices (RMSEA and SRMR) even indicate good model fit and the CFI is not considered good but acceptable. In the fully fixed model, RMSEA also signifies acceptable model fit. Changing weight *a* from 2.5 to 2 leads to the results presented in the fifth and sixth rows. This change leads to a minor improvement in the fit of the hybrid model so that RMSEA and SRMR are good, while CFI as well as NNFI are not good but acceptable. The fully fixed model shows a considerable decrease in χ^2. Its RMSEA is good and its SRMR not good but acceptable. In sum, in both types of models, the consideration of the speed latent variable substantially improves model fit.

The fully fixed model profited most from changing weight *a*. After the change, the difference in RMSEA signifies equivalency of the models. However, the difference in CFI suggests superiority of the hybrid model, while the Akaike information criterion (AIC), which takes model complexity into consideration, indicates superiority of the fully fixed model. Taken together, these results suggest that the two models are more or less equivalently efficient.

In the next step, the factor loadings were analyzed. Table 10.2 (see also Equation 1) provides the standardized factor loading (λ) and residuals (δ). Standardization, a post hoc modification that is conducted to improve interpretation, applies to both estimates and fixations. The first column of this table gives the item number, with the first to ninth items excluded due to

Table 10.2 Standardized factor loadings and remainders

	Hybrid model			Fully fixed model		
Item	Attribute factor	Speed factor	Remainder	Attribute factor	Speed factor	Remainder
10	0.255	0.007	0.935	0.380	0.007	0.855
11	0.215	0.012	0.954	0.373	0.011	0.860
12	0.423	0.020	0.820	0.390	0.019	0.848
13	0.313	0.032	0.901	0.381	0.030	0.854
14	0.405	0.052	0.833	0.386	0.049	0.848
15	0.372	0.083	0.855	0.381	0.077	0.849
16	0.566	0.132	0.662	0.402	0.128	0.822
17	0.629	0.200	0.565	0.402	0.196	0.800
18	0.325	0.295	0.807	0.382	0.274	0.779
19	0.392	0.414	0.675	0.383	0.386	0.704
20	0.079	0.545	0.697	0.351	0.469	0.657

insufficient variance for the analysis of variances and covariances. The second column provides the factor loadings on the attribute latent variable of the hybrid model, with the largest loadings observed on Item 16 and Item 17. The third column includes the factor loadings on the speed latent variable with a monotonic increase from virtually zero to over 0.5. The fourth column comprises the residuals, with two residuals (Items 10 and 11) indicating negligible contributions. The results for the fully fixed model can be found in columns five to seven. The factor loadings on the attribute latent variable of the fifth column vary between 0.351 and 0.402. The factor loadings on the speed latent variable start from virtually zero and end up at 0.469. The remainders show variation between 0.657 and 0.860. The only observation of concern is that in the hybrid model, two items are virtually excluded, while the other items behave as expected. This means that under the assumption of each item being an essential part of the scale, the hybrid model is less well suited for the investigation.

Finally, the latent variance explained by the factors was investigated. This investigation requires the scaling of latent variables (Schweizer & Troche, 2019; Schweizer et al., 2019). The scaled estimates of the variance parameters of the latent variables serve as estimates of the latent variances. In the case of the hybrid model, the free factor loadings need to be replaced for this purpose by the observed estimates as fixation before scaling.

In the hybrid model, the estimation of the variance parameter reveals $\phi_{attribute} = 0.313$ ($t = 5.05$, $p = .000$) for the attribute latent variable, and $\phi_{speed} = 0.105$ ($t = 2.76$, $p = .003$) for the cognitive speed latent variable. In the fully fixed model $\phi_{attribute} = 0.254$ ($t = 4.63$, $p = .000$) for the attribute latent variable and $\phi_{speed} = 0.092$ ($t = 2.29$, $p = .011$) for the cognitive speed latent variable. These results show that more latent variation is captured by the hybrid model (0.418) than by the fully fixed model (0.346). However, the percentages of latent variance captured by the attribute latent variable and the cognitive speed latent variable are quite similar, at 74.9% and 73.4%, on the one hand, and 25.1% and 26.6%, on the other hand.

To sum up, in data collected by a speeded test, CFA measurement models with a speed latent variable provide a substantially better account of the data than CFA measurement models without such a latent variable. Further, it is not necessary to construct replacements for missing data in order to demonstrate structural validity that can potentially lead to distortion. Only the CFA measurement models with a speed latent variable provide evidence of an underlying attribute dimension; otherwise there is model misfit. Furthermore, investigation of the latent variance revealed the attribute as the primary contributor to respondents' performance.

Concluding Remarks

This chapter has focused on missing data due to a time limit in testing that is only one type of MNAR. We like to argue that generalization to other types of missing data is easily achievable. What distinguishes the different types are the characteristic courses across the sequence of items for representing missing data. For example, in the case of missing data because of a planned missing data design, the complex course reflecting cognitive speed just needs to be replaced by a course that reflects the characteristics of the design (Schweizer, Gold, & Krampen, 2023; Schweizer, Gold et al., 2020). Therefore, we hope that the detailed description of the investigation of this somewhat more complex type of missing data will equip future users with sufficient guidance for dealing with missing data.

Since most statistical methods demand complete data, the need to deal with missings is an essential challenge to data analysis. In many cases, a replacement method is selected to deal with this challenge. For example, missing data can be replaced by the *full information maximum likelihood estimation method* (Enders, 2013) or alternatively by following the *multiple-imputation approach* (van Buuren, 2018). Such replacement provides a basis for investigating data by all kinds of methods. However, since in the ideal case, replacement requires prediction of the systematic influence on performance as well as of the random influence that cannot be predicted, by definition, there is no guarantee that such replacement yields responses that otherwise would be observed, and it means that there is always the danger of a distortion of structure. The approach to dealing with missing data that has been described here avoids this kind of possible distortion and in this respect enriches the pool of methods for dealing with missing data.

References

Borter, N., Schlegel, K., & Troche, S. (2023). How speededness of a reasoning test and the complexity of mental speed tasks influence the relation between mental speed and reasoning ability. *Journal of Intelligence, 11*(5), 89. https://doi.org/10.3390/jintelligence11050089

Byrne, B. M. (2016). Using multitrait-multimethod analysis in testing for evidence of construct validity. In K. Schweizer & C. DiStefano (Eds.), *Principles and methods of test construction* (pp. 288–307). Hogrefe Publishing.

Campbell, D. T., & Fiske, D. W. (1959). Convergent and discriminant validation by the multitrait-multimethod matrix. *Psychological Bulletin, 56*(2), 81–105. https://doi.org/10.1037/h0046016

Campbell, D. T., & Stanley, J. C. (1966). *Experimental and quasi-experimental designs for research for research.* Rand McNally.

Cheung, G. W., & Rensvold, R. B. (2002). Evaluating goodness-of-fit indexes for testing measurement invariance. *Structural Equation Modeling, 9*, 233–255. https://doi.org/10.1207/S15328007SEM0902_5

Cintron, D. W. (2021). Methods for measuring speededness: chronology, classification, and ensuing research and development (ETS Research Report: ETS-RR-21-22). E. T. Service. https://doi.org/10.1002/ets2.12337

DiStefano, C. (2016). Examining fit with structural equation models. In K. Schweizer & C. DiStefano (Eds.), *Principles and methods of test construction* (pp. 166–193). Hogrefe.

Enders, C. K. (2013). Analyzing structural equation models with missing data. In G. R. Hancock & R. O. Mueller (Eds.), *Structural equation modeling: A second course* (pp. 493–519). Information Age.

Fischer, H. (2011). *A history of the central limit theorem.* Springer. https://doi.org/10.1007/978-0-387-87857-7

Graham, J. M. (2006). Congeneric and (essentially) tau-equivalent estimates of score reliability. *Educational and Psychological Measurement, 66*(6), 930–944. https://doi.org/10.1177/0013164406288165

Gulliksen, H. (1950). Speed versus power tests. In H. Gulliksen (Ed.), *Theory of mental tests* (pp. 230–244). Wiley. https://doi.org/10.1037/13240-017

Hartig, J., Hölzel, B., & Moosbrugger, H. (2007). A confirmatory analysis of item reliability trends (CAIRT): Differentiating true score and error variance in the analysis of item context effects. *Multivariate Behavioral Research, 42*(1), 157–183. https://doi.org/10.1080/00273170701341266

Hu, L., & Bentler, P. M. (1999). Cutoff criteria for fit indexes in covariance structure analysis: Conventional criteria versus new alternatives. *Structural Equation Modeling, 6*, 1–55. https://doi.org/10.1080/10705519909540118

Jöreskog, K. G. (1970). A general method for analysis of covariance structure. *Biometrika, 57*(2), 239–257. https://doi.org/10.2307/2334833

Jöreskog, K. G., & Sörbom, D. (2006). *LISREL 8.80*. Scientific Software International.

Knowles, E. S. (1988). Item context effects on personality scales: Measuring changes the measure. *Journal of Personality and Social Psychology, 55*(2), 312–320. https://doi.org/10.1037/0022-3514.55.2.312

Little, R. J. A., & Rubin, D. B. (2002). *Statistical analysis with missing data* (2nd ed.). Wiley.
Lord, F. M. (1965). A note on the normal ogive or logistic curve in item analysis. *Psychometrika, 30*(3), 371–372. https://doi.org/10.1007/BF02289500
Lu, Y., & Sireci, S. G. (2007). Validity issues in test speededness. *Educational Measurement, 26*(4), 29–37. https://doi.org/10.1111/j.1745-3992.2007.00106.x
Maul, A. (2013). Method effects and the meaning of measurement. *Frontiers in Psychology, 4*, 169. https://doi.org/10.3389/fpsyg.2013.00169
McArdle, J. J. (2009). Latent variable modeling of differences and change with longitudinal data. *Annual Review Psychology, 60*, 577–605. https://doi.org/10.1146/annurev.psych.60.110707.163612
McCullagh, P., & Nelder, J. A. (1985). *Generalized linear models.* Chapman and Hall.
Nelder, J. A., & Wedderburn, R. W. M. (1972). Generalized linear models. *Journal of the Royal Statistical Society – Series A, 135*, 370–384. https://doi.org/10.2307/2344614
Oommen, E. (2023). *Ethical research practices for research with human subjects.* https://paperpal.com/blog/researcher-resources/ethical-research-practices-for-research-with-human-subjects
Oshima, T. C. (1994). The effect of speededness on parameter estimation in item response theory. *Journal of Educational Measurement, 31*, 200–219. https://doi.org/10.1111/j.1745-3984.1994.tb00443.x
Partchev, I., De Boeck, P., & Steyer, R. (2013). How much power and speed is measured in this test? *Assessment, 20*, 242–252. https://doi.org/10.1177/1073191111411658
Podsakoff, P. M., MacKenzie, S. B., Lee, J. Y., & Podsakoff, N. P. (2003). Common method biases in behavioral research: A critical review of the literature and recommended remedies. *Journal of Applied Psychology, 88*, 879–903. https://doi.org/10.1037/0021-9010.88.5.879
Reise, S. P. (2012). The rediscovery of bifactor measurement models. *Multivariate Behavioral Research, 47*(5), 667–696. https://doi.org/10.1080/00273171.2012.715555
Ren, X., Wang, T., Sun, S., Deng, M., & Schweizer, K. (2017). Speeded testing in the assessment of intelligence gives rise to a speed factor. *Intelligence, 66*, 64–71. https://doi.org/10.1016/j.intell.2017.11004
Rhemtulla, M., & Hancock, G. R. (2016). Planned missing data designs in educational psychology research. *Educational Psychology, 51*, 305–316. https://doi.org/10.1080/00461520.2016.1208094
Rindler, S. E. (1979). Pitfalls in assessing test speededness. *Journal of Educational Measurement, 16*(4), 261–270. https://doi.org/10.1111/j.1745-3984.1979.tb00107.x
Rioux, C., Lewin, A., Odejimi, O. A., & Little, T. D. (2020). Reflection on modern methods: planned missing data design for epidemiological research. *International Journal of Epidemiology, 49*(5), 1702–1711. https://doi.org/10.1093/ije/dyaa042
Rubin, D. B. (1976). Inference and missing data. *Biometrika, 63*(3), 581–592. https://doi.org/10.2307/2335739
Schmitt, N., & Kuljanin, G. (2008). Measurement invariance: Review of practice and implications. *Human Resources in Management, 18*, 210–222. https://doi.org/10.1016/j.hrmr.2008.03.003
Schweizer, K. (2012). The position effect in reasoning items considered from the CFA perspective. *International Journal of Educational and Psychological Assessment, 11*, 44–58.
Schweizer, K. (2020). Method effects in psychological assessment. *Psychological Test and Assessment Modeling, 64*, 337–343.
Schweizer, K., Gold, A., & Krampen, D. (2020). A semi-hierarchical confirmatory factor model for speeded data. *Structural Equation Modeling, 27*(5), 773–780. https://doi.org/10.1080/10705511.2019.1707083
Schweizer, K., Gold, A., & Krampen, D. (2023). On modeling missing data in structural investigations based on tetrachoric correlations with free and fixed factor loadings. *Educational and Psychological Measurement, 83*(6), 1113–1138. https://doi.org/10.1177/00131644221143145
Schweizer, K., Gold, A., Krampen, D., & Wang, T., (2020). On modeling missing data of an incomplete design in the CFA framework. *Frontiers in Psychology, 11,* Article 581709. https://doi.org/10.3389/fpsyg.2020.581709
Schweizer, K., Reiß, S., Ren, X., Wang, T., & Troche, S. (2019). Speed effect analysis using the CFA framework. *Frontiers in Psychology, 10*, ArtID 239. https://doi.org/10.3389/fpsyg.2019.00239
Schweizer, K. & Ren, X., (2013). The position effect in tests with a time limit: the consideration of interruption and working speed. *Psychological Test and Assessment Modeling, 55*, 62–78.

Schweizer, K., Ren, X., & Wang, T. (2024). Negativity of factor correlations biases the sizes of factor variances in bifactor CFA models. *Frontiers in Applied Mathematics and Statistics, 10*, Article 1423726. https://doi.org/10.3389/fams.2024.1423726

Schweizer, K., & Troche, S. (2019). The EV scaling method for variances of latent variables. *Methodology, 15*(4), 175–184. https://doi.org/10.1027/1614-2241/a000179

Schweizer, K., Troche, S., & DiStefano, C. (2019). Scaling the variance of a latent variable while assuring constancy of the model. *Frontiers in Psychology, 10*, Article 887. https://doi.org/10.3389/fpsyg.2019.00887

Schweizer, K., Troche, S., & Reiß, S. (2019). Does the effect of a time limit for testing impair structural investigations by means of confirmatory factor models? *Educational and Psychological Measurement, 79*, 40–64. https://doi.org/10.1177/0013164418770824

Stankov, L. (2010). Capacity versus speed in intelligence and ageing. *Australian Psychologist, 34*(2), 138–143. http://doi.org/10.1080/0005006990857443

Stenlund, T., Lyrén, P.-E., & Eklöf, H. (2018). The successful test taker: Exploring test-taking behavior profiles through cluster analysis. *European Journal of Psychology of Education, 33*(2), 403–417. https://doi.org/10.1007/s10212-017-0332-2

Tallis, G. M. (1962). The maximum likelihood estimation of correlation from contingency tables. *Biometrics, 18*(3), 342–353. https://doi.org/10.2307/2527476

van Buuren, S. (2018). *Flexible imputation of missing data* (2nd ed.). CRC Press; Chapman & Hall.

Wilhelm, O., & Schulze, R. (2002). The relation of speeded and unspeeded reasoning with mental speed. *Intelligence, 30*, 537-554. https://doi.org/10.1016/j.intell.2017.11004

Wise, S. L. (2017). Rapid guessing behavior: Its identification, interpretation, and implications. *Educational Measurement, 36*(4), 52–61. https://doi.org/10.1111/emip.12165

Zeller, F., Reiss, S., & Schweizer, K. (2017). Is the item-position effect in achievement measures induced by increasing item difficulty? *Structural Equation Modeling, 24*(2), 745-754. https://doi.org/10.1080/10705511.2017.1306706

Zeller, F., Reiss, S., & Schweizer, K. (2020). Does speededness in collecting reasoning data lead to a speed factor? *European Journal of Psychological Assessment, 36*, 96-104. https://doi.org/10.1027/1015-5759/a000498

Appendix

Speed Effect Analysis: An Example With Fully Fixed Factor Loadings

```
DA NI=11 NO=120 MA=CM
LA
I10 I11 I12 I13 I14 I15 I16 I17 I18 I19 I20
CM
0.040
0.012 0.097
0.006 0.019 0.055
0.018 0.005 0.010 0.097
0.019 0.006 0.031 0.022 0.222
-0.003 0.021 0.026 0.004 0.044 0.196
0.009 0.017 0.011 0.033 0.022 0.056 0.236
0.010 0.004 0.030 0.020 0.067 0.048 0.104 0.227
0.014 0.028 0.011 0.019 0.028 0.022 0.061 0.050 0.222
0.006 -0.012 0.012 0.021 0.025 0.027 0.093 0.081 0.058 0.228
0.005 -0.004 -0.002 0.004 0.006 0.014 0.028 0.024 0.028 0.034 0.103
MO NX=11 NK=2 TD=DI,FR PH=FU,FI
LK
Attribute Speed
! Fixed loadings on attribute latent variable
VA 0.200000000 LX 1 1
VA 0.311448230 LX 2 1
VA 0.234520788 LX 3 1
VA 0.311448230 LX 4 1
VA 0.471168760 LX 5 1
VA 0.442718872 LX 6 1
VA 0.485798312 LX 7 1
VA 0.476445170 LX 8 1
VA 0.471168760 LX 9 1
VA 0.477493455 LX 10 1
VA 0.320936131 LX 11 1
! Fixed loadings on speed latent variable
VA 0.001338561 LX 1 2
VA 0.003421862 LX 2 2
VA 0.00421814 LX 3 2
VA 0.009129241 LX 4 2
VA 0.022345561 LX 5 2
VA 0.033583811 LX 6 2
VA 0.057908472 LX 7 2
VA 0.086915709 LX 8 2
VA 0.126716685 LX 9 2
```

```
VA 0.180273076 LX 10 2
VA 0.160468065 LX 11 2
FR PH 1 1
FR PH 2 2
PD
OU ML SC IT=1000 AD=OFF ND=3
```

The code for the hybrid model only differs in a few points from the fully fixed model. See below:

```
! Free loadings on attribute latent variable
FR LX 1 1
..............................
FR LX 11 1
```

... instead of ...

```
! Fixed loadings on attribute latent variable
VA 0.200000000 LX 1 1
..............................
VA 0.320936131 LX 11 1
```

... and ...

```
VA 1 PH 1 1
```

... instead of ...

```
FR PH 1 1
```

Chapter 11

Carryover and Item Position Effects

Stefan J. Troche and Helene M. von Gugelberg

Abstract

This chapter provides an overview of the literature on carryover and item position effects in psychometric reasoning tests. Carryover effects are considered at the level of test scores and describe how test scores increase through repeated test administration. In contrast, item position effects are considered at the item level and refer to the dependency of item responses on the position of the respective item within the item series of a test. Methodological approaches for mapping and controlling item position effects using confirmatory factor analysis (CFA), item response theory (IRT) approaches, and multilevel modeling (MLM) are described. Findings on the psychological meaning of the item position effect in terms of learning, practice, and fatigue effects are presented. These findings underline the fact that the item position effect is not merely a method effect but can contain psychologically relevant information. Ignoring the item position effect can impact the accuracy of person parameter estimation and the interpretation of test scores in reasoning tests. This also applies to carryover effects. Test administrators should be aware of these effects when repeatedly applying reasoning tests to the same participants or interpreting test scores as indicators of reasoning ability.

Carryover Effects in Repeated Tests

In experimental repeated-measures designs, *order effects* are well-known to be a potential challenge when participation in the first experimental condition influences the behavior in a second condition. For example, participants might become tired or more familiar with the experimental situation in the second condition, so they show different behaviors in the two conditions due to the experimental manipulation *and* the order of the two conditions. In this case, the effects of the experimental manipulation are confounded with what are referred to as *carryover effects*. Thus, carryover effects refer to the influence of an earlier examination on participants' experience, behavior, or performance in a later examination. To avoid such carryover effects, it is recommended that conditions be counterbalanced in experimental research (Goodhew & Edwards, 2019).

One example where counterbalancing is impossible is in the psychometric investigation of *test-retest reliability*. In these investigations, the same test is administered twice to the same sample with a given test-retest interval of minutes, hours, days, or even years. The test scores from the two test administrations are then correlated. The resulting correlation coefficient directly reveals the test's reliability (Reynolds et al., 2021).

This conclusion, however, is only accurate when the "true" scores do not change from the first to the second test administration (i.e., the measured trait must be stable) and when the two administrations are independent. The requirement of unchanged "true" scores is of particular importance for developmental tests or neuropsychological tests. In these settings, the construct to be measured might indeed change from the first to the second administration, maybe due to children's natural development, the progression of a neurological disease, or recovery from the consequences of an accident.

The requirement of two independent test administrations is of more general relevance, because it proceeds from the assumption that the first test administration does not affect the second one in the sense of a carryover effect. Especially for psychometric performance tests, this seems to be a challenging assumption, as in many investigations of test-retest reliability, the test scores in the second administration are substantially higher than in the first administration.

A similar but less pronounced effect is usually found in the investigation of *parallel test reliability*, where test scores also increase from the first to the second test administration, even though this can be controlled by counterbalancing the order of presenting the two parallel test versions. This increase in test scores from a first to a second administration of the same or a parallel test without a systematic change in the measured trait, refers to the carryover effect described in this chapter.

In their meta-analysis on carryover effects in test-retest investigations of cognitive ability tests, Scharfen et al. (2018) reported an average increase in test scores of 0.33 standard deviations from the first to the second testing. This effect decreased with increasing test-retest intervals, but it did not depend on whether the tests tapped clerical speed or reasoning abilities.

Lievens et al. (2007) summarized three possible reasons for this increase in retest scores. First, the cognitive ability might increase due to the testing. Second, the first test experience might decrease interferences in the retest because participants are less anxious or need less time to understand the tasks, leading to better performance in the retest. Third, participants memorize item content and solutions and acquire test-specific knowledge and skills during the first testing and, hence, benefit from the first testing during the second testing. The last explanation does not assume that the construct (e.g., reasoning ability) changes, but that participants develop a kind of test-wiseness. In their study, Lievens et al. (2007) could not explain retest effects by increases in the construct but found empirical evidence for the third explanation. Similarly, Hayes et al. (2015) reported that changes in test-taking strategy explained a substantial portion of the variance in score gains from a first to a second test administration. Therefore, these authors assumed that the carryover effect reflects a kind of skill acquisition. This line of argument is consistent with Arendasy and Sommer (2017), who explained the carryover effect primarily by learning and refining solution strategies during the first test administration.

The role of mere memory effects on the retest effect has been investigated by McKelvie (1992), who implemented different retest conditions to determine the test-retest reliability of the Wonderlic Personnel Test (Wonderlic, 1983) with a test-retest interval of three weeks. Participants in the *standard condition* were asked to just perform the test a second time. In the *reassess condition*, they were instructed to explicitly reevaluate the items even when they thought they could remember the responses from the first administration. Participants in the *memory condition* were asked to duplicate their responses from the first administration as well as they could. Finally, participants were instructed to do the same in the *pure memory condition* but, in contrast to the memory condition, explicitly requested not to reevaluate the items. The test-retest reliability in the pure memory condition, but not in the memory and the reassess condition, was significantly lower than in the standard condition, indicating that explicit response recall was unlikely to inflate test-retest reliability artificially. Furthermore, an increase in test scores from the first to the second test administration was found in the standard, the memory, and the reassess condition, but not in the pure memory condition. This latter finding indicates that practice effects are essential to understanding the carryover effects in the repeated administration of cognitive ability tests.

The finding that practice effects contribute to carryover effects is also supported by Scharfen et al.'s (2018) meta-analysis. They determined significant score gains of 0.15 standard deviations when parallel forms of the same cognitive ability test were used in the first and the second test administration. This estimation was somewhat smaller than in a previous meta-analysis by Hausknecht et al. (2007), who obtained an effect size of 0.24. When alternate test forms are used, the mere remembering of items and their solution can be ruled out to explain the score gains. Instead, the acquisition of test-specific knowledge and skills is the more plausible explanation for these carryover effects from one test version in the first to its parallel version in the second test administration.

Although the causes underlying carryover effects are still unclear, there is good evidence that test repetition changes the validity of the test scores when variance is added to the scores, which is unrelated to the measured construct (Lievens et al., 2007). Therefore, awareness of carryover effects and understanding their underlying processes in cognitive ability tests are essential.

In sum, carryover effects are commonly observed when cognitive ability tests are administered more than once. These effects are reflected in increased test scores in the second compared with the first test administration – irrespective of whether the same test or a parallel form is used in the second administration. Since the increase in test scores is associated with changes in validity (in terms of the construct to be measured and predictions to be made), test administrators should take these effects seriously and consider them appropriately when making decisions based on test scores obtained by a repeated measure. Learning and skill acquisition are promising explanations for carryover effects. Thus, in a neuropsychological investigation, for example, a higher test score in the second test administration compared to the first might reflect this learning, instead of recovery from a disease or from the consequences of an accident. Even if the specific underlying reasons for carryover effects are unknown for a given test, knowledge about the existence of a carryover effect (and, if possible, about its size) might help frame a score gain of an individual in a repeated measure as a carryover effect or as an actual change in the construct – if the gain in score exceeds what could be expected due to the carryover effect.

Item Position Effect in Reasoning Tests

A well-known fact in psychology is that an item's position within a series of items affects its processing. *Primacy* and *recency effects*, for example, have been observed highly consistently in serial-recall tasks, indicating that items at the beginning or the end of a list can be better remembered than items in the middle of the list (Ebbinghaus, 1885; Oberauer et al., 2018). Another example is the *attentional blink*, which describes how, in a stream of rapidly presented stimuli, the processing of a first target impedes the processing of a second target (Raymond et al., 1992).

Priming paradigms have also revealed that the processing of previous stimuli can (positively or negatively) affect the processing of a following stimulus (Frings et al., 2015).

Against the background of these findings from cognitive psychology, it is not surprising that *item position effects* have also received attention in psychometric tests and questionnaires. In psychometrics, an item position effect is present when the responses to an item in a test are influenced not only by the attribute the test is supposed to measure but also by the position in which the item is presented within the series of test items. Thus, in contrast to carryover effects as described in the previous section, item position effects do not involve a focus on test scores but rather on response behavior at the item level. These effects on items can be expected to bias the test scores as estimations of the latent trait.

Item position effects have been demonstrated in various personality tests (e.g., Knowles, 1988), psychometric performance tests (e.g., Schweizer, 2012), and educational achievement tests (e.g., Debeer & Janssen, 2013). Both the numerous approaches for representing these effects in empirical data and the conceptual explanations for item position effects vary depending on the type of tests being examined. This chapter briefly touches upon item position effects in educational tests to illustrate the *item response theory* (IRT) approaches (see the section "Item Position Effects in the IRT"), while the primary focus is on item position effects in reasoning tests. These have most frequently been examined through *confirmatory factor analysis* (CFA). In the following paragraphs, we will present this approach in more detail before introducing alternative approaches based on IRT and *multilevel modeling* (MLM).

Challenged Unidimensionality of Reasoning Tests

Logical reasoning can be defined as drawing (the correct) conclusions or inferences from given information (Lakin & Kell, 2020). A common distinction is made between inductive and deductive reasoning. *Inductive reasoning* refers to the process of drawing conclusions from the recognition of particular facts to a general rule, in which these facts are summarized (Beckmann, 2001). In contrast, in *deductive reasoning*, the (unambiguously) correct consequences are derived from premises or combinations of premises (Beckmann, 2001; Carroll, 1993). Psychometrically, inductive and deductive reasoning seem closely related (Wilhelm, 2005). Therefore, in the following section, we will refer to *reasoning ability* when referring to tests that measure individual differences in the ability to draw conclusions from given information.

In hierarchical intelligence models such as the *three stratum model* of Carroll (1993), reasoning tests tap an essential component of *fluid intelligence* as a broad ability at the second stratum. Fluid intelligence, in turn, is closely related to *general intelligence* (Gustafsson, 1984; Kan et al., 2011; Kvist & Gustafsson, 2008). Therefore, reasoning tests are commonly administered in research and applied psychology as part of intelligence test batteries, or when general intelligence is supposed to be measured by a single test instead of a test battery (Roth & Herzberg, 2008; Urbina, 2011).

Typical features of reasoning tests are a relatively large number of items and highly homogeneous item material. This can be seen in Raven's Standard Progressive Matrices (RSPM) or Raven's Advanced Progressive Matrices (RAPM; Raven & Court, 1998), two of the most frequently used reasoning tests, which differ primarily in their difficulty.

RSPM are appropriate for individuals with average ability, while RAPM better differentiate between individuals with above-average ability. Each of the 36 items in Set II of the RAPM

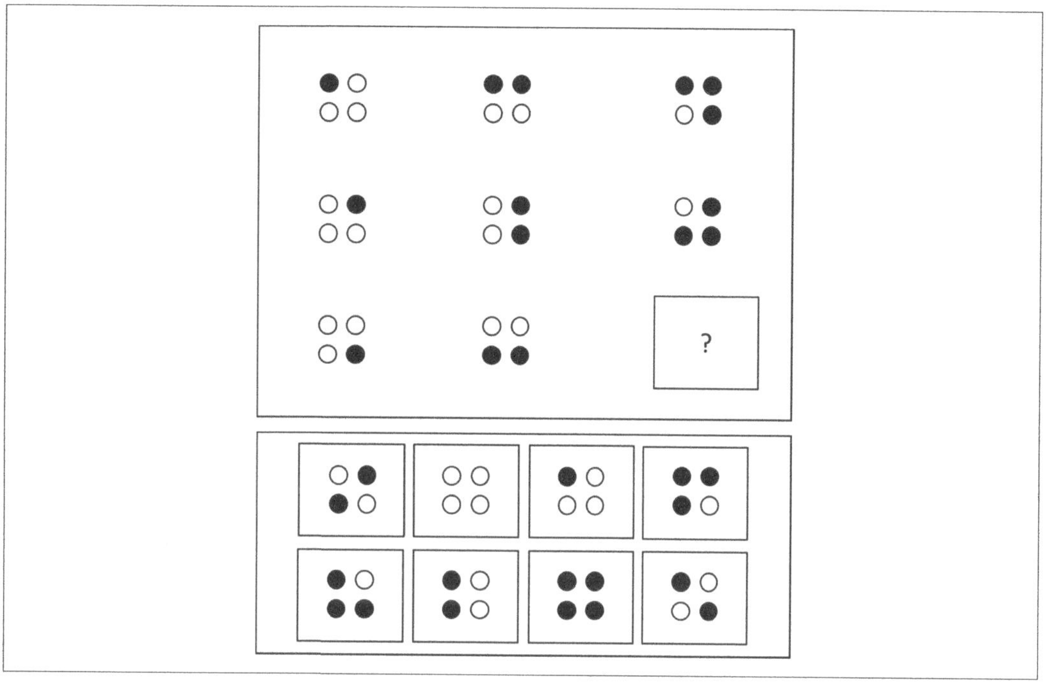

Figure 11.1 A fictitious reasoning ability item of a matrices test. The rule in the first two rows has to be identified and transferred to the third row of the upper stimulus matrix to fill the entry with the question mark. The first option in the second row of the response alternatives in the lower part is the correct response.

comprises a 3 × 3 matrix. Figural stimuli are presented in eight matrix entries, while the lower right entry is missing (see Figure 11.1 for a fictional example similar to but not taken from Raven's matrices). Participants' task is to identify the rule (or rules) underlying the given entries of the matrix and to choose the missing entry from eight possible response alternatives. A correct response is interpreted as a successful act of reasoning.

Examples of other commonly used reasoning tests are Cattell's Culture Fair Tests (Cattell & Cattell, 1963) and the Vienna Matrices Test (Formann & Piswanger, 1979). Furthermore, most intelligence test batteries contain one or more reasoning tests (e.g., Jäger et al., 1997).

Despite the very similar item material of established reasoning tests and the very similar demands in each task – for example, identifying the rule(s) underlying the matrix – psychometric analyses have frequently failed to demonstrate a good fit for a one-dimensional model (Dillon et al., 1981; Embretson, 1995; Van der Ven & Ellis, 2000; Vigneau & Bors, 2008). Thus, the assumption that only reasoning ability accounts for the variance and covariance of items of a given reasoning test does not seem tenable.

As potential reasons for the heterogeneity of reasoning tests, Embretson (1995) suggested the differential influence of general control processing and working memory capacity on different items, while DeShon et al. (1995) pointed out the distinction between items that required visuospatial processing and items that required verbal-analytical processing. Other authors have argued that methodological reasons, such as differences in the skewness of items (Vigneau & Bors, 2008) or the item position effect (Schweizer, 2012), might contribute to the lack of homogeneity of reasoning test items.

Item Position Effect in Confirmatory Bifactor Models

The basic logic of studies using the CFA approach to examine the presence of an item position effect in data obtained from a reasoning test is as follows: In the first step, it is probed how well a one-factor model (i.e., the assumption of a single latent variable) describes the variance-covariance matrix of the test items. In terms of measurement models, a test is made for whether a *one-factor congeneric model* or, even better, an (essentially) *tau-equivalent measurement model* fits the observed data (see Figure 11.2, Panel A). In the congeneric model, the factor loadings are freely estimated, while they are fixed to the same value for all items in the (essentially) tau-equivalent model. The latter model has clear advantages over the congeneric model because, for example, test score differences better correspond to individual differences in the latent variable (Graham, 2006). However, the tau-equivalent model is not a prerequisite for studying the item position effect.

The second step examines the item position effect by adding a second latent variable to the one-factor model. This transforms the one-factor model into a bifactor model (see Figure 11.2, Panel B). Extracting two latent variables from the same set of items in a bifactor model necessitates fixing the factor loadings on at least one latent variable. Especially for the item position effect, it is important to ensure that the latent variable is indeed associated with the items' positions. Therefore, the factor loadings are fixed according to the items' positions or, alternatively, according to a linear or quadratic transformation of their positions. Therefore, this model is henceforth denoted as the *item position effect model* (IPE model) in this chapter and this approach is, more generally, called *fixed-links modeling approach*. The latent reasoning variable's factor loadings should be treated the same way as in the one-factor model - that is, fixed to the same value (essentially tau-equivalent) or freely estimated (congeneric). We will use fixed factor loadings on both latent variables in the following.

The model fit of the one-factor and the IPE model can now be compared. If the IPE model describes the data better than the one-factor model, this is evidence for the presence of an item position effect (Schweizer, 2012).

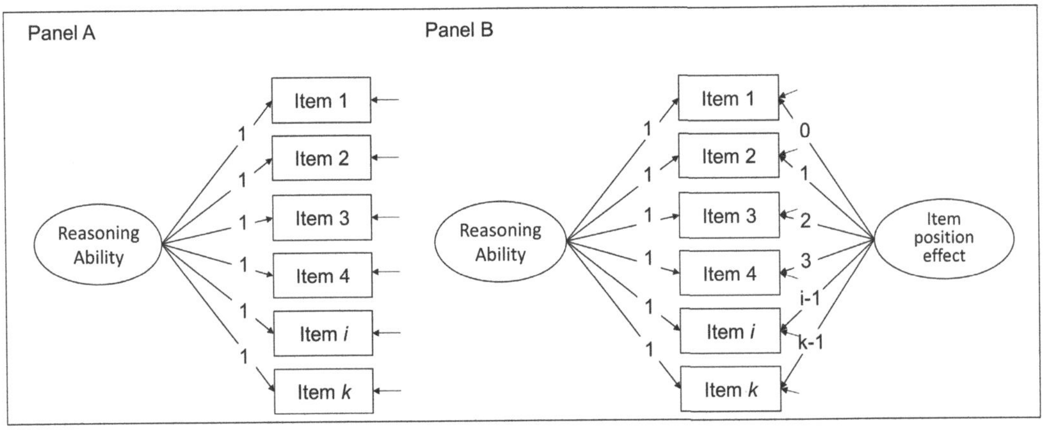

Figure 11.2 Illustration of measurement models for a reasoning test with and without the item-position effect. Panel A shows an essentially tau-equivalent measurement model with all factor loadings fixed to the same value ("1"). The bifactorial model in Panel B describes an item position effect (IPE) model, with an essentially tau-equivalent measurement model for reasoning ability and an additional latent variable representing the IPE, where the factor loadings linearly increase from the first to the last item.

The ideas in the preceding paragraph can be formalized as follows. The first step tests whether a one-dimensional model can describe the data obtained with a reasoning test (see Panel A of Figure 11.2). In accordance with Jöreskog (1971), the empirical variance-covariance matrix $\mathbf{\Sigma}$ of k items i of the test is explained by a single latent variable ("reasoning ability") with the variance parameter ϕ and the factor loadings represented in the vector $\boldsymbol{\lambda}$ with k entries (one factor loading for each of the k items). Variance and covariance, which the latent variable cannot explain, are depicted in the $k \times k$ residual matrix $\mathbf{\Theta}$, which should have zeros offside the diagonal if the correlations between items are only due to the latent variable:

$$\mathbf{\Sigma} = \boldsymbol{\lambda} \cdot \phi \cdot \boldsymbol{\lambda}' + \mathbf{\Theta}. \tag{1}$$

In the case of two latent variables (see Panel B of Figure 11.2), Equation 1 changes to the more general Equation 2:

$$\mathbf{\Sigma} = \mathbf{\Lambda} \cdot \mathbf{\Phi} \cdot \mathbf{\Lambda}' + \mathbf{\Theta}. \tag{2}$$

Here, the factor loadings on the two latent variables are represented in the $k \times 2$ matrix $\mathbf{\Lambda}$ and its transposition $\mathbf{\Lambda}'$, where at least one entry (i.e., one factor loading) must be constrained to yield a computational solution.

$$\Lambda = \begin{pmatrix} \lambda_{11} & \lambda_{21} \\ \lambda_{12} & \lambda_{22} \\ \cdots & \cdots \\ \lambda_{1i} & \lambda_{2i} \\ \lambda_{1k} & \lambda_{2k} \end{pmatrix} \quad \text{and} \quad \Lambda' = \begin{pmatrix} \lambda_{11} & \lambda_{12} & \cdots & \lambda_{1i} & \lambda_{1k} \\ \lambda_{21} & \lambda_{22} & \cdots & \lambda_{2i} & \lambda_{2k} \end{pmatrix}. \tag{3}$$

The matrix $\mathbf{\Phi}$ contains the variance parameters of the two latent variables and their covariance, which can be set to zero when it is assumed that the item position effect is independent of reasoning ability:

$$\Phi = \begin{pmatrix} \phi_{11} & 0 \\ 0 & \phi_{22} \end{pmatrix}. \tag{4}$$

In many CFA applications, factor loadings are estimated. Consequently, the variance parameters are restrained (e.g., to 1) to yield a solution for Equation 1 or Equation 2. Thus, Equation 2 might be specified as follows in Equation 5:

$$\Sigma = \begin{pmatrix} \lambda_{11} & \lambda_{21} \\ \lambda_{12} & \lambda_{22} \\ \cdots & \cdots \\ \lambda_{1i} & \lambda_{2i} \\ \lambda_{1k} & \lambda_{2k} \end{pmatrix} \cdot \begin{pmatrix} 1 & 0 \\ 0 & 1 \end{pmatrix} \cdot \begin{pmatrix} \lambda_{11} & \lambda_{12} & \cdots & \lambda_{1i} & \lambda_{1k} \\ \lambda_{21} & \lambda_{22} & \cdots & \lambda_{2i} & \lambda_{2k} \end{pmatrix} + \begin{pmatrix} \theta_{11} & 0 & 0 & 0 & 0 \\ 0 & \theta_{22} & 0 & 0 & 0 \\ 0 & 0 & \cdots & 0 & 0 \\ 0 & 0 & 0 & \theta_{ii} & 0 \\ 0 & 0 & 0 & 0 & \theta_{kk} \end{pmatrix}. \tag{5}$$

If, however, the factor loadings are fixed (for example, "1" for the latent reasoning variable and in a linearly increasing way for the latent variable describing the item position effect), then the estimation of the variance parameters becomes mandatory to yield a solution for Equation 2. Thus, Equation 2 can be specified as follows:

$$\Sigma = \begin{pmatrix} 1 & 1 \\ 1 & 2 \\ 1 & 3 \\ \dots & i \\ 1 & k \end{pmatrix} \cdot \begin{pmatrix} \phi_{11} & 0 \\ 0 & \phi_{22} \end{pmatrix} \cdot \begin{pmatrix} 1 & 1 & \dots & 1 & 1 \\ 1 & 2 & \dots & i & k \end{pmatrix} + \begin{pmatrix} \theta_{11} & 0 & 0 & 0 & 0 \\ 0 & \theta_{22} & 0 & 0 & 0 \\ 0 & 0 & \dots & 0 & 0 \\ 0 & 0 & 0 & \theta_{ii} & 0 \\ 0 & 0 & 0 & 0 & \theta_{kk} \end{pmatrix}. \quad (6)$$

Equation 6 represents the outset for investigations of the item position effect in the CFA framework, and two comments should be made on this equation. First, we recommend testing whether the factor loading of the first item on the item position effect latent variable should be "0" or "1." This decision can be based on content-related considerations or statistical ones. Suppose the item position effect is a practice effect due to the processing of earlier items. This effect cannot apply to the first item because no prior items were completed. Thus, the "0" is an appropriate beginning. However, fixing the first factor loading to "1" might be justified if practice items were presented before the actual test. From a statistical perspective, the first item's variance should be critically considered. In most reasoning tests (and for some samples), the first item is so easy that its variance is very small and cannot be meaningfully divided into reasoning- and position-related parts, so that "0" leads to better model–data fit. In any case, the beginning of the course of factor loadings should be chosen carefully.

The second comment on Equation 6 refers to the overall height of the factor loadings. At first glance, it might be unclear whether a course of [1, 2, 3, ..., *k*] or a course of [0.1, 0.2, 0.3, ..., *k*/10] is more appropriate. Both these linear courses, however, lead to the same outcome, since any multiplication of the matrix **Λ** by an arbitrary factor *c* is compensated for by multiplying **Φ** with $\frac{1}{c^2}$ during the estimation process. Thus, the only consequence is a change in the estimates of the variance parameters, which is accompanied by a corresponding change of the standard errors so that the decision regarding their statistical significance is not affected. Schweizer et al. (2009) recommended choosing a course of factor loadings with "1" as the maximum at the end. Thus, assuming that the course of factor loadings is a *linear* function of the position leads to the two possible functions when *i* represents the item position and *k* the total of items:

$$f_{\text{linear (starting with 1)}} = \frac{i}{k} \text{ or } f_{\text{linear (starting with 0)}} = \frac{i-1}{k-1}. \quad (7)$$

If it is assumed that the course of factor loadings is a *quadratic* function of the items' positions, then the two possible functions change respectively:

$$f_{\text{quadratic (starting with 1)}} = \frac{i^2}{k^2} \text{ or } f_{\text{quadratic (starting with 0)}} = \frac{(i-1)^2}{(k-1)^2}. \quad (8)$$

Please note that changing the factor loadings from $f = i$ to $f = \frac{i}{k}$ does not affect the model fit, as explained above. If, however, the relation between the factor loadings is changed beyond a simple multiplication (e.g., from $f = i$ to $f = \frac{i-1}{k-1}$), the model fit will also change.

To date, it is unknown why sometimes a linear (Lozano, 2015; von Gugelberg et al., 2021) and sometimes a quadratic course of factor loadings (Ren, Schweizer, et al., 2017; Troche et al., 2016; Zeller et al., 2017) better describes the item position effect. Therefore, it seems necessary to contrast the two courses when looking for the item position effect in empirical data, to determine which course better describes a potential item position effect. In both cases, Equation 6 provides the mathematical description of the IPE model in Figure 11.2, with two latent variables representing reasoning ability and the item position effect to describe the variance-covariance matrix **Σ** for the *k* items of a reasoning test.

Input to CFA With Binary Data

Most commonly, CFA with binary data is based on tetrachoric correlations, with the assumption that, despite the dichotomy of the responses, the latent construct underlying the responses to the items is continuous. In the computation of tetrachoric correlations, thresholds are estimated to link the binary data with the continuous latent variable. These thresholds describe the point on the continuum (i.e., ability) that must be exceeded to answer an item correctly rather than incorrectly. A stable estimation of these thresholds, however, requires large sample sizes. With smaller samples, the threshold estimates become less precise, and the model fit might become unacceptable even if the model is valid. Therefore, Schweizer (2013) proposed a threshold-free approach using probability-based covariances as input.

$$Cov(x, y) = Pr(X = 1 \wedge Y = 1) - [Pr(Y = 1) \cdot Pr(X = 1)]. \tag{9}$$

These covariances are equal to "conventional" covariances computed with binary data (for proof of this statement, see the Appendix). In the R package *lavaan*, this equation is used for CFA when no declaration is added that the data are binary or categorical - although, actually, *lavaan* automatically rescales the covariances and uses $(n - 1)$ as the denominator, which can be avoided by specifying the command with "sample.cov.rescale = FALSE."

In contrast to tetrachoric correlations, however, probability-based covariances do not provide a link between the binary data and the continuous latent variable. Therefore, it is necessary to include this link in the model. Weighting the factor loadings in the CFA by the standard deviation of the respective item can provide such a link (Schweizer, 2013). Thus, for the fixation of the factor loadings, the constraints (such as the constant factor loadings in the tau-equivalent model or the linearly increasing constraints for depicting the item position effect) must be multiplied by the standard deviation of the respective item.

A decisive advantage of probability-based covariances is the possibility of using the *maximum likelihood* (ML) estimation in the CFA. In contrast, tetrachoric correlations require an estimation method based on *weighted least squares* (WLS). This difference can be of particular interest if continuous variables (such as response times) are to be added later to the measurement model of the reasoning test to investigate their relationships with reasoning ability or the item position effect. These variables can be better modeled with ML-based estimation methods compared with WLS-based estimation methods. Thus, using probability-based covariances is especially advantageous when the measurement model of the reasoning test is embedded in more complex structural equation models.

Example of Specifying an IPE Model in R

On the Center for Open Science website (https://osf.io/zb8uf), a dataset example from 203 participants is available, along with an R script (Example_IPE.R), to demonstrate how an IPE model, as presented in Figure 11.2, can be specified. The R packages *lavaan* (Rosseel, 2012) and *semTools* (Jorgensen et al., 2018) are required for the following analyses. The R code "Example_IPE_tetrachoric.R" specifies the following example when tetrachoric correlations are used as input to the CFA. This will not be further commented on below. However, running this code shows a similar pattern of results to that presented in the following paragraphs when probability-based covariances are used as input.

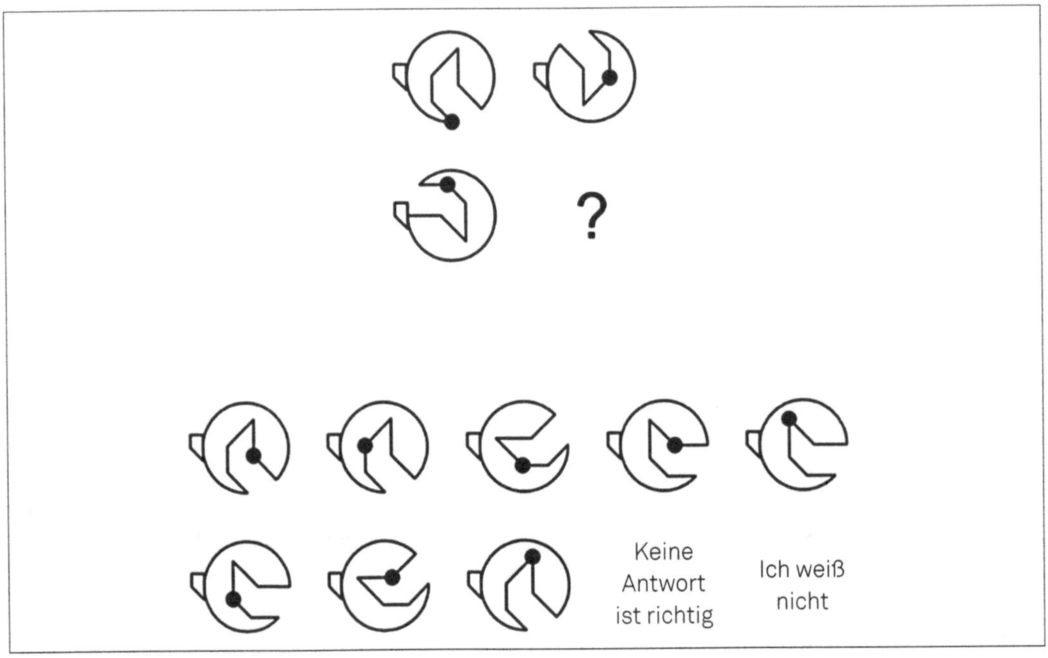

Figure 11.3 Example item from the Test of Figural Analogies (TFA) constructed with the R package Imak of Blum and Holling (2018). From the left to the right entry in the upper row of the stimulus matrix, the main shape is rotated by 180°, the black dot moves inwards by two corners, and the trapezium does not move. The task is to apply the same rule(s) to the lower row. The correct response alternative is the fifth entry of the upper row of response alternatives. ("*Keine Antwort ist richtig*" means "*No response alternative is correct*"; "*Ich weiß nicht*" means "*I don't know*").

The example data were collected with 24 items of a Test of Figural Analogies (TFA). The TFA was constructed with the R package *IMak* (Blum & Holling, 2018) as a reasoning ability test (von Gugelberg et al., 2025). Each reasoning item was composed of a 2 × 2 matrix with a question mark for the lower right entry (see Figure 11.3 for an example item). From the relation between the two elements in the first row or the two elements in the left column, the correct solution to substitute the question mark had to be chosen from eight response alternatives. All participants responded to all items, and completion time was not limited. Correct responses were coded "1" and incorrect responses "0." Prior to the 24 items, participants completed three practice items.

To examine whether the series of 24 items caused an item position effect, the (essentially) tau-equivalent model served as a starting point, which assumed that only one latent variable was the source of systematic variance and covariance in the data, and the factor loadings were restricted to be equal. In the R code, the specification of the (essentially) tau-equivalent model was given from Line 24 to Line 60, with each item assigned to the latent reasoning variable. The relations between items and the latent variable were weighted by 1 * SD_i (* indicates multiplication in R; see Lines 30 to 53), where SD_i refers to the standard deviation of item *i*. In the fit command (Line 57), the estimator was set to ML estimation (estimation = "ml") but could have been easily changed to the Satorra-Bentler corrected ML estimation (estimation = "mlm"). It was not specified that the data were binary, so the CFA was computed with probability-based covariances. In this case, the fit command (Line 57 in the R code) must include "sample.cov. rescale = FALSE" to compute the covariances with n instead of $(n - 1)$ as the denominator.

The summary command in Line 60 returned the model fit for the (essentially) tau-equivalent model, which is also summarized in Table 11.1. A model fit is usually considered good (or acceptable) when the CFI is ≥ 0.95 (0.90), the root-mean-square error of approximation (RMSEA) is ≤ 0.06 (0.08), and the SRMR is < 0.08 (0.11); see DiStefano (2016) and Schweizer (2010). Given these criteria, the tau-equivalent model did not fit the data well (see the upper part of Table 11.1). Using the Satorra-Bentler correction, however, led to an acceptable model fit (see lower part of Table 11.1).

If an item position effect was present in the data, an IPE model (see Panel B in Figure 11.2) should have described the data better than an (essentially) tau-equivalent model. Thus, the model specified from Line 69 to Line 123 is a bifactor IPE model including two latent variables: the latent variable representing reasoning ability (specified as in the essentially tau-equivalent model) and the latent variable representing the item position effect. All 24 items have factor loadings on both latent variables. However, the constraints for the factor loadings on the latent variable representing the item position effect increased linearly from 1 to 24 (and were weighted by the standard deviation; see Lines 97 to 120).

Estimating the IPE model with ML and executing the summary command, R provides the model fit, the factor loadings, and the variances of the manifest and latent variables. The model fit indices are summarized in Table 11.1. According to RMSEA and SRMR, the model can be evaluated as good. The CFI, however, indicates an acceptable model fit. Using the MLM estimation, the IPE model fit is good, and even the χ^2 value is statistically insignificant.

For comparing the IPE model with the (essentially) tau-equivalent model, a χ^2-difference test is inappropriate because the two models are not hierarchically nested. However, the better fit of the IPE model compared with the (essentially) tau-equivalent model is indicated by the smaller AIC and the more than 0.010 larger CFI (Chen, 2007).

Table 11.1 Fit indices of the tau-equivalent and IPE measurement models in the example data and variance parameter(ϕ) of the latent variables.

Model	χ^2	*df*	*p*	CFI	RMSEA	SRMR	AIC	$\phi_{reasoning}$	ϕ_{IPE}
ML									
tau-equivalent model	373.969	275	< .001	0.883	0.042	0.089	4635.53	.28***	–
IPE model	341.380	274	.003	0.920	0.035	0.076	4604.94	.160***	0.000***
$ML_{Satorra\text{-}Bentler}$									
tau-equivalent model	314.813	275	.049	0.940	0.029	0.089	4635.53	.218***	–
IPE model	286.791	274	.286	0.981	0.017	0.076	4604.94	.160***	0.000***

Note. Fit indices for the (essentially) tau-equivalent and the item position effect (IPE) model, as well as variance parameters (ϕ) of the latent variable representing reasoning ability and the item position effect, with the upper part of the table giving the results from maximum likelihood (ML) estimation and the lower part giving the results from the Satorra-Bentler corrected ML estimation ($ML_{Satorra\text{-}Bentler}$). Analyses were run with *lavaan* version 0.6-17. N = 203. AIC = Akaike information criterion; CFI = comparative fit index; *df* = degrees of freedom; RMSEA = root-mean-square error of approximation; SRMR = standardized root mean square residual. *** $p < .001$

The variances of the two latent variables are reported in the last two lines of the R output from the summary command and in the last two columns of Table 11.1. The variance parameters of both latent variables in the IPE model reached statistical significance. This indicates that both latent variables explained substantial variance in the response behavior, underscoring their meaning when interpreting the test results. However, the variance of the item position effect was shown to be .000. Dividing each factor loading for the item position effect variable by 10 (i.e., 0.1; 0.2; ..., 2.4) results in the same model fit, but the estimated variance parameter changes to 0.034. The variance parameter of the reasoning variable remains unchanged. This illustrates that the size of variance parameters depends on the size of the chosen factor loadings. Furthermore, the two variance parameters cannot be directly compared with each other when the size of factor loadings is not considered. Therefore, it is necessary to scale the variance parameters before comparing them.

Different methods for scaling have been proposed, and each suits a different purpose, such as comparing the variance parameters between two or more samples (Little et al., 2006). For the present purpose, where the variance parameters of two latent variables are concurrently extracted from the same set of manifest variables, Schweizer and Troche (2019) proposed a scaling method that yields variance estimates related to eigenvalues (*EV scaling*). The procedure of EV scaling is demonstrated in the Excel file EV Scaling of Variance Parameters.xlsx on the Center for Open Science website (https://osf.io/zb8uf). Each original factor loading (as used in the R code explained above) is first squared and then divided by the sum of squared factor loadings for the respective latent variable. Afterwards, the square root is taken, resulting in new factor loadings. As can be taken from Line 61 in the Excel file (cells C61 and I61), the sum of the squared factor loadings is now 1 for both the reasoning and the item position effect latent variable. This ensures that the variance parameters of the two latent variables can be compared with each other when these values are used to fix the factor loadings.

The IPE model is analyzed a second time in the R code (Line 150ff) but with the new factor loadings. The resulting model fit is the same as in Table 11.1 with the original factor loadings. The variance parameters, however, now refer to the same sum of squared factor loadings (i.e., 1 for both latent variables). As can be taken from the output, the scaled variance parameters are 0.699 and 0.342 for the latent variables representing reasoning ability and the item position effect, respectively. Thus, the item position effect explains about one third of the latent variance – that is, 0.342 / (0.699+0.342) = 0.329. This illustrates that the item position effect should not be ignored when individual differences are interpreted for this test.

Meaning of the Item Position Effect in the CFA Approach

Identifying the item position effect and its representation in terms of a latent variable in a reasoning test does not reveal anything about its psychological nature. In the following paragraphs, we introduce and evaluate the most common explanations of the item position effect: *item difficulty* and *rule learning*. These explanations refer to the CFA-based fixed-links modeling approach presented above, where the item position effect is represented by its impact on the factor loadings on a latent variable. Some other less elaborated explanations will also be addressed. Later in this chapter, we will show that the item position effect can also be investigated within IRT and MLM frameworks. Within these frameworks, the item position effect might require explanations other than those presented in this section for reasoning tests.

Item Difficulty

The items of reasoning tests are commonly arranged with increasing difficulty to avoid participants losing their motivation when confronted with items that are too difficult at the beginning of the test. Therefore, the item position effect might reflect the increasing difficulty of the items or, in other words, might be a difficulty factor (see Schweizer et al., Chapter 14, this book). However, the pure difficulty of test items does not necessarily result in different factor loadings, but may rather lead to different intercepts of the semipartial regressions between a latent and a manifest variable.

In the first study on this question, Zeller et al. (2017) used two modified versions of the RAPM. Both versions consisted of 18 items with a similar range of difficulty (Mackintosh & Bennett, 2005). In one version (RAPM 1), the items were ordered according to their difficulty, whereas they were presented in a pseudorandomized order in the other version (RAPM 2). A sample of 266 university students completed both RAPM versions. In both RAPM versions, a second latent variable representing the item position effect explained a significant portion of variance besides reasoning ability. Furthermore, in RAPM 2, a third latent variable representing item difficulty (with factor loadings referring to the items' difficulty) further improved the model–data fit. Such a difficulty factor could not be found in RAPM 1, most likely because item position and difficulty were confounded.

When Zeller et al. (2017) combined the measurement models of the two RAPM versions, the two latent variables representing reasoning ability could be combined into a single latent variable. This is plausible since both RAPM versions should measure the same ability. Additionally, the latent variable representing the item position effect in RAPM 1 was highly correlated with the item position effect but not with the difficulty factor in RAPM 2 ($r = .004$; NS). The difficulty factor in RAPM 2 illustrated that the item position effect in RAPM 1 may have coincided with or been amplified by a difficulty factor. Nevertheless, the results for RAPM 2 indicated that the item position effect can occur independently of item difficulty, hence, item difficulty is not a sufficient explanation of the item position effect.

The second study on dissociating the item position effect from item difficulty used simulated data (Schweizer & Troche, 2018). Data generation was based on an empirical dataset, which included the responses of 300 participants on the 36 RAPM items. In this empirical dataset, the item position effect was observed, providing an ideal starting point to investigate whether it might be explained by item difficulty. The simulated data had the same number of participants and the same number of items as the empirical dataset. Additionally, the overall level of the covariances between the items was the same as in the empirical data. However, the *range* of item difficulty was set to zero in the simulated data so that all items had the same difficulty. In nearly all 1,200 simulated datasets, a second (item position related) latent variable with increasing factor loadings could be identified. This latent variable could not be explained by item difficulty, because item difficulty did not vary and therefore did not covary with item position. Thus, the second latent variable referred to the item position effect but not to item difficulty. In sum, the studies by Zeller et al. (2017) and Schweizer and Troche (2018) make it unlikely that the item position effect, as described by a latent variable in the fixed-links approach, can be ascribed to the increasing difficulty of items in reasoning tests, although item difficulty might amplify it.

Learning

Reasoning test items usually rely on a limited number of rules (Carpenter et al., 1990). Variations and combinations of these rules are used to construct different items with varying complexity and difficulty. Consequently, participants repeatedly face the same rule(s) during test completion. It seems plausible that the rules become more familiar with each repetition and are learned by the participants. Before focusing on the relationship between rule learning and the item position effect, we introduce key findings from research on learning while completing psychometric tests.

Carlstedt et al. (2000) presented the items of three different reasoning tests to two groups of participants in different ways. The first group completed the three tests, and the items for each test were presented as a coherent series. For the second group, the items of the three tests were intermixed. The main finding for the present purpose was that the first group correctly solved the later items of each test more often than the second group. Carlstedt et al. (2000), therefore, assumed that the presentation of similar items facilitated learning the (limited number of) underlying rules, and participants benefitted from this learning when completing later items.

Further evidence for a learning effect in reasoning tests was provided by Verguts and De Boeck (2002). These authors modified items of the RAPM so that two rules could be learned by completing the earlier (and easier) items, and applied later to the more difficult items. When one of the rules was presented more frequently than the other rule in earlier items, the probability of choosing the more frequently presented rule in later items was higher than the probability of choosing the less frequently presented rule. This finding indicated that the rule was indeed learned during the earlier items. Since this pattern of results was obtained for both rules, Verguts and De Boeck (2002) argued that this learning effect was rule-specific and could not be explained by pure familiarity with the item material.

Bui and Birney (2014) also focused on rule learning in participants completing the RAPM. In their study, participants completed one of three *learning sets*, each consisting of 13 RAPM items. The sets were identical except for one specific rule, which was not present in the first set, but four times in the second set and 10 times in the third set. Afterward, participants in all three groups completed a *transfer set* containing three items with the specific underlying rule. Thus, participants had different learning opportunities in the three conditions. If learning of the specific rule occurred, performance should increase from the group with the first learning set (no learning opportunity) to the group with the third learning set (10 items with learning opportunities). The three groups did not differ in their overall performance on the transfer set. However, in a regression model, the number of correct solutions for items with the specific rule predicted performance in the transfer set. Thus, performance did not differ between the groups, but on an individual level, correct solutions mattered. This effect also interacted positively with fluid intelligence. The authors concluded that learning occurred during the completion of test items, but this was triggered by correct solutions, not merely by the exposure to a rule. Furthermore, the learning effect was more pronounced in individuals with higher fluid intelligence – but was not identical to fluid intelligence. This result suggests that learning during test completion represents an ability distinct from reasoning ability, rather than a change of it.

The studies mentioned above indicate that a kind of (continuous) learning takes place during test taking since the same or similar rules are used repeatedly. Proceeding from this idea, Ren et al. (2014) investigated whether the item position effect was systematically related to associative and complex learning. In the *associative learning task*, participants were supposed to learn the meaning of 20 artificial words. After a learning phase, word-meaning combinations were presented, and participants indicated for each word-meaning combination whether it had been learned in the learning phase as associated or not. The *complex learning task* consisted of five conditions, where different rules had to be learned during the learning phase. The rules referred to strings of two to three "x" and "o" symbols and their arrangement. For example, the *change rule* stated that the correct answer was "o" if two neighboring stimuli were different (e.g., "xoo"). During the testing stage, participants were given five sets of four tasks (each set requiring a different rule). They had to solve the tasks by applying the previously learned rules. Separate latent variables representing associative learning and complex learning were extracted from the learning tasks. Furthermore, latent variables representing reasoning ability and the item position effect were derived from the participants' RAPM data. Reasoning ability was significantly related to associative learning ($\beta = .28$), while the item position effect showed a remarkably high relation to complex learning ($\beta = .78$).

In a conceptual replication of this study by Schweizer et al. (2021), a shortened version of the RAPM with 18 items was implemented. The items were presented in a pseudorandomized order, ensuring that item position and difficulty were not confounded. This allowed for extracting three latent variables representing reasoning ability, the item position effect, and difficulty. For measuring learning, the same complex learning task as in the study by Ren et al. (2014) was used, but an additional distinction was made between learning simple and difficult rules. The core results are presented in Figure 11.4. Learning easier rules correlated with reasoning ability and the difficulty factor. Learning of difficult rules was significantly correlated with reasoning ability, $r = .21$, but mainly with the item position effect, $r = .42$.

The findings from Ren et al. (2014) and Schweizer et al. (2021) indicate that the item position effect is functionally related to rule learning. Together with the above-outlined evidence

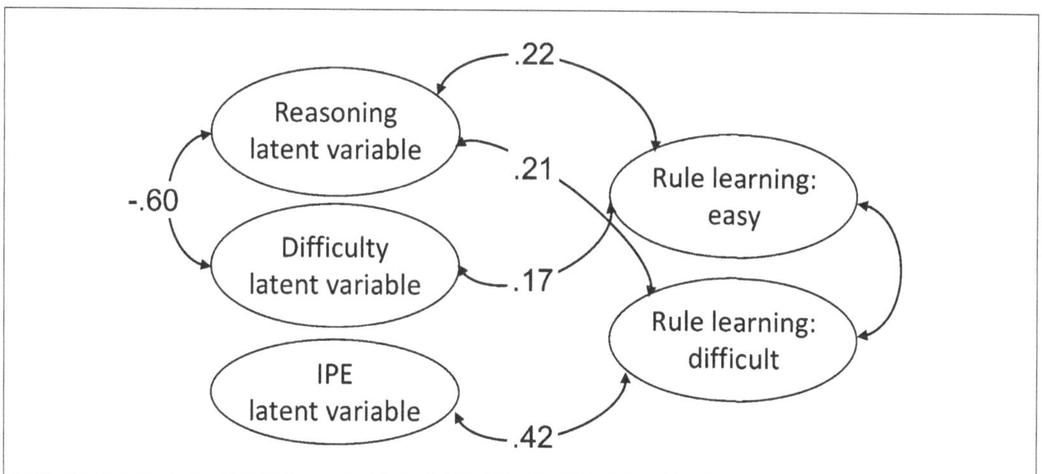

Figure 11.4 The core of the structural equation model of Schweizer et al. (2021) with a substantial correlation between complex rule learning and the latent variable representing the item position effect. Adapted with permission under license CC BY-NC-ND 4.0 from Schweizer, K., Troche, S., Rammsayer, T., & Zeller, F. (2021). Inductive reasoning and its underlying structure: Support for difficulty and item position effects. *Advances in Cognitive Psychology*, *17*(4), p. 280.

that rules are continuously learned during test taking (Carlstedt et al., 2000; Verguts & De Boeck, 2002; Bui & Birney, 2014), the item position effect might represent individual differences in the continuous learning of the rules underlying reasoning test items.

Most recently, the learning hypothesis was supported by the finding that the item position effect could be identified across all 24 items of the figural analogies as used in our empirical example. However, if the underlying rules changed after the 18th item in a second condition, the item position effect was disrupted (von Gugelberg et al., 2025). Thus, the repetition of rules seems to be a necessary condition for the item position effect in this reasoning test.

When analyzing the relationship between the item position effect and learning, it should be remembered that they are based on correlational studies (except for the study by von Gugelberg et al., 2025). Consequently, other constructs may be driving these associations. This latter argument is further supported by the fact that the item position effect in the RAPM seems to correlate with executive functions such as working-memory updating and shifting (Ren et al., 2017; but see Schweizer et al., 2021, who could not replicate the association with working-memory updating). The precise interplay among reasoning ability, the continuous learning of the rules underlying test items, and executive functions remains unclear from these correlational data. Nonetheless, it is a plausible hypothesis that executive functions or proactive cognitive control (von Gugelberg et al., 2021) facilitate the continuous learning of rules while completing a reasoning test.

Impulsivity

Proceeding from the relationship between the item position effect and executive functions, as explained above, Lozano (2015) assumed that individuals with higher impulsivity would have a less pronounced item position effect due to their lower attentional resources. Indeed, Lozano (2015) found a substantial relationship between the item position effect in the RAPM and impulsivity of about $r = -.50$. However, Ren, Gong, et al. (2017) could not replicate this finding. In their study, the correlation between the item position effect and impulsivity was not statistically significant, $r = .14$, although the item position effect was strongly related to executive attention, $r = .62$.

Item Position Effects in the IRT

The item position effect has also been explored in the IRT framework. Most of these studies proceeded from (extensions of) the *Rasch model* (Rasch, 1960), where the probability of a correct response to item i ($X_i = 1$) depends on the difficulty of item i (σ_i) and the ability of the test taker v as expressed in the person parameter ξ_v: The more ξ_v exceeds σ_i, the higher is the probability of a correct response.

$$Pr\left(X_{vi} = 1 | \xi_v, \sigma_i\right) = \frac{e^{(\xi_v - \sigma_i)}}{1+e^{(\xi_v - \sigma_i)}}. \tag{10}$$

Item Position and Item Difficulty

The Rasch model assumes that the response to an item is independent of the responses to other items in the test and, therefore, also independent of the item's position within the test. Item position effects challenge this assumption. For instance, if preceding items provide a context to the participants, this could increase or decrease the difficulty of a subsequent item, depending on whether the context is confusing or helpful. Additionally, in reasoning tests where a limited set of rules underlies the items, these rules could be learned from items presented earlier, easing the processing of later items. A similar effect might result from increasing familiarity with the stimulus material. These phenomena (learning and familiarity) can be categorized under *practice effects*. *Fatigue effects*, in contrast, are also conceivable, especially in long tests, leading to increased difficulty parameters of items presented at later positions in the test.

The *two-step procedure* is one possible design to examine the presence of item position effects in the IRT framework (see Debeer & Janssen, 2013). In the first step of this design, identical items are presented in two or more test forms, which differ in item ordering. Thus, in one test form, a given item is presented more at the beginning of the test, while the same item is presented at a later position in other test forms. The item difficulty parameters are determined separately for each form.

In the second step, the difficulty parameters of the same items are assessed across test forms to determine whether the difficulty parameters differ when the items are presented in different positions (Kingston & Dorans, 1984; Meyers et al., 2008). Hartig and Buchholz (2012), for example, reported higher difficulty parameters when items of the OECD Program for International Student Assessment (PISA) science test were presented in a later position (rather than an earlier one), and they interpreted this finding as an indication of a fatigue effect.

The consideration of the item position effect, thus becomes relevant when different individuals face the same items at different positions within a test. If the item's difficulty varies for individuals, this can impact the estimates of their person parameters, leading to inaccurate assessments. This is particularly problematic when items from the same test are presented in different forms with varying sequences, as is frequently done in educational tests (Debeer & Janssen, 2013; Hartig & Buchholz, 2012).

Adaptive testing is another example where it is problematic when the item difficulty parameters vary with the items' position. For adaptive tests, the difficulty parameters are usually determined in a nonadaptive standard administration during the test construction. In the adaptive (tailored) test administration, the person parameter of a test taker is estimated anew after each response to an item. The next adaptively presented item is then selected on the basis of this estimation, with the difficulty parameter of the next item being as similar as possible to the current person parameter estimation. Thus, the items in adaptive tests are not presented in a fixed order, but their order differs between test takers. In this case, the position at which an item is presented should not affect the item's difficulty parameter, so that the (a priori determined) difficulty parameter is still an adequate criterion for selecting the next item. Otherwise, the position-dependent variability in the difficulty parameters should be considered during the adaptive administration (Frey et al., 2017).

For such a consideration of the influence of an item's position on its difficulty parameter, the extension of the Rasch model to the *linear logistic test model* (LLTM) of Fischer (1972) can be used. In the LLTM, the difficulty σ_i of each item i, as used in Equation 10, is expressed as a linear combination of p different elementary parameters η_j, as shown in Equation 11:

$$\sigma_i = \Sigma_j^p \omega_{ij} \eta_j. \tag{11}$$

The number of p elementary parameters must be smaller than the number of k items in the test, and ω_{ij} represents a weighting variable.

The LLTM can be applied to a wide range of research questions. For example, an elementary parameter could be a specific rule underlying the respective items. Of particular importance for the present purpose is the item's position, which can also be used as an elementary parameter in the LLTM. Thus, with the LLTM, the influence of the item position on the item difficulty parameter can be modeled in one step, so Debeer and Janssen (2013) refer to this design as the *one-step procedure*.

Kubinger (2009), for example, used the LLTM to investigate whether the difficulty parameters in the subtest Applied Computing from the Adaptive Intelligence Diagnosticum (Kubinger & Wurst, 2000) varied as a function of the items' position. For this purpose, Kubinger replaced the item difficulty parameter with a linear combination of the "root" difficulty (as determined in a standard administration) and the position of the item in the adaptive test. If the items' positions influenced their difficulty parameter, the LLTM, including item position, should better describe the data than an LLTM neglecting the possible influence of item position. For the Applied Computing subtest, the two LLTMs did not differ significantly in the study by Kubinger (2009), indicating that item position did not significantly influence the items' difficulty. Thus, the person parameter estimation with this adaptive test was not challenged by the fact that the same items were presented for different persons at different positions.

In other studies the focus has been on investigating whether learning through the processing of earlier items would influence the difficulty parameters of later items in psychometric performance tests. This concept is analogous to the item position effect, as the number of items previously encountered determines an item's position within a (homogenous) test. However, some authors proposed that only correctly answered items contribute to a learning effect (contingent learning). This leads to a distinction between models that consider *contingent learning* (Kempf, 1977; Verguts & De Boeck, 2000), *noncontingent learning* (Fischer & Formann, 1982), or both types separately (Lozano & Revuelta, 2021). Lozano and Revuelta (2021) provide a detailed overview of these and further models.

Lozano and Revuelta (2020) explored various of these models to describe the responses of 293 participants to the RAPM items. They investigated whether items became easier with the total number of preceding items with the same underlying rule(s), or with the number of preceding items with the same underlying rule(s) that had been solved correctly. A remarkable finding of this study was that the repetitions of the rules led to increased item difficulty, which the authors interpreted as evidence of fatigue effects.

However, Lozano and Revuelta (2020) also applied the models to the drawing principles or figural properties of the RAPM items as classified by Embretson (2002). For two of the three figural properties, they found practice effects. In other words, the repeated presentation of items with the same figural properties led to a learning or practice process, but not the repetition of items with the same (abstract) rule(s).

The above-mentioned investigations focused on the general effect of item position on item difficulty. Other studies also considered individual differences in this effect (Debeer & Janssen, 2013; Kempf, 1977). In the model put forward by Debeer and Janssen (2013), which built on the work of Rijmen et al. (2002), for example, an overall fixed effect of position on item difficulty is extended to a person-specific random effect representing individual differences in the item position effect. Debeer and Janssen (2013) applied this model to a PISA test consisting of science, math, and reading item clusters. They found items to become more difficult when presented later in the test, and this effect was less pronounced in individuals with higher ability.

Item Position and Item Discrimination

In Equation 10, it is assumed that the probability of a correct solution increases for all items in the same way with an increase in the latent trait. In other words, the item characteristic curves of the *k* items of a test all have the same slope. In a more general version of Equation 10 (see Equation 12), however, differences in the slope can be considered to lead to what is referred to as a *two-parameter logistic (2-PL) model* (Birnbaum, 1968), where α_i represents the slope of the item characteristic slope of item *i*:

$$Pr(X_{vi} = 1|\xi_v, \sigma_i) = \frac{e^{\alpha_i(\xi_v - \sigma_i)}}{1+e^{\alpha_i(\xi_v - \sigma_i)}}. \quad (12)$$

Some authors have examined whether item position might affect not only the item difficulty but also the item discrimination parameter of an item (Debeer & Janssen, 2013; Hamilton & Shuminsky, 1990; Knowles, 1988; Steinberg, 1994). Nagy et al. (2018) proposed a model with representations of position effects on the discrimination and difficulty parameters. This model was applied to a reading comprehension test, presented to 2,774 participants in nine different versions with varying item sequences. Nagy et al. (2018) found a negative item position effect on the item difficulty parameters, with marked individual differences in this effect. This effect was interpreted as an indication of (individual differences in) persistence during test taking. Furthermore, the item discrimination parameters decreased from the earlier to the later items. According to Nagy et al. (2018), this effect suggested that *reading comprehension* measured at the beginning of the test was gradually replaced by another ability – for example, persistence during test taking. To our knowledge, such modeling of variation in the item discrimination parameters as a function of item position has not yet been applied to reasoning tests.

Item Position Effect as a Second Trait

In a seminal paper, Embretson (1991) recommended representing the change in a latent trait as a second latent variable and, therefore, as a second dimension instead of a change of the person parameter. This idea can be implemented in the IRT framework through multidimensional models.

In the study by Lozano and Revuelta (2020), for example, multidimensional models were examined in addition to the unidimensional models already described above. In these multidimensional models, a second person parameter ξ_{2v} was introduced alongside the first person parameter ξ_{1v} to represent individual differences in the position-related change (practice or fatigue effect) during the test. However, Lozano and Revuelta (2020) found that this additional person parameter did not describe the RAPM data better than the unidimensional models. Therefore, the authors concluded that the assumption of an additional dimension was not necessary to represent practice effects in the RAPM.

This is in sharp contrast to studies using the fixed-links modeling approach, where a second latent variable representing the item position effect in the RAPM consistently improved the model fit (e.g., Lozano, 2015; Ren, Gong, et al., 2017; Schweizer, 2012). This apparent contradiction might be explained by the fact that Lozano and Revuelta (2020) investigated how item position influenced item difficulty and not item discrimination parameters, which would be the counterparts to the factor loadings in the fixed-links modeling approach.

In sum, different IRT-based models and procedures have been developed to examine the item position effect and have been applied primarily to educational tests (e.g., from PISA studies). While CFA-based investigations of the item position effect in reasoning tests provide evidence for learning as an explanation of the item position effect, IRT-based studies on educational tests supported fatigue and persistence as explanations. Educational tests are often long and demand more persistence than (relatively short) reasoning tests. Furthermore, it is not easy to imagine how learning takes place during an educational knowledge test. Therefore, differences between the kinds of tests might explain the divergent results. However, the CFA- and the IRT-based approaches also differ in their focus on item difficulty, item discrimination, and the number of assumed traits. These conceptual (not only methodological) differences in investigating the item position effect from the CFA or the IRT perspective might also lead to different results, which should attract more attention in future studies.

Item Position Effects in MLM

Birney et al. (2017) introduced MLM as another methodological approach to investigate the item position effect. MLM is a statistical approach to analyzing data that includes multiple levels of information. Compared with multivariate analysis of variance, the MLM can better deal with missing data, leading to less biased results due to dropouts. Furthermore, it explicitly considers that individuals can randomly deviate from the overall average (Gueorguieva & Krystal, 2004), and data do not have to be aggregated. Therefore, changes in response behavior across single trials or items can be analyzed.

Birney and Beckmann (2022) suggested the use of a logistic MLM to describe responses to RAPM items (or items of other reasoning tests) depending on intraindividual differences as well as interindividual differences as two levels of the MLM. *Intraindividual* variability, for example, can be caused at the first level by item difficulty or item position when an individual's response behavior changes depending on the position or difficulty of an item. *Interindividual* variability, such as differences in reasoning ability or personality traits, is included at the second level. Following Birney and Beckmann (2022), the basic idea of such a model can be described as follows:

Level 1:

$$Y_{iv} = \pi_{0v} + \pi_{1v} \cdot X_{iv} + \pi_{2v} \cdot Z_{iv}. \tag{13}$$

Level 2:

$$\pi_{0v} = \beta_{00} + \beta_{01} \cdot W_v + \beta_{02} \cdot V_v + r_{0v}. \tag{14}$$

$$\pi_{1v} = \beta_{10} + \beta_{11} \cdot W_v + r_{1v}. \tag{15}$$

$$\pi_{2v} = \beta_{20} + \beta_{21} \cdot W_v + r_{2v}. \tag{16}$$

In Equation 13, Y_{iv} represents the observed response of individual v on item i as a function of the mean score for individual v across all items (π_{0v}) and the change in variables X (π_{1v}) and Z (π_{2v}), which could, for example, represent item position and item difficulty.

At Level 2, the parameters π_{0v}, π_{1v}, and π_{2v} are specified (see Equation 14, Equation 15, and Equation 16) to consider individual differences in the respective parameters. The parameter β_{00} is the mean intercept in the sample, while the parameters β_{01} and β_{02} represent individual differences in the intercept due to the variables W_v and V_v, respectively (e.g., reasoning ability and neuroticism).

The slope parameters π_{1v} and π_{2v} at the first level are decomposed into the sample's mean slopes (β_{10} and β_{20}, respectively) and the effect of individual differences on the slopes (β_{11} and β_{22}, respectively) related to variable W_v. It should be noted that it is not necessary to assume all slopes and intercepts are affected by all Level 2 variables. As can be seen from Equation 14, Equation 15, and Equation 16, variable V_v is assumed to influence the Level 1 intercept π_{0v} but not the slopes π_{1v} and π_{2v}.

Using an MLM, Birney et al. (2017) analyzed the responses of 311 managers to the 36 RAPM items. The model defined item position and difficulty as Level 1 variables. As Level 2 variables, reasoning ability (assessed as the weighted mean of scores in three additional reasoning tests) and a grouping variable (confidence judgment) were defined. This grouping variable was necessary because one subgroup of the sample was required to judge their confidence in the responses while the other subgroup had no such requirement. In this *base model*, an external measure of reasoning ability (besides the RAPM), and the grouping variable (confidence judgment) had a significant effect on the probability of correct responses. This was also true for item difficulty but not for item position. The last finding calls into question whether item position substantially influences the probability of solving an item correctly.

However, additional moderator models, including measures of personality, revealed that for individuals with higher neuroticism, the odds of solving an item correctly decreased with increasing item position, but increased for individuals with low neuroticism (Birney et al., 2017). The authors suggested that worry and anxiety (as indicative for individuals with high neuroticism) possibly impeded continuous learning during the test and, therefore, a positive slope could only be found for individuals with low neuroticism.

To the very best of our knowledge, the study by Birney et al. (2017) is the only one that has applied MLM to investigate the item position effect. The depiction of position-related intraindividual variability in the response behavior is an important step to learning more about processes *within* individuals during test completion and about the multiple facets of the item position effect.

Summary, Conclusions, and Outlook

Since the beginning of psychometric research, it has became clear that reliable and valid measures can only be obtained when scales consist of more than one item. Therefore, psychometric measures are usually composed of a series of items, which should be tau-equivalent or parallel indicators of the attribute being measured. Research on the item position effect has revealed that this well-founded practice can lead to problems when the processing of earlier items changes the processing of later items. As pointed out by Werner Heisenberg (2002) in the context of quantum physics, "we cannot observe without disturbing the phenomenon to be observed" (p. 126; translated by the authors). This also seems to apply to psychometric measures.

A couple of methodological approaches have, however, been developed to control for the systematic change in response behavior as well as for individual differences in this change. Studies using IRT approaches to modeling the item position effect are primarily interested in the position-related bias of item difficulties in educational tests. These tests often have different versions that vary in the order of item presentation. When estimating person parameters under these conditions, it is important to examine item difficulties for invariance across different test versions and to consider the potential influence of item position.

Investigations of reasoning tests in this context are less common (but see, e.g., Lozano & Revuelta, 2020; Verguts & De Boeck, 2002). For the studies available, there is no consistent pattern of results regarding item difficulty parameters in reasoning tests (cf. Kubinger, 2009; Lozano & Revuelta, 2020; Verguts & De Boeck, 2002). Possible reasons for the inconsistencies are different reasoning tests, different samples from different populations, and differences in the methodological approach to examining the item position effect.

Studies investigating multidimensionality and changes in item discrimination parameters due to item position are even rarer. This complicates a systematic comparison of these results with the results on the item position effect based on fixed-links modeling within the CFA framework. CFA-based studies on the item position effect have focused on a latent variable representing it via the continuous increase of factor loadings with item position. This line of research has revealed that controlling the item position effect in reasoning tests has implications for construct validity since reasoning ability and item position effect are differently related to cognitive processes such as executive functions, cognitive control, or learning. Also, the prediction of achievement in daily life based on reasoning tests has been reported to rely mainly on the item position effect (Ren et al., 2014). Even the relationship between reasoning ability and general intelligence has been found to be influenced by the item position effect (Schweizer et al., 2011, 2018).

Although there is good progress in identifying the psychological sources of the item position effect in terms of practice and fatigue effects, much work is yet to be done to move beyond the inconsistencies in the literature, to a more comprehensive understanding of the item position effect. Of particular interest are the conditions under which practice and learning effects or fatigue effects emerge in reasoning tests; how they affect item difficulty and item discrimination (or factor loadings) in different ways; and whether the representation of an item position effect requires a second latent variable. This endeavor can be supported by a better understanding of the intraindividual differences during test completion as addressed by the MLM approach (Birney et al., 2017).

Test administrators are well-advised to consider the possible influence of both carryover and item position effects when using reasoning tests. In the case of repeated test administration to assess systematic change in a construct (e.g., progressive illnesses, rehabilitation measures, or training and interventions), carryover effects can lead to an overestimation of improvements and an underestimation of deterioration. In the context of research, carryover and item position effects can be controlled for, with sufficiently large samples and appropriate designs. In individual diagnostics, it is difficult to control for these effects. Increasing digitalization could provide a remedy for this dilemma, when, for example, individual test and item scores are analyzed and interpreted with computer assistance, under consideration of the data from (suitable) norm samples and modeling approaches as introduced above to provide a more accurate test interpretation. However, such future developments also require that test users have a basic understanding of the challenges carryover and item position effects pose to test score interpretation, as well as possibilities to control them within the CFA, IRT, and MLM frameworks.

Disclosures

While preparing this manuscript, we used ChatGPT (https://chat.openai.com/), deepl.com, and Grammarly (https://www.grammarly.com) to improve language and readability. We have always carefully reviewed AI suggestions and take full responsibility for the contents of this chapter.

References

Arendasy, M. E. & Sommer, M. (2017). Reducing the effect size of the retest effect: Examining different approaches. *Intelligence, 62,* 89–98. https://doi.org/10.1016/j.intell.2017.03.003

Beckmann, J. F. (2001). *Zur Validität des Konstrukts des intellektuellen Veränderungspotentials* [On the validity of the constructs of intellectual potential for change]. Logos Verlag.

Birnbaum, A. (1968). Some latent trait models and their use in inferring an examinee's ability. In F. M. Lord & M. R. Novick (Eds.), *Statistical theories of mental test scores* (pp. 392–479). Addison-Wesley.

Birney, D. P., & Beckmann, J. F. (2022). Intelligence IS cognitive flexibility: Why multilevel models of within-individual processes are needed to realise this. *Journal of Intelligence, 10*(3), 49. https://doi.org/10.3390/jintelligence10030049

Birney, D. P., Beckmann, J. F., Beckmann, N., & Double, K. S. (2017). Beyond the intellect: Complexity and learning trajectories in Raven's Progressive Matrices depend on self-regulatory processes and conative dispositions. *Intelligence, 61,* 63–77. https://doi.org/10.1016/j.intell.2017.01.005

Blum, D., & Holling, H. (2018). Automatic generation of figural analogies with the IMak package. *Frontiers in Psychology, 9,* Article 1286. https://doi.org/10.3389/fpsyg.2018.01286

Bui, M., & Birney, D. P. (2014). Learning and individual differences in Gf processes and Raven's. *Learning and Individual Differences, 32,* 104–113. https://doi.org/10.1016/j.lindif.2014.03.008

Carlstedt, B., Gustafsson, J.-E., & Ullstadius, E. (2000). Item sequencing effects on the measurement of fluid intelligence. *Intelligence, 28*(2), 145–160. https://doi.org/10.1016/S0160-2896(00)00034-9

Carpenter, P. A., Just, M. A., & Shell, P. (1990). What one intelligence test measures: A theoretical account of the processing in the Raven Progressive Matrices Test. *Psychological Review, 97*(3), 404–431. https://doi.org/10.1037/0033-295X.97.3.404

Carroll, J. B. (1993). *Human cognitive abilities - A survey of factoranalytic studies.* Cambridge University Press.

Cattell, R. B., & Cattell, A. K. S. (1963). *Culture fair intelligence test.* Institute for Personality and Ability Testing.

Chen, F. F. (2007). Sensitivity of goodness of fit indexes to lack of measurement invariance. *Structural Equation Modeling, 14*(3), 464–504. https://doi.org/10.1080/10705510701301834

Debeer, D., & Janssen, R. (2013). Modeling item-position effects within an IRT framework. *Journal of Educational Measurement, 50*(2), 164–185. https://doi.org/10.1111/jedm.12009

DeShon, R. P., Chan, D., & Weissbein, D. A. (1995). Verbal overshadowing effects on Raven's Advanced Progressive Matrices: Evidence for multidimensional performance determinants. *Intelligence, 21*(2), 135–155. https://doi.org/10.1016/0160-2896(95)90023-3

Dillon, R. F., Pohlmann, J. T., & Lohman, D. F. (1981). A factor analysis of Raven's Advanced Progressive Matrices freed of difficulty factors. *Educational and Psychological Measurement, 41*(4), 1295–1302. https://doi.org/10.1177/001316448104100438

DiStefano, C. (2016). Examining fit with structural equation models. In K. Schweizer & C. DiStefano (Eds.), *Principles and methods of test construction* (pp. 166–193). Hogrefe.

Ebbinghaus, H. (1885). *Über das Gedächtnis* [About memory]. Dunker.

Embretson, S. E. (1991). A multidimensional latent trait model for measuring learning and change. *Psychometrika, 56,* 495–515. https://doi.org/10.1007/BF02294487

Embretson, S. E. (1995). The role of working memory capacity and general control processes in intelligence. *Intelligence, 20*(2), 169–189. https://doi.org/10.1016/0160-2896(95)90031-4

Embretson, S. E. (2002). Generating abstract reasoning items with cognitive theory. In S. Irvine & P. C. Kyllonen (Eds.), *Generating items for cognitive tests: Theory and practice* (pp. 219–250). Erlbaum.

Fischer, G. H. (1972). *Conditional maximum-likelihood estimations of item parameters for a linear logistic test model* (Research Bulletin 9). University of Vienna, Psychological Institute.

Fischer, G. H., & Formann, A. K. (1982). Some applications of logistic latent trait models with linear constraints on the parameters. *Applied Psychological Measurement, 6*(4), 397–416. https://doi.org/10.1177/014662168200600403

Formann, A. K., & Piswanger, K. (1979). *Wiener Matrizen-Test* [Vienna matrices test]. Beltz.

Frey, A., Bernhardt, R., & Born, S. (2017). Umgang mit Itempositionseffekten bei der Entwicklung computerisierter adaptiver Tests [The treatment of item position effects in the development of computerized adaptive tests]. *Diagnostica, 63*(3), 167–178. https://doi.org/10.1026/0012-1924/a000173

Frings, C., Schneider, K. K., & Fox, E. (2015). The negative priming paradigm: An update and implications for selective attention. *Psychonomic Bulletin & Review, 22*(6), 1577–1597. https://doi.org/10.3758/s13423-015-0841-4

Goodhew, S. C., & Edwards, M. (2019). Translating experimental paradigms into individual-differences research: Contributions, challenges, and practical recommendations. *Consciousness and Cognition, 69,* 14–25. https://doi.org/10.1016/j.concog.2019.01.008

Graham, J. M. (2006). Congeneric and (essentially) tau-equivalent estimates of score reliability: What they are and how to use them. *Educational and Psychological Measurement, 66*(6), 930–944. https://doi.org/10.1177/0013164406288165

Gueorguieva, R., & Krystal, J. H. (2004). Move over ANOVA: Progress in analyzing repeated-measures data and its reflection in papers published in the archives of general psychiatry. *Archives of General Psychiatry, 61*(3), 310–317. https://doi.org/10.1001/archpsyc.61.3.310

Gustafsson, J.-E. (1984). A unifying model for the structure of intellectual abilities. *Intelligence, 8*(3), 179–203. https://doi.org/10.1016/0160-2896(84)90008-4

Hamilton, J. C., & Shuminsky, T. R. (1990). Self-awareness mediates the relationship between serial position and item reliability. *Journal of Personality and Social Psychology, 59*(6), 1301–1307. https://doi.org/10.1037/0022-3514.59.6.1301

Hartig, J., & Buchholz, J. (2012). A multilevel item response model for item position effects and individual persistence. *Psychological Test and Assessment Modeling, 54*(4), 418–431.

Hausknecht, J. P., Halpert, J. A., Di Paolo, N. T., & Moriarty Gerrard, M. O. (2007). Retesting in selection: A meta-analysis of coaching and practice effects for tests of cognitive ability. *Journal of Applied Psychology, 92*(2), 373–385. https://doi.org/10.1037/0021-9010.92.2.373

Hayes, T. R., Petrov, A. A., & Sederberg, P. B. (2015). Do we really become smarter when our fluid-intelligence test scores improve? *Intelligence, 48,* 1-14. https://doi.org/10.1016/j.intell.2014.10.005

Heisenberg, W. (2002). *Der Teil und das Ganze. Gespräche im Umkreis der Atomphysik* [Physics and beyond] (7th ed.). Piper.

Jäger, A. O., Süß, H.-M., & Beauducel, A. (1997). *Berliner Intelligenzstruktur-Test – Form 4* [Berlin Intelligence Structure Test]. Hogrefe.

Jöreskog, K. G. (1971). Statistical analysis of sets of congeneric tests. *Psychometrika, 36*(2), 109–133. https://doi.org/10.1007/BF02291393

Jorgensen, T. D., Pornprasertmanit, S., Schoemann, A. M., Rosseel, Y., Miller, P., Quick, C., & Garnier-Villarreal, M. (2018). *semTools: Useful tools for structural equation modeling* (R Package Version 0.5, 1).

Kan, K.-J., Kievit, R. A., Dolan, C., & van der Maas, H. (2011). On the interpretation of the CHC factor Gc. *Intelligence, 39*(5), 292–302. https://doi.org/10.1016/j.intell.2011.05.003

Kempf, W. (1977). Dynamic models for the measurement of traits in social behavior. In W. Kempf & B. H. Repp (Eds.), *Mathematical models for social psychology* (pp. 14–58). Huber.

Kingston, N. M., & Dorans, N. J. (1984). Item location effects and their implications for IRT equating and adaptive testing. *Applied Psychological Measurement, 8*(2), 147–154. https://doi.org/10.1177/014662168400800202

Knowles, E. S. (1988). Item context effects on personality scales: Measuring changes the measure. *Journal of Personality and Social Psychology, 55*(2), 312–320. https://doi.org/10.1037/0022-3514.55.2.312

Kubinger, K. D. (2009). Applications of the linear logistic test model in psychometric research. *Educational and Psychological Measurement, 69*(2), 232–244. https://doi.org/10.1177/0013164408322021

Kubinger, K. D., & Wurst, E. (2000). *Adaptives Intelligenz Diagnostikum-Version 2.1 (AID 2)* [Adaptive Intelligence Diagnosticum]. Beltz.

Kvist, A. V., & Gustafsson, J.-E. (2008). The relation between fluid intelligence and the general factor as a function of cultural background: A test of Cattell's Investment theory. *Intelligence, 36*(5), 422–436. https://doi.org/10.1016/j.intell.2007.08.004

Lakin, J. M., & Kell, H. J. (2020). Intelligence and reasoning. In R. J. Sternberg (Ed.), *The Cambridge handbook of intelligence* (2nd ed.). Cambridge University Press. https://doi.org/10.1017/9781108770422.023

Lievens, F., Reeve, C. L., & Heggestad, E. D. (2007). An examination of psychometric bias due to retesting on cognitive ability tests in selection settings. *Journal of Applied Psychology, 92*(6), Article 6. https://doi.org/10.1037/0021-9010.92.6.1672

Little, T. D., Slegers, D. W., & Card, N. A. (2006). A non-arbitrary method of identifying and scaling latent variables in SEM and MACS models. *Structural Equation Modeling, 13,* 59–72. https://doi.org/10.1207/s15328007sem1301_3

Lozano, J. H. (2015). Are impulsivity and intelligence truly related constructs? Evidence based on the fixed-links model. *Personality and Individual Differences, 85,* 192–198. https://doi.org/10.1016/j.paid.2015.04.049

Lozano, J. H., & Revuelta, J. (2020). Investigating operation-specific learning effects in the Raven's Advanced Progressive Matrices: A linear logistic test modeling approach. *Intelligence, 82,* 101468. https://doi.org/10.1016/j.intell.2020.101468

Lozano, J. H., & Revuelta, J. (2021). A Bayesian generalized explanatory item response model to account for learning during the test. *Psychometrika, 86*(4), 994–1015. https://doi.org/10.1007/s11336-021-09786-x

Mackintosh, N. J., & Bennett, E. S. (2005). What do Raven's Matrices measure? An analysis in terms of sex differences. *Intelligence, 33*(6), 663–674. https://doi.org/10.1016/j.intell.2005.03.004

McKelvie, S. J. (1992). Does memory contaminate test-retest reliability? *Journal of General Psychology, 119*(1), Article 1. https://doi.org/10.1080/00221309.1992.9921158

Meyers, J. L., Miller, G. E., & Way, W. D. (2008). Item position and item difficulty change in an IRT-based common item equating design. *Applied Measurement in Education, 22*(1), 38–60. https://doi.org/10.1080/08957340802558342

Nagy, G., Nagengast, B., Becker, M., Rose, N., & Frey, A. (2018). Item position effects in a reading comprehension test: An IRT study of individual differences and individual correlates. *Psychological Test and Assessment Modeling, 60*(2), 165–187.

Oberauer, K., Lewandowsky, S., Awh, E., Brown, G. D. A., Conway, A., Cowan, N., Donkin, C., Farrell, S., Hitch, G. J., Hurlstone, M. J., Ma, W. J., Morey, C. C., Nee, D. E., Schweppe, J., Vergauwe, E., & Ward, G. (2018). Benchmarks for models of short-term and working memory. *Psychological Bulletin, 144*(9), Article 9. http://dx.doi.org/10.1037/bul0000153

Rasch, G. (1960). *Probabilistic models for some intelligence and attainment tests.* Danish Institute for Educational Research.

Raven, J. C., & Court, J. H. (1998). *Raven's progressive matrices and vocabulary scales.* Oxford Psychologists Press.

Raymond, J. E., Shapiro, K. L., & Arnell, K. M. (1992). Temporary suppression of visual processing in an RSVP task: An attentional blink? *Journal of Experimental Psychology: Human Perception and Performance, 18,* 849–860. https://doi.org/10.1037/0096-1523.18.3.849

Ren, X., Gong, Q., Chu, P., & Wang, T. (2017). Impulsivity is not related to the ability and position components of intelligence: A comment on Lozano (2015). *Personality and Individual Differences, 104,* 533–537. http://dx.doi.org/10.1016/j.paid.2016.09.007 https://doi.org/10.1016/j.paid.2016.09.007

Ren, X., Schweizer, K., Wang, T., Chu, P., & Gong, Q. (2017). On the relationship between executive functions of working memory and components derived from fluid intelligence measures. *Acta Psychologica, 180,* 79–87. http://dx.doi.org/10.1016/j.actpsy.2017.09.002

Ren, X., Wang, T., Altmeyer, M., & Schweizer, K. (2014). A learning-based account of fluid intelligence from the perspective of the position effect. *Learning and Individual Differences, 31,* 30–35. https://doi.org/10.1016/j.lindif.2014.01.002

Reynolds, C. R., Altmann, R. A., & Allen, D. N. (2021). *Mastering modern psychological testing: Theory and methods* (2nd ed.). Springer. https://doi.org/10.1007/978-3-030-59455-8

Rijmen, F., De Boeck, P., & Leuven, K. U. (2002). The random weights linear logistic test model. *Applied Psychological Measurement, 26*(3), 271–285. https://doi.org/10.1177/0146621602026003003

Rosseel, Y. (2012). lavaan: An R package for structural equation modeling. *Journal of Statistical Software, 48*(2), 1–36. https://doi.org/10.18637/jss.v048.i02

Roth, M., & Herzberg, P. Y. (2008). Psychodiagnostik in der Praxis: State of the Art? [Psychodiagnostics in practice: state of the art?]. *Klinische Diagnostik und Evaluation, 1*(1), 5–18.

Scharfen, J., Peters, J. M., & Holling, H. (2018). Retest effects in cognitive ability tests: A meta-analysis. *Intelligence, 67,* 44–66. https://doi.org/10.1016/j.intell.2018.01.003

Schweizer, K. (2010). Some guidelines concerning the modeling of traits and abilities in test construction [Editorial]. *European Journal of Psychological Assessment, 26*(1), Article 1. https://doi.org/10.1027/1015-5759/a000001

Schweizer, K. (2012). The position effect in reasoning items considered from the CFA perspective. *International Journal of Educational and Psychological Assessment*, 11(2), 44–58. Schweizer, K. (2013). A threshold-free approach to the study of the structure of binary data. *International Journal of Statistics and Probability, 2*(2), 67. https://doi.org/10.5539/ijsp.v2n2p67

Schweizer, K. (2013). A threshold-free approach to the study of the structure of binary data. *International Journal of Statistics and Probability, 2*(2), 67–76. https://doi.org/10.5539/ijsp.v2n2p67

Schweizer, K., Schreiner, M., & Gold, A. (2009). The confirmatory investigation of APM items with loadings as a function of the position and easiness of items: A two-dimensional model of APM. *Psychology Science Quarterly, 51*(1), 47–64.

Schweizer, K., & Troche, S. (2018). Is the factor observed in investigations on the item-position effect actually the difficulty factor? *Educational and Psychological Measurement, 78*(1), 46–69. https://doi.org/10.1177/0013164416670711

Schweizer, K., & Troche, S. (2019). The EV scaling method for variances of latent variables. *Methodology, 15*(4), 175–184. https://doi.org/10.1027/1614-2241/a000179

Schweizer, K., Troche, S. J., & Rammsayer, T. H. (2011). On the special relationship between fluid and general intelligence: New evidence obtained by considering the position effect. *Personality and Individual Differences, 50,* 1249–1254. https://doi.org/10.1016/j.paid.2011.02.019

Schweizer, K., Troche, S. J., & Rammsayer, T. H. (2018). Does processing speed exert an influence on the special relationship of fluid and general intelligence? *Personality and Individual Differences, 131,* 57–60. https://doi.org/10.1016/j.paid.2018.04.022

Schweizer, K., Troche, S., Rammsayer, T., & Zeller, F. (2021). Inductive reasoning and its underlying structure: Support for difficulty and item position effects. *Advances in Cognitive Psychology, 17*(4), 274–283. https://doi.org/10.5709/acp-0336-5

Steinberg, L. (1994). Context and serial-order effects in personality measurement: Limits on the generality of measuring changes the measure. *Journal of Personality and Social Psychology, 66*(2), 341–349. https://doi.org/10.1037/0022-3514.66.2.341

Tabachnick, B. G., & Fidell, L. S. (2001). *Using multivariate statistics* (4th ed.). Allyn & Bacon.

Troche, S. J., Wagner, F. L., Schweizer, K., & Rammsayer, T. H. (2016). The structural validity of the culture fair test under consideration of the item-position effect. *European Journal of Psychological Assessment, 35*(2), 182–189. https://doi.org/10.1027/1015-5759/a000384

Urbina, S. (2011). Tests of intelligence. In R. J. Sternberg & S. B. Kaufmann (Eds.), *The Cambridge handbook of intelligence* (pp. 20–38). Cambridge University Press. https://doi.org/10.1017/CBO9780511977244.003

Van der Ven, A. H. G. S., & Ellis, J. L. (2000). A Rasch analysis of Raven's standard progressive matrices. *Personality and Individual Differences, 29*(1), 45–64. https://doi.org/10.1016/S0191-8869(99)00177-4

Verguts, T., & De Boeck, P. (2002). The induction of solution rules in Raven's Progressive Matrices Test. *European Journal of Cognitive Psychology, 14*(4), 521–547. https://doi.org/10.1080/09541440143000230

Verguts, T., & De Boeck, P. (2000). A Rasch model for detecting learning while solving an intelligence test. *Applied Psychological Measurement, 24*(2), 151–162. https://doi.org/10.1177/01466210022031589

Vigneau, F., & Bors, D. A. (2008). The quest for item types based on information processing: An analysis of Raven's Advanced Progressive Matrices, with a consideration of gender differences. *Intelligence, 36*(6), 702–710. https://doi.org/10.1016/j.intell.2008.04.004

von Gugelberg, H. M., Schweizer, K., & Troche, S. J. (2021). The dual mechanisms of cognitive control and their relation to reasoning and the item-position effect. *Acta Psychologica, 221,* 103448. https://doi.org/10.1016/j.actpsy.2021.103448

von Gugelberg, H. M., Schweizer, K., & Troche, S. J. (2025). Experimental evidence for rule learning as the underlying source of the item-position effect in reasoning ability measures. *Learning and Individual Differences, 118,* 102622. https://doi.org/10.1016/j.lindif.2024.102622

Wilhelm, O. (2005). Measuring reasoning ability. In O. Wilhelm & R. W. Engle (Eds.), *Handbook of understanding and measuring intelligence* (pp. 373–392). Sage. https://doi.org/10.4135/9781452233529.n21

Wonderlic, E. F. (1983). *Wonderlic Personnel Test manual.* E. F. Wonderlic & Associates.

Zeller, F., Reiß, S., & Schweizer, K. (2017). Is the item-position effect in achievement measures induced by increasing item difficulty? *Structural Equation Modeling, 24*(5), 745–754. https://doi.org/10.1080/10705511.2017.1306706

Appendix

Schweizer (2013) proposed using probability-based covariances as input to a bifactor CFA as a threshold-free approach. Here, we will show that these covariances are equal to *conventional* covariances computed with binary data.

The *conventional* equation of the covariance is defined as follows (Tabachnick & Fidell, 2001):

$$Cov(x,y) = \frac{\sum[(x-\overline{x})\cdot(y-\overline{y})]}{n}. \tag{A1}$$

If x and y are two dichotomous variables with possible values of 0 (*wrong response*) and 1 (*correct response*), $\overline{x}$ and $\overline{y}$ refer to the relative frequency (or probability, Pr) of a correct response, then they can be rewritten as $Pr(X=1)$ and $Pr(Y=1)$ in Equation A2:

$$Cov(x,y) = \frac{\sum[(X-Pr(X=1))\cdot(Y-Pr(Y=1))}{n}. \tag{A2}$$

This equation, in turn, can be reformulated as follows:

$$Cov(x,y) = \frac{\sum\left[(X\cdot Y - X\cdot\left(Pr(Y=1)\right) - (Pr(X=1)\cdot Y) + (Pr(X=1)\cdot Pr(Y=1))\right]}{n}.$$

$$Cov(x,y) = \frac{\sum(X\cdot Y)}{n} - \frac{\sum\left(X\cdot Pr(Y=1)\right)}{n} - \frac{\sum\left(Y\cdot Pr(X=1)\right)}{n} + \frac{\sum\left(Pr(Y=1)\cdot Pr(X=1)\right)}{n}.$$

Thus, the covariance consists of four terms with the following characteristics when the data consist of zeros and ones: In the second and the third term, the probabilities $Pr(Y=1)$ and $Pr(X=1)$ are constant so that they can be taken in front of the respective sigma sign.

$$Cov(x,y) = \frac{\sum(X\cdot Y)}{n} - \frac{Pr(Y=1)\cdot\sum(X)}{n} - \frac{Pr(X=1)\cdot\sum(Y)}{n} + \frac{\sum\left(Pr(Y=1)\cdot Pr(X=1)\right)}{n}.$$

The sum of X and the sum of Y (in the second and the third term, respectively) refer to the total number of correct responses and are divided by n so that this ratio represents the probability of a correct response X and Y, respectively. These two terms can be rewritten as $[Pr(Y=1)\cdot Pr(X=1)]$, respectively. The last term consists of n times the product of two constants divided by n. Thus, the last three terms are identical for binary data. The first term does not equal zero only if $X=1$ and $Y=1$ and, therefore, represents the probability that participants respond correctly to both items. The equation can again be rewritten:

$$Cov(x,y) = Pr(X=1 \wedge Y=1) - [Pr(Y=1)\cdot Pr(X=1)]. \tag{A3}$$

Thus, if the data are not classified as "ordered" or "categorical" in *lavaan*, the program will use these probability-based covariances as input for the CFA, when the command is specified with "sample.cov.rescale = FALSE." This avoids that *lavaan* automatically rescales the covariances and uses $(n-1)$ instead of n as the denominator in Equation A1.

Chapter 12

Ecological Fallacy and Multilevel Modeling

Damian P. Birney and Richard Morris

Abstract

This chapter first reviews research showing how the degree and direction of associations between variables can markedly differ depending on the level of aggregation at which the attributes of interest are observed and measured. We describe William S. Robinson's observed distinction between *individual-level correlations* and what he referred to as *ecological correlations*, and outline the implications of misinterpreting one as the other, which is referred to as an *ecological fallacy*. We draw from examples in psychology, education, and business, where these issues challenge theory development. *Multilevel-modeling* (MLM) methods can address the complexity of such data, and we demonstrate how this is achieved. Finally, the chapter outlines how the risk of committing an ecological fallacy also exists in cases where repeated within-individual observations of an individual are aggregated to make between-individual comparisons, and reflects on the implications of using MLM to derive estimates of latent constructs under these conditions.

> *If the correlation between two traits, A and B (say, poverty and delinquency), in* n *groups (say, the residents of w districts) has a certain value, K, the correlation between A and B in the individuals or the families composing the groups need not be K and will not be, save in very special circumstances. It will usually be very much nearer zero. This is easily demonstrable, yet some able teachers have been guilty of thinking that the two correlations will be closely similar, or of leaving their students relatively unprotected against thinking so. And it is to be feared that many readers with little knowledge of correlation often misapply correlations between features of states, counties, cities, wards, classes, etc. to their constituent units.*
>
> E. L. Thorndike (1939, p. 122)

Introduction

This chapter has two objectives. First, it will review how the degree and direction of associations between variables can differ markedly depending on the level at which the attributes of interest are observed and measured, and in relation to what constitutes the appropriate unit of analysis. When overlooked, this has significant implications for the conclusions that can be drawn from the data. The reader is reminded of William S. Robinson's distinction between *individual-level correlations* and what he referred to as *ecological correlations* (Robinson, 1950), and the chapter will include an outline of the implications of misinterpreting the latter as if they were the former – that is, of committing an *ecological fallacy*, as Selvin (1958) subsequently coined it.

Although the ecological fallacy was recognized in some form as early as the 1930s (e.g., Thorndike, 1939), it remains an important methodological concept to be aware of and appropriately consider, especially when dealing with clustered data. It can also take on different forms whenever some level of aggregation is involved.

Multilevel-modeling (MLM) methods have been developed in large part to address the complexity of such data (Curran & Bauer, 2011), and the second objective of this chapter is to outline and demonstrate how this has been achieved. We will draw from examples in psychology, education, and business where these issues present substantive challenges to research and theory development. As the focus of this edited volume is to consider method effects in assessment, we will also outline how the risk of ecological fallacy also exists when repeated within-individual observations of an individual are aggregated to make between-individual comparisons, and the implications of using MLM methods to derive estimates of latent constructs. Readers interested in this methodological approach, will find R scripts for the presented examples on the Center for Open Science website (https://osf.io/63hae). But first the foundational concerns are reviewed.

Robinson Effect and the Ecological Fallacy

Robinson (1950) provided a cautionary note to those attempting to make inferences about individuals from aggregated group-level data. In doing so, he was, according to Curran and Bauer (2011), the first to clearly demarcate the distinction between individual correlations and ecological correlations. An individual correlation is defined as a relationship between attributes where the statistical object of analysis is an *indivisible unit*; in Robinson's case, this was a person. In contrast, the statistical object of ecological correlations exists at the level of a group or cluster of people. Examples of groupings include students clustered within classrooms, or citizens clustered within geographical regions, such as states or community districts. Robinson (1950) showed that use of ecological correlations between group level attributes can grossly misrepresent the true relationship between individual attributes.

A variety of exemplars have been presented in the literature, some we report on below, but let's begin with the data that Robinson (1950) used to demonstrate his point. Based on race and illiteracy data available from the 1930 US census in nine different geographic regions (referred to as *divisions*), Robinson calculated a correlation between the percentage of divisional populations 10 years or older that were Black, and the percentage of the same divisional populations that were illiterate. Thus, the data consisted of nine points, and the observed correlation between them was $r = .946$, indicating a very strong relationship between illiteracy and race. Because the data was aggregated or clustered by geographic division, rather than derived from the individual level, this was an ecological correlation.

When instead, Robinson used state-level data groupings (rather than divisional groupings), a different ecological correlation was obtained, $r = .773$. When attributes at the individual level within areas were considered, rather than relying on group-level marginal means, the observed correlation was $r = .203$. Although the underlying data were the same in each case (Grotenhuis et al., 2011, identified some anomalies in Robinson's original calculations, but the general commentary regarding ecological versus individual correlations still holds), the choice of level of aggregation led to substantively different interpretations of the nature of the association, with concordant substantive implications.

Going further, in another example in the same paper, Robinson used illiteracy data comparing those who were foreign-born versus native-born, and from this derived an individual level correlation of $r = .118$, with foreign-born citizens showing higher illiteracy. This small but positive correlation was consistent with expectations of the time that educational standards were lower for foreign-born individuals. In contrast, ecological correlations were substantially negative; the divisional-level ecological correlation was $r = -.619$, and the state-level ecological correlation was $r = -.526$. Not only were the ecological correlations greater in magnitude, they were also in the opposite direction. Robinson (1950) surmised, "there need be no correspondence between the individual correlation and the ecological correlation" (p. 354), and indeed, they may even be in opposite directions.

This special case, where the direction of the association differed across levels, was later to become more specifically known as *Simpson's paradox* (Blythe, 1972), after Simpson (1951). Pearl (2014) and Kievit et al. (2013) reflected on the nature of this paradox, and how differing correlations can be expected when data is aggregated at individual and group levels. We will highlight this in our later examples.

What Robinson was dealing with here was a hierarchy of nesting, where individuals were clustered within states, and states clustered within geographic divisions. This sort of clustering is pervasive. Once we start looking, we will see multilevel data everywhere – within education we can think of repeated measures clustered within students who are clustered within different classrooms; and different classrooms might be clustered within schools, and different schools might be clustered within districts. Elsewhere, researchers might be interested in, say, cell function clustered within different anatomical regions, or crop yields as a function of differences in plant varieties, climates, and soil conditions within and between countries.

Robinson's contribution was to highlight the fact that multilevel data have dependencies that single-level analyses are not necessarily well suited to. In elementary school, for instance, children within the same class are often observed to be more like each other on a range of outcome variables than they are to children from other classes, simply because they are in the same class. They have the same teacher, similar classroom experiences, and the same students sitting around them every day. In evaluating student outcomes, if we treat all students within and across classrooms as independent observations and not take their dependencies into account, we are very likely to misestimate the effects of important individual- and classroom-level factors.

This is particularly the case when relationships between variables within clusters differ between clusters – that is, when there is heterogeneity of covariance. The importance of dependency is also recognized in research endeavors, where different research papers can be clustered within research groups. If we do not take into consideration dependencies within labs, as well as differences across labs, we can misestimate true effects here too. Meta-analytic tools employing MLM techniques have been developed to evaluate and adjust for such dependencies (Schwarzer et al., 2015).

Unfortunately (perhaps), there is no one best solution for how to deal with clustered data, because it is not always appropriate to consider everything at the lowest indivisible unit.

Subramanian et al. (2009) report that the increased awareness of the ecological fallacy and the mantra that correlations should only be based on individual level data were soon challenged, leading to the introduction of the *individualistic fallacy* by Alker (1969). Subramanian et al. (2009) also note that Susser (1973) referred to this as the *atomistic fallacy*, where researchers attempt to generalize from observations of the individual to the group, when it is not appropriate to do so.

At the crux of the issue is that much of the way the world works entails a series of interactions with entities that operate at different levels, and we need appropriate theories and methods that take this complexity into consideration. Multilevel statistical methods have been developed to deal with such data from real-world problems. However, the application of these models also requires a strong grasp of the theoretical rationale for considering analyses at one level over another. Consistent with Pearl (2014), there is nothing in the data in and of itself that tells us which level to model. It is the responsibility of the researcher to explicate (and test) hypotheses regarding what they expect the *true* causal pathways to be. This is where the true complexity of the ecological fallacy problem often lies (Kievit et al., 2013).

The View From Management and Education Sciences

Mathieu and Chen (2011) provide an illuminating review of the etiology of multilevel models in management research. One focus of their work was to reflect on different levels of consideration that span the range from *micro*, which they define as the study of person-level processes, to *macro*, which focuses on questions at the level of firms and organizational systems. *Meso* level processes draw on groupings that exist in between. Questions at this intermediate level often have cross-level theoretical integration as their goal.

An example those questions present is related to organizational culture which can operate both at the level of the individual and the level of the organization. For instance, it seems intuitively apparent that the values of individuals within an organization may impact and change the culture and behaviors of that organization. Similarly, the culture of the organization might impact and change the values and behaviors of individuals (e.g., Mathieu & Chen, 2011; Ostroff et al., 2012). Importantly, these two sets of causal processes, one coming from the individual and the other from the organization, are unlikely to be independent and unidirectional, but instead entail cause-and-effect feedback loops within and across levels.

This type of cross-level influence is also seen in educational data. Say we are interested in knowing how to maximize a student's achievement. An obvious starting point is the individual. However, the broader context in which the student is learning needs to be taken into consideration – general characteristics of the group and classroom that the student is a member of are known to be important (Burstein, 1980; Fang et al., 2018; Marsh & Parker, 1984). For instance, a low-ability individual may achieve differently in a classroom with peers of high ability than in a classroom with low-ability peers. Knowing that, on average, high-ability classes excel relative to low-ability classes implies that the only important feature for achievement is the separate individuals' ability. However, multiple levels of information confound this interpretation. A high-ability student may flounder in a low-ability school because the group context might not support higher levels of curiosity and inquisitiveness, despite the student's own ability. The opposite has also been observed, where low-ability students may do better in classes with on average a larger number of high achievers who as a group, implicitly motivate learning.

In relation to this, Marsh and colleagues (Marsh & Parker, 1984; Nagengast & Marsh, 2011) proposed the *big-fish-little-pond effect*, which suggests that students with similar underlying abilities have higher self-concepts when they are part of a less capable group. In other words, the academic self-concept of a high achiever will be greater in a regular classroom than in a gifted one. To the extent that academic self-concept drives achievement motivation, differences in academic performance can emerge as a function of the group context somewhat independently of the students' ability. Again, regardless of the specific details, our point here is that investigating the interplay between individual and group level effects must be considered inherently as a multilevel problem.

With the increased accessibility of MLM tools, questions about how processes operate at different levels can be asked in ways that are not possible for single-level approaches. Conceiving of, and being able to, model data across levels has allowed for more authentic theories to be developed and tested, and this has propagated a need for researchers to better formalize their methodological paradigms in terms of *theory, measurement, and analysis* (Rousseau, 1985).

The theoretical imperative relates to the level at which researchers intend to frame their interpretations. Measurement and analysis relate to the observational units that are the focal point of consideration. Although Mathieu and Chen (2011) largely address organizational contexts, the nature of groupings is more or less analogous to the individual, state, and district groupings considered by Robinson (1950), as previously described. Where they may differ is in relation to additional challenges from the observational units (e.g., people) not necessarily being neatly hierarchically nested and instead having the potential to belong to multiple clusters at the same time.

Unit of Analysis and Clustering Levels

When the level of measurement does not align with the level of analysis, researchers must have an underlying theory that guides their data aggregation – namely, they need to provide different types of validity evidence to justify their aggregation of scores.

Mathieu and Chen (2011, p. 618)

Mathieu and Chen (2011) highlighted the importance of allowing for flexibility in conceptualizing different levels of data, in that they do not necessarily need to be strictly hierarchical, and that in fact, in authentic situations, often are not. For instance, within an organization, individuals can simultaneously be members of multiple groups and hold different roles, meaning that decision making based on analyses assuming simple hierarchical nesting can be problematic. We also see this in education. For instance, university students may be enrolled in multiple classes, some with the same teacher, and some with different teachers. It is important to understand the implications of such cross classifications, because different questions and problems present themselves at different levels, and it is therefore not sufficient to simply ask whether one level (e.g., individual) is better than another (e.g., group) without consideration of the broader context of dependencies.

While the statistical foundations of multilevel analyses are rapidly developing, the approaches to dealing with cross classifications and complex nesting are still in rather nascent form. Until these challenges are resolved, even current MLMs, as sophisticated as they are, are unlikely to fully represent reality.

Another challenge in multilevel environments is that the cycling of change in observational units can occur at different rates in the different levels. For instance, in psychology, personality *states* (e.g., momentary fluctuations in emotional stability) may change across the course of an hour, day, or week, and be influenced by contemporaneous situational factors (e.g., Wood et al., 2019). On the other hand, changes in personality *traits* may evolve across years and decades, and be influenced by higher level shifts, such as leaving home, parenthood, chronic illnesses or disability, or the impact of aging itself (e.g., Bleidorn et al., 2018). In general, lower-level factors (e.g., personality states) are likely to cycle more rapidly than higher-level factors (e.g., personality traits), so an assumption that temporal patterns are comparable across different levels of analysis is most likely to be unsubstantiated in practice (Kozlowski & Klein, 2000; Mathieu & Chen, 2011). Heterogeneity needs to be embraced, rather than treated as noise and distilled out.

As Mathieu and Chen (2011) point out, if one is to well-represent and apply MLM models appropriately, one needs to approach research in a systematic way. Just as Thorndike (1939) and Robinson (1950) noted before them, Mathieu and Chen (2011) remind us that we need to ask ourselves why the particular level of analysis we have chosen is appropriate and not others, and what are the implications of its corollary – that other levels will be ignored. This is not a matter of researcher preference, rather they argue that the multilevel paradigm obliges us to articulate this from the outset in planning data collection. Such formalizations facilitate statistical analyses, but are also a priori critical for authentic theoretical developments (Navarro, 2021). The following sections will outline basic aspects of MLM.

Multilevel Modeling

The goal of MLM is to appropriately deal with data that is nested or clustered in some way. MLM provides a formal way to incorporate homogeneity (fixed effects) and heterogeneity (random effects) of means, variances, and covariances at theoretically appropriate levels of aggregation. While the goal here is not to go into the full nuanced statistical detail of MLM, a brief introduction to the idea is useful for the issues raised regarding assessment, in the final section.

Representing Clustered Data

To assist in understanding the hierarchical structure of multilevel analyses, it is common to conceptually frame the approach as a series of separate regression models at each level of the hierarchy (Raudenbush & Bryk, 2002), as represented in the left panel of Figure 12.1. The Level 1 model parameterizes an intercept and one or more predictors. If there are no predictors at Level 1, then the analysis entails an intercepts-only model. At Level 2, each of the Level 1 parameters (intercepts and slopes) are represented as dependent variables in separate regression models. If three levels are considered, there are analogous Level 3 models for each Level 2 parameter.

For our first example, we consider an example where, as shown in Figure 12.1, the lowest level is at Level 2 and the highest level is at Level 3, as was the case for Robinson (1950). We begin by describing the parameters of the model, and then we will apply it to a small, simulated dataset.

A. Three level model

Level 1 (multiple measures)

$$Y_{ijk} = \pi_{0jk} + \pi_{1jk}W_1 + e_{ijk}$$

Level 2 (multiple individuals)

$$\pi_{0jk} = \beta_{00k} + \beta_{01k}.X_1 + r_{0jk}$$
$$\pi_{1jk} = \beta_{10k} + \beta_{11k}.X_1 + r_{1jk}$$

Level 3 (multiple groups)

$$\beta_{00k} = \gamma_{000} + \gamma_{001}.Z_1 + u_{00k}$$
$$\beta_{01k} = \gamma_{010} + \gamma_{011}.Z_1 + u_{01k}$$
$$\beta_{10k} = \gamma_{100} + \gamma_{101}.Z_1 + u_{10k}$$
$$\beta_{11k} = \gamma_{110} + \gamma_{111}.Z_1 + u_{11k}$$

B. Example of 3-level clustering

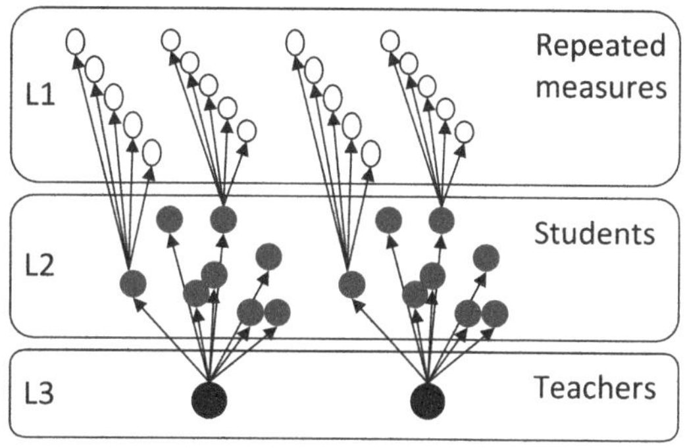

Figure 12.1 Three-level hierarchical model represented in (A) equations and (B) graphically. Where Y_{ijk} = observation on occasion i for student j with teacher k; the π coefficients are the Level 1 (L1) intercept (π_{0jk}) and slopes (π_{1jk}); β for Level 2 (L2) intercepts (β_{00}, β_{10}) and slopes (β_{10}, β_{11}); γ for Level 3 (L3) intercepts (γ_{000}, γ_{010}, γ_{100}, γ_{110}) and slopes (γ_{001}, γ_{011}, γ_{101}, γ_{111}); e_{ijk} is the within-person residual; and the r and **u** terms are the person- and group-level residual terms, respectively.

Two-Level Multilevel Model

Consider the case of measures of academic performance and self-confidence in academic success (collected before doing the test) for individual students at Level 1 which are clustered within classrooms at Level 2, where classrooms are either taught with English as a second language (ESL) focus or not. We have simulated grades and confidence data for 25 students in each of six classrooms. A quick inspection of the data plotted in Figure 12.3 suggests an overall positive relationship between confidence and grades when we ignore classroom clustering, but a negative relationship within classrooms. This is an example of Simpson's paradox, where the within-classroom level association is in the opposite direction from the overall effect. We will reflect on the theoretical implications of this shortly. The hierarchical model is described below (Figure 12.2; where the regression coefficients are analogous to those reported in Figure 12.1 for two levels, rather than three levels).

In MLM regression models, the dependent variable (DV) is always observed at the lowest level, Level 1. The intercept, β_{0j}, is the estimated grade for classroom *j* when the Level 1 predictor in the model is 0 – that is, when confidence (X_{ij}) = 0, and is conditional on effects of Level 2 predictor effect of class type (Z_j); and β_{1j} is the corresponding confidence slope for classroom *j*, again, conditional on the class type (Z_j) effect. The meaning of 0 will depend on whether we center confidence, and if we do, whether we are doing so at the classroom level – referred to as *group-mean centering* – or at the individual level – referred to as *grand-mean centering*. Figure 12.3 demonstrates this in our simulated data.

Relative to the uncentered (raw) data (Figure 12.3A), when confidence is group-mean centered (Figure 12.3C), the mean confidence for each of the *J* classrooms is scaled to be 0, while the within-classroom variance remains unchanged. The implication of this is that the

Level 1 (multiple individuals)

$$Y_{ij} = \beta_{0j} + \beta_{1j}X_{ij} + r_{ij} \quad (1)$$

Level 2 (multiple groups)

$$\beta_{0j} = \gamma_{00} + \gamma_{01}.Z_j + u_{0j} \quad (2)$$

$$\beta_{1j} = \gamma_{10} + \gamma_{11}.Z_j + u_{1j} \quad (3)$$

Where,

Y_{ij} = exam grade for student *i* in class *j*

X_{ij} = self-rated academic confidence for student *i* in class *j*

Z_j = class *j* indicator, 1 = English as second language (ESL) class, 0 = non-ESL class

Combined Model

Obtained by substituting level 2 equations (2) and (3) into level 1 equation (1)

$$Y_{ij} = (\gamma_{00} + \gamma_{01}.Z_j) + (\gamma_{10}X_{ij}) + (\gamma_{11}.Z_jX_{ij}) + [(u_{0j} + u_{1j}X_{ij}) + r_{ij}]$$

lme4 R code: lmer(Y ~ 1 + X + Z + Z:X + (1 + Z |class), data = data)

Figure 12.2 Representation of hierarchical model of exam grade as a function of academic confidence measured at Level 1 and class type measured at Level 2.

group-centered confidence variable can only contain *within-classroom variance*, because the classes no longer differ in mean confidence. Thus, classroom differences in confidence are removed as a source of Level 2 variation from the model, somewhat purifying parameter estimates to their different levels. Similarly, the fixed-effect slopes of any Level 2 predictor (e.g., ESL) can only be a between-classroom Level 2 effect, because there is no between-group variance in *Level 1* confidence.

Another type of centering is grand-mean centering (Figure 12.3B), which maintains between-classroom differences (for discussions on the importance and nuance of centering, see Hoffman & Walters, 2022). The data in the following examples are hypothetical and simulated to

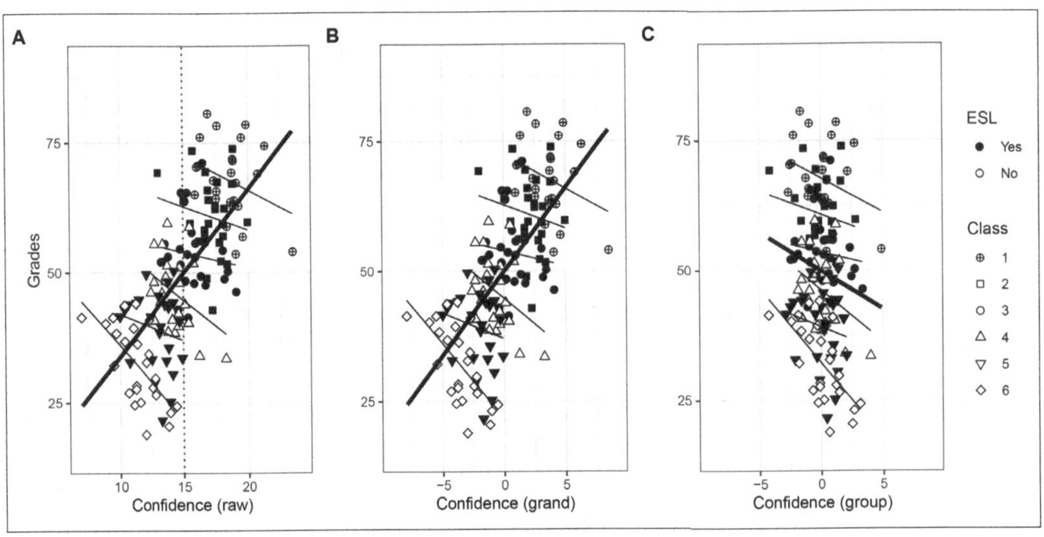

Figure 12.3 Demonstration of Level 1 variable centering: (A) raw uncentered, (B) grand-mean centered, and (C) group-mean centered.

reproduce Simpson's paradox (where, for Grades: within-class means range = 32–68, within-class SD range 12–17; Confidence: within-class means range 11–19, within-class SD range 2–4; and within-class grades to confidence correlation range: -.1 to -.7).

Each plotted point represents one student, and students from the same class are of the same marker type. The thick black line represents the standard ordinary least squares (OLS) regression estimate ignoring class – with regression coefficients for confidence (A) = 3.23; (B) = 3.23, (C) = -1.49. The thin lines are the within-class OLS confidence slopes. Filled markers indicate English as a second language (ESL) class, unfilled markers indicate a non-ESL class.

Conceptually, a Level 1 regression equation will be estimated for each classroom j. Level 1 residuals, represented by r_{ij}, are assumed to be normally distributed with mean = 0 and variance = σ^2. At Level 2, variation in β_{0j} (Figure 12.2, Equation 2) and β_{1j} (Figure 12.2, Equation 3) is modeled as a function of Level 2 predictors (e.g., Z_j). Level 2 predictors are variables that are invariant within classrooms (i.e., constant for each student), but varying across classrooms. Examples may include teacher characteristics (e.g., tenure), classroom characteristics (e.g., class size, year level), or even aggregated student level factors (e.g., average class self-confidence), which as described before, can have distinct impacts on academic achievement over and above the impact of the students' specific status on these as Level 1 variables (Fang et al., 2018).

For our example, Z_j is an indicator of whether the class is for ESL students or not. At Level 2, the different γ coefficients represent the fixed-effect regression parameters. As represented in Figure 12.2, Equation 2, γ_{00} is the overall intercept (mean) implied by the modeled variable centering (i.e., wherever zero is set for the predictors). The Level 2 ESL slope is represented by γ_{01}, which because ESL is a binary variable, represents the overall difference in exam performance between ESL and non-ESL classrooms. The random effect residual parameter, u_{0j}, represents for each j, how much their estimated grade (β_{0j}) deviates from the model's prediction (γ_{00}). If u_{0j} were to be excluded (or set to 0), each of the lower-level effects for students will be constant at the value of the fixed effects (γ_{00}); there are no random effects. Level 2 residuals of the intercepts (u_{0j}) and slopes (u_{1j}) are assumed to be normally distributed with mean = 0 and variance = τ_{00} and τ_{11} (for the intercepts and slopes, respectively). Each Level 1 predictor modeled with a random effect will have a Level-2 τ. The covariance of u_{0j} and u_{1j} is τ_{01}.

In Figure 12.2, Equation 3, γ_{10} is the overall mean of the β_{1j}, the linear relationship between grades and confidence (X_{ij}) across the J classrooms, while γ_{11} is the cross-level interaction of confidence (X) and ESL status (Z_j) on exam performance. This represents how much the association between confidence and grades (β_{1j}) differs for those in ESL classrooms compared with those who are in non-ESL classrooms.

Analyses

Single-Level Perspective

Table 12.1 reports class-level statistics from these data. Classroom mean performance ranges from 32.21 to 67.78, and mean confidence ranges from 11.34 to 18.58. If one were to correlate the mean grade and confidence values for each classroom reported in Table 12.1, we would have an estimate of an ecological correlation. In this sample, this correlation is almost perfect (i.e.,

$r = .99$), coincidently similar to Robinson (1950). Within classrooms, all correlations between grades and confidence are negative, ranging between $r = -.63$ and $r = -.13$ (the average across the six classrooms, another type of ecological correlation, is $r = -.30$). Finally, if we were to ignore class membership and treat the 150 students as entirely independent observations, the individual correlation between exam performance and confidence was $r = .66$ (the unstandardized ordinary least squares [OLS] regression coefficient $b = 3.23$ is consistent in direction; Table 12.2).

Table 12.1 OLS and MLM classroom level statistics (*SD*s in parentheses) and total effects.

Single Level Statistics							MLM Random Effects			
Class	**Grades**		**Confidence**		***r***	b_j	$\gamma_{0j\ raw}$	$\gamma_{1j\ raw}$	$\gamma_{0j\ gmc}$	$\gamma_{1j\ gmc}$
Class 1	67.78	(7.39)	18.58	(1.73)	−0.31	−1.32	80.32	−0.68	67.53	−0.82
Class 2	60.84	(7.44)	17.16	(1.40)	−0.17	−0.90	76.59	−0.92	60.73	−1.08
Class 3	53.57	(7.07)	15.71	(1.54)	−0.13	−0.60	72.35	−1.19	53.60	−1.36
Class 4	46.21	(7.09)	14.29	(1.32)	−0.37	−2.00	67.61	−1.50	46.23	−1.65
Class 5	39.15	(7.59)	12.86	(1.42)	−0.19	−0.99	62.65	−1.82	39.34	−1.92
Class 6	32.21	(7.66)	11.34	(1.67)	−0.63	−2.88	57.00	−2.18	32.33	−2.19
Totals & fixed effects:	49.96	(14.24)	14.99	(2.89)	0.66	3.23	69.42	−1.38	49.96	−1.50

Note. raw = uncentered confidence data, gmc = group (class) centered confidence; b_j is the OLS unstandardised regression coefficient; γ_{0j} = intercept; and γ_{1j} = confidence slope, where j = 1 to J classrooms.

An obvious question is what does the negative within-class correlation imply (relative to the overall positive correlation), and what might be its cause? On the surface, it seems to suggest that there may be within-classroom factors impacting the alignment between students' confidence in their *future* grades and what they end up achieving. It is quite a difficult test, Figure 12.3 shows many of our simulated students scored below 50, and this may have been contrary to their expectations which are reflected in their confidence ratings. We have already alluded to the work of Marsh and colleagues (Marsh & Parker, 1984; Nagengast & Marsh, 2011) on the big-fish–little-pond effect, where individual level effects can be influenced by group level factors contrary to expectations. In terms of the confidence–performance relationship, there are further examples in the literature of meaningful counterintuitive findings. For instance, Jackson et al. (2017) showed that although undergraduate psychology students with higher trait confidence tended to make more decisive decisions in problem-solving tasks, their accuracy was impacted negatively by higher-levels of recklessness. The core point of our example is that data viewed at only one level can obscure meaningful complexity.

In sum, one can derive several measures of association from the data that span different levels, each with different values and interpretations. First, the ecological correlation suggests a perfect positive relationship between grades and confidence. Second, at the level of the individual (ignoring the classroom clustering), the association is more moderate, and still positive.

Table 12.2 Multilevel models.

	OLS		MLM.0-Base		MLM.1-raw		MLM.2-grmc		MLM.3-gmc		MLM.4-esl	
Fixed Effects	*b*	*p*	γ	*p*	γ	*p*	γ	*p*	γ	*p*	γ	*p*
Intercept (γ_{00})	1.56	0.74	49.96	<.001	69.42	<.001	48.70	<.001	49.96	<.001	51.19	<.001
Confidence (γ_{10})	3.23	<.001			-1.38	.002	-1.38	.002	-1.50	.001	-0.82	.205
ESL (γ_{01})											-2.45	.840
Confidence x ESL (γ_{11})											-1.27	.152
Random Effects[a]												
σ^2 (within)			54.42		48.99		48.99		49.04		48.58	
τ_{00} (between – intercept)			176.80		77.21		296.36		177.01		219.53	
τ_{11} (between – slope)					0.32		0.32		0.27		0.28	

Note. a = although not reported here, some statistical packages will test whether the random-effect variance are statistically different from zero. OLS = Ordinary Least Squares regression, *lm(grades ~ 1 + conf, data=data)*; MLM.0-Base = intercept-only MLM model, *lmer(grades ~ 1 + (1 | class), data=data))*, MLM.1-raw = random-intercept and random-slope of raw confidence, *lmer(grades ~ 1 + conf + (1 + conf | class), data=data)); MLM.2-grmc* = random-intercept and random-slope of confidence grand-mean centered, *lmer(grades ~ 1 + grmc+ (1 + grmc| class), data=data))*, where *grmc=conf-mean(conf)*; MLM.3-gmc = random-intercept and random-slope of confidence group-mean centered, *lmer(grades ~ 1 + gmc + (1+ gmc | class), data=data))*, where gmc is derived *as group_by(class) %>% mutate(gmc=conf-mean(conf))*; MLM.4-esl = random-intercept and random-slope of confidence group-mean centered and English as second language class (esl) as a fixed-effect, *lmer(grades ~ 1 + gmc*esl.c + (1+ gmc | class), data=data))*, where *esl.c* is *esl* contrast-coded (non-esl class = −0.5, esl class = 0.5). *b* = unstandardized OLS regression coefficients, p = statistical p-value, γ = MLM regression coefficient (subscripting as per Figure 12.2).

Finally, if we look at each classroom separately, there are weak negative associations between grades and confidence. Each of these measures of association are influenced (or confounded) in some way by the clustering context. Appropriately applied, MLM helps us to resolve this confounding, but again, the decision as to which level to focus on depends on one's purpose, and the way to manage this is to be explicit in specifying this purpose.

Multilevel Perspective

The impact of classroom clustering can be demonstrated using several MLMs. First, we begin with an unconditional model with no predictors and with the intercept as a random effect (Table 12.2; MLM.0-Base). The fixed effect in this model (γ_{00}) is 49.96, and this coincides with the mean grade across all students (Table 12.1). This baseline model simply decomposes the total variability in the outcome data (grades) into variance between classes (τ_{00} = 176.80) and variance within classes (σ^2 = 54.42), without considering the influence of other Level 1 or 2 predictors. The sum of these variance components, 231.22, is the total variance in the data. The intraclass correlation (ICC = .765) is the proportion of variance between clusters relative to the total variance, and indicates 76.5% of the variability in student grades is due to Level 2 variability – that is, differences between classrooms. The remaining variability (23.5%) is due to within-classroom differences.

The next step is to consider the relationship between grades and confidence more closely. As noted above, we have a decision to make about whether to center the variable, and if so, how. For illustration, we report the analyses with three versions of the confidence variable, uncentered (raw), grand-mean centered (grmc), and group-mean centered (gmc). In model MLM.1, the data are not centered (i.e., raw) as shown in Figure 12.3A. Note that no student responded with a confidence score less than about 7. Therefore, the interpretation of the fixed effect of the intercept (γ_{00} = 69.42) is for a hypothetical person (who does not exist in the data) reporting a confidence score of 0. There are reasonable grounds to be wary of situations like this, not least of which is that other parameters are also influenced by the zero point of the predictor. For instance, not only is the estimated intercept conditional on the zero point, so too is the estimate of the variance of the intercepts (τ_{00} = 77.21). When there is sparsity (or absence) of data at these critical points, reliability/stability of estimates will be impacted.

Model MLM.2 addresses the data sparsity issue by grand-mean centering the confidence score. This is achieved by subtracting the grand-mean of confidence (14.99) from each student's response. Of course, as represented in Figure 12.3B, this is just a linear shift in the confidence scale and thus the confidence slopes (associations with grades) remain the same. This is reflected in comparisons of model MLM.1 and MLM.2. The fixed effect and variance of the confidence slope are the same (γ_{10} = –1.38; and τ_{11} = 0.32 in both models); whereas the MLM.2 intercepts (γ_{00} = 48.70) and their variance (τ_{00} = 296.36) differ relative to MLM.1.

The third model, MLM.3 includes confidence group-mean centered, which as we outlined before, more clearly demarcates sources of within-class variance from between-class variance. Because we have removed between-class variance due to confidence, the fixed effect of the intercept (γ_{00} = 49.96) is equivalent to the intercept fixed effect in the baseline model (MLM.0) when confidence was not included. The fixed effect of the confidence slope (γ_{10} = –1.50) is now considered a more reliable estimate of the *true* within-class association between confidence and grades (Hoffman & Walters, 2022).

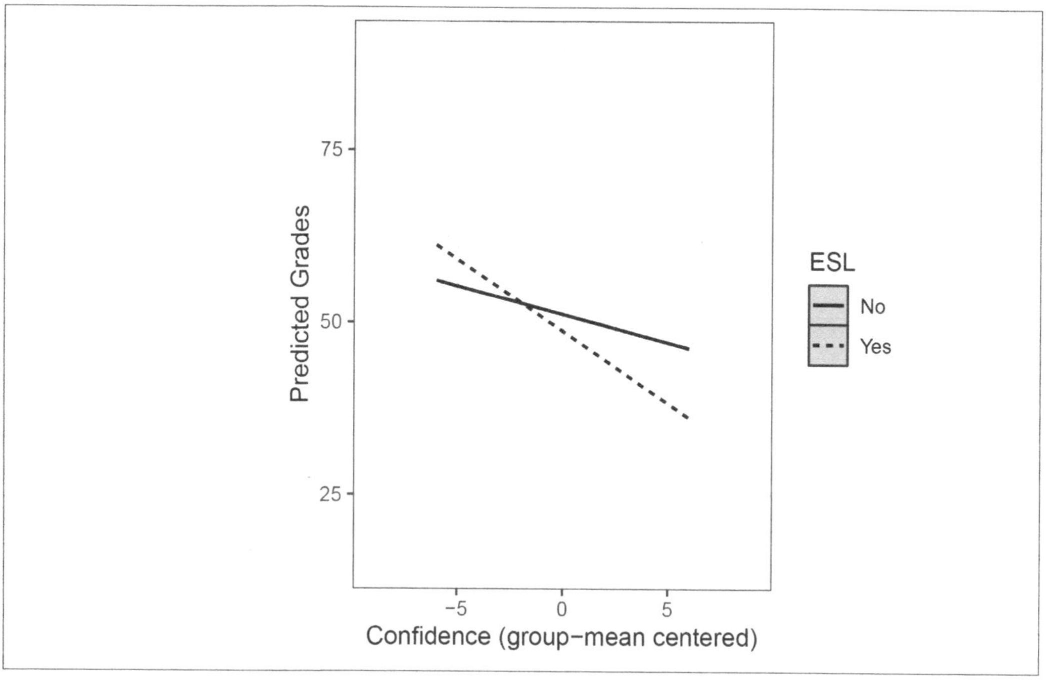

Figure 12.4 Cross-level interaction between confidence and English as a second language (ESL) class status on academic performance.

Finally, for completeness, we consider the Level 2 classroom-related variable ESL. It is important to understand where 0 is set for the predictors in all regression analyses, this is true for MLMs as well. ESL classrooms were coded as 1 and non-ESL classrooms coded as 0. If we consider this raw data, the relevant regression coefficients (intercepts and confidence slopes) would be interpreted as the effect for non-ESL classrooms. Alternative coding schemes for different purposes can also be considered. We could use a standard contrast coding to center ESL (i.e., 0 = –.5, 1 = .5). If there were an unbalanced number of classrooms for each ESL type, we might consider some weighted-effect coding (Grotenhuis et al., 2017). We report the original data coding in model MLM.4 because it is illustrative to remind ourselves of zero-point interpretations.

In MLM.4, the intercept ($\gamma_{00} = 51.19$) represents the estimated grade for non-ELS classrooms (ESL = 0) with average confidence for the classroom the student is in (average = 0). The confidence slope ($\gamma_{10} = -0.82$) is the fixed effect association between confidence and grades for people in non-ESL classrooms. The interaction term ($\gamma_{11} = -1.27$) is the cross-level interaction between confidence and ESL, as plotted in Figure 12.4. It is the difference in the Level 1 confidence slopes in the non-ESL relative to the ESL classrooms, thus we can deduce that the confidence slope for the ESL classrooms is ($\gamma_{10} = -0.82$) + ($\gamma_{11} = -1.27$) = -2.09.

Some Additional Considerations

In all models, the variance of the confidence slopes (τ_{11} range: 0.27–0.32) is small relative to the variability of the classroom intercepts (τ_{00} range: 77.21–296.36). What this suggests is that there are small differences between the classroom slopes. For practical reasons one might argue that we do not need to include random effects for confidence in our modeling, because the fixed effect is sufficient. Removing random effects from the model reduces the number of parameters to be estimated, and all else being equal, leads to better estimates of the remaining parameters (Raudenbush & Bryk, 2002). But of course, if we had not tested this first, and just assumed there were no random effects, we would not have known this.

Ecological Fallacy and Repeated Measures

A repeated measures MLM design entails repeated measures of the same person (i.e., Levels 1 and 2 of Figure 12.1). Typical exemplars of such designs are longitudinal studies, where an attribute of some sort (e.g., affective responses, such as sadness or anxiety; Kuppens & Verduyn, 2017) is measured repeatedly in order to study the nature of the attribute's stability and fluctuation (MacCann et al., 2020) and other influencing factors. These designs are common in dynamic personality and emotion regulation research, in which between-person stability in traditional trait-level measures are now broadly accepted to coexist with within-person change in concomitant state-level reactions to different situations over time (Geukes et al., 2017; Minbashian et al., 2010; Vazire & Sherman, 2017).

It is not just the means of traits and states that are the focus of MLM research. MLM has revitalized interest in understanding *variability of responses* to different test items clustered within individuals as a trait in and of itself, and as distinct from typical sum score aggregates. For instance, Beckmann et al. (2020) investigated within-individual variability in people's responses to different items of the same personality scale. They observed systematic patterns of homogeneity and heterogeneity in this variability as a function of different personality dimensions, different contexts (at work or at home), and different perspectives (self-ratings vs. other-ratings). Their aim was to uncover what is obscured in traditional observational designs and single-level analyses, which aggregate across item responses, and in doing so, treat within-person variability as noise to be weeded out. Again, multilevel approaches have been critical in allowing this nuance to be uncovered.

Ecological Correlations and Ergodicity

Failing to take systematic between-person differences in within-person variability into consideration can also be conceived of as an instance of the ecological fallacy. In contrast to Robinson (1950) who considered the individual as the lowest unit of analysis, here the lowest unit is the measurement occasion. Furthermore, the grouping variable is not a state or division as it was for Robinson, rather it is the individual themselves, which define the clusters. In the repeated measures context, the lowest level an ecological correlation can exist is at the between-individual level, because it is here that the abstraction occurs (i.e., across within-person measurement occasions).

An alternative way to understand the concept of an ecological correlation at the level of the individual is to consider how it is related to the conceptually similar notion of *ergodicity*. Ergodicity holds when relationships between attributes observed at one level can be directly mapped to different levels (Molenaar, 2004, 2013). In such situations, ecological correlations are the same as individual correlations. The ergodic assumption (or fallacy, some might say) exists when we make the implicit supposition that the structural relationship between different attributes identified across different people also holds within each person as the same quality in the same proportions.

For instance, we make an ergodic assumption when we imply that the five-factor structure of personality exists within each and every person in the same way as it exists between people. This is made explicit when we report and interpret five-factor personality profiles of different people, effectively ignoring the possibility that one person might have, say, a four-factor internal personality structure, and another a six-factor structure. Such differences bring into question the validity of psychological measurement, generally, when it is based on single-level theorizing. Several researchers have demonstrated that ergodicity is not only theoretically questionable, but also often logically untenable (Borsboom et al., 2003; Molenaar, 2013).

This type of challenge is recognized in psychology and education, but often not at the level of the individual. For instance, it is common for test developers to consider measurement invariance across different populations as an important part of test validation strategies (Putnick & Bornstein, 2016). For instance, we might investigate the extent to which the five-factor personality structure holds in different populations, such as countries or cultures, as Lui et al. (2020) did. If measurement invariance fails, then validity is at risk, and it is incumbent upon the research community to investigate further.

At the level of the individual, measurement invariance is typically not explored. Historically, there are numerous pragmatic and statistical challenges in doing this. It entails many repeated administrations of the personality test on the same individual that may not even be feasible, and then testing measurement invariance across multiple people (Molenaar, 2013). In such a model, the between-person structure would be the fixed effect, and each persons' within-person structure the random effect. This is not an easy study to run; however, as a thought experiment in extending the notion of ecological correlations to the level of measurement of an individual, it holds some weight. In the meantime, less ambitious investigations are possible, which we will reflect on next.

Autocorrelations

In the classroom example (see Figure 12.2), we framed MLM as a series of regression models at different levels, where the intercepts and slopes of Level 1 predictors (i.e., as inputs) are used as dependent variables (i.e., as outputs) at Level 2. However, in practice, these regressions are run simultaneously. This can be demonstrated by substituting the Level 2 equations into the Level 1 model. The resulting mixed-model equation for our repeated measures design is shown as Equation 4:

$$Y_{ij} = \beta_{00} + \beta_{01}.X_j + \beta_{10}.W_{ij} + \beta_{11}.X_j.W_{ij} + [(\mathrm{r}_{0j} + \mathrm{r}_{1j}.\mathrm{W}_{ij}) + \mathrm{e}_{ij}] \quad (4)$$

The mixed model demonstrates that parameters are estimated simultaneously. As we described earlier, r_{0j} is typically assumed to be normally distributed with a mean = 0 and a variance = τ_{00}. Similarly, r_{1j} is assumed to be normal with mean = 0 and variance = τ_{11}. Relative to clusters of observations of individuals (in, say, classrooms), clusters of observations within individuals often have stronger interdependency (because they come from the same person). Observations of the same individual closer in time can be more similar than observations that are more distal. This can lead to substantive autocorrelations which can weaken confidence in some of the typical assumptions (e.g., of normality of residuals). There are statistical approaches, including Bayesian models (Kéry, 2010; Rouder & Haaf, 2019), that allow for different degrees of autocorrelations, nonnormal distributions, and more complex designs.

Partial Pooling and Shrinkage: Improving Reliability of Parameters

As has been alluded to, another instantiation of the ecological fallacy is assuming that the random effects are equal to the fixed effect, and not investigating further. As we have seen in the previous example, estimates of means and associations can be influenced by the perspective and level chosen for consideration.

The relative reliability or precision of the estimates can also differ when estimates are based on more or fewer observations. One of the powerful features of MLM is that the full distribution of data *within* and *between* groupings is used to estimate model parameters through partial *pooling*. In contrast to full pooling, which is what we are doing when all of the data are combined to estimate intercepts (means) and slopes irrespective of clustering (e.g., individual level correlations), partial pooling combines information about means and variances within clusters, with information about means and variances between clusters, to derive more reliable estimates of both fixed and random effects.

Partial pooling in MLM leads to some advantages compared with OLS regression (Brunner & Austin, 2009). When used to derive contrast estimates for hypothesis testing, MLM results in greater precision and lower Type 1 error rates (Gelman et al., 2012). This is the case because partial pooling leads to what is often referred to as *shrinkage*, which under certain circumstances results in a shift of parameter estimates and their associated standard errors toward mean parameter coefficients in the complete data (the intercept and slope fixed effects). This has the desirable effect of shrinking coefficients that are estimated with lower accuracy more than those estimated with higher accuracy (Hox, 2010).

The amount of shrinkage observed is a function of the relative precision of group estimates, which is influenced by between-cluster variability (τ), and the residual error (within-group variance, σ^2), which is influenced by cluster sample size (n). Figure 12.5 reports a simulation of these factors.

In Figure 12.5, scores for each of 24 people (*a* to *x*) with $n = 5$, 10, or 30 repeated measures, and with low between-cluster variance ($\tau = 1.5$) and high between-cluster variance ($\tau = 7.5$) is simulated and plotted. Shrinkage can be observed by the degree to which the black circles in Figure 12.5B (which are the raw OLS cluster means) are weighted toward the overall fixed effect obtained from the full data (here represented by the straight line in Figure 12.5B).

What we observe is that less shrinkage occurs as τ increases. This makes sense, because τ represents variation around the Level 2 fixed effect, and it is conceptually reasonable to have less trust in this fixed effect when τ is large, and not shrunken toward it.

Second, less shrinkage also occurs as cluster sample size increases. All else being equal, generally the larger the number of observations, the smaller the variance will be. Conceptually, a smaller within-cluster sample leads to less information about within-cluster variability (σ^2) on which to estimate the cluster means – put simply, we have less confidence in means derived from small samples. Because MLM partially pools information from the multiple clusters available in the data, the precision of the within-cluster estimate for a cluster with a small sample can be improved. This is achieved by shrinking random effects toward the overall fixed effect (Harrison et al., 2018; Rouder & Haaf, 2019).

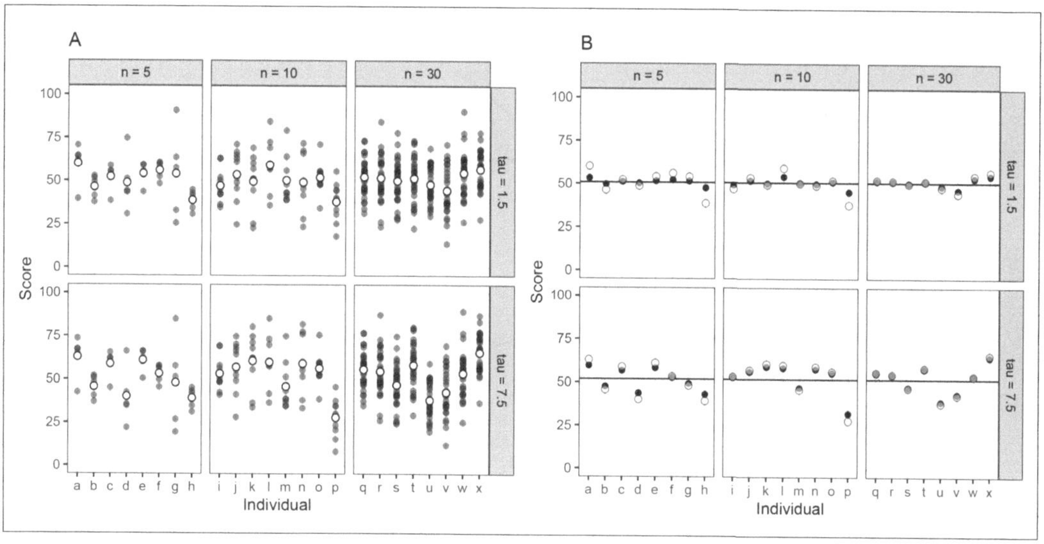

Figure 12.5 Simulation of shrinkage. (A) Raw data distribution for repeated measures of each individual and their estimated unpooled means (white circles), and (B) modeled effects with unpooled means (white circles) and partially pooled means (random effects; black circles).

Shrinkage and Within-Person Slopes

While overall and cluster-specific means are important, we can also consider shrinkage with regard to slopes. In Figure 12.6A, the data from six employees is plotted with different markers where the DV is work-based productivity measured repeatedly over time, and the covariate of interest is anxiety, also measured repeatedly over time.

Every line in Figure 12.6A represents a different form of the anxiety-productivity relationship. The solid lines represent relationships estimated by single-level analyses (i.e., OLS regression). The dashed and dotted lines represent relationships estimated by an MLM analysis. The thin lines represent the within-individual relationships between anxiety and productivity; there is one set for each employee. The thick lines represent overall relationships.

First, consider the solid lines. The solid thick line is the OLS regression for all measures for all employees ignoring the cluster dependency. It is a positive relationship (slope = 3.17), suggesting that as anxiety increases, productivity also increases. In Robinson's terms, this is an association at the level of the individual (Robinson, 1950). If we look at the solid thin lines numbered for each employee, these are also OLS regression slopes, and are all negative (Figure 12.6B); for a given employee, as anxiety increases productivity falls (which intuitively, seems more consistent than a positive relationship).

Now consider the dashed and dotted lines, which represent estimated MLM associations that take into consideration the clustering of measures within employees. The thick dashed line is the anxiety fixed effect slope (−1.09) from the MLM analysis. It takes into consideration the different (negative) within-group effects, and thus is also negative. The thin dotted lines represent the anxiety random slopes for each employee. The extent to which the random slopes (Figure 12.6A and 12.6B) differ from the OLS slopes is due to shrinkage toward the fixed effect.

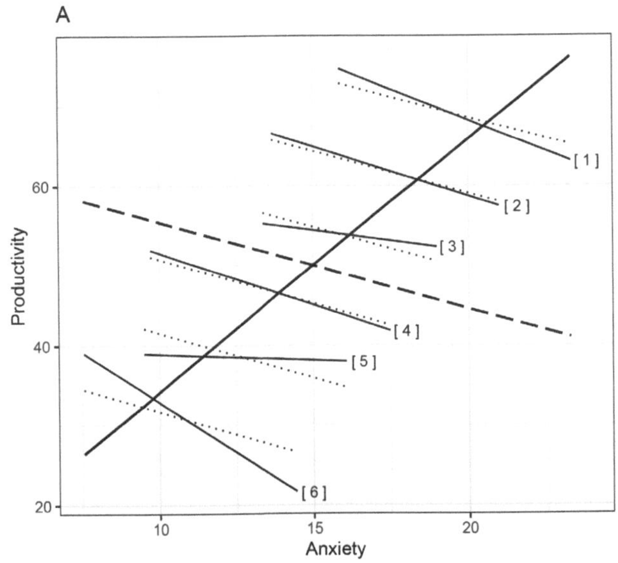

B

Employee	OLS slope	Random effect
1	−1.57	−1.04
2	−1.25	−1.06
3	−0.52	−1.08
4	−1.30	−1.10
5	−0.15	−1.13
6	−2.52	−1.15
Total/Fixed Effect	3.17	−1.09

Figure 12.6 Shrinkage and random slope effects with (A) plotted data and (B) effect estimates.

For the reasons outlined above, all else being equal, the MLM estimates are a more precise estimate of the true relations because they draw on information available in the full data – that is, information from within groups as well as information between groups. That being the case, one might ask whether random-effects are more reliable estimates of individual-level traits, both in terms of means (intercepts) and correlations (slopes) than scores that come from single-level analyses. This is the last issue we will consider.

Random Effects as Measures of Traits

Given the advantageous aspects of MLM analyses, in terms of demarcating within- and between-group variance, a reasonable question is whether we can extract the random effects that have been shrunk toward the fixed effect from MLM and use them as measures of individual traits. Before we consider this, let us take a brief look at the typical psychometric approach to measurement of individual traits.

Within psychology, the *measure* often used to estimate a person's level on some attribute will be an aggregate function of their responses to the test items they have answered – for example, a total sum score. No matter how rigorously a test is developed, it is readily accepted that all observed test scores are variously imperfect indicators of the unobservable, true level of the latent attribute they are intended to measure. Because of this, observed scores always include some error (which is also unobservable and therefore latent).

Classical test theory proposes that under the right circumstances (Birney et al., 2022), between-person variation in the observed score (X) can be decomposed into systematic variation due to differences in peoples' true scores (T) and variation due to nonsystematic error (E). We recognize this as: X = T + E; and when framed in terms of variances, as: var(X) = var(T + var(E) + 2·cov(T,E). Because it is typically assumed that true scores and errors are uncorrelated, the last term equates to 0, and we have the basis of classical formulations of reliability, as shown in Equation 5 and Equation 6:

$$\text{var}(X) = \text{var}(T) + \text{var}(E) \tag{5}$$

$$\text{reliability} = \text{var}(T)/\text{var}(X) \tag{6}$$

Simply stated, reliability is the proportion of total observed variation in the measure that is due to true score variation, and this is why the interpretation of a reliability coefficient of, say, 0.8, is that 80% of variation in the data is systematic and the remaining 20% is noise.

This simple measurement model is very often the basis of ever more complex methods and tools for estimating true score variance, including structural equation modelling and to some extent, item response theory. These statistical methods facilitate estimation of *true* latent level relationships between multiple latent variables that have been *purified* from their inherent unreliability (Bollen, 1989). Just as we can extract random effects from MLM models, we can also extract person-level estimates of true scores from these measurement models. However, it is important to recognize that while relationships observed in the statistical models can be interpreted at the level of latent variables, the extracted values are not the true latent scores; they are estimates which by definition are also imperfect (see e.g., Lechner et al., 2021; Zitzmann et al., 2024). In these models, often the best we can hope for is to be able to derive reliable estimates that are not biased; however, even this is not always guaranteed (Lechner et al., 2021). MLM analyses are not immune to these issues, but shrinkage does provide some advantages.

Reliability of Difference Scores as Latent Trait Measures

Rouder and Haaf (2019) investigated the issue associated with shrinkage and the use of within-person difference scores (i.e., slopes between two measurement points). Difference scores are central to many psychological concepts, such as inhibition. The *Stroop task* is a classic inhibition task where participants are required to name the font color of different color words. Congruent trials are when the font color and meaning of the word align – for example, the word "blue" printed in blue ink. Incongruent trials are when the font color and the color word do not align – for instance, the word "red" printed in blue ink. The correct response in both cases is blue; however, responses are slower and more error prone in incongruent trials because of the over-learnt tendency to read words rather than name the color of the font they are printed in. The inhibition trait score is typically some composite of the difference in performance on congruent versus incongruent trials.

Researchers have observed for some time that a variety of tests designed to measure inhibition using difference scores tend not to be correlated with each other as highly as would be expected, and that part of the problem has to do with unreliability of these scores (Hedge et al., 2018). Rouder and Haaf (2019) demonstrated that in these tasks, small numbers of within-person trials (i.e., observations) can attenuate effect sizes and correlations between tasks. They showed that an application of MLM can improve on concepts like reliability and correlation needed for studying individual differences. This was achieved through the process of shrinkage, which was outlined above. As expected, the precision benefits were greatest when there were small numbers of within-person trials, which for pragmatic reasons is quite common in the inhibition research literature. Interestingly, correlations between different inhibition tasks remained low even using multilevel methods to derive scores, suggesting there are deeper reasons for low correlations, other than reliability.

Concluding Comment: An Aggregation Problem

All of the challenges discussed can be thought of generally as a special case of the problem of aggregation. Measures of central tendency (e.g., mean, median, and mode), variation (e.g., standard deviation, skewness, and range), and covariation (e.g., correlation and moderation) are straightforward examples of aggregation. These statistics are intended as reductive summaries of a larger set of data, and except for in a rather unique circumstance (one such exception being when the data are constant, with zero variation), it is well accepted that they cannot represent nuance at the unit of observation. This is not a major problem in and of itself, as long as one remains cognizant of the level of aggregation, as Robinson (1950) and those before and after him have pointed out. Long before the opportunity to take formal classes in statistics, we learn from our everyday experiences with the world, that concepts like mean and variance can be very useful. For instance, we learn that some things vary more under some situations than others (e.g., heterogeneity of variance and covariance). We may also learn that there may be no single instance in a set of data, such as children's ages (e.g., ages 6, 4, 3, 7, 2, and 8), that takes the value of its mean (i.e., 5). Aggregation is the cornerstone of science's search for general principles; experimental and correlational research designs assume validity of aggregates used in statistical analyses ranging from *t* tests to factor analysis, and in deriving comparative differences in means or associations as effect sizes. However, as we hope to have demonstrated here, unchecked, aggregates have a tendency to obscure meaningful heterogeneity and foster homogenization of complexity, and this is the crux of the problem. The challenge is knowing when and under which circumstances aggregation is problematic.

Krammer (2023) have suggested that the historical tendency in education and psychology to rely on aggregation and to build theories around mean effects, has led to a systemic undervaluing of heterogeneity. Bryan et al. (2021) make similar observations. They argue that behavioral science has focused too much on mean effects (such as fixed effects, in MLM parlance) and Type 1 errors, at the cost of not embracing the possible heterogeneity of these effects (e.g., random effects in MLM and Type 2 errors). They argue for moderation, as well as for sample and population effects to be incorporated much more broadly into our theorizing. In other words, they suggest we start with the assumption of heterogeneity and complexity and then actively seek out opportunities to observe situations and conditions where effects may not hold, rather than assuming homogeneity exists across observations by default. This is at the heart of Robinson's observation (Robinson, 1950).

We have covered several rather complex concepts in this brief consideration of the ecological fallacy and the value of multilevel regression models in illuminating it. It only remains to end with what we think is a rather apt quote regarding one of the more important attributes of the researcher:

In order to become an intelligent consumer of research, not to mention a competent researcher, it is essential that you develop knowledge and skills in various aspects of the research endeavor. However, *no amount of technical proficiency will do you any good if you do not think* (Pedhazuer & Schmelkin, 1991, p. 2).

Supplementary Information

R code is provided for all examples and analyses in the supplementary files for this book, on the Center for Open Science website (https://osf.io/63hae). The core analysis R packages used are *lme4* (Bates et al., 2015) and *lmerTest* (Kuznetsova et al., 2016). Plots were generated with *ggplot2* (Wickham, 2016).

References

Alker, H. R. (1969). A typology of ecological fallacies. In M. Dogan & S. Rokkan (Eds.), *Quantitative ecological analysis in the spatial science* (pp. 69–86). MIT Press.

Bates, D., Maechler, M., Bolker, B., & Walker, S. (2015). Fitting Linear Mixed-Effects Models Using lme4. *Journal of Statistical Software, 67*(1), 1–48. https://doi.org/10.18637/jss.v067.i01

Beckmann, N., Birney, D. P., Beckmann, J. F., Wood, R. E., Sojo, V., & Bowman, D. B. (2020). Inter-individual differences in intra-individual variability in personality within and across contexts. *Journal of Research in Personality, 85*, 1–22. https://doi.org/10.1016/j.jrp.2019.103909

Birney, D. P., Beckmann, J. F., Beckmann, N., & Stemler, S. E. (2022). Sophisticated statistics cannot compensate for method effects if quantifiable structure is compromised. *Frontiers in Psychology: Quantitative Psychology and Measurement, 13*, 812963, 1–13. https://doi.org/10.3389/fpsyg.2022.812963

Bleidorn, W., Hopwood, C., & Lucas, R. (2018). Life events and personality trait change. *Journal of Personality, 86*(1), 83–96. https://doi.org/10.1111/jopy.12286

Blythe, C. (1972). On Simpson's paradox and the sure-thing principle. *Journal of the American Statistical Association, 67*(338), 364–366. https://doi.org/10.1080/01621459.1972.10482387

Bollen, K. A. (1989). *Structural equations with latent variables.* Wiley. https://doi.org/10.1002/9781118619179

Borsboom, D., Mellenbergh, G. J., & van Heerden, J. (2003). The theoretical status of latent variables. *Psychological Review, 110*(2), 203–219. https://doi.org/10.1037/0033-295X.110.2.203

Brunner, J., & Austin, P. C. (2009). Inflation of Type I error rates in multiple regression when independent variables are measured with error. *Canadian Journal of Statistics, 37*(1), 33–46. https://doi.org/10.1002/cjs.10004

Bryan, C. J., Titon, E., & Yeager, D. S. (2021). Behavioural science is unlikely to change the world witout a heterogeneity revolution. *Nature Human Behaviour, 5*, 980–989. https://doi.org/https://doi.org/10.1038/s41562-021-01143-3

Burstein, L. (1980). The analysis of multilevel data in educational research and evaluation. *Review of Research in Education, 8*(4), 158–233. https://doi.org/10.2307/1167125

Curran, P. J., & Bauer, D. J. (2011). The disaggregation of within-person and between-person effects in longitudinal models of change. *Annual Review of Psychology, 62*, 583–619. https://doi.org/10.1146/annurev.psych.093008.100356

Fang, J., Huang, X., Zhang, M., Huang, F., Li, Z., & Yuan, Q. (2018). The Big-Fish-Little-Pond Effect on academic self-concept: A meta-analysis. *Frontiers in Psychology, 9*(1569), 1–11. https://doi.org/10.3389/fpsyg.2018.01569

Gelman, A., Hill, J., & Yajima, M. (2012). Why we (usually) don't have to worry about multiple comparisons. *Journal of Research on Educational Effectiveness, 5*, 189–211. https://doi.org/10.1080/19345747.2011.618213

Geukes, K., Nestler, S., Hutteman, R., Küfner, A. C. P., & Back, M. D. (2017). Trait personality and state variability: Predicting individual differences in within- and cross-context fluctuations in affect, self-evaluations, and behavior in everyday life. *Journal of Research in Personality, 69*, 124–138. https://doi.org/10.1016/j.jrp.2016.06.003

Grotenhuis, M., Eisinga, R., & Subramanian, S. V. (2011). Robinson's ecological correlations and the behavior of individuals: Methodological corrections. *International Journal of Epidemiology, 40*(5), 1123–1125. https://doi.org/10.1093/ije/dyr081

Grotenhuis, M., Pelzer, B., Esinga, R., Nieuwenhuis, R., Schmidt-Catran, A., & Konig, R. (2017). When size matters: advantages of weighted effect coding in observational studies. *International Journal of Public Health, 62*, 163–167. https://doi.org/10.1007/s00038-016-0901-1

Harrison, X. A., Donaldson, L., Correa-Cano, M. E., Evans, J., Fisher, D. N., Goodwin, C. E. D., Robinson, B. S., Hodgson, D. J., & Inger, R. (2018). A brief introduction to mixed effects modelling and multi-model inference in ecology. *Peerj, 6*, e4794. https://doi.org/10.7717/peerj.4794

Hedge, C., Powell, G., & Sumner, P. (2018). The reliability paradox: Why robust cognitive tasks do not produce reliable individual differences. *Behavior Research Methods, 50*(3), 1166–1186. https://doi.org/10.3758/s13428-017-0935-1

Hoffman, L., & Walters, R. W. (2022). Catching up on multilevel modeling. *Annual Review of Psychology, 73*, 659–689. https://doi.org/10.1146/annurev-psych-020821-103525

Hox, J. J. (2010). *Multilevel analysis: Techniques and applications* (2nd ed.). Routledge.

Jackson, S. A., Kleitman, S., Stankov, L., & Howie, P. (2017). Individual differences in decision making depend on cognitive abilities, monitoring and control. *Journal of Behavioral Decision Making, 30*, 209–223. https://doi.org/10.1002/bdm.1939

Kéry, M. (2010). *Introduction to WinBUGS for ecologists: Bayesian approach to regression, ANOVA, mixed models and related analyses*. Academic Press. https://doi.org/10.1016/C2009-0-30639-X

Kievit, R. A., Frankenhuis, W. E., Waldorp, L. J., & Borsboom, D. (2013). Simpson's paradox in psychological science: A practical guide. *Frontiers in Psychology: Quantitative Psychology and Measurement, 4*(513), 1–14. https://doi.org/10.3389/fpsyg.2013.00513

Kozlowski, S. W. J., & Klein, K. J. (2000). A multi-level approach to theory and research in organizations: Contextual, temporal, and emergent processes. In K. J. Klein & S. W. J. Kozlowski (Eds.), *Multilevel theory, research, and methods in organizations* (pp. 3–90). Jossey-Bass.

Krammer, G. (2023). A cautionary note on aggregation in educational psychology and beyond. *Theory & Psychology, 33*(5), 681–700. https://doi.org/10.1177/09593543231172495

Kuppens, P., & Verduyn, P. (2017). Emotion dynamics. *Current Opinion in Psychology, 17*, 22–26. https://doi.org/10.1016/j.copsyc.2017.06.004

Kuznetsova, A., Brockhoff, P. B., & Christensen, R. H. B. (2016). lmerTest: Tests in linear mixed effects models. *Journal of Statistical Software, 82*(13), 1–26. https://doi.org/10.18637/jss.v082.i13

Lechner, C. M., Bhaktha, N., Groskurth, K., & Bluemke, M. (2021). Why ability point estimates can be pointless: a primer on using skill measures from large-scale assessments in secondary analyses. *Measurement Instruments for the Social Sciences, 3*(3). https://doi.org/10.1186/s42409-020-00020-5

Lui, P. P., Samuel, D. B., Rollock, D., Leong, F. T. L., & Chang, E. C. (2020). Measurement invariance of the five factor model of personality: Facet-level analyses among Euro and Asian Americans. *Assessment, 27*(5), 887–902. https://doi.org/10.1177/1073191119873978

MacCann, C., Jiang, Y., Brown, L. E. R., Double, K. S., Bucich, M., & Minbashian, A. (2020). Emotional intelligence predicts academic performance: A meta-analysis. *Psychological Bulletin, 146*(2), 150–186. https://doi.org/10.1037/bul0000219

Marsh, H. W., & Parker, J. (1984). Determinants of student self-concept: Is it better to be a relatively large fish in a small pond even if you don't learn to swim as well? *Journal of Personality and Social Psychology, 47*(1), 213–231. https://doi.org/10.1037/0022-3514.47.1.213

Mathieu, J. E., & Chen, G. (2011). The etiology of the multilevel paradigm in management research. *Journal of Management, 37*(2), 610–641. https://doi.org/10.1177/0149206310364663

Minbashian, A., Wood, R. E., & Beckmann, N. (2010). Task-contingent conscientiousness as a unit of personality at work. *Journal of Applied Psychology, 9*(5), 793–806. https://doi.org/10.1037/a0020016

Molenaar, P. C. M. (2004). Manifesto on psychology as idiographic science: Bringing the person back into scientific psychology, This time forever. *Measurement, 2*(4), 201–218. https://doi.org/10.1207/s15366359mea0204_1

Molenaar, P. C. M. (2013). On the necessity to use person-specific data analysis approaches in psychology. *European Journal of Developmental Psychology, 10*(1), 29–39. https://doi.org/10.1080/17405629.2012.747435

Nagengast, B., & Marsh, H. W. (2011). The negative effect of school-average ability on science self-concept in the UK, the UK countries and the world: The Big-Fish-Little-Pond-Effect for PISA 2006. *Educational Psychology, 31*(5), 629–656. https://doi.org/10.1080/01443410.2011.586416

Navarro, D. (2021). If mathematical psychology did not exist we might need to invent it: A comment on theory building in psychol. *Perspectives on Psychological Science, 16*(4), 707–716. https://doi.org/10.1177/1745691620974769

Ostroff, C., Kinicki, A. J., & Muhammad, R. S. (2012). Organizational Culture and Climate. In I. Weiner, N.W. Schmitt & S. Highhouse (Eds.), *Handbook of Psychology*, 2nd edition (pp. 643–676). https://doi.org/10.1002/9781118133880.hop212024

Pearl, J. (2014). Comment: Understanding Simpson's paradox. *American Statistician, 68*(1), 8–13. https://doi.org/10.1080/00031305.2014.876829

Pedhazuer, E. J., & Schmelkin, L. P. (1991). *Measurement, design, and analysis: An integrated approach*. Lawrence Erlbaum.

Putnick, D., & Bornstein, M. (2016). Measurement invariance conventions and reporting: The state of the art and future directions for psychological research. *Developmental Review, 41*, 71–90. https://doi.org/10.1016/j.dr.2016.06.004

Raudenbush, S. W., & Bryk, A. S. (2002). *Hierarchical linear model: Applications and data analysis methods* (2nd ed.). Sage.

Robinson, W. S. (1950). Ecological correlations and the behavior of individuals. *American Sociological Review, 15*(3), 351–357. https://doi.org/10.2307/2087176

Rouder, J. N., & Haaf, J. M. (2019). A psychometrics of individual differences in experimental tasks. *Psychonomic Bulletin and Review, 26*, 452–467. https://doi.org/10.3758/s13423-018-1558-y

Rousseau, D. M. (1985). Issues of level in organizational research: Multi-level and cross-level perspectives. *Research in Organizational Behavior, 7*, 1–37.

Schwarzer, G., Carpenter, J. R., & Rücker, G. (2015). Fixed effect and random effects meta-analysis. In *Meta-analysis with R* (pp. 21–53). Springer. https://doi.org/10.1007/978-3-319-21416-0_2

Selvin, H. (1958). Durkheim's suicide and problems of empirical research. *American Journal of Sociology, 63*(6), 607–619. https://doi.org/https://doi.org/10.1086/222356

Simpson, E. (1951). The interpretation of interaction in contingency tables. *Journal of the Royal Statistical Society. Series B (Methodological), 13*(2), 238–241. https://www.jstor.org/stable/2984065 https://doi.org/10.1111/j.2517-6161.1951.tb00088.x

Subramanian, S. V., Jones, K., Kaddour, A., & Krieger, N. (2009). Revisiting Robinson: The perils of individualistic and ecologic fallacy. *International Journal of Epidemiology, 38*(2), 342–360. https://doi.org/10.1093/ije/dyn359

Susser, M. (1973). *Causal thinking in the health sciences*. Oxford University Press.

Thorndike, E. L. (1939). On the fallacy of imputing the correlations found for groups to the individuals or smaller groups composing them. *American Journal of Psychology, 52*(1), 122–124. https://doi.org/https://doi.org/10.2307/1416673

Vazire, S., & Sherman, R. A. (2017). Introduction to the special issue on within-person variability in personality. *Journal of Research in Personality, 69*, 1–3. https://doi.org/10.1016/j.jrp.2017.07.004

Wickham, H. (2016). *ggplot2: Elegant graphics for data analysis*. Springer-Verlag.

Wood, R. E., Beckmann, N., Birney, D. P., Minbashian, A., Beckmann, J. F., & Chau, R. (2019). Situation-contingent units of personality at work. *Personality & Individual Differences, 136*(1), 113–121. https://doi.org/10.1016/j.paid.2018.01.026

Zitzmann, S., Bardach, L., Horstmann, K. T., Ziegler, M., & Hecht, M. (2024). Quantifying individual personality change more accurately by regression-based change scores. *Structural Equation Modeling: A Multidisciplinary Journal, 31*(5), 909–922. https://doi.org/10.1080/10705511.2023.2274800

Chapter 13

Bias Through Selection and Restriction

Thomas Ostermann, Dennis Anheyer, and Sebastian Appelbaum

Abstract

Bias through selection is a well-known phenomenon, not only in psychology. In most cases, it refers to a distortion in the composition of samples that can lead to biased data and incorrect estimates of statistics in surveys or studies. Selection biases are not necessarily immediately apparent or recognizable from the study protocol and often only become apparent when the sample is examined in detail. *Bottom* or *ceiling effects*, *scale shrinkage*, and *regression to the mean* have been identified as methodological challenges. This chapter attempts to lay the foundations for dealing with these three essential forms of bias. In addition to theoretical aspects, the problems are explained using examples based on data, and the methodological approaches known from the literature are presented. In some cases, graphical examples are also used to illustrate the phenomena.

Introduction

Assessments measuring the ability of a person to perform tasks have been an integral part of research from the very beginning of psychology, starting in 1890 with Cattell's "Mental Tests and Measurements," including classical tasks such as a letter memory test (Cattell, 1890), and followed in 1904 with Binet's test for intelligence (Binet & Simon, 1904). The fact that people with very low or very high results on such tests are often target groups in psychological research can lead to serious problems. Conversely, a test developed for such extreme groups cannot simply be applied to the normal population. In both cases, three problems can arise:

- bottom or ceiling effects,
- scale shrinkage,
- regression to the mean.

These will be examined in more detail in this chapter.

Bottom or Ceiling Effects

Due to their construction, psychological and physiological tests often have a predefined upper or lower bound, or limit. In the case of physiological tests, this is due to the boundaries given by the biological system: for example, oxygen uptake in sports is limited and cannot be infinitely improved. In psychological tests, there is also a boundary primarily due to the finite number of questions on a specific topic or the construction of, for example, rating or visual analog scales. In the case of the Minnesota Multiphasic Personality Inventory (MMPI; Buchanan, 1994), the subscales, such as the D-scale for depression, are scaled with a minimum of 0 and a maximum of 120 points. Thus, participants cannot obtain higher or lower scores once they reach the ceiling of 120 or the bottom of 0, respectively.

Methodological issues dealing with this type of effect are accordingly called *bottom* or *ceiling effects*. Although the effect is symmetrical from a mathematical point of view, the literature often only refers to the "ceiling effect." We will follow this common practice in this chapter and will primarily focus on ceiling effects as examples. First, however, we will look at formal definitions of this effect. Taylor (2010) described the ceiling effect as the observation that the highest possible score, or a score close to it, is reached on a test or measurement instrument. A ceiling effect can occur with questionnaires, standardized tests, or other measurements used in research studies. In terms of intervention, and more statistically, Garin (2014, p. 631) puts it this way: "The ceiling effect refers to the point at which an independent variable no longer has an effect on a dependent variable, when a kind of saturation has been reached."

Ceiling effects may have different causes and effects, which can be categorized as follows:

- task-related effects,
- ceiling effects and interventions, and
- skewed responses.

Task-Related Effects

Task-related effects can be split into two main dimensions: the appropriateness of the task for the domain being measured, and the difficulty of the task for the participants.

In the first case of the appropriateness of the task, the task might be too easy or too difficult for a given dimension. In the case of measuring quality of life, this is also known as the "no problems" problem. In the European Quality of Life 5-Dimension 5-Level (EQ-5D-5L) questionnaire instrument measuring health-related quality of life with five questions (score value "1" for *no problems*), almost one third of the participants of a large German cohort reported their health state as "1, 1, 1, 1, and 1" (Konnopka & Koenig, 2017).

In the second case, regarding difficulty of the EQ-5D-5L, the task may be appropriate in theory, but the participants do not show the intended variance. An example of a task that is too easy is provided by a validation of the Cognitive Abilities Screening Instrument (CASI; Teng et al., 1994) for people suffering from dementia (McCurry et al., 1999). Between 22.4% and 39.7% of the participants reached the highest possible scores on the subscales Long-Term Memory, Attention, Language, and Visual Construction. Jian et al. (2021) concluded that these ceiling effects "may result from the high percentage of our sample having less severe dementia" (p. 4), with 72.4% of the participants having a *Clinical Dementia Rating* (CDR) less than 1.

A very intuitive example of both bottom and ceiling effects is illustrated in Figure 13.1 using a weightlifting task. Figure 13.1A describes a task that is either too easy (see top panel) or too difficult (see middle panel) weightlifting task applied to a mixed population where individuals with different levels of muscle strength achieve identical results, whereas in Figure 13.1B, a

Figure 13.1
Bottom and ceiling effects. Top and middle panels (A): Bottom and ceiling effects related to a task: Strong and weak persons for muscle strength are equally successful. Bottom panel (B): Bottom and ceiling effects related to a population: A differentiated weightlifting task is applied to a group of well-trained athletes, who can lift all weights. Illustrations reproduced with permission. © 2025 Dr. med. Patrick Rebacz

differentiated weightlifting task is applied to a group of well-trained athletes who lift all available weights.

In both examples, this will cause less variation in the data and, in the case of repeated measures, an unintended high degree of correlation, or no correlation if the variance is restricted or approaches toward zero. Exactly the opposite effect may occur when the relationship of two independent variables is considered – for example, through linear regression models as illustrated by McBee (2010) in the field of educational research. Here, performance measures tend to produce strong ceiling effects due to an insufficient range of possible scores. To illustrate this, McBee (2010) gives the following example:

> Imagine two students taking a third-grade reading test. The first student reads at a fifth-grade level, whereas the second student reads at a seventh-grade level. Both students earn perfect scores on the third-grade test, but their actual levels of reading ability are not the same. (McBee, 2010, p. 314)

Figure 13.2 illustrates where potential reading ability (open circles) is downgraded to the maximum score (solid circles). This is known as a type of censoring, where a value outside the range of a measuring instrument is assigned the maximum value.

In our example, the two regression lines acting as markers for correlation show how ceiling effects may lead to an underestimation of correlations in such cases: while the dashed line represents the potential reading ability including the open circles ("uncensored data"), the solid line results from the censored data of the solid circles.

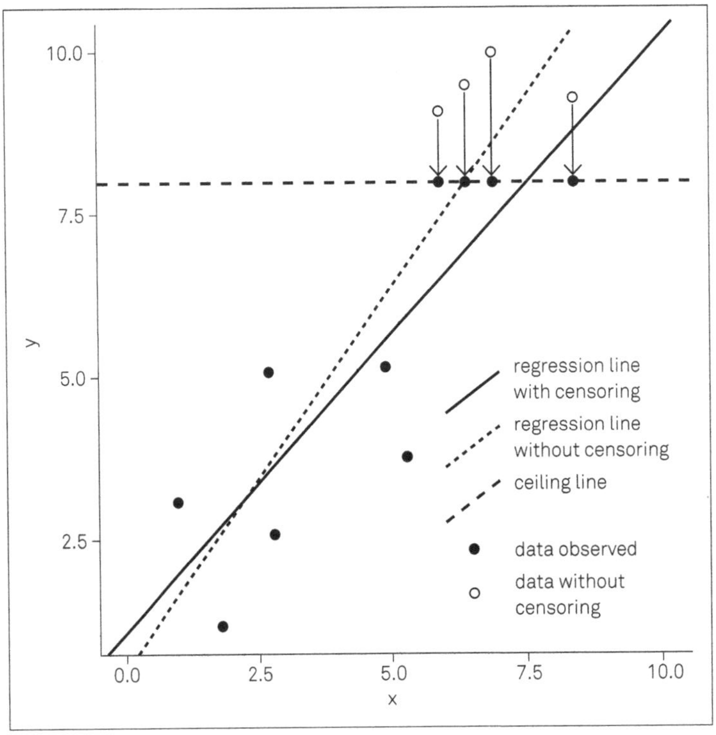

Figure 13.2
Regression lines with and without censoring due to ceiling effects.

Ceiling Effects and Interventions

Bottom and ceiling effects can also unintentionally affect an intervention's outcome and the evaluation of its success. The following example illustrates this scenario: A company wants to improve the mental health of its employees. In the wake of the COVID-19 pandemic and the associated challenges to the work situation, several employees have increasingly complained of excessive stress and associated illnesses. The employee representatives approach the company management with a request to initiate an occupational health management provision. For this purpose, an external service provider is commissioned to offer a stress management and prevention program for employees.

In order to evaluate the success of the program, the participants are asked to complete a questionnaire to assess their health-related quality of life with the Short-Form 36 Health Survey (SF-36). The items of the SF-36 can be divided into a physical dimension (21 items) and a mental health dimension of quality of life (14 items), and a single item on self-reported global health. For the two dimensions of physical and mental health, raw scores can be transformed to T-scaled norm values with a mean of 50 and a standard deviation of 10 points. Questionnaires are administered before the intervention and after the 8-week intervention.

In our baseline scenario, 40 employees participate in the stress prevention program and complete the questionnaires accordingly. With an average score of 40 on the mental health subscale of the SF-36 at the beginning of the intervention, the employees did indeed suffer from a mental health limitation, since their mean T-score was one standard deviation below the population mean of T = 50, which in this case serves as the ceiling value.

In our hypothetical scenario, we now simulate a ceiling effect by gradually replacing scores of employees with mental health limitations (i.e., scores of T = 40) with average scores of (approximately) 50 on this subscale. As a result, similar to the task-related effects described in Figure 13.1B, these newly introduced scores show little to no change in mental health status after the intervention, because the replacement scores were already close to the normative average, leaving little room for further improvement.

This, of course, directly impacts the observed effect of the intervention. Using Cohen's *d* for repeated measures as a standardized measure of effect, the effect size is more than halved when a ceiling effect occurs in 10 of the 40 participants. With a rising number of participants exhibiting a ceiling effect, the intervention effect starts to decline (Figure 13.3A), and the variance (here: the 95% confidence interval) diminishes. Consequently, the statistical significance of this effect turns into nonsignificance (Figure 13.3B). In our case, this holds true once approximately 17 participants exhibit a ceiling effect, where the measured effect of the intervention is no longer statistically significant (Figure 13.3B).

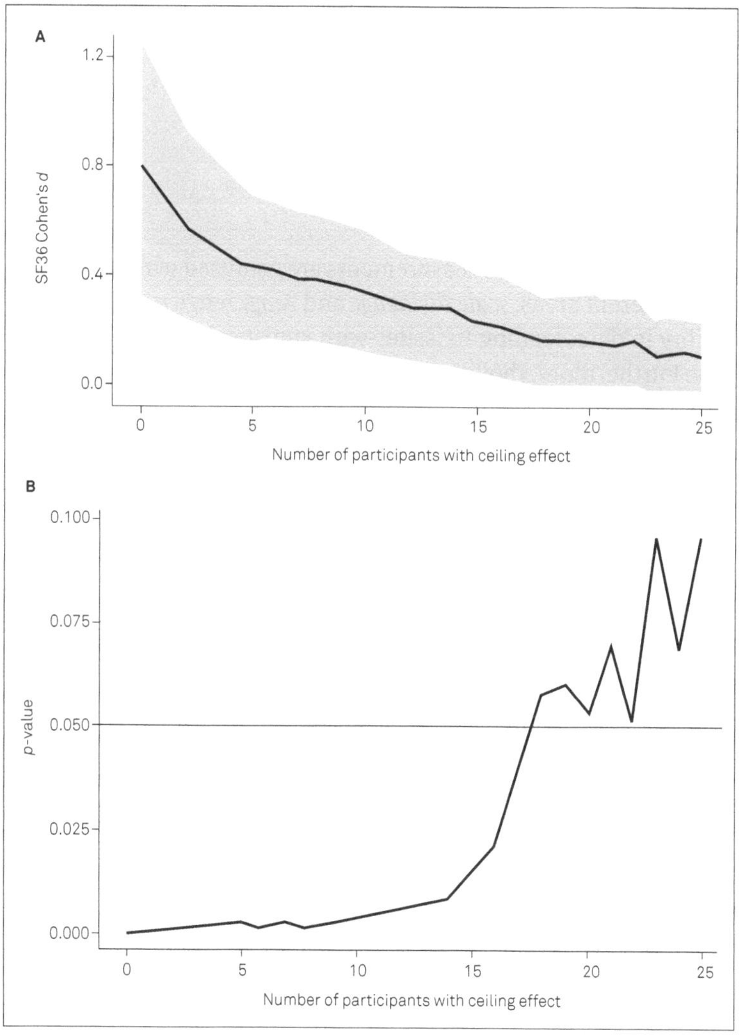

Figure 13.3
Relationship between ceiling effects and interventional effects. A) Effect of the intervention from baseline to 2 months after the end of the intervention measured using Cohen's *d*. The light shade corresponds to the 95% confidence interval. B) Significance of the interventional effect on SF-36 mental health score from the baseline to 2 months after the end of the intervention measured by a *t*-test for repeated measures. The horizontal line represents the 5% significance level.

Of course, it is trivial that if initial values are adjusted to the post-intervention values, differences will shrink. However, this problem exactly arises if a high percentage of participants with ceiling effects are present at baseline. Even if the intervention is potentially helpful, this cannot be observed or statistically proven due to ceiling effects. This phenomenon will be addressed again later when scale shrinkage is discussed.

Response Bias (Skewed Response)

Finally, bottom and ceiling effects can be caused by a response bias among participants. Beyond motivational aspects (Hjortskov et al., 2023), a response bias often occurs in questionnaire surveys on attitudes in which respondents believe the socially desirable response to be the maximum (e.g., in the case of satisfaction surveys) or minimum (e.g., in the reporting of smoking habits) reportable value, leading to a compression of data points at the upper (or lower) edge of the scale. Furthermore, even if there is no such intentional bias, survey respondents often tend to select what is written on the left side of the response scale (referred to as the *left-side selection bias*), which in cases of a uniform direction of items (i.e., from *very unsatisfied* to *very satisfied*) also leads to a clustering of data inherent to the basic design of the measure (Chyung et al., 2018).

Scale Shrinkage and Range Restriction

Two other phenomena that often occur in repeated measurements are confused with each other, although they concern two quite different areas: *scale shrinkage* and *range restriction*. Both phenomena can reduce the variability in data, leading to issues with statistical power, effect size estimation, and generalizability. Furthermore, they can also reduce the ability to detect meaningful relationships between variables. First, we will look at scale shrinkage.

Scale Shrinkage

Scale shrinkage typically occurs in repeated measurements following an intervention, such as a training session. This concept can also be illustrated using the weightlifting task (Figure 13.4). Participants with lower baseline muscle mass achieve better results in weightlifting during the course of training as their muscle mass increases, whereas those participants who already possess high muscle mass show little improvement and tend to remain in the upper range. Consequently, while individual results increase, the total range and thus the variance decreases.

To our knowledge, the term *scale shrinkage* was first introduced in the 1980s and became popular with a paper by Yen (1985), who documented an increase in the mean values but shrunken variance in ability testing of students for different grades.

In the ideal case of each interventional study, it is intended that interventions – for example, learning or training – lead to an improvement in performance. In such scenarios, the confounding effect of scale shrinkage is rarely apparent at first glance. It becomes evident when results are clustered, such as students who are grouped by their grades. Students who are already well

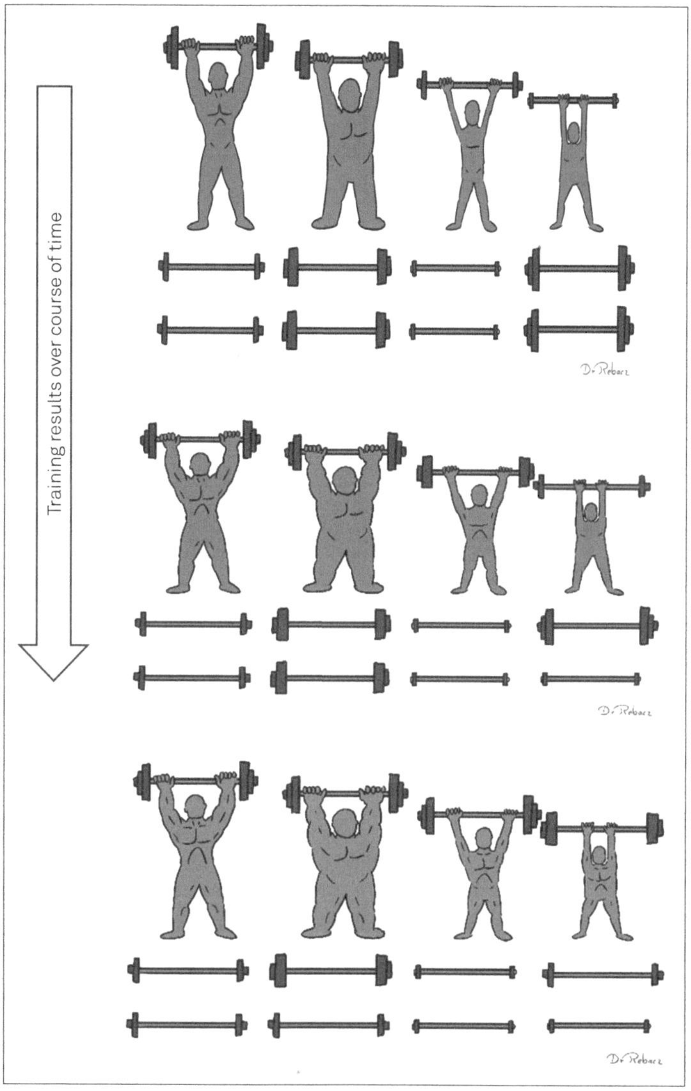

Figure 13.4
Weightlifting task to demonstrate scale shrinkage over the course of time. Illustrations reproduced with permission. © 2025 Dr. med. Patrick Rebacz.

trained or have higher performance at the beginning of the training show a smaller intervention effect, while this effect can be larger for students with lower baseline performance. As a result, in repeated measurements the mean value increases while the variance decreases: The scale seems to shrink. This is also used as an explanation in an early paper of Camilli (1988) on the relationship between scale shrinkage and the estimation of latent distribution parameters: "Students are becoming less diverse in ability over the course of the school year; perhaps schooling is having a homogenizing effect" (p. 228).

Based on the data provided by Yen (1985), a more detailed illustration was presented by Camilli et al. (1993), as displayed in Figure 13.5.

Although Camilli originally used medians instead of mean values, the idea of scale shrinkage is apparent for the two dimensions of Math Concepts and Math Computations.

A feasible way to consider both the mean ($\bar{x}$) and the standard deviation (s) is the coefficient of variation (CV): $CV = \frac{s}{\bar{x}}$. When measuring longitudinal changes in human performance, the

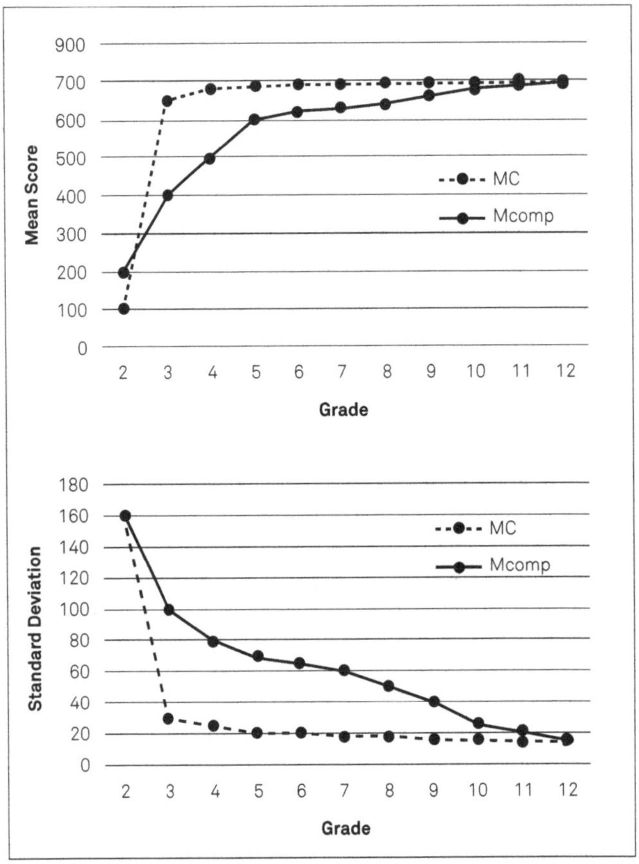

Figure 13.5
Hypothetic score means and standard deviations by year at school for Math Concepts and Math Computations based on the idea of shrinkage in Camilli et al. (1993).
MC = Math Concept, dashed lines; Mcomp = Math Computations, solid lines.

CV, according to Shechtman (2013), can be used to determine whether an intervention was successful in improving performance and/or in the homogenization of the sample. To illustrate this idea, the data from Figure 13.5 were used to calculate the CV. The result is displayed in Figure 13.6.

A more pronounced scale shrinkage leads to a visible "elbow" in the graph as can be seen in the dashed line in Figure 13.6. Unfortunately, there is no established statistical procedure to

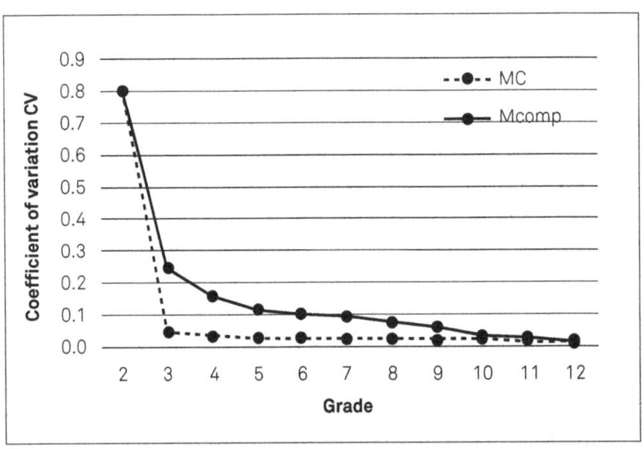

Figure 13.6
Coefficient of variation (CV) from the example in Figure 13.5.
MC = Math Concept, dashed lines; Mcomp = Math Computations, solid lines.

quantify this visible elbow. Within the statistical literature, there are only test procedures and an R package for CVs of independent samples and for a test of a CV against a given value (Feltz & Miller, 1996; Forkman, 2009; Krishnamoorthy & Lee, 2014; Marwick & Krishnamoorthy, 2019).

The specific case of repeated measurements remains unaddressed, and no corresponding statistical test could be identified in the literature.

Range Restriction

Range restriction, according to a recent definition of the American Psychological Association (APA), denotes "the limitation [...] of the full range of total possible scores that may be obtained to only a narrow portion of that total" (American Psychological Association, 2024, response to entering "range restriction"). Thus, at first glance, range restriction seems to be a quite similar phenomenon to scale shrinkage, which, however, has one important difference. In contrast to scale shrinkage, range restriction needs at least one other variable – for example, a sampling parameter, a study center, or another aspect of the experimental design that limits the range of possible outcomes.

For example, in a meta-analysis of the grade point averages (GPA) of university students, restriction of range might occur if only students with a prior course in MBSR are included, which according to Ostermann et al. (2022) may influence the scoring of the GPA and may lead to an observation bias. More specifically, this might also have an effect when it comes to correlating variables, which was first pointed out by Pearson (1903) and expanded by Thorndike (1949) to three cases in his famous book, *Personnel Selection: Test and Measurement Techniques.* We will explain the effect of range restriction due to selection on either X or Y and the range restriction due to a third Variable Z in more detail and will follow the typology and framework of Sackett and Yang (2000).

Range Restriction Due to Selection: No Third Variable

This scenario has already been mentioned in the GPA example above: two variables X and Y are examined, and one of those variables (in this case, X) is restricted with respect to the other variable (here, Y). If, in this case (known as *Thorndike's Case 2*), the unrestricted standard deviation, S_x, and the restricted standard deviations of X, s_x, and the correlation coefficient r_{xy} obtained from the restricted sample are known, then Equation 1 can be used to estimate the unrestricted correlationt $\tilde{\rho}_{xy}$ as first described in Pearson (1903, p. 23):

$$\tilde{\rho}_{xy} = \frac{\left(S_x/s_x\right) r_{xy}}{\sqrt{1 + r_{xy}^2\left(S_x^2/s_x^2 - 1\right)}} \tag{1}$$

In the case where $S_x = s_x$, it is evident that $\tilde{\rho}_{xy}$ equals r_{xy}. However, in scenarios involving systematic – that is, nonrandom – selection, $\tilde{\rho}_{xy}$ differs from a certain extent r_{xy}. The example in the following section illustrates this effect.

Example: Correlation of Physical Activity and Anxiety

There are a number of studies demonstrating that physical activity and anxiety are negatively correlated (McDowell et al., 2019). In a validation study for the Herdecke Quality of Life Questionnaire (HLQ), the correlation of the physical activity subscale (HLQ-Physical Activity) was correlated with the Hospital Anxiety and Depression Scale values for Anxiety (HADS-A; Kröz et al., 2008). The original correlation in the unrestricted data, in Kröz et al. (2008), was $\tilde{\rho}_{xy} = -0.504$, as illustrated in Figure 13.7A. To illustrate our case of restriction, Figure 13.7B displays only the data where HLQ-Physical Activity ≥ 40.

For the example of restricted data in Figure 13.7B, the following values were obtained (x = HLQ-Physical Activity; y = HADS-Anxiety): $r_{xy} = -0.39$, $S_x = 18.74$, $s_x = 13.82$, which leads to the following estimation of the unrestricted correlation shown in Equation 2:

$$\tilde{\rho}_{xy} = \frac{-\left(18.74/_{13.82}\right)0.39}{\sqrt{1+(-0.39)^2\left(18.74^2/_{13.82^2}-1\right)}} = -0.498 \tag{2}$$

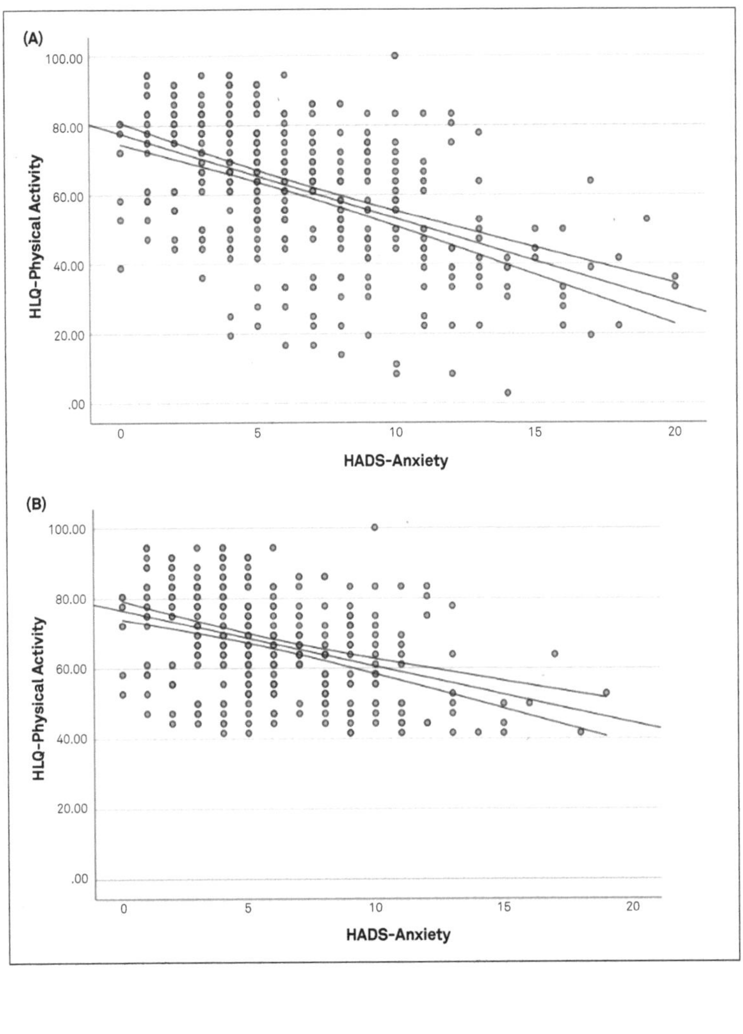

Figure 13.7
Bivariate scatter plot with line depicting the correlation between physical activity measured with the Herdecke Quality of Life Questionnaire–Physical Activity (HLQ-PA) and anxiety measured with the Hospital Anxiety and Depression Scale values for Anxiety (HADS-A). (A) with no restriction and (B) with selection based on physical activity by excluding all data points with scores less than 40. The central lines represent the regression slopes, surrounded by their 95% confidence intervals. Based on the data from Kröz et al. (2008).

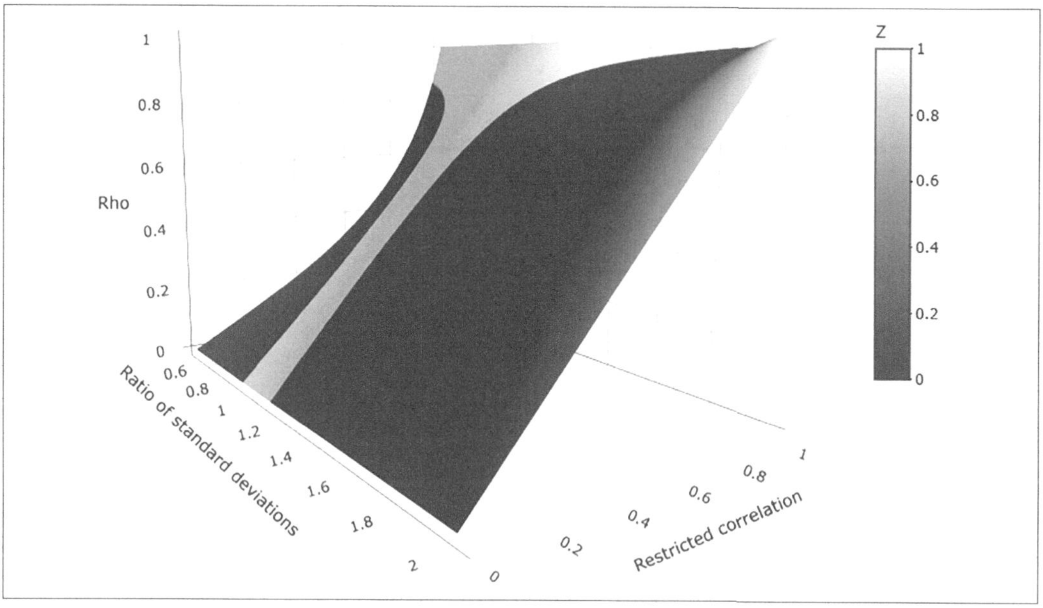

Figure 13.8 Correlation with no restriction (rho, ρ_{xy}) together with the ratio of standard deviations S_x/s_x, and restricted correlation r_{xy}. The light grey area denotes a 10% difference of ρ compared with r_{xy}.

As can be seen, this is a remarkably close approximation of the original correlation, of $\tilde{\rho}_{xy} = -0.504$. The change in correlation in the formula depends on two parameters: the ratio of restricted and unrestricted standard deviations S_x/s_x and the correlation coefficient r_{xy} of the restricted sample. For the range of positive correlations (interval [0,1]) and of standard deviations ratio of 1:2 or 2:1 (interval [0.5, 2]), the corrected correlation coefficients are obtained as presented in Figure 13.8.

As observed in Figure 13.8, S_x/s_x has a substantial corrective effect on the approximated correlation of the whole population, if the restricted correlation r_{xy} is low, while for high correlations the influence of the ratio of standard deviations S_x/s_x vanishes (light grey in Figure 13.8).

Equation 2 does not require a normality assumption (Lawley, 1943) but, like all correlation coefficients, it assumes a linear relationship between X and Y and requires homoscedasticity – meaning, equal error terms in the restricted sample and in the population. Finally, this formula is not applicable if a two-dimensional selection process is applied, such as when an elliptic region is omitted (Figure 13.9).

Selection on a Third Variable *Z*

Another case in the typology of Sackett and Yang (2000) deals with the case of when there is no selection with respect to X or Y, but the selection is controlled by a third variable Z. In this case, a distinction must be made between whether Z is empirically measurable or not. Examples of both scenarios are given in the following sections.

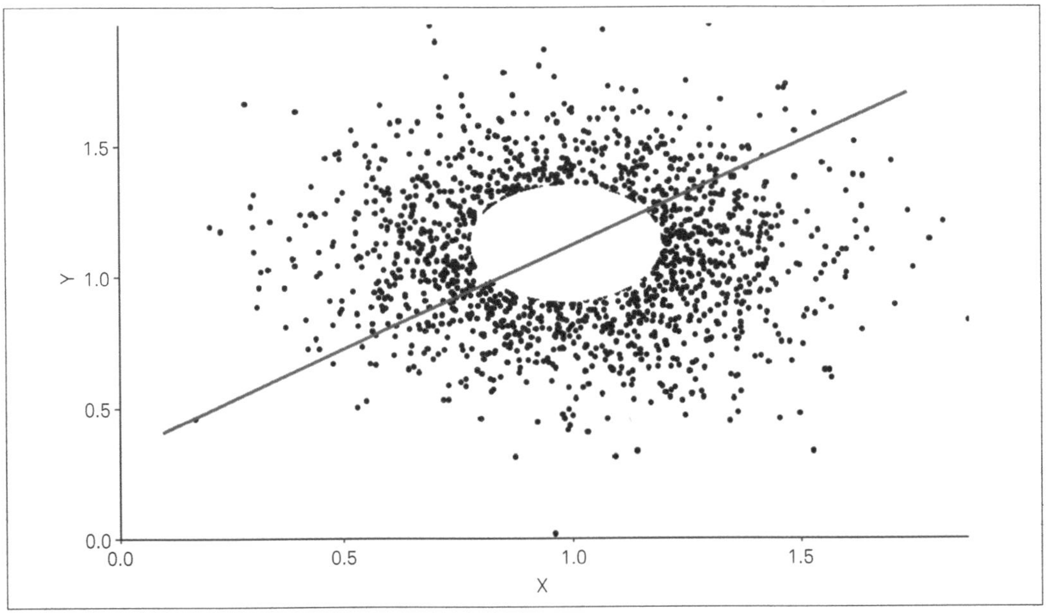

Figure 13.9 Correlation with an elliptic selection based on X and Y.

Z Is Measurable

In the case of a measurable third variable *Z* (Thorndike's Case 3), the unrestricted correlation is estimated using Equation 3:

$$\tilde{\rho}_{xy} = \frac{r_{xy}+r_{zx}r_{zy}\left(S_Z^2/s_Z^2-1\right)}{\sqrt{1+r_{zx}^2\left(S_Z^2/s_Z^2-1\right)}\sqrt{1+r_{zy}^2\left(S_Z^2/s_Z^2-1\right)}} \quad (3)$$

which shares structural similarities with the formula in the first scenario but includes correlations and standard deviations related to the variable *Z*.

As an example, we utilize the same data of Kröz et al. (2008) on physical activity and anxiety and restrict the sample based on age as a third variable *Z*: only patients aged between 40 and 60 are included in our analyses.

The following correlations emerge from the restricted sample: $r_{xy} = -0.56$, $r_{zy} = -0.105$, and $r_{zx} = -0.045$. Combined with the standard deviations of the age $S_z = 13.64$ of the total population and $s_z = 5.77$ of the restricted sample, we obtain the result shown in Equation 4:

$$\tilde{\rho}_{xy} = \frac{-0.56+(-0.105\cdot-0.045)\left(13.64^2/5.77^2-1\right)}{\sqrt{1+(-0.045)^2\left(13.64^2/5.77^2-1\right)}\sqrt{1+(-0.105)^2\left(13.64^2/5.77^2-1\right)}} = -0.523 \quad (4)$$

Again, the formula is symmetric with respect to *X* and *Y* and effectively adjusts the correlation of the restricted sample in the correct direction, with the *true* correlation being $\tilde{\rho}_{xy} = -0.504$.

Z Unknown, Unrestricted and Restricted Variances Known for *X* and *Y*

This scenario is not uncommon: a selection variable is not measurable, but for the variables *X* and *Y* there are extensive data available from representative samples or even from populations. Combined with the parameters of the restricted sample, Equation 5 can be used to estimate the unrestricted correlation:

$$\tilde{\rho}_{xy} = r_{xy}\left({}^{S_x}/_{s_x}\right)\left({}^{S_y}/_{s_y}\right) \pm \sqrt{\left(1 - {}^{s_x^2}/_{S_x^2}\right)\left(1 - {}^{s_y^2}/_{S_y^2}\right)} \qquad (5)$$

The sign ± of this formula is positive if both correlations $\tilde{\rho}_{zx}$ and $\tilde{\rho}_{zy}$ have the same direction, and negative if they have opposite directions. Again, our age-restricted data from the last example give the statistics needed here: $r_{xy} = -0.56$; $S_x = 18.74$; $S_y = 3.90$; $s_x = 20.40$; and $s_y = 4.00$.

Substituting these values into Equation 6 yields

$$\tilde{\rho}_{xy} = -0.56\left({}^{20.40}/_{18.74}\right)\left({}^{4.00}/_{3.90}\right) + \sqrt{\left(1 - {}^{20.40^2}/_{18.74^2}\right)\left(1 - {}^{4.00^2}/_{3.90^2}\right)} = -0.527 \qquad (6)$$

which is almost identical to the range restricted correlation for the scenario of measurable *Z*.

Regardless of the case regarding range restriction, this phenomenon, as demonstrated above, has a considerable influence on questions of reliability and factorial or meta-analytical validity (for further reading, see Bobko et al., 2001; Fife et al., 2012; Franco-Martínez et al., 2023; Hunter et al., 2006; Johnson et al., 2018; Le & Schmidt, 2006).

Regression to the Mean

Another phenomenon that occurs when variables are selected, is *regression to the mean* (RTM). It occurs in repeated measures taken from selected populations. In these cases, shifts in means or reductions in variance are observed that could be misinterpreted as treatment effects, although they are only due to the selection process. Figure 13.10 illustrates this concept based on two normally distributed repeated measures Y_1 and Y_2.

A classic example of this effect is found in psychological assessment or medical screening situations – for example, for prostate cancer (Van Poppel et al., 2022). Typically, participants or

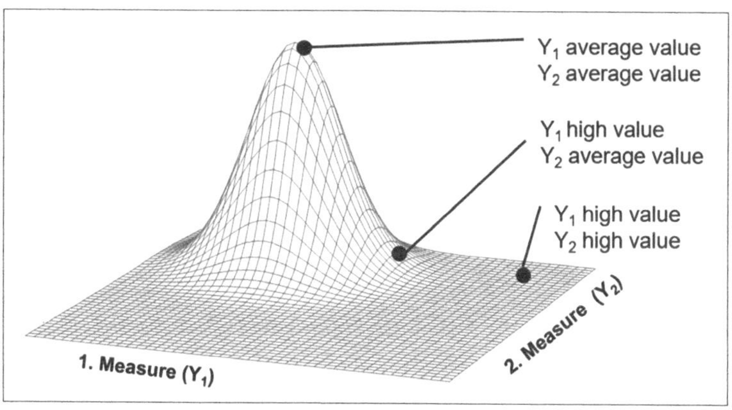

Figure 13.10
Illustration of regression to the mean, based on normally distributed data.

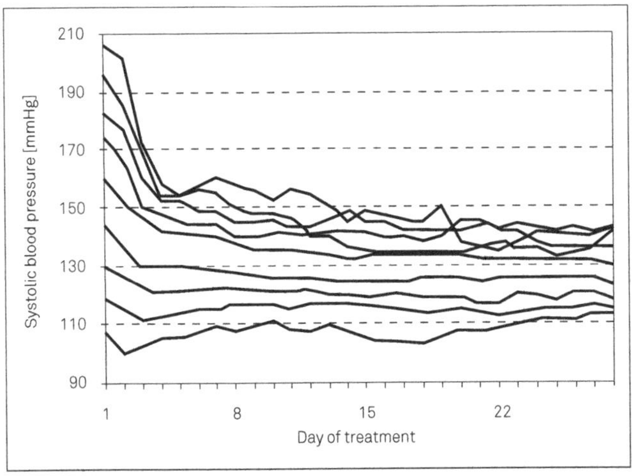

Figure 13.11
Blood pressure curves taken from Ostermann, Willich, and Lüdtke, 2008, *BMC Medical Research Methodology*, *8*(52), Figure 3. Published under the terms of the Creative Commons Attribution License (https://creativecommons.org/licenses/by/2.0).

patients within the normal limits of – for example, blood parameters – are exempted from further evaluation. Conversely, if participants show elevated values, an action follows that is, in the simplest case, watchful waiting with renewed (repeated) measurement. Repeated measurements are therefore only performed on a selected patient population – in this case on patients with extreme values during the initial measurement.

Extreme values, however, not only occur in patients with a confirmed clinical diagnosis but also, albeit rarely, in healthy individuals. In these cases, one would expect the elevated values to normalize in a repeated measurement – that is, to move within the normal limits again. This, and nothing more, is RTM: Elevated parameter values have a tendency to be lower on subsequent measurement occasions.

The same applies to lowered values, where an increase is statistically expected if the distribution is not heavily skewed (Lüdtke & Ostermann, 2005). Several examples in the literature, however, exist in which such results are interpreted as a kind of "normalization" (Gutenbrunner & Ruppel, 1992; Kümmell, 1982). This misinterpretation predominantly occurs when patients are clustered into groups defined by baseline values. In Figure 13.11, the progression of blood pressure measurements of patients during a spa treatment is shown (Gutenbrunner & Ruppel, 1992). The individual courses were clustered in relation to their baseline values in intervals of 10 mmHg, so that nine subgroup blood pressure courses can be seen. A slight increase is observed in the lower blood pressure curve and a significant decrease in the upper groups over time.

This systematic convergence, however, has no intrinsic meaning in the sense of causality and can be generated purely mathematically by selecting random numbers using any conventional spreadsheet program (Lüdtke & Ostermann, 2005) or within the R software environment. A simple example in R with uniformly distributed random numbers to illustrate this regression to the mean is provided in the Appendix.

Example of RTM

To provide an empirical example of RTM, normally distributed blood pressure values were simulated based on the data displayed in Figure 13.11. As mean values and standard deviations were not available in the original publication (Gutenbrunner & Ruppel, 1992), they were estimated from the figure as follows: baseline: 151 ± 21 mmHg, end of treatment: 127 ± 18 mmHg, which is similar to data obtained in a study on blood pressure lowering by hydrotherapy (Jacob & Volger, 2009). Based on the assumption of normally distributed blood pressure values and by grouping the data into systolic blood pressure intervals of 10 mmHg between 100 and 200 mmHg at baseline, the following results were obtained using a modified version of the R script shown in the Appendix:

A simple look at the changes in the subgroups of Figure 13.12 actually suggests a kind of normalization: High values fall significantly, while low values tend to rise and values close to the mean are unchanged. However, a similar figure (Figure 13.13) is obtained even when there is no change in the outcome (baseline: 151 ± 21 mmHg; end of treatment: 151 ± 21 mmHg).

Figure 13.13 is a perfect example of RTM: even if there is no change, a change can be suggested by selecting data at the tails of the distribution and displaying it accordingly. A straightforward solution to correct for RTM in repeated measurements is given by a practical correction of the *t* test for repeated measures by Mee and Chua (1991). Mee and Chua's (1991) test involves regressing the outcome values Y_2 after therapy on $X = Y_1 - \mu$, where μ is assumed to be a known population mean. By applying simple linear regression techniques, the intercept $\beta_0 = \mu + \tau$ and the slope β_1 are estimated. Subsequently, using *t*-test statistics, the hypothesis is tested that the intervention has an additive benefit – that is, H_0: $\beta_0 = \mu$ is tested against H_1: $\beta_0 = \mu + \tau$ where $\tau \neq 0$. Mee and Chua's original approach then leads to Equation 7:

$$t(\mu) = \sqrt{n(n-2)}\,\frac{s_{Y_1}^2 \bar{Y}_2 - s_{Y_1Y_2}\bar{Y}_1 + (s_{Y_1Y_2} - s_{Y_1}^2)\mu}{\sqrt{\left(s_{Y_1}^2 s_{Y_2}^2 - s_{Y_1Y_2}^2\right)\left((n-1)s_{Y_1}^2 + n(\bar{Y}_1 - \mu)^2\right)}} \tag{7}$$

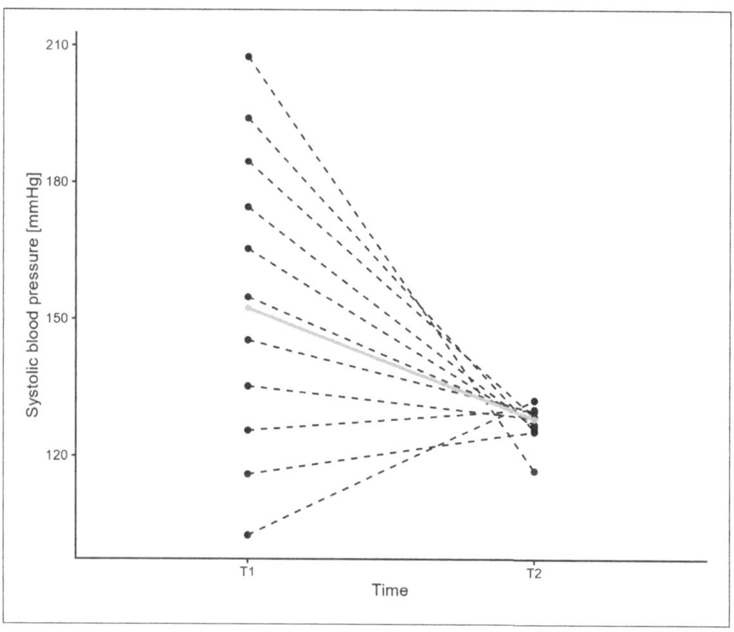

Figure 13.12
Systolic blood pressure dynamics from baseline (T1; M + SD: 151 ± 21 mmHg) to the end of treatment (T2; M + SD: 127 ± 18 mmHg) when clustered into intervals of 10. The solid line displays the overall mean.

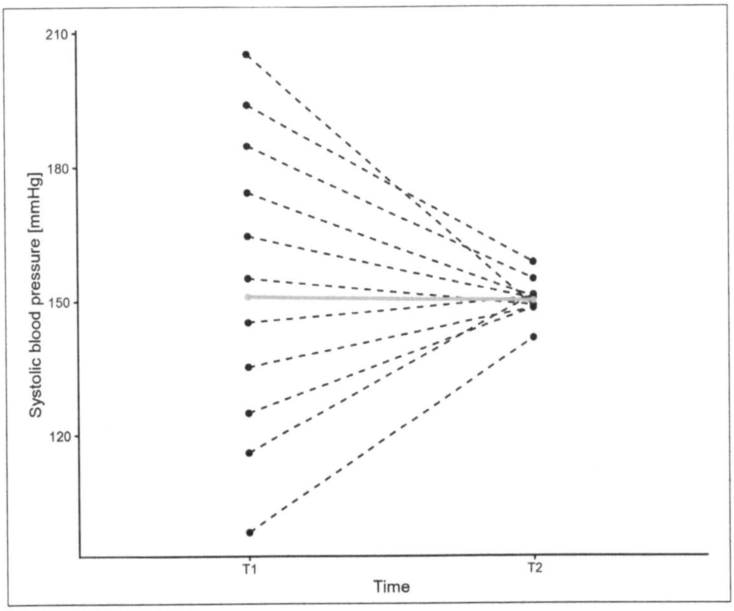

Figure 13.13
Systolic blood pressure dynamics when clustered into intervals of 10. Baseline: 151 ± 21 mmHg; end of treatment: 151 ± 21 mmHg. The solid line displays the overall mean.

An SAS macro and an Excel template for this approach are provided by Ostermann, Willich et al. (2008); an R package called *regtomean* is currently being prepared (Recchia et al., 2025).

This framework has successfully been applied in epidemiological and uncontrolled studies (Ostermann & Lüdtke, 2009; Ostermann, Willich et al., 2008, 2016; Stapinski et al., 2013). In contrast to alternative methods to control for RTM, this approach is straightforward and does not require stringent statistical assumptions. It can be used to differentiate true treatment effects from statistical artifacts when one has to interpret the results of uncontrolled studies. In meta-analyses, health technology reports, or systematic reviews, this approach may be helpful to clarify the evidence derived from uncontrolled observational studies or to detect a potential placebo effect (Anheyer et al., 2023).

Conclusion

This chapter has delved into the intricacies of several challenges that test users and researchers encounter in their empirical journey. These challenges, while often subtle, wield significant influence over the scientific process.

Firstly, floor and ceiling effects have been described as phenomena where data gravitate toward extreme values, potentially masking the true underlying patterns. Understanding and addressing these effects is paramount to ensuring that research findings accurately represent the nuances of the phenomena studied.

Scale shrinkage emphasizes the delicate balance between preserving data variability and capturing the essence of repeated measures. Researchers must navigate this terrain skillfully to avoid pitfalls such as reduced statistical power and distorted effect size estimations.

Range restriction, the silent disruptor, reminds us to be vigilant in constructing representative samples that mirror the full range of variation within the population. Neglecting this challenge can severely limit generalizability and introduce bias into statistical analyses.

Lastly, the elusive phenomenon of RTM has been highlighted, where extreme scores tend to regress toward the population mean upon retesting. Researchers must account for this effect to accurately interpret changes over time and avoid drawing unwarranted conclusions based on spurious trends.

By recognizing and proactively addressing these challenges, researchers significantly enhance the robustness and validity of their findings, ultimately contributing to the advancement of scientific knowledge. As we close this chapter, these challenges should be viewed not as obstacles, but as opportunities for refinement and growth in the pursuit of empirical understanding.

Acknowledgment

We want to thank Dr. med. Patrick Rebacz (https://visionom.de/) for the illustrations of the weightlifting tasks in Figure 13.1 and Figure 13.4.

References

American Psychological Association. (2024). *APA dictionary of psychology* (2nd ed.). https://dictionary.apa.org/restriction-of-range

Anheyer, D., Bugaj, T. J., Lüdtke, R., Appelbaum, S., Trübel, H., & Ostermann, T. (2023). No placebo effect beyond regression to the mean on the six minute walk test in pulmonary arterial hypertension trials. *International Journal of Molecular Sciences, 24*(2), 1069. https://doi.org/10.3390/ijms24021069

Binet, A., & Simon, T. (1904). Méthodes nouvelles pour le diagnostic du niveau intellectuel des anormaux. [New research on measuring the intellectual level of school children] *L'année Psychologique, 11*(1), 191–244. https://doi.org/10.3406/psy.1904.3675

Bobko, P., Roth, P. L., & Bobko, C. (2001). Correcting the effect size of d for range restriction and unreliability. *Organizational Research Methods, 4*(1), 46–61. https://doi.org/10.1177/109442810141003

Buchanan, R. D. (1994). The development of the Minnesota multiphasic personality inventory. *Journal of the History of the Behavioral Sciences, 30*(2), 148–161. https://doi.org/10.1002/1520-6696(199404)30:2<148::AID-JHBS2300300204>3.0.CO;2-9

Camilli, G. (1988). Scale shrinkage and the estimation of latent distribution parameters. *Journal of Educational Statistics, 13*(3), 227–241. https://doi.org/10.3102/10769986013003227

Camilli, G., Yamamoto, K., & Wang, M. M. (1993). Scale shrinkage in vertical equating. *Applied Psychological Measurement, 17*(4), 379–388. https://doi.org/10.1177/014662169301700407

Cattell, J. McK. (1890). Mental tests and measurements. *Mind, 15*(59), 373–381. https://doi.org/10.1093/mind/os-XV.59.373

Chyung, S. Y., Kennedy, M., & Campbell, I. (2018). Evidence-based survey design: The use of ascending or descending order of Likert-type response options. *Performance Improvement, 57*(9), 9–16. https://doi.org/10.1002/pfi.21800

Feltz, C. J., & Miller, G. E. (1996). An asymptotic test for the equality of coefficients of variation from k populations. *Statistics in Medicine, 15*(6), 647–658. https://doi.org/10.1002/(SICI)1097-0258(19960330)15:6<647::AID-SIM184>3.0.CO;2-P

Fife, D. A., Mendoza, J. L., & Terry, R. (2012). The assessment of reliability under range restriction: A comparison of α, ω, and test-retest reliability for dichotomous data. *Educational and Psychological Measurement, 72*(5), 862–888. https://doi.org/10.1177/0013164411430225

Forkman, J. (2009). Estimator and tests for common coefficients of variation in normal distributions. *Communications in Statistics – Theory and Methods, 38*(2), 233–251. https://doi.org/10.1080/03610920802187448

Franco-Martínez, A., Alvarado, J. M., & Sorrel, M. A. (2023). Range restriction affects factor analysis: Normality, estimation, fit, loadings, and reliability. *Educational and Psychological Measurement, 83*(2), 262–293. https://doi.org/10.1177/00131644221081867

Garin, O. (2014). Ceiling effect. In A.C. Michalos (Ed.), *Encyclopedia of quality of life and well-being research.* Springer. https://doi.org/10.1007/978-94-007-0753-5_296

Gutenbrunner, C., & Ruppel, K. (1992). Zur Frage der adaptiven Blutdrucknormalisierung im Verlauf von komplexen Bäderkuren unter besonderer Berücksichtigung von Homogenisierungseffekten und Lebensalter [On adaptive normalization of the blood pressure in the course of complex balneotherapy, with regard to homogenization and age]. *Physikalische Medizin, Rehabilitationsmedizin, Kurortmedizin, 2,* 58–64. https://doi.org/10.1055/s-2008-1062104

Hjortskov, M., Jacobsen, C. B., & Kjeldsen, A. M. (2023). Choir of believers? Experimental and longitudinal evidence on survey participation, response bias, and public service motivation. *International Public Management Journal, 26*(2), 281–304. https://doi.org/10.1080/10967494.2023.2166635

Hunter, J. E., Schmidt, F. L., & Le, H. (2006). Implications of direct and indirect range restriction for meta-analysis methods and findings. *Journal of Applied Psychology, 91*(3), 594–612. https://doi.org/10.1037/0021-9010.91.3.594

Jacob, E. M., & Volger, E. (2009). Blutdrucksenkung durch Hydrotherapie: Eine randomisierte, kontrollierte Studie bei leichter bis mittelschwerer Hypertonie [Blood pressure lowering by hydrotherapy: A randomised, controlled trail in mild to moderate hypertension]. *Physikalische Medizin, Rehabilitationsmedizin, Kurortmedizin, 19*(03), 162–168. https://doi.org/10.1055/s-0029-1202769

Jian, Z. H., Li, C. P., & Chiu, E. C. (2021). Ecological, convergent, and discriminative validities of the cognitive abilities screening instrument in people with dementia. *Medicine, 100*(11). e25225. https://doi.org/10.1097/MD.0000000000025225

Johnson, W., Deary, I. J., & Bouchard, T. J., Jr. (2018). Have standard formulas correcting correlations for range restriction been adequately tested? Minor sampling distribution quirks distort them. *Educational and Psychological Measurement, 78*(6), 1021–1055. https://doi.org/10.1177/0013164417736092

Konnopka, A., & Koenig, H. H. (2017). The "no problems"-problem: An empirical analysis of ceiling effects on the EQ-5D 5L. *Quality of Life Research, 26*(8), 2079–2084. https://doi.org/10.1007/s11136-017-1551-3

Krishnamoorthy, K., & Lee, M. (2014). Improved tests for the equality of normal coefficients of variation. *Computational Statistics, 29,* 215–232. https://doi.org/10.1007/s00180-013-0445-2

Kröz, M., Büssing, A., Girke, M., Heckmann, C., & Ostermann, T. (2008). Adaptation of the Herdecke Quality of Life questionnaire towards quality of life of cancer patients. *European Journal of Cancer Care, 17*(6), 593–600. https://doi.org/10.1111/j.1365-2354.2007.00913.x

Kümmell, H. C. (1982). Untersuchung zur Therapie mit Crataegus [Study on therapy with Crataegus]. *Herzmedizin, 5,* 157–165.

Lawley, D. N. (1943). A note on Karl Pearson's selection formulae. *Proceedings of the Royal Society of Edinburgh, LX/I-Part 1*(1), 28–30.

Le, H., & Schmidt, F. L. (2006). Correcting for indirect range restriction in meta-analysis: testing a new meta-analytic procedure. *Psychological Methods, 11*(4), 416–438. https://doi.org/10.1037/1082-989X.11.4.416

Lüdtke, R., & Ostermann, T. (2005). Regression zur Mitte – ein Thema in der Krebsforschung? [Regression to the mean – a topic in cancer research?] *Deutsche Zeitschrift für Onkologie, 37*(04), 169–175. https://doi.org/10.1055/s-2005-918020

Marwick, B., & Krishnamoorthy, K. (2019). *cvequality: Tests for the equality of coefficients of variation from multiple groups* (R software package version 0.1, 3). https://github.com/benmarwick/cvequalityon

McBee, M. (2010). Modeling outcomes with floor or ceiling effects: An introduction to the Tobit model. *Gifted Child Quarterly, 54*(4), 314–320. https://doi.org/10.1177/0016986210379095

McCurry, S. M., Edland, S. D., Teri, L., Kukull, W. A., Bowen, J. D., McCormick, W. C., & Larson, E. B. (1999). The cognitive abilities screening instrument (CASI): Data from a cohort of 2524 cognitively intact elderly. *International Journal of Geriatric Psychiatry, 14*(10), 882–888. https://doi.org/10.1002/(SICI)1099-1166(199910)14:10<882::AID-GPS42>3.0.CO;2-D

McDowell, C. P., Dishman, R. K., Gordon, B. R., & Herring, M. P. (2019). Physical activity and anxiety: A systematic review and meta-analysis of prospective cohort studies. *American Journal of Preventive Medicine, 57*(4), 545–556. https://doi.org/10.1016/j.amepre.2019.05.012

Mee, R. W. & Chua, T. C. (1991). Regression toward the mean and the paired sample *t* test. *The American Statistician, 45*(1), 39–42. https://doi.org/10.2307/2685237

Ostermann, T., Boehm, K., & Kusatz, M. (2016). Evaluation of 5536 patients treated in an integrative outpatient tinnitus treatment center: Immediate effects and a modeling approach for sustainability. *BMC Health Services Research, 16,* 1–9. https://doi.org/10.1186/s12913-016-1644-7

Ostermann, T., & Lüdtke, R. (2009). Zur Analyse von Wahlergebnissen in Parteihochburgen unter Berücksichtigung von Regressionsphänomenen [Methodological contribution to the analysis of election results in party stronholds]. *Methoden, Daten, Analysen (mda), 3*(2), 187–201.

Ostermann, T., Pawelkiwitz, M., & Cramer, H. (2022). The influence of mindfulness-based interventions on the academic performance of students measured by their GPA: A systematic review and meta-analysis. *Frontiers in Behavioral Neuroscience, 16,* Article 961070. https://doi.org/10.3389/fnbeh.2022.961070

Ostermann, T., Willich, S. N., & Lüdtke, R. (2008). Regression toward the mean: A detection method for unknown population mean based on Mee and Chua's algorithm. *BMC Medical Research Methodology, 8*(1), 1–9. https://doi.org/10.1186/1471-2288-8-52

Pearson, K. (1903). Mathematical contributions to the theory of evolution. XI. On the influence of natural selection on the variability and correlation of organs. *Philosophical Transactions, 200*(321–330), 1–66.

Recchia, D., Ostermann, T., & Recchia, M. D. (2025). *Package 'regtomean.'* https://mirror.marwan.ma/cran/web/packages/regtomean/regtomean.pdf

Sackett, P. R., & Yang, H. (2000). Correction for range restriction: An expanded typology. *Journal of Applied Psychology, 85*(1), 112–118. https://doi.org/10.1037/0021-9010.85.1.112

Shechtman, O. (2013). The Coefficient of Variation as an Index of Measurement Reliability. In S. Doi, & G. Williams (Eds.), *Methods of Clinical Epidemiology* (pp. 39–49). Springer Series on Epidemiology and Public Health. Springer. https://doi.org/10.1007/978-3-642-37131-8_4

Stapinski, L. A., Montgomery, A. A., Heron, J., Jerrim, J., Vignoles, A., & Araya, R. (2013). Depression symptom trajectories and associated risk factors among adolescents in Chile. *Plos One, 8*(10), e78323. https://doi.org/10.1371/journal.pone.0078323

Taylor, T. H. (2010). Ceiling effect. In N. J. Salkind (Ed.), *Encyclopedia of research design* (pp. 133–134). SAGE Publications.

Teng, E. L., Hasegawa, K., Homma, A., Imai, Y., Larson, E., Graves, A., Sugimoto, K., Yamaguchi, T., Sasaki, H., Chiu, D. & White, L. R. (1994). The Cognitive Abilities Screening Instrument (CASI): A practical test for cross-cultural epidemiological studies of dementia. *International Psychogeriatrics, 6*(1), 45–58. https://doi.org/10.1037/t28521-000

Thorndike, R. L. (1949). *Personnel selection: Test and measurement techniques.* Wiley.

Van Poppel, H., Albreht, T., Basu, P., Hogenhout, R., Collen, S., & Roobol, M. (2022). Serum PSA-based early detection of prostate cancer in Europe and globally: Past, present and future. *Nature Reviews Urology, 19*(9), 562–572. https://doi.org/10.1038/s41585-022-00638-6

Yen, W. M. (1985). Increasing item complexity: A possible cause of scale shrinkage for unidimensional item response theory. *Psychometrika, 50*(4), 399-410. https://doi.org/10.1007/BF02296259

Appendix

R Code to Visualize the Regression-to-the-Mean Effect

```
# 1. Create two data columns x1 and x2 with random numbers between 0 and 1,000.
set.seed(123)
ID <- 1:1000
x1 <- sample(0:1000, 1000, replace = TRUE)
x2 <- sample(0:1000, 1000, replace = TRUE)

# 2. Choose the selection criterion (Grouping).
dat <- data.frame(ID, x1, x2)
ID_up_700 <- dat$ID[dat$x1>700]
ID_low_300 <- dat$ID[dat$x1<300]

# 3. Determine the mean values in the groups and in the total sample.
mean(dat$x1[ID_up_700])
mean(dat$x2[ID_up_700])
#
mean(dat$x1[ID_low_300])
mean(dat$x2[ID_low_300])
#
mean(dat$x1)
mean(dat$x2)

# 4. Graphical representation of the mean values.
dat_plot <- data.frame(x=c(mean(dat$x1[ID_up_700]), mean(dat$x1[ID_low_300]),
mean(dat$x1),
   mean(dat$x2[ID_up_700]), mean(dat$x2[ID_low_300]), mean(dat$x2)),
   time=rep(1:2, each=3),
   group = c("x>700", "x<300", "Total", "x>700", "x<300", "Total"))

library(ggplot2)
p <- ggplot(data = dat_plot, aes(x=time, y=x, color = group)) + geom_point() + geom_line(linetype
= "dashed")
p <- p+theme_classic()+theme(legend.title = element_blank())
```

A graph of the following form should then be produced:

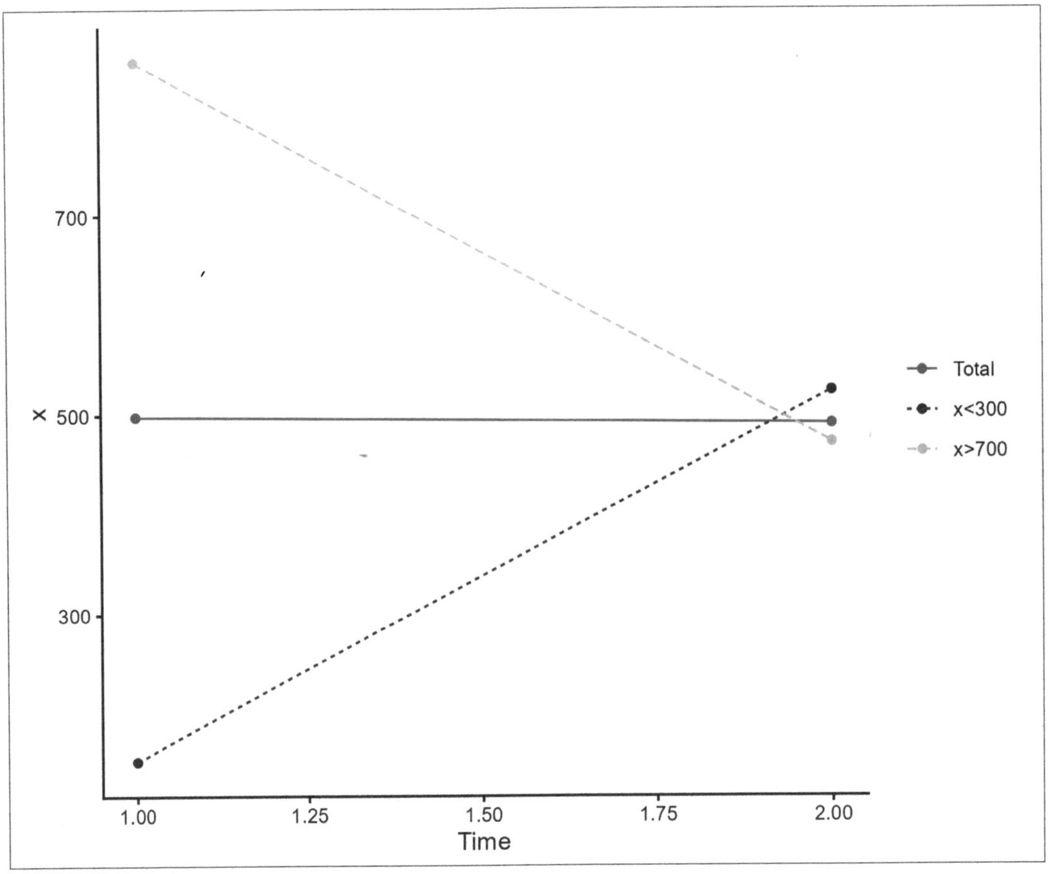

Figure 13.A1 Illustration of regression to the mean. Mean values at baseline and follow-up for participants with extreme baseline values (>700 or <300) and for the total sample.

Row 1 (light grey dotted line) shows the regression to the mean for baseline values > 700, Row 2 (black dotted line) shows the regression to the mean for baseline values < 300, Row 3 (solid line) reflects the mean values of the total data set.

Chapter 14

Difficulty Factors as Method Effects

Karl Schweizer, Christine DiStefano, and Stefan J. Troche

Abstract

A *difficulty factor* is defined as a factor where factor loadings reflect item difficulties rather than the construct of interest and, therefore, do not allow for conclusive interpretation. Observations suggest binary data and an extreme degree, as well as a broad range of item difficulty, as preconditions for the presence of a difficulty factor. In addition, a random process associated with extreme difficulty can create common systematic variation, which may finally give rise to a weak difficulty factor. This phenomenon is mostly observed in combination with an attribute factor that accounts for a major part of the common systematic variation. In cases of a close negative relationship between a difficulty and an attribute factor, a booster mechanism can enhance the amount of common systematic variation for which a difficulty factor accounts.

Introduction

Within the measurement literature, difficulty factors have been discussed for roughly 75 years. A *difficulty factor* is defined as a situation where factor loadings reflect item difficulties rather than the construct of interest; this artifact is primarily observed when binary (or dichotomous) data are analyzed. One of the first demonstrations of a difficulty factor was reported by Guilford (1941) when investigating the structure of the Seashore Test of Pitch Discrimination. Guilford's observation started a scientific discussion on possible reasons that lead to the observation of a difficulty factor. This discussion culminated in a proposal by McDonald (1965) that a difficulty factor follows from a nonlinear relationship between observed data, on the one hand, and a factor representing an underlying dimension, on the other. However, researchers have also debated whether the presence of a difficulty factor might either suggest a lack of unidimensionality, represent a distinct ability, or occur due to respondents' guessing of a correct response (Hattie, 1985).

Although the discussion of difficulty factors is common in the measurement literature, reports of such factors in practice became rare and have recently been almost completely restricted to investigations of overfactoring (e.g., Green, 1983; Green et al., 1997; Revuelta et al., 2022), while rarely addressing difficulty factors explicitly (e.g., Schweizer & Reiß, 2019). The neglect of this topic may partly be explained by the preferred use of a one-factor *confirmatory factor analysis* (CFA) measurement model (Brown, 2015) in test construction and validation in recent decades. The unidimensional CFA model aims to demonstrate one underlying dimension giving rise to the common systematic variation of data. The consideration of an additional factor without sound theoretical foundation would call into question the confirmatory nature of this approach. Thus, in a number of cases, a possible contribution of a difficulty factor might have been neglected or not considered as a viable explanation of additional systematic variation in response behavior.

The characteristics of a difficulty factor (e.g., broad range of item difficulties; Ferguson, 1941) suggest that there are specific areas where such a factor is more likely to be observed than otherwise. These are areas where items with both a very high or very low degree of difficulty and also a broad range of difficulties can be found. Such features are more likely to characterize a performance or aptitude test than a personality or attitude scale. Considering a difficulty factor in data collected by means of a performance or aptitude test can be useful for capturing common systematic variation that otherwise would lead to a model misfit. It appears that it is not the content of a test or scale per se that matters, but the empirical characteristics of the set of items.

Most of the research on the difficulty factor was conducted at times when exploratory factor analyses dominated research on test construction and evaluation. In the meantime, developments in theory and technology have reshaped the conditions for research on the difficulty factor, which is apparent in the switch from exploratory factor analysis to CFA.

Furthermore, there is an increasing concern about method effects distorting the underlying structure of data (Maul, 2013; Schweizer, 2020), regarding systematic variation that is unrelated to the systematic variation associated with the measured attribute. *Multitrait-multimethod* (MTMM) models have been utilized (Byrne, 2016; see also Chapter 3: "MTMM Construct Validity Using SEM," by Ziegler & Horstmann, in this present work) for controlling systematic variation associated with a specific type of method effects known to impair the validity of measurement. Additionally, an advanced version of CFA, the bifactor model (e.g., Reise, 2012), has become available, enabling the investigation of method effects that does not fit with the MTMM framework. Because of the discussion of difficulty factors in the measurement literature, a reexamination of this condition is warranted in light of advancements in both measurement theory and computational resources.

Defining a Difficulty Factor

The defining characteristic of a difficulty factor is the correlation between the items' factor loadings on a latent variable and the items' difficulties. But that may not be the sole reason; furthermore, it has never been defined how large the correlation of loadings and difficulties should be. The present concept of a difficulty factor appears to have been mainly shaped by the research of McDonald (1965, 1967; McDonald & Ahlawat, 1974). In McDonald's research, a difficulty factor is conceptualized as part of a complex situation. This characteristic does not occur in isolation but is observed in concordance with another factor when investigating the structure of data collected by a set of items tapping the same source. A difficulty factor is characterized as a weak factor that accompanies a strong factor; here, weak and strong refer to the amount of explained latent variance. In describing the state of the art (at the time), McDonald and Ahlawat (1974) referred to these two factors as the *genuine factor of content* and the *spurious factor*. These two factors are assumed to play different roles: The role of the genuine factor is to account for the systematic variation of the data (i.e., variation associated with the trait of interest) while the role of the spurious factor appears to be the reflection of the items' difficulty level. But it is not the difficulty level as "measured by the proportion of examinees passing each item" (McDonald & Ahlawat, 1974, p. 84), which is considered to be the source of this factor. Rather, it is the range of the variability of the difficulty levels (Ferguson, 1941; Gibson, 1959, 1960). This characterization of a difficulty factor as a spurious factor suggests that the source of a difficulty factor lies outside of what is traditionally considered to be the source of systematic variation of data giving rise to a factor.

It should be noted that research on difficulty factors has revealed further characteristics of possible relevance. These include the binary nature of the items, which has been suggested to make it more likely that this effect is observed (Floyd & Widaman, 1995; McDonald & Ahlawat, 1974). The variances of binary variables that are directly or indirectly part of the input to factor analysis show an especially strong (nonlinear) relationship with the items' difficulty levels. As factors account for variation within data, this relationship may be reflected by the similarity of factor loadings and difficulty levels.

Another observation was that the presence of items with extreme difficulty levels (especially high probabilities of a correct response) among other items with moderate difficulty levels may play a key role in the generation of a difficulty factor (Bandalos & Gerstner, 2016; Schweizer & Reiß, 2019; Schweizer & Troche, 2018). If data are binary and the difficulty level is extreme (i.e., very hard or very easy items), the item variance is likely to be very small and may not be captured well by a broad attribute factor.

Previous investigations have also posited that the presence of a difficulty factor might be due to an "incorrect" correlational input (i.e., phi correlations vs. tetrachoric correlations) used for analyses (Hattie, 1985). Under these conceptualizations, the difficulty factor represents an artifact of measurement, separated from the substantive content under study.

As is apparent, some circularity characterizes the concepts involved in the definition of a difficulty factor: Item difficulty and difficulty factor are interdependent in the sense that the identification of a difficulty factor is not possible without items of different degrees of difficulty. If all item difficulties are equal, there cannot be a difficulty factor. Thus, a broad range of item difficulties is one implicit precondition for observing a difficulty factor. Furthermore, estimates of factor loadings of different sizes are another precondition for the detection of a difficulty factor. Given correspondence of the rank orders, eventually a difficulty factor can be identified this way.

Scientific Discussion of Difficulty Factors

The scientific discussion surrounding difficulty factors has mainly focused on two different problems inherent in factor analysis. The first problem concerns the type of systematic variation captured by a difficulty factor. Factor analysis, as developed in the tradition of the explanatory approach of Spearman (1904), assumes that a factor captures systematic variation of data originating from a latent source driving responses to the item(s). By means of this approach, Spearman identified *general intelligence* as a major source of all cognitive performance. Under this framework, a factor should not be possible without corresponding systematic variation, nor should systematic variation be possible without a latent source. One exception is a factor based on a method effect, describing the presence of systematic variation other than the variation due to the latent source.

For example, in the investigation of the structure of MTMM data, factors may capture systematic variation caused by the methods used to collect the data (e.g., observer ratings, self-reports) – independent from the systematic variation associated with the traits of interest (e.g., Byrne, 2016; Widaman, 1985; Ziegler & Horstmann, Chapter 3: "MTMM Construct Validity Using SEM," in this present work). Previous studies have investigated the possibility that method effects could contribute to the presence of a difficulty factor. For example, studies have examined the effect of variability of item difficulties (Ferguson, 1941) and the effect of inappropriate correlation coefficients serving as input to factor analysis (Wherry & Gaylord, 1944).

The second problem addressed in scientific discussions concerns two parts: on the one hand, the relationship of binary and binomially distributed data, and on the other, a factor that is defined as a continuous and normally distributed variable. This problem can be summarized by the following question: How can the binomial distributions of binary data (i.e., the manifest variables) relate to the normal distribution of a continuous factor? This problem played a major role when McDonald (1965, 1967) considered nonlinear regression of manifest variables on continuous and normally distributed factors, and described the relationships by curves that differed for manifest variables of different difficulty levels. This novel approach developed into nonlinear factor analysis, a branch of factor analysis that takes into consideration this special relationship of observed variables to factors (Wall & Amemiya, 2007).

Other research along this line of inquiry established the idea of the *generalized linear model* (Dupuy, 2018; Nelder & Wedderburn, 1972; Skrondal & Rabe-Hesketh, 2004). The generalized linear model differs from the linear model by the inclusion of a link transformation which relates different types of distributions to each other. Nowadays, there are established procedures available to conduct such transformations (e.g., probit or logistic link).

The search by McDonald (1965; McDonald & Ahlawat, 1974) for the sources underlying the genuine and difficulty (i.e., spurious) factors led to the assumption of a nonlinear latent dimension giving rise to both factors. In other words, there is a latent dimension, which is not a straight line when perceived from the perspective of the Cartesian coordinate system. Within this system, the nonlinear dimension cannot be described by means of one axis only; instead, a plane is needed for its description, or two axes instead of one are required. Perceiving these axes as factors means that two (orthogonal) factors are necessary for its description. These two factors reflect the same latent dimension although they may capture different portions of latent systematic variation associated with the same latent dimension.

Especially, the relationships between manifest variables and the difficulty factor were assumed to be nonlinear. McDonald and Ahlawat (1974, p. 98) referred to a difficulty factor as a "factor due to nonlinearity," thus reflecting the nonlinearity of the assumed underlying structure. This conceptualization enables a difficulty factor and a genuine factor to originate from the same latent dimension and justifies the characterization of a difficulty factor as a spurious factor.

Difficulty Factors Due to Random Processes

In this section, we provide an account of the occurrence of a difficulty factor that is based on what is known about difficulty factors to date. As outlined in the previous sections, conditions potentially leading to (or facilitating the occurrence of) a difficulty factor are:

- the binary or dichotomous nature of data (Floyd & Widaman, 1995; McDonald & Ahlawat, 1974);
- a broad range of difficulty levels of the items of the scale used in collecting data (Ferguson, 1941; Gibson, 1959, 1960);
- items showing extreme difficulty levels (Bandalos & Gerstner, 2016; Schweizer & Reiß, 2019; Schweizer, DiStefano et al., 2021; Schweizer & Troche, 2018).

Furthermore, it has to be taken into consideration that, in no case, do the three conditions predict the observation of a difficulty factor with a high probability, meaning that an additional but unknown process must also be active.

The outset of these considerations is provided by the situation that is reached after completing parameter and fit estimation in CFA. This situation is described by Equation 1:

$$min = F[\mathbf{\Sigma}(\vartheta), \mathbf{S}] \tag{1}$$

indicating that the iterative estimation process involving the fitting function, F, has reached the point of minimum discrepancy between the model-implied covariance matrix, $\mathbf{\Sigma}$, specified by the set of parameter values represented by ϑ, and the empirical covariance matrix, $\mathbf{S}$. $\mathbf{\Sigma}$ represents common systematic variation for which the latent variable accounts and unique systematic variation. Considered in more detail, the off-diagonal elements of the empirical covariance matric, $s_{ij} \in \mathbf{S}$ $(i{\neq}j)$, are reproduced as well as possible by the off-diagonal elements of the model-implied covariance matrix, $\sigma_{ij} \in \mathbf{\Sigma}$ $(i{\neq}j)$, which consists of the product of factor loadings, λ_i and λ_j, and the variance parameter, ϕ.

In the ideal situation – that is, where minimization according to Equation 1 leads to good model fit, the p factor loadings on the latent variable of the one-factor CFA measurement model account for the $p(p\text{-}1)/2$ different off-diagonal elements of $\mathbf{S}$. This is possible if all s_{ij} $(i,j=1,...,p,$ $i{\neq}j)$ are of more or less the same size. In this case, all s_{ij} can be reproduced by λ_i and λ_j $(i,j=1,...,p,$ $i{\neq}j)$ that are of more or less the same size. We represent this situation by stating that the probability (Pr) of all s_{ij} $(i,j=1,...,p,$ $i{\neq}j)$ to stay within the interval limited by l_b and u_b is the same, as shown in Equation 2:

$$\text{const} = Pr(l_b < s_{ij} < u_b) \tag{2}$$

for a reasonable small difference between u_b and l_b. Such a situation is possible in continuous and normally distributed data where s_{ij} is rather independent of difficulty.

The situation changes for the one-factor CFA measurement model if the described condition does not hold for all s_{ij}. Besides s_{ij}, the empirical covariance matrix may also include a few elements with a decreased probability of staying within the range between l_b and u_b, $s^*_{ij} \in \mathbf{S}$, as is indicated by Equation 3:

$$Pr(l_b < s^*_{ij} < u_b) < Pr(l_b < s_{ij} < u_b). \tag{3}$$

The smaller probability characterizing s^*_{ij} may not mean a dramatic change but allow for occasional large transgressions of l_b or u_b. In the case of a transgression of u_b, the genuine factor can become insufficient for accounting for the common systematic variation of data. In such a case, an additional factor can be necessary to reach good model fit.

That such a situation can exist and that it includes binary data and extreme difficulties is demonstrated by an empirical study using simulated data (Schweizer et al., 2022). That study investigated how the difficulty level established by dichotomization influenced the sizes of correlations that constitute systematic variation for which a latent variable may account in CFA since a specific effect of dichotomization of continuous data on the latent structure of data had already been demonstrated (Schweizer, Gold et al., 2021). Continuous random data with a latent structure were generated in such a way that the expected correlation between the columns of the data matrix was 0.1225; the sample size was 300 matrices. Subsequently, the data were dichotomized in different ways to obtain different probabilities of a "correct response" (in a metaphorical sense), since it was expected to modify the relationships of the columns underlying the common systematic variation for which a latent variable accounts. The dichotomized columns displayed moderate or extreme difficulties (probabilities of a "correct response") that were .75 and .975.

After computing correlations among the columns of moderate probability and among columns of extreme probability, results were categorized according to their sizes and counted. The categories were [−1 to −.75[, [−.75 to −.5[, [−.5 to −.25[, [−.25 to 0[, [0 to .25],].25 to .5],].5 to .75], and].75 to 1]. Figure 14.1 illustrates the frequencies observed for these categories.

The expected category was the category ranging from 0 to 0.25, since it included the expected correlation as mean. Correlations computed from data with moderate probability were more likely to fall into this category than the other correlations. The correlations computed from columns dichotomized according to the extreme probability, were more likely than others to fall outside of this range. In other words, correlations obtained from extremely difficult items displayed an increased likelihood of deviating from the expected size of correlations. What

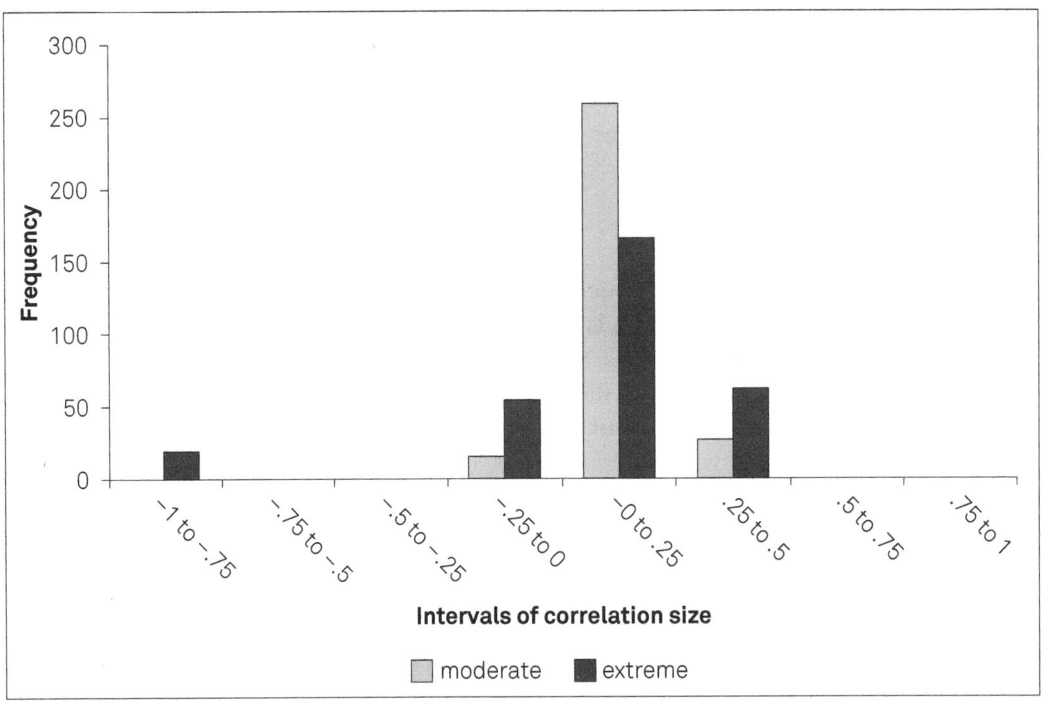

Figure 14.1 Frequency distribution of correlations categorized according to their sizes into moderately difficult (.75) and extremely difficult (.975) columns.

should also be clear at this point is that such cases were not predictable; they were the result of random processes.

In sum, binary or dichotomous data with an extreme difficulty level display the tendency to occasionally lead to larger-than-expected correlations that are not predictable, since they originate from random data. If a few such correlations are combined with a larger number of correlations originating from data with moderate difficulty levels, so that a broad range of difficulty levels is given, a genuine latent variable may not be sufficient to account for the common systematic variation. In this situation, a difficulty factor that accounts for the covariation of the extreme items may be required to reach good model fit.

The Booster of a Difficulty Factor

A difficulty-dependent random process can only serve as the basis of a weak difficulty factor, such as a spurious factor that may be dismissed as insufficient. Yet, given that difficulty factors have been observed that account for a sufficient degree of factor variance, there must be another influence that contributes to reaching such a degree. Therefore, this section is concerned with a mechanism that can transform a weak factor into a strong factor, termed the *booster mechanism*. This mechanism is outlined below. The basic idea is that a virtually negligible difficulty factor can account for a major amount of systematic variation if it is allowed to enter into a negative relationship with a genuine factor (Schweizer, DiStefano et al., 2021; Schweizer et al., 2024).

We start by presenting the linear measurement model of CFA (Brown, 2015) that is extended to include two latent variables (= factors), ξ_{genuine} and ξ_{spurious}. This is defined as:

$$\mathbf{x} = \boldsymbol{\lambda}_{\text{genuine}}\, \xi_{\text{genuine}} + \boldsymbol{\lambda}_{\text{spurious}}\, \xi_{\text{spurious}} + \boldsymbol{\delta} \tag{4}$$

where $\mathbf{x}$ is the $p \times 1$ vector of centered manifest variables, $\boldsymbol{\lambda}_{\text{genuine}}$ and $\boldsymbol{\lambda}_{\text{spurious}}$ are the $p \times 1$ vectors of factor loadings, ξ_{genuine} and ξ_{spurious} are the latent variables, and $\boldsymbol{\delta}$ is the $p \times 1$ vector of residuals. In order to facilitate the following reasoning, we assume that all entries of $\boldsymbol{\lambda}_{\text{genuine}}$ and $\boldsymbol{\lambda}_{\text{spurious}}$ are positive.

This model is transformed into the $p \times p$ model of the covariance matrix, $\boldsymbol{\Sigma}$, for parameter estimation and the investigation of model fit (Gumedze & Dunne, 2011; Jöreskog, 1970). The covariance model is defined as in Equation 5:

$$\boldsymbol{\Sigma} = \boldsymbol{\Lambda\Phi\Lambda}' + \boldsymbol{\Theta} \tag{5}$$

where $\boldsymbol{\Lambda}$ is the $p \times q$ matrix of factor loadings, $\boldsymbol{\Phi}$ is the $q \times q$ matrix of variances and covariances of latent variables, and $\boldsymbol{\Theta}$ is the $p \times p$ diagonal matrix of residuals. Of special importance are $\boldsymbol{\Lambda}$ and $\boldsymbol{\Phi}$. Starting from Equation 5 and assuming two latent variables ($q = 2$), $\boldsymbol{\Lambda}$ is defined in Equation 6 and $\boldsymbol{\Phi}$ in Equation 7 as:

$$\boldsymbol{\Lambda} = \left[\boldsymbol{\lambda}_{\text{genuine}}, \boldsymbol{\lambda}_{\text{spurious}}\right]. \tag{6}$$

$$\boldsymbol{\Phi} = \begin{bmatrix} \phi_{\text{genuine}} & \phi_{\text{genuine}\times\text{spurious}} \\ \phi_{\text{genuine}\times\text{spurious}} & \phi_{\text{spurious}} \end{bmatrix}. \tag{7}$$

Note. Since $\mathbf{\Phi}$ is expected to be a symmetric matrix along the main diagonal, the off-diagonal entries show the same subscripts.

This means in Equation 8:

$$\mathbf{\Sigma} = \mathbf{\Lambda\Phi\Lambda}' + \mathbf{\Theta} = \left[\boldsymbol{\lambda}_{\text{geniune}}, \boldsymbol{\lambda}_{\text{spurious}}\right] \times \begin{bmatrix} \phi_{\text{genuine}} & \phi_{\text{genuine}\times\text{spurious}} \\ \phi_{\text{genuine}\times\text{spurious}} & \phi_{\text{spurious}} \end{bmatrix} \times \left[\boldsymbol{\lambda}_{\text{geniune}}, \boldsymbol{\lambda}_{\text{spurious}}\right]' + \mathbf{\Theta}. \quad (8)$$

In order to restrict the spatial size of Equation 8, the intermediate step is omitted and the subscripts are shortened (subscript g replaces genuine and subscript s replaces spurious) so that Equation 9 is

$$\mathbf{\Sigma} = \left[\boldsymbol{\lambda}_g, \boldsymbol{\lambda}_s\right] \times \begin{bmatrix} \phi_g & \phi_{g\times s} \\ \phi_{g\times s} & \phi_s \end{bmatrix} \times \left[\boldsymbol{\lambda}_g, \boldsymbol{\lambda}_s\right]' + \mathbf{\Theta}. \quad (9)$$

Further reasoning requires that this product is transformed into a sum. Matrix multiplication is conducted for this purpose. It yields Equation 10:

$$\mathbf{\Sigma} = \left[\phi_g\boldsymbol{\lambda}_g\boldsymbol{\lambda}_g' + \phi_{g\times s}\boldsymbol{\lambda}_s\boldsymbol{\lambda}_s' + \phi_{g\times s}\boldsymbol{\lambda}_g\boldsymbol{\lambda}_g' + \phi_s\boldsymbol{\lambda}_s\boldsymbol{\lambda}_s'\right] + \mathbf{\Theta} \quad (10)$$

(see Schweizer et al., 2024). Since the product of a column vector and a row vector is a matrix, $\boldsymbol{\lambda}_g \times \boldsymbol{\lambda}_g'$ is replaced by $\mathbf{M}_g$ and $\boldsymbol{\lambda}_s \times \boldsymbol{\lambda}_s'$ by $\mathbf{M}_s$ in Equation 11:

$$\mathbf{\Sigma} = \left[\phi_g\mathbf{M}_g + \phi_{g\times s}\mathbf{M}_s + \phi_{g\times s}\mathbf{M}_g + \phi_s\mathbf{M}_s\right] + \mathbf{\Theta} \quad (11)$$

that is a matrix composed of several matrices. Because of the explicit assumption of positive factor loadings (Equation 4), it can be assumed that all entries of the matrices are also positive.

The right-hand part of Equation 11 includes two types of matrices ($\mathbf{M}_g$ and $\mathbf{M}_s$), two types of variance parameters (ϕ_g and ϕ_s), and one covariance parameter ($\phi_{g\times s}$). The matrices are positive because of an assumption (see Equation 4) and the variances because of their definition. In contrast, $\phi_{g\times s}$ can be both positive and negative. It suggests distinguishing between two versions of $\mathbf{\Sigma}$.

In the first version, it is assumed that $\phi_{g\times s} = 0$. After dissolving the right-hand part of Equation 11 into individual matrices and the removal of the two matrices multiplied by $\phi_{g\times s}$, Equation 12 is available:

$$\mathbf{\Sigma} = \phi_g\mathbf{M}_g + \phi_s\mathbf{M}_s + \mathbf{\Theta}. \quad (12)$$

In the other version, it is assumed that $\phi_{g\times s} \neq 0$. After dissolving the right-hand part into individual matrices and some rearrangements, Equation 13 becomes available:

$$\mathbf{\Sigma} = \phi_g\mathbf{M}_g + \phi_{g\times s}\left(\mathbf{M}_g + \mathbf{M}_s\right) + \phi_s\mathbf{M}_s + \mathbf{\Theta}. \quad (13)$$

It is important to realize that all the entries of $\mathbf{\Phi}$ (Equation 8) are scalars but show different ranges. While $\phi_g \geq 0$ and $\phi_s \geq 0$ because they represent variances, $\phi_{g\times s}$ is not restricted to either zero or positive values. In the following, we investigate the consequences of different values of $\phi_{g\times s}$ for ϕ_g and ϕ_s. In this investigation, we omit $\mathbf{\Theta}$ since it does not represent common systematic variation captured by factors. Consequently, the left-hand parts of Equation 12 and Equation 13 ($\mathbf{\Sigma}$) reduce to $\mathbf{\Lambda\Phi\Lambda'}$. The following investigation is expected to yield information on the ranges within which ϕ_g, ϕ_s, and $\phi_{g\times s}$ can vary while $\mathbf{\Lambda\Phi\Lambda'}$ stays constant.

Version 1: $\phi_{g\times s} = 0$. It is the version based on Equation 12 but does not include $\mathbf{\Theta}$.

$$\mathbf{\Lambda\Phi\Lambda'} = \phi_g\mathbf{M}_g + \phi_s\mathbf{M}_s. \tag{14}$$

In this variant, each component of the right-hand part contributes positively to the sum. Furthermore, no entry of the right-hand matrices of Equation 14 can become larger than the corresponding entry of the left-hand matrix ($\mathbf{\Lambda\Phi\Lambda'}$) since $\phi_g \geq 0$ and $\phi_s \geq 0$ (for all entries of matrices). This means that there are strict limitations to the sizes of ϕ_g and ϕ_s.

Version 2a: $\phi_{g\times s} > 0$. The interaction component is retained and assumed to be positive. We make this obvious by adding a superscript + to ϕ (ϕ^+) in Equation 15:

$$\mathbf{\Lambda\Phi\Lambda'} = \phi_g\mathbf{M}_g + \phi^+_{g\times s}\left(\mathbf{M}_g + \mathbf{M}_s\right) + \phi_s\mathbf{M}_s. \tag{15}$$

Again, each entry of a matrix of the right-hand part contributes positively to the sum. Furthermore, no entry of the right-hand matrices can become larger than the corresponding entry of the left-hand matrix ($\mathbf{\Lambda\Phi\Lambda'}$) because neither ϕ_g nor ϕ_s nor $\phi_{g\times s}$ can be negative.

Version 2b: $\phi_{g\times s} < 0$. The overall structure of Equation 13 (with the exception of $\mathbf{\Theta}$) is retained. In this version, however, the interaction component is no longer positive. We make this obvious by adding a superscript – to ϕ (ϕ^-) in Equation 16:

$$\mathbf{\Lambda\Phi\Lambda'} = \phi_g\mathbf{M}_g + \phi^-_{g\times s}\left(\mathbf{M}_g + \mathbf{M}_s\right) + \phi_s\mathbf{M}_s. \tag{16}$$

This means $(\phi_g\, m_{g\_ij}) > 0$ ($m_g \in \mathbf{M}_g$) for all $i,j = 1, \ldots, p$ and also $(\phi_s\, m_{s\_ij}) > 0$ ($m_s \in \mathbf{M}_s$) for all $i,j = 1, \ldots, p$ but $[\phi_{g\times s}\,(m_{g\_ij} + m_{s\_ij})] < 0$ for all $i,j = 1, \ldots, p$.

Version 2b differs from Versions 1 and 2a by a change of the restrictions for the sizes of the variance parameters. To demonstrate this change, the interaction component is shifted from the right-hand part to the left-hand part so that the interaction component is subtracted from $\mathbf{\Lambda\Phi\Lambda'}$ in Equation 17:

$$\mathbf{\Lambda\Phi\Lambda'} - \phi^-_{g\times s}\left(\mathbf{M}_g + \mathbf{M}_s\right) = \phi_g\mathbf{M}_g + \phi_s\mathbf{M}_s. \tag{17}$$

Since $\phi_{g\times s}$ is negative, the (weighted) sum of two matrices is added to $\mathbf{\Lambda\Phi\Lambda'}$ instead of subtracted. To make this change obvious, we replace – by + and compensate for this change by replacing $\phi_{g\times s}$ by its absolute value in Equation 18:

$$\mathbf{\Lambda\Phi\Lambda'} + \left|\phi^-_{g\times s}\right| \times \left(\mathbf{M}_g + \mathbf{M}_s\right) = \phi_g\mathbf{M}_g + \phi_s\mathbf{M}_s. \tag{18}$$

Now, the right-hand parts of Equation 14 and Equation 18 formally correspond exactly, whereas there is a striking difference between the left-hand parts of these equations. From comparing the left-hand parts, it becomes obvious that the right-hand part of Equation 18 can become larger than the right-hand part of Equation 14 depending on the (negative) size of $\phi_{g\times s}$: There is even the theoretical possibility that $\phi_g, \phi_s \mapsto +\infty$ for $\phi_{g\times s} \mapsto -\infty$.

The insight provided by Equation 18 is that a large (negative) $\phi_{g\times s}$ must be associated with especially large size(s) of variance parameter(s), ϕ_g and/or ϕ_s, since otherwise equality does not hold. These variance estimates can become much larger than the variance estimates that are possible within the frameworks of Version 1 (Equation 12) and Version 2a (Equation 13). There can be overestimation of the variance parameters that is compensated by the negative covariance (see also the analysis of the negativity of factor correlation; Schweizer et al., 2024). We refer to this way of increasing of factor variance due to compensation as a booster mechanism. However, the outlined increases are only a possibility. Whether this possibility becomes reality depends on the characteristics of the available data.

Evidence Supporting the Assumed Booster Mechanism

To demonstrate the effect of the booster mechanism, two studies are described that were presented at the Ninth European Conference on Methodology in 2021 held at Valencia, Spain. The two studies investigated the booster mechanism using simulated data in Study 1 (Schweizer & Troche, 2018) and real data in Study 2 (Schweizer, DiStefano et al., 2022). In both studies, variance estimates of genuine and difficulty factors were computed and appropriately scaled.

A Simulation Study

In a simulated data study, five hundred 500 × 20 matrices of random data were generated in accordance with three relational patterns using PRELIS (Jöreskog & Sörbom, 2001) – that is, 1,500 matrices of random data were generated for this study. Note that this study is rooted in the previous studies using the same methodology but is optimized for providing a clearcut case. The continuous, normally distributed data of the generated matrices were dichotomized to produce binary data, since difficulty factors have been observed primarily for binary data (Floyd & Widaman, 1995). By following the specifications outlined in previous research, the researchers were confident to observe a sufficient number of difficulty factors in the major difficulty condition of the current investigation.

Three 20 × 20 relational patterns included diagonal entries of 1.00, and off-diagonal entries were selected to be reproducible by a one-factor model with factor loadings of either 0.37, 0.40, or 0.45 to demonstrate generality over a range of interest. These values are referred to as *weak latent source*, *medium latent source,* and *strong latent source*, respectively.

The probabilities of the preferred values (a correct response) of generated data matrices in dichotomization varied between 0.50 and 0.80 in the basic version of the data. The manipulation for increasing the chance of observing a difficulty factor consisted of increasing the probabilities for the 5th, 10th, and 15th columns of the matrices in the same way. These columns were selected since observing a difficulty factor did not require a special ordering of columns according to difficulty levels, as is the case regarding a position effect factor (Troche & von Gugelberg, Chapter 11: "Carry-Over and Item Position Effects," in this present book; Zeller et al., 2017). Since extreme difficulty values were expected to give rise to such a factor, the probabilities for the three selected columns were either 0.925 (*minor difficulty treatment*) or 0.975 (*major difficulty treatment*).

CFA models with fixed factor loadings were constructed. Factor loadings for items on the genuine factor were fixed with values set to equal sizes (to 1) while the factor loadings on the difficulty (= spurious) factor corresponded to the numbers used in data generation. The input to CFA was achieved by computing probability-based covariances (Schweizer, 2013). A link transformation of the factor loadings was also performed because of the difference between the binomial distribution of the data and the normal distribution of the latent variables of the models (McCullagh & Nelder, 1985; Schweizer et al., 2015).

The employed models included either one or two factors, where the two factors were either uncorrelated or correlated. The variance (and covariance) parameters of the latent variables were set free for estimation to enable the fitting of the model to the data. Furthermore, the variances of the latent variables were scaled to allow for comparing the variances of the genuine and difficulty factors (Schweizer et al., 2019; Schweizer & Troche, 2019).

Models were estimated using the LISREL software package (Jöreskog & Sörbom, 2006) with maximum likelihood estimation as the estimator. We used the following fit indices and criteria (in parenthesis) for investigating results: χ^2, root-mean-square error of approximation (RMSEA ≤ 0.06), standardized root mean square residual (SRMR ≤ 0.08), comparative fit index (CFI ≥ 0.95), and Tucker-Lewis Index (TLI ≥ 0.95); see DiStefano (2016). The CFI difference was used to compare models.

Results

The investigation of model fit in models with one factor, two uncorrelated factors, and two correlated factors led to the results presented in Table 14.1. Some two-factor model applications were omitted because further improvement of model fit over the degree already achieved for the one-factor model was not required – that is, a model that fits should not be made more complex (simplicity principle). All statistics are means.

Table 14.1 reveals an overall good model fit according to RMSEA and SRMR, while some one-factor models missed the cutoffs for good model fit regarding TLI and CFI. The results for data with minor difficulty treatment (0.925) revealed a generally good model fit when investigated by the one-factor model and, therefore, were excluded from further investigations by two-factor models.

The comparison of the fit estimates for the one-factor and two-factor models applied to data with major difficulty treatment (0.975) revealed substantial differences, suggesting improvement in model fit according to the CFI difference for uncorrelated and correlated factors ($CFI_{diff} \geq 0.01$). Thus, there was justification for the consideration of a difficulty factor besides the genuine factor. But the two-factor models did not differ from each other.

Next, scaled variances and corresponding covariances were estimated. Figure 14.2, Panels A–C, includes bars representing the mean variance and covariance estimates. Figure 14.2A shows the results for the variance of the genuine factor. There is an increase in the size of the variance from the one-factor model to the model with two unrelated factors and, again, to the model with two correlated factors. On average the variance of the genuine factor in the model with two correlated factors is 7.7 times larger than the variance of the one-factor model.

Figure 14.2B illustrates the results for the variance of the difficulty factor. In the model with two unrelated factors, the variance estimate is negative, while it is positive in the model with two correlated factors. Since variances are defined to be positive, the results for the model with two unrelated factors are invalid. Such invalid results can occur if the computation of variances is not conducted according to the original definition as the sum of squared deviation.

Table 14.1 Mean fit results for models with difficulty factors

Model	Extreme difficulty level	Source type	χ^2	*df*	RMSEA	SRMR	TLI	CFI	AIC
One factor	0.975	Strong	233.3	189	0.021	0.051	0.955	0.955	277.3
		Medium	225.0	189	0.018	0.049	0.942	0.941	267.0
		Weak	218.7	189	0.016	0.047	0.931	0.930	260.7
	0.925	Strong	211.4	189	0.014	0.046	0.978	0.977	253.4
		Medium	205.7	189	0.012	0.045	0.973	0.970	247.7
		Weak	202.6	189	0.010	0.044	0.968	0.964	244.6
Two factors unrelated	0.975	Strong	216.3	188	0.016	0.046	0.969	0.969	260.3
		Medium	209.6	188	0.013	0.045	0.963	0.961	253.6
		Weak	207.1	188	0.012	0.044	0.953	0.950	251.1
Two factors related	0.975	Strong	212.5	187	0.015	0.046	0.972	0.972	258.5
		Medium	207.0	187	0.013	0.045	0.965	0.963	253.0
		Weak	205.2	187	0.012	0.044	0.955	0.952	251.2

Note. AIC = Akaike information criterion; CFI = comparative fit index; TLI = Tucker-Lewis Index; RMSEA = root-mean-square error of approximation; SRMR = standardized root mean square residual.

Furthermore, in the model with two correlated factors, the scaled variance of the difficulty factor is quite large. It is larger than the variance of the genuine factor in the one-factor model (see left set of columns in Figure 14.2A).

Figure 14.2C for covariances illustrates negative covariances depicted as bars pointing downwards, as is characteristic of the booster mechanism. Further, large negative covariances (Figure 14.2C) are associated with larger factor variances (Figure 14.2A and B) and small negative covariances (Figure 14.2C) with small factor variances (Figure 14.2A and B).

In sum, these results confirm the expectations based on the booster mechanism: Genuine and difficulty (= spurious) factors account for larger parts of systematic variation when the correlation among them is set free for estimation than otherwise. The covariances among the factors emerge as negative values. The variance sizes observed in combination with an estimated covariance surmount the estimates for the genuine factor as part of a one-factor model.

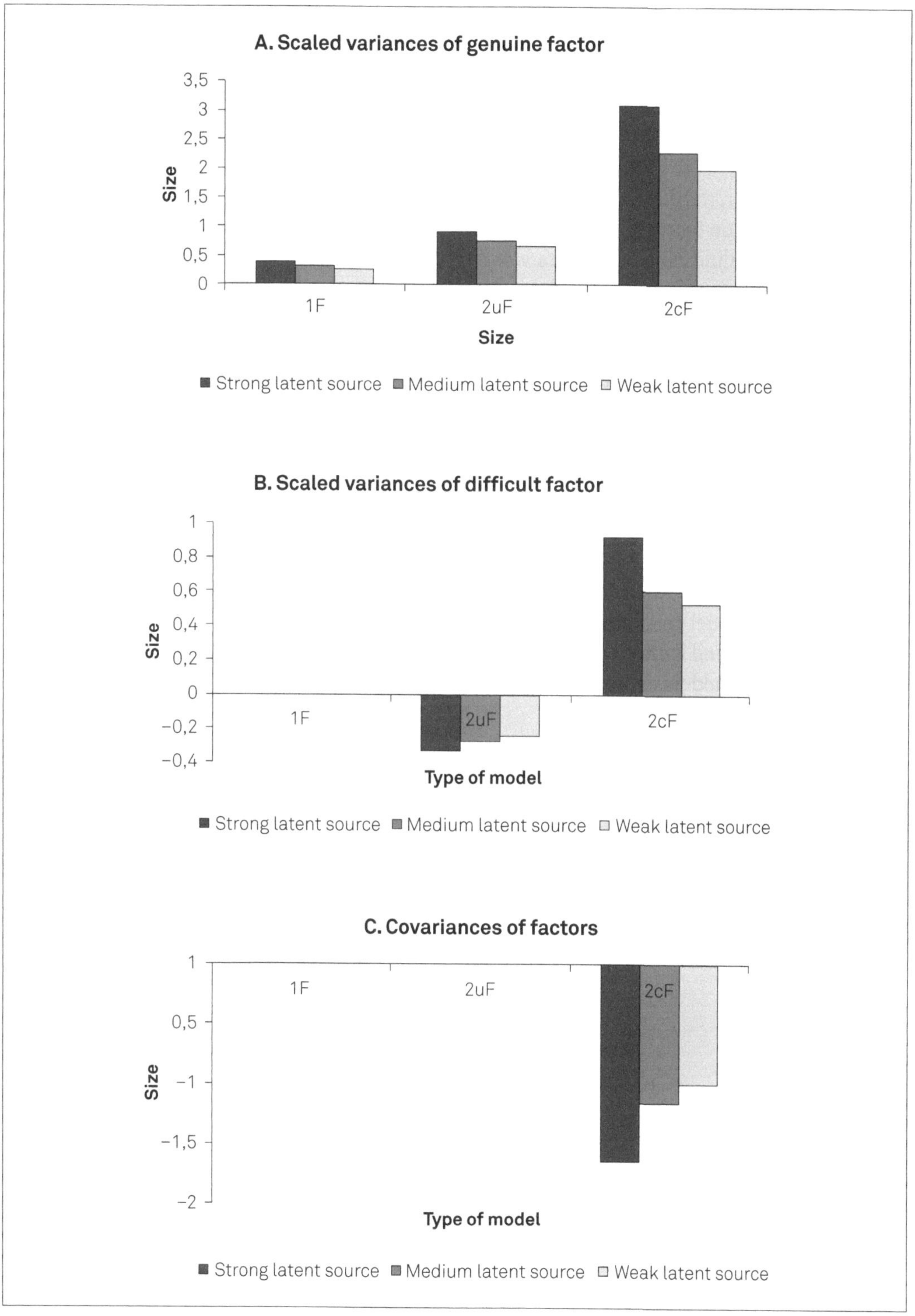

Figure 14.2 Illustration of mean variances and covariances observed by models with one-factor (1F), two uncorrelated factors (2uF), or two correlated factors (2cF). Panel A: Scaled variances of genuine factor. Panel B: Scaled variances of difficulty factor. Panel C: Covariances of factors.

Empirical Study

This study served the investigation of the structure of the short version of *Advanced Progressive Matrices* (APM; the short-version described by Mackintosh & Bennett, 2005). Data were collected from a sample of 287 university students (Schweizer et al., 2022). Please note, that it is not the aim of this section to discredit APM but to reveal general problems of this type of assessment: as we suggest, the difficulty factor is due to characteristics of the sample, and the also considered item-position factor is a problem shared by all multi-item scales. Since APM is an established measure of fluid reasoning, data were expected to show systematic variation that could be explained by a one-factor CFA model (M1). However, the model fit was not good for all of the considered fit indices (especially not for CFI and TLI). Including two method factors was necessary for reaching an overall good model fit. These factors were the difficulty factor and the item position effect factor. The difficulty factor was realized by fixing the factor loadings according to the difficulty levels (probabilities of responding correctly) of the corresponding items. For the item position effect factor, the factor loadings were fixed according to the items' position in the sequence of items. Finally, all factor loadings for the fluid reasoning factor were fixed to the same value, which was 1. (NB: Afterwards, factor scaling occurred as additional step.)

The measurement models included the reasoning factor alone (M1); reasoning factor and the difficulty factor (M2); or the reasoning factor, the difficulty factor, and the item position effect factor (M3). Further versions were created by specifying the relationships between the factors. There were model versions with correlations between the difficulty and the reasoning factors (Mc2 and Mc3) and without such correlations (Mu2 and Mu3). The scaled variance estimates obtained by these models are depicted as bars in Figure 14.3.

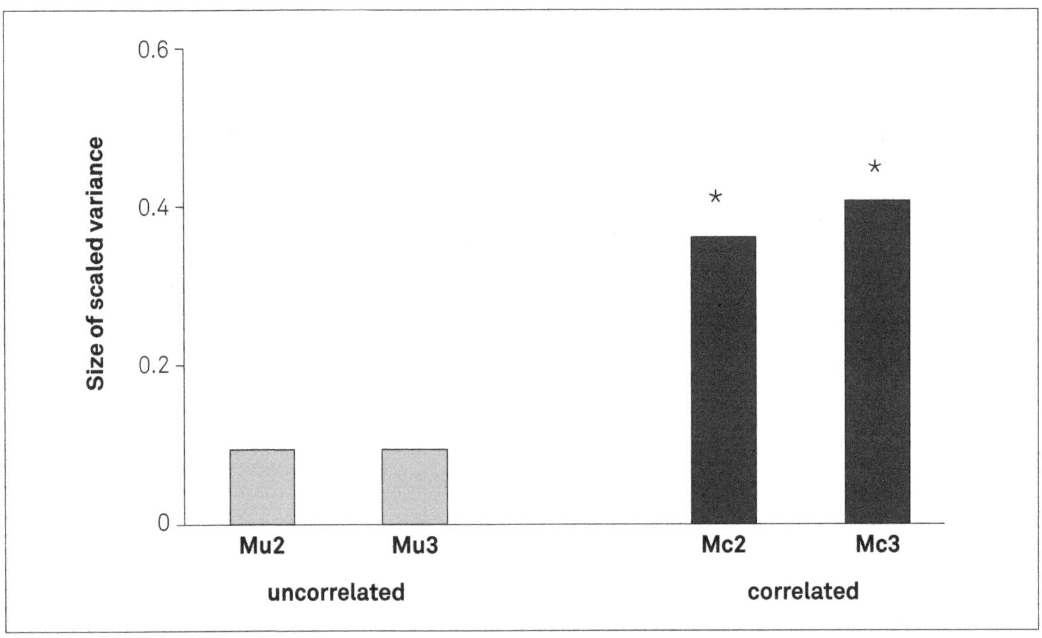

Figure 14.3 Scaled variance estimates of the difficulty factor illustrated as bars. Asterisk on top of a bar signifies significance obtained by two-factor and three-factor confirmatory factor analysis (CFA) models (Mu2: model with two uncorrelated factors, Mu3: model with three uncorrelated factors, Mc2: model with two correlated factors, Mc3: model with three correlated factors).

In cases where the factors were not allowed to correlate (Mu2 and Mu3), the variance estimate of a difficulty factor was small and did not reach significance. This means that there was no evidence of a difficulty factor. However, when there was a correlation between the reasoning factor and the difficulty factor, the variance estimate for the difficulty factor was large and reached significance (Mc2: $\phi_{\text{difficulty}} = 0.36$, $t = 3.05$, $p < .05$; Mc3: $\phi_{\text{difficulty}} = 0.40$, $t = 3.36$, $p < .05$). Also, the variances estimated for the other factor(s) increased. In all of the measurement models with the factor correlation set free for estimation, the correlation turned out to be negative and to be quite large (Mc2: $r = -.59$, $t = 2.66$, $p < .05$; Mc3: $r = -.55$, $t = 2.65$, $p < .05$).

In sum, a difficulty factor is unlikely to account for a large part of the systematic variation when it is realized as independent factor. However, it can turn into a substantial contribution to good model fit when it is allowed to negatively correlate with a genuine factor. Considering a difficulty factor as a method effect can enable the accounting for additional common systematic variation that otherwise prevents reaching a good model fit. The Appendix describes in more detail how a difficulty factor can be included in a measurement model and demonstrates the positive effect on the model fit of the measurement model using an example data set. The corresponding R script and the variance and covariance matrix are provided on the Center for Open Science website (https://osf.io/fhukz).

Concluding Remarks

Unlike other method effects, a difficulty factor appears to be a rather unstable phenomenon. While other method effects can be observed regularly, difficulty factors are observed rarely. The preconditions of observing a difficulty factor described in the literature do not guarantee the observation of such a factor. They just make one aware of situations with an increased likelihood of observing such a factor. This suggests that a difficulty-dependent random process may be an important ingredient in observing a difficulty factor. Such a process is unlikely to lead to a difficulty factor that accounts for a large amount of systematic variation of its own.

To reach significance, a difficulty factor appears to need the neighborhood of a genuine factor, as suggested by the approach to explaining a difficulty factor of McDonald and Ahlawat (1974). The combination with such a genuine factor can create a booster mechanism that increases the latent variances of both the genuine and the difficulty factors. A characteristic of this mechanism is the negative correlation observed between genuine and difficulty factors. It can transform an otherwise negligible difficulty factor into a factor that substantially contributes to good model fit in structural investigations. The Appendix includes the program code used in investigating the APM data.

Observation-based reports and results of empirical investigations lead us to propose the combination of difficulty-dependent random processes and a booster mechanism, as forces driving the observation of a difficulty factor. It appears that many of the rare observations of a difficulty factor can be explained this way (e.g., Schweizer & Reiß, 2019).

In summary, the notion of a difficulty factor has been discussed in the measurement literature for roughly 75 years. This phenomenon may occur under specific circumstances related to components in the analysis, such as item difficulty values, metric level of data analyzed, and tested model. Understanding what factors may cause a difficulty factor to occur, gives researchers greater potential for controlling such factors so that the focus remains on the construct under investigation.

References

Bandalos, D. L., & Gerstner, J. J. (2016). Using factor analysis in test construction. In K. Schweizer & C. DiStefano (Eds.), *Principles and methods of test construction* (pp. 26–51). Hogrefe.

Brown, T. A. (2015). *Confirmatory factor analysis for applied research* (2nd ed.). Guilford Press.

Byrne, B. M. (2016). Using multitrait-multimethod analysis in testing for evidence of construct validity. In K. Schweizer & C. DiStefano (Eds.), *Principles and methods of test construction* (pp. 288–307). Hogrefe.

DiStefano, C. (2016). Examining fit with structural equation models. In K. Schweizer & C. DiStefano (Eds.), *Principles and methods of test construction* (pp. 166–193). Hogrefe.

Dupuy, J.-F. (2018). *Statistical methods for overdispersed count data*. ISTE Press; Elsevier.

Ferguson, G. A. (1941). The factorial interpretation of test difficulty. *Psychometrika, 6*(5), 323–329. https://doi.org/10.1007/BF02288588

Floyd, F. J., & Widaman, K. F. (1995). Factor analysis in the development and refinement of clinical assessment instruments. *Psychological Assessment, 7*(3), 286–299. https://doi.org/10.1037/1040-3590.7.3.286

Gibson, W. A. (1959). Three multivariate models: Factor analysis, latent structure analysis, and latent profile analysis. *Psychometrika, 24*(3), 229–252. https://doi.org/10.1007/BF02289845

Gibson, W. A. (1960). Nonlinear factors in two dimensions. *Psychometrika, 25*(4), 381–392. https://doi.org/10.1007/BF02289755

Green, S. B. (1983). Identifiability of spurious factors using linear factor analysis with binary items. *Applied Psychological Measurement, 7*(2), 139–147. https://doi.org/10.1177/014662168300700202

Green, S. B., Akey, T. M., Fleming, K. K., Hershberger, S. L., & Marquis, J. G. (1997). Effect of number of scale points on chi-square fit indices in confirmatory factor analysis. *Structural Equation Modeling, 4*(2), 108–120. https://doi.org/10.1080/10705519709540064

Guilford, J. P. (1941). The difficulty of a test and its factor composition. *Psychometrika, 6*(2), 67–77. https://doi.org/10.1007/BF02292175

Gumedze, F. N., & Dunne, T. T. (2011). Parameter estimation and inference in the linear mixed model. *Linear Algebra and its Application, 435*, 1920–1944. https://doi.org/10.1016/j.laa.2011.04.015

Hattie, J. (1985). Methodological review: Assessing unidimensionality of tests and items. *Applied Psychological Measurement, 9*(2), 139–164. https://doi.org/10.1177/014662168500900204

Jöreskog, K. G. (1970). A general method for analysis of covariance structure. *Biometrika, 57*(2), 239–251. https://doi.org/10.1093/biomet/57.2.239

Jöreskog, K. G., & Sörbom, D. (2001). *Interactive LISREL: User's guide*. Scientific Software International.

Jöreskog, K. G., & Sörbom, D. (2006). *LISREL 8.80: User's reference guide*. Scientific Software International.

Mackintosh, N. J., & Bennett, E. S. (2005). What do Raven's Matrices measure? An analysis in terms of sex differences. *Intelligence, 33*(6), 663–674. https://doi.org/10.1016/j.intell.2005.03.004

Maul, A. (2013). Method effects and the meaning of measurement. *Frontiers in Psychology, 4*, Article 169. https://doi.org/10.3389/fpsyg.2013.00169

McCullagh, P., & Nelder, J. A. (1985). *Generalized linear models*. Chapman and Hall.

McDonald, R. P. (1965). Difficulty factors and nonlinear factor analysis. *British Journal of Mathematical and Statistical Psychology, 18*(1), 11–23. https://doi.org/10.1111/j.2044-8317.1965.tb00690.x

McDonald, R. P. (1967). Non-linear factor analysis. *Psychometric Monograph, 15*, 167.

McDonald, R. P., & Ahlawat, K. S. (1974). Difficulty factors in binary data. *British Journal of Mathematical and Statistical Psychology, 27*(1), 82–99. https://doi.org/10.1111/j.2044-8317.1974.tb00530.x

Nelder, J. A., & Wedderburn, R. W. M. (1972). Generalized linear models. *Journal of the Royal Statistical Society, A, 135*, 370–384. https://doi.org/10.2307/2344614

Reise, S. P. (2012). The rediscovery of bifactor measurement models. *Multivariate Behavioral Research, 47*(5), 667–696. https://doi.org/10.1080/00273171.2012.715555

Revuelta, J., Ximenez, C., & Minaya, N. (2022). Overfactoring in rating scale data: a comparison between factor analysis and item response theory. *Frontiers in Psychology, 13*, Article 982137. https://doi.org/10.3389/fpsyg.2022.982137

Schweizer, K. (2013). A threshold-free approach to the study of the structure of binary data. *International Journal of Statistics and Probability, 2*, 67–75. https://doi.org/10.5539/ijsp.v2n2p67

Schweizer, K. (2020). Method effects in psychological assessment. *Psychological Test and Assessment Modeling, 64*(3), 337–343.

Schweizer, K., DiStefano, C., & Troche, S. (2021). Conditions leading to the observation of a difficulty effect and its consequence for confirmatory factor analysis. *Psychological Test and Assessment Modeling, 63*(4), 469–483.

Schweizer, K., DiStefano, C., & Troche, S. (2022). The identification of the difficulty factor using variance estimates. *Proceedings from the 9th European Congress of Methodology* (pp. 52–57). University de Valencia. https://doi.org/10.7203/PUV-OA-438-5

Schweizer, K., Gold, A., & Krampen, D. (2021). Effect of dichotomization on the latent structure of data. *Frontiers in Applied Mathematics and Statistics, 7,* 723258. https://doi.org/10.3389/fams.2021.723258

Schweizer, K., & Reiß, S. (2019). On the contextual conditions driving a difficulty factor. *International Journal of Statistics and Probability, 8*(5), 1–12. https://doi.org/10.5539/ijsp.v8n5p1

Schweizer, K., Ren, X., & Wang, T. (2015). A comparison of confirmatory factor analysis of binary data on the basis of tetrachoric correlations and of probability-based covariances: A simulation study. In R.E. Millsap, D.M. Bolt, L.A. van der Ark, & W.-C. Wang (Eds.), *Quantitative psychology research* (pp. 273–292). Springer. https://doi.org/10.1007/978-3-319-07503-7_17

Schweizer, K., Ren, X., & Wang, T. (2024). Negativity of factor correlations biases the sizes of factor variances in bifactor CFA models. *Frontiers in Applied Mathematics and Statistics, 10,* 1423726. https://doi.org/10.3389/fams.2024.1423726

Schweizer, K., & Troche, S. (2018). Is the factor observed in investigations of the item-position effect actually the difficulty factor? *Educational and Psychological Measurement, 78,* 46–69. https://doi.org/10.1177/0013164416670711

Schweizer, K., & Troche, S. (2019). The EV scaling method for variances of latent variables. *Methodology, 15*(4), 175–184. https://doi.org/10.1027/1614-2241/a000179

Schweizer, K., Troche, S., & DiStefano, C. (2019). Scaling the variance of a latent variable while assuring constancy of the model. *Frontiers in Psychology, 10,* Article 887. https://doi.org/10.3389/fpsyg

Skrondal, A., & Rabe-Hesketh, S. (2004). *Generalized latent variable modelling: Multilevel, longitudinal and structural equation models.* Chapman & Hall; CRC Press.

Spearman, C. (1904). "General intelligence" objectively determined and measured. *American Journal of Psychology, 15,* 201–293. https://doi.org/10.2307/1412107

Wall, M. M., & Amemiya, Y. (2007). A review of nonlinear factor analysis and nonlinear structural equation modeling. In R. Cudeck & R.C. MacCallum (Eds.), *Factor analysis at 100: historical developments and future directions* (pp. 337–361). Lawrence Erlbaum.

Wherry, R. I., & Gaylord, R. H. (1944). Factor pattern of test items and tests as a function of the correlation coefficient: content, difficulty and constant error factors. *Psychometrika, 9*(4), 237–244. https://doi.org/10.1007/BF02288734

Widaman, K. F. (1985). Hierarchically nested covariance structure models for multitrait-multimethod data. *Applied Psychological Measurement, 9,* 1–26. https://doi.org/10.1177/014662168500900101

Zeller, F., Reiss, S., & Schweizer, K. (2017). Is the item-position effect in achievement measures induced by increasing item difficulty? *Structural Equation Modeling, 24*(2), 745–754. https://doi.org/10.1080/10705511.2017.1306706

Appendix

CFA-Based Measurement Model Including a Difficulty Factor

To demonstrate how the difficulty factor can be included in a CFA-based measurement model, we used the data collected with the nine odd-numbered APM items (out of the total of 18 items version by Mackintosh & Bennett, 2005) from the study by Schweizer et al. (2022) reported in this chapter as an empirical study (see the section "Empirical Study"). However, we restricted ourselves to a subsample of 250 participants for the purpose of demonstration and did not include the item position effect as reported above.

For the CFAs, probability-based covariances are used as input and the variance-covariance matrix for the nine items is provided at https://osf.io/fhukz. An R script ("Difficulty Factor.R") can be found in the same place, which entails the following analyses.

After the data are imported (Lines 11 to 14), the one-factor model is specified in Lines 18ff. As the variance-covariance matrix consists of probability-based covariances, a link transformation is required for the specification of the factor loadings. This is achieved by multiplying the factor loadings by the transformation weight, $w_i = \sqrt{Pr(X_i = 1) \times [1 - Pr(X_i = 1)]}$. These weights are reported in Table 14.A1 and used as fixations of the factor loadings in the R script (Lines 20 to 28).

Table 14.A1 Difficulty levels, transformation weights, and fixations for factor loadings.

Item number	Difficulty levels	Transformation weights (also fixations for genuine factor)	Fixations for factor loading (difficulty factor)
1	0.7108	0.4534	0.3223
2	0.3449	0.4753	0.1639
3	0.9230	0.2666	0.2461
4	0.4130	0.4924	0.2033
5	0.3220	0.4672	0.1505
6	0.8800	0.3250	0.2860
7	0.5050	0.5000	0.2525
8	0.2560	0.4364	0.1117
9	0.1889	0.3914	0.0739

The one-factor model leads to an appropriate (and regarding some fit indices even a good) model fit, as can be taken from Table 14.A2. Nevertheless, we probed whether the inclusion of a difficulty factor leads to an improved data description in a bifactor model (Line 37ff.). For this purpose, the same attribute factor ("genuine factor") is specified first, then the difficulty factor ("spurious factor"). Here, each factor loading is fixed by the difficulty level as reported in the second column of Table 14.A1. Afterwards, these fixations are also weighted with the same transformation link as the factor loadings of the genuine factor. This multiplication results in the final fixations reported in the last column of Table 14.A1, which refer to the fixations reported in the R script (Lines 50 to 58). The correlation between the two factors is restricted to zero to return the second model in Table 14.A2. The resulting model fit is somewhat better compared with the one-factor model. However, the R output clearly reveals that the variance of the difficulty factor is not statistically significant. Therefore, the inclusion of the difficulty factor seems not necessary here.

However, if the correlation between the two factors is freely estimated (just delete "0*" in Line 60 and rerun the model), the variance parameter becomes statistically significant. Furthermore, a substantial negative correlation can be observed ($r = -.65$, $z = -2.36$, $p < .05$), as is characteristic of the booster mechanism. The model fit, as reported in Table A2, of this bifactor model considering the difficulty effect is now substantially better than the fit of the one-factor model. This is especially obvious from the comparison of the AIC values, the CFI values, and the RMSEA values.

Table 14.A2 Fit results of one-factor and two-factor CFA models.

No. of factors	Factor correlation	χ^2	*df*	RMSEA	SRMR	TLI	CFI	AIC
1	–	44.47	35	0.033	0.066	0.920	0.922	2336.6
2	No	41.78	34	0.030	0.065	0.932	0.936	2335.9
2	Yes	34.92	33	0.015	0.061	0.983	0.984	2331.0

Note. Fit results of one-factor and two-factor CFA models with the second factor specified as difficulty factor with the correlation between the two factors restricted to zero (Line 2) or freely estimated (Line 3). AIC = Akaike information criterion; CFA = confirmatory factor analysis; CFI = comparative fit index; TLI = Tucker-Lewis Index; RMSEA = root-mean-square error of approximation; SRMR = standardized root mean square residual.

Contributors

Dennis Anheyer
Department of Psychology and Psychotherapy
Witten/Herdecke University
58455 Witten
Institute for General Practice and
Interprofessional Care
University Hospital Tübingen
72076 Tübingen
Germany

Sebastian Appelbaum
Department of Psychology and Psychotherapy
Witten/Herdecke University
58455 Witten
Germany

Natalie Badstuber
Psychology Department
Paris Lodron University
5020 Salzburg
Austria

Damian P. Birney
School of Psychology
University of Sydney
Sydney, NSW 2006
Australia

Sonja Breuer
Psychology Department
Paris Lodron University
5020 Salzburg
Austria

Clara Cuevas
Research Institute for Personnel Psychology,
Organizational Development, and Quality of
Working Life (IDOCAL)
Universitat de València
46010 Valencia
Spain

Rudolf Debelak
Machine Learning and Optimization Laboratory
École Polytechnique Fédérale de Lausanne
1015 Lausanne
Institute of Education
University of Zurich
8001 Zurich
Switzerland

Christine DiStefano
Educational and Developmental Science
University of South Carolina
Columbia, SC 29208
USA

Jungsun Go
Educational and Developmental Science
University of South Carolina
Columbia, SC 29208
USA

Samuel Greiff
School of Social Sciences & Technology
Technical University Munich
80333 Munich
Germany

Ana Hernández
Research Institute for Personnel Psychology,
Organizational Development, and Quality of
Working Life (IDOCAL)
Department of Methodology of the Behavioral
Sciences
Universitat de València
46010 Valencia
Spain

Kai T. Horstmann
Department of Psychology
University of Siegen
57072 Siegen
Germany

Dragos Iliescu
Department of Psychology and Cognitive Science
University of Bucharest
050663 Bucharest
Romania
Department of Industrial Psychology
Stellenbosch University
South Africa

Andrei Ion
Department of Psychology and Cognitive Science
University of Bucharest
050663 Bucharest
Romania

Richard Morris
Brain and Mind Centre
University of Sydney
Sydney, NSW 2006
Australia

Geophrey Odero
Department of Statistics
University of South Carolina
Columbia, SC 29208
USA

Tuulia M. Ortner
Psychology Department
Paris Lodron University
5020 Salzburg
Austria

Thomas Ostermann
Department of Psychology and Psychotherapy
Witten/Herdecke University
58455 Witten
Germany

Xuezhu Ren
School for Education
Huazhong University of Science & Technology
Wuhan 430074
PR China

Norman Rose
Institute of Infectious Diseases and Infection Control
Jena University Hospital
07747 Jena
Germany

Karl Schweizer
Institute for Psychology
Goethe University Frankfurt
60323 Frankfurt a.M.
Germany

Carolin Strobl
Department of Psychology
University of Zurich
8050 Zurich
Switzerland

Inés Tomás
Research Institute for Personnel Psychology, Organizational Development, and Quality of Working Life (IDOCAL) Department of Methodology of the Behavioral Sciences
Universitat de Valencia
46010 Valencia
Spain

Stefan J. Troche
Institute of Psychology
University of Bern
3012 Bern
Switzerland

Helene M. von Gugelberg
Institute of Education
University of Zurich
8001 Zurich
Switzerland

Tengfei Wang
Department of Psychology and Behavioral Sciences
Zhejiang University
Hangzhou
PR China

Matthias Ziegler
Department of Psychology
Humboldt-Universität zu Berlin
10099 Berlin
Germany

Peer Commentaries

This edited volume is a highly recommended resource for understanding how method effects can compromise the validity of psychological measurement when they are not properly addressed. Featuring contributions from leading experts, each chapter clearly explains specific sources of distortion and offers evidence-based strategies for controlling them during test development and evaluation. Whether you are developing a new scientifically sound instrument or assessing existing measures of psychological constructs, this volume provides the rigorous, state-of-the-art guidance needed to ensure that your instruments truly reflect the constructs they are intended to capture.

Axel Meyer, PhD, Professor for Psychological Methods and Evaluation, Department of Psychology, University of Bielefeld, Germany

This accessible and engaging book addresses an important but often neglected topic in psychological measurement. The chapters provide up to date and well-researched information on a wide variety of topics ranging from types of method effects and their underlying psychological processes to the detection and modeling of these effects. This book should be in the library of anyone interested in measurement issues in the behavioral sciences.

Deborah L. Bandalos, PhD, Professor Emerita, Department of Graduate Psychology, James Madison University, Harrisonburg, VA